A
CHECKLIST OF
AMERICAN IMPRINTS
for
1837

Items 42653-48672

compiled by

CAROL RINDERKNECHT

The Scarecrow Press, Inc.
Metuchen, N.J., & London
1986

Library of Congress Catalog Card No. 64-11784

ISBN 0-8108-1841-8

ABC buch, und lese und denk-
uebungen bei dem ersten unter-
richt der kinder. New York,
1837. 36 p. DLC; OO; PPULC.
42653

Abbot Academy, Andover, Mass.
Catalogue of the trustees,
teachers and pupils of the Abbot
Female Academy, Andover, for
the year ending Sept. 20, 1837.
Andover, Gould and Newman,
printers, 1837. 12 p. MAnA.
42654

Abbott, Benjamin, 1732-1796.
The Experience And Gospel
Labours Of The Rev. Benjamin
Abbott, To Which Is Annexed
A Narrative Of His Life And
Death. Also, Extracts From The
Journal Of The Rev. John Wesley.
Second English Edition. Phila-
delphia: S. Conrad, 1837.
309 p. MBNMHi. 42655

Abbott, Jacob, 1803-1879.
The Mount Vernon Reader; a
course of reading lessons, selected with reference to their
moral influence on the hearts
and lives of the young ... New
York, Collins, Keese and Co.,
1837. CtY; MH. 42656

---- Rollo learning to read; or,
Easy stories for young children.
By the author of little scholar
learning to talk. Boston, Otis

Broaders, and Co., New York,
Jas. H. Weeks, 1837. 180 p.
ViU. 42657

Abercrombie, John, 1780-1844.
The harmony of Christian
faith and Christian character.
9th ed. E. W. Whyte, 1837.
102 p. C-S; MH. 42658

---- Inquiries concerning the intellectual powers and the investigation of truth. By J. Abercrombie. New York, Harper and
bros., 1837. 376 p. FTa; IaK;
NbCrD; NNF; OWoC; TNP.
42659

---- The philosophy of the moral
feelings. By John Abercrombie
.... from the 2d Edinburgh ed.
with questions for the examination
of students. New York, Harper
and Brothers, 1837. 236 p.
DLC; FTa; IaU; MH; MMh.
42660

Académie Nathionale de Medecine,
Paris.
Commission chargee de l'examen du magnetisme animal. Animal magnestism ... 2d ed. Philadelphia, H. Perkins, 1837. CtY.
42661

Academy of natural sciences of
Philadelphia.
Catalogue of the library of
the Academy of natural sciences
of Philadelphia. Philadelphia,

1

J. Dobson, n. pr., 1837. 300 p.
CtY; MH; NjR; PU; RPB. 42662

---- List of members and cor-
respondents of the Academy of
natural sciences of Philadelphia.
From the origin of the society
on the 25th of January, 1812,
to the 1st of November, 1837.
Philadelphia, Rackliff & King,
printers, 1837. 18 p. CSfCW;
DLC; MBat; PPULC; PU. 42663

---- Notice of the academy of
natural sciences of Philadelphia.
Fourth ed. Philadelphia, Rackliff and King, 1837. v. p.
DLC; MH; MnSH; PPAmP; PPL.
42664
An account of the loss of the
Wesleyan missionaries, Messrs.
White, Hillier, Truscott, Oke
and Jones, with Mrs. White and
Mrs. Truscott, and their children and servants in the Maria
mailboat, off the island of An-
tigua, in the West Indies, February 28, 1826, by Mrs. Jones,
the only survivor on that mourn-
ful occasion. From the fifth
London edition. N.Y., pub. by
T. Mason and G. Lane, for the
Methodist Episcopal church, at
the conference office, 1837.
23 p. CL; IEG.   42665

An account of the proceedings
of the celebration of St. Patrick's
day, 1837, at the hall of the
Franklin institute, Masonic hall,
and the oration, delivered by
Joseph M. Doran, esq., at the
Adelphi. Philadelphia, M.
Fithian [1837]. 29 p. DLC;
MdBLC.   42666

Account of the rate of silver
... Concord, New Hampshire,
1837. MB.   42667

Adam, Alexander, 1741-1809.

Adams Latin grammar; with
numerous additions and improvements, designed to assist the
more advanced students.... Elu-
cidations of the Latin classics;
stereotype edition. Philadelphia,
William Marshall & company; Hartford, D. Burgess & co., 1837.
330 p. InHan; GMM; NN; OO;
PPM.   42668

---- Roman antiquities; or, An
account of the manners and customs of the Romans; designed to
illustrate the Latin classics. ...
By Alexander Adam ... Seventh
New York edition, with additional notes by Lorenzo L. Da Ponte
... New York, Collins, Keese &
co., 1837. 439 p. GEU; KHi;
MdBD; NNUT; OZaN.   42669

Adam, M. T.
The millennium; being a series
of discourses illustrative of its
nature, the means by which it
will be introduced and the time
of its commencement. By the
Rev. M. T. Adam. New York,
Robert Carter, 1837. GDecCT;
ICP; NCH; NjPT; TxDaTS.
42670
Adams, Charles, 1808-1890.
A funeral discourse delivered
at Great Fall, N.H. ... July,
1837. occasioned by the death
of Rev. A. Medcalf ... By Rev.
Charles Adams, A.M. Concord,
N.H. Printed by Roby, Kimball,
and Merrill, 1837. (3), 4-24 p.
IEG; MH; Nh; Nh-Hi; PU.
42671
Adams, Charles Francis, 1807-
1886.
Further reflections upon the
States of the Currency in the
United States. By C. F. Adams.
Boston, Published by William D.
Ticknor, 1837. 41 p. CtY:
MBAt; MWA; PU; WHi.   42672

---- Reflections upon the present state of currency in the United States. Boston, Printed by E. Lincoln, 1837. 34 p. CtY; LU; MWA; OO; PU.   42673

Adams, Daniel, 1773-1864.
Adam's new arithmetic; arithmetic, in which the principles of operating by numbers are analytically explained & synthetically applied ... designed for the use of schools & academies in the U.S. Keene, N.H., Prentiss, 1837. 262 p. DLC; MH; Nh; PU; MiU.   42674

Adams, Jasper, 1793-1841.
Elements of moral philosophy. By the Rev. Jasper Adams ... Cambridge [Mass] Folsom, Wells, and Thurston, 1837. 492 p. AU; CoDI; DLC; MiD; NNut.   42675

---- ---- New York, Wiley and Putnam, 1837. 492 p. CtB; LN; MnU; OAkU; TMeSC.   42676

---- ---- Philadelphia, E. L. Carey and A. Hart, 1837. 492 p. GDecCt; LNT; MdBJ; NjP; VtU.   42677

---- A Lecture delivered before the American Institution of Instruction, at Worcester, Massachusetts, Aug. 29, 1837. Boston, 1837. 22 p. NcD.   42678

Adams, John Quincy, 1767-1848.
The jubilee of the constitution. A discourse delivered at the request of the N.Y. historical society in the city of New York on Tuesday, April 30th, 1839. .... O. New York, 1837. 136 p. OCY.   42679

---- Letters from John Quincy Adams, to his constituents of the twelfth Congressional district in Massachusetts, to which is added his speech in Congress, delivered February 9, 1837. Boston, Isaac Knapp, 1837. 72 p. MBAt; MTop; MWA; PHi; OO.   42680

---- An oration delivered before the inhabitants of the town of Newburyport, at their request, on the sixty-first anniversary of the Declaration of independence, July 4th, 1837. By John Quincy Adams ... Newburyport [Mass.] Printed by Morss and Brewster [1837]. 68 p. CtSoP; MeB; MDecP; Nh-Hi; RPB.   42681

Adams, Nehemiah, 1806-1878.
The baptized child. Ed. 3. Boston, Massachusetts Sabbath Bost. 1837. School society, 1837. 24, 36-192 p. T. ICMe; InCW; MeBat; MWA; WHi.   42682

Adams, Thomas F.
Typographia: a brief sketch of the origin, rise, and progress of the typographic art; with practical directions for conducting every department in an office. By Thomas F. Adams, typographer. Philadelphia, The compiler, 1837. [3]-372, [8] p. IaU; MB; MnU; TxU; WM.   42683

Addicks, Barbara O'Sullivan.
Essay on education; in which the subject is treated as a natural science, in a series of familiar lectures. With notes. By Mrs. Barbara O'Sullivan Addicks ... New York, Protestant Episcopal press, print., 1837. 48 p. CtY; DHEW; MWA; NNG; ScU.   42684

Addison, Alvin.
Eveline Mandeville. By Alvin

Addison, Author of "The Rival
Hunters." Cincinnati: Published by U. P. James, [1837].
100 p. TxU.   42685

Addison, Joseph.
  The works of Joseph Addison;
complete in three volumes, embracing the whole of the "Spectator." New York, Herper &
brothers, 1837. 3 v. FSa;
IaHi; NNUT; RPaw; WAsN. 42686

Address of the Worcester Convention to the Electors of Massachusetts. Worcester, 1837.
N.   42687

Address ... to the citizens of
the U.S. Philadelphia, 1837.
PPL.   42688

Admirari, Nil. See Shelton,
Frederick William.

Advantages and disadvantages of
the marriage state; an allegory.
Springfield, 1837. CtHWatk.
                              42689
Adventures of a Bachelor; or,
Stolen Vigils. [Quotation.]
Philadelphia, Grigg & Elliot,
1837. 163 p. CtY; DLC; LNH.
                              42690
The adventures of Puss in boots.
Baltimore. Published by Bayly
& Burns, 1837. [2] p., 6 l.,
[2] p. MdHi.   42691

Advertisement; showing the nature and character of the theological writings of Emenuel
Swedenborg; and of the doctrines of the New Jerusalem
church. Columbus, Citler &
Pilsbury, 1837. 6 p. PBa;
PPULC.   42692

Advice and Select Hymns, for
The Instruction of Little Children.
Seventh Series. No. 10. Pub.

by (Atwood) & Browne. Concord, 1837. 16 p. MHi; Nh-Hi.
                              42693

The Advocate of Peace. v. 1,
June, 1837. Boston, Mass.,
American Peace Society, [etc.,
etc.], 1837-. LNH; MBAt; MiU;
PP; TxU.   42694

Aeschylus.
  The Prometheus of Aeschylus,
with notes, for the use of col-
leges in the United States. By
T. D. Woolsey ... Boston, J.
Munroe and co., 1837. 90 p.
CtY; IJI; OO; RPB; ViU.
                              42695

Aesopus.
  Aesop's fables, translated
into English; with a print before each fable. Abridged for
the amusement and instruction
of youth. Cooperstown, H. and
E. Phinney, 1837. 5-30 p. DLC.
                              42696
---- ---- Philadelphia, De Silver,
Thompson & Co., 1837. 12 &
228 p. CtNbT; NNC-T; OCX.
                              42697
The Affecting History of the
Children in the Wood. See English, Clara.

Affecting scenes; being passages
from the diary of a physician.
New York, Harper & Bros., 1837.
2 v. PPHa.   42698

The African glen, from the Colos-
seum, London, now at the Zoological institute....A description
of the views of the British settlement of Graham's Town....to-
gether with an extensive collection....by A. Steedman....
New York, Allanson, 1837. 36 p.
NjP; NN.   42699

The age of humbugs: The grand
tour, and other original poems,

by the author of the "Snowy daughter." ... Wheeling, E. W. Newton, printer, 1837. 52 p. RPB.   42700

Aged gipsey, The. Boston, 1837. MBAt.   42701

Agrarian stories No. 1. Fanny Forrester. Philadelphia, 1837. 36 p. DLC; MB.   42702

Agricultural almanac. Lancaster, Pa., Printed by John Bear, 1837. 36 p. IaHA.   42703

Aikin, William E. A., 1807-1888. ... Catalogue of Phaenogamous plants and ferns, native or naturalized, growing in the vicinity of Baltimore, Maryland, by William E. A. Aikin. ... [Baltimore, 1837]. 55-92 p. CtY; DLC; MdBJ; MH; PU.   42704

---- An introductory lecture before the medical class of the University of Maryland, Nov. 1837. By William E. A. Aikin ...Baltimore, printed by John D. Toy, 1837. 20 p. DLC; McHi; MWA; MdUM; PPCP.   42705

Ainsworth, Luther. Practical mercantile arithmetic in which the theory and practice of arithmetic are familiarly explained and illustrated by a great variety of mercantile, mechanical, and mathematical problems. Second edition, revised and improved by the addition of mental exercises. By Luther Ainsworth. Providence, Published by B. Cranston & Co.; Boston, Gould, Kendall & Lincoln; New-York, Robinson, Pratt & Co., F. J. Huntington & Co....1837. 272 p. CtHWatk; MWHi; NN.   42706

---- A practical system of English grammar, in which the principles of the language are plainly and familiarly taught by questions and answers, and illustrated by a copious variety of practical examples. By Luther Ainsworth, ... Providence, B. Cranston & co., John E. Brown, 1837. 144 p. DLC; NNc.   42707

Ainsworth, Robert, 1660-1743. An abridgement of Ainsworth's dictionary, English and Latin, designed for the use of schools. By Thomas Morell, D.D. Carefully corrected and improved from the last London quarto edition by John Carey, LL.D. Philadelphia, Published by Uriah Hunt; New York, J. & J. Harper, and Collins & Hannay; Boston, Richardson & Lord, and Hilliard, Gray & co., 1837. 1028 p. IaHi; FU; KyU; PU; WaPS.   42708

Ainsworth, William Harrison, 1805-1882. Crichton. By W. Harrison Ainsworth, Esq., author of "Bookwood." ... In two volumes. New York, Harper & Brothers, 1837. 2 v. FSa; MB; MeB; OCl; PPL.   42709

Alabama. General Assembly, 1836. Journal of the Senate, of the State of Alabama, Begun and Held in the Town of Tuscaloosa, on the First Monday in November, 1836. Being the Eighteenth Annual Session of the General Assembly of Said State. Tuscaloosa, David Ferguson, Printer, 1837. 128 p. A-SC.   42710

---- ---- 1837. Journal of the House of Reps., of the Legislature of Alabama at the Called Session. Begun and held at the

Town of Tuscaloosa, on the
Second Monday in June 1837,
Tuscaloosa. Printed by Fergu-
son & Eaton, 1837. 91 p.
A-SC.   42711

---- ---- House.
Journal of the House of
Representatives at a Session of
the General Assembly of the
State of Alabama, Begun and
Held at the City of Tuscaloosa,
on the First Monday in November, 1837. Tuscaloosa, Ferguson & Eaton, Printers, 1837.
208 p. A-SC.   42712

---- ---- Joint Committee on
the State Bank.
Report of the joint examining
committee, of both branches of
the legislature of Alabama, on the
condition and affairs of the state
bank and branches: 1837. in
House of rep. - read, and 3000
copies ordered to be printed.
In senate - read, and 3000
copies ordered to be printed.
Tuskaloosa, printed by Slade-
at his Despatch Printing Office,
1837. 7 p. ABBS; NN.   42713

---- ---- Senate.
Journal of the Senate, of
the Legislature of Alabama, at
the Called Session Begun and
Held at the Town of Tuscaloosa,
on the Second Monday in June,
1837. Tuscaloosa, Printed by
Ferguson & Eaton, 1837. 40 p.
A-SC.   42714

---- Governor, 1835-1837.
(Clement C. Clay)
Message of Governor Clay,
to the general assembly of the
state of Alabama, at the called
session, which commenced in
June, 1837. Tuscaloosa, [1837].
11 p. TxU.   42715

---- Laws, Statutes, etc.
An act to extend the time of
indebtedness to the bank of the
state of Alabama and its branches,
and legalizing the suspension of
specie payments; and for other
purposes. Passed at the called
session of the legislature, June
12, 1837. Mobile, printed by
Cooper & Leavens, 1837. 14 p.
ABBS; ABS.   42716

---- ---- Acts of the legislature
in relation to the bank of the
state of Alabama and its branches
[Mobile, 1837?]. 8 p. ABS.
                               42717
---- ---- Acts passed at the annual session of the general assembly of the state of Alabama,
begun and held in the town of
Tuscaloosa, on the first Monday
in November, one thousand eight
hundred and thirty-six. Clement
C. Clay, governor. Hugh Mc-
Vay, president of the senate.
A. P. Bagby, speaker of the
house of representatives. Tuscaloosa, David Ferguson, state
printer, 1837. 152 p. DLC;
IaU-L; In-SC; MH-L; RPL.
                               42718
---- ---- Acts passed at the
called session of the general assembly of the state of Alabama,
begun and held in the town of
Tuscaloosa, on the 12 day of
June, 1837. Tuscaloosa, Ferguson & Eaton, state printers,
1837. 42 p. In-SC; MdBB;
MH-L; Nj; RPL.   42719

---- University.
Catalogue of the officers and
students, of the University of
Alabama; for the year 1837.
Tuscaloosa, printed at the In-
telligencer Office, 1837. 8 p.
A-Ar; DLC; MHi.   42720

---- ---- Ordinances and resolu-

tions of the board of trustees
of the University of Alabama,
which are of a general and public nature--passed since the
close of their session in January, 1831--up to the close of
the August session, 1837. Tuskaloosa, Printed by Marmaduke
J. Slade, 1837. 46 p. AU;
GEU; MH.   42721

---- ---- Library.
A catalogue of the library of
the University of Alabama. Tuskaloosa, Marmaduke J. Slade,
printer, 1837. 54 p. A-Ar;
AU; NcD.   42722

---- ---- Trustees.
Report of the trustees, of
the University of Alabama. To
the honorable senate and house
of representatives of the stage
of Alabama in general assembly
convened. Tuscaloosa, David
Eerguson [sic], printer, 1837.
7 p. A-AR; AB; MB; NcD.
                           42723
Alabama, eine geographisch-
statistich topographische skizze
fuer einwanderer und freunde
der laender und voelkerkunde.
Baltimore, Scheld, 1837. 22 p.
IU; MdBSHG; PU.   42724

Albany, N.Y. Second Presbyterian Church.
Catalogue of communicants,
Jan., 1837. Albany, 1837.
26 pp. MB.   42725

Albany Academy, Albany, N.Y.
The statutes of the Albany
academy. Revised and passed,
October 9, 1829. Reprinted,
with amendments and alterations,
November, 1837. Albany, Printed
by E. W. and C. Skinner, 1837.
36 p. MH; MiU-C.   42726

Albany Military Association.

Constitution & By-Laws ..
Albany, 1837. 62 p. CtY; N.
                           42727
Albion Female Seminary.
Catalogue of the Members of
the Albion Female Seminary, for
the Academic Year, Commencing
Sept. I, 1836, & closing July 20,
1837, Together with Terms of
Admittance &c. Albion, N.Y.,
Printed by T. C. Strong, 1837.
8 p. NAlbi.   42728

Alcott, Amos Bronson, 1799-1888.
New Connecticut. An auto-
biographical poem. By A. Bronson Alcott. Ed. by F. B. Sanborn. Boston, Roberts brothers,
1837. 3 p. 1., [v]-xxvi, 247 p.
front. (port.) OClW.   42729

Alcott, William Alexander. See
Alcott, William Andrus, 1798-1859.

Alcott, William Andrus, 1798-1859.
(An) address delivered before
the Amer. Physiological society,
March 7, 1837 ... Boston, 1837.
36 p. CtMW; DLC; MB; MBAt.
                           42730
---- The cedars of Lebanon, in
conversations between a mother
and her daughters. Boston,
Massachusetts Sabbath School
Society, 1837. DLC; MBC.
                           42731
---- The house I live in; or,
The human body, for the use of
families and schools. By Wm. A.
Alcott... Second edition - en-
larged. Boston, Light & Stearns,
1837. 13-246 p. CtY; MeB;
NNUT; PU; ScOrC.   42732

---- The Library of health, and
teacher on the human constitution.
Wm. A. Alcott, editor. Boston,
George W. Light, 1837-. v. 1-
CoDMS; IEG; MBarn; MBBC;
NNNAM.   42733

---- The shepherd boy and
the giant. Boston, 1837.
MBC.   42734

---- Ways of living on small
means.... Boston, Light and
Stearns, 1837. 106 p. CtY;
ICU; MB.   42735

---- ---- Second edition. Boston, Light & Stearns, 1837.
106 p. ICU; MB; MNa.   42736

---- ---- 4th ed. Boston, 1837.
CtY; MB; NN.   42737

---- ---- 5th ed. Enl. and
imp. Boston, Light and Stearns,
1837. (3) 4-5 (2) 8-10 (1) 12-
134 (10) p. CtMW   42738

---- ---- 6th ed. enl. and improved. Boston, Light, 1837.
134 p. CtHWatk; CtMW; MBC.
                           42739
---- (The) young missionary;
exemplied in the life of Timothy.... Boston, Massachusetts
sabbath school society, 1837.
175 p. DLC; OC; OO.   42740

---- The young wife, or Duties
of woman in the marriage rela-
tion. By Wm. A. Alcott ... 2d
Stereotupe ed. Boston, G. W.
Light, 1837. 376 p. CtY; IEG;
MWA; NjMD; PLFM.   42741

Alden, Ebenezer, 1788-1881.
Memoir and Correspondence
of Mrs. Mary Ann Odeorne
Clark... Bost., Massachusetts
Sabbath School society, 1837.
226 p. DLC; GMiluC;
MiD-B; OMC; TxHR.   42742

Alden (J   ).
Cartagraphers chart of
Georges shoal and bank, sur-
veyed by Charles Wilkes, lieut.
Commander [and others] in

U.S. brig. Porpoise, schooners
Maria & Hadassah ... engraved
by S. Stiles, Sherman & Smith,
N.Y. by order of ... Mahlon
Dickerson, Secretary of the navy.
[New York, pub. under direc-
tion of the navy commissioners,
1837.] ScC.   42743

Alexander, Archibald, 1772-1851.
Evidences of the authenticity
inspiration and canonical authority of the Holy Scriptures.
Philadelphia, Pennsylvania, Presbyterian Board of Publication,
1837. 308 p. ODaB.   42744

---- A treatise on Justification
by Faith. By Archibald Alexander, D.D. Professor of Didactic
and Polemic Theology in the Theological Seminary at Princeton,
New Jersey. Philadelphia, Printed
and for sale by Wm. S. Martien
for the Presbyterian Tract and
Sunday-School Society, 1837.
50 p. ICP; MBC; NCH; PPM;
ViRut.   42745

[Alexander, John Henry].
Map of the proposed rail road
from Frederick town to Emmitsburg. Baltimore, E. Weber &
co. [1837?]. MdBE.   42746

Alexandria Boarding School,
Alexandria, Va.
Catalogue of teachers and
students, 1837-1842. Alexandria,
1837-42. 8 v. DLC.   42747

Alford, Julius C.
Speech....on the resolution
of Mr. Thompson, to censure the
Hon. John Quincy Adams, delivered in the House of Representatives, Feb. 7, 1837. Washington, Printed by Gales and
Seaton, 1837. 8 p. WHi.
                           42748
Allegany City Company.

Articles of association...
together with a description of
the property, etc. January 10,
1837. New York, Marine, 1837.
20 p. DLC; MB; NRHi. 42749

Alleine, Joseph, 1634-1668.
An Alarm to UnConverted
Sinners: in A Serious treatise
on Conversion by Joseph Alleine.
New York, American Tract Society, 1837. 168 p. KyD.
42750

Allen, Benjamin, d. 1836.
An oration, in defence of divine revelation; together with
the valedictory addresses; delivered in the Baptist meeting-
house, in Providence, at the
commencement of Rhode Island
college, September 6, A.D.
1797. By Benjamin Allen, A.B.
Published by request. Providence, Printed by Carter and
Wilkinson, [1837]. 16 p. CSt.
42751

[Allen, George, comp.] 1792-
1883.
Hymns for the hospital chapel,
Worcester. Worcester, Mirick
and Bartlett, 1837. MB; MBC;
MWHi; NNUT. 42752

Allen, James.
Narrative of the life of James
Allen, alias George Walton, alias
Jonas Pierce, alias James H.
York, alias Burley Grove the
highway man, being his death-
bed confession, to the Warden
of the Massachusetts State
Prison. Boston, Harrington and
Co., Publisher, 1837. 32 p.
DLC; MBAt; MBM; MoU; MWA.
42753

Allen, Joseph, 1790-1873.
Questions on select portions
of the four Evangelists. Part
second comprising the principal
discourses and parables of our
Lord. Designed for the higher

classes in Sunday Schools.
Fourth edition. By Joseph Allen .... Boston, Benjamin H.
Greene, 1837. 118 p. PMA.
42754

Allen, Joseph D.
Report of Joseph D. Allen,
chief engineer, to the board of
directors. New York, T. & C.
Wood Printer, 1837. 23 p. CSt;
NBuG; NN; NUtHi; ScU. 42755

Allen, William, 1784-1868.
Memoir of Rev. E. Whulock
D.D. founder of Dartmouth Col-
lege. [Boston, 1837] 32 p.
ICN. 42756

Allen, William, 1803-1879.
Speech of the Honorable William Allen delivered at the great
Democratic festival held at Lancaster, Ohio on the 29th day of
August 1837. Lancaster, printed
by J. and C. H. Brough, 1837.
16 p. DLC; IEN; MiD; OClWHi.
42757

Alpha Delta Phi.
Catalogue. Address. Printed
in New York, R. B. Brooks and
Company, 1837-. 25 p. DLC;
NGH; OOxM; PHi; RPB. 42758

Alrich, W. P.
Anniversary address .... before the Union literary society
of Washington college .... n.pl.
John Grayson, printer, 1837.
16 p. IU; NjR; PHi; PPM;
PPPrHi. 42759

Alsop, Samuel, 1813-1888.
A complete key to Gummere's
Surveying; in which the operations of all the examples, not
solved in that work, are exhibited
at large ... By Samuel Alsop.
Philadelphia, Kimber & Sharpless,
1837. 84 p. ICMS; KyLo; NjP;
OrSaW; PWcHi. 42760

Alvarado, J. B.
El C. Juan B. Alvarado
gobernador interino del estado
libre y soberano de la Alta
California, á sus habitantes ...
Monterey, May 10, 1837.
Cu-B.   42761

Amenia Seminary.
Catalogue of the officers and
students of Amenia Seminary,
Amenia, N.Y., 1837-38. Poughkeepsie, Killey ' Lossing, 1837.
14 p. NP.   42762

The American Almanac, for the
year 1838. Boston, Pub. by
Charles Bowen, (1837). IaHA
324 p.; MWHi 336 p.   42763

American and Foreign Bible Society.
Proceedings of the Bible convention, which met in Philadelphia, April 26, 27, 28, and 29,
1837; together with the report
of the board of managers of the
American and foreign Bible society, embracing the period of
its provisional organization.
New York, printed for the
American and foreign Bible society by John Gray, (1837).
88 p. ICP; MB; MiD-B;
OClWHi; RPA.   42764

....The American Anti-Slavery
Almanac, for 1837, ... Vol. 1.
No. 2. - Boston, Pub. by N.
Southard and D. K. Hitchcock,
[1837]. 34 p. MiU; RNHi.
                          42765
....The American anti-slavery
Almanac, for 1838.... N. South-
ard, ed. Boston, published by
D. T. Hitchcock, [1837]. 48 p.
MMal; MPeHi; MWA; WHi. 42766

---- Adapted to most parts of
the United States. ... N. Southard, editor. vol. 1 No. 3.

Boston, Published by Isaac Knapp,
(1837). (46) p. Ct; MBAt;
MWA; OO.   42767

American Anti-slavery society.
An appeal to abolitionists.
New York [MS dating: Sept.
27, 1837] 3 p. OClWHi.
                          42768
---- Colonization. (Compiled,
chiefly from recent publications.)
New York, (1837?). 24 p. MH.
                          42769
---- The declaration of senti-
ments and constitution of the
American Anti-Slavery Society.
With an address to the public
by the executive committee....
New York, Published by the
American Anti-Slavery Society....
1837. 16 p. CtY; ICN; MToP;
OClWHi; RP.   42770

---- Human Rights - Extra.
New York, September, 1837.
Office of the American Anti-
Slavery Society New York, Sept.
11, 1837. ... Broadsheet. MH.
                          42771
---- St. Domingo. (Compiled,
chiefly, from recent publications)
New York [1837?] 24 p. MH.
                          42772
American archives: consisting of
a collection of authentic records,
state papers, debates, and letters and other notices of publick
affairs....In six series. By
Peter Force. Prepared and published under authority of an act
of Congress. Washington, 1837-
53. 9 v. CSmH; FU; MdU;
TMeB; WU.   42773

American association for the supply of teachers, Philadelphia.
[Officers, constitution, and regu-
lations] 1837. [Philadelphia,
1837] 8 p. MiU-C; PHi.
                          42774
The American Baptist and gospel

light. New Series. V. 1-.
New York and Philadelphia, P.
Relyea and Co., 1837-. CtY.
42775
American Baptist Publication
Society.
The Baptist Manual: A Se-
lection from the Series of Pub-
lications of the Baptist General
Tract Society, designed for the
Use of Families; and as an ex-
position of the Distinguishing
sentiments of the Denomination.
Philadelphia, Published at the
Tract Depository, No. 21.
192 p. ICNB; MH; PPL. 42776

American Bible Society. Library.
Catalogue of editions of the
Holy Scriptures in various
languages, and other biblical
works, in the library of the
American Bible society. New
York, Printed for the Society
by Daniel Fanshaw, 1837. 31 p.
CtY; MB; NjP; NNUT; PPDrop.
42777
American Board of Commissioners
for Foreign Missions.
Manual for Missionary candidates of the American board of
commissioners for foreign Missions. Boston, [Printed by
Crocker and Brewster,] 1837.
34 p. CBPSR; RPB; WHi.
42778
The American coast pilot: containing directions ... harbors,
capes and headlands, ... coasts
of North and South America:
... by Edmund M. Blunt. 13th.
Ed., improved, ... New York,
Published by Edmund and
George W. Blunt, 1837. 720,
(2) p. MB; MeHi; MH; MNan;
MWhB. 42778a

---- American Comic Almanac for
1838. Philadelphia, Pa., Sold by
Grigg & Elliot, (1837.) MWA
42779

American Comic Almanack, 1838.
Boston, Mass., Sold by Thomas
Groom, (1837.) MWA; NN; WHi.
42780
American Exchange Company,
New York.
... Articles of association,
and deed of trust. New-York,
1837. 24 p. CtY. 42781

The American Farmer's Almanac
for the year of Our Lord 1837;
Boston, Published and sold by
Allen & Company, 1837. 30 p.
MH; MHi; MWA; RNHi; RPB.
42782
The American gentleman's med-
ical pocket-book and health-
adviser ... By the author of The
Lady's medical pocket-book.
Philadelphia, J. Kay Jun. and
brother; Pittsburgh, J. L. Kay
and Co., [1837]. 254 p.
MdBJ-W; ViU. 42783

American Institute of Architects.
Constitution and By-Laws of
the American Institute of Architects, instituted 1836. Philadelphia, Printed by Lydia R.
Bailey, North Fifth St., 1837.
11 p. NNNM. 42784

American Institute of Instruction.
Memorial to the Directors relative
to the better preparation of the
teachers of the schools of the
commonwealth. [Boston, 1837]
18 p. MB; MBC; RPB. 42785

The American juvenile keepsake
... Bristol, R. I. J. Gladding
and co. (1837?) 3-252 p. MB;
RPB. 42786

The American juvenile primer,
and first step to learning, carefully arranged on a new, simple
and interesting principle. Philadelphia, Turner & Fisher, 1837.
2-23 p. 42787

American ladies' magazine; containing original tales, essays, poetry and music, with plates and fashions; by Mrs. Sarah J. Hale. Boston, 1837. 576 p. CtHWatk; DLC; VtU.   42788

The American Medical Intelligencer. A concentrated record of medical science and literature. By Robley Dunglison, M.D. ... Philadelphia, Published by A. Waldie; J. J. Haswell, 1837-1842. 5 v. CoFS; MiU; Nh; PPL; ViU.   42789

American moral reform society. Minutes and proceedings of the first annual meeting of the American Moral Reform Society. Philadelphia, Merrihew and Gunn, 1837. DHU; MHi; RP.
                                    42790
American Naval Battles: being a complete history of the battles fought by the navy of the United States, from its establishment in 1794, to the present time.... Boston, Printed and Published by Charles Gaylord, 1837. 278 p. CSmlt; DLC; MeHi; ViRU; WaS.   42791

American philosophical society and the Franklin institute. Directions for making meteorogical observations... [Philadelphia], 1837. CtY; MB; NN; PPAN.   42792

American Physiological Society. First annual report of the American physiological society. Boston, Marsh, Capen, and Lyon, 1837. 148 p. CtMW; MB; OC; PPAN; WU-M.   42793

---- Constitution of Am. Physiol. Soc. co. Catalogue of Members & officers. Prefixed, Summary explanation of the objects of

the Society. Boston, Marsh, Capen and Lyon, 1837. 19 p. CtMW; DLC; MBAt; OO; TxU.
                                    42794
The American practical navigator: being an epitome of navigation ...By Nathaniel Bowditch...9th new stereotype ed. New York, E. & G. W. Blunt, 1837. xv, (1), 317, 439 p. MB; PPAmP; RPB.   42795

---- Tenth Edition. New York. J. M. Elliot, Print. Stereotyped At The Boston Type And Stereotype Foundry. Published By E & G. W. Blunt, Proprietors, 1837. 439 p. MB; MSaP; MWfo; NjP; NNA.   42796

American Seamen's Friend Society.
Seamen's devotional assistant, and mariner's hymns; prepared under direction of the American seamen's friend society. New York, By the society, 1837. 510 p. MdBD.   42797

The American society for the diffusion of useful knowledge. Established October 17, 1836. Prospectus... New York, Published by the committee, 1837. 1 p., 1., 38, 15 p. CBPSR; ICP; KyDC; MB; NNUT.   42798

American Sunday-School union. Descriptive catalogue of books and other publications for Sunday-schools and parish libraries. Philadelphia, 1837. 68 p. MW; MHi.   42799

---- Questions and stories on the commandments, with grace and prayers. Written for the American Sunday School Union, and revised by the Committee of publication. Philadelphia, [1837]. 24 p. NNC.   42800

---- The Sad history of James
Parker. Philadelphia, 1837.
13 p. RPB.   42800a

---- Second reading book....By
the association for the improvement of the juvenile books.
Second edition. Philadelphia,
Published by T. Ellwood Chapman, 1837. 180 p. PLFM.
                          42801
---- The Sunday-school teacher's dream. Philadelphia, American Sunday-school union, (1837).
58 p. IU; MH; PPPrHi.   42802

---- The Thornton family. Revised by the committee of publication of the American Sunday
School Union. Philadelphia,
American Sunday School Union,
[1837]. 153 p. CtY; ICBB;
MBC.   42803

---- The union annual. 1837.
Philadelphia, American Sunday
school union, 1837. [9]-269 p.
CSmH; IU; MH; NjR; PU.   42804

---- The union primer, or,
First book for children. Pre-
pared for the American Sunday
School Union, and revised by
the Committee of publication,
Philadelphia, American Sunday
School Union, [1837]. CaBVaU;
DLC; ICBB.   42805

---- Union questions; or, Questions on select portions of
Scripture from the Old and New
Testaments, v. 9, being a continuation of v. 7, comprising
the history of the Israelites from
the Babylonian captivity to the
end of the Old Testament, &
including the books of Daniel,
Ezra, Esther & Nehemiah.
Philadelphia, Am. S.S.U., 1837.
144 p. AmSSchU; IEC; MH.
                          42806

American Temperance Union.
Journal. [Philadelphia, New
York, V. 1-. Jan. 1837-]
CU; MBAt; NjP; PPL; PU.
                          42807
Americanischer Stadt und Land
Calender auf das 1838ste Jahr
Christi....Philadelphia: Gedruckt
und zu haben bey Conrad Zent-
ler....[1837]. 28 p. MWA;
PReaHi.   42808

Americanisches roth- und hulfs-
buchlein, enthaltend hausmittel
und recepte...Osnaburg, Stark
Co., Ohio, Heinrich Kurz, 1837.
57, [3] p. OClWHi.   42809

(Der) Amerikanisch Deutsche
Hausfreund und Baltimore Calen-
dar for 1838. Baltimore, Md.,
Johann T. Hanzsche, [1837].
MWA.   42810

Ames, Julius Rubens, 1801-1850.
"Liberty"...By Julius R.
Ames. New York, American anti-
slavery society, 1837. 231 p.
IEG; MBAt; NB; NcD; RP.
                          42811

---- ---- Philadelphia, n. pub.,
1837. 231 p. MnHi; OO.
                          42812
Amherst College, Amherst, Mass.
Amherst college catalogue of
the officers and students, November, 1837. Northampton,
(Mass.), Metcalf, pr., 1837.
20 p. CoU; IaGG; MeB; MS;
NN.   42813

Amory, John H.
Almanac, or the golden rule,
a tale of the sea. Boston, Weeks,
Jordan and Co., etc, etc, 1837.
144 p. NN.   42814

---- ---- Cleveland, O., Jewett,
Proctor, and Worthington, 1837.
144 p. DLC; TNF.   42815

---- Old Ironside. First number, The story of a shipwreck.
Boston, B. B. Mussey, 1837.
144 p. CtY; MH.   42816

Anabaptism Disproved, and The
Validity and Sufficiency of Infant Baptism Asserted in two
letters from a minister to his
friend. New York, J. Collord,
1837. Various pages. IEG;
LNB; MBNMHI; NjPT; RPB.
42817
Anapolis [sic], Maryland.
Mayor (John Miller).
Report of the Mayor of Annapolis to the corporation, accompanied by the Treasurer's
general reports for the years
ending April 1836 and 1837.
Annapolis, 1837. MdBP.   42818

The anatomy of a humbug, of
the genus germanicus, species
homoeopathia ... New York,
The author, 1837. 28 p.
CSt-L; CtY; DLC; PPL; PU.
42819
Andover Theological Seminary.
Annals. 1837. NjP.   42820

---- Catalogue of the officers
and students of the Theological
seminary, Andover, Mass ....
Andover, n. pub. Printed by
Gould and Newman, 1837. 12 p.
NjR.   42821

---- Laws of the theological in-
stitution in Andover. Andover
[Mass.], Printed by Gould and
Newman, 1837. 31 p. CSmH;
MH; MiD-B; MnSM; TxU.   42822

Andrews, -
Eliza M. Westall & Wm. G.
Hill, vs. James F. Perry, &
Wife, Argument; Andrews for
Plaintiffs. The question at is-
sue before the court, arises on
the construction of a single

clause in the last will of Stephen
F. Austin... [Texas? 1837?]
52 p. WHi.   42823

Andrews, Ethan Allen, 1787-
1858.
First lessons in Latin; or,
An introduction to Andrews and
Stoddard's Latin grammar. By
Prof. E. A. Andrews. Boston,
Crocker and Brewster; New-
York, Leavitt, Lord, and co.,
1837. [19]-208, [2] p. DLC;
MiU; MWHi; PMA; RPB.   42824

---- The first part of Jacobs
and Doring's Latin reader:
adapted to Andrews and Stod-
dard's Latin grammar. By Prof.
E. A. Andrews. Boston,
Crocker and Brewster; New York,
Leavitt, Lord, and co., 1837.
MH; NjPT; TxU-T.   42825

---- ---- 2 ed. Boston, Crocker & Brewster, pubs., 1837.
266 p. RPB.   42826

---- A grammar of the Latin language; for the use of schools,
and colleges. 3d. ed. Boston,
Crocker and Brewster, 1837.
323 p. LNDil; MBAt; MH;
WBeloHi.   42827

---- Latin exercises; adapted to
Andrews and Stoddard's Latin
grammar. By Prof. E. A. Andrews. Boston, Published by
Crocker & Brewster, 1837.
308 p. CSansS; CtY; MB; MH;
RPB; TxU-T.   42828

Andrews (L. F. W.).
The "two opinions"; or, Salvation and damination, being an inquiry into the truth of certain
theological tenets prevalent in
the year of our Lord 1837. By
L. F. W. Andrews. Macon (Ga),
printed for the author, 1837.

(6, 7)-195 p. AfIT; MMet-Hi;
NjPT; PPL; ScNC.   42829

Andrews, Silas M.
    The Sabbath at home. By
the Rev. Silas M. Andrews.
Philadelphia, Presbyterian Tract
and Sunday School Society,
1837. 18 p. ICU; MsSC: NjPT;
PPPrHi; WHi.   42830

Andrews, W.
    An address delivered on oc-
casion of the Festival of St.
John, December 27th, 1837, be-
fore the officers and members
of Macon Lodge, No. 19, ... By
Brother L. F. W. Andrews.
Macon, Geo., 1837. 12 p.
NNNFM.   42831

Andrews, William Eusebius,
1773-1837.
    The Catholic school book.
Revised by John Simmons.
Philadelphia, E. Cummiskey,
(1837). MH   42332

Ann Arbor Land Company.
    Splendid sale of real estate
in Ann Arbor, at auction!!
The undersigned will offer at
public auction on the 8th day
of June next, at the Ann Arbor
exchange, in this village, on
the most liberal terms, 1000 lots,
... Also, 100 out lots of from 1
to 10 acres each, lying within
one mile of the village; ... Also
a number of improved farms....
Argus Office Print--Ann Arbor,
Mich., [1837]. Broadside.
MiU; MiU-C; MiU-Hi.   42833

Anniversary of the booksellers'
dinner, Mch. 30, 1837. (N.Y.,
1837.) 23 p. MH.   42834

The annual Monitor, and memorandum book for 1837. York,
Printed and Published by W.

Alexander and Co. and others,
1837. 144 p. PSC-Hi.   42835

Anthony, Henry Bowen, 1815-
1884.
    The Fancy Ball. A Sketch.
Printed for private circulation.
Pulaski House, Savannah, March
31st. (Savannah, W. T. Williams),
1837. 12 p. MH; NcD; RPB.
                           42836
Anti-masonic state committee of
Pennsylvania.
    Circular letter addressed...
to the committees of other states.
Harrisburg, Penn'a, June 20,
1837. 1 p. MHi.   42837

Anti Slavery Association. Re-
port 2nd Convention Mt. Pleasant,
Jefferson Co. O. April 27, 1837.
Cincinnati, 1837. OCHP.   42838

Anti slavery convention of American women. New York, 1837.
    An address to free colored
Americans, issued by the Anti-
slavery convention of American
women, held in the city of New
York, by adjournments from the
9th to 12th May, 1837. N.Y.,
Dorr, 1837. 32 p. ICN; MB;
OO; TxU; WHi.   42839

---- An appeal to the women of
the nominally free states, issued
by an Anti-slavery convention
of American women, held by adjournments from the 9th to the
12th of May, 1837 ... New York,
W. S. Dorr, printer, 1837. 68 p.
DLC; MiU; PHi; OO; TxU.
                           42840
---- Proceedings of the Anti-
slavery convention of American
women, held in the city of New-
York, May 9th, 10th, 11th, and
12th, 1837. New-York, Printed
by W. S. Dorr, 1837. 23 p.
ICN; MB; PHC; RP; TxU: WHi.
                           42841

Apes, William, b. 1798.
Eulogy on King Philip, as pronounced at the Odeon, in Federal street, Boston, 2nd ed...Boston, The author, 1837. 48 p. CSmH; MBAt; MdHi; PHi.   42842

---- Experience of five Christian Indians of the Pequod tribe; second edition. By Wm. Apess....Boston, William Apess, 1837. 47 p. CtSoP; ICN; MWA; NjR; OMC.   42843

Apostolic Fathers.
The Apostolic Fathers, Polycarp and Ignatius. If any one ....let him read the Apostolic Fathers, Dr. Murdock. Burlington, N.J., J. L. Powell; Missionary press, (1837). 48 p. CtHT; IaDuU; MdBD; NNG; PHi.   42844

Appeal of clerical abolitionists on anti-slavery measures (Signed by Charles Fitch and 4 others.) -Reply by editor pro.tem. of the Liberator-A layman's (W. L. Garrison) reply to a Clerical appeal-Reply to the appeal by A. A. Phelps-.Declaration of abolitionists in the theological seminary at Andover, Mass. [Boston, 1837] 26 p. MH; OO.
                                  42845
An appeal to matter of fact and common sense; or, A rational demonstration of man's corrupt and lost estate... New York, T. Mason and G. Lane, publisher, J. Collard, printer, 1837. 66 p. GDecCT; ICBB.
                                  42846
An Appeal to the ... legislature of the state of New York, by a native American n.p. 1837. 11 p.   42847

An appeal to the members elect of the legislature of the state of New-York, by a native American. n.pl., n.pub., n.pr. 1837. 11 p. DLC; NjR.   42848

An appeal to the Presbyterian Church by the minority of the late General Assembly, convened at Philadelphia, May, 1837. New York, 1837. 20 p. NcMHi; NjR; PPPrHi.   42849

An appendix to the exposition of the pretended claims of William Vans on the Estate of John Codman; containing original documents, correspondence and other evidence. Boston, Samuel N. Dickinson, 1837. viii, 420 p. MBNEH; MdBB; MFi; MHi.
                                  42850
Appleton, Jesse.
The works of Rev. Jesse Appleton, D.D. ... with a memoir. In two vols. ... Andover, Gould and Newman, 1837. 2 v. IEG; MAnP; NcU; RBr; WNaE. 42851

Appleton academy, New Ipswich, N.H.
A catalogue of the officers, instructors, and students ... 1836/37. New Ipswich, J. Garfield, printer, 1837. 1 v. CSmH.   42852

Arabian nights.
Arabian nights entertainments tr. from the Arabic by M. Gollard, Ithaca, Mack, 1837. 262 p. N; ScGrvGWC.   42853

Arguments in favour of a reformed system of currency, by a private gentleman to a member of Congress in 1834. And the outline of a system proposed. Columbia, 1837. 40, (3) p. CtY; NcD.   42854

Aristophanes.

The Knights of Aristophanes, translated by T. Mitchell, A.M., late fellow of Sidney Sussex college, Cambridge, 1st Amer. ed. Washington, D.C., Garret Anderson, 1837. 160 p. WLac. 42855

Arkansas. Auditor.
Report of the auditor of state for the period Sept. 12, 1836 - Oct. 31, 1837. Little Rock, Reed & Budd, printers, 1837. 8 p. TxU. 42856

No entry 42857

---- Bank of the State.
Report of the Bank of the State of Arkansas, made to the General Assembly, November 7, 1837. [n.p., 1837?] 8 p. TxU. 42858

---- Commissioner of public buildings.
Report of the commissioner of public buildings. [Little Rock, 1837.] 3 p. TxU. 42859

---- ---- Report of the special agent, who settled the accounts of ex-governor Pope. [Little Rock, 1837.] 4 p. TxU. 42860

---- General Assembly.
Journals of the first session of the General Assembly of the State of Arkansas, begun and held at the city of Little Rock, in said state, on the twelfth day of September, in the year of Christ, one thousand eight hundred and thirty-six, and of the independence of the United States of America the sixty-second.

Little Rock, Printed by Woodruff & Pew, Printers to the State, 1837. Ar-Hi; ArU; DLC; ICU; NcU. 42861

---- ---- Auditor (Elias Newton Conway).
Report of the auditor of the state of Arkansas. [Little Rock, 1837.] 8 p. TxU. 42862

---- ---- Joint Committee on Auditor's and treasurer's books. Report [Little Rock? 1837?] 4 p. TxU. 42863

---- ---- Joint committee on banks.
Report of the joint committee on banks. Saturday, Nov. 18, 1837. [Little Rock, 1837] 4 p. TxU. 42864

---- Governor (James S. Conway).
A proclamation, by the governor of the State of Arkansas. Printers, Woodruff & Pew, 1837. Broadside. DNA. 42865

---- Laws, Statutes, etc.
Acts passed at the first-- session of the general assembly of the state of Arkansas.--1836. Little Rock, 1837. Ar-SC; ArU; DLC; RPL; WaU. 42866

---- Real estate bank.
Report of the president of the real estate bank of the State of Arkansas. [n.p., 1837?] 8 p. TxU. 42867

---- Treasurer.
Report of the treasurer of the state of Arkansas. Little Rock. John H. Reed and John J. Budd, printers, 1837. 8 p. TxU. 42868

Armstrong, John, 1784-1829.
Lectures on the morbid anatomy,

nature, and treatment of acute
and chronic diseases; by the
late John Armstrong ... Edited
by Joseph Rix ... 1st American
ed.: with an account of the life
and writings of Dr. Armstrong,
by John Bell ... Philadelphia,
Desilver, Thomas & co., 1837.
2 v. Cst-L; DSG; PPA; ScSp;
TCh.   42869

Armstrong, Robert G.
   Memoir of Hannah Hobbie; or,
Christian activity, and triumph
in suffering. By Rev.
Robert G. Armstrong ... New-
York, American tract society
[1837?] [3]-255 p. CSmH;
IaGG; MHi; NeU; PWW.   42870

Arnold, George B.
   Mr. Arnold's seventh semi-
annual report of his service as
minister at large, in New York.
Published by the Book and tract
society of the First Congregational church, N.Y., 1837.
James Van Norden, printer,
1837. 34 p. MWA; WHi.   42871

Arnold, Seth S.
   The family choir: a selection
of hymns set to music, to which
a few plain psalms and hymn
tunes are appended: the whole
designed particularly as an assistant to family worship, and
intended to accompany "Family
hymns" published by the American Tract Society. Boston, Kidder and Wright, 1837. 35 p.
IEN; NNUT; NRU.   42872

Arnold, Thomas Kerchever,
1806-1853
   First Greek Lessons. By
Thomas Kerchever Arnold, M.A.
From The Third London Edition.
New York, D. Appleton & Co.,
Publishers, 1837. 232 p.
MNBedf   42873

Arnold, W. A.
   Arnold's patent yankee cooking stove. Northampton, 1837.
8 p. MWHi.   42874

Ash, Thomas T. Guide to the
lions of Philadelphia.... See
under title.

Aspden, Matthias.
   Letters and other Documents,
Produced in the Case of the
Succession of Matthias Aspden,
and Ordered to be Printed.
Philadelphia, (Privately printed),
1837. 316 p. MB; Nh-Hi; NN;
PHi; PP; PPL.   42875

Associate Reformed Synod of the
West. Ohio.
   Extracts from the Minutes of
the Proceedings of the Associate
Reformed Synod of the West
Held at Chillicothe, October 18th
1837, and continued by adjourn-
ment. Hamilton, Ohio, Printed
by I. M. Walters, 1837. (2),
36 p. ICP; NcMHi; NN; PPiXT.
                           42876
Association for the Benefit of
Colored Orphans, New York.
   First, 3d, 16th annual report,
1837, 1839, 1853. New York,
1837-53. 3 v. MBAt.   42877

Atkinson Academy. Atkinson,
N.H.
   Catalogue of the officers and
students of Atkinson academy,
Atkinson, N.H. for the term end-
ing August 16, 1837. Haverhill,
from the press of J. H. Harris
Gazette Office, 1837. 8 p. MHa.
                           42878
Atlantic Company of Baltimore.
   The charter of the Atlantic
company of Baltimore. Baltimore,
Printed by William Wooddy, 1837.
9 p. MdHi.   42879

Atlas of the United States Printed

for the Use of the Blind. at the
expense of John C. Cray; under
the direction of S. G. Howe. at
the N.E. Institution for the
Education of the Blind. Boston,
1837. NLan; ScC.   42880

Atwill, Winthrop.
The treason of Benedict Arn-
old, a lecture delivered before
a society of young men in
Northampton. By Winthrop
Atwill. Northampton, J. H.
Butler, 1837. 45 pp. CtY;
DLC; MH; OclWHi; WHi.   42881

Auburn and Rochester Railroad
Company.
... Report. See Higham,
Robert. CSmH   42882

Auburn & Syracuse Railroad
Company.
Report of a committee to the
board of directors; and of E. F.
Johnson, Esq. chief engineer of
the Auburn & Syracuse Railroad
Company. [Auburn? 1837.]
16 p. DBRE, DIC; DLC; NNE;
NRU.   42883

Auburn Theological Seminary.
Catalogue of the officers and
students of the Theological Seminary at Auburn, N.Y., January, 1837. Auburn, Oliphant &
Skinner, printers, 1837. 8 p.
MBC; MH; N; NAuHi.   42884

Auctor Incertus, pseud.
Characters and characteristics of Middlebury college; by
Auctor incertus. Middlebury,
1837. 22 p. RPB; VtHi; VtU.
                         42885
The Augsburgh confession with
explanatory notes.... See
Hartwick Synod of the Evangelical Lutheran Church in
the state of New York.

Augusta College. Augusta, Ky.
By-Laws and course of instruction established at Augusta College. Published by order of the
trustees. Cincinnati, R. P.
Thompson, 1837. 19 p. KyU.
                         42886
(Austin, James Trecothick) 1784-
1870.
Review of Dr. Channing's letter to Hon. Henry Clay ... Boston, N.D. Ticknor, 1837. 24 p.
MB; MH; NHi.   42886a

---- Speech delivered in Faneuil
Hall, December 8, 1837, at a
meeting of citizens called on the
petition of William E. Channing
and others. By James T. Austin,
Attorney General of Massachusetts.
Boston, John H. Eastburn, printer, 1837. 13 p. DLC; MB;
MHi; MnSM; MWA.   42887

Austin, Stephen Fuller, 1793-
1836.
Map of Texas with parts of
the adjoining states, compiled by
Stephen F. Austin. Philadelphia,
H. S. Tanner, 1837. TxU.
                         42888
---- Translation of the laws,
orders and contracts, on colonization, from January 1821, up
to 1829; in virtue of which, Col.
Stephen F. Austin introduced
and settled foreign emigrants
in Texas. With an explanatory
introduction. Columbia, Reprinted
by Borden & Moore, public printers, 1837. 81 p. CU; DLC;
NHi; NNLI; TxU.   42889

Auto-biography of Sam Simple,
giving an account of the administration of the affairs of the Simple
family, from the year 1829 to
1837, by his aunt, Deborah Crab-
stick....A political allegory.
Boston, 1837. 36 p. DLC; MB;
Me; MHi.   42890

Autumn leaves, a collection of miscellaneous poems, from various authors ... New York, John S. Taylor, 1837. 203 p. CtHT; KHi; MB; MBBC; RPB.
42891

Aydelott, B(enjamin) P(arham).
American education or The education we need; an address delivered at the close of the sessions of 1836-7, of the Woodward College, and Woodward high school. (Cincinnati, Kendall and Henry printers, 1837.) MH.
42892

---- Report on the study of the Bible in common schools; ... Cincinnati, Printed by N. S. Johnson, 1837. 7 p. CSmH; CtY; MWA; NjPT; OClWHi.
42893

B

B., N.
Manual of private prayer, or Closest devotions. Charleston, 1837. DLC.
42894

Bache, Alexander Dallas, 1806-1867.
... Observations to determine the magnetic dip at Baltimore, Philadelphia, New York, West Point, Providence, Springfield and Albany ... [Philadelphia, 1837] 209-215 p. DLC; PPULC; UU.
42895

Bachman, John, 1790-1874.
Sermon on the doctrines and discipline of the Evangelical Lutheran church, preached at Charleston, S.C. November 12th 1837. Charleston, Burges, 1837. 37 p. MBC; Mh-And; PPAmP; PPLT; ScCMu.
42896

Back, George, 1796-1878.

Narrative of the Artic land expedition to the mouth of the Great Fish River, and along the shores of the Arctic Ocean, in the years 1833, 1834 and 1835... By Captain Back ... Philadelphia, E. L. Carey & A. Hart, 1837. ICU; MdBJ; MH; MLy; ViU.
42897

---- ---- 2 ed. Philadelphia, E. C. Dorsey, printer, 1837. 456 p. CtMW; MWA; NUt; OCY; RPB.
42898

The backwoodsman.
Proposals for publishing at Grafton, Greene County, Illinois, the Backwoodsman, a weekly paper, devoted to political intelligence, the current news of the day, literature, agriculture, &c. &c. Edited by John Russell, of Bluffdale. [Alton? 1837.] Broadside. I.
42899

Bacon, Henry.
The Religious education of the young. A sermon by Henry Bacon. East Cambridge, 1837. 19, (1) p. MMeT-Hi.
42900

---- ... A Sermon by Henry Bacon ... East Cambridge, [Boston, J. N. Bangs, printer], 1837. 20 p. MMeT-Hi.
42901

Bacon, Leonard.
The duties connected with the present commercial distress. A sermon, preached in the Center church, New Haven, May 21, 1837, and repeated May 23. New Haven, Printed by Hitchcock & Stafford, 1837. 18 p. CoCsC; ICP; MB; NjR; ScU.
42902

Bacon, William Thompson, 1812-1881.
The influence of nature on the individual mind: poem before the senior class of Yale College,

New Haven, 1837. 30 p. MBC.
42903
---- A poem (The influence of
nature on the individual mind)
and the Valedictory oration by
Charles Andrew Johnson, pronounced before the senior class
of Yale college July 5, 1837.
New Haven, B. L. Hamlen, 1837.
42 p. CtB; IU; MH; PHi; RPB.
42904
---- Poems, by William Thompson
Bacon. Boston, Weeks, Jordan
& co., 1837. [13]-134 p. CSmH;
ICU; MeBat; NBuG; TxU. 42905

Badgley, Jonathan.
The principles of English
grammar in familiar lectures;
accompanied by amusing dialogues, ... By Jonathan Badgley. Whitesboro, Printed at the
office of the friend of man,
1837. 191, (1) p. DLC; NUt.
42906
Bagley, William.
The practice at the chambers
of the judges, of the courts of
common law, in civil actions.
... From the London edition.
Philadelphia, John S. Littell,
1837. 192 p. Cu-Law; KyLxT;
OO; PP; ViU-L. 42907

Bailey, Ebenezer.
First lessons in algebra,
being an easy introduction to
that science designed for the
use of academies and common
schools. By Ebenezer Bailey,
... Improved stereotype edition.
Boston, American stationers;
company, John B. Russell, 1837.
252 p. CSt; KyLo; MB; MH;
MShM. 42908

---- 23d ed. Boston, 1837.
MB. 42909

---- A Key to the First lessons
in algebra containing the answers

to the questions, with numerous
explanations and solutions. Boston, John B. Russell, 1837. MH.
42910
---- The young ladies' class
book; a selection of lessons for
reading in prose and verse. By
Ebenezer Bailey ... sixteenth
stereotype edition Boston, Gould,
Kendall, and Lincoln, 1837.
408 p. MNBedf; PPL. 42911

Bailey, Rufus William, 1793-1863.
The family preacher; or,
Domestic duties. Illustrated and
enforced in eight discourses by
Rev. Rufus William Bailey. New
York, John S. Taylor, 1837.
158, 24 p. CSansS; GDecCT;
MeBat; NcU; PPM. 42912

--- The issue, presented in a
series of letters on slavery. By
Rev. Rufus Wm. Bailey, of South
Carolina. New-York, J. S.
Taylor, 1837. 110 p. CSmH;
ICN; NUt; TxU; VtU. 42913

---- A mother's request answered
in letters of a father to his daughters. Philadelphia, Joseph
Wheatham, 1837. 270 p. GDecCt;
NjMD; TBriK; WvED. 42914

Baird, Robert, 1798-1863.
Memoir of Anna Jane Linnard,
by Rev. Robert Baird; with an
introduction by the Hon. Theodore Frelinghuysen, and a letter from the Rev. William Neill
....2d ed. Philadelphia, Henry
Perkins. n.pr., 1837. 231 p.
IEG; MB; NjR; MB; NjMD.
42915
Baker, Joseph S.
Calls to ministerial improvement: A sermon; delivered before the Baptist education society of Virginia, at its annual
meeting, June 3, 1837. Richmond, Wm. Sands, 1837. 14 p.

MBC; MNtCA; NjR; OClWHi;
ViRU.   42916

Baker, R. P.
Report of Major R. P. Baker,
engineer in chief of the Lake
Washington and Deer Creek
railroad on the subject of its
extension across the valley of
the Mississippi to the town of
Tchula. Published by order of
the board of directors. [N.p.]
1837. 23 p. NN; PPF.   42917

Baker, Samuel George.
University of Maryland ....
an introductory lecture, delivered before the medical class
of the university, ... by Samuel George Baker, M.D....
Baltimore, Printed by John D.
Toy, 1837. 32 p. DLC; DSG;
MB; MdHi; PPL; NNNAM.   42918

Baldwin, Elihu Whittlesey, 1789-
1840.
Address on the encourage-
ment of emulation in the education of youth, delivered before the
Education convention of Indiana.
By Elihu W. Baldwin ... December 27, 1837. Published by
order of the Senate. Indianapolis, Douglass & Noell, printers, 1837. 12 p. DLC; ICHi;
In; InU.   12919

---- A sermon at the dedication
of they Presbyterian church in
Madison street, New York, Aug.
27, 1837. New York, 1837.
20 p. MH-AH; NjR: PHi;
PPPrHi.   42920

Baldwin, Henry, 1780-1844.
A general view of the origin
and nature of the Constitution
and government of the United
States, deduced from the political history and condition of
the colonies and states, from

1774 until 1788. And the decisions of the Supreme court of
the United States. Together
with opinions in the cases decided at January term, 1837,
arising on the restraints on the
powers of the states. By Henry
Baldwin ... Philadelphia, Printed
by J. C. Clark, 1837. 197 p.
CtY; DLC; IaU; MdHi; PPM.
                          42921
---- Remonstrance against ...
abolishing or regulating tolls on
vessels passing through the lock
and canal at Baldwinville. ...
Albany, March 23, 1836. 31 p. N.
                          42922
Baldwin, Loammi, 1780-1838.
Report on the Brunswick canal
with rail road, Glynn County,
Georgia. With an appendix containing the character and com-
missioner's report. By Loammi
Baldwin ... Boston, J. H. East-
burn, printer, 1837. 48 p.
CSt; ICU; MBAt; MeU; NcD.
                          42923
Baldwin, Thomas.
Narrative of the massacre by
the Savages of (his) wife and
children, etc. By Thomas Bald-
win of Kentucky. New York,
Martin and Perry, 1837. DLC;
ICN; MBAt.   42924

Ball, Charles.
Slavery in the U.S. A narrative of the life and adventures
of Charles Ball. A black man,
who lived forty years in Maryland, South Carolina and Georgia, as a slave ... New York,
J. S. Taylor, 1837. 517 p.
GEU; IC; MH-And; MnHi; ViRVU.
                          42925
Ball, Edward. See Fitzball, Edward.

Ballou, Adin, 1803-1890.
A discourse on the subject of
American slavery, delivered in

the First Congregational meeting house, in Mendon, Mass.,
July 4, 1837. By Adin Ballou,
published by request of the
hearer. Boston, Printed by
Isaac Knapp, 1837. 88 p. MB;
MdBJ; MWA; NN-Sc; OO.   42926

---- The Touchstone, Exhibiting
Universalism and Restorationism
as they are, Moral Contraries.
By a consistent Restorationist.
Providence, Printed by B. Cran-
ston & Co., 1837. 32 p. MB;
MH; MnU; NCaS; RPB.   42927

Ballou, H. F.
   On Revivals and Protracted
Meetings. A sermon, delivered
in Whitingham, Vermont, on Sunday, Oct. 22, 1837. By H. F.
Ballou, pastor of the Universalist Societies in Whitingham and
Wilmington...Boston, Abel Tomkins...J. N. Bang, printer,
1837. 16 p. MMeT-Hi; PPL;
PPULC.   42928

---- A sermon, on religious ex-
citements and protracted meetings; elicited by a protracted
meeting attended by the author,
in Whitingham, Vt. Delivered
in Whitingham, on Sunday, Oct.
22, 1837. By H. F. Ballou,
Pastor of the Universalist Societies in Whitingham and Wilmington. Published by request. Boston, Abel Tompkins, J. N. Bang,
Printer, 1837. (3)-16 p. MiD-B.
   42929

Ballou, Hosea, 1771-1850.
   A Collection of psalms and
hymns for the use of Universal-
ist societies and families. By
Hosea Ballou, 2d. Boston,
Benjamin B. Mussey, 1837. (3),
29-538 p. IG; IGK; MB; MBUPH;
MMeT-Hi.   42930

Baltimore.

Report of the engineer appointed by the commissioners of
the mayor and city council of
Baltimore, on the subject of the
Maryland Canal. Baltimore,
Printed by Lucas & Deaver, 1837.
27 p. MdHi; NNE.   42931

---- Board of Trade.
   Memorial of the Board of trade
of the city of Baltimore, to the
Legislature of Maryland. Annapolis, Jeremiah Hughes, printer,
1837. 5 p. MdHi.   42932

---- Citizens.
   Proceedings of the Great
Meeting of the Friends of Civil
and Religious Liberty, held in
Baltimore, 1837. Baltimore,
Bull and Tuttle, 1837. DLC.
   42933
---- (Ecclesiastical Province)
Council.
   Pastoral letter of the most
reverend the Archbishop of
Baltimore, and the right rever-
end, The Bishops of the Roman
Catholic Church, in the United
States of America; assembled in
provincial council, in the city
of Baltimore, in the month of
April 1837, to the clergy and
laity of their charge. Baltimore,
Published by Fielding Lucas Jr.,
1837. 43 p. ICLay; M; MdBLC;
NNF.   42934

---- Ordinances.
   Journal of the proceedings
of the First Branch of the City
Council of Baltimore. January
session, 1837. Baltimore, printed
by Sands & Neilson, 1837. 4-
363 p. MdBB; MdHi.   42935

---- ---- The ordinances of the
Mayor and City Council of Baltimore, passed at the January session, 1837. To which is annexed Sundry Acts of Assembly

passed at December session,
1837; Baltimore, Printed by
Lucas & Deaver, 1837. 93,
134 p. MdBB; MdHi; MH-L;
MdLR.   42936

---- ---- Revised ordinances
for the City of Baltimore.
Baltimore, Printed by Lucas &
Deaver, 1837. 136 p. MdBLC.
                               42937
Baltimore & Susquehanna Railroad Company.
   Memorial of the president &
directors. Baltimore, 1835. 7
p. Phi.   42938

Balzac, Honore de.
   About Catharine de' Medice
and Gambara. With photo-
gravures. By Honore de Balzac. Boston, E. B. Hall and
Locke Co., 1837. (XIV), 391 p.
NJost.   42939

---- The lily of the valley and
the firm of Nucingen. With
photogravures. By Honore de
Balzac. Boston, E. B. Hall
and Locke Co., 1837. 359 p.
NJost.   42940

---- Modeste Mignon and other
stories. With photogravures.
By Honore de Balzac. Boston,
E. B. Hall and Locke Co.,
1837. (IV), 396 p. NJost.
                               42941
Bancroft, George, 1800-1891.
   History of the colonization
of the United States. By George
Bancroft ... Boston, Bowen,
1837-41. 3 v. V. 1, 2d ed.;
V. 3, 7th ed. pub. by Little.
CtHT.   42942

---- History of the United
States from the discovery of
the American continent....Bos-
ton, Little, Brown & Co.,
1837-74. 10 v. Mi; MnDu;

MWiW; NbOC; OT; TMeT.
                               42943
Bancroft, Mark.
   American tales. Philadelphia,
Atkinson, 1837. 304 p. PWcHi.
                               42944
Bangor, Maine. Classical Insti-
tute.
   Catalogue of the Classical In-
stitute, Bangor, Maine. 1836-
37. Bangor, 1837. 11 p.
IaGG; MeB.   42945

Bangor Journal of Literature.
   Bangor Journal of Literature,
Science, Morals, and Religion,
from June 1, 1837, to May 24,
1838. Ed. by Rev. Thomas
Curtis. Bangor, 1837-38. 4to.
                               42946
Bangor Medical Association.
   Constitution of the Bangor
medical association, together with
the rules and regulations of po-
lice (sic) and practice. Bangor,
S. S. Smith, 1837. 12 p.
CBPSR.   42947

Bangs, Nathan, 1778-1862.
   An original Church of Christ:
Or a scriptural Vindication of
the orders and powers of the
ministry of the Methodist Episcopal Church. New York, New
York, T. Mason and G. Lane,
1837. 388 p. CtY; MoS; ODaB;
TNP; WHi.   42948

---- ---- 2d ed. rev. New York,
Mason, 1837. 388 p. CJ; CtMW;
GDecCT; NjMD; TxU; WaPs; IRA.
                               42949
[Banin John] 1799-1842.
   Damon and Pythias; or, the
test of friendship, a play. Phila-
delphia, Frederick Turner, (1837).
58 p. MB; RPB.   42950

Bank convention. New York,
1837.
   List of delegates, to the bank

convention, New York, November 27, 1837. [New York, 1837?] 2 p. TxU.   42951

---- Minutes of the proceedings of the Bank Convention, held in the city of New York, on the twenty-seventh of November, 1837. New York, Bowen & co., [1837]. 24 p. CtY; ICJ; MH; PU; RNR.   42952

---- Report of the delegates of the banks of the City of New-York, to the bank convention, held at New York, on 27th November to 1st December, 1837. Published by order of the General committee of the city banks. New York, A. DeCamp & co., 1837. 14 p. ICU; MB; MH; MiU-C; NNC; TxU.   42953

Bank of Kentucky.
Charter of the Bank of Kentucky, Louisville, Ky., Shadrach Penn, Jr., 1837. 34 p. KyBgW; NjP.   42954

Bank of New Jersey, Newark.
Charter of the Bank of New Jersey, passed in council .... 1837.... Newark, N.J., Guest, 1837. 12 p. MH-BA; NjP.   42955

Bank of Tennessee.
Charter of the State bank of Tennessee. Passed January 19th, 1838. Nashville, S. Nye and company, printers, 1837. 27 p. NNC; THi.   42956

Bank of the state of Arkansaw. Branch, Arkansas Post.
Charter of the Branch Bank of the State of Arkansas, at Arkansas Post. Passed December 15, 1837. [Little Rock, 1837.] 4 p. TxU.   42957

Banks, Ephraim.

Speech of Ephraim Banks, esq., of Mifflin, delivered in the Convention, to amend the constitution of Pennsylvania, December 22, 1837. In support of an amendment to prohibit banks from issuing notes of a less denomination than ten dollars, as offered by Mr. Read of Susquehanna. Philadelphia, Printed by J. Wilbank, 1837. 15 p. DLC; MWA; NjR; P; PPi.   42958

Bannister, Nathaniel Harrington, 1813-1847.
England's iron days. A tragedy, in five acts; by Nathaniel Harrington Bannister ... New Orleans, W. McKean & co., 1837. 57 p. DLC; ICU; MH; PU; WM.   42959

Baptists. Alabama. Union Association.
Minutes of the second session of the Union Association, convened at Big Creek meeting house, Pickens county, Alabama. From 22d to 26th September, 1837. Tuscaloosa, printed by Ferguson & Eaton, at the office of the "Flag of the Union," 1837. 8 p. NHC-S.   42960

---- Connecticut.
... Infant church membership vindicated and explained. By a committee of the Black River Association. D. Watertown, 1837. CBPSR; Ct; N; NjPT.   42961

---- ---- New London Association.
Minutes of the twentieth anniversary of the New London Baptist Association, held with the Baptist Church in Chester, September 27th and 28th, 1837. New London, Ebenezer Williams, Printer, [1837.] 14 p. NHC-S; PCA.   42962

---- ---- Stonington Union Association.

The minutes of the twentieth anniversary of the Stonington Union Association, held at Sterling Conn. June 21st and 22nd, A.D. 1837. Norwich, Printed by M. B. Young, 1837. 8 p. NHC-S; PCA; RWe. 42963

---- Georgia. Georgia Association.

Minutes of the Georgia Baptist association, held at Newford, Wilkes County, Ga., on the 6th, 7th, and 9th of October, 1837. Washington, Ga., Printed at the Christian Index office, 1837. 16 p. NHC-S.
42964

---- Iowa. Coffee Creek Association.

Minutes of the eleventh annual meeting of the Coffee Creek association of Baptists; begun and held at Elizabeth Meeting house, Clark county, Ia. on the second, third, and fourth days of September, 1837. Printed at the Vernon Visitor office, [1837?] 6 p. TxDaHi.
42965

---- Illinois. Blue River Association.

Minutes of the fourth annual meeting of the Blue River Association of United Baptists, held with the Pleasant Vale Church, Pike County, Illinois, August 25th and days following, 1837. Upper Alton, Printed at the Pioneer office, 1837. 4 p. ISB; NRCR-S. 42966

---- ---- Illinois River Association.

Minutes, second annual meeting ... at the courthouse, Peoria, Oct. 6, 1837. Upper Alton, Pioneer Office, 1837. 7 p. ISB.
42967

---- ---- North District Association.

Minutes of the sixth annual meeting of the North District Baptist Association, Friends of Humanity; held with the Island Grove Church, Sangamon County, Illinois, September 8th, 9th and 10th, 1837. Upper Alton, Printed at the Pioneer office, 1837. 8 p. ISB; NRCR-S. 42968

---- ---- Salem Association.

Minutes of the Fourth Annual Meeting of the Salem Association of United Baptists, held with the Newhope Church, McDonough County, Illinois, September 1st and days following, 1837. Upper Alton, Printed at the Pioneer office, 1837. 7 p. ISB; PCA.
42969

---- Kentucky. Bethel Association.

Minutes of the thirteenth Bethel Baptist Association, held at Mt. Zoin, Todd county, Kentucky, on the 23d, 24th, and 25th days of Sept., 1837. Saturday an introductory sermon was delivered by Robert Anderson, from Titus, 2nd chap. 11--14, "For the grace of God that bringeth salvation both appeared to all men....: Russellville, Printed by W. Green Pillow, 1837. 8 p. LNB. 42970

---- ---- General association.

Minutes of the General association of Baptists in Kentucky which met for organization in Louisville, on Friday October 20, 1837... introductory sermon by elder Wm. Vaughan. Louisville, 1837. 19 p. MB; MHi; LNB; KyLoS; TxU; ViRU. 42971

---- Maine. Bowdoinham Association.

Minutes of the fifty-first anniversary of the Bowdoinham Association, holden at Greene, Wednesday and Thursday. Sept.

27th & 28th, 1837. Hallowell,
William Noyes, Printer, [1837.]
8 p. PCA.   42972

---- ---- Hancock Association.
Minutes of the third anniver-
sary of the Hancock Baptist
Association, held in the Baptist
Meeting-House in Sedgwick, on
Tuesday and Wednesday, Sep-
tember 26th and 27th, 1837.
Ellsworth, Joseph H. Jordan....
Printer, 1837. 16 p. PCA.
                             42973
---- ---- Penobscot Association.
Twelfth anniversary. Min-
utes of the Penobscot Baptist
Association, held in the First
Baptist Meeting House, Hamp-
den, Wednesday and Thursday,
Sept. 20 & 21, 1837. Belfast,
F. P. Ingalls....Printer, 1837.
17 p. PCA.   42974

---- ---- Convention
[Thirteenth anniversary.]
Minutes of the Maine Baptist
Convention, holden in Bath,
October 4th and 5th, 1837.
Portland, Charles Day and Co.,
Printers, 1837. 16 p. PCA.
                             42975
---- ---- Cumberland Associa-
tion.
Minutes of the twenty-sixth
anniversary of the Cumberland
Baptist Association, held at the
Meeting House of the Baptist
Church in New-Gloucester, Me.,
on Tuesday and Wednesday
August 29 & 30, 1837. Port-
land, Printed by Charles Day
& Co., 1837. 15 p. MeHi;
PCA.   42976

---- ---- Kennebec Association.
Minutes of the eighth anniversary of the Kennebec Baptist Association, held at the
Baptist Meeting House in Waterville, September 6 and 7, 1837.

With a summary view of the
Churches. Portland, Charles
Day and Co., Printers, 1837.
16 p. PCA.   42977

---- ---- Washington Association.
Minutes of the third anniversary of the Washington Baptist Association, held in the Baptist Meeting-House in Calais, on
Thursday and Friday, September
28th and 29th, 1837. Ellsworth,
Me., Joseph H. Jordan....Print-
er, 1837. 16 p. PCA.   42978

---- ---- Waldo Association.
Minutes of the ninth anniversary of the Waldo Baptist
Association, held in the Baptist
Meeting-House in Hope, Thursday and Friday, Sept. 14th and
15th, 1837. Belfast, Maine,
F. P. Ingalls....Printer, 1837.
12 p. PCA.   42979

---- Maryland. Baptist union
association.
Minutes of the ... annual
meeting ... Baltimore, Ptd. by
J. W. Woods, 1837. 13 p.
MiD-B; PCA; ViRU.   42980

---- ---- Baltimore Association.
Minutes of the Baltimore Baptist Association, held by appointment with the Harford Baptist
Church, Harford County, Md.,
May 18, 19 and 20, 1837. Alexandria, Gilbert Beebe, Printer,
1837. 12 p. PCA; PHi. 42981

---- Massachusetts. Barn-
stable Baptist Association.
6th anniversary. ... Yarmouth,
(Mass.) Garmouth register, 1837.
16 p. DLC.   42982

---- ---- Boston association.
Minutes...meeting at Charleston. Boston, Gould, Kendall &

Lincoln, 1837.   27 p.   MiD-B.
42983
---- ---- Convention.
Annual report of the Massachusetts Baptist Convention, presented by the Board of Directors, at their thirty-fifth anniversary in Boston, June 1, A.D. 1837. Boston, Press of J. Howe, 1837. 52 p. PCA.
42984
---- ---- Franklin County Association.
Minutes of the Franklin County Baptist Association, held at the Baptist Meeting House in Conway, Mass., September 13 and 14, 1837. Seventh anniversary. Greenfield, Mass., Printed by Phelps and Ingersoll, 1837. 12 p. NRC-R; PCA.
42985

---- - -- Millers River, formerly Wendell Association.
Minutes of the thirteenth anniversary of the Wendell Baptist Association, held with the Baptist Church in Athol, Massachusetts, September 27 & 28, 1837. Amherst, J. S. & C. Adams, Printers, 1837. 15, [1] p. PCA.
42986

---- ---- Old Colony Ass'n.
Fifteenth anniversary. Minutes of the Old Colony Baptist Association, held with the Central Baptist Church in Middleboro, Wednesday and Thursday, Oct., 4th and 5th, 1837. Boston, Press of John Putnam, 1837. 16 p. MNtcA; PCA.
42987
---- ---- Salem Association.
Minutes of the tenth anniversary of the Salem Baptist Association and the twenty-fifth anniversary of the Salem Bible Translation and Foreign Mission Society: held in...

Methuen,...September 27 and 28, A.D. 1837. Lowell, Leonard Huntress, printer, 1837. 18 p. MBevHi; PCA.
42988

---- ---- Sturbridge Association.
Minutes of the Sturbridge Association held in various towns. 1837-1854. Worcester, Printed by Henry J. Howland, 1837-1854. MNtcA; PCA.
42989

---- ---- Taunton Association.
Minutes of the Taunton Baptist Association, held at the Baptist Meeting-House in Taunton, on Wednesday and Thursday, Oct. 19 and 20, 1836. New-Bedford, printed by J. C. Parmenter, 1837. 8 p. MNBedF.
42990

---- Michigan. Lagrange Association.
Minutes of the fourth anniversary of the Lagrange Baptist Association, held at the meeting-house in Whitmanville, Michigan, on the nineteenth and twentieth of October, 1836. Kalamazoo, H. Gilbert, printer, 1837. 18 p. NHC-S; PCA.
42991

---- ---- ---- Minutes of the fifth anniversary of the Lagrange Baptist Association, held in Comstock, on Wednesday and Thursday June 21st and 22d, 1837. 8 p. NHC-S; PCA; PCC.
42992
---- ---- State Convention.
Report of the proceedings of the Baptist convention of the State of Michigan, held at Saline, September 6 & 7, 1837. Together with the list of officers for the ensuing year, and their address to the churches. Ann Arbor, Printed at the Journal Office, 1837. 16 p. PCA; PCC.
42993

---- Mississippi. Mississippi

association.

Minutes of the Mississippi
Baptist association ... 1837.
Natchez [Miss.] Printed at the
Free trader office, 1837. 1 v.
CSmH; LNB; NHC-S.   42994

---- ---- Convention.

Proceedings of a meeting to
consider the propriety of forming
a Baptist State Convention, held
in the Baptist Meeting House,
at Washington, Mississippi, 23d
and 24th December, 1836.
Natchez, Printed by Stanton &
Besancon, 1837. 16 p. NHC-S.
42995

--- --- --- Proceedings of the
first annual meeting of the convention of the Baptist denomination of the State of Mississippi,
held at Palestine, Hinds County,
Miss., on the 5th and 6th days
of May, 1837. Natchez, Printed
at the Free Trader Office, 1837.
28 p. MoSM; NHC-S; NN.
42996

---- ---- Mississippi association.

Minutes of the Mississippi
Baptist association ... 1837.
Natchez [Miss.] Printed at the
Free trader office, 1837. 1 v.
CSmH; LNB; NHC-S.   42997

---- ---- Pearl River Association.

Minutes of the eighteenth
anniversary session of the Pearl
River Baptist Association, convened at Ebenezer church,
Covington county, Miss., on
the 9th, 10th, and 11th days
of Sept. Monticello, Printed
by Cohea and Cameron, 1837.
13 p. LNB.   42998

---- Missouri. District Association of Baptized Churches.

Minutes of the ninth annual
meeting of the Missouri District

Association of Baptized Churches,
Friends to Humanity, held with
Sugar-Creek Church, Jefferson
County, Mo., August 12th, and
days following, 1837. 4 p. PCA.
42999

---- ---- Salem Association.

Minutes of the Salem Association, held at the Rocky Fork
church, Boone county, Mo. on
the 2d and 3d day of September.
1837. [n.p., n.d.] 3 p. MoHi.
43000

---- New Hampshire. State Convention.

Proceedings of the New Hamp-
shire Baptist State Convention,
New Hampshire branch of the
N.B. Education Society. New
Hampshire Baptist S.S. Union,
New Hampshire Foreign Bible
Society, and the New Hampshire
branch of the Baptist General
Tract Society at their annual
meetings at East Sanbornton,
October 24, 25, & 26, 1837.
Concord, Charles Young, Printer,
1837. 54 p. PCA.   43001

---- New Jersey. State Convention.

Minutes of the eighth annual
meeting of the New Jersey Baptist State Convention for missionary purposes, held at the meeting house of the Burlington Baptist Church, November 1 & 2,
1837. Trenton, Printed by Phillips and Boswell, 1837. 16 p.
PCA.   43002

---- New York. Berkshire County
Association.

Tenth anniversary. Minutes
of the tenth anniversary of the
Berkshire County Baptist Asso-
ciation, and the first anniver-
sary of the Berkshire County
Baptist Bible Society, held in the
Baptist Meeting-House in Otis, on
Wednesday and Thursday, Oct.

11, and 12, 1837. Troy, N.Y.,
Printed at Budget Office, 1837.
18 p. PCA.   43003

---- ---- Black River Association.
    Black River Association, In-
fant Church Membership Vindicated and explained. Watertown?, Pr. by Knowlton & Rice,
1837. 24 p. NcWfC.   43004

---- ---- Broome & Tioga Association.
    Minutes of the fourteenth an-
niversary of the Broome & Tioga
Baptist Association, held with
the 2d Church in Spencer, N.Y.,
June 14th & 15th, 1837. Utica,
Printed by Bennett & Bright,
1837. 16 p. NRC-R.   43005

---- ---- Canisteo River Association.
    Minutes of the Second Anni-
versary of the Canisteo River
Baptist Association, held at
Woodhull on the 13th and 14th
days of September, 1837; together with their Circular Letter. Bath, Printed by Charles
Adams, 1837. 12 p. PCA.
                              43006

---- ---- Cattaraugus Ass.
    Proceedings of the Cattarau-
gus Association at their First
Anniversary held at Franklinville
on the Twenty-second and twenty-
third of June, 1836 Rochester,
N.Y. Printed by William Alling
& Co., Sign of the Bible, Exchange St., 1837. 12 p.
NHC-S.   43007

---- ---- Cayuga Baptist Association.
    Minutes of the thirty-seventh
anniversary of the Cayuga Baptist Association. Convened at
Port Byron, Cayuga County,
N.Y. September 21-22, 1837.

Auburn, Printed by Allen &
Lounsbury, 1837. 15 p. NHC-S.
                              43008
---- ---- Central Association.
    Minutes of the Seventh-Day
Baptist Central Association, held
at Brookfield, Madison Co., N.Y.
June 7, 1837. DeRuyter, Printed
by J. & C. H. Maxson, 1837.
16, 9 p. NAlf.   43009

---- ---- Convention.
    Proceedings of the Sixteenth
Anniversary of the Baptist Mis-
sionary Convention of the State
of New York, held at Rochester,
Oct. 18 & 19, 1837; with the
Report of the Board, Treasurer's
Report, Address to the Churches,
Constitution, List of Life Members,
&c, &c. Utica, Printed by Ben-
nett & Bright, 1837. 60 p.
PCA.   43010

---- ---- Education Society.
    Twentieth annual meeting of
the Baptist Education Society of
the state of New York; with the
reports of the board, treasurer,
accountant, agent, &c. Utica,
press of Bennett & Bright, 1837.
28 p. DLC; ICU; MWA; NRC-R.
                              43011
---- ---- Franklin Association.
    Minutes of the Twenty-sixth
Anniversary of the Franklin Baptist Association, held at Franklin, Delaware County, N.Y.
June 28 and 29, 1837. Delhi,
Printed by Paine & Clark, 1837.
22 p. PCA.   43012

---- ---- General Conference.
    Minutes of the Seventh-Day
Baptist General Conference, held
at Berlin, Renselaer Co., N.Y.
September 1837. together with
the Minutes of the Missionary,
Pract, & Education Societies,
whose annual sessions were held
at the same time and place. De-

Ruyter, Printed by J. & C. H. Maxson, 1837. 22 p. NAlf.

43013

---- ---- Genesee Association.

Minutes of the Ninteenth Anniversary of the Genesee Baptist Association, held at La Grange, Genesee Co., June 5 & 6, 1837. Perry, Printed by Mitchell & Lewis, American Citizen Office, 1837. 16 p. PCA.

43014

---- ---- Holland Purchase Association.

Minutes of the Twenty-second Anniversary of the Holland Purchase Baptist Association; held with the Baptist Church, in Hamburgh, Erie County, N.Y. On the 23d and 24th of August, 1837. Buffalo, Press of Salisbury, Manchester & Co., 1837. 16 p. NHC; PCA; NBu.

43015

---- ---- Hudson River Association.

The Twenty-second Anniversary of the Hudson River Baptist Association - statement of belief - held in the Meeting House of the Mount Pleasant Baptist Church, N.Y., June 20, 21, & 22, 1837. New York, Printed by John Gray, 1837. 24 p. PCA.

43016

---- ---- Livingston Association.

Minutes of the Sixth Anniversary of the Livingston Baptist Association, held with the Church in Livonia on the Twenty-eighth and twenty-ninth of June, 1837. Rochester, N.Y., Printed by William Alling, 1837. 10 p. NHC-S; PCA.

43017

---- ---- Missionary Convention.

Proceedings of the sixteenth anniversary of the Baptist Missionary Convention of the state of New York, held at Rochester, Oct. 18, & 19, 1837; with the report of the board, treasurer's report, address to the churches, constitution, list of life members, &c, &c. Utica, Printed by Bennett & Bright, 1837. 60 p. N; PCA.

43018

---- ---- Monroe Association.

Tenth Annual Publication. 1837. Minutes of the Tenth Anniversary of the Monroe Baptist Association - statement of belief - held at the Baptist Meeting House, in Sweden, Oct. 3 and 4, 1837. Rochester, Printed by Shepard Strong & Dawson, 1837. 16 p. NRCR; PCA.

43019

---- ---- New-York Association.

Minutes of the Forty-Seventh Anniversary of the New-York Baptist Association, held at the Meeting-House of the M'Dougal-Street Baptist Church, in New-York, on Tuesday, Wednesday and Thursday, May 30, 31, and June 1, 1837. New-York, Printed by Henry Ludwig, 1837. 32 p. PCA.

43020

---- ---- Niagra Association.

Reprint of the Minutes of the Fourteenth Anniversary of the Niagra Baptist Association, held at the Baptist Meeting House in Hartland, June 14th and 15th, 1837. Albion, Printed originally by Timothy C. Strong, 1837. 12 p. PCA.

43021

---- ---- Ontario Association.

Minutes of the Twenty-Fourth Anniversary of the Ontario Association, held with the Church in Canandaigua Village, Ontario Co., N.Y. September 28th and 29th, 1837. Canandaigua, Printed by David C. M. Rupp, 1837. 12 p. NHC-S; NRCR; PCA.

43022

---- ---- Oswego Association.

Proceedings of the fifth anniversary of the Oswego Baptist association, held in the meeting-house of the Oswego Baptist church, N.Y. Wednesday and Thursday, June 21 & 22, 1837. Utica, printed by Bennett & Bright, 1837. 16 p. NRCR.   43023

---- ---- Otsego Association.

Minutes of the forty-second annual meeting of the Otsego Baptist Association, held at Litchfield, Herkimer Co., N.Y., on Wednesday and Thursday, August 30 & 31, 1837. Utica, Printed by Bennett & Bright, 1837. 16 p. NHC-S; NRCR; PCA.   43024

---- ---- Seneca Baptist Association.

Minutes of the fifteenth Annual Session ... held at Mecklenburgh, with the Second Church in Hector, Tompkins Co. On Wednesday and Thursday the seventh and eighth days of June, 1837. Periodical: ... A copy of your minutes is requested. Ithaca, Printed ay [sic] Mack, Andrus, & Woodruff, 1837. 12 p. CSmH.
                                43025

---- ---- Stephentown Association.

The Sixth Anniversary of the Stephentown Baptist Association, held in the Meeting House of the Baptist Church in Berlin, N.Y., September 13 & 14, 1837. Kinderhock, Printed at the Office of the Kinderhock Sentinel, 1837. 14 p. PCA.   43026

---- ---- Worcester Association.

Minutes of the Seventh Anniversary of the Worcester Baptist Association, held at the Baptist Meeting House, in Leesville, Schoharie Co. N.Y. September 27th & 28th, 1837. Cooperstown, Printed by Holroyd and Barber, 1837. 12 p. NRCR; PCA.   43027

---- North Carolina. Convention.

Proceedings of the sixth annual meeting of the Baptist State Convention of North Carolina, held at County Line M.H., Caswell County, November 11-15, 1836. Newborn, Printed at the Recorder Office, 1837. 35 p. PCA.   43028

---- ---- Liberty Association.

Proceedings of the fifth annual meeting of the Liberty Association, held at Lick Creek Meeting House, Davidson County, N.C., on the 12th and 14th days of August, 1837. Salem, Printed by Blum & Son, 1837. 8 p. PCA.   43029

---- ---- Raleigh Bap't Ass'n.

Minutes of the Raleigh Baptist Association held at Liberty meeting....house Wake County, North Carolina on Sat. the first Lord's Day in Oct. 1836, and the days following. Raleigh, Gales, 1837. 22 p. NcU; PCA.   43030

---- Ohio. Bloomfield Ass'n.

Minutes ... 1st anniversary ... Bloomfield, Saturday preceding the second Sunday in August [Aug. 12], 1837. Danville, Loveless & Delay, 1837. 7 p. ISB.
                                43031

---- ---- Columbus Regular Association.

Minutes of the Nineteenth Anniversary of the Columbus Regular Baptist Association, Held with the Berlin Church, Delaware

County, Ohio, September 2 &
4, 1837. Columbus, O.,
Printed by Cutler & Pillsbury,
1837. 8 p. PCA.   43032

---- ---- Convention.
Proceedings of the Tenth Annual Meeting, Held at Granville,
May 21-24, 1836. Caption title.
Cincinnati, Printed by N. S.
Johnson, 1837. 10 p. PCA.
43033
---- ---- ---- Proceedings of
the Eleventh Anniversary, held
at Marietta, May 27th-30, 1837.
Caption title. Cincinnati, Printed
by N. S. Johnson, 1837. 14 p.
PCA.   43034

---- ---- Geanga Baptist Assn.
Minutes of the Third Session
of the Geanga Baptist Association, Held with the Baptist
Church In Chardon, Geanga
County, Ohio, on Wednesday and
Thursday, June 14th and 15th,
1837. Painesville, 1837. 12 p.
OClWHi.   43035

---- ---- Huron Association.
Minutes of the Sixteenth Anniversary of the Huron Baptist
Association, Held at Fairfield,
Huron County, Ohio, August
30 & 31, 1837. Norwalk, Ohio,
Printed by S & C. A. Preston,
1837. 16 p. OClWHi; PCA.
43036
---- ---- Mad river association.
Minutes of the Twenty-fifth
Anniversary of the Mad River
Baptist Association, held with
the Kings Creek Church, September 15, 16, 17 & 18, 1837.
Troy, Ohio, John T. Tullis,
Printer, 1837. 14 p. CSmH;
PCA.   43037

---- ---- Maumee River Baptist
Ass'n.
Minutes of the third anniver-

sary of the Sandusky river baptist Association; held at Seneca,
Seneca County, Ohio, Sept. 15th
and 16th, 1837. 10 p. OClWHi.
43038
---- ---- Miami Association.
Minutes of the Miami Baptist
Association. Held at Tapscott
Meeting House, Warren County,
Ohio, on the eighth, ninth and
tenth of September, 1837. Rossville, Ohio, Printed by Franklin
Stokes, 1837. 8 p. OClWHi; PCA.
43039
---- ---- Portage association.
No. 5. Periodical. Minutes
of the Portage Baptist association.
Streetsborough, Sept. 27th &
28th, 1837. James Lowry, printer. Cuyahoga Falls, Ohio. [3],
4-14, [2] p. OClWHi.   43040

---- ---- Rocky River Baptist
Ass'n.
...The minutes of the sixth
anniversary of the Rocky River
Baptist association, held at Cleveland, Ohio, June 21 and 22,
1837, with their circular and
corresponding letters. Wednesday, June 21. Rocky River
Baptist Association, 1837. Cleveland, Penniman and Bemis, 1837.
16 p. OClWHi.   43041

---- ---- Salem Baptist Ass'n.
Minutes of the Salem Baptist
Association, held at Graham Station, Meigs county, Ohio, on
the 23rd, 24th and 25th Days of
September, 1837. Athens, Ohio,
Printed by Ayan Vorhes, 1837.
7 p. OClWHi.   43042

---- ---- Scioto Association.
Minutes of the Scioto Association; held at Jonathan's creek
church, Licking county, O. August 19th, 20th and 21st, 1837.
Lancaster, Printed by J. & C. H.
Brough, 1837. 7 p. OClWHi.
43043

No entry   43044

---- ---- Scioto Predestinarian
Baptist.
Minutes of the Scioto Baptist
Association; held at Jonathan's
Creek Church, Licking County,
O. August 19th, 20th and 21st,
1837. Lancaster, Printed by
J. & C. H. Brough, 1837. 7 p.
OClWHi.   43045

---- Pennsylvania. Baptist mis-
sionary association.
Minutes of the annual Bap-
tist Missionary assn. of Penn.
With the annual reports of the
Board of Mgrs. and the Consti-
tution of the Soc. Phila., T. W.
Ustick, 1833-35, 36. Phila.,
C. Sherman, 1837. C.   43046

---- ---- Central Union Assn.
Minutes of the fifth annual
session of the Central Union
Association of Independent Bap-
tist Churches, held in the
meeting house of the First Bap-
tist Church of Philadelphia,
May 30 and 31st, 1837. Phila-
delphia, Joseph & William Kite,
Printed, 1837. 16 p. PCA.
                                  43047
---- ---- Centre Association.
Minutes of the Centre Baptist
Association, at their seventh annual meeting, held in the meeting of the Cambria and Clearfield
Church, Clearfield County,
Penna. August 25th and 26th,
1837. Bellefonte, Penna.,
Printed by Wm. A. Kinslow,
1837. 8 p. PCA; PScrHi.
                                  43048
---- ---- Convention
Minutes of the convention
of delegates of Baptist associa-
tions in Pennsylvania, for the
formation of a state conven-
tion for domestic missions....
Together with an appendix con-

taining the tenth annual report
of the Baptist missionary association of Pennsylvania. Philadelphia, C. Sherman & co.,
printers, 1837-. 24 p. MiD-B;
PBcrHi.   43049

---- ---- Monongahela Associa-
tion.
Minutes of the fifth anniver-
sary of the Monongahela Baptist
Association, held with the George
Creek Church, at Smithfield,
Fayette County, Pennsylvania,
May 26th, 27th, and 28th, A.D.
1837. Pittsburgh, Printed by
Alexander Jaynes, Irwin's Row,
1837. 8 p. PCA.   43050

---- ---- Philadelphia Association.
Minutes of the 130th anniversary of the Philadelphia Baptist Association, held by appointment in the meeting house of the
Third Baptist church, Philadelphia, October 3, 1837. Philadelphia, Baptist General Tract.
Depository, 1837. 28 p. PHi;
PPL; PCA.   43051

---- ---- Philadelphia Female
Bible Association.
First annual report of the
Baptist Female Bible Association
of Philadelphia. Philadelphia,
Rackliff & Jones, Printers, 1837.
11, [1] p. PCA.   43052

---- Rhode Island. Convention.
Report of the Baptist Conven-
tion of Rhode Island and vicinity,
presented at the annual meeting
in Pawtucket, on Wednesday,
April 12, 1837. Providence,
H. H., Brown, 1837. 19 p.
PCA.   43053

---- ---- Warren Assn.
Seventieth anniversary. Minutes of the Warren Baptist Asso-

ciation, held at the First Baptist
Meeting-House, in Pawtucket, on
Wednesday and Thursday, September 13 and 14, 1837. Providence, H. H. Brown, 1837.
16 p. PCA; RHi.   43054

---- Tennessee. Concord Association.
    Minutes of the Concord Bap-
tist Association, held at Bradley's Creek M. H. Rutherford
County, Tenn., September 2,
3 & 4, 1837. [Nashville, J. C.
Carpenter & co, printers, 1837.]
4 p. NHC-S.   43055

---- ---- Hiwassee Association.
    Minutes of the fourteenth
annual session of the Hiwassee
Association of the United Baptist.
Began and held at Pisgah meeting house, Meigs County, E.
Tennessee, the Friday before
the fourth Saturday in September, 1837. [Madisonville, Johnstown & Edwards, 1837.] 4 p.
NHC-S.   43056

---- ---- West Tennessee State
Convention.
    Minutes of the third annual
meeting of the Baptist State Convention for West Tennessee, and
of the second annual meeting of
the West Tennessee Baptist Education Society, held at Paris,
Henry County, Tenn., on the
4th, 5th, 6th and 7th of August, A.D. 1837. Carpenter
& Co. Printers, Nashville, Tenn.,
1837. 32 p. NHC-S.   43057

---- Vermont. Addison County
Association.
    Minutes of the Addison Co.
Baptist Association, held at
the Baptist Meeting-House in
Addison, on Wednesday and
Thursday, September 27 and
28, 1837. Brandon, Vt., Ver-

mont Telegraph Press, 1837. 6,
[2] p. PCA.   43058

---- ---- Vermont Association.
    Minutes of the fifty-second
anniversary of the Vermont Baptist Association, held at the
Baptist Meeting House in Ira, on
Wednesday and Thursday, October 4th. and 5th., 1837. Brandon, Vermont Telegraph Press,
1837. 7 [1] p. MNtCA; PCA;
MNtCA.   43059

---- ---- Woodstock Association.
    Woodstock Baptist Association,
Minutes of the (Fifty-Third An-
niversary) at their Meeting in
Rockingham, Sept. 27 & 28; 1837;
together with the Doings of the
Young Men's Education Society,
at their First Anniversary.
Windsor, Vt., Printed at the
Chronicle Press, (1837). 8 v.
16 p. XE.   43060

---- Virginia. Dover Association.
    Minutes of the Dover Baptist
Association, convened at Matthews
Church, Matthews County, Vir-
ginia, on Saturday, Sunday, and
Monday, October 7-9, 1837, Rich-
mond, printed by Wm. Sands, at
the Herald office, 1837. 16 p.
ViRU.   43061

---- Virginia Goshen Association.
    Minutes of The Goshen Baptist
Association, Held at Mount Gilead
M.H., Goochland County, Vir-
ginia, Commencing on the 9th of
September, 1837. Richmond,
Printed By Wm. Sands, at The
Herald Office, 1837. [3]-11 p.
ViRu.   43062

---- Virginia Shiloh Baptist Association.
    Twenty-Fifth Annual Minutes
of the Shiloh Baptist Association,
Held at Mount Salem Meeting-

House, Rappahannock County,
Virginia. September 2nd, and
4th, 1837. Fredericksburg,
Arena Printing Office, 1837.
[11]-16 p. ViRu.   43063

Baraga, Friedrich, 1797-1868.
   Abinedjiiag omasinaiganiwan.
Buffalo, Press of Oliver G.
Steele, 1837. 8 p. MBAt.
                                43064
Barbauld, Anna Letitia (Aiken)
1743-1825.
   Hymns in prose; for little
children. By Mrs. Barbauld.
New Haven, S. Babcock, 1837.
16 p. CtY; PP; PPULC.   43065

---- Lessons for children. By
Mrs. (Anna Letitia) Barbauld;
with engravings and four original tales. Newark, N.J., Benjamin Olds, 1837. 180 p. NjR.
                                43066
Barber, John Warner, 1798-1885.
   Connecticut historical collections, containing a general collection of interesting facts,
traditions, biographical sketches,
anecdotes, etc., relating to
the history and antiquities of
every town in Connecticut with
geographical descriptions. Illustrated by 190 engravings.
By John Warner Barber. 2d
ed. New Haven, Durrie &
Peck and J. W. Barber, 1837.
viii, [9]-560 p., map. CU;
DLC; MB; PPL; ViU.   43067

---- Elements of general history: being a collection of
facts relating to the history of
man, empires, states & king-
doms, from the earliest period
to the present time for the use
of schools. New Haven, Durrie
& Peck, 1837. 288 p. Ct;
OClW.   43068

Barbour, Oliver Lorenzo, 1811-
1889.

   An analytical digest of the
equity cases decided in the
courts of the several states, and
of the United States, from the
earliest period and of the decisions in equity, in the courts of
chancery and exchequer,...
down to 1836. By O. L. Barbour, and E. B. Harrington. In
three volumes.... Springfield,
Mass., Published by G. and C.
Merriam, 1837. 3 v. ArCH;
CtMW; MdBB; OrU; PP.   43069

Bardsley, James Lomax.
   The retrospective address ...
July 19, 1837. Worcester, Deigh-
ton & Co., [1837.] 55 p. DSG;
MBV.   43070

Barker, John, 1813-1860.
   An address, delivered before
the students of the Genesee Wesleyan seminary, on the sixty-
first anniversary of American independence, July 4, 1837. ...
Rochester [N.Y.] Printed by
Shepard, Strong and Dawson,
1837. 20 p. CSmH; NRU.
                                43071
Barnard, Charles Francis, 1808-
1884.
   1st annual report to the proprietors of Warren St., Chapel,
Jan. 1, 1837. [Boston, 1837.]
MBAt.   43072

---- ---- Chapel hymn-book.
See under title.

---- Tracts, stories, etc., Boston, 1837. MH.   43073

Barnard, Daniel Dewey, 1797-
1861.
   An address delivered before
the Philoclean and Peithessopian
societies of Rutgers college, ...
July 18, 1837; ... Albany, Printed
by Hoffman & White, 1837. 46 p.
CSmH; DLC; NjR; NNG; TxU.
                                43074

---- A discourse pronounced at Schenectady, before the New-York Alpha of the society of Phi Beta Kappa, July 25th, 1837, by D. D. Barnard. Albany, Printed by Hoffman & White, 1837. 51 p. CtSoP; MH; NNUT; OOxM; TNP. 43075

---- Lecture on the character and services of James Madison, delivered before the young men's association for mutual improvement in the city of Albany ... Albany, Hoffman and White, 1837. CSt; ICN; MBAt; PHi; RPB. 43076

Barnard, Frederick Augustus Porter.
A compendious view of the remarkable facts and recent discoveries in electro-magnetism ...by Frederick A. P. Barnard, A.M. New York, George Dearborn and co., 1837. (1), 28 p. CtY; IU; NNNAM; PPULC. 43077

Barnard, Henry, 1811-1900.
Remarks...May 23d, 1837, on the proposed amendment to the constitution, limiting the tenure of office of the judges of the Supreme and Superior Courts. n.p., n.d. (Hartford, 1837?) 8 p. CtHWatk; MB; NN. 43078

Barnard Memorial, Boston.
Report of the committee of the contributors to the chapel. [Boston] [1837]. 1 vol. MH-AH. 43079

Barnes, Wm., M.A., F.S.A. Rector of Richmond.
Selection of Psalms and Hymns ... new ed. rev. Richmond, 1837. CtY. 43080

Barnes & Carroll, Philadelphia.
Tariff; or, Rates of duty, from and after the 31st of December, 1833, until the 30th of June, 1842, containing, also, rules and examples of calculating duties on goods, paying either a specific or ad valorem duty, together with the most concise rules and tables, for ascertaining duties on British goods. Comp. and calculated by Barnes & Carroll, ship brokers ... Philadelphia. 2d ed. [Philadelphia] Printed by J. Young, 1837. 128 p. DLC; MiD; PPFrankI; PPi. 43081

Barnstable Conference, Mass.
The conference of churches and anniversaries of Barnstable County, Holden ... 1837-38. Boston, 1837-38. 2 pt. MBC. 43082

Barnum, H. L.
Reply to the president of the Ohio and Indianapolis Railroad Company. Jeffersonville, Ia., Robert R. Lindsey, printer, 1837. In; InHi; NN. 43083

Barr, John, 1749-1831.
A New and Complete General Index and Concise Directory of the Bible. ... Published by the Brattleboro Typographic Company ... Brattleboro, Vermont, 1837. 63 p. MeAu. 43084

---- ---- New York, Mason and G. Lane, 1837. 177 p. CtMW; ILM; MiU. 43085

---- ---- ---- 210 p. ICU; PCC; PPLT; ViU; NcSaIL. 43086

Barrett, Joseph Appleton, 1813-1833.
The literary remains of J. A. Barrett and Emily Maria Barrett. Boston, Munroe and Francis, 1837. 119 p. CtY; MB; MH; RPB. 43087

Barrett, Solomon.
The principles of language:
containing a full grammatical
analysis of English poetry,
... By Solomon Barrett, Jun.
lll Albany, Published by O.
Steele, 1837. 120 p. CSt;
IU; MiJa; NN; OMC.   43088

Barrow, John, 1764-1848.
A Memoir of the life of Peter
the Great by John Barrow,
Esq. Secretary, to the Admir-
alty, Author of "Pitcairn's
Island and its Inhabitants,"
&c. New York, Published by
Harper & Brothers, 1837.
319 p. MH; MNt; NN; NNot;
OMC.   43089

(Barstow, George)
The times, or the pressure
and its causes examined. By
a citizen of Mass. Boston,
1837. 24 p. CtY; ScU;
MH.   43090

Bartlett, H. M.
A discourse delivered in the
Church of Bristol Parish, Petersburg, Virginia, November,
1836, By H. M. Bartlett. Petersburg, Printed at the office
of the Farmers Register, 1837.
21 p. CtHT; MdBD.   43091

Bartlett, John Stephen, d. 1840.
Letter to the president,
counsellors, etc., of the Massachusetts Med. Soc., May 31,
1837. Boston, 1837. 12 p.
DLC; DNLM; MBAt; MH.   43092

Bartlett, Montgomery Robert.
A statistical and chronological
view of the United States of
North America, and the several
states and territories ... Rochester, N.Y., C. S. Underwood,
printer, 1837. 48 p. CSmH;
MiU; NN; OCHP.   43093

Bartlett, Richard, 1794-1837.
Remarks and Documents Re-
lating to the Preservation and
Keeping of the Public Archives.
By Richard Bartlett, Esq. Mem-
ber of the New-Hampshire His-
torical Society. Concord,
Printed by Asa M'Farland, 1837.
72 p. CSmH; ICJ; MH; Nh-Hi;
TxU.   43094

Barton, Edward Hall, d. 1859.
A discourse on temperance,
and of the applicability of stimu-
lants in a warm climate, de-
livered before the New Orleans
Temperance Society... New Or-
leans, T. Rea, 1837. 32 p.
CtY; DNLM; LU; MH; PPC.
                          43095
---- Introductory lecture on ac-
climation, delivered at the opening of the third session of the
Medical College of Louisiana.
By E. H. Barton... Published at
the request of the class. New
Orleans, Commercial bulletin
print., 1837. 17 p. CtY; DLC;
DNLM; LU; MB; MBAt; TxU.
                          43096
Bartrum, Joseph P.
Arithmetic in the Ancient
Order, ... prepared for superior
schools; and forming a complete
guide to self-instruction by persons beyond the term of pu-
pilage. By Joseph P. Bartrum.
Boston, William D. Ticknor,
1837. 316 p. DAU; MH.
                          43097
Bassett, William, 1803-1871.
Letter to a member of the society of Friends, in reply to objections against joining anti-
slavery societies. By William
Bassett.... Boston, Isaac Knapp,
1837. 41 p. CtSop; MWA; NjR;
OO; TNF.   43098

Bates, Benjamin.
A Letter Addressed To A

Member Of The Legislature Of
Virginia. By Benjamin Bates.
New-Bedford, (Mass.), Re-
Printed By J. C. Parmenter,
1837. 11 p. CBPac; MNBedf;
MWA; NN.   43099

Bates, Elisha.
    An examination of certain
proceedings and principles of
the Society of Friends, called
Quakers. By Elisha Bates ...
St. Clairsville [O.] Printed for
the author by Horton J. Howard, 1837. 309 p. DLC; IEG;
NjR; OClWHi; PHC.   43100

---- Proceedings and principles
of friends. St. Clairville,
1837. PSC-Hi.   43101

---- Reasons for receiving the
ordinance of Christian baptism;... St. Clairsville, O.,
Printed by Horton J. Howard,
from the first London edition,
1837. KyLx; LexPL.   43102

---- A Refutation Of the Docu-
ment of the Meeting for Suf-
ferings of Ohio Yearly Meeting.
St. Clairsville, Printed for the
Author by Horton J. Howard,
1837. 40 p. KyLx; PSC-Hi.
                            43103
---- Water baptism and the
Lord's Supper. See Crewdson,
Isaac.   43104

Bates, Joshua, 1776-1854.
    Moral education. A lecture
delivered before the American
institute of instruction, Aug.
26, 1837. By Joshua Bates,
president of Middlebury college.
Boston, I. R. Butts, 1837.
21 [3] p. CBPSR; ICU; MH;
MiU-C; WHi.   43105

Battle-axe and weapons of War.
Vol. 1. nos. 1-4 (July 1837-

Aug. 1840) Philadelphia, 1837-
1840. NN; PHi; PPULC. 43106

Battles of Mexico. Survey of
the line of operations of the U.S.
army, 1837. (Map.) PPL.
                            43107
[Bautain, Louis Eugene Marie]
1796-1867.
    An epitome of the history of
philosophy....By C. S. Henry.
In 2 vols.... New York, Harper
and bros., 1837. 2 v. FTa.
                            43108
Baxter, Richard, 1615-1691.
    The reformed pastor; showing
the nature of the pastoral work.
By the Rev. Richard Baxter.
New York, T. Mason and G.
Lane, publishers, 1837. 298 p.
CtHT; GAGTh; IEG; NNMHi;
OkOk; TChU.   43109

---- The saints everlasting rest;
or, A treatise of the blessed
state of the saints....from the
works of Mr. Richard Baxter.
By John Wesley. New York,
N.Y., published by T. Mason
and G. Lane, 1837. 333 p.
FLiS.   43110

---- ---- Philadelphia, Desilver,
Thomas & co., 1837. 320 p.
GBar; IaFayU; OCan.   43111

Bayard, Richard Henry, 1796-
1868.
    Speech on Mr. Benton's mo-
tion to expunge from the Journal
of the Senate The Resolution of
March 28th, 1834. Delivered in
the Senate of the United States
January 16, 1837. Wilmington,
Del., R. & J. B. Porter, 1837.
15 p. DeWI; MBAt; MWA; WHi.
                            43112
---- Speech on the Bill Imposing
Additional Duties, as Depositories
in Certain Cases, on Public Officers. Delivered in the Senate

of the United States, Oct. 2,
1837. Wilmington, Printed by
R. & J. B. Porter, 1837.
20 p. MWA; P; PPL.   43113

Bayle, A[ntoine] L[aurent]
J[esse], 1799-1858.
An elementary treatise on
anatomy. By A. L. J. Bayle
... Tr. from the 4th ed. of the
French. By A. Sidney Doane
... New York, Harper & broth-
ers, 1837. 470 p. CSt-L; CU;
GU-M; MNF; PU.   43114

Bayle-Mouillard, Elisabeth Fe-
licie (Canard), 1796-1865.
Gentleman & lady's book of
politeness & propriety of de-
portment dedicated to the youth
of both sexes, tr. from the 6th
Paris edition, enlarged & improved. Amer. ed. 4. Boston,
Ticknor, 1837. 214 p. DLC;
PPULC; PU.   43115

Baylies, Francis, 1783-1852.
Speech of the Hon. Francis
Baylies, before the Whigs of
Taunton, on the 13th of Sept.,
1837. Taunton [Mass.] By
Bradford & Amesbury, 1837.
16 p. CSmH; DLC; MB; MWA;
NjR.   43116

Bayly, Thomas Haynes, 1797-
1839.
Flowers of loveliness; twelve
groups of female figures, em-
blematic of flowers; designed
by various artists; with poetical
illustrations, by Thomas Haynes
Bayly.... New York, W. Jackson, 1837. DLC; NNC; PP;
PPULC; ViU.   43117

Beach, George.
To the stockholders of the
Phoenix bank. (By George
Beach). [Hartford,] Case,
Tiffany & co., pr., 1837. 23 p.

Ct; DLC; MB; NjR; NN. 43118

Beaconsfield, Benjamin, Disraeli,
1st earl of, 1804-1881.
Henrietta Temple, a love story,
by the Right Hon. Benjamin Disraeli, earl of Beaconsfield. New
York, George Routledge and sons,
[1837]. CO; GAuY.   43119

---- ---- Philadelphia, E. L.
Carey and A. Hart, 1837. 2 v.
in 1. AMob; CtHt; OBog; PU.
                         43120
---- Venetia. Philadelphia, E. L.
Carey and A. Hart, 1837. 2 v.
MdBd; NGcA; NN; NNC; PPULC.
                         43121
---- The works of D'Israeli the
younger, in one volume. Phila-
delphia, E. L. Carey and A.
Hart, 1837. (2), (13)-1038 p.
LNL; MdBJ; NjP.   43122

Bean, Joseph.
A Sermon preached before the
congregation of the First church
and parish of Wrentham, on a
day of public humiliations, fasting and prayer, A.D. 1755. by
Rev. Joseph Bean, pastor of said
church. Providence, H. H. Brown,
1837. 23 p. MWeyhi; RHi.
                         43123
Beard, John, jr.
An address delivered at the
request of the literary societies
of Davidson College at the close
of the examination on the 1st
July, 1837, ... Salisbury, N.C.,
Western Carolinian Office, 1837.
12 p. DLC; NcDaD.   43124

Beaumont, Francis, 1584-1616.
... The bridal; a tragedy in
five acts adapted for representation (with three original scenes
written by James Sheridan
Knowles ...) from the Maid's
tragedy of Beaumont and Fletcher ... N.Y., S. French, [1837?]
67 p. C; OCl.   43125

A'Beckett, Gilbert Abbott, 1811-
1856.
The assignation; or, what
will my wife say; a drama in
two acts. 36 [1] p. N.Y.,
Samuel French & son, [1837].
OCl.   43126

Beebee, Pierre Ogilvie.
An analysis of common law
practice; in questions adapted
to Mr. Graham's treatise on the
practice of the New York Supreme Court. By Pierre Ogilvie Beebee, esq. ... Multum
in Parvo. New York, printed
for the author, 1837. 282 p.
DLC; NNLI; OCLaw; PU-L.
                            43127
---- An analysis of Mr. Anthon's Abridgement and synopsis of Sir William Blackstone's
Commentaries on the laws of
England. By Pierre Ogilvie
Beebee... New York, The author, 1837. [25]-232 p. CtY-L;
DLC; MPiB; OO; PPULC. 43128

Beecher, Catherine Esther,
1800-1878.
An essay on slavery and
abolitionism, with reference to
the duty of American females.
By Catherine E. Beecher.
Philadelphia, H. Perkins; Boston, Perkins & Marvin, 1837.
152 p. CU; IGK; MWA; PHC;
WHi.   43129

---- ---- Second ed. Philadelphia, Henry Perkins; Boston,
Perkins & Marvin, 1837. (3),
4-151 p. MPiB; NjP; PSC-Hi;
TxU; Vi.   43130

Bell, John.
Animal magnetism: past fic-
tions - present science. By
John Bell, M.D., Lecturer on
the institutes of medicine and
medical jurisprudence; member
of the college of physicians of
Philadelphia, and of the Amer.
Philos. Soc., etc. From the
Select medical library and elec-
tric journal of medicine, Vol. 11,
No. 1. for November, 1837.
Philadelphia, Haswell, Barrington,
and Haswell, 1837. 16 p. MBM;
MWA; PP; PPL-R; ScU. 43131

---- Speech of Mr. Bell, of Tennessee, on the bill to secure the
freedom of elections: Delivered
in the House of representatives,
January, 1837. Washington,
Printed by William W. Moore,
1837. 29 p. CtY; ICU; NcD;
PHi; TxU.   43132

---- Substance of Mr. Bell's
speech, upon the bill authorising
the secretary of the Treasury to
issue treasury notes to the amount
of ten millions of dollars, in the
House of representatives, October 7th, 1837. Washington,
Printed by Jacob Gideon, jr.,
1837. 24 p. Phi; T.   43133

Bell, T. L.
Don Guzman; or A Legend of
the Piscataqua. By T. L. Bell.
Portsmouth, Printed by Thomas
Whittem, 1837. 12 p. Nh.
                            43134
Bell, Thomas, 1792-1880.
The anatomy, physiology, and
diseases of the teeth. By Thomas
Bell...3d American ed., with
numerous plates. Philadelphia,
Carey, Lea and Blanchard, 1837.
351 p. ICJ; MOS; OClW; PPWa;
ViU.   43135

Bellarmino, Robert Francesco
Romolo, 1542-1621.
The felicity of the saints. By
Cardinal Robert Bellarmino of the
society of Jesus. Tr. by the
Rt. Rev. Dr. David ... Balti-
more, F. Lucas, Jr., [1837].

303 p. IaDuMtC; MBBCHS;
NNF; ODau.   43136

Bellenger, William A.
Conversational phrases and
dialogues, in French and English. Comp. chiefly from the
18th and last Paris ed....
Boston, J. Munroe and Co.,
1837. 121 p. CtY; DLC; MB;
MH; OFH.   43137

Bellini, Vincenzo.
Come, brave the sea with
me, love. From Il Puritani.
Arranged as a song & adapted
for the piano forte, by S. Mi-
lon. New York, Hewitt, 1837.
9 p. CtY; NN; PPL; ViU.
                             43138
---- I bring to thee a faded
wreath. (Song.) Arranged
for the pianoforte. Philadelphia, Fiot. Meigneu & Co.,
(1837). 3 p. MB.   43139

Bells Point shoal in Core sound,
N.C... a map. Washington?,
1837. PPAmP; PPL; PPULC.
                             43140
Beman, Nathan S. S.
Punctuality in the payment
of debts. A sermon. New
York, 1837. 14 p. MH-And.
                             43141
Beman, Samuel.
The kingdom of heaven is at
hand. By Samuel Beman...
New York, Leavitt, Lord & co.,
(etc. etc.), 1837. 276 p. CtY;
MeBat; MWiW; NNUT; OO. 43142

Ben Lomond Coal Company.
Proposals for incorporating
the Ben Lomond Coal Company.
Richmond, T. W. White Printer,
... 1837. CSmH.   43143

Benezet, Anthony.
Plain path to Christian perfection. Philadelphia, Printed

by Joseph Rakeshaw, 1837. (iv)-
107 p. MdW; NcGu.   43144

Bennet, James Arlington.
The American system of practical book-keeping,.... By James
Bennett, A. & M. Eighteenth
edition. New York, Collins Keese
& co., 1837. 36, 104 p. MH;
NNC.   43145

Bennett, [John Cook]
The accoucheur's vade mecum,
by Doctor Bennett, of the Big-
Hocking Ohio medical society.
Buffalo, New York, Salisbury,
Manchester & co., printers,
1837. 32 p. MHi; OClWHi.
                             43146
Benson, Joseph, 1749-1821.
The life of the Rev. John W.
De La Flechere: compiled from
the narrative of Rev. Mr. Wes-
ley; the biographical notes of
Rev. Mr. Gilpin; from his own
letters, and other authentic docu-
ments, many of which were never
before published. By Joseph
Benson. New York, J. Collord,
printer, 1837. 356 p. IaFayU;
InGrD; IU; MB; MWA.   43147

Bentham, Jeremy, 1748-1832.
Defence of usury; shewing
the impolicy of the present legal
restraints on the terms of pecuniary bargains ... To which
is added A letter to Adam Smith,
Esq. L.L.D. on the discourage-
ments opposed by the above restraints to the progress of in-
ventive industry. Albany, printed
by Croswell, Van Benthusyen and
Burt, 1837. 61 p. CSmH; Ia;
MB; NNut; RNR.   43148

---- ---- New York, T. Foster,
1837. 48 p. CtY; DLC; MnHi;
OO; PPM.   43149

Benton, C.

A statistical view of the number of sheep in the several towns and counties in Maine, New Hampshire, Vermont, Massachusetts, Rhode Island, Connecticut, New York, Pennsylvania and Ohio: ... Cambridge (Mass.), Folsom, Wells and Thurston, 1837. vi, (7), 143 p. DLC; MBAt; NhD; OCo; RPB. 43150

Benton, Thomas Hart, 1782–1858.

Speech on the bill designating and limiting the funds receivable for the revenues of the United States; delivered in the senate of the United States, Jan. 27, 1837. Washington, 1837. 23 p. [Pamphlet]. DLC; InHi; MBAt; WHi. 43151

———— Speech of Mr. Benton, of Missouri, on Mr. Calhoun's amendment...Delivered in Senate U.S. September 22, 1837. Montpelier, Patriot office, 1837. 15 p. OClWHi; PPM; PPFRB. 43152

———— Speech on Mr. Calhoun's amendment to the bill to provide the collection, keeping and disbursement of the public moneys, without the agency of banks, Delivered in the senate of the United States, Sept. 22, 1837. Washington, 1837. 15 p. [pamphlet] CtY; DLC; InHi; TxU; WHi. 43153

———— Speech on the expunging resolution [in relation to President Jackson and the removal of the deposits]. Delivered in the senate, January 12, 1837. [Washington, 1837]. 7 p. DLC; MoHi; PPL-R; PPM; WHi. 43154

———— Speech..on the Resolution

of Mr. Ewing, for rescinding the Treasury Order (of July 11, 1836, for excluding Paper Money from the Land Offices, etc.) delivered in the Senate, Dec. 1836. Washington, 1837. 28 p. CtSoP; DLC; IU; MiD; NjR. 43155

Bernard, Stephen.

The beginner's new and easy French grammar, divided into sixty lessons...Designed for the use of schools and academies. ...2d. ed. ... greatly improved. Baltimore, Cushing & sons, 1837. [5]-166 p. MdHi; MH; OO; ViU. 43156

———— A complete treatise on the French verbs ... with notes & illustrations. ... By Stephen Bernard. 2d ed. ... greatly improved. Baltimore, 1837. 112 p. MdHi. 43157

———— New and easy French grammar, divided into sixty lessons, with a complete treatise on the regular, irregular and defective verbs. By Stephen Bernard. 2d ed. remodelled, corrected and greatly improved. Baltimore, 1837. NjPT. 43158

Best, William.

Concise system of logic, rev. by W. Mann. Philadelphia, Massey and Boate, 1837. 5-95 p. MB; MBAt; NN. 43159

Bethune, George Washington, 1805-1862.

Genius. An address delivered before the literary societies of Union college, Schenectady, N.Y. July, 1837. By George W. Bethune.... Philadelphia, G. W. Mentz & son; John C. Clark, printer, 1837. 40 p. CtSoP; ICN; MH; PPL; TNP. 43160

Bever, John.

[Last will and testament].
Of Columbiana Co., Ohio....
1837. 7 leave, printed on one
side. OClWHi.   43161

Beverly, Mass.
By-laws and regulations of
the town of Beverly. Adopted
March 13, 1837. [Salem, Mass.]
Salem gazette press, 1837.
24 p. CSmH; MBevHi.   43162

Beverly Mechanic Association.
Constitution...Adopted March
22, 1836. Revised April 4,
1837. Salem: Printed at the
Gazette Office, 1837. 8 p.
MBevHi.   43163

Bible.
Die Bibel; oder, Die ganze
Heilige Schrift des Alten and
Neuen Testments. Nach r.
Martin Luther's uebersetzung,
12. aufl. Stereotypirt von J.
Howe, Philadelphia, New York,
Amerikanische Bibel-gesells-
chaft, 1837. 2 v. in 1. CU;
MBGCT; MH-AH; NjPT; OrSaW;
PPL.   43164

---- Book of Proverbs. New
York, American Tract Society
[1837?] 90 p. ICRL.   43165

---- Book of Psalms. Printed
for the blind. (Braille). Boston, 1837. MB; MBAt; MWA.
                             43166
---- The Book of Psalms, translated out of the original Hebrew,
and with the former translation
diligently compared and rev.
New York, American Bible Society, 1837. 112 p. ICU; NN.
                             43167
---- The comprehensive Bible
containing the old and new Testaments, according to the authorized version.... Hartford
(Conn.), Judd, Loomis & Co.,

1837. 1460 p. MBD; PRosC;
TNP; VtMidSM.   43168

---- The comprehensive commentary on the Holy Bible; containing
the text according to the author-
ised version; with marginal references; Matthew Henry's commentary, condensed ...; the practical observations of Rev. Thomas
Scott, D.C., with extensive explanatory, critical, and philological notes, selected from Scott,
Doddridge [etc.] ... conveniently
arranged for family and private
reading, and at the same time
particularly adapted to the wants
of Sabbath school teachers and
Bible classes ... Edited by Rev.
William Jenks ... Embellished
with engravings, on wood and
steel ... Brattleboro, [Vt.],
Brattleboro' typographic company,
1836-38. 6 vols. NBuG; NjPT;
PPL; TJaU; WAsN.   43169

---- The Cottage Bible and Family Expositor; containing the Old
and New Testaments,....refer-
ences and marginal readings of
the Polyglott Bible....and a valuable chronological index....Em-
bellished with maps and engravings. Ed. by Rev. William Patton. Complete in two volumes.
Hartford, D. F. Robinson & H. F.
Sumner, 1837. 2 v. NcWsS;
NN; OKentU.   43170

---- ... The English version of
the Polyglott Bible containing the
Old and New testaments, with
the marginal readings, and a full
and original selection of references to parallel and illustrative
passages, arr. in a manner
hitherto unattempted. Brattleboro, Vt., Brattleboro typograph-
ical Company, 1837. 1254 p.
CtY; KWiU; MeL; MeLew; MwAU.
                             43171

---- ---- Philadelphia, Desilver, Thomas & Co., 1837. vii, 587, 189 p. CoU; DCU; KyLoSH; MH; MWA. 43172

---- The English version of the polyglott Bible, containing the Old and New Testaments; with original selections of references to parallel and illustrative passages; and marginal readings ... designed to facilitate the acquisition of Scripture knowledge in Bible classes, Sunday Schools, &c. Baltimore, Armstrong & Berry, 1837. 2 v. in 1. Mi; MiU; NN; PPPrHi; ViU. 43173

---- Explanatory notes upon the New Testament by John Wesley, M.A. late fellow of Lincoln College Oxford. New York, printed by J. Collord, 1837. 734 p. CtY; Ia; LNH; NBuG; NcRP. 43174

---- An exposition of the Gospels of St. Matthew and St. Mark, and of some other. Detached parts of Holy Scripture .... New York, published by L. Mason and G. Lane, J. Collord, printer, 1837. 538 p. ABBS; CBPSR; MH-AH; NcD; TxAbM. 43175

---- The four Gospels, translated from the Greek with preliminary dissertations, and notes, critical and explanatory. By George Campbell. In two volumes. Andover, Printed & published by Gould & Newman, 1837. 2 v. KyLoS; MiU; NjMD; OClWHi; ViLC. 43176

---- ---- Boston, Gould, 1837. 2 v. DLC; IaCrC; MBC. 43177

---- The four Gospels, with notes, chiefly explanatory; designed for teachers in Sabbath Schools, and bible classes, and as an aid to family instruction. In two vols., containing Matthew and Mark. Boston, Gould, Kendall and Lincoln, 1837. 2 v. DLC; KyLoS; MDux. 43178

---- Gospel of St. John. Ed. by J. Hamilton. Schenectady, 1837. 2 v. in 1. MB. 43179

---- The Greek testament, with English notes, critical, philological, and exegetical, partly selected and arranged from the lest commentators, ancient and modern, but chiefly original. 1st. American from the 2nd London ed., in 2 vols. Boston, Perkins & Marvin, etc., etc., 1837. 2 v. ICJ; MiU; OO; ViW; WaPS. 43180

---- The history of our lord and saviour Jesus Christ; comprehending all that the four evangelists have recorded concerning him; .... translated into the Delaware language, in 1806, by Rev. David Zeisberger, missionary of the United Brethren. Retranslated, so as to conform to the present idiom of the language, by I. D. Blanchard. J. Meeker, printer, Shawanoe Baptist Mission, 1837. 221 p. KHi; MoS; PU-Mus. 43181

---- The Holy Bible.... [Baltimore, Armstrong & Berry, 1837.] 920-281 p. NN. 43182

---- Boston, O. Clapp, 1837. 2 p.l., 3-510, 162 p. NNAB. 43183

---- ---- Hartford, Ct., Judd, Loomis & Co., 1837. x, 11-729, 225 p., 16 pl. DLC; NN; NNAB. 43184

---- ---- New York, stereotyped by A. Chandler, for the
American Bible Society, 1837.
669 p. NNAB.   43185

---- ---- Sandbornton, Wilson
And Giles, printer, Charles
Lane, publisher, 1837. 755,
(1), 30 p. MAbD.   43186

---- The Holy Bible, containing
the Old and New Testaments,
according to the authorized
version; with explanatory notes,
practical observations, and copious marginal references. By
Thomas Scott. New York, Collins and Hannay, 1837. 2 v.
TxBrdD.   43187

---- The Holy Bible containing
the old and New Testament.
The Text carefully printed
from the most correct copies of
the present authorized translation, including the marginal
readings and parallel texts:
with a commentary and critical
notes...by A. Clarke. New
York, T. Mason and G. Lane,
1837-1854. 6 v. CBPac; MMeT;
MWA; NN; ODW.   43188

---- The Holy Bible: containing the Old and New Testaments:
together with the Apocrypha:
translated out of the original
tongues...with Canne's marginal notes and references...
Added an index; an alphabetical
table of all the names in the Old
and New Testaments, with their
significations.... Woodstock,
Vt., Haskell, 1836. 927, (4) pp.
MB.   43189

---- The Holy Bible, containing
the Old and New Testaments:
translated out of the original
tongues, and with the former
translation diligently compared

and revised. Stereotype Company's Power Press, 1837. 486,
162 p. MAtt; Nh-Hi; PPiPT.
                           43190

---- ---- Cooperstown, N.Y.,
H. & E. Phinney, 1837. 768 p.
CtY; DLC; MWA; MWeA; NNAB.
                           43191

---- ---- Hartford, Con., Andrus, Judd, & Franklin, 1837.
CSt-L; DLC.   43192

---- ---- New-York, Stereotyped
by A. Chandler, and printed by
D. Fanshaw for the American
Bible Society, 1837. 1043 p.
DLC.   43193

---- ---- New York, American
Bible society, 1837. 831, [1]
254 p. NN.   43194

---- ---- New-York, Stereotyped
by A. Chandler for the American Bible Society, 1837. 1213 p.
TxU.   43195

---- The Holy Bible, containing
the Old and New Testaments...
With Canne's marginal references.
Together with the Apocrypha and
concordance. To which are
added, an index, a table of texts,
and...an account of the lives
and martyrdom of the apostles
and evangelists. With plates.
The text corrected according to
the standard of the American
Bible Society. Stereotyped by
J. Connor, New-York. New-
York, published by T. Mason &
G. Lane, for the Methodist Episcopal Church, 1837. 527 (1),
78, 168 p., 12 pl. CtMW; NN.
                           43196

---- The Holy Bible, translated
from the Latin Vulgate: ... With
the approbation of the Provincial
Council. Baltimore, Published
by Fielding Lucas, Jr., [1837].

810, [2], 5-214, [1] p. CStolU;
DGU; IMunS; NN; Wa.   43197

---- The Holy Bible, translated
from the Latin Vulgate... The
Old Testament, first published by
the English college at Doway,
A.D. 1609. And the New Testament, first published by the
English college at Rhemes, A.D.
1582. With annotations, references, and a historical and
chronological index. First
stereotype, from the fifth Dub-
lin edition. Newly revised and
corrected according to the
Clementin edition of the Scriptures. Philadelphia, E. Cummiskey, 1837. 691 p., 4 ℓ.,
5-191 (1) p., 1 ℓ. IU;
NcWsW; NN.   43198

---- The ministry of Jesus
Christ: compiled and arranged
from the four Gospels, for
families and Sunday schools...
By T. B. Fox...Boston, Weeks,
Jordan and Co.; Portsmouth,
J. W. Foster, 1837. 2 v.
CU; DLC; MB; MH; OOC. 43199

---- Minuajimouin gainajimot
au St. Luke. Anishinabe en-
net giizhianikvnotabivng au S.
Hall...gaie au George Copway.
Boston, 1837. 110 p. BrMus;
CSmH; MB.   43200

---- Das Neue Testament...
unsers herrn und Heilandes
Jesu Christi. New York, stereotypirt von Rees für die Amerikanische Bibel-gesellschaft,
1837. 472 p. CtMW; MiD.
                           43201
---- ---- New York, D. Fanshaw, 1837. PPeSchw.   43202

---- ---- Von Joseph Franz
Ullioli. New York and Cincinnati, Drud und Berlag von

Friedrich Pustet, (1837). 464 p.
MoU; MWH.   43203

---- ---- Philadelphia, George
W. Menz, 1837. 272 p. PPCS;
PReaAT.   43204

---- A New hieroglyphical bible:
...containing four hundred cuts,
by Adams. New York, Harper
& Brothers, 1837. 210 p. DLC;
MBAt; MNBedf; NjP; NPV.
                           43205
---- The New Testament ...
Published by the Brattleboro
Typographic Company ... Brat-
tleboro, Vermont, 1837. 216 p.
KWiU; MeAu.   43206

---- The New Testament, arranged in historical and chronological order; with copious notes
on the principal subjects in theology; ... Revised...by T. W.
Coit. Boston, Perkins & Marvin,
1837. 455, 472 p. CtHC; MMeT;
MoSpD; OSand; TChU.   43207

---- The New Testament of Our
Lord and Saviour Jesus Christ.
By William Tyndale, the martyr.
The original edition, 1526, being
the first vernacular translation
from the Greek. With a memoir
of his life and writings. To
which are annexed, the essential
variations of Coverdale's, Thomas
Matthew's, Cranmer's, the Gene-
van, and the Bishops' Bibles, as
marginal readings. By J. P.
Dabney. Andover [Mass.] New
York, Printed and published by
Gould & Newman, from the London edition of Bagster, 1837.
105, [530] p. C-S; InCW; LNB;
MAnP; NboP; RPB.   43208

---- The New Testament of our
Lord and Saviour Jesus Christ.
The text carefully printed from
the most correct copies of the

present authorized translation
...A new ed. with author's
final corrections...New York,
T. Mason & G. Lane, 1837.
2 v. CoU; PCC; TJaU; WaPS.
                              43209

---- The New Testament of
our Lord and Savior Jesus
Christ, translated from the
Latin Vulgate...With the approbation of the provincial council. Baltimore, Fielding Lucas,
[1837]. 809-10, 5-214, [1] p.
DGU.   43210

---- The New Testament of our
Lord and Savior Jesus Christ,
translated from the original
Greek...Charleston, S. Bab-
cock and Co., 1837. 288 p.
NN.   43211

---- ---- Concord, N.H., Roby,
Kimball and Merrill, 1837.
390 p. CCSC; MCET; Nh-Hi.
                              43212

---- ---- Hartford, Judd,
Loomis and Co., 1837. 251 p.
Ct; NN.   43213

---- ---- New York, American
Bible society, 1837. 112 p.
NjP.   43214

---- ---- New York, American
Bible Society, 1837. 431 p.
ICU; MH-AH.   43215

---- ---- New York, New York,
The American Bible Society,
1837. 543 p. ODaB.   43216

---- ---- 35th ed. New York,
American Bible Society, 1837.
344 p. NNAB.   43217

---- ---- New York, Published
by T. Mason and G. Lane, for
the Methodist Episcopal Church,
1837. [2]-556 p. CStcr; CtY;
NNUT.   43218

---- ---- Newark, N.J., B. Olds,
1837. 344 p. NN.   43219

---- ---- Philadelphia, A. I.
Dickinson and C. Word, 1837.
453 p. NN.   43219a

---- ---- Philadelphia, Desilver,
Thomas & Co., 1837. 190 p.
MoSpD.   43220

---- ---- Philadelphia, M'Carty
and Davis, 1837. 256 p. NN.
                              43221
---- ---- Trenton, Davenport,
1837. 239 p. PU.   43222

---- The New Testament, of our
Lord and Saviour Jesus Christ;
with original selections of reference to parallel and illustrative
passages, and marginal readings:
together with other valuable
additions. Baltimore, Published
by Armstrong and Berry, 1837.
902, 281 p. MLawL.   43223

---- A new translation of the
Hebrew prophets, arranged in
chronological order. By George
R. Noyes ... Boston, J. Munroe
and company, 1837-43. 3 v.
CLU; IEG; MB-FA; NN; PPP.
                              43224
---- ---- Second edition....
Boston, James Munroe and Co.,
1837-1843. 3 v. CtY-D;
MBBCHS; MB-FA; PMA; VtFah.
                              43225
---- Notes, critical and practical
on the book. Judges designed
as a general help to biblical
reading and instruction by George
Bush, professor of Hebrew and
Oriental Literature, N.Y.C. Uni-
versity. New York, Ivison, &
Phinney, 1837. (11)-257 p.
MCNC.   43226

---- Notes explanatory and practical, on the Acts of the Apostles.

Designed for Bible classes and Sunday-Schools. By Albert Barnes. Seventh edition. New York, Leavitt Lord and Co., 1837. 356 p. GHi; MB; MH; NcD; NcWC.   43227

---- Notes, explanatory and practical, on the First Epistle of Paul to the Corinthians. New York, Harper and brothers, 1837. 357 p. NcD; OrU.   43228

---- El Nuevo Testamento Traducido Al Espanol Por El R. P. Felipe Scio De S. Miguel ....Nueva York, Edicion Estereotipica Por F. F. Ripley.... Formada en Nueva York, A.D. 1816. Imprenta de D. Fanshaw, 1837. (2), 477 p. MB; MeLewB; MH; Mid-B; MWA.   43229

---- The Old & New Testament, arranged in historical and chronological order...by George Townsend. Boston and Philadelphia, 1837-1838. 2 v. CtY; MiU.   43230

---- Psalms, in metre, selected from the Psalms of David.... Philadelphia, Desilver, Thomas and Co....1837. 110 p. MiGr; TNP.   43231

---- Psalms in metre, selected from the Psalms of David; suited to the feasts, and fasts of the church, and other occasions of public worship. Philadelphia, Protestant Episcopal Female Prayer-book Society, 1837. 248 p. MiU-C; NNU-W.   43232

---- Psalms, in metre, selected from the psalms of David; with hymns .... New York, Swords, Stanford & Co., 1837. "139p, 132p." NHem.   43233

---- The Psalms of David in metre: translated and diligently compared with the original text ...Philadelphia, Desilver Jr., & Thomas, 1837. 62 p. CSansS.   43234

---- Psalms of David initiated in the language of the New Testament, and applied to Christian use and worship. By Isaac Watts...Timothy Dwight...at the request of the General Association of Connecticut. New Haven, Durrie and Peck, 1837. 505 p. CtY; OCA.   43235

---- ---- New Haven, Durrie and Peck, 1837. 633 p. CtY; CU; OCA.   43236

Bible and Common Prayer Book Society of the central part of the state of New York. Formed in 1820. Utica, Hobart Press, R. Beresford, printer, 1837. 8 p. NUt.   43237

Bible characters, instructive and entertaining. Compiled for the Use of young children. 3rd ed. New York, M. Day, 1837. 277 p. DLC.   43238

Bible colporter and magazine. (American and foreign Bible society.) v. 1-54. New York, 1837-1857? NRAB; PCA.   43239

A biblical and theological dictionary explanatory of the history, manners and customs of the Jews. New York, Pub. by T. Mason & G. Lane. J. Collord, printer, 1837. 1003 p. NcGB.   43240

Bicknell, Robert T.
    Bicknell's Counterfeit Detector & Bank note list....Philadelphia, 1837. 32 p. MiU.   43241

Biddle, Edward C.

Recommendatory notices of
the Indian history and biography,
now publishing, by E. C. Biddle...with a list of subscribers
to March 1, 1837. [Phila.,
Biddle, 1837]. 42 p. FOc;
NN; PPAmP; PPULC; TxU.
43242

Biddle, James C.
Annual oration...Philomathi-
an Society of the University...
Philadelphia, 1837. PPL. 43243

Biddle, Owen, 1774-1806.
An improved and enlarged
edition of Biddle's young carpenter's assistant; being a complete system of archetecture for
carpenters, joiners...Particular-
ly adapted to country use by
John Haviland...Philadelphia,
M'Carty and Davis, 1837. 52 p.
DLC; NNC-A; OCU; PPULC.
43244

Biddle, Richard, 1796-1847.
Remarks of Mr. Biddle of
Pennsylvania on the bill to postpone the fourth instalment payable under the Deposit Act delivered in the House of Representatives, September, 1837.
Washington, Printed by Gales
and Seaton, 1837. 10 p. CtY;
DLC; ICN; MWA; PHi; P. 43245

---- Speech of Mr. Biddle, of
Pennsylvania, on the bill authorizing the issue of treasury
notes. Delivered in the House
of Representatives, October 4,
1837. Washington, Printed by
Gales and Seaton, 1837. 23 p.
DLC; PPM; MWA. 43246

Biernatski, Johann Christoph,
1795-1840.
The hallig. tr. by Mrs.
Marsh. Boston, 1837. MB.
43247

Bigelow, John Prescott, 1797-
1872.

Abstract of Massachusetts
School Returns, for 1836. ...
Boston, 1837. DLC. 43248

Billington, Linus W., 1802-
Discourse....April 11, 1837,
at the funeral of Othello P.
Hawkes. Canandaigua, 1837.
13 p. DLC; RPB. 43249

.... Billy Barlow: Zip Coon:
Banks of Brandywine. Philadelphia, n. pub., n. pr., 1837.
8 p. NjP. 43250

Bingham, Caleb, 1757-1817.
The American preceptor improved; being a new selection of
lessons for reading and speaking. Designed for the use of
schools. By Caleb Bingham,
A.M. Sixty-eight (eighth improved) edition. Boston, by
J. H. A. Frost, Lincoln and
Edwards (and others), 1837.
(5)-178 p. KyLxT; M; MH; MiD;
NN; TxH. 43251

---- The Columbian orator: containing a variety of original and
selected pieces; together with
rules; calculated to improve
youth and others in the ornamental and useful art of eloquence.
By Caleb Bingham ... Boston,
J. H. A. Frost, [etc. etc.],
1837. vi, [7]-300 p. ILM; OMC;
TNP; PPeSchw. 43252

Binney, Amos, 1803-1847.
A Monograph of the helices
of the United States, by Amos
Binney, M.D. ... (Extracted
from the Boston Journal of Natural History) Boston, printed by
Freeman and Bolles, [1837].
32 p. CU; IN; MSaP; PPAN;
VtU. 43253

Binney, Horace, 1780-1875.
Eulogium on Wm. Tilghman...

Philadelphia, 1837. 26 p. PHi.
43254
Biographic sketch of Mohammed Ali ... Washington, P.
Force, 1837. 16 p. DLC.
43255
Biography of Santa Anna, derived from various sources;
with an account of the battle
of San Jacinto, where he was
taken prisoner, by the Texians.
Philadelphia, Printed by J.
Thompson, 1837. 7 p. DLC;
PU.   43256

Birch, Thomas.
Account of (his) imprison-
ment for contempt of court. New
York, 1837. MBAt.   43257

Bird, Francis William, 1809-
1894.
Physiological reform. An ad-
dress delivered before the
American physiological Society
at their first annual meeting,
June 1, 1837. Boston, Marsh,
Capen & Lyon, 1837. 48 p.
DLC; MB; MBAt; MH; MH-M.
43258
Bird, Robert Montgomery,
1806-1854.
Calavar; or the Knight of
the Conquest; A Romance of
Mexico. By Robert M. Bird.
In Two Vols. Third Edition.
Philadelphia, Carey, Lea &
Blanchard, 1837. 2 v. CtY;
MeB; TKL; TxD-W; ViU. 43259

---- Nick of the woods, or The
Jibbenainosay. A tale of Kentucky, by the author of "Calavar" ... Philadelphia, Carey,
Lea & Blanchard, 1837. 2 v.
DeWi; ICU; MWA; PU; RPB.
43260
Bishop, Robert Hamilton, 1777-
1855.
A tribute of respect to departed friends, and a word of

encouragement to their sons ...
Oxford [O], R. H. Bishop, jun.,
1837. 17 p. CSmH; ICU; MH;
OClWHi; ODa.   43261

Blagden, George Washington,
1802-1884.
Principles on which a preacher
should condemn sin; a sermon at
the ordination of Robert B. Hall
in Plymouth, August 23, 1837.
Boston, Crocker & Brewster,
1837. 40 p. DLC; ICN; MBAt;
MHi; RPB.   43262

---- A Sermon, preached at the
ordination of Rev. Robert B.
Hall, over the Third Congregational church and society in
Plymouth, Ms., Aug. 23, 1837.
By George W. Blagden, pastor
of the Old South church, Boston.
1837. 45 p. MH-And; MiD-B;
MTa.   43263

Blair, Hugh, 1718-1800.
An abridgment of lectures on
rhetoric. By Hugh, Blair D.D.
New edition, with appropriate
questions to each chapter, by
a teacher of Philadelphia. Philadelphia, Charles, Bell, 1837.
230 p. InStmaS; MH; OCX;
OOxM; NcGw.   43264

---- Lectures on Rhetoric.
Philadelphia, Chas. Bell, 1837.
PPeSchw.   43265

---- Lectures on Rhetoric and
Belles Lettres. New York, 1837.
InCW.   43266

Blair, Robert
The grave and other selected
poems on the common lot of man.
By Drs. Blair, Gray, Cowper,
Wordsworth, and James Mont-
gomery. Boston, published by
Isaac Knapp, 1837. 53 p. CtHT;
MWey; NGif; NN; RP.   43267

Blake, John Lauris, 1788-1857.
Conversations on natural philosophy. See Marcet, Jane (Hallimand).

---- Conversations on vegetable physiology. See Marcet, Jane (Hallimand).

---- First book in astronomy, adopted to the use of common schools. Illustrated with steel plate engravings. By Rev. J. L. Blake, A.M....Stereotyped edition with additions and improvements. Boston, Gould, Kendall and Lincoln.... 1837. CTHWatk; In; MHa; MoSU; ScCrwl.   43268

---- The historical reader, designed for the use of schools and families. On a new plan ....Rochester, N.Y., Hoyt and Porter, 1837. 372 p. IaAS; RPB.
                                  43269
---- Parlor book; or, Family encyclopedia of useful knowledge and general litearture. New York, John L. Piper and company, 1837. 960 p. MB; NjHo; NN.   43270

---- ---- 4th edition. New York, 1837. MB; MoS.   43271

Blake, S. H.
An Address Delivered before the Assn. of Teachers, and Friends of Popular Education, at Exeter, Dec. 28, 1836. By S. H. Blake. Published by the association. Bangor, Printed by S. S. Smith, 1837. 23, (1) p. CBPSR; MeBat; MH; MWA; Nh.   43272

Blanchard, Henri Louis.
La dillettante. Oh! would I were a happy rover. A vocal fantasia with imitation of Tyrolian, Spanish, Italian & German Melodies. Philadelphia, Fiot, Meignen & co., [1837]. 9 p. MB.
                                  43273
Blatchford, Richard M.
Extracts from a report to the trustees of the Apalachicola land Company, by Richard M. Blatchford, president of the board of directors, and special agent of said Company, appointed to examine and report upon the situation of the property of the company. Made May 17, 1837. [New York? 1837] 16 p. DLC; FSaHi.   43274

Blessington, Marguerite (Power) Farmer Gardiner, 1789-1849.
The honey-moon: by the Countess of Blessington and other tales.... Philadelphia, E. L. Carey and A. Hart, 1837. 2 v. in 1. KU; Mi; DSH; NN; TNP.
                                  43275
---- The victims of society. Philadelphia, 1837. 2 v. MBL; NjPT; PPL.   43276

The blind made happy.... New York, Scofield and Voorhies; Boston, Whipple & Damrell, 1837. 108 p. DLC; MH; MWatP; PPAmP; PPULC.   43277

Blodgett, Constantine, 1802-1879.
A sermon, preached ... on the late fast, September 1st. 1837. ... Pawtucket, Mass., Robert Sherman, printer, 1837. 1 p.l., 20 p. CSmH; MiD-B; MoSpD.   43278

Bloore, Joshua.
Oration at the Young Men's Union Celebration, 4th July 1837, at Waterford, Saratoga Co., N.Y. Saratoga Springs, 1837. 12 p. N.   43279

Blunt, John James, 1794-1856.

Sketch of the reformation in
England; with an introductory
letter to the editor by G. W.
Doane. Philadelphia, William
Marshall & co., 1837. 14, 298 p.
MdBD; NBuDD; PP; ScDuE;
WGr.   43280

Blunt, Joseph, 1792-1860.
Shipmaster's assistant and
commercial digest, containing
information useful to merchants,
owners and masters of ships;
with the tariff of 1832. New
York, 1837. DLC; IU; MBAt;
MH; RPB.   43281

---- ---- [2nd ed.] New York,
E. & G. W. Blunt, 1837.
686 p. LNLL; MdBP; NRAL;
RPB.   43282

Blythewood, D.
An essay; embracing first
the divine authority of marriage. Charleston, W. Riley,
1837. 20 p. DLC.   43283

Boardman, Henry Augustus.
Vanity of a life of fashion-
able pleasure. By Henry A.
Boardman. Philadelphia, Pa.,
Martien, 1837. 41 p. PPins.
                                  43284
(Boddington, Mary)
Janet Hamilton and other
tales. By the author of "Slight
reminiscences." Philadelphia,
Carey, Lea & Blanchard, 1837.
2 v. MBL; MH.   43285

Boeuf, Joseph F. A.
A new and complete grammar
of the French tongue...4th ed.,
cor., enl., and improved. By
Joseph F. A. Boeuf. ... New-
York, [H. Ludwig, printer],
1837. 15-143 p. MB; MH; OFH.
                                  43286
Bohuszewicz, E. B.
Boston grand march. For

the pianoforte. Boston, Parker
& Ditson, 1837. 3 p. MB.
                                  43287
Bokum, Hermann, 1807-1878.
Never despair: a tale of the
emigrants. Founded on fact...
New York, Scofield and Voorhies,
1837. 104 p. CtY; ICN; MH;
PPULC.   43288

Bolles, John Augustus.
A Treatise on Usury and
Usury Laws, by John A. Bolles,
Boston, James Munroe and Com-
pany, 1837. 75 p. DLC; ICU;
MBAt; MWA; PPL.   43289

Bolles, William.
A spelling book containing exercises in orthography, pronunciation, and reading. Revised
and enlarged. Stereotyped by
A. Pell & Bro. New-London,
W. & J. Bolles, 1837. MH;
                                  43290
Bolmar, Antoine.
A Collection of colloquial
phrases on every topic necessary
to maintain conversation: arranged under different heads;
with numerous remarks...a new
ed., rev., and cor. Philadelphia, Carey, Lea, and Blanchard,
1837. 208 p. KyU; NN; OO;
ViU.   43291

---- A theoretical and practical
grammar of the French tongue.
With numerous additions and improvements, and with the addition of a complete treatise on the
genders of French nouns, as
also with the addition of all the
French verbs by A. Bolmar.
5th ed., corr. by the author.
Philadelphia, E. L. Carey & A.
Hart, 1837. MH; PLFM; ViRU;
ViU; WGr.   43292

Bolton, Mass? Evangelical Church.
The confession of faith and

covenant, adopted by the Evangelical Church of Bolton, Lancaster, Sterling, and Stow, March, 1830. Boston, Printed by Tuttle, Dennett & Chisholm, 1837. 20 p. ICP. 43293

Bond, Samuel Miller.
A short account of some remarkable incidents in the life of Dr. William C. Daniell, of Savannah, Georgia...[Savannah?] 1837. 81 p. DLC; GU-De. 43294

Bond, Thomas Emerson, 1813-1872.
Anniversary address, delivered before the Oratorical society of Dickinson institute, Carlisle, July 17, 1837. By Thomas E. Bond ... Baltimore, J. D. Toy, 1837. 24 p. CSmH; CSt-L; NjR; MdHi; MnHi. 43295

Bondage a moral institution, sanctioned by the scriptures of the Old and New Testaments, and the preaching and practice of the Savior and His apostles. By a Southern Farmer. .... printed by Griffin & Purse, Macon, 1837. 78 p. CU; MB; MdBP; TxU; WHi. 43296

Bonneville, B. L. E. The Rocky Mountains;... See Irving, Washington.

Bonnycastle, Charles, 1792-1840.
A lecture, introductory to the course of mathematics, of the University of Virginia, delivered at the commencement of the session of 1837. By Charles Bonnycastle. Charlottesville, printed by Tompkins and Noel, 1837. 15 p. DLC; MB; NjPT; PPULC; ViU. 43297

Bonnycastle, John, 1750?-1821.
An introduction to algebra. 8th New York, from the last London ed. Revised, corrected, and enl. New York, W. E. Dean, etc., 1837. MH. 43298

---- A key to the last N.Y. ed. of Bonnycastle's algebra. ... New York, W. E. Dean, 1837. 261, (1) p. ICBB; MiU: NjR; NPStA. 43299

Book of Birds. New York, Mahlon Day, 1837. 22 p. CtY; DLC. 43300

The book of commerce by sea and land, exhibiting its connection which agriculture, the arts, and manufactures to which are added a history of commerce, and a chronological table. Philadelphia, Uriah Hunt, 1837. 185 p. ICBB; MH; MiU; NNG; PHi. 43301

The book of conversation; a guide for the tongue ... Tr. from the French. Charleston, S. Babcock & Co., 1837. 251 p. DLC; NeWfC. 43302

Book of letters, and pictures. Northampton, J. Metcalf, 1837. 8 p. NUt. 43303

Book of Mormon.
The book of Mormon: an account written by the hand of Mormon, upon plates taken from the plates of Nephi ... Tr. by Joseph Smith, jr. Kirtland, Ohio, Printed by O. Cowdery & co. for P. P. Pratt and J. Goodson, 1837. 619 p. CU-B; MH; OO; ViU; WaU. 43304

---- ---- 2nd ed. Kirtland, Ohio, Printed by O. Cowdery & co., for P. P. Pratt and J. Goodsen, 1837. 620 p. ArLSJ; DLC; MHoly; MiU-C; NNP. 43305

A book of public prayer, by
John Calvin and others. New
York, Charles Scribner, 1837.
NjMD.   43306

The Book of Songs; or the
Northern, Eastern, Western and
Southern vocalist: comprising
American, English, Scotch
Irish, naval, hunting, comick
and sentimental selections....
Watertown, New York, Knowlton
& Rice, 1837. 72 p. NRU;
RPB.   43307

Book of trees. New York,
1837. 22 p. MB.   43308

Books of cuts, designed for
the amusement and instruction
of young people. New York,
1837. 23 p. RPB.   43309

Boone, William Jones.
    Address in behalf of the
China mission, by the Rev.
William J. Boone ... published by
order of the Foreign committee
of the Board of missions. New-
York, W. Osborn, 1837. 21 p.
M; MdBD; NIC; NNG; WHi.
                                 43310
Bordentown Institute, Borden-
town, N.J.
    Catalogue of the officers and
students of the Bordentown Insti-
tute, for the year ending Dec.
31, 1836. Burlington, J. L.
Powell, 1837. 15 p. CSmH;
MdBD.   43311

Bossuet, Jacques Benigné
    Elevations to God. From the
French of Bossuet, Bishop of
Meaux. Norwich, Thomas
Robinson, 1837. 104 p.   43312

Boston.
    Order of services for the or-
dination of Rev. John T. Sargent, as Minister at large for
this city. Sunday evening, October 29, 1837. Boston: Printed
by Tuttle, Dennett and Chisholm,
1837. 4 p. MWA.   43313

---- Associated Banks of the
City of Boston.
    Report of Committee made to
the Board of Commissioners at
its meeting June 26, 1837. (Boston, 1837.) 2 p. MHi.   43314

---- Bowdoin Street Church.
    The Articles of Faith and
Covenant of the...Boston: with
a list of the members. Boston,
1837. 57 p. MB; MHi.   43315

---- Chamber of Commerce.
    Report and plan recommended
by Com. on Assignment law.
Boston, 1837. MB; MH-BA.
                                 43316
---- Christian Church.
    A Brief Statement of the
Causes which led to a Division
of the Christian Church in Summer Street, and the Establishment of another Meeting at the
Lyceum Hall in Hanover Street,
etc. [Boston, 1837.] 12 p.
                                 43317
---- City Council.
    Circular, City of Boston,
February 16, 1837 to accompany
certain resolutions which have
been adopted by the City Council, together with several copies
of Nomenclature of diseases and
of blank returns for deaths.
[Boston, 1837.] 1 p. MHi.
                                 43318
---- ---- ...(Report of the Joint
Committee instructed to revise
the City Charter. Dated Oct.
16, 1837. Boston, 1837.) 24 p.
DLC; IU; MH.   43319

---- ---- Joint committee on hospitals for small-pox.
    Report made by a joint com-

mittee of the City council of
the city of Boston, ... Boston,
J. H. Eastburn, ... printer,
1837. 15 p. CSmH; IU; MBAt;
MB; MHi.   43320

---- Clarendon St. Baptist
Church.
King's daughter's cookbook,
containing five hundred favorite
recipes, collected and published
by whatsoever circle of King's
daughters of Clarendon St.
Baptist Church, Boston, Mass.
1st ed. Boston, [1837?] 150 p.
LU.   43321

---- Commissioners to devise a
plan for supplying the city with
pure water.
Report of the commissioners
appointed under an order of
the City council, of March 16,
1837, to devise a plan for supplying the city of Boston with
pure water. Boston, J. H.
Eastburn, printer, 1837. 95 p.
ICU; MiD-B; OO; TxDaM; WHi.
                            43322

---- Committee.
Report of the committee appointed to consider what disposition shall be made of the
Court House on Court Square.
1837. 4 p. MBC.   43323

---- Common Council.
Rules and orders of the common council of the city of Boston, and city charter; together
with a list of city officers.
Boston, John H. Eastburn, city
printer, 1837. 76 p. MoS.
                            43324

---- Federal Street Baptist
Church.
The declaration of faith, with
the church covenant and list
of members, of the Federal street
Baptist Church, Bost. ... 4th
ed. Boston, Gould, Kendall

and Lincoln, 1837. 38 p. ICN;
MiD-B.   43325

---- Fifth Universalist Church.
The confession of faith and
form of Church Government of
the Fifth Universalist Church in
Boston. Boston, O. Brewer,
1837. MB-FA.   43326

---- Hancock Enging Co. No.
10.
By-laws. Boston, 1837.
MB.   43327

---- House of Employment.
House of employment ... juvenile offenders 1836. (Boston,
1837.) MB.   43328

---- House of Industry.
House of industry. Rules
and regulations. [Boston, 1837.]
MB.   43329

---- Mason Street Sabbath School
Library.
Descriptive catalogue of books
in the Mason street sabbath
school library...Boston, Printed
by Perkins & Marvin, 1837.
63 p. WHi.   43330

---- Mason Street Sabbath School.
Reports of the superintendent.
[Boston], 1837. 20 p. CtY.
                            43331
---- Mayor. 1837-1839 (Samuel
A. Eliot).
Communication of the Mayor
... relative to overseers of the
poor. Mar. 30, 1837. Boston,
1837. MB.   43332

---- Public Schools. Report on
the memorial of the Boston Acad-
emy of Music, August, 1837.
(Boston, 1837). 20 p. MHi.
                            43333
---- School committee.
Report of the School Committee

of the city of Boston, on the
expediency of introducing
musical instruction into the public schools of the city. [Bos-
ton, 1837?]. 7 p. MB; MBAt;
MHi; NNT-C.   43334

---- ---- ....Report on the
distribution of the pupils in
the grammar schools of the city
of Boston. Boston, J. H. Eastburn, city printer, 1837. 12 p.
CtY; ICU; MB; MH; MiD-B.
                              43335
---- Second Baptist Church.
A summary declaration of
the faith and practice of the
Second Baptist Church of
Christ, in Boston, which was
agreed to by the church in
1743, when under the pastoral
care of the Rev. Ephrain Bound.
... Boston, Gould, Kendall &
Lincoln, 1837. 11 p. Nh;
PCA.   43336

---- Twelfth Congregational
Society.
Rules and regulations of the
Sunday school in the Twelfth
Congregational Society. Rev.
and arranged, 1837. School
instituted March, 1837. Boston, Tuttle, Dennett & Chisholm, 1837. 17 p. MH.   43337

---- Warren Street Chapel.
Circular, April 17, 1837.
Boston, 1837. Bdse.
MHi.   43338

---- ---- Proceedings. 1, 2,
5-23, 25-27, 30-43, 60-71.
Boston, 1837-1907. 5 vols. &
cover. MB.   43339

---- ---- Rep. of Com. of
Contributors. (Boston, 1837.)
MB.   43340

Boston Academy of Music.

The Boston Academy's collection of church music: consisting
of the most popular Psalm and
hymn tunes, anthems, sentences,
chants, &c. Old and New; together with many beautiful pieces,
tunes and anthems, selected from
the masses and other works of
Haydn, Mozart, Beethoven, Pergo-
lesi, Righini, ... including, also,
original compositions by German,
English and American authors.
Published under the direction of
the Boston Academy of Music.
fifth edition. Boston, Published
by J. H. Wilkins and R. B. Carter, 1837. 357 p. MB; MBAt;
MnM; RPB; KCoLu.   43341

---- Extracts from the quarterly
report, November, 1837. Boston, 1837. 7 p. MHi.   43342

---- Extracts from the report,
Nov. 18, 1837. Boston, 1837.
MBAt.   43343

---- Sixth concert by the choir
and orchestra of the academy,
at the Odeon, Febr. 1, 1837.
[Boston, 1837?]. 12 p. CtY.
                              43344
---- Eighth concert, March 8,
1837. Boston, 1837. [Boston,
1837?]. 23 p. MHi.   43345

---- Ninth concert (and last one
for the season) by the choir and
orchestra of the academy, at the
Odeon, Wednesday evening,
March 15, 1837. Boston, Per-
kins, 1837. 20 p. MH-And.
                              43346
---- ... Tenth concert (and last
for the season) by the choir and
orchestra of the academy, at the
Odeon, March 22, 1837. Boston,
Perkins and Marvin, 1837. 18 p.
MHi; RPB.   43347

The Boston Almanac, for the year

1838. Volume I. no. 3. Boston, printed by S. N. Dickinson, [1837]. 103 p. IaHi; MeB; MWA; MWo; RNHi.   43348

Boston and New York Coal Company.
  Charter and bye-laws. New York, Booth, 1837. 21 p. CtY; MB.   43349

---- Report of the examination and survey of the coal fields and iron ore belonging to the Boston and New York Coal Company at Frostburg, Alleghany County, in the state of Maryland. New York, E. B. Clayton, printer, 1837. 18 p. DLC.   43350

Boston Anthenaeum.
  Catalogue of the eleventh exhibition of paintings in the Anthenieum gallery. Boston, John N. Eastburn, printer, 1837. 8 p. IaDaP; MWHi; MWo.   43351

The Boston book, being specimens of metropolitan literature. Ed. by B. B. Thatcher. Boston, Light and Stearns, 1837. (2nd Vol. of a set which began in 1836.) 360 p. GDecCT; MB; MWA; PHi; TxU.   43352

Boston Children's Friend Society.
  An Act of incorporation, constitution and by-laws of the Boston Children's Friend Society.... Boston, Press of J. Howe, 1837. 23 p. MB; MWA.   43353
---- Order of exercises at the anniversary of the Children's Friend Society, Boston, Dec. 10, 1837. [Boston, Press of J. Howe, 1837] Broadside. MB.   43354

Boston Courier. V. 1 - Boston, Jan. 16, 1837-. (Was Boston Weekly Courier) CtY; MBAt.   43355

Boston Fire dept.
  Great meeting of the Fire department. (July 7, 1837.) Boston, 1837. MB.   43356

Boston Dispensary.
  Institution of the Boston Dispensary for the medical relief of the poor. Incorporated 1801. (Containing the Act of Incorporation, the rules and the list of contributors.) Boston, 1837. DLC; DNLM; M; MHi.   43357

Boston Irish Protestant Association.
  Circular letter to their brethren of Boston and vicinity. 2d ed. Boston, 1837. MB; MBAt.   43358
Boston journal of natural history, containing papers and communications read to the Boston society of natural hsitory, 1834-1863. Boston, Hilliard, Gray & Co., (etc.), 1837-1863. 7 v. CSt; ICU; MeB; OrCS; PPWA.   43359
Boston reading lessons for primary schools. Boston, 1837. CtHWatK; MB.   43360

Boston Society of Natural History. Library.
  Catalogue of the library of the Boston society of natural history. Boston, Printed by Freeman and Bolles, 1837(-41?). 27 p. CtY; MBM; MWA; NhD; WHi.   43361

Boston Type and Stereotype Foundry.
  Specimen of modern printing types, cast at the letter foundry of the Boston Type and Stereotype Company. Boston, 1837. ICU; MBC.   43362

Boston Universalist Young Men's Institute.

Constitution of the Boston Universalist Young Men's Institute, with a list of members, and a catalogue of the library. Boston, Printed by George P. Oakes, 1837. (3), 4-12 p. MMeT.   43363

Boston Wharf Company.

Report of the board of directors to the stockholders, submitting the 1st annual report of their agents. Boston, 1837. MB; MBAt.   43364

Bostwick, David, 1721-1763.

A fair & rational vindication of the right of infants to the ordinance of baptism being the substances of several discourses from Acts.II.39...New York, Carter, 1837. 58 p. CSansS; CSmH; NjR; NjPT; PPPrHi. 43365

Boswell, James, 1740-1795.

The life of Samuel Johnson, including a journal of a tour to the Hebrides, by James Boswell, Esq., A new edition, with numerous additions and notes, by John Wilson LL.D. F.R.S. New York, Dearborn and Co., 1837. 2 v. MB; MdW; PBm; PPDrop; ViU.   43366

Botham, P. E. Bates.

Common School Arithmetic. 7th ed., revised & improved. Hartford, Conn., H. Benton, 1837. MH; MiU.   43367

Botta, Carlo Giuseppe Guglielmo, 1766-1837.

History of the war of the independence of the United States of America. By Charles Botta.... 5th ed., in two volumes, rev. and cor. New-Haven, Published and printed

by Nathan Whiting, [1837.] 2 v. FG; MiD-B; NcD; TBRi; TU.
43368

Boudinot, Elias, d. 1839.

Cherokee affairs, authorized by John Ross. By E. Boudinot, formerly editor of the Cherokee Phoenix, Athens, printed in the office of the Southern Banner, 1837. 66 p. WAnHi.   43369

---- Letters and other papers relating to Cherokee affairs; being in reply to sundry publications authorized by John Ross... Athens, printed at the office of the "Southern Banner," 1837. 66 p. CtHWatk; WHi.
43370

Boudinot, Elias, 1740-1821.

The man in a trance; or, Life of the Rev. William Tennent, late pastor of the Presbyterian church at Freehold, New Jersey,...Improved ed. Dayton, Published by B. F. Ella; Madison Ind., James McMillan; Cincinnati, George Conclin, 1837. 60 p. OCHP; WHi.   43371

Bouilland, Jean Baptiste, 1796-1881.

New researches on acute articular rheumatism in general, and especially on the law of coincidence of pericarditis and endocarditis with this disease, as well as on the efficacy of the method of treating it by repeated bloodlettings at short intervals. By J. Bouilland ... Translated by James Kitchen, M.D. Philadelphia, Haswell, Barrington, and Haswell, 1837. [9]-64 p. CSt-L; MdBJ; NjP; PP; ViU.
43372

Bouilly, Jean Nicolas, 1763-1842.

Savings bank, and other stories: illustrating true independence and domestic economy. New York, S. Coleman, 1837. 140 p. ICU; MBC.   43373

Bouldin, James Wood.
Speech of ... on the bill to authorize the issue of treasury notes. Delivered in the House, September 26, 1837. Washington, printed at the globe office, 1837. 7 p. DLC; NNC; PPM.
43374

Bourdon, Louis Pierre Marie.
Elements of algebra. See Davies, Charles, 1798-1876.
43375

[Bourne, George] 1780-1845.
Slavery illustrated in its effect upon woman and domestic society ... Boston, I. Knapp, 1837. [9]-127 p. GEU; IaU; MB; PPL; RP.
43376

Bouton, Nathaniel, 1797-1878.
Temporal prosperity; an address delivered before the Concord temperance society, March 30, 1837. Concord (N.H.), A. M'Farland, 1837. 22 p. CtB; ICU; MH-And; MWA; NhD.
43377

Bowdoin College.
Laws of Bowdoin College in the State of Maine. Brunswick, Press of Joseph Griffin, 1837. 30 p. CSmH; MeB; MeHi.
43378
---- Class of 1837.
Reunion. Class of 1837, Bowdoin college, June 22, 1837. [Brunswick, Brunswick telegraph job press, 1837?] 21 p. DLC; MeB; RPB.
43379

[Bowen, Abel], 1790-1850, comp.
The naval monument, containing official and other accounts of all the battles fought between the navies of the United States and Great Britain during the late war; and an account of the war with Algiers ... To which is annexed a naval register of the United States, re-vised and corrected, and brought down to the year 1836. New York, Nafis & Cornish; St. Louis, Van Dien & McDonald, 1837. 326 p. CSmH; NN; MoS; OCl.
43380

Bowman, Samuel,1800-1861.
The form of sound words; a sermon preached at St. Andrew's church, Philadelphia, at the opening of the convention of the Protestant Episcopal church in the diocese of Pennsylvania, May 17th, 1837....[Pennsylvania, 1837.] 9 p. WHi.   43381

Bowring, John.
Minor Morals For Young People. Illustrated In Tales And Travels. By John Bowring, Philadelphia, Carey, Lea & Blanchard, 1837. 262, 8 p. ICBB; MBL; MLow; NCH; NPStA.   43382

Boyd, James.
Address delivered before the charitable Irish society in, Boston, at the celebration of their centennial anniversary, March 17, 1837. By James Boyd, ... Boston, Published by James B. Dow, 1837. 40 p. CtSoP; MB; Nh; PPM; RPB.   43383

Boyer, Abel, 1667-1729.
Boyer's French dictionary: .... with a table of French verbs, etc. Boston, Published by Hilliard Gray & Co., 1837. 250 p. CSfCMM.   43384

Boylston Circulating Library.
Catalogue. Boston, Francis, 1837. 83 p. MB.   43385

The boys' manual; comprising a summary view of the studies, accomplishments, and principles of conducts.... New York, D. Appleton & company, n.pr., 1837. 288 p. MB; MnU; NjR; RPAt.   43386

Bozman, John Leeds, 1757-1823.
The history of Maryland,
from its first settlement, in
1633, to the restoration, in
1660, with a copious introduction, and notes and illustrations.
By John Leeds Bozman. Baltimore, J. Lucas & E. K. Deaver,
1837. 2 v. KyLoF; MdBE;
NjPT; OrP; PHC; TxU.   43387

Bracht, Tieleman Janszoon van,
1625-1664.
The bloody theatre, or,
Martyrs' mirror, of the defence-
less Christians, who suffered
and were put to death ...
from the time of Christ until the
year A.D. 1660. Formerly compiled from various authentic
chronicles and testimonies published in the Dutch language,
by Thielem J. von Bracht.
Carefully translated ... by I.
Daniel Rupp...(Lancaster) Published by David Miller, 1837.
1048 p. CSt; IaPeC; MBAt;
PHi; ViRU.   43388

Bradbury, Charles, 1798-1864.
History of Kennebunkport,
[Me.] from its first discovery
by Bartholomew Gosnold, May
14, 1602 to A.D. 1837 ...
Kennebunk, J. K. Remich,
1837. 301 p. CtSoP; InCW;
Me; MWA; OC.   43389

Bradford, Duncan.
The Wonders of the Heavens,
being a popular view of Astron-
omy, including a full illustra-
tion of the Mechanism of the
heavens; embracing the sun,
moon, and stars. By Duncan
Bradford. Boston, American
Stationers Company, John B.
Russell, 1837. 371 p. IU;
KyLoF; NjP; RPaw; WaPS.
                          43390
Bradford, Thomas Gamaliel.

Illustrated Atlas of the United
States, etc. Boston, 1837.
MBAt.   43391

Bradford Junior College. Brad-
ford, Mass.
A catalogue of the corporation,
office and students of Bradford,
(Vt.) academy, the term ending
May 12, 1837. Haverhill, N.H.,
Printed by J. R. Reding, 1837.
[12] p. MnHi.   43392

Bradley, Eliza.
An Authentick narrative of
the shipwreck and sufferings of
Mrs. Eliza Bradley, the wife of
Capt. James Bradley of Liver-
pool, England, commander of the
British ship Sally, which was
wrecked on the coast of Barbary,
in June, 1818. Written by her-
self. Ithaca, Mack, Andrus,
& Woodruff, 1837. 90 p. MWA.
                          43393
Brainerd, Thomas.
A sermon delivered at the
opening of the new lecture room
in the Third Presbyterian church
of Philadelphia June 16, 1837 by
Thomas Brainerd. Philadelphia,
Printed by Wm. F. Geddes, 1837.
14 p. CtY; OCHP; PPL; TxDaM.
                          43394
Bramwell, William.
Short account of the life of
Ann Cutler. New York, 1837.
20 p. MWA.   43395

Branagan, J.
The pleasures of paradise; or
a glimpse of the sovereign beauty. To which is added the
guardian genius of the federal
union. Philadelphia, 1837. PPL,
PPL-R.   43396

Brandreth, Benjamin, 1807-1880.
Philip Von Artaveld the people's friend, an historical play,
in three acts. New York, printed

for the author, 1837. 73 p.
MH.   43397

Brantly, William Theophilus.
    Objections to a Baptist ver-
sion of the New Testament.
By William T. Brantly ... With
additional reasons for preferring
the English Bible as it is. By
Octavius Winslow ... New York,
J. P. Callender, 1837. 66 p.
IEG; MeBaT; NbCrD; NcSaiL;
NHC-S; NNUT.   43398

---- Themes for meditation, en-
larged in several sermons, doc-
trinal and practical by William
T. Brantly. Philadelphia, C.
Sherman & Co., 1837. 400 p.
ICU; KyLoS; MsWJ; PCA;
ViRut.   43399

Bray, John, 1782-1822.
    The tooth-ache; or, Mistakes
of a morning, a petit comedy,
in one act, a free translation
from the french. Philadelphia,
C. Neal, 1837. 21 p. MH.
                                       43400
Brazer, John, 1787-1846.
    Lessons of the past. A ser-
mon, on the anniversary of
ordination, preached to the
North society, in Salem, Mass.
Sunday, November 19th, 1837.
By John Brazer. Salem, printed
at the Gazette office, 1837.
22 p. CSmH; ICMe; OClWHi;
RPB; WHi.   43401

Breckinridge, Robert Jefferson,
1800-1871.
    Discourse on the formation
and development of the American mind; delivered before the
literary societies of Lafayette
college, Easton, Pa., Sept. 20,
1837. Baltimore, Richard J.
Matchett, printer, 1837. 40 p.
CtY; ICU; MBAt; NjP; PPL.
                                       43402

Brewster, Charles Warren.
    National standard of costume.
A lecture on the changes of
fashion, delivered before the
Portsmouth lyceum, by Charles
W. Brewster ... [Portsmouth,
N.H.] Portsmouth journal press,
1837. 15 p. CSmH; KU; MB;
MiD-B; MWA.   43403

Brewster, David, 1781-1868.
    A treatise on optics. By
Sir David Brewster. ... New
ed. With an appendix, containing an elementary view of the
application of analysis to reflex-
ion and refraction, by A. D.
Bache...Philadelphia, Carey Lea
& Blanchard, 1837. 323, viii,
[9]-95 p. IaB; MiU; MWA;
PAtM; ScC.   43404

Bricheteau, Isidora, 1789-1861.
    ... Medical clinics of the Hos-
pital Necker; or, Researches and
observations on the nature, treatment, and physical causes of
diseases. By I. Bricheteau.
... Translated from the French
... Philadelphia, A. Waldie, 1837.
141 p. ICJ; MB; MeB; Nh; PP.
                                       43405
Bridge, B.
    The American Speaker. Com-
prising elegant Selections....
Cincinnati, E. Morgan, and Son,
etc., 1837. OCHP; OClWHi.
                                       43406
Bridgeman, Thomas.
    The young gardener's assist-
ant containing a catalogue of
garden and flower seeds, with
direction for the cultivation of
culinary vegetable and flowers,
fruit trees the grape vine, etc.
7th ed. New York, Milchel &
Turner, printers, 1837. ICJ;
MH; MWA; NjPT.   43407

Bridgewater Treatises. Philadelphia, 1837-1839. 3 v. PHi;
PPULC.   43408

A Brief Outline for a National Bank. By a Native Citizen. Cincinnati, Paul & Dodd, Printer, Sept., 1837. 8 p. DLC.
43409

A brief outline of the rise, progress, and failure of the revolutionary scheme of the nineteen Van Buren electors of the state of Maryland...Baltimore, Ptd. by Sands and Neilson, 1837. 90 p. MdHi; MiD-B; RPB; ScU.
43410

Brief sketch of the life and military services of Arthur P. Hayne, of Charleston, South Carolina. Philadelphia, Printed by T. K. & P. G. Collins, No. 1 Lodge Alley, 1837. 16 p. DLC; ICN; ScHi; ViU; ViW.
43411

Brief thoughts on five systems of doctrine. In a letter to a friend. Boston, Published by Fairfield and Pitman, 1837. 16 p. MB.
43412

Brinsmade, Horatio Nelson.
A sermon, preached at the funeral of the Hon. Joshua Danforth, who died at Pittsfield, January 30, 1837, on the seventy-eighth year of his age. By H. N. Brinsmade ... Pittsfield [Mass.], Printed by Phineas Allen and son, [1837?]. 24 p. CSmH; CtY; MW; NjR; RPB.
43413

Bristol Academy. Taunton, Mass. Trustees.
Replies of trustees ... and a letter from the president of the board; occasioned by the publications of Mr. Frederick Crafts, (late preceptor of the school) on the subject of his dismission. Taunton, [Mass], Bradford and Amsbury, 1837. 12 p. RPB.
43414

The British drama: a collection of the most esteemed tragedies, comedies, operas, and farces, in the English language. Philadelphia, Desilver, Thomas & co., 1837. 2 v. Mi; NbOM; PBm; PPULC; ViU.
43415

Brockenbrough, William Henry, 1812-1850.
The right of instruction. The Virginia doctrine considered. Being an answer to the letters of Judge Joseph Hopkins, originally published in the Southern literary messenger. By W. H. Brockenbrough. Charlottesville, James Alexander, 1837. 54 p. NcD; TxU; ViU; WHi.
43416

[Bromme, Traugott], 1802-1866.
Louisiana. Ein taschenbuch für auswandered und freunde der länder-und Völkerkunde. Baltimore, Md., C. Scheld und co., 1837. 54 p. IU; MdBE; MiU; MoS; Tx.
43417

---- Mississippi und Alabama. Taschenbuch für einwanderer und freunde der lander- und völkerkunde. Baltimore, Md., C. Scheld und co., (W. Einhorn), 1837. 4 p. ℓ., 24 p., 4 ℓ., 22 p. MdBE; MiU; MoSM; Tx; WHi.
43418

---- Reise durch die Florida's, von St. Augustine durch die halbinsel nach Pensacola. (Aus Bromme's Reisen besonders abgedruckt)....Baltimore, Md., C. Scheld und co., 1837. (3)-80 p. ICJ; ICN; MdBE; MoSM; TX.
43419

Brook, Mary (Brotherton), 1726-1782.
Reasons for the necessity of silent waiting, in order to the solemn worship of God ... New York, N.Y., Yearly meeting of

Friends, 1837. 34 p. CtY;
MBC; NjPT.   43420

Brooklyn City Temperance Society.
    Constitution, by-laws &c.
of the Brooklyn City Temperance Society. November, 1837.
8 p. NSmb.   43421

Brooks, Charles, 1795-1872.
    Elementary instruction. An
address delivered before the
schools and the citizens, of the
town of Quincy, July 4, 1837.
By Charles Brooks ... Quincy,
Printed by J. A. Green, 1837.
20 p. DLC; MB; MeU; NjPT;
PPL.   43422

---- A Family Prayer Book,
and private manual. ... By
Charles Brooks. Tenth edition.
Boston, James Munroe and
Company; New York, C. S.
Francis, 1837. 348 p. MB;
MHi; MHingHi; MWA.   43423

---- A Lecture delivered before the American Institute of
Instruction, at Worcester, August 25, 1837. By Charles
Brooks, of Hingham, Massachusetts. Published by request.
Printed by I. R. Butts, 1837.
19 p. MWA.   43424

---- Prayers for children and
young persons. Extracted from
The family prayer book. 1
pam. Hingham, 1837. 12 p.
MH; MH-AH.   43425

---- School reform or Teacher's seminaries; a lecture delivered before the American Institute of instruction at Worcester, August 25, 1837. Boston, I. R. Butts, 1837. 19 p.
CtHWatk; MH.   43426

Brooks, Nathan Covington, 1809-
1898.
    Scriptural anthology; or, Bib-
lical illustrations: designed as a
present for all seasons. By
Nathan C. Brooks, A.M. Philadelphia, W. Marshall & co.;
Baltimore, Bayly & Burns, 1837.
[9]-180 p. DLC; MdBLC; MdBP;
PPLT; RPB.   43427

Brother Jonathan's Almanac, for
1838. Philadelphia, Pa., Thomas
L. Bonsal, (1837). MWA.
                             43428
Brown, David Paul, 1795-1872.
    Eulogium upon William Rawle,
L.L.D., delivered on the 31st
of December, 1836, by David Paul
Brown. Philadelphia, E. L.
Carey & A. Hart, 1837. 45 p.
DLC; ICN; MBAt; MH; PPA.
                             43429
Brown, (G.)
    The institutes of English gram-
mar. New York, 1837. MB.
                             43430
Brown, Isaac Van Arsdale, 1784-
1861.
    A sermon on the work of the
Holy Spirit; delivered in Easton,
Pa., before the synod of New
Jersey Oct. 17, 1837....New
York, R. Carter, 1837. 35 p.
DLC; MB; NjP; PHi; PPPrHi.
                             43431
Brown, James.
    The American system of Eng-
lish syntax, developing the con-
structive principles of the Eng-
lish phrenod or language ...
By James Brown. Philadelphia,
J. Blackmarr, 1837. 33-442 p.
DLC; MP; PHi; PPAmP; OO.
                             43432
Brown, John.
    Historical notices of St.
George's church, Newburgh, in
a sermon, delivered in said
church January 1, 1837. By the
Rev. John Brown... New-York,

Swords, Stanford & co., 1837.
30 p. NBLIHI; MnHi; MWA;
NjR; NNG.   43433

Brown, John, 1722-1787.
A concordance to the Holy
Scriptures of the Old and New
Testaments: ...By John Brown,
... Published by the Brattle-
boro Typographic Company...
Brattleboro, Vermont, 1837.
84, (4) p. KWiU; MeAu.   43434

---- ---- Hartford, Con.,
Thrall, 1837. 272 p. MB; OO.
                             43435
Brown, John, 1784-1858.
The Christian pastor's man-
ual: a selection of tracts on
the duties, difficulties and en-
couragements of the Christian
ministry, ed. by John Brown...
1st American ed. from the
Edinburgh, ed. Philadelphia,
J. Whetham, 1837. 420 p.
CoD; ICP; PPP; NbOP; WaPS.
                             43436
Brown, John A., 1810.
The family guide to health,
containing a description of the
Botanic Thomsonian system of
medicine with a biographical
sketch of the author. By J. A.
Brown....Providence, B. T.
Albro, printer, 1837. 224 p.
IEN-M; MBM; MoSMed; RHi;
RPB.   43437

---- Supplement to the family
guide to health containing directions for compounding botanic
medicines, also some remarks
... Providence, B. T. Albro,
1837. 32 p. DLC; OClW;
OClWHi.   43438

Brown, John Newton, 1803-1868.
Encyclopedia of religious
knowledge: or, Dictionary of
the Bible, theology, religious
biography. All religions, ec-

clesiastical history and missions.
Brattleboro, Vt., Brattleboro
Typographic Co., 1837. (7)-
1275 p. ArLP; LNH; NbOP;
OSW; TNWI.   43439

Brown, Jonathan.
The history and present con-
dition of St. Domingo. By J.
Brown ... Philadelphia, W.
Marshall and co., 1837. 2 v.
DeWi; GHi; IaDaP; MMal; RP.
                             43440
Brown University.
A Catalogue of the Library of
the United Brothers' Society of
Brown University, with the
Names of the Members. Founded,
A.D. 1806. Providence, printed
by Knowles, Vose & Co., 1837.
40 p. MBAt; MBC.   43441

---- Catalogue of the Officers
and Students of Brown University, for the Academical Year
1837-38. Providence, H. H.
Brown, 1837. 21 p. MiU-C.
                             43442
Browne, Peter Arrell, 1782-1860.
An essay on Indian corn.
By Peter A. Browne ... Philadelphia, Printed by J. Thompson,
1837. 32 p. CtY; DLC; IU;
NN; PHi.   43443

---- An essay on the veterinary
art; setting forth its great usefulness, giving an account of
the veterinary colleges in France
and England, and exhibiting the
facility and utility of instituting
similar schools in the United
States. To which is added, a
few hints upon the propriety of
connecting therewith an insurance upon the lives of horses.
By Peter A. Browne ... Philadelphia, Printed by J. Thompson,
1837. 22 p. CtY; DLC; MWA;
NjR; PU.   43444

---- An essay upon the theory
and operation of the steam engine. Philadelphia, I. Ashmead and Co., 1837. 35 p.
DBRE. 43445

Browning, Robert, 1812-1889.
The king and the Cook,
from the authors revised text.
New York, 1837. PPL. 43446

Brownlee, William Craig, 1784-
1860.
The Christian father at home;
or, A manual of parental instruction; in two parts: I.
on the necessity of salvation;
2. on the way of salvation.
New York, Robert Carter (New
York, printed by Scratcherd
and Adams), 1837. DLC; ICU;
MeBat; MPiB; PPPrHi. 43447

---- Lights and Shadows of
Christian Life....by William
Craig Brownlee, D.D. New
York, John S. Taylor, ...
1837. 388 p. GHi; ICU;
MeBat; NhD; PPPrHi. 43448

Brown's literary omnibus.
News, books entire, sketches,
reviews, tales, miscellaneous
intelligence. V.1-2; Jan. 6,
1837-July 20, 1838. Philadelphia, A. Waldie [etc.], 1837-
38. 2 v. in 1. CtY; DLC;
NcD; RPB. 43449

Brownson, Orestes Augustus,
1803-1876.
An address on popular edu-
cation. Delivered in Winnisim-
met village, on Sunday evening,
July 23, 1837. By O. A.
Brownson. Printed by request.
Boston, Press of J. Putnam,
1837. 15 p. CtY; MH; MHi;
Nh; TNP. 43450

---- Babylon is falling. A discourse preached in the Masonic
temple, to the Society for christian union and progress, on Sunday morning, May 28, 1837. Boston, I. R. Butts, 1837. 22 p.
CtY; ICMe; MBC; MnHi; NN.
43451
---- The spirit of gain, or the
fall of Babylon, a discourse on
the times, delivered before the
Society for christian union and
progress. Boston, 1837. 22 p.
MBC. 43452

Bruce, Nathaniel F.
A discourse delivered in St.
Luke's church, Rochester, on
Sunday evening, February 5th,
1837, and in Grace church, Sun-
day the 12th, after the admini-
stration of Holy Eucharist. By
Nathaniel F. Bruce. Rochester,
N.Y., Hoyt & Porter, 1837.
CU; NR; NRHi; NRU. 43453

Bruce, Robert, 1776-1846.
An introductory lecture, delivered before the Institute of
arts and sciences, Pittsburgh, on
the 20th December, 1836. By
the Rev. R. Bruce, D.D. [Pitts-
burgh, Pa.], Printed by Johnston
& Stockton ... 1837. 24 p.
CSmH; MiD-B; OClWHi. 43454

Bruce's (George) Son and Com-
pany, New York.
A specimen of printing types
cast by Geo. Bruce & Co. New
York. (New York), 1837. 277 ℓ.
NN; NNC; NNC-Atf. 43455

Bruckner, G.
Handbuch...erdbeschreibung.
Hildbunghausen, Amsterda., New
York bibliographischen institute,
1837. PPeSchw. 43456

Brunson, Alfred.
The sweet singer of Israel:
a collection of hymns and spiritual

songs, usually sung at camp, prayer, and social meetings, and in revivals of religion. Selected and compiled, at the request of the publishers. By the Rev. Alfred Brunson, and the Rev. Charles Pitman.... Pittsburgh, Published by John I. Kay & Co., 1837. 320 p. ICN; NL; PWCHi. 43457

Brunswick Land and Canal Companies.
Trust Deed & By-laws. Boston, John H. Eastburn, printer, 1837. 15 p. MH-BA. 43458

Brunswick Land Company (Georgia).
Public sale. The Brunswick land company offer at public sale, from one to two hundred well selected lots. The sale will commence...on Thursday, the twenty-fifth day of May (1837). By order of the directors. Edward Eldredge, general agent. (Brunswick? 1837). 11 p. GHi; MB; MH; NN. 43459

---- (Trust deed and By-Laws) Prospectus. Boston, Eastburn's press, 1837. 12 p. Mh-BA. 43460

Buchanan, James, 1791-1868.
Speech of Mr. Buchanan, on the Bill imposing additional duties, as depositories in certain cases, on public officers. Delivered in Senate U.S. September, 29, 1837. Washington, printed at the Globe Office, 1837. 22 p. InHi; MdHi; MH; PPM; TxH. 43461

---- Speech of Mr. Buchanan on the resolution of Col. Benton, to expunge from the journal of the senate, the resolution of the 28th of March, 1834; de-

livered in the senate of the U.S. January 16, 1837. Washington, D.C., printed at the Globe office, 1837. 13 p. CtSoP; ICN; MoS. 43462

Buck, Charles, 1771-1815.
A theological dictionary, containing definitions of all religious terms ... Philadelphia, Printed by Woodward, 1837. 472 p. CBPac; ICNBT; NStc; PAlt; OCY. 43463

Buckingham, G.
The Bible vindicated from the charge of sustaining slavery. Columbus, Ohio, Temperance office advocate office, 1837. 24 p. ODa; OO; TNF. 43464

Buckingham, James Silk, 1786-1855.
Mr. Buckingham's address to the people of the United States. New York. Oct. 25, 1837. New York, W. Molineux, Printer, [1837]. (4) p. DLC; MB; MnHi; PPL; TU. 43465

Buckland, William, 1784-1856.
Geology and mineralogy considered with reference to natural theology. By the Rev. William Buckland ... Philadelphia, Carey, Lea and Blanchard, 1837. 2 v. DLC; IaK; ICU; PPA; ViRut. 43466

Buel, Jesse, 1778-1839.
An address delivered before the Berkshire agriculture society, October 5, 1837, being its twenty-seventh anniversary. By Jesse Buel; printed at the request of the society. Pittsfield, Phinebas Allen & son, Alfred Southwick, pr., 1837. 34 p. DLC; MBHo; MPiB; NjR. 43467

Buffalo and Erie railroad company.
Report of the chief engineer, on the preliminary surveys, of

the Buffalo and Erie railroad,
printed by order of the Board
of Directors. Dunkirk, (N.Y.),
J. I. Bruce, printer, 1837.
DBRE; DLC; PPULC.   43468

Buffalo Boarding School.
First Annual Catalogue of
the Buffalo Boarding School.
P. G. Cooke, Principal, E. S.
Hawley, Assistant. Buffalo,
Printed by Charles Faxon, 1837.
MH; NBuHi.   43469

Buffalo Library, Buffalo, N.Y.
A catalogue of books in the
library of the Young Men's As-
sociation of the city of Buffalo.
Founded 22d February, 1836.
Incorporated March 3d, 1837.
Buffalo, press of Oliver G.
Steele, 1837. 42 p. 8 v.
ICLaw; NBu.   43470

---- First annual report of the
executive committee of the Young
Men's Association of the city of
Buffalo. Reported and adopted
Feb. 8, 1837. Buffalo, press
of Oliver G. Steele, 1837.
13 p. CSmH; ICU; NBu; WHi.
                         43471
Bulfinch, Stephen Greenleaf.
An introductory discourse,
delivered on recommencing the
services of the unitarian church
in Pittsburgh. Pittsburgh,
1837. 16 p. ICMe; MBAt;
MH; MH-And; PPAmP.   43472

Bullions, Peter, 1791-1864.
The principles of English
grammar; comprising the substance of the most approved
English grammars extant. With
copious exercises in parsing
and syntax, for the use of
academies and common schools.
(On the plan of Murray's grammar) 2d ed. rev. and cor-
rected. By the Rev. Peter

Bullions....New York, Robert
Carter, 1837. CTHWatk; DLC;
MWHi; RPB; TxU-T.   43473

Bungay, George Washington,
1818-1892.
Acrostics and miscellaneous
poems by G. W. Bungay. New
York, John W. Oliver, Printer,
1837. 128 p. NBuG; NIC; RPB;
ViU.   43474

Bunting, Hannah Syng, 1801-
1832.
Memoir, diary and letters of
Hannah Syng Bunting, of Phila-
delphia, who departed this life
May 25, 1832, in the thirty-first
year of her age. Compiled by Rev.
Timothy Merritt. New York,
Pub. by Carlton & Porter, Sunday-school union....1837. 2 v.
DLC; MBC; NIC; NNMHi; PPM.
                         43475
Bunyan, John, 1628-1688.
Der Heilige Krieg, wie der-
selbe gefuehrt wird von Christo
Jesu, dem Sohne des El Schaddai,
des ewigen und allmaechtigen
Koenigs, wider den teufel. Oder:
das verlieren und wiedererobern
der beruehmten Stadt mensch
seele. Beschreiben von Johann
Bunian, Prediger zu Bedford.
Mit sechs bildren geziert. Harrisburg, Pa., Gedruckt und zu
haben bei G. G. Peters, 1837.
288 p. IaDuW; P; PHi; PPG.
                         43476
---- The holy war made by
King Shaddai upon Diabolus to
regain the metropolis of the
world. ...With explanatory,...
notes by the Rev. G. Burder.
Exeter, J. and B. Williams,
1837. (9)-240 p. CSmH; InNob;
MWA; NHC-S; TNP.   43477

---- The pilgrim's progress, from
this world, to that which is to
come. Delivered under the

similitude of a dream....Cincinnati, Morgan & Sanxay, 1837. 2 v. in 1. MnU; OC; OClWHi. 43478

---- ---- Hartford, Judd, Loomis and Co., 1837. 368 p. CtHT; CtY; MiJa; PPF; VtCaS. 43479

---- ---- New York, Harper & Bros., 1837. 348, (2) p. ILM; LNT; MiU; NPla; PU. 43480

Burchardism vs. Christianity. (Philadelphia? printed by Platt & Ranney, 1837.) 16 p. NNUT. 43481

Burdett, Samuel.
Catalogue of his stock of books, sold in Boston [Boston] 1837. MBAt. 43482

Burford, Robert.
Description of a view of the city of Jerusalem, and the surrounding country....Boston, Richard, Lord & Holbrook, 1837. 12 p. CtY; DLC; MH-And; PHi; RPB. 43483

---- Description of a View of the Falls of Niagara. Now Exhibiting at the Panorama, Charles Street, Boston. Boston, 1837. 12 p. MHi; MWA. 43484

Burges, Tristam, 1770-1853.
A brief of the remarks made before the Committee on railways and canals, on the petition of the Seekonk branch railroad co....[Boston? 1837?]. 37 p. CSmH; DLC; ICJ; MWA; NN. 43485

Burgess, Archibald.
Baptism considered in relation to its mode and subjects, in a series of discourses. Boston, Perkins & Marvin, 1837. 258 p. InCW; NbOP; OO; PPPrHi; ViRUt. 43486

Burke, Edmund, 1729-1797.
The Works of Edmund Burke, with a memoir. In three vols. New-York, published by Harper & Brothers, 1837. 3 v. AMob; MAnP; OClW; PPC; ScU. 43487

Burke, William, 1752-1836.
Memoir of William Burke, a soldier of the revolution. Reformed from intemperance, and for many years a consistent and devoted Christian. Carefully prepared from a journal kept by himself. To which is added an extract from a sermon preached at his funeral, by Rev. N. Miner. Hartford, Case, Tiffany, and co., 1837. CtSoP; MdBE; MiD-B; RHi; WHi. 43488

Burnap, George Washington.
The voice of the times; a sermon delivered in the First Independent Church of Baltimore, on Sunday, May 14, 1837. By George W. Burnap....Baltimore, John D. Toy, Pr., 1837. 16 p. MBAt; MdBLC; NIC; PPM. 43489

Burnap, U. C.
A Sermon preached in Chester, Vermont, June 19, 1837, at the funeral of Ichabod Onion, Esq. By U. C. Burnap. Published by Mrs. J. Onion, as a Memorial for the Family. Lowell, Leonard Huntress, Printer, 1837. [3]-13 p. MiD-B; MW; PPL. 43490

Burnham, Charles Guildford.
A new system of arithmetic, on the cancelling plan: ... and all proportional questions in one rule applicable to the whole. The process greatly simplified and abridged. By Charles G. Burnham, A.M. Boston, Published by Marsh, Capen & Lyon; New-York, Daniel Appleton & co., 1837. 14-256 p. CtHWatk; MH; MiU; Nh; RPB. 43491

Burns, John, 1774-1850.

The Principles of Midwifery; Including the Diseases of women and children. By John Burns, M.D., F.R.S. Regius professor of surgery in the Univ. of Glascow, etc. From the eighth London ed; Rev. and greatly enl.; with improvements and notes, by T. C. James, M.D. Prof. of Midwifery in the Univ. of Penn. N.Y., Charles S. Francis; Boston, Mass., Jas. H. Francis, 1837. 804 p. DSG; KyLoJM; NSYU; PPHa.   43492

Burns, Robert, 1759-1796.

The works of Robert Burns; containing his life, by John Lockhart .... the poetry and correspondence of Dr. Currie's ed; biographical sketches of the poet by himself, Gilbert Burns, professor Stewart, and others....Hartford, Judd, Loomis & co., 1837. 425 p. DLC; IaK; MWA; OCan; ScNC.   43493
---- The works of Robert Burns: with an account of his life, and criticism on his writings. To which are prefixed, some observations on the character and condition of the Scottish peasantry. Philadelphia, J. Crissy, 1837. NBuG.   43494

Burr, Aaron, 1756-1836.

Memoirs of Aaron Burr, with miscellaneous selections from his correspondence, by Matthew L. Davis. New York, Published by Harper & Brothers, 1837. 2 v. CoU; GMM; MWA; ScCC; THi.   43495

Burr, David.

Report of the improvement at the Grand Rapids of the Wabash River....November 28,

1837. Indianapolis? 1837? MiU.
                                     43496
Burr, David H.

Plan of the hall of the House of Representatives of the United States. engraved by J. V. N. Throop. [Washington, D.C., 1837?] MB; NCD; PPULC.
                                     43497
Burritt, Elijah Hinsdale, 1794-1838.

The geography of the heavens, and class book of astronomy, accompanied by a celestial atlas... 4th ed., with an introduction, by Thomas Dick... New-York, F. J. Huntington & co., 1837. CtY; KyLoF; MH; NjR.   43498

Burrowes, John Freckleton, 1787-1852.

The thorough-base primer, containing explanations and examples of the rudiments of harmony, with fifty exercises. 3d American, improved from the London edition. Boston, J. Loring, 1837. 112 p. InCW; MeB; MH; MWHi; Nh-Hi.   43499

---- ---- 9th ed., with additions. London, Published by the author; New York, Republished by Firth and Hall, 1837. 95, 36 p. MB; MWA; NBu; NN; ViU.   43500

Burton, Warren.

White slavery: A new emancipation cause, presented to the people of the United States. By Warren Burton, author of "the district school as it was." Worcester, M. D. Phillips. Boston, C. C. Little & Co. And B. H. Mussey, 1837. 199 p. MWHi.
                                     43501
Burton, William Evans, d. 1860.

Burton's comic songster; being entirely a new collection of original and popular songs, as sung by Mr. Burton, Mr. Tyrone

Power, Mr. John Reeve, Mr.
Hadaway. Ed by W. E. Bur-
ton. With twelve engravings.
Philadelphia, J. Kayjun; Pittsburgh, J. I. Kay and Co.,
1837. 320 p. CtHT; MH;
NSchU.   43502

Burton's gentleman's magazine
and American monthly review.
Philadelphia, Set comprises vol.
1-7. July 1837-Dec. 1840.
AAP; DLC; MH; PPULC; TxU.
                          43503
Burts, Robert, d. 1839.
   The Scourge of the Ocean:
A Story of the Atlantic, by an
Officer of the U.S. Navy...
(anon.). Philadelphia, E. L.
Carey & A. Hart, 1837. 2 v.
in 1. MsJPED; TNP; TxU.
                          43504
Bury, Charlotte [Susan Maria
(Campbell)] 1775-1861.
   The divorced. By Lary
Charlotte Bury ... Philadelphia,
E. L. Carey & A. Hart, 1837.
2 v. in 1. AU; DLC; PPL;
PPULC.   43505

Bush, George, 1796-1859.
   Life of Mohammed; founder
of the religion of Islam, and of
the empire of the Saracens.
New York, Harper & Bros.,
1837. 261 p. FTa; IEG; MB;
MoK; ScC.   43506

Bushe, George.
   Plates illustrating a treatise
on the malformations, injuries,
and diseases of the rectum and
anus, by George Bushe...
New-York, French & Adlard,
1837. 10 ℓ., 9 pl. DLC;
KyLxT; MBAt; NBuG; ViRA.
                          43507
Bushe, George Macartney,
1797?-1836.
   A catalogue of the valuable
library of the late Dr. Geo. M.

Bushe, comprising a selection of
the best works on anatomy, surgery and medicine, published in
England, France and the United
States....[New York, W. Osborn, printer, 1837]. 23 p.
DLC; MB; PPULC.   43508

---- A treatise on the malformations, injuries, and diseases of
the rectum and anus ... By
George Bushe ... New York,
French & Adlard, 1837. 299,
[1] p. Cu-M; ICJ; LyLxT;
MnU; PPCP.   43509

Bushnell, Horace, 1802-1876.
   An oration, pronounced before the society of Phi beta kappa,
at New Haven, on the principles
of national greatness, August 15,
1837. By Horace Bushnell.
New Haven, Herrick and Noyes,
1837. 27 p. CBPSR; CtY;
MeHi; MH-And; TNP.   43510

Bustard, John.
   A memoir of Miss Mary Helen
Bingham, who died on the fourth
of June, 1825, in the seventeenth
year of her age. From the London Edition. Revised by the
editors. New York, published
by T. Mason and G. Lane, J.
Collord, Printer, 1837. 229 p.
NcD; MBNMHi; ODW.   43511

Butler, Joseph, 1692-1752.
   The analogy of religion, natural
and revealed, to the constitution
and course of nature...New York,
Published by Leavitt, 1837.
105-348 p. IaU; MoS; MWA;
OrALc; PPPrHi; ScCliJ.   43512

Butler, Mann, 1784-1852.
   An appeal from the misrepresentations of James Hall, respecting the history of Kentucky and
the West....To which is annexed
a chronology of the principal

events....in the history of the western country of the United States from the earliest Spanish and French explorations to 1806. Frankfort, Ky., A. G. Hodges, 1837. 32 p. DLC; ICU; MWA; OCHP; WHi.   43513

---- An Oration on National Independence, delivered ... on the Fourth of July, 1837, at Fort Gibson, Mississippi, consisting principally, of a Sketch of the Rise of the State of Mississippi, from the Exploration of De Soto, in 1539, to the present time. .... Frankfort, Ky., Albert G. Hodges, 1837. 23 p. MH; OCHP; WHi.   43514

Butler, William Archer.
    Sermons, doctrinal and practical. By the Rev. William Archer Butler, M.A. Ed. from the author's mss. By James Amiraux Jeremie, D.D., 1st American, from the 3d. Cambridge ed. Philadelphia, (T. K. & P. G. Collins, printer), 1837. 399 p. MTop.   43515

Butter, Henry.
    Scholar's companion...guide to...English language. 6th ed. Philadelphia, H. Perkins, etc., etc., 1837. MH.   43516

---- ---- Ed. 7. Philadelphia, Perkins, 1837. 274 p. CtHWatk; NcWsS; OClWHi; OO; PU.   43517

The Buzzard; published every other Thursday by Jebediah Brown-Bread, Esq. v. 1, no. 1-v. 1, no. 26. Akron, O., S. A. Lane, 1837-38. OClWHi.   43518

Byerly, Stephen.
    Byerly's new American spelling-book, ... Compiled by Stephen Byerly, ... Revised

edition. ... Philadelphia, M'Carty & Davis, 1837. 167 p. MiU-C.   43519

Byington, Cyrus, 1793-1868.
    Chakta Almanac. Union, Okla., Mission Press, 1837. MWA.   43520

Byles, John Barnard, 1801-1884.
    A practical treatise on the law of bills of exchange, promissory notes, banknotes, bankers' cashnotes, and checks...From the last London ed. greatly enl. ... Philadelphia, Littell, 1837. 180 p. MdBB; Nb; OO; PP; ViU.   43521

Byron, George Gordon Noël Byron, 1788-1824.
    Letters, journals and other prose writings of Lord Byron, with notices of his life, by Thomas Moore...New York, G. Dearborn, 1837. 2 v. MdW; NN; NR.   43522

---- The works of Lord Byron; in verse and prose. Including his letters, journals, etc. With a sketch of his life. New-York, Alexander V. Blake....1837. 319, 627 p. IP; GauY; MB; NbOP; PU.   43523

C

Caesar, C. Julius.
    Caesar, translated by William Duncan. In two volumes. New York, Published by Harper & Bros., 1837. 2 v. NPotN.   43524

---- The commentaries of Caesar. Translated into English: To which is prefixed a discourse concerning the Roman art of war. By William Duncan, ... Philadelphia, Thomas Wardle, 1837. vi, 366 p. CtY; DLC; LNH; MBBC; PMA.   43525

Cain, John.

The officer's guide and farmer's manual, containing a comprehensive collection of judicial and business forms adapted to the jurisprudence of Indiana, with an explanation of law phrases and technical terms both Latin and French; to which is prefixed the Declaration of independence, the Constitution of the U. States, and the Constitution of Indiana. By John Cain, esq. Revised by a member of the bar. 2d ed., with the school act of 1837. Indianapolis, Stacy and Williams, 1837. [5]-418 p. CSmH; DLC; In; MH-L. 43526

Cairo City and Canal Company.

An act to incorporate the Cairo City and Canal Company, in the state of Illinois. Alton, Printed by L. A. Parks, 1837. 7 p. MH. 43527

---- Deed of trust, Cairo City and Canal Company, to the New New York Life Insurance and Trust Company, for the benefit of the holders of bonds. New York, James Narine, printer, no. 11 Wall Street, corner of Broad, 1837.

11 p., following with 11 p. of miscellaneous letters, extracts, and reports, and 3 p. "City of Cairo." (Published by the proprietors, A.D. 1818.)

Contains also 2 fold maps pertaining to Cairo, 1838. ICHi. 43528

Calder, Frederick.

Memoirs of Simon Epescopius, the celebrated pupil of Arminius, and subsequently Doctor of Divinity and professor of theology in the University of Leyden....brief account of

the synod of Dort; and of the sufferings to which the followers of Arminius were exposed.... New York, Mason & Lane, 1837. 478 p. KyDC; MiU; NcD; OO; PMA. 43529

Caldwell, Charles, 1772-1853.

Thoughts on schools of medicine, their means of instruction, and modes of administration, with references to the schools of Louisville and Lexington. By Charles Caldwell, M.D. Louisville, Prentice and Weissinger, 1837. 31 p. DLC; MWA; NNNAM; OCLloyd. 43530

Caldwell, William.

Union harmony: or Family musician. Being a choice selection of tunes, selected from the works of the most eminent authors, ancient and modern, together with a large number of original tunre, composed and harmonized by the author, to which is prefixed a comprehensive view of the rudiments of music, abridged and adapted to the capacity of the young. By William Caldwell. Printed by F. A. Parham. Maryville, Ten., 1837. 151, [10] p. NcMHi; T; TKL-Mc. 43531

Caledonian March, arranged for the pianoforte by a professor. Philadelphia, Willig, 1837. (1) p. MB. 43532

Calhoun, John Caldwell, 1782-1850.

Remarks of Mr. Calhoun, in the Senate of the United States, on the bill authorizing an issue of treasury notes, on the 19th September, 1837. [Washington, 1837]. 21 p. CU; MiU-C; MoS; OClWHi; WHi. 43533

---- Remarks of Mr. John C.
Calhoun, of South Carolina, on
his proposition to cede the
Public Lands to the new States,
... In the Senate of the United
States, February 7, 1837.
Washington, Printed by William
B. Moore & Co., 1837. 15 p.
MeB.   43534

---- Remarks of Mr. Calhoun, on
the bill authorizing an issue of
treasury notes: delivered in
the Senate of the United States,
September 19, 1837. Washington, Blair and Rives, 1837.
16 p. CSmH; DLC; MdBJ; MHi.
                              43535
---- Remarks....on the reception of abolition petitions, delivered in the Senate of the
United States, February, 1837.
Washington, D.C., printed by
W. W. Moore & Co., 1837. 7 p.
DLC; WHi.   43536

---- Speech of the Hon. John
C. Calhoun, on his amendment
to separate the government from
the banks. Delivered in the
Senate of the United States,
October 3, 1837. Washington,
1837. 12 p. CU; CtY; DLC;
MdBJ; MWA.   43537

---- Speeches of Mr. Calhoun
....on....the admission of
Michigan, delivered in the
Senate....January, 1837.
Wash., Ptd. by Duff Green,
1837. 13 p. DLC; MBAt;
MiD-B; O; WHi.   43538

Calhoun, William Barron.
    Speech of William B. Cal-
houn, of Massachusetts, on the
currency questions, submitted
to Congress at the Extra session. Delivered in Committee of
the whole, Oct. 12th, 1837.
Springfield [Mass.], Printed at

the office of the Republican and
journal, [1837?]. 15 p. CSmH;
InHi; MWA; PPL.   43539

Call, Moses v. Clark, A. S.
    Report of the case Call vs.
Clark, tried before the Supreme
Judicial Court of Maine, contain-
ing a full statement of the Testi-
mony of more than fifty witnesses.
By A. S. Clark, M.D. First
Edition. - Copy Right Secured.
Bath, Elisha Clarke, 1837. 48 p.
N-L.   43540

Calling things by their right
names. A brief reply to an
article under that title in the
Southern Watchman of May 19,
1837. By a Unitarian Layman...
Charleston, Printed by Walker
& James, 1837. 12 p. MB; MMeT-
Hi; NcD.   43541

Callot, Alexander G., b. 1796.
    Progressive interlinear French
reader; on Lock's plan of instruction ... By A. G. Collot ... The
whole to be used as a key to
"Collot's pronouncing French
reader," and in conjunction
therewith. Philadelphia, J. Kay,
jun. and brother; New York,
Collins, Keese & co.; [etc., etc.],
1837. ViU.   43542

---- Progressive pronouncing
French reader ... By A. G.
Callot ... Philadelphia, J. Kay,
jun. and brother; New York,
Collins, Keese & co.; [etc. etc.[,
1837. xix, [1], 300 p. ViU.
                              43543
Calmet, Augustin, 1672-1757.
    Calmet's dictionary of the
Holy Bible as published by the
Late Mr. Charles Taylor, condensed and arranged in alphabetical order. Eighth ed. Revised with large additions by Edward Robinson. By Augustus

Calmet. Boston, Cracker and
Brewster, 1837. 989 p. ICU;
MTop; MWA; ScNC.   43544

---- ---- Eighth edition revised
with large additions, by Edward
Robinson. Boston, Crocker
and Brewster; New York,
Leavitt Lord & Co., 1837. [1]-
1003 p. DLC; ICU; LNB;
NRSB; ViU.   43545

Calvert, Frederic.
   A treatise upon the law respecting parties to suits in
equity. By Frederick Calvert,
esq. From the London edition-
1837. Philadelphia, John S.
Littell, 1837. xxx, 228, 317 p.
CoU; MdBB; NNLI; PPB; ScSC.
                          43546
Cambreleng, Churchill Caldom,
1786-1862.
   Speech of Mr. Cambreleng, on
the bill imposing additional
duties, as depositories in certain cases, on public officers.
Delivered in the house of representatives, October 13, 1837.
Washington, printed by Blair
and Rives, 1837. 25 p. DLC;
MdHi; NNC; PPULC.   43547

Cambridge, Mass.
   Annual report of the receipts
and expenditures of the town.
March, 1837-46. (Cambridge
1837-46.) 10 reports in 1 vol.
MB; MH.   43548

---- Cambridgeport Parish Sunday School. Hymn. Written
for the children of the Cambridgeport Parish Sunday
School, and sung by them at
their meeting, Christmas Eve,
1837. Broadside. MH.   43549

Cambridge Lyceum.
   Constitution and by-laws as
revised and adopted, Nov. 1837.
Boston, (1837?) MH.   43550

Campbell, Alexander, 1788-1866.
   A debate on the Roman Catholic religion, held in the Syca-
more street meeting house, Cincinnati, from the 13th to the
21st of Jan. 1837, between Alexander Campbell of Bethany, Va.,
and Rt. Rev. John B. Purcell,
bp. of Cincinnati. Taken down
by reporters and revised by the
parties. New York, Benzinger
Bros., (1837). 360 p. CU;
IaDuC; LNH; NNUT; PPiD.
                          43551
---- ---- St. Louis, Mo., Christian Board of Publications, 1837.
360 p. IaU; MoS; OCl; WaSpG.
                          43552
Campbell, H. R.
   Report of surveys made to
avoid the inclined plane upon
and for the improvement of the
Eastern division of the Columbus
Phila. R.R. Philadelphia, 1837.
14 p. PHi.   43553

Campbell, James.
   Tariff. or rates of duties payable on goods, wares & merchandise, imported into the United
States of America, after the first
day of January, 1836, until Dec.
31, 1837. With the rates of
duty of the tariff of 1828. And,
an appendix, containing several
important laws of the United
States & state of New-York, relating to commerce. Rev. & cor.
by James Campbell, deputy collector of the port of New-York.
New-York, M. Day, [1837].
(6), 164 p. MH-BA; O. 43554

Campbell, Randolph.
   The Rules of discipline, Covenant, and articles of faith, of the
fourth Church in Newburyport.
Rev. Randolph Campbell, Pastor.
A.D. Newburyport, Hiram Tozer, printer, 1837. 8 p. MNe.
                          43555

Campbell, S. M.
Across the desert, a life of
Moses. Philadelphia, Presbyterian board of publication,
1837. 342 p. ICMe.   43556

---- The Poetical works of
Thomas Campbell: including
Theodric, and many other
pieces not contained in any
former edition. Philadelphia,
J. Crissy, 1837. vi, 7-183,
(38) p. ArL; KyBC; MeB;
NIC; OUr.   43557

Canfield, Russell.
The Besom of Truth; or, a
brief reply to the question, "is
the resurrection of Christ from
the dead, so taught in the
Bible as to be a subject of rational belief?" Boston, Geo. A.
Chapman, 1837. 12 p. MH-
And; OC.   43558

[Carey, David], 1782-1824.
Life in Paris; or, The
rambles and sprees, of Dick
Wilk fire...Squire Jenkins and
Captain O' Shuffleton...in the
French metropolis...New Or-
leans [etc.], 1837. 2 v. CtY;
MB; MH; PPUnC; WGr.   43559

Carey, Eustace, 1791-1855.
Memoir of William Carey,
D.D., late missionary to Bengal;
professor of Oriental languages
in the college of Fort William,
Calcutta. By Eustace Carey.
With an introductory essay, by
Jeremiah Chaplin ... Hartford,
Canfield and Robins, 1837.
468 p. ICU; LNB; NcD; OMC;
PserHi.   43560

Carey, Henry Charles, 1793-
1879.
Principles of political economy ... By H. C. Carey ...
Philadelphia, Carey, Lea &

Blanchard, 1837-40. 4 pts. in
3 v. InGrD; LU; MH; PPA.
RPAt.   43561

Carey, Mathew, 1760-1839.
Autobiography of M. Carey.
Addressed to a friend. [Phila-
delphia? 1837?]. 122, 12 p.
CSmH.   43562

---- Plea for the poor, particularly females an inquiry how far
the charges alleged against them
of improvidence idleness & dissi-
pation are founded in truth, by
a citizen of Phila., 6th ed. Philadelphia, Bailey, 1837. 16 p.
Phi; PPULC; PU.   43563

---- ---- 7th ed. Philadelphia,
printed by L. R. Bailey.-Decem-
ber 20, 1837. 20 p. MWA; NPV;
PPULC; PU.   43564

---- A solemn address to the
mothers, wives, sisters and daughters of citizens of Philadelphia,
whose influence if zealously and
adequately exerted would greatly
mitigate the unmerited sufferings
of hundreds of their townswomen
writhing in penury and distress
...by a citizen of Philadelphia.
Philadelphiia, 1837. 11 p. MBAt;
PHi; WHi.   43565

... Carleton's new handbook of
popular quotations; a book of
ready reference for such familiar
words, phrases and expressions
as are oftenest quoted and met
with in general literature; together with their authorship and
position in the original. Also a
list of familiar quotations from
the Latin, French and other languages ... N.Y., Dillingham,
1837. 160 p. CWoY.   43566

Carlyle, Thomas, 1795-1881.
The diamond necklace and mira-

beau by Thomas Carlyle. New
York, John W. Lovell Company,
1837? OkEnP.   43567

---- The French revolution: a
history.... Boston, Charles C.
Little and James Brown, [1837].
3 v. in 2 (20 books). CoDR;
IES; KHi; MH; OCad.   43568

---- ---- Boston, Estes and
Lauriat, 1837. 2 v. IaMu;
KWiU; LNX; WHori.   43569

---- ---- New York, Charles
Scribner's Sons, 1837. 3 vols.
CL; KyLo-C; MTop.   43570

---- ---- New York, International
Book company, 1837. 2 v.
(420, 461 p.). MdMwM; MiEalC;
NmStM.   43571

---- ---- New York, John W.
Lovell Company, publishers,
(1837). 2 v. IES; KEm; MBrSA;
NRSB; USlW.   43572

---- ---- New York, United
States Book Co., 1837. 2 v.
IaTip.   43573

---- ---- New York, University
press company, publishers,
(1837). 2 v. MoMM.   43574

---- The life of Friedrich
Schiller. Comprehending an
examination of his works ...
From the London ed. New York,
G. Dearborn & co., 1837.
294 p. CtHT; DLC; GDecCT;
MdBG; NNUT.   43575

---- Sartor resartus. In three
books. 2d ed. Boston, J.
Munroe and company; Philadelphia, J. Kay, jun. & brother;
[etc., etc.], 1837. 300 p.
CU; KyU; MeB; NjP; NN.
                              43576

Carmichael, William M.
An Address delivered at the
funeral of forty-three emigrants,
chiefly from England and Ireland,
whose remains were recovered
and unclaimed from the Barque
Mexico, wrecked on Hempstead
Beach, on the night of January
2, 1837...Hempstead, Printed by
James C. Watts, [1837]. NSmb.
                              43577

Carne, John, 1789-1844.
A history of the missions in
Greenland and Labrador. From
Carne's Lives of eminent mission-
aries. New York, T. Mason and
G. Lane, for the Sunday school
union of the Methodist Episcopal
Church, 1837. 218 p. NBuG.
                              43578

Cartee, Cornelius Soule.
The Souvenir Minstrel; A
Choice Collection of The Most
Admired Songs, Duets, Glees,
Choruses, etc. etc...Philadelphia,
William Marshall & Co., 1837.
256 p. CtHWatk; OClWHi; RPB.
                              43579

Carter, C. C.
Hymns for children on the
Lord's Prayer, our duty towards
God, and scripture history.
Derby, 1837. 52 p. CtY.
                              43580

Carter, J. E.
The botanic physician, or
family medical adviser: being an
improved system founded on correct physiological principles.
Comprising a brief view of anatomy, physiology, pathology, hy-
giene, or art of preserving
health: a materia medica....
To which is added a dispensatory,
embracing more than two hundred
recipes for preparing and admin-
istering medicine. Madisonville,
Tenn., B. Parker & Co., 1837.
688 p. InI; MnU; NcD; TNP;
TU.   43581

Carter, James Gordon.

Speech of Mr. Carter, of Lancaster, delivered in the House of Representatives of Massachusetts, February 2, 1837, ... (on) the Bill "concerning the deposite; the Surplus Revenue;" ... (and the appropriation of one half the said Surplus Revenue to the Common Schools, ... Boston, Light & Stearns, 1837. 30 p. CtY; MBAt; MHi; MiD-B; MWA.
43582

Cathage [Ill.] Female Benevolent Society.

The constitution of the Carthage Female Benevolent Society. Carthage, Th. Gregg, Printer, 1837. 7 p. IHi.
43583

Carus, William.

The treasure in earthern vessels: a sermon ... at the ordination held by the ... Bishop of Winchester, at Farnham ... Dec. 17, 1837, Cambridge, J. & J. J. Deighton & T. Stevenson, 1837. 23 p. CtY; MBC.
43584

Carvosso, William, 1750-1834.

The great efficacy of simple faith in the atonement of Christ, exemplified in a memoir of Mr. William Carvosso...Edited by his son. New-York, T. Mason & G. Lane, 1837. 348 p. KSalW; MH; NNMHi; OClWHi; PPM.
43585

---- Life of William Carvosso, sixty years a class leader ... A memoir ... written by himself and ed. by his son ... New York, Mason and Lane, 1837. [27]-348 p. MnSH; WKen.
43586

(Cass, Lewis), 1782-1866.

To the public. (Washington? n. imp. 1837). 8 p.

MdHi; MiU; ScU.   43587

Castle, Thomas, 1804?-1840?

A manual of surgery, founded upon the principles and practice lately taught by Sir Astley Cooper & Joseph Henry Green. Boston, 4th Amer. ed., enl., 1837. 467 p. PPJ; PPULC; RPM.
43588

Catalogue of medicinal plants and vegetable medicines, to which is affixed their most prominent medical properties. Prepared in the United society, Watervliet, N.Y... Orders to be directed to Watervliet, N.Y. Albany, Printed by Packard & Van Benthuysen, 1837. 8 p. OClWHi.   43589

A catechism for the Deist; in which the divine authenticity of the Bible is proved. By the author of the Cottage dialogues. New York, Tract society of the M.E. church, 1837. 16 p. IEG; OClWHi; PCA.   43590

A catechism, to be used by the teachers in the religious instruction of persons of colour: to which are prefixed, easy instructions for coloured persons ... Prepared in conformity to a resolution of the convention, under the direction of the bishop. Charleston, A. E. Miller, 1837. 106 p. DLC; NcD; NNG; ScFl.
43591

Catlin, George, 1796-1872.

Catalogue of Catlin's Indian Gallery of Portraits, Landscapes, Manners and Customs, Costumes, &c. ... New York, Piercy and Reed, 1837. 36 p. MdHi; MH; PHi; PPL; ScU.   43592

Catskill Association.

Catskill Association, formed for the Purpose of improving the Town of Catskill, in the County

of Greene, State of New York, and other Purposes. December 28, 1836. New York, Mitchell & Turner, 1837. 47 p. DLC; MiD-B; MiU; NN; PHi.
43593

Causes of the present crisis: shown by an examiner: originally published in the daily newspapers. Philadelphia, 1837. 23 p. CtY; IU; MBC; MiU-C; ScC.
43594

"Cavendish." See Neale, William Johnson.

The central Presbyterian. v. 1- 1837- Richmond, Va., 1837- . CtY; MBAt.
43595

Cervante Saavedra, Miguel de, 1547-1616.
El ingenioso hidalgo Don Quijote de la Mancha, compuesto por Miguel de Cervantes Saavedra. Nueva edicion clasica ilustrada con notas historicas, gramaticales y criticas por la Academia espanola sus individuos de número Pellicer arrieta y clemencin. Eumendada y corregida por Francisco Sales...Seg unda edicion. Boston, Perkins Y Marvin (etc.) 1837. 2 v. CtY; IaGG; MH.
43596
---- The life and exploits of Don Quixote de la Mancha translated from the original Spanish of Mignel de cevantes Saavedra, by Charles Jarvis, Esq. in four volumes. Exeter, J. & B. Williams .... 1837. 4 v. 43597

Challoner, Richard, 1691-1781.
The Catholic Christian, instructed in the sacraments, sacrifice, ceremonies and observations of the church.... New York, Kelly, 1837. MBAt; OClStM.
43598

---- Grounds of the Catholic Doctrine, contained in the Profession of Faith, published by Pope Pius the IVth, and now in use for the reception of converts into the church, By way of question and answer, thirteenth edition, To which are added. Reasons why a Roman Catholic cannot conform to the Protestant Religion. Baltimore, Fielding Lucas, Jr.; Philadelphia, E. Cummiskey, 1837. MdW; MiDSH; NPStA.
43599

---- Think well on't; or, Reflections on the great truths of the christian religion. Philadelphia, E. Cummiskey, 1837. 264 p. IaDuMtC; MBBC; MiD. 43600

Chalmers, Thomas, 1780-1847.
Scripture references, designed for the use of parents, teachers and private christians. 1st. Amer. fr. 7th Glasgow ed. Boston, E. F. Adams, 1837. 36 p. MBC; MHi; MWA; OO.
43601

Chambers, Robert, 1802-1871.
History of the English language and literature. By Robert Chambers. To which is added a history of American contributions to the English language and literature. By Rev. Royal Robbins. Hartford, E. Hopkins, 1837. [9]-328 p. CU; ICBB; MdBP; PWW; TxU. 43602

Chambers, Thomas Jefferson, 1802-1865.
Reply of Major-general T. Jefferson Chambers, T.A. to the newspaper attack made against him by David G. Burnet, late president ad interim of the Republic of Texas.... Houston, printed at the office of the telegraphy, 1837. 81 p. CtY; NN; TxU. 43603

Chambers, William, 1800-1883.
The winter Evening Book.
New York, C. S. Francis,
1837. 9-334 p. MdCatS; MH;
NN.   43604

Chamier, Frederick, 1796-1870.
The Arethusa. A naval
story. By Captain Chamier ...
Philadelphia, E. L. Carey & A.
Hart, 1837. 2 v. MsNF; RPB.
43605
Champneys, Benjamin, 1800-
1871.
An oration, delivered before
the Goethean and Diagnothean
literary societies, of Marshall
college, Mercersburg, Pennsylvania, at their annual celebration, September 26, 1837, by
B. Champneys ... Lancaster,
Bryson and Forney, printers,
1837. 23 p. InU; N; P; PHi;
PU.   43606

Channing, William Ellery, 1780-
1842.
An address on temperance,
by William E. Channing, delivered by request of the Council of the Massachusetts temperance society ... Feb. 28, 1837
... Boston, Weeks, Jordan and
co., 1837. 117 p. CtY; LNP;
MWA; NjMD; RNR.   43607

---- ---- (2nd ed.) Boston,
Weeks, Jordan & Company, 1837.
119 p. MH; MWA.   43608

---- ---- (Third edition.) Boston, Weeks, Jordan & company,
1837. 119 p. MH; NNUT;
RPB.   43609

---- Discourses, reviews, and
miscellanies, by William Ellery
Channing. 4th ed. Boston,
Charles J. Hendee, 1837.
603 p. IaHoL; LNH; Mi; MoS;
PHi.   43610

---- Letter of William E. Channing to James G. Birney. Boston, James Munroe and co.,
1837. 36 p. CtY; MBAU; MiD-
B; PSC-Hi; TxDaM.   43611

---- A letter to the abolitionists,
with comments. First published
in the Liberator, December 22,
1837. Boston, printed by Isaac
Knapp, 1837. 32 p. MH; MPiB;
OO; PHi; RHi.   43612

---- A letter to the Hon. Henry
Clay, on the annexation of Tex-
as to the United States...Boston,
J. Munroe and company, 1837.
72 p. CSmH; ICU; MeHi; NNUT;
RPB; ScC.   43613

---- ---- 2d ed. By William E.
Channing. Boston, J. Munroe
and company, 1837. 72 p. CtY;
MWA; OclWHi; PU; RP. 43614

---- ---- 3rd ed. Boston,
James Munroe and Company, 1837.
72 p. CtY; MdHi; MiD-B; PHi;
RHi.   43615

---- ---- 4th ed. Boston, James
Munroe and Company, 1837. 72
p. CU; MPiB; PHC; RPB;
TxW.   43616

---- ---- 5th ed. Bost., James
Munroe & co., 1837. 72 p. CtY;
ICU; MdHi; PHi; TxH. 43617

---- ---- [6th ed.]. Boston,
James Munroe and company,
1837. 72 p. CSt; CtHWatk;
MoSHi; MTop; NIC.   43618

---- Remarks on creeds, intoler-
ance, and exclusion, by William
E. Channing, D.D. Printed for
the American Unitarian association.
Boston, James Munroe & co., 1837.

20 p. MCon; MeB; MeBat;
MH-And; RHi.   43619

---- Rewards on Creeds, In-
tolerance, and Exclusion. By
William E. Channing, D.D.
Printed for the American Unitarian Association. Boston,
James Munroe & Co., September, 1837. 20 p. ICMe.   43620

---- The Sunday School. A
Discourse pronounced before
the Sunday School Society. By
William E. Channing. Boston,
James Munroe & Co., 1837.
34 p. CBPac; ICMe; MB;
MeB; MeBat.   43621

---- A tribute to the memory
of the Rev. Noah Worcester,
D.D. in a discourse delivered
in Boston, November 12, 1837,
by William E. Channing. Bos-
ton, Published by Joseph Dowe,
1837. (5) 6-28 p. CSmH;
ICMe; KHi; MH-And; TxDaM.
                                43622
The Chapel Hymn Book. 2d
edition Prepared for Warren
St., and Pitts St. Chapels by
Mr. Barnard, Ezra Weston,
Jr., and Fredk. T. Gray.
Boston, 1837. 288 p. MB;
MHi.   43623

Chapin, A. B.
    Chronicle of the church ...
ed. by A. B. Chapin. New
Haven, 1837-8. 2 v. in 1.
CtMW.   43624

Chapin, Graham Hurd, 1799-
1843.
    Speech...on the motion to
amend the bill to provide for
harbors on the western lakes.
Delivered in the House of Reps.,
Feb. 27, 1837. Washington,
Ptd. at the Globe office, 1837.
7 p. MiD-B; MiGr.   43625

Chapin, Horace Billings.
    The penalty of the divine law.
A sermon. By Rev. H. B. Cha-
pin ... Northampton [Mass.]
John Metcalf, printer, 1837. 20,
23, [1] p. CSmH; CtY; ICN;
MBC; MNF.   43626

---- Women forbidden to speak
in the church. Northampton,
Mass. (J. Metcalf, printer),
(1837). 23 p. CtY; MBC; MHi;
MNF; NjR.   43627

Chapin, Stephen.
    Divine economy in raising up
great men. A sermon delivered
in the first Baptist church, before the board of trustees of the
Columbian college, D.D., with
an obituary notice of its principal founder, the Rev. Luther
Rice. By Stephen Chapin...
Washington, Peter Force, 1837.
24 p. ICU; MAnP; MNtCA; PCA;
RPB.   43628

Chaplin, Jeremiah.
    Causes of religious declension,
particularly those which have
occasioned the present low state
of religion, among different denominations of Christians, by
Jeremiah Chaplin, D.D., ...
Hartford, Canfield and Robins,
1837. ICP; InCW; MB; NjPT;
ViRU.   43629

Chapman, Jonathan.
    An Oration delivered before
the Citizens of Boston, on the
61st Anniversary of American
Independence, July 4, 1837.
Printed by request of the City
Authorities. Boston, John H.
Eastburn, City Printer, 1837.
24 p. CtSoP; MBAt; MH; PHi;
RPB.   43630

Charleston, S.C. Citizens and
City Council.

The proceedings of the Citizens and City Council of Charleston in relation to the destruction of the Steamboat Home. Charleston, S.C., Printed by T. J. Eccles, 1837. 39 p. MH; MiD-B; NcD; PPAmP; ScCC.   43631

---- Mayor.
Annual report. Charleston, 1837-76. DLC.   43632

---- ---- Report of the proceedings of the City authorities of Charleston, during the past year, ending September 1st, 1837; with suggestions for the improvement of the city. By R. Y. Hayne, Mayor. Printed by order of Council. Charleston, Printed by A. E. Miller. No. 4 Broad-Street, 1837. 40 p.   CU; DLC; ScC; ScHi; ScSp.   43633

---- Medical college. Charleston.
Announcement of the annual course of lectures by the faculty of the Medical college of South-Carolina ... under the direction of the Medical society of South-Carolina, for the year 1837-38. Charleston, Printed by Edward C. Councell ... 1837-. 1 v. CSmH.   43634

---- Ordinances, etc.
Ordinances of the city of Charleston: from the 5th Feb., 1833, to the 9th May, 1837. Together with such of the acts and clauses of acts of the legislature of South-Carolina as relate to Charleston, passed since December, 1832. Published by a resolution of Council. Charleston, Printed by A. E. Miller, 1837.   173 p.   DLC; MB; NN; ScU; WHi.   43635

---- Second Presbyterian Church.
Rules of the association ... for the temperal government, of the church. As revised by the Association in 1837. [Charleston, 1837?]   99 p.   TxU.   43636

Chase, Heber.
The final report of the committee of the Philadelphia medical society ... in the radical cure of hernia; ... With notes illustrations, ... By Heber Chase, M.D. ... Philadelphia, Published by J. G. Auner, 1837. 243 p. CU; Ia; LNOP; MB; Nh. 43637

Chase, Leslie.
Oration delivered before the corps of cadets, at West Point, July 4, 1837. By Cadet Leslie Chase, of New York. Newburgh, n. pub.; J. D. Spalding, printer, 1837. 22 p. Nh-Hi; NjPT.
43638
Chase, Philander, bp. 1775-1852.
Bishop Chase's pastoral letter to his diocese of Illinois: read in Springfield, Sangamon county, at his first meeting of his convention, May 14, A.D. 1837. Peoria, printed at the register office, 1837. 25 p. CtHT; IES; NCU; NGH; OClWHi.   43639

Chase, Salmon Portland, 1808-1873.
Speech of Salmon P. Chase, in the case of the colored woman, Matilda, who was brought before the Court of common pleas of Hamilton County, Ohio, by writ of habeas corpus: March 11, 1837. Cincinnati, Pugh & Dodd, printers, 1837. 40 p. CSmH; DHU; InHi; MdBJ; NjP. 43640

Chatham Academy, Savannah.
Catalogue of the trustees, officers & students of Chatham

Academy, Savannah, 1835-6.
Savannah, 1837. 19 p. PHi;
PPULC.   43641

Cheever, George Barrell, 1807-
1890.
The American common place
book of prose; a collection of
eloquent and interesting extracts
from the writing of American Authors. Boston, Published by
American Stationers Co., 1837.
468 p. CtB; MiToC; MH; NjP;
OrPr.   43642

Chesapeake & Ohio Canal Company.
Letter from Geo. C. Washington, Esq., President Chesapeake
& Ohio Canal Co. to the Governor of Maryland. Annapolis,
William M'Neir, printer, 1837.
9 p. MdHi.   43643

---- Special report of the president and directors of the Chesapeake and Ohio canal company,
to the stockholders in general
meeting. Made under the resolution of the stockholders of
the 31st of March, 1837, on
the subject of slack-water navigation, &c, presented April 21,
1837. Washington, Printed by
Gales and Seaton, 1837. 24 p.
MdBE; MdHi; MiD-B; Vi. 43644

Chicago. Charters.
An act to incorporate the
city of Chicago, passed March
4, 1837. Chicago, Printed at
the office of the Chicago
democrat, 1837. 23 p. ICHi.
                                     43645
---- Ordinances.
The laws and ordinances of
the city of Chicago; passed
in Common council. Chicago,
Printed at the office of the
Chicago democrat, 1837. 21 p.
ICHi.   43646

Chichester, Samuel.
The analytical spelling, pro-
nouncing, and defining book;
... By Samuel Chichester, ...
New-York, Published by the
author, 1837. 180 p. NNC.
                                     43647
Chidlaw, Benjamin Williams.
...An address on the exi-
gences and responsibilities of
the present age. Delivered be-
fore the Hamilton & Roasville Sab-
bath schools, on the fourth of
July, 1837.... Hamilton, Ohio,
I. M. Walter, 1837. 8 p. OClWHi.
                                     43648
Child, Lydia Maria (Francis),
1802-1880.
The family nurse; or com-
panion of the frugal housewife.
Boston, Charles J. Hindee, 1837.
156 p. CSmH; InGrD; MMal;
NbU; TxU.   43649

---- The Little Girl's Own Book.
Boston American Stationers Com-
pany. John B. Russell. Carter,
Hendee, & Babcock. Cambridge,
Folsom Wells and Thurston, Print-
ers to the University, 1837.
(5), 14-288 p. MWat; NcWsS.
                                     43650
Childers, W. W.
An Oration delivered before
the Philomathesian and Euzelian
Societies of the Wake Forest
Institute.... July 4, 1837. By
W. W. Childers. Raleigh, N.C.,
Pr. by Gales & Son, office of
Raleigh Register, 1837. NcWfC;
NN.   43651

Childhood the spring of life...
Bost., 1837. 35 p. DLC.
                                     43652
Children in the Wood. The
Children in the woods. 7 series.
Concord, Brown, 1837. 16 p.
DLC.   43653

---- The Children in the wood.

An effecting tale. Cooperstown, H. E. Phinney, 1837.
31 p. NNC.   43654

---- The Children in the Wood-
To which is added My Mother's
Grave, a pathetic Story. New
York, Day, 1837. 3-23 p. DLC;
MB.   43655

Childs, H. H.
    A synopsis of the course of
lectures, general principles by
H. H. Childs, M.D., at the
Maine medical school. Press of
J. Griffin, [Brunswick] 1837.
MB; OCGHM.   43656

Childs, Isaac.
    The vision of Isaac Child;
with explanatory notes, from
another hand. To which is
prefixed a biographical sketch
of his life. Sandy Hill (Now
Hudson Falls, N.Y.) Republished by Griffen, Mabbet and
Company, 1837. 15 p. N.
                              43657
Childs, Ward.
    Five sermons on sanctifica-
tion. By Rev. Ward Childs,
pastor of the church at Strykers-
ville. Published by request of
said church. Buffalo, printed
at the Spectator office, 1837.
32 p. MiD.   43658

The Child's Annual. Boston,
1837. 192 p. PHi.   43659

The Child's book ... Windsor,
Vt., P. Merrifield, [1837].
[3]-10 p. CtY.   43660

The child's book of American
geography: ... and eighteen
maps,...second edition. Boston, James B. Dow, 1837.
64 p. front. 18 maps. NNC.
See Goodrich, Samuel G.

The childs first book: or An
easy introduction to the spelling
book ... according to the orthography and pronunciation of
Noah Webster. Hartford, R.
White, 1837. 5-66 p. DLC.
                              43661
Chipman, Daniel, 1765-1850.
    Speech of Hon. Daniel Chip-
man, delivered in the Convention
holden at Montpelier, on the
sixth of January, 1836, while in
committee of the whole on the
proposed articles of amendment
to the Constitution, constituting
a senate. Middlebury, Printed
by E. R. Jewett, 1837. 25 p.
MH-L; MHi; MiD-B; VtMidSM.
                              43662
Chittenden, Nathaniel W.
    Influence of woman upon the
destinies of a people; oration,
commencement of Columbia Coll.,
Oct. 3. New York, 1837. MBAt.
                              43663
Chitty, Joseph, 1776-1841.
    A treatise on the parties to
actions and on pleading, with
second and third volumes, containing precedents of pleadings,
and copious directory notes.
... By Joseph Chitty, ... and
Thomas Chitty, ... 7th American
ed., ... Springfield, Mass., G.
and C. Merriam, 1837. 3 v.
CSt; KyU-L; PP; TMeB; WaU.
                              43664
Chivers, Thomas Holley, 1809-
1858.
    Nacoochee; or, The beautiful
star, with other poems. New
York, W. E. Dean, printer,
1837. 143 p. CtHWatk; MWA;
NbU; OMC; TxU.   43665

Christ and Him crucified. A
sermon, preached to the Second
Baptist Church, in Wilmington,
Del., By the pastor of the said
church. September 8, 1836.
Published by request. New York,

J. P. Callender, 1837. 40 p.
PCA.   43666

Christian, E.
A plea for episcopacy. A
discourse delivered in Charlottesville, March 5, 1837. By the
Rev. E. Christian,...Charlottes-
ville, James Alexander, printer, 1837. 22 p. CSmH; MBD;
TKL-Mc.   43667

The Christian almanac for Connecticut for the year 1837,
1839-40. Hartford, [1837-
40]. 3 v. MBAt.   43668

The Christian almanac for Kentucky, for the year of Our
Lord and Saviour Jesus Christ,
1837. Lexington, Published
by A. T. Skillman, 1837.
46 p. MHi; OC.   43669

The Christian Almanac for New
England, for the year 1837,
Boston, Published for the
American Tract Society, and
for Gould, Kendall & Lincoln,
1837. 48 p. MMedHi; RNHi.
                            43670
The Christian almanac for New
England...1838 Boston...Pub-
lished for the American tract
society...and for Gould, Ken-
dall & Lincoln...[1837]. 48 p.
ICMcHi; MeHi; WHi.   43671

Christian Almanac for Pennsyl-
vania and Delaware for 1838.
Philadelphia, Pa., Pennsylvania
Branch of the American Tract
Society, [1837]. MWA.   43672

Christian Almanac for Pennsylvania and the Middle States for
1838. Philadelphia, Pa., Philadelphia Tract Society, [1837].
MWA; PHi.   43673

Christian Almanack for 1838.

Boston, Mass., Published for
the American Tract Society, and
for Gould, Kendall & Lincoln,
[1837]. MWA.   43674

The Christian index, and Baptist
miscellany, devoted to the diffusion of truth and piety. By
Jesse Mercer and W. H. Stokes.
Washington, Ga., M. J. Kappel,
1837. GMiluC; OOxM.   43675

The Christian offering. Boston,
Dow, 1837. 231 p. LNH; MBC;
MWA.   43676

Christian politeness. Written
for the American Sunday-school
union and revised by the committee of publication. Philadelphia, American Sunday-school
union [1837]. 102 p. ICBB;
MA.   43677

The Christian Review. V. 1-29;
March 1836-Oct. 1863. Boston,
Gould, Kendal & Lincoln; [etc.
etc.], 1837. 28 v. CoCsC;
KyLoS; NjR; PPEB; WaS.
                            43678
Christian supports under the
troubles of this world, unto
which are added, prayers and
meditations suitable for all persons afflicted in mind, body or
estate, and selections from the
daily companion. 20th ed.
Phil. Bailey, 1837. viii, (9)-
126 p. CtHT.   43679

Christian Witness. Boston,
1837-9. MBC.   43680

The Christmas box and New Year's
gift for 1837; a collection of
amusement and instruction for
the young.... Philadelphia,
Thomas T. Ash & Henry F. An-
ners, (1837). 185 p. NjR.
                            43681
Chronicles of Mt. Benedict. A

tale of the Ursuline convent,
the quasi production of Mary
Magdalen...Boston, 1837.
191 p. DLC; IU; MB; MdBJ;
MH.   43682

[Church, Edward].
  Notice on the beet sugar:
containing 1st. A description
of the culture and preservation
of the plant. 2d. An explanation of the process of extract-
ing its sugar. Preceded by a
few remarks on the origin and
present state of the indigenous
sugar manufactories of France.
Translated from the works of
Dubrunfaut, De Domballe, and
others. Northampton, J. H.
Butler; Boston, Hilliard, Gray,
& co.. [etc., etc.], 1837.
[7]-54 p. DLC; LNH; NhD;
PU; RPAt.   43683

The Church catechism, with
explanation of vestival and
fasts, and some brief directions for behavior in church.
Lowell, Daniel Bixby, 1837.
40 p. MBD.   43684

The Churchman's Almanac For
The Year Of Our Lord 1837;
Being The First After Leap-
Year, The 61-62d Of American
Independence, And The 52d
Since The Organization Of The
Protestant Episcopal Church In
The United States Of America:
Containing, Besides The Usual
Calendar And Celestial Phe-
nomena, Various Items Of Use-
ful Information, And Condensed
Views And Statistical Tables Of
The Present State Of The
Church and her Institutions,
Together With A Complete Alpha-
betical List Of The Clergy.
First Edition. New York, Prot-
estant Episcopal Press, [1837].
NBuG.   43685

---- Second edition. New York,
Protestant Episcopal press, 1837.
36 p. MWA; NBuDD.   43686

The churchman's almanac for
1838. ... 1st ed. New York,
Protestant Episcopal press,
[1837]. 36 p. NNA.   43687

---- Third Edition. New York,
N.Y., Protestant Episcopal
Press, [1837]. MWA.   43688

---- Fourth Edition. New York,
N.Y., Protestant Episcopal
Press, [1837]. MWA.   43689

Churchman's Almanack. By D.
Young. New York, Protestant
Episcopal Press, 1834. 4th ed.
MWA.   43690

Cicero, Marcus Tullius.
  De claris oratoribus liber
qui dicitur Brutus. Edited by
Charles Beck. Cambridge,
(Mass.), J. Owen, 1837. vi,
(2), 145 p. IEG; MCR; MH;
MME; RPB.   43691

---- M. T. Ciceronis De officiis
libri tres. Ex editionibus Oliveti et Ernesti. Accedunt notae
anglicae. Cura C. K. Dillaway,
A. N. Bostoniae, Perkins et
Marvin; Philadelphia, H. Perkins,
1837. 297 p. IP; MB; MeB;
MH; ViU.   43692

---- The orations translated by
Duncan, the offices by Cockman,
and the cato and laelive by Mel-
moth. New York, Published by
Harper & Brothers, 1837. 3 v.
LMD; MoSpD; NBLIHI; OCh.
                         43693
---- Select orations of Cicero:
With an English commentary, and
historical, geographical, and legal
indexes, by Charles Anthon,
LL.D. New York, Harper &

Brothers, 1837. 518 p. MBC;
MH; PPL; RNR; TxD-T.   43694

---- De Senectute et de ami-
citia, ex editionibus Oliveti et
Ernesti. Accedunt notae
Anglicae. Cura C. K. Dillaway. Bostoniae, Perkins et
Marvin, [etc., etc.], 1837.
158 p. MH; MiU; PBa; PU.
                              43695
---- M. T. Cicero De senectute
et De amicitia.... Bostoniae,
Sumptibus Hilliard, Gray, et
soc., 1837. 478 p. RPB.
                              43696
Cincinnati. Commercial Bank.
    Commercial Bank of Cinti
Regulation adopted by the
Board of Directors to increase
the Capitol Stock Feb. 14,
1833. Statement of Condition
of the...Jan. 1837. OCHP.
                              43697
Cincinnati and Whitewater Canal
Company.
    An act to incorporate the
Cincinnati and Whitewater canal
company ... Cincinnati, Looker,
Ramsey & Co., ptrs., 1837.
12 p. OC; OCHP; MiD-B.
                              43698
Cincinnati college.
    A catalogue of the officers
and students in the medical
and law departments of Cincinnati college, ... session, 1837-
38. ... Published under the
direction of the board. Cincinnati, Ohio, Printed by N. S.
Johnson, 1837. 12 p. MB;
NNNAM; OCGHM; OCHP.   43699

---- Circular of Cincinnati
College, including the requisites
for admission: the course of
studies: discipline and internal
regulations. Cincinnati, Pugh
and Dodd, 1837. 16 p. NN.
                              43700
Cincinnati Fuel Gas Light &

Coke Company, Cincinnati.
    An Act to incorporate the ....
1837. OCHP.   43701

Cinderella; or, The little glass
slipper. Baltimore, pub. by
Bayly & Burns, 1837. (9) p.
TxU.   43702

Citizen's Almanack for 1838.
Philadelphia, Pa., Griggs & Co.,
[1837]. MWA.   43703

Citizen's and Farmer's Almanac
for 1838. Calculations by Nathan Bassett. Baltimore, Md.,
Plaskitt, Fite & Co., [1837].
DLC; MWA.   43704

---- Philadelphia, Pa., Griggs
& Co., [1837]. MWA.   43705

Citizens' Bank of Louisiana, New
Orleans.
    Report of the Joint Committee
on the Affairs of the Citizens'
Bank of Louisiana. Submitted
to the Legislature Jan. 1837.
New Orleans, 1837. AU.
                              43706
City and Country Almanac.
By Chas. F. Egelmann. Balti-
more, W. & J. Neal, 1837. MWA.
                              43707
City bank, New Haven.
    Special committee concerning
the City bank, of New Haven.
Report ... Hartford, 1837.
22 p. CtY.   43708

City of Prairie du Chien Company.
    Articles of agreement and as-
sociation of the City of Prairie
du Chien Company. Instituted
April 1st, 1837. Ann Arbor,
Printed at the Office of the
Michigan Argus, 1837. 8 p.
DLC; KHi.   43709

Claiborne, John Francis Ham-
tranck.

Argument, submitted by
Messrs. Claiborne and Gholson,
representatives from the state
of Mississippi, to the Committee of elections. City of Washington, Blair & Rives, printers,
1837. 14 p. MiU-C.   43710

---- Remarks of Mr. Claiborne,
of Mississippi, in defence of
the Settlers of the Public Lands.
Delivered in the House of
Representatives, January, 1837.
Washington, Blair & Rives,
Printers, 1837. 7 p. MsJS.
                            43711
---- Speech of Mr. Claiborne.
of Mississippi on the motion to
arrest Reuben M. Whitney. Esq.
of Washington City for an alleged contempt. delivered in
the house of representatives of
the United States. Feb. 10, 1837.
Washington, printed by Jacob
Gideon, 1837. 22 p. MsJs;
OCLaw; TxU.   43712

Clamorgan land association.
   Title papers of the Clamorgan
grant of 536,904 arpens of alluvial lands in Missouri and
Arkansas. Washington, Printed
by Gales and Seaton, 1837. 20,
8 p. CU; ICN; LNH; MdHi;
WHi.   43713

Clancy, James.
   A treatise of the rights,
duties and liabilities of hus-
bands and wife at law and in
equity. By James Clancy, Esq.
New York, Printed and Published at the Law Press, 1837.
684 p. MH-L; NRAL; PAtM;
PP; PU-L.   43714

---- ---- 2d American from
last London ed. New York,
Printed and published at the
Law press, 1837. 684 p.
CoU; IU; NNC-L; TMeB; W.
                            43715

Clark, Daniel A.
   Sermons. By Rev. Daniel
A. Clark. ... New York, pub-
lished by John S. Taylor, Brick
Church Chapel, 1837. 9-324,
(8) p. MLow; MNe; ScOrC.
                            43716
Clark, John Alonzo, 1801-1843.
   The young disciple; or, A
memoir of Anzonetta R. Peters.
By Rev. John A. Clark...
Philadelphia, William Marshall
& co., 1837. 328 p. GDecCt;
MH; NcGu; PPL; RBa.   43717

Clark, Mary.
   A concise history of Massa-
chusetts, from its first settle-
ment,...By Mary Clark. New
York, published by Daniel and
George F. Cooledge; Boston,
Munroe And Francis, 1837. 180
p. MAbD; MH; MiD-B.   43718

Clark, Willis Gaylord, 1808-1841.
   The Parlour Scrap Book:
Comprising fourteen engravings
with poetical illustrations.
Philadelphia, Carey, Lea, and
Blanchard, 1837. 72 p. ICU;
KyU; MH; PU; RPB.   43719

Clarke, Adam, 1760?-1832.
   An account of the religions
& literary life of Adam Clarke...
Ed. by the Rev. J. B. B. Clarke
...New York, Pub. by T. Mason
& G. Lane, for the Methodist
Episcopal church, 1837. 3 v. in
1. GAGTh; IaWel; MnSH; NBuG;
NNUT.   43720

---- Christian Theology. By
Adam Clarke, L.L.D., F.A.S.
selected from his published and
unpublished writings, and systematically arranged. With a life
of the author, by Samuel Dunn
....New York, Published by T.
Mason and G. Lane, J. Collord,
printer, 1837. 438 p. DLC;

IaDmD; KyWA; OO; TNS.
43721

---- Clavis Biblica: or, A compendium of Scriptural knowledge: containing a general view of the contents of the Old and New Testaments ... with directions how to read most profitably the Holy Bible. Originally drawn up for the instruction of two high priests of Budhoo ... by Adam Clarke ... New York, T. Mason and G. Lane, 1837. 235 p. GaGTh; IaScW; MdW; NNG. 43722

---- Christian theology; by Adam Clarke, selected from his published and unpublished writings and systematically arranged, with a life of the author by Samuel Dunn. New York, Mason and G. Lane, 1837. 438 p. DLC; KyWA; OO. 43723

---- ---- "Second edition." New York, T. Mason and G. Lane, 1837. 438 p. OO. 43724

---- Doctrine of salvation by faith proved, or, an answer to the important question, What must I do to be saved. New York, T. Mason & G. Lane, 1837. IEG; MBC; NNMHi; PPL; ScSpW. 43725

---- Manners of the Ancient Israelites. See Fleury, Claude, 1640-1723.

---- The preachers; manual: Including Clavis biblica, and a letter to a Methodist preacher. By Adam Clarke, L.L.D., F.A.S.; also, four discourses on the duties of a minister of the gospel. By Thomas Coke, L.L.D. .... New York, Published by T. Mason and G. Lane, 1837. 235 p. KSalW;

NcD; OO; TChU. 43726

---- A sermon on the love of God to a lost world, by Adam Clarke, L.L.D., F.A.S. ... New-York, Published by T. Mason and G. Lane, ... 1837. 28 p. DLC; IEG; MWA; NNMHi; ScSpW. 43727

Clarke, James, b. 1784?
Speech of James Clarke, esq. of Indiana [County] delivered in the Convention, to amend the constitution of Pennsylvania, on the first of December, 1837. In support of an amendment to prohibit banks from issuing notes of a less denomination than ten dollars, for the present, and less than twenty dollars, from and after the year 1842. Philadelphia, Printed by J. Wilbank, 1837. 16 p. DLC; InU; OClWHi; PHi; PPM. 43728

Clarke, John, 1755-1798.
An Answer to the question, Why are you a Christian? By John Clark, D.D., Hartford, published by Peter B. Gleason and Co., 1837. (7)-54 p. Ct; MBC; MWeA. 43729

Clark's Troy Almanac for 1838. Calculated by C. H. Anthony. Troy, N.Y., N. Tuttle, [1837]. MWA; NN. 43730

Clarkson, Thomas, 1760-1846.
On water baptism, & the Lord's Supper ... Extracted from ... The portraiture of Quakerism. New York, 1837. CtY; PHC; PSC-Hi; PPULC. 43731

Clay, Clement Comer, 1789-1866.
Speech of Mr. Clay, of Alabama, on the bill imposing additional duties, as depositories in certain cases, on public officers. Delivered in Senate United States.

Oct. 4, 1837. Washington,
1837. 16 p. CtY; InHi; PPM;
TxU.   43732

Clay, Henry, 1777-1852.
  An address of Henry Clay,
to the public, containing certain
testimony in refutation of the
charges against him, made by
General Andrew Jackson, touching the presidential election in
1825. Lexington, Ky., Re-
printed by E. Bryant, Intelligencer office, 1837. 66 p.
CSmH; DLC; MoU.   43733

---- Speech of Henry Clay of
Kentucky on the Bill imposing
additional duties, as depositories
in certain cases, on public
officers, "in the Senate of the
United States, Sept. 23, 1837."
Boston, Benjamin H. Green,
1837. 19 p. ICU; LNT; MHi;
MiD-B; OCHP.   43734

---- Speech of Mr. Clay, of
Kentucky, on the resolution to
expunge a part of the journal
for the session of 1833-1834.
Delivered in the senate of the
United States, January, 1837.
Washington, printed by William
W. Moore, 1837. 14 p. MdHi;
MH.   43735

---- Speech of Mr. Clay of
Kentucky on the Specie circular. Delivered in the Senate
of the United States, January
11, 1837. Washington,
Printed by Duff Green, 1837.
13 p. DLC; MBAt; MH; MWA;
NjR.   43736

---- Speech upon the tariff;
Wm. B. Giles speech in answer
to above; also his speech in
reply to Gen. Taylor.... Richmond, 1837. 118 p. PHi.
                                  43737

---- Speeches of Henry Clay &
Daniel Webster, in Senate of the
United States, Sept. 25, 1837,
on the Sub-Treasury Bill. Nor-
wich, J. Dunham, (1837). 48 p.
CSmH; Ct; NN.   43738

Cleveland, A. B.
  Studies in poetry and prose:
... 2d ed. Baltimore, Bayly
and Burns, 1837. 480 p. MdHi.
                                  43739
Clifton, William.
  Back side Albany: comic ballad....by M. Hawkins, arr. (for
v & pf.). New York, 1837.
CtY.   43740

Clinton County (N.Y.) Anti-
slavery Society.
  Anti-Slavery Convention, Proceedings of, to which is appended the call of the said Convention, the Plattsburgh protest,
and the reply, directed by the
Convention. Held at Beekman-
town, Apr. 25 and 26. Plattsburgh, Platt & Blanchard, Printers, 1837. 31 p. CSmH; FC.
                                  43741
Clowes, John, 1743-1831.
  The Golden wedding ring; or,
observations on the Institution
of marriage. Albany, W. C. Little, 1837. 48 p. MB; WHi.
                                  43742
Cobb, Jonathan Holmes, 1799-
1882.
  A manual containing information respecting the growth of
the mulberry tree, with suitable
directions for the culture of
silk; in three parts. Boston,
Carter, Hendee, 1837. 98 p.
MHa.   43743

Cobb, Lyman, 1800-1864.
  Cobb's arithmetical rules and
tables designed for the use of
small children in families and
schools. Indianapolis, Henkie,
1837. 35 p. IaU.   43744

---- Cobb's juvenile reader....
containing interesting, moral,
& instructive reading lessons
....Designed for the use of
small children....Indpls., Henkle
& Chamberlain, 1837. 144 p.
In.   43745

---- Cobb's juvenile reader,
no. 1: containing interesting,
moral, and instructive reading
lessons, composed of easy words
of one and two syllables. Designed for the use of small
children, in families and
schools. By Lyman Cobb ...
Ithaca, N.Y., Mack, Andrus
and Woodruff, 1837. CtY.
                             43746
---- ---- Washington, D.C.,
D. Howard, 1837. vi, [7]-72 p.
DLC; ViU.   43747

---- Cobb's juvenile reader, no.
3; containing interesting, historical, moral, and instructive
reading lessons composed of
words of a greater number of
syllables than the lessons in
nos. I and II - To which are
prefixed observations on the
principles of good reading -
Ithaca, N.Y., Mack, Andrus and
Woodruff. Stereotyped by J.
Conner, N.Y., 1837. [25]-216
p. N.   43748

---- ---- New York, Collins,
Keese, & co., Dean, print.,
1837. 214 p. WHi.   43749

---- .... The reticule and
pocket companion; or, miniature
lexicon of the English language,
by Lyman Cobb. New York,
Harper & Brothers, 1837.
816 p. NHem.   43750

---- Cobb's sequel to the juvenile readers; comprising a selection of lessons in prose and

poetry, from highly esteemed
American and English writers...
St. Clairsville, O., Horton J.
Howard, 1837. 215 p. OClWHi.
                             43751
---- Cobb's spelling book by
Lyman Cobb. Cleveland, Jones,
1837. 168 p. MiMarsHi. 43752

---- Cobb's spelling book, being
a just standard for pronouncing
the English language; containing
the rudiments of the English
language, arranged in catechetical
order; an organization of the alphabet.... Ithaca, N.Y., Printed
and published by Mack, Andrus
& Woodruff, 1837. 168 p. NIC;
NIDHI; PReaHi.   43753

Cobbett, William, 1763-1835.
  A French Grammar; or, plain
instruction for the learning of
French, by William Cobbett.
New York, Published by John
Doyle, 1837. 368 p. MB; MsNF;
PPM; RNR; TxU-T.   43754

---- A grammar of the English
language, in a series of letters
.... New York, Published by
John Doyle, 1837. 213 p. CSmH;
CtHWatk; VtU.   43755

---- Life of Andrew Jackson,
president of the United States
of America.... New York, Harper
& brothers, 1837. [9]-206 p.
CSmH; IHi; MBevHi; MikT; THi.
                             43756
(Codman, John), 1782-1847.
  An exposition of the pretended claims of William Vans on
the estate of John Codman; with
an appendix of original documents,
correspondence and other evidence. Boston, S. N. Dickinson, 1837. 438 p. CtY; MBAt;
MeB; MLy; MWA.   43757

---- The succession of the pas-

toral office. A sermon delivered May 24, 1837, at the
installation of the Rev. Samuel
W. Cozzens, ... By John Codman, D.D. ... Boston,
Printed by Perkins and Marvin,
1837. (3)-38 p. MBC; McBat;
MWA; NcMHi; RPB.   43758

Cogswell, William, 1787-1850.
  Christian philanthropist, or,
Harbinger of the millenium.
With an introductory essay by
James Matheson, 2d ed. Bos-
ton, Perkins, 1837. 2, 394 p.
OO.   43759

---- Letters to young men preparing for the Christian ministry. By William Cogswell.
Boston, Perkins & Marvin;
Philadelphia, Henry Perkins,
1837. 236 p. CtY; IaPeC;
MeB; Nh-Hi; OClW.   43760

Coke, Richard Henry.
  An address delivered before
the graduates of the Erodelphian
society of Miami university, August 9th, 1837. By Richard
Henry Coke....Oxford [O.],
Printed by R. H. Bishop, 1837.
15 p. ICU; MWA; OClWHi;
OHi; PPiXT.   43761

Colburn, Warren, 1793-1833.
  Arithmetic upon the inductive
method of instruction being a
sequel to intellectual arithmetic.
Boston, published by Hilliard,
Gray & Co., 1837. 245 p.
OMC; MH.   43762

---- First lessons; intellectual
arithmetic, upon the inductive
method of instruction, by Warren Colburn, A.M. Concord,
Published by Oliver L. Sanborn,
1837. 172 p. MB; RNR. 43763

---- Intellectual arithmetic upon

the inductive method of instruc-
tion... Concord, N.H., Oliver
L. Sanborn, 1837. [13], 178 p.
IGK; MB; MnHi; InU.   43764

---- An introduction to Algebra
upon the inductive method of
instruction. By Warren Colburn. Boston, Hilliard, Gray
& Co., 1837. 276 p. MH.
                        43765
---- Key, containing answers
to examples in the sequel to intellectual arithmetic. Boston,
Hilliard, Gray & co., 1837.
MNS.   43766

Cole, George Washington.
  A thanksgiving discourse, de-
livered at Clinton, December 1,
1836. By Rev. Geo. Washington
Cole, rector of St. Peter's Church,
Tecumseh, and of St. Patrick's,
Clinton. Published by request
of the vestry of St. Patrick's
Church, Clinton. Detroit, Printed
by Geo. L. Whitney, 1837. 26 p.
CSmH; MWA; MiD-B; NBuDD.
                        43767
Cole, Jonathan.
  Meditations for the Sick....
Boston, James Munroe and Co.,
1837. ICMe; MFm; MBC; MH;
MWA.   43768

Coleman, Henry, 1785-1849.
  Letter to the farmers of Massachusetts, on the subjects of
an agricultural survey of the
state by the authority of the
legislature....Boston, Weeks,
Jordan and company, 1837. 18
p. CLCM; CtY; MB; MH; MWA.
                        43769
[Coleman, Robert M], d.1837.
  Houston displayed; or, Who
won the battle of San Jacinto?
By a farmer in the army. Velasco,
1837. 38 p. Tx; TxU. 43770

Coleridge, Samuel Taylor, 1772-
1834.

The Poetical works of Coleridge, Shelley and Keats. Complete in one volume, stereotyped by J. Howe. Philadelphia, Desilver, Thomas and Company, 1837. 607 p. MH; MoJc; MoSW; RPAt.
43771

Colgate University.
Catalogue of the corporation, officers, and students, of Hamilton College. Clinton, 1837-8. [Utica, 1837.] 19 p. N; NCH.
43772

---- Catalogus senatus academici, et eorum qui munera et officia academica gesserunt, quique aliquo gradu exornati fuerunt, in Collegio Hamiltoniensi, Comitatus Oneidensis, in republica Neo-Eboracensi. Uticae, Typis Bennett et Bright, [1837]. 16 p. CSmH; NN.
43773

---- Report of the Society for Inquiry of the Hamilton Literary & Theological Institution, March, 1837. Utica, Printed by Bennett & Bright, 1837. 20 p. NRC-R.
43774

---- Theta Chi fraternity. The subscript. The silver anniversary. A twenty-five year history of the Iota Chapter of the Theta Chi fraternity. Hamilton, N.Y., 1837. 87 p. NHC-S.
43775

Colles, Abraham, 1773-1843.
... Practical observations on the veneral disease, and on the use of mercury, by Abraham Colles ... Philadelphia, A. Waldie, 1837. 211 p. CtY; NNN; PU; RNR; ViU.
43776

Collot, Alexander G., b. 1796.
Progressive interlinear French reader; on Locke's plan of instruction: a course of interesting and instructive

lessons in French literature.... By A. G. Collot,... Philadelphia, James Kay, jun. and brother....1837. xx, 283 p. CoU; CTHWatk; MH; NbOM; TMeG.
43777

---- Progressive pronouncing French reader; on a plan new, simple and effective...to be used in conjunction with "Collot's Interlinear French reader." Philadelphia, J. Kay, etc. 1837, 1859. CTHWatk; MH; OBerB; PHi; TxU-T.
43778

Colman, George, 1762-1836.
Jonathan in England, (altered from George Colmans comedy of "Who wants a guinea?"), a comedy in 3 acts. ... New York, S. French, [1837]. 32 p. C.
43779

---- ... The review. A comic operatic farce. In two acts. By George Colman, the younger ... Correctly printed from the most approved acting copy ... as now performed in the London and American theatres. Embellished with a portrait of Thomas H. Hadaway. Philadelphia, New-York, Turner & Fisher, (1837?). 2 p. L., (9)-37 p. CtY; NIC.
43780

Colman, Henry, 1785-1849.
Letter to the Farmers of Massachusetts on the subject of an Agricultural Survey of the State by the authority of the legislature. By Henry Colman, commissioner for such survey. Boston, Weeks, Jordan and Company, Literary Rooms, 1837. 18 p. CtY; DLC; MBAt; MHi.
43781

---- The times, a discourse delivered in the Hollis Street Church, Boston, on Sunday June 11, 1837 ... Boston, Published by Weeks, Jordan and Co. (etc.), 1837. 28 p. ICMe; MBC; MiD-B; NNUT; PPAmP.
43782

The Colored American.

Established for and devoted to the moral, mental, and political improvement of the people of color. Vol. 1, No. 1-8, Jan. 7 -Feb. 25, 1837. New York, 1837. CtY; NIC.   43783

Colton, Chauncey, 1800-1876.
On the religious state of the country. New York, 1837. PHi.
                   43784
Columbia and Philadelphia Railroad.

Report of surveys made to avoid the inclined plane upon and for the improvement of the Eastern Division...by order of the Canal Commissioners of the state of Pennsylvania. By H. R. Campbell, Civil Engineer. Philadelphia, Printed by A. Seyfert & Co., Jan. 1837. 14 p. MB; MH-BA; PPFrankl.
                   43785
Columbia Hose Company.
Construction and by-laws. Philadelphia, 1837. 16 p. PHi.   43786

Columbia University.
An account of the celebration of the first semi-centennial anniversary of the incorporation of Columbia college, by the legislature of New York; with the oration and poem delivered on the occasion...New York, G. & C. Carvill & co., 1837. 62 p. CtY; CU; MiD; MWA; RPB.   43787

Columbian Almanac for 1837, being the first after bissextile, or, leap year; containing 365 days, and the sixty-first year of American independence. Philadelphia, Published by Jos. McDowell, 1837. 34 p. NjR; PHDHi.   43788

Columbian Almanac for 1838. Philadelphia, Pa., Jos. M'Dowell, [1837]. MWA.   43789

Columbus Almanac for 1838. By W. Lusk. Columbus, Ohio, E. Glover, [1837]. MWA.   43790

Combe, Andrew.
The Physiology of Digestion, considered with relation to the principles of Dietetics. By Andrew Combe, M.D. ... Fourth American edition. Boston, Marsh, Capen & Lyon; New York, Daniel, Appleton & Co., 1837. 12-310 p. CU; ICU; MBM; MeB; OClM.   43791

Combe, George, 1788-1858.
The Constitution of man considered in relation to external objects, by George Combe. ... Boston, Marsh, Capen, & Lyon; New-York, Daniel Appleton & Co., 1837. 436 p. MSher.
                   43792
---- ---- 4th American from the 2d English ed., cor. 2nd enl. Boston, Marsh, 1837. 412 p. DHU; DLC.   43793

---- ---- 5th American from the 2d English ed., cor. and enl. Boston, W. D. Ticknor, 1837. 412 p. CtMMHi; MdBE; MHi; WaS.   43794

---- ---- 8th Amer. ed., materially rev. and enl. Boston, March, Capen & Lyon; New York, Daniel Appleton & Co., 1837. 436 p. GEU; IEG; MB; Mh-Z; MBrigStG; MoSpD.   43795

---- Lectures on popular education; delivered to the Edinburgh philosophical association, in April and November 1833 ... 2d ed., cor. and enl. Edinburgh, Boston (etc., etc.), 1837. CtY; ICN; NB.   43796

---- A system of phrenology,
by G. Combe ... 4th American
from the 3d Edinburgh ed.,
rev. and enl. by the author.
Boston, Marsh, Capen, and
Lyon, 1837. 664 p. CL; CSt-
L; InThE; MB; NBMS.   43797

Comer, Thomas.
Cap't. Austin's quickstep.
Boston, Diston, 1837. 2 p. MB.
                               43798
---- A Yankee ship and a
Yankee crew. Nautical song.
(Accomp. for pianoforte.)
Boston, Parker & Ditson, 1837.
5 p. MB.   43799

Comic Texas oldmanick, 1837.
New York, 1837. DLC.   43800

Comly, John, 1773-1850.
New spelling book adapted
to different classes of pupils;
compiled with a view to render
the arts of spelling and reading easy and pleasant to children. Philadelphia, 1837. In.
                               43801
Commercial herald, Philadelphia.
The carriers of the Commercial Herald to their patrons.
Philadelphia, 1837. PPL.   43802

The Common School Library of
useful and entertaining knowledge. New York, D. Appleton
and Co., 1837-43. 25 v.
MBBC; NN.   43803

"Common sense." Especially addressed to the most suffering
portion of our fellow-citizens,
the "bone and sinew" of our
country--the mechanics. By
a mechanic. Philadelphia, C.
Bell, 1837. 31 p. DLC; IU;
PHi.   43804

Compendium of Jewish history
exhibited in the form of a

Catechism, designed for the use
of Sabbath schools. Ed. 2. Boston, Tompkins, 1837. 50 p.
OCH; PHi.   43805

Comstock, Andrew, 1795-1874.
Fish & his institution ex-
posed. Remarks on stammering.
Philadelphia, 1837. 2 parts.
PPL-R.   43806

---- Practical elocution, or a
system of vocal gymnastics, comprising diagrams illustrative of
the subject and exercises. By
Andrew Comstock, M.D. Second
edition. Philadelphia, Kay and
Brother, 1837. 311 p. CtY;
MB; ODaU; PMA; PU.   43807

---- Remarks on stammering,
from a lecture on elocution delivered before the American Lyceum, May 6, 1837. Philadelphia,
1837. 7 p. MB; MBM; PPAmP.
                               43808
Comstock, John Lee, 1789-1858.
Elements of chemistry. 19th
ed. Pub. by Robinson, Pratt,
& Co. New York, 1837. 356 p.
MWHi.   43809

---- ---- Twentieth Edition.
New York, Published by Robinson, Pratt & Co., 1837. 356 p.
MeLewB; MoSU; OU; PBed.
                               43810
---- An introduction to mineralogy; adapted to the use of schools
& private students illustrated by
nearly two hundred wood cuts.
3rd. edition, improved. New
York, Robinson, 1837.
AU; IaDaM; MB; NcEd; PPM.
                               43811
---- An introduction to the study
of botany, including a treatise
on vegetable physiology, and
descriptions of the most common
plants in the middle and northern
states .... 4th ed. New York,

Robinson, Pratt & co., 1837.
[9]-464 p. IaDL; MH; MoU;
PU; WU.   43812

---- Outlines of geology: intended as a popular treatise on
the most interesting parts of the
science. Together with an
examination of the question,
whether the days of creation
were indefinite periods. Designed for the use of schools
and general readers. By J. L.
Comstock...3d ed. New York,
Robinson, Pratt, & co., 1837.
384 p. NBuB; NNUT; NRU;
PFal.   43813

---- Outlines of Physiology,
both comparative and human;
in which are described the
mechanical animal, vital and
sensorial organs and functions;
also the application of these
principles to muscular exercise
and female fashions and de-
formities; Intended for the use
of schools and heads of families,
together with a synopsis of human anatomy. By John L.
Comstock. 2nd ed. New York,
Robinson, Pratt and Co., 1837.
12, 310 p. MH; MiGr; NcD;
OUrC; PPCP.   43814

---- A system of natural philosophy; in which the principles of
mechanics, optics, astronomy, hydraulics, pneumatics, acoustics,
hydrostatics, astronomy, electricity, and magnetism are familiarly explained....40th ed.
By J. L. Comstock....New York,
Robinson, Pratt and co., 1837.
(9)-295. Cst; MB; MH; MoU; Nh.
                                 43815
---- ---- Forty-fifth edition.
By J. L. Comstock, M.D. ...
New York, Published by Robinson, Pratt & Co., 1837.
CTHWatk; IaKn.   43816

---- A treatise on mathematical
and physical geography. Intended for the use of schools,
academies, and general readers.
By J. L. Comstock.... Hartford, Packard and Brown, 1837.
309 p. InCW; KWiU; OCX; PU;
TxU-T.   43817

Concord, N.H. - Baptist Church.
A short summary and declaration of faith of the Baptist
Church in Concord. To which
is added the church covenant.
Concord, Young & Worth, 1837.
22 p. MH.   43818

Concord Female Anti-Slavery
Society, Concord, N.H.
The constitution of the Society,
organized 15, November, 1834
with a list of the names of members. Concord, A. M. Farland,
1837. 8 p. MH.   43819

Confessions, trials & biographical
sketches of the most cold blooded
murderers, who have been executed in this country from its
first settlement... Boston,
Thomson, 1837. 408 p. MB;
MBs; NPla; OCLaw; PP.   43820

Congregational Churches in Connecticut.
A Confession of faith, owned
and consented to by the elders
and messengers of the churches
in the colony of Connecticut,...
New-Lond., Ptd., 1710. Hartford, Reptd., by P. B. Gleason
& Co., 1837. 126 p. MiD-B.
                                 43821
---- Consociation of Windham
county.
Rules of the Consociation of
Windham county, Connecticut,
adopted October 4th, 1836. Hartford, Printed by P. Canfield,
1837. 12 p. CSmH; NNUT.
                                 43822

---- General Association.

General Association of Connecticut. Minutes of, at their meeting in New Milford, June 1837; with the report of the state of religion, etc. Hartford, 1837. IEG; MB; NcMHi; PPPrHi. 43823

---- ---- Pastoral letter of the General association of Connecticut. (Norfolk? 1836). 8 p. CtY. 43824

Congregational Churches in Mass. Barnstable Asso. Conf.

The conference of churches and anniversaries of the County of Orleans, April 26, 1837. Boston, Torrey & Blair, printers, 1837. 24 p. M; MTA. 43825

---- General Assoc.

Minutes of the General Association of Massachusetts, at their meeting at North Brookfield, June 28, 1837; with the narrative of the state of religion, and the Pastoral Letter. Printed by Crocker & Brewster, Boston, 1837. 46, (1) p. MeBat. 43826

Cong. Churches in N.H. General Asso.

Minutes of the General Association of New Hampshire, At Their Meeting In Claremont, August, 1837. Published By Order Of The Association. Gilmanton, Printed By Alfred Prescott, 1837. 28 p. ICN. 43827

---- Piscataqua Association.

Articles of faith and form of covenant, adopted by the Piscataqua Association of Ministers, at their meeting, July 16, 1834. Portsmouth, C. W. Brewster, 1837. 8 p. MBC; MiD-B. 43828

Congregational Churches in Rhode Island. Evangelical Consociation.

Proceedings of the Evangelical consocation and Home Missionary Society of Congregational Churches in Rhode Island.... Providence, B. Cranston & Co., 1837. 24 p. IEG; RP. 43829

Congregational Church in U.S.

Constitution, articles of faith and rules of order of the New York Congregational Association, Adopted May 3, 1837. New York, Benedict, 1837. IEG; MBC; OO; PPPrHi. 43830

Congregational churches in Vermont - General convention.

Extracts from the minutes of the General convention...at their session at Springfield, Sept. 1837. Windsor, Chronicle Press, 1837. 16 p. MiD-B. 43831

Congregational Publishing Society.

Gift for scholars.... Boston, 1837. 80 p. CtHWatk. 43832

Congress of nations. Dissertation on the subject, by a friend of peace. New York, 1837. MBC. 43833

Connecticut, General assembly, Committee to visit and examine the banks in Conn.

Report of the Committee appointed by the legislature to visit and examine the banks in Connecticut, made at May session, 1837. Hartford, 1837. 23 p. CSmH; Ct; CtY; MB. 43834

---- ---- House. Journal. Hartford, 1837-. DLC; GU; LU; NjP; ViU-L. 43835

---- ---- Special Committee concerning the City Bank, of New

Haven.

Report of the Special Committee, concerning the City Bank, of New Haven. Published by Order of the General Assembly. Hartford, Russell and Jones, printers, 1837. 22, (3) p. Ct; CTHWatk; CtSoP; MH-BA.
                              43836

---- Geological survey.

A report on the geological survey of Connecticut. By Charles Upham Shepard, M.D. Published under the direction of His Excellency, Henry W. Edwards, governor of the state. New Haven, printed by B. L. Hamlen, 1837. 188 p. CSt; IaDaM; MB; NhD; ScC.   43837

---- Governor (Henry W. Edwards).

Message of the governor to the General Assembly of Connecticut, May session, 1837. Hartford, Russell & Jones, (1837?) 7 p. Ct.   43838

---- Laws, statutes, etc.

An act relating to joint stock corporations. Hartford, 1837. 7 (1) p. CtY.   43839

---- ---- Public Acts of the State of Connecticut...Hartford, printed by John L. Boswell, 1837(-76). 24 v. CtMW; MBU-L; PHi.   43840

---- ---- The public statute laws of the state of Connecticut, passed at the May and December sessions, 1836 and the May session of the General assembly, 1837. Hartford, John L. Boswell, 1837. 109 p. IaU-L; MB; Mi-L; Nj; PU.   43841

---- ---- Resolves and private acts of the State of Connecticut, passed May Session, 1837. Pub-

lished agreeably to a resolve of the General Assembly, under the superintendence of the Secretary of said State. State of Connecticut, SS. Hartford, Printed by John L. Boswell, 1837. 72 p. CtB; MdBB; NNLI; RPL; Wa-L.
                              43842

---- ---- Resolves and private laws of the state of Connecticut, from the year 1789 to the year 1836. Published by authority of resolutions of the General assembly, passed May 1835 and 1836, under the supervision of special committee.... Hartford, John B. Eldredge, printer, 1837. V. 1-. Ar-SC; CoU; Ky; MB; Nb.   43843

---- Legislature.

Rules of the House of Representatives, and Joint Rules of Proceedings of the Senate and House of Representatives of Connecticut. Printed by order of the House. Hartford, Russell and Jones, Printers, 1837. [3]- 8 p. MiD-B.   43844

---- State Prison.

Report of the directors of the Connecticut State Prison, to the General Assembly May session, 1837. Published by order of the General Assembly. Hartford, Printed by Russell and Jones, 1837. 24 p. Ct.   43845

(Connecticut and Passumpsic Rivers Railroad).

Report of the Engineer on the survey of the Valley Railroad in Vermont. Montpelier, William Clark, 1837. 37 p. MH-BA; NN; PPF.   43846

The Connecticut Annual Register and United States Calendar, for 1837; to which is prefixed An Almanack....No. 47. Published

by Samuel Green. New-London,
and Canfield & Robins, Hartford. Samuel Green......
printer. (1837). 160 p. Ct.
43847

Connecticut State Medical So-
ciety.
  Proceedings of the President
and Fellows of the Connecticut
Medical Society, in Convention,
May, 1837: ... with a List of
the Members of the Society.
New Haven, Printed by B. S.
Hamlen, 1837. 16 p. Ct;
CtHWatk; MH; NNNAM; WU-M.
43848

Conner, firm, type founders,
New York.
  [Supplement to the specimen of printing types and
ornaments from the type and
stereotype foundry of Conner
and Cooke. New York, 1837?]
NNC.   43849

Considerations on the eastern
diocese. By a presbyter of
the Diocese of Mass. Boston,
Dutton and Wentworth, Printers, 1837. 35 p. MBD; MBAt;
NNG; PPL; RP.   43850

Convention of a number of citizens of Pennsylvania, praying
Congress to construct a
Macadmized Road from a National Road to Erie, September
7, 1837. Laid on the table,
and ordered to be printed.
Washington, Blair and Rives,
printers, 1837. 2 p. R; Sc.
43851

Convention of Friends of constitutional reform, New York.
  The address, and draft of a
proposed constitution, submitted to the people of the
state of New York, by a convention of Friends of constitutional reform, held at Utica,
September, 1837. New York,

The Convention, 1837. 4, 8 p.
MH-L; MoSHi; NN; RPB. 43852

Conversations of a father with
his children. Vol. II. First
American from the third London
edition. Boston, Benjamin H.
Greene, Otis, Broaders and co.,
New York, J. H. Weeks, 1837.
191 p. fronts. IaDaP; MB;
MBAt; WHi.   43853

Conversations on the art of glass
blowing. New-York, M. Day,
1837. (1)6-23 p. DLC; MB;
NN.   43854

Conversations on the memoirs of
pious children, including the history of Julia Chase, of Barnstable, Mass. Philadelphia, American Sunday-school union, [1837].
[5]-50 p. DLC; PPAmS. 43855

Cook, Zeb.
  (Interrogationies by Zeb.
Cook, Jr. Pres. Mass. Mining
Co. to Gen. Samuel Chandler,
Supt. of that company, concern-
ing the Geology of the Mass.
Mining Co., Mansfield, Mass.)
N.P.N. imp. (1837?) 6 p. MiD-
B.   43856

Cooke, Parsons, 1800-1864.
  Female preaching, unlawful
and inexpedient. A sermon, by
Parsons Cooke, pastor of the
First Church in Lynn. Lynn,
printed and published by James
R. Newhall, 1837. 19 p. ICU;
MBC; MH-And; MWA; PPPrHi.
43857
---- A Sermon preached at the
installation of Rev. Randolph
Campbell, as pastor of the fourth
church and society in Newbury-
port. October 12, 1837. By
Rev. Parsons Cooke, pastor of
the First Church in Lynn. ...
Newburyport, Hiram Tozer,

Printer, 1837. 32 p. CU; MBC;
MiD-B; NjR; RPB.   43858

Cooley, Timothy Mather, 1772-
1859.
    Memoir of Mary West. Bos-
ton, 1837. MBC.   43859

---- Sketches of the life and
character of the Rev. Lemuel
Haynes, A.M. for many years
pastor of a church in Rutland,
Vt., and late in Granville,
New York...New-York, Harper
& bros., 1837. 345 p. CtHT;
KU; MWA; OClWHi; PHi; VtB.
                          43860
Cooly, Byron.
    Memoirs, compiled from his
papers and conversations while
under sentence of death. Cincinnati, R. P. Brooks and co.,
printers, 1837. 42 p. MnH;
MnHi.   43861

(Cooper, Edward C).
    An inquiry into the spirit of
truth; being some serious considerations....of the natural immortality of mans present physical existence. With an appendix,
entitled Religion as it is....New
York, printed for the author,
1837. 38 p. MB.   43862

Cooper, James Fenimore, 1789-
1851.
    Gleamings in Europe, Eng-
land: By an American. Philadelphia, Carey, Lea and Blanchard, 1837. 2 v. CoU; InU;
KHi; MoSU; PNt.   43863

---- The Water-witch; or, The
Skimmer of the seas. The works
of James Fenimore Cooper. New
York and London, G. P. Putnam's sons, the Knickerbocker
press, 1837. 444 p. MTop; NN.
                          43864
---- Wept of wish-ton-wish. By

J. Fenimore Cooper. New York,
John W. Lovell & Co., 1837.
362 p. MPeaI.   43865

Cooper, Thomas, 1759-1839.
    On the connection between
geology and the Pentateuch, in
a letter to Professor Silliman,
from Thomas Cooper, M.D. To
which is added an appendix.
Boston, Aber Kneeland, 1837.
83 p. IU; MiU; NcD; MWA.
                          43866
Cooper, William, 1810-1877.
    Researches on the cheiroptera
of the United States by William
Cooper. Extracted from the annals of the lyceum of natural
history. New York, George P.
Scott & co., printers, 1837.
[53]-276 p. CLCM; CU; DLC;
DNLM; PPAmP; PPAN.   43867

Coote, Richard Holmes.
    A treatise on the law of mort-
gages. By Richard Holmes Coote,
... Philadelphia, John S. Littell.
...New York, Halsted and Voor-
hies, 1837. 320 p. MH; NcU;
PP; Sc-SC; ViU-L; WaU. 43868

Corbett, M.
    The Oriental key to the Sa-
cred Scriptures, as they are illustrated by the existing rites,
usages, and domestic manners of
eastern countries; with a short
account of the different books
and writers of the sacred volume. By M. Corbett. The introduction by the author of
"Oriental annual." Philadelphia,
Joseph Whetham, 1837. 336 p.
CtY; ICU; MdBD; NNUT; PPP.
                          43869
Core sound, North Carolina,
surveyed, 1837. Washington,
[1837?] (Map) PPL-R.   43870

---- No. 2. Washington, 1837.
                          43871

Cornelius (Elias.), 1794-1832.
The Little Osaga Captive (Lydia Carter), an authentic narrative; to which are added some...letters, written by Indians. Third edition. Boston, 1837. 72 p. MWA.   43872

Corning & Blossburg Railroad.
Report, made to the directors of the Tioga Coal, Iron, Mining and Manufacturing Company, by Miller Fox, engineer, and other documents relating to the road. Geneva, N.Y., J. Taylor Bradt, Printer, 1837. 37 p. CSmH; DLC; PPF. 43873

Correspondence between E. C. Delavan and the Rev. Dr. Sprague. Albany, n. pub., n. pr., 1837. 8 p. MB; NjR.
43874

Corwin, Thomas.
Speech on the bill from the Committee of ways and means, to reduce the revenue of the U.S. As the wants of the Government. Delivered in the House of Representatives of the U.S. Jan. 12, 1837. Washington, 1837. 15 p. CtY; ICU; MBAt; MH-And; MWA.
43875

Cottage Dialogues; or Conversations on Camp Meetings and Other Subjects, between William James and Others. Methodist Tracts. New York, 1837. IEG; PCA.   43876

The cottage stories, or Henry Acton's maxims to his son William. Being a sequel to "Woodland Cottage," Salem, Ives & Jewett, 1837. MB; MH.   43877

Cottom's Virginia & North Carolina Almanack for 1838. Calculations by David Richardson. Richmond, Va., Peter

Cottom, [1837]. MWA; Vi.
43878
The court and camp of Bonaparte. New York, Harper and bros., 1837. 396 p. DLC; FTU; MH; NN; OO.   43879

Covel, James.
Questions on the historical books of the New Testament; designed for Bible classes and Sabbath schools. By Rev. James Covel, jun. ... New York, Published by T. Mason and G. Lane, 1837. 152 p. NNMhi.   43880

Coventry (Conn.) Second Congregational Church.
Historical notice, with articles of faith, covenant, and catalogue of members. Hartford, 1837. 16 p. CtSoP.   43881

Cox, Francis Augustus, 1783-1853.
The Baptists in America; a narrative of the deputation from the Baptist Union in England to the United States and Canada. New York, Leavitt, Lord, 1837. 476 p. IObNB; ViU.   43882

Cox, Robert.
The life of the Rev. John William Fletcher, vicar of Madeley.... First American edition; with an introduction, and a selection from the correspondence of Wm. Fletcher, by the Rev. George A. Smith. Philadelphia, George & Byington, 1837. 240 p. DLC; LNH; MdBP; NAlf. 43883

Coxe, Arthur Cleveland, 1818-1896.
Advent, a mystery. By Arthur Cleveland Cox. New York, J. S. Taylor, 1837. [11]-132 p. CSmH; ICN; MH; NCH; TxU.   43884

Cozzens, Samuel Woodworth.
A sermon occassioned by the
death of the Hon. William Reed,
delivered Feb. 26, 1837. By
Samuel W. Cozzens.... Boston,
Printed by Crocker and Brew-
ster, 1837. 27 p. CtSoP;
IEG; MHi; MeHi; RPB.   43885

Crabb, George, 1778-1851.
English synonyms with copi-
ous illustrations and explana-
tions, drawn from the best
writers. By George Crabb.
New York, Published by Harper
& Brothers, 1837. 65-535 p.
ICU; KyLoCP; LNB; NN; ViU.
                          43886
Crabbe, George, 1785-1857.
The life of the Rev. George
Crabbe. By his son, the Rev.
George Crabbe, A.M. New York,
George Dearborn & Co., 1837.
311 p. MHolli; Ms; MsSC; NN;
RP.   43887

Cramer's Louisiana & Mississippi
almanac for 1837. By George
R. Perkins. Natchez, Published
by Pearce and Berancon, Stanton and Berancon, printers,
1837. 30 p. MS-Ar; MsJS.
                          43888
The Cranberry Meadow; a
Temperance tale, founded on
fact. By the Author of "The
Poor Man's House Repaired."
Published by the council of the
Massachusetts temperance society. Boston, printed by Cassady and March, 1837. 16 p.
MH; MPeHi; NNC; RPB.   43889

Crandall, Phineas.
The true faith vindicated;
or, Strictures on "The true believer's defence;" a work written by the Rev. Charles Morgridge, ... against the divinity
and deity of Christ, and doctrine
of the Trinity. By Phineas

Crandall, ... New Bedford, Sidney Underwood, 1837. CBPac;
MBC; MBNMHi; MH-And; TxDaM.
                          43890
Creek Nation.
Memorial of the Creek delegation in relation to funds due
the "Creek Orphans" under the
Creek treaty of 1832. and the
act of March 3, 1837...Washing-
ton, Printed by John L. Guick,
1837. MdBJ;   43891

Cressey, Timothy Robinson,
1800-1870.
Address before the Ohio Bap-
tist education society, at their
Annual meeting, held in Gran-
ville, August, 1837. [Granville,
O., The society, 1837.] 16 p.
OHi.   43892

Crewdson, Isaac, 1780-1844.
Water baptism and the Lord's
Supper. Scriptural arguments
in behalf of the perpetual obli-
gation of these ordinances. By
Isaac Crewdson, Elisha Bates,
and a few additional remarks, by
Iota. Philadelphia, W. Stavely,
1837. 100 p. CtHT; InRchE;
OrPD; PSC-Hi.   43893

Crichton, Andrew.
The history of Arabia....By
Andrew Crichton. In 2 vols....
New York, Harper and bros.,
1837. 2 v. FTa; IU; MH; PMA;
WU.   43894

The cries of London. New York,
Mahlon Day, 1837. PPRF.
                          43895
Crockett, David, 1786-1836.
An account of Col. Crockett's
tour to the North and down East,
in the year of our Lord one
thousand eight hundred and thirty-
four. His object being to examine the grand manufacturing
establishments of the country ...

the condition of its literature and morals, the extent of its commerce ... 10th ed. Philadelphia, E. L. Carey and A. Hart, 1837. 234 p. KHi; MnDu; OFH; MnHi; T.   43896

---- ... Exploits and adventures in Texas. See Smith, Richard Penn, 1799-1834.

---- The life of Martin Van Buren ... with a concise history of the events ... that have occasioned his unparalleled elevation; together with a review of his policy as a statesman ... 16th ed. Philadelphia, 1837. 209 p. CtY; LU; MH; NhD; WaU.   43897

---- A narrative of the life of David Crockett, of the State of Tennessee.... Written by himself. 24th ed. Philadelphia, E. L. Carey and A. Hart; New York, Collins, Keese & co., 1837. [4], 211 p. MnU; NRU; O; TKL-Mc.   43898

Crockett, John Wesley, 1807-1852.
    Speech of John W. Crockett, of Tennessee, on the bill to authorize the issuing of Treasury notes. Delivered in the House of representatives, October 5, 1837. [Washington, 1837]. 8 p. CtY; NN.   43899

Crockett's Free-and-easy song book. Philadelphia, 1837. 128 p. DLC; MB.   43900

Crockett's Texas Almanack. New York, Turner & Fisher, 1837. MWA.   43901

Croly, George, 1780-1860.
    Life and times of His Majesty, George the Fourth, with anec-

dotes of distinguished persons of the last fifty years. By Rev. George Croly. New York, Harper and bros., 1837. 414 p. FTU; LNT; NNUT; PHi; PMA.   43902

Croom, Hardy Bryan, 1798-1837.
    A catalogue of plants, native or naturalized, in the vicinity of Newbern, North Carolina, ... by H. B. Croom, A.M., esq. ... New-York, G. P. Scott and co., printers, 1837. (3), 52 p. DLC; MH; Nh; NNNBC; PU.   43903

---- Observations on the genus Sarracenia; with an account of a new species. New York, G. P. Scott & Co., 1837. 104 p. DLC.   43904

Croserio, Camille, 1786-1855.
    On homeopathic medicine, illustrating its superiority over the other medical doctrines... Tran. from the French by C. Neidhard. Philadelphia, Kiderlen, 1837. 89 p. DLC; MWA; NNC-M; PHi; RPB.   43905

Cross, James Conquest.
    An Inaugural discourse on the value of time, and the importance of study to the physician. Lexington, Finnell & Zimmerman, Printers, 1837. 34 p. IEN-M; KyLxT; MB; NjPT; OC.   43906

Crothers, Samuel.
    The gospel of the jubilee. An explanation of the typical priveleges secured to the congregation and pious strangers, by the atonement on the morning of the jubilee. Hamilton, O., Printed by I. M. Waters, 1837. 84 p. DLC; ICP; InPerM; MdBJ; OClWHi.   43907

Cruden, Alexander, 1701-1770.
    A complete concordance to the holy scriptures of the Old and

New Testaments; in two parts,
with an original life of the author. By Alexander Cruden.
New York, Dodd, Mead & co.,
[1837?] 856 p. GAM-R.   43908

Cruse, C.
     Introductory lecture delivered
at the opening of the Lancaster
Conservatory of the Arts and
Sciences, and City Lyceum, on
the evening of July 3d, 1837.
Lancaster, Pa., Printed by C.
M'Cleary, 1837. 28 p. PLT;
PPHa.   43909

Cudworth, Ralph, 1617-1688.
     The true intellectual system
of the universe.... 1st American ed.; with references to
the several quotations in The intellectual system; and an account of the life and writings
of the author by Thomas Birch.
By Ralph Cudworth. New
York, Andover, Gould & Newman, 1837-1838. 2 v. ArCH;
CU; IaGG; NjR; WaPS.   43910

Culbertson, James.
     An address delivered in
Zanesville, on the Fourth of
July, 1837. At the request of
the Zanesville and Putnam
colonization society. By the
Rev. James Culbertson. Zanesville, Printed by Adam Peters,
1837. 16 p. OCHP.   43911

Culbreth, Thomas.
     (Document No. 10.) Letter
from Thomas Culbreth, Clerk
of the Council, to Josiah Baily,
esq. Attorney general. Annapolis, William M'Neir, printer,
1837. 4 p. MdHi.   43912

.... Cumberland almanac, for
the year of our Lord 1838:
calculated for the horizon of
Nashville, Tenn. Nashville,

Printed by S. Nye and co. at
the Republican banner office,
[1837]. [36] p. MWA; T.
                              43913
Cumberland Presbyterian Church.
     The constitution of the Cum-
berland Presbyterian Church.
containing the confession of
faith, catechism, and a directory
for the worship of God; together
with the form of government
and discipline, as revised and
adopted by the general assembly
at Princeton, Ky. May 1829.
fourth edition. Nashville, Printed
at Smith's Steam Press, 1837.
[3], iv-v, [2], 8-296, [4] p.
AU; MH-AH; PPPrHi.   43914

Cumberland Valley Rail Road
Company.
     Second report of William Milnor
Roberts, chief engineer of the
Cumberland Valley Railroad Com-
pany, made to the Board, on the
29th December 1836. Chambers-
burg, Pa., Printed by Hickok &
Blood, 1837. 10 p. DLC; DBRE;
MdLR; NN; WHi.   43915

Cuming, Francis H.
     The children of the resurrec-
tion; or, The believer consoled
under the loss of relatives and
friends who have not died in the
Lord. A sermon preached on
the afternoon of Easter, March
26, 1837, in Calvary Church,
New York, N.Y., 1837. 24 p.
CtHT; MeB; MH-And; MWA; NjPT.
                              43916
Cummings, Samuel.
     The western pilot: containing
charts of the Ohio River and of
the Mississippi,....Accompanied
with directions for navigating
the same and a gazetteer, or
description of the towns on their
banks, tributary streams, etc....
with a table of distances from
town to town on all the above

rivers. By Samuel Cumings (!)
Cincinnati, G. Conclin, 1837.
CSmH; MoHi; OClWHi.   43917

Cunnabell, J. L.
Selection of airs, marches,
etc. Boston, Published by R. H.
Blake, Kidder & Wright printers,
1837. 40 p. MWHi.   43918

Cunningham, Allan.
The lives of the most emi-
nent British painters and
sculptors. In three volumes.
New York, published by Harper
and brothers, 1837. 3 v.
IaDa; MH; MWA; OClWHi;
ScCliP.   43919

---- A wet sheet and a flowing
sea. A nautical song...written
by Allan Cunningham. Adapted
& arranged by Thomas Walton.
(With accompaniment for pianoforte.) Philadelphia, Hewitt
& Co., 1837. 3 p. MB.   43920

Curling, Thomas Blizard, 1811-
1888.
A treatise on tetanus, being
the essay for which the Jack-
sonian prize, for the year
1834, was awarded, by the
Royal College of surgeons, in
London. By Thomas Blizard
Curling ... Philadelphia, Haswell, Barrington, and Haswell,
1837. 126 p. CtY; KyU;
MdBJ; PP; ViU.   43921

Curr, Joseph.
Familiar instructions in the
faith and morality of the Catholic church ... By the Rev.
Joseph Curr. Philadelphia,
pub. ... by Patrick J. Fallon,
1837. 211 p. DLC.   43922

A Cursory Examination of the
Respective Pretensions of the
Colonizationists and Abolition-

ists. ... New-York, 1837. 12 p.
ICN; MB; MWA; OClWHi; TNF.
43923

Curtis, Alva, 1797-1881.
Lectures on midwifery and
the forms of disease peculiar to
women and children. Columbus,
Jonathan Phillips, 1837. 389 p.
DSG; MdBM; MH-M; NBMS; ODa.
43924

Cushing, Abel.
Speech .... on resolves to
the action of Congress upon anti-
slavery petitions .... By Abel
Cushing. Boston, n. pub.
printed by Beals & Greene, 1837.
23 p. DLC; MB; MBAt; NjR;
PPL.   43925

Cushing, Caleb, 1800-1879.
Letters to ... Edward Ever-
ett, ... on the question of the
North Eastern Boundary. ....
(Boston, 1837.) 8 p. MHi.
43926

---- Speech of Mr. Cushing, of
Massachusetts, on the bill making appropriations for the current expenses of the Indian department. Delivered in the
House of Representatives, Feb.
1, 1837. Washington, Gales and
Seaton, 1837. 14 p. MBAt; MH;
MiD-B; MWA.   43927

---- Speech on executive powers,
delivered in the House of Representatives, Dec. 19, 1837.
(Washington, 1837). 8 p. MH;
PHi.   43928

---- Speech of Mr. Cushing, on
the message of the President of
the United States, at the opening of the twenty-fifth Congress.
Delivered in the House of representatives, Sept. 25, 1837.
Washington, 1837. 34 p. CtY;
ICN; MBAt; NN; OClWHi.
43929

---- Speech of Mr. Cushing of

Massachusetts on the proposition to censure Mr. John Quincy Adams, for an alleged disrespect to the House of Representatives. (Washington, 1837.) 15 p. MB; MH; MWA.   43930

Cushing, Luther S.
    Inquiry into the present state of the remedial law of Mass. for its reform. Boston, Hilliard, Gray & Co., 1837. 52 p. MB; MWCL.   43931

The customs and manner of the Bedouin Arabs: designed especially to illustrate the early Scripture history. ... Written for the American Sunday-school union, and revised by the Committee of publication. Philadelphia, American Sunday-school union, [1837]. 160 p. DLC; GDecCT; OCl; TxLocC.   43932

Cutler, Ann.
    Short account of life of Ann Cutler. N.Y., 1837. 20 p. MWA.   43933

Cutting, Sewall Sylvester, 1813-1882.
    Influence of Christianity on government and slavery: a discourse, delivered in the Baptist Church, in West Boylston, Mass. January 15, 1837. By Sewall S. Cutting, pastor. Worcester, printed by Henry J. Howland, 1837. 14 p. ICU; MBC; MiD-B; MWA; RPB.   43934

D

Daboll, Nathan, 1750-1818.
    ... A key to Daboll's arithmetic...to which is added, a new method of solving the irreducible case of cubic equations...also 250 curious and abstruse arithmetical, mathematical and philosophical questions ...by John D. Williams...New York, H. & S. Raynor, 1837. [5]-180 p. DLC.   43935

Daboll, Nathan, 1782-1863.
    Daboll's schoolmaster's assistant, improved and enlarged. Being a plain practical system of arithmetic, adapted to the United States. By Nathan Daboll. With an addition of the farmer's and merchant's best method of bookkeeping, designed as a compensation to Daboll's arithmetic by Samuel Green. Ithaca, N.Y., Printed and Published by Mac, Andrus and Woodruff, 1837. 228, 12 p. ICJ; MH; NNC; OClWHi; RPB.   43936

---- ---- Utica, G. Tracy, 1837. 240 p. ICN; MH; MiU; NBuG; OClWHi.   43937

The Dade asylum: or, Mental monument to Major Dade & those who have fallen in the Florida war. Charleston, S.C., Thomas J. Eccles, 1837. 40 p. PHi; TxU.   43938

Daggett's perpetual almanac, and arithmetical navigator. Calculated for the entire nineteenth century. By Samuel Daggett.... Printed at New Bedford, for the author....1837. 12 p. MNBedf.   43939

Daily, William Mitchel, 1812-1877.
    A sermon on education, Delivered in the Methodist church, at Bloomington, Ia. Feby 26, 1837. ... (n.p.) Pub. at the Special request of the Congregation, Indiana, (1837). 20 p. MHi.   43940

The Daily chronicle and convention journal: containing the sub-

stance and spirit of the proceedings of the convention
which assembled at the state
capitol in Harrisburg, May 2,
1837, to alter and amend the
constitution of the state of
Pennsylvania; having been published for the same ... Harrisburg, E. Guyer, 1837. 3 v.
in 1. DLC; ICU; MBAt; P;
PWW; TxU.   43941

Dale, Benjamin.
    An examination of Mr. Ran-
toul's report for abolishing
capital punishment in Massachusetts. ... Boston, printed
for the author [Fairfield &
Pitman's Print], 1837. 72 p.
WHi.   43942

Dallas, George M.
    Opinion on the claim of
Charles F. Sibbald. Philadelphia,
1837. 4 p. PHi.   43943

Dalling and Bulwer, William
Henry Lytton Earle Bulwer,
1801-1872.
    The Lords, the government
and the country; a letter on
the present state of affairs.
Exeter, 1837. MBAt; NN.
                                43944

Dalzel, Andrew, 1742-1806.
    .... sive, Collectanea graeca
majora, ad usum academicae
juventutis accomodata; cum notis
philologicis, quas partim col-
legit, partim scripsit Andreas
Dalzel... Ed. 4. americana,
ex auctoribus correcta priori-
bus emendatior, cum notis
aliquot interjectis. Boston,
Hilliard, Gray & co.; Philadelphia, Kimber & Sharpless, 1837.
2 v. CtY; IaDaP; NjMD; TU;
WHi.   43945

Damon, Norwood.
    The Chronicles of Mount

Benedict: A Tale of the Ursuline Convent ... (anon.). Boston, printed for the publisher,
1837. 191 p. DLC; M; MB; MH.
                                43946
Dana, Daniel, 1771-1859.
    A sermon delivered at the
annual election. January 4,
1837.... Before the legislature
of Massachusetts.... Boston,
n. pub. Dutton and Wentworth,
printers, 1837. 44 p. CSmH;
ICU; MAnP; NjR; PPL.   43947

Dana, James Dwight, 1813-1895.
    A system of Mineralogy: in-
cluding an extended treatise on
crystallography: .... By James
Dwight Dana, A.M. .... New
Haven, Published by Durrie &
Peck and Herrick & Noyes, 1837.
452, 119 p. AzU; KyDC; NjR;
PPi; RNR.   43948

Dance, Charles, 1794-1863.
    Advice gratis; a farce, in one
act. New York, Samuel French,
[1837?] 26 p. OCl.   43949

---- The Bengal tiger; a farce,
in one act. 23 p. New York,
... Samuel French, [1837?]
OCl.   43950

---- The country squire; or,
two days at the hall; an original
comedy in 2 acts, by Charles
Dance ... correctly marked and
arranged by J. B. Wright ...
New York, S. French, 1837.
42 p. C; OCl; PPL.   43951

Danforth, Joshua Noble.
    Memoir of William C. Walton,
late pastor of the Second Pres-
byterian church in Alexandria
D.C. and of the Free church in
Hartford, Conn. .... Hartford,
D. Burgress and co.; New York,
J. S. Taylor, 1837. 319 p.
CtSoP; ICU; MWA; NNUT; OO;
RPB.   43952

Darlington, William, 1782-1863.

Flora cestrica: an attempt to enumerate and describe the flowering and filicoid plants of Chester county, in the State of Pennsylvania. By William Darlington. West-Chester, printed for the author by S. Siegfried, 1837. 620 p. A-GS; MH; NjP; PP; RPB.   43953

Dartmouth College.

Catalogue senatus academici collegii Dartmuthensis in re-publica Neo-Hantoniensi.... Bostoniae, typis Perkins et Marvin, 1837. 68 p. CtY; DLC.   43954

D'Arusmont, Francis (Wright).

History of the bankrupt purseholder, presenting a general view of the origin and rise of whiggery, with its policy and achievements from its birth unto the present hour. Philadelphia, New York, Boston, Cincinnati, 1837. 32 p. MnHi.   43955

Daunou, Pierre Claude Francois, 1761-1840.

Outlines of a history of the Court of Rome and of the temporal power of the Popes, translated from the French. Philadelphia, Joseph Whethan, 1837. xix, 328, (2) p. CtY; IEG; MB; MWA; PPL.   43956

Davenport, Bishop.

History of the United States, containing all the events necessary to be committed to memory; with the Declaration of Independence, the Constitution of the United States, and a table of chronology, for the use of schools...A new ed. revised, improved. Philadelphia, William Marshall & Co., 1837. 173 p.

DLC; RPB.   43957

---- A pocket gazetteer, or Traveller's guide through North America and the West Indies, Comp....By Bishop Davenport. Baltimore, Cushing & sons. (etc.), 1837. 468 p. DLC; MiD-B.   43958

Davenport, Thomas, 1802-1851.

Electro-Magnetism. History of Davenport's Invention of the Application of Electro-Magnetism to Machinery; with Remarks on the Same ... by Professor Silliman. ... New-York, G. & C. Carville & Co., and Geo F. Hopkins & Son, 1837. 94 p. ICU; MB; MdBP; OkU; PPM.   43959

David, J. C.

An Introduction to universal language, and progenitive distinctions of families. [Washington, 1837.] 32 p. DLC.   43960

Davies, Charles, 1798-1876.

The common school arithmetic, prepared for the use of academies and common schools in the United States, and also for the young gentlemen who may be preparing to enter the military academy at West Point. By Charles Davies.... Geneva, J. & J. N. Bogert, n. pr., 1837. 270 p. NCanHi; NjR.   43961

---- Elements of algebra: translated from the French of M. Bourdon. Revised and adapted to the course of mathematical instruction in the United States. By Charles Davies....New York, Wiley & Long, 1837. 353 p. IaHi; NjP; OClW; PAtM.   43962

---- Elements of geometry and trigonometry. By Charles Davis. New York, Pub. by A. S. Barnes and co., Cincinnati, Rickey,

Mallory and Webb, 1837. GAuY.
43963

---- Elements of surveying,
including a description of the
instruments and the necessary
tables. Revised and adapted to
the course of mathmatical instruction in the United States.
New York, Wiley, and Long,
1837. v.p. Ia; MvC; MH.
43964

Davies, Samuel R.
A refutation of sundry un-
founded accusations, contended
in letters and conversations
from Dr. Daniel Drake, to a
committee of the third district
Medical Society. To the public. Cincinnati? n.p. n.d.,
1837? 8 p. OClWHi.   43965

Davis, Alexander Jackson, 1803-
1892.
Architectural scraps. New
York, (1837). Partly mss.
MBAt.   43966

---- Rural residences, etc.,
consisting of designs, original
and selected, for cottages, farm
houses, villas, village churches.
New York, 1837. MBAt; MdBP;
MnU-Ag; NN.   43967

Davis, E.
The Franklin intellectual arithmetic: for the use of schools.
By E. Davis, A.M. ... Stereotyped edition. Springfield,
Published by G. & C. Merriam,
1837. 108 p.   43968

Davis, Emerson, 1798-1866.
A Thriving town. A sermon,
preached at the annual fast,
April 6, 1837, in Westfield,
Mass. By Emerson Davis.
Springfield, printed by Mer-
riam, Wood and Co., 1837.
16 p. MH-And; MSHi; MWeA;
MWo; NN.   43969

Davis, Gustavus Fellowes, 1797-
1836.
Memoir of Rev. Gustavus F.
Davis ... with six sermons on
the peculiar sentiments of the
Baptist denomination, preached
by him before his congregation,
1834-5. By Abigail L. Davis.
Hartford, Canfield, & Robins,
1837. 167, 152 p. CBB; IN;
MWA; NNUT; RPB.   43970

Davis, James M.
Universalism unmasked, or
the spurious gospel exposed: ...
By James M. Davis. Philadel-
phia, Printed by I. Ashmead &
Co., 1837. 294 p. CtSoP;
KyLoP; MH; MoS; PPL.   43971

Davis, John, 1774-1854.
Captain Smith and Princess
Pocahontas an Indian tale. New
ed. rev. & cor. Dayton, [O.],
Ells., 1837. 128 p. OC; ViU.
43972

Davis, John Anthony Gardner,
1801-1840.
An exposition of the principles
which distinguish estates tail
from other limitations. By
J. A. G. Davis ... Designed
for the use of the senior law
class of the University. Charlottesville [Va.], Printed by
Tompkins & Noel, 1837. 32 p.
CSmH; Vi; ViU.   43973

Davis, Matthew, 1766-1850.
Memoirs of Aaron Burr. See
Burr, Aaron.

Davis, Owen.
Sketches of sermons, delivered
by Rev. Owen Davis in the First
Free Bethal Church, in West
Centre Street, Boston. Boston,
printed for the author, 1837.
12 p. DLC; MNtcA; MWA.
43974

Davis, Robert, b. 1798?

The Canadian farmer's travels in the United States of America, in which remarks are made on the arbitrary colonial policy practiced in Canada, and the free and equal rights and happy effects of the liberal institutions and astonishing enterprise of the United States. By Robert Davis. Buffalo, printed for the author, [Steele's Press.], 1837. 107 p. CaT; CaOTU; CtY; InU.   43975

Davis, S. A.

The Western Universalist hymn book, designed for public and private worship, compiled from various authors. By S. A. Davis & M. A. Chappell. ... Pittsburgh, printed by W. F. Stewart, 1837. 192 p. MMeT-Hi.   43976

Davis, Solomon.

Prayer book in the language of the Six Nations of Indians. See Protestant Episcopal Church in the U.S.A. Book of Common prayer. Oneida.

Davison, Gideon Miner, 1791-1869.

The traveller's guide through the middle and northern states, and the provinces of Canada. .... 7th ed. Saratoga Springs, G. M. Davison; New-York, S. S. & W. Wood, 1837. 465 p. CSmH; ICN; LNH; MB; PPM.   43977

Davy Crockett, or, The Nimrod of the West, the only cure for the hard times; a poem, by a friend to the Colonel. New York, Printed for the Author, 1837. CSmH; DLC; OMC; RPB.   43978

Davy Crockett's almanack, 1838,

of wild sports in the West, ... Nashville, Tennessee. Published by the heirs of Col. Crockett, [1837]. CSmH; WHi.   43979

Dawson, William Crosby, 1798-1856.

Speech of Mr. Dawson, of Georgia, on the bill to postpone the fourth instalment payable under the deposite act. Delivered in the House of representatives, September 27, 1837. Washington, 1837. 14 p. CtY; NN.   43980

Day, Jeremiah, 1773-1867.

An introduction to Algebra, being the first part of a course of mathmatics adapted to the method of instruction in the American colleges....By Jeremiah Day, D.D., LL.D....Thirtieth edition ....New Haven, (Conn.), Published by Hezekial Howe, 1837. 333 p. MH; NIC; WOshT; IaDuU.   43981

---- ---- 28th ed. New Haven, H. Howe, 1837. 332 p. CtY; MH.   43982

---- ---- Twenty Ninth Edition. New Haven, 1837. 332 p. NbOM. NBuDC; NbOM.   43983

Day, Thomas, 1748-1789.

History of Sanford & Merton, a work intended for the use of schools, & juvenile readers; a new stereotype edition; three volumes in one. Baltimore, Neal, 1837. 391 p. Ct; NNC.   43984

Day's City and Country Almanac, for 1838. By David Young, Philomath. New York, N.Y., Mahlon Day, (1837.) MWA.   43985

Day's New York Pocket Almanac for 1838. New York, N.Y., M. Day, (1837.) Imprint varies. MWA.   43986

De La Beche, Henry Thomas,
1796-1855.
Researches in theoretical
geology. By H. T. De La
Beche ... with a preface and
notes by Prof. Edward Hitchcock ... New York, F. J.
Huntington & co.; Philadelphia,
Desilver, Thomas & co., 1837.
342 p. CU; IaGG; NNC; OClW;
PPi.   43987

De Lancey, William H.
Farewell address of Rev.
William H. De Lancey ... To
the congregation of St. Peter's
Church, Jan. 16, 1837. Philadelphia, [1837]. 7 p. PHi; PPL.
                              43987a
De Pui, James.
Evil effects of angry excite-
ment: a sermon delivered before
the congregation of Saint Paul's
church. Alton, Illinois, Bail-
hache and Parks, 1837. 12 p.
NN.   43988

Decoigne City and Canal Co.
Articles of Association, and
other documents relating to
Decoigne City Canal Company.
Alton, (Ill.), Hessin and
Sawyer, Printers, 1837. 11 p.
MHi; Ci.   43989

Dedham, Mass. Convention of
Common School Education.
An Address To the People
of the County of Norfolk, on
Common School Education, Pre-
pared by a Committee of the
Convention on the subject of
Education, holder at Dedham
Nov. 3, 1837 ... Advertiser
Press - Dedham, [1837].
Broadside. MH.   43990

---- South Church.
Confession of faith, covenant
(and names of members). Dedham, 1837. NBLiHi.   43991

Defoe, Daniel, 1660-1731.
The life and adventures of
Robinson Crusoe.... Cincinnati,
J. W. Ely, 1837. InU.   43992

---- ---- Hartford, Published by
Andrus and Judd, 1837. 2 v.
CtY; MWA; NNowi.   43993

---- New Robinson Crusoe, Designed for youth. Ornamented
with plates. Cooperstown,
1837. 27 p. MWA.   43994

---- The political history of the
devil. The history of the devil,
as well as ancient as modern...
2d ed. Philadelphia, 1837. 2
v. in 1. CtY.   43995

Delafield, Edward.
Introductory address to the
students of medicine of the Col-
lege of physicians and surgeons
of the university of the state
of New York. ... by Edward
Delafield, M.D., ... New York,
Published by the students, 1837.
44 p. MBM; NNNAM; NNC-M.
                              43996
Delafield, Richard, 1798-1873.
Letter of Capt. Richard Dela-
field, of the U.S. engineer
corps, to Matthew Newkirk, Esq.
... Philadelphia, Printed by
S. C. Atkinson, 1837. 10 p.
DBRE; MdHi; NbO; PHi; PPM.
                              43997
---- Letters and documents,
relative to his application to con-
nect League Island with the main
land. Harrisburg, 1837. NN.
                              43998
Delavan, Edward Cornelius.
Correspondence with Rev. Dr.
Sprague. Albany, 1837. 8 p.
MB; MBAt; OO.   43999

Delaware. Court Reports.
Reports of the cases argued
& adjudged in the Superior court

& Court of errors & appeals
of...Del; fr. the organization
of those courts under the
amended constitutions...
Wilmington, Del., Cann brothers and Kindig inc.; [etc., etc.]
1837-1919. V. 1-. DeWI; I;
NcD; Ok; PU-L.   44000

---- General Assembly. Senate.
Journal of the Senate of
the state of Delaware, at a
session commenced and held at
Dover on Tuesday, the third
day of Jan. 1837; and the
sixty-first year of the Independence of the United States
of America. Dover, Del.,
Samuel Kimmey, 1837. 182 p.
IaHi.   44001

---- Laws, statues, etc.
Laws of the State of Delaware, passed at a session of
the general assembly, commenced and held at Dover, on
Tuesday the third day of January, in the year of our Lord,
one thousand eight hundred
and thirty-seven, and of the
independence of the United
States, the sixty first. By
authority. Dover, Samuel Kimmey, printer, 1837. [57]-590 p.
Ky; Mi-L; Nj; R; W.   44002

Delaware and Hudson Canal
Company.
Annual report(s) of the
board of managers ... to the
stockholders. New York,
printed by John M. Elliott,
1837-58. MH-BA.   44003

Delaware Rail Road Company.
Charter .. with the report
of the commissioners and engineers, acting by order of
the legislative and the estimates and proposed route of the
road. Dover, Del., Kimmey,

1837. 54 p. CtY; DeWi; DLC.
                          44004
Deleuze, Joseph Philippe Francois, 1753-1835.
Practical instruction in animal
magnetism. Trans. by T. C.
Hartshorn...With an appendix
of notes by the translator, and
letters from eminent physicians
& others, descriptive of cases
in the United States. Providence, Cranston, 1837. 106-36
p. CtY; MB; MH; MH-M; PPCP.
                          44005
---- ---- 2d ed. Providence,
B. Cranston, & Co., 1837.
(9)-262, 204 p. CSmH; MdBP;
PaHosp; RPB; RHi.   44006

Dell, William Clarkson Brook.
The doctrine of Baptisms reduced from its ancient and
modern corruption; and restored
to its primitive soundness and
integrity. ... By Wm. Dell,
Philadelphia, J. Richards, Printer, 1837. 36 p. NjR; OClWHi;
OO; PHi; PSC-Hi.   44007

---- ---- 11th ed. New York,
1837. PSC-Hi.   44008

Deming, Elizur, 1797-1855.
Address before Philomathean
Society of Wabash College. n.p.
1837? 16 p. In.   44009

(Democratic party.)
Proceedings and address of
Democratic Republicans, opposed
to the sub-treasury & special deposit schemes, at a meeting held
in the city of New York, Jan. 2,
1838. New York, J. Booth &
son, 1837. 30 p. MH-BA.
                          44010
---- Monroe County. Michigan.
Democratic meeting. A meeting
of the electors of Monroe County,
who are willing to adopt the following as the fundamental creed

of their political sentiments, and who are disposed to support candidates for office whose views are in known accordance therewith, is requested at Loranger's hotel, in the City of Monroe, on Friday evening next, at 6 o'clock.... Monroe, Oct. 3, 1837. [Monroe, 1837]. Broadside. MiD-B.   44011

---- New York (City).
Declaration of rights and constitution and by-laws, adopted at the county meeting, July 1837. N.Y., 1837. 12 p. NNC. 44012

---- New York (State).
Republican legislative address. At a meeting of the Democratic Republican members of the senate and assembly of the state of New York....May 24, 1836. [New York, 1837?]
                                   44013
---- Virginia. 1st Congressional District, 1837.
Proceedings of the republican convention held in Suffolk on the 13th March, 1837. Norfolk, Printed by Shields, Asburn & Grigsby, 1837. 8 p. DLC; Vi.
                                   44014
Dempster, William Richardson.
"Oh! come with me." A ballad [T. accomp. for pianoforte.] Philadelphia, Munns, [1837.] 7 p. MB.   44015

(Denison, Charles W.)
Christ and him crucified; a sermon. By Charles W. Denison. New York, J. P. Callender, pub. Piercy and Reed, pr., 1837. 40 p. NjPT. 44016

Denison university, Granville, O.
General information respecting the internal arrangements of the Granville literary and theological institution.

Columbus, 1837. ICN.   44017

Derby, John Barton, 1793?-1867.
Musings of a recluse. ...
Boston, The author, 1837. 180 p. CSmH; CtMH; MFm; MH; RPB.   44018

A description of Georgia, by A grutteman who has resided there upward of seven years, and was one of the first settlers. London, Corbet, 1741. Washington, P. Force, 1837. DLC; MBBC; MnHi; OClWHi; TxU.   44019

Desecration of the Sabbath; to the Pastors and Congregations under the Synod of Philadelphia, 1837. 4 p. PHi.   44020

Desilver's United States Register and Almanac. Phila., Pa. R. Desilver, 1837. MWA.   44021

De[troit almanac and] Mich[igan register] for the year 1838: being the second after bissextile or leap year, and of American independence, till July 4, the 62nd year. Astronomical calculations by William W. McLouth. Detroit, Printed and sold, wholesale and retail, by Burger & Stevens (successors to Morse & Brother), [1837]. 24 p. MiD-B.
                                   44022
Detroit Democrat and Emigrant's Western Guide.
Prospectus of a new journal to be styled the Detroit Democrat, and Emigrant's Western Guide. [57 lines]. Detroit, November 23, 1837. [Detroit, 1837]. Broadside. MiD-B.
                                   44023
Deutscher Massigkeits Calender. Phila., Pa., 1837. MWA. 44024

Devil's Comical Almanac. New York, Turner & Fisher, 1837. MWA.   44025

Dewees, William Potts, 1768-
1841.

A compendious system of
midwifery, chiefly designed to
facilitate the inquiries of those
who may be pursuing this
branch of study. Illustrated
by occasional cases, and many
engravings. Eighth edition,
with additions and improvements. By William P. Dewees
... Philadelphia, Lea, Carey
& Blanchard, 1837. 660 p.
ArU-M; CtY; ICJ; MB; MdBJ;
NBMS.   44026

---- A treatise on the dis-
eases of females, by William
P. Dewees...6th ed. rev. and
cor. Philadelphia, Carey Lea
& Blanchard, 1837. [13]-591 p.
CSt-L; InU-M; NhD; PPCP;
RPM.   44027

Dewey, Orville, 1794-1882.

An address delivered before
the members of the American
institute, in the city of New-
York, by the Rev. Orville
Dewey, October 19, 1837 ...
New-York, Printed by J. Van
Norden, 1837. 16 p. DLC;
MBAU; MWA; PPAmP; PPM.
                             44028

Dexter, Andrew Alfred.

Appeal on behalf of the Montgomery railroad addressed to all
interested ... Montgomery (Ala.),
1837. 16 p. NNC.   44029

A dialogue between Telemachus
and Mentor on the rights of
conscience and military requisi-
tions. Philadelphia, John Richards, 1837. 20 p. NjR;
OClWHi; PPM; PSC-Hi; PU.
                             44030

Dialogue between three Sunday
scholars ... New York, Pub.
by T. Mason and G. Lane, for
the Sunday school union of the

Methodist Episcopal church, 1837.
8 p. DLC.   44031

The diary; or, Yeoman's calen-
dar and manufacturer's almanac
for the year...1838. By Edward
Symmes. Lowell, printed by
Journal press, (1837). DLC; MB;
MHi; MWA.   44032

Dick, John.

Lectures on theology. By
the late Rev. John Dick. Published under the superintendency
of his son. With a preface
memoir & etc. by the American
editor. Philadelphia, Edward C.
Biddle, 1837. 2 v. ABBS; InHu;
NcElon; PU; ViRut; TWcW.
                             44033

Dick, Thomas, 1774-1857.

Celestial scenery; or, The
wonders of the planetary system
displayed, illustrating the per-
fections of deity and a plurality
of worlds. New York, Harper
& brothers, [1837?] 422 p.
InCW; MCli; NBuDD; WHi.
                             44034

---- The Christian philosopher;
or, The Connexion (sic) of science and philosophy with religion.
Hartford, H. T. Sumner & Co.,
1837. 162 p. MBC.   44035

---- ---- Milton, Pa., Published
by S. Wilson and T. C. Slack.
Printed by Stephen Wilson, 1837.
476 p. OSW; P; PSt; PWmpDS.
                             44036

---- An essay on the sin and
the evils of covetousness, and
the happy effects that would
flow from a spirit of Christian
beneficence.... By Thomas
Dick. Philadelphia, Edward C.
Biddle, 1837. 10-204 p. CtMW;
MChi; MWA; OrU; RNR.   44037

---- On the improvement of society by the diffusion of knowledge:

an illustration of the adven-
tages which would result from
a more general dissemination of
rational and scientific information among all ranks...By
Thomas Dick...Hartford, H. F.
Sumner & co.; New-York,
Robinson, Pratt & co., 1837.
GHi; InGrD; MNF; NT; TxD-T.
44038

---- The Philosophy of a fu-
ture state. Hartford, H. F.
Sumner & Co., 1837. 127 p.
MBC. 44039

---- The Philosophy of religion;
or, An Illustration of the moral
laws of the universe. Hartford, H. B. Sumner & Co.,
1837. 186 p. MBC. 44040

Dickens, Charles, 1812-1870.
Child's History of England.
By Chas. Dickens. New York,
International Book Co., 1837.
374 p. FTa; WySH. 44041

---- Oliver Twist: .... Phila-
delphia, Carey, Lea and
Blanchard, 1837. 186 p.
CtMW; DLC; MH. 44042

---- The Pickwick Papers. By
Charles Dickens, "Boz." With
forty eight illustrations on
steel, from designs by Phiz
and Cruikshank. In two volumes. Philadelphia, T. B.
Peterson, 1837. 2 v. IaCrM;
InGo; OZaN; PU; WBoy. 44043

---- Posthumous papers on the
Pickwick club; containing a
faithful record of the perambu-
lations, perils, travels, adventures, and sporting transactions
of the corresponding members,
ed by Boz. 1st. Am. ed.
Philadelphia, Carey, Lea &
Blanchard, 1837. 5 v. OMC;
OO. 44044

---- ---- 2d ed. Philadelphia,
Carey, Lea & Blanchard: (Dickinson & Ward, printers.), 1837.
2 v. MH; MWA; NjR; PHi;
PLFM. 44045

---- ---- 3rd ed. Philadelphia,
Carey, Lea & Blanchard, 1837.
5 v. CU-S; ICU; IU; PMA.
44046
---- ---- 4th ed. Philadelphia,
Carey, Lea & Blanchard, 1837.
5 v. CtY; MB; MH; NNC; PP.
44047
---- Public life of Mr. Tulrumble,
once Mayor of Mudfog. By Boz
(pseud.) With other tales and
sketches, from Bentley's miscellany, and the library of fiction.
Philadelphia, Carey, Lea and
Blanchard, 1837. 208 p. CLU;
ICN; MeB; PFal. 44048

---- Sketches of "Boz." Illustrative of everyday life and
every-day people. By Charles
Dickens. Philadelphia, Carey,
Lea & Blanchard, 1837. [9]-
203 p. GU; MdBP; MWA; ScNC;
WGr. 44049

---- The Tugg's at Ramsgate,
and other sketches illustrative
of everyday life and every-day
people, by Boz....to which is
added the pantomime of life by
the same author. Philadelphia,
Carey, Lea and Blanchard, 1837.
[9]-204 p. CSmH; MB; MH;
NcAS; NCH. 44050

Dickinson, Daniel S.
Speech on the Repeal of the
Usury Laws, delivered...on the
10th & 11th February, 1837;
by the Hon. D. S. Dickinson,...
New York, Printed by William H.
Colyer, 1837. 30 p. CSmH;
CtY; MWA. 44051

Dickinson, Peard.

Memoir of the Rev. Peard
Dickinson: in which the dis-
pensations of Providence and
Grace toward individuals are
exemplified in some remarkable
instances. Written by himself.
New York, T. Mason & G.
Lane, 1837. 192 p. DLC;
GAGTh; MBNMHi; MnSH.   44052

Dickinson college, Carlisle, Pa.
Belles lettres society.
    Catalogue of the members of
the Belles lettres society, of
Dickinson college, from its
foundation, February 22, 1786,
to February 22, 1837. Baltimore, Printed by J. W. Woods,
1837. 21 p. MdBP; NN; PPL;
PU.   44053

Dillingham, William Henry, 1790-
1854.
    Oration delivered before the
National Grays and their fellow
citizens, at the Court House
in West Chester, Pa., on the
22d of February, 1837. By
Wm. H. Dillingham, Esq....
Philadelphia, Brown and Sinquet,
Printers, 1837. 18 p. CSmH;
CtY; MWiW; PHi; PPM.   44054

A Directory for the City of
Buffalo containing the names
and residence of the heads of
families, householders, and oth-
er inhabitants, in said city,
on the 1st of May, 1837.
Buffalo, S. Crary, 1837.
CSmH; DLC; MiD; NBu; NRU.
                           44055
A Directory of the Cities of
Cleveland and Ohio, for the
Years 1837-38. See MacCabe,
Julius P. Bolivar.

The discussion: or, The character, education, prerogatives,
and moral influence of woman.
Boston, C. C. Little & J.

Brown, 1837. DLC; MH; NhD;
PU; RPAt.   44056

Disraeli, Benjamin. See Beacon-
field, Benjamin Disraeli, 1804-
1881.

Dissertation on the Subject of a
Congress of Nations, for the Adjustment of International Disputes
without Recourse to Arms. By
a Friend of Peace. New York,
Ezra Collier, 1837. 156 p. DAU;
IEN; ODaB; PHC; TxU.   44057

Disturnell, John, 1801-1877.
    The classified mercantile di-
rectory for the cities of New
York and Brooklyn. New York,
J. Disturnell, 1837. CtMW;
MdBP; MH; NBLIHI; OCIWHi.
                           44058
---- A guide between New York,
Philadelphia, Baltimore and Wash-
ington. Containing a description
of the principal places on the
route, and tables of distances...
New York, J. Disturnell, 1837.
16 p. DLC.   44059

---- Guide to the City of New
York; containing an Alphabetical
List of Streets etc. Accompanied
by a correct map. New York,
Published by J. Disturnell, 1837?
14, (2) p. MH; MHi; NBu.
                           44060
---- The Hudson river guide;
containing a description of all
the landings and principal places
on the Hudson river, as far as
navigable; stage canal, and railroad routes. Accompanied by a
correct map...New York, Disturnell, 1837? 16 p. ICN; MB;
MBAt; PPL.   44061

Dix, John Adams, 1798-1879.
    Decisions of the superintendent
of common schools of the state of
New York. Selected and arranged

by John A. Dix, superintendent.
Together with the laws relating
to common schools, and the
forms and regulations prescribed for their government.
Pub. by authority of the
Legislature. Albany, printed
by Croswell, Van Benthuysen
& Burt, 1837. (2), 479 p.
CtY; IaU; NjR; OO; TxU.
44062

Doane, Augustus Sidney, 1808-
1852.
Surgery illustrated. Com-
piled from the works of Cutler,
Hind, Velpeau, and Blasius,
with fifty-two plates. By A.
Sidney Doane...2d ed. New
York, Harper & brothers,
1837. 200 p. MBM; MoSW-M;
OC; PPCP; ViU. 44063

Doane, George Washington,
1799-1859.
The apostolical commission,
the missionary charter of the
church: the sermon at the
ordination of Mr. Joseph Wolff
... by the Rt. Rev. George
Washington Doane ... Burlington, [N.J.], J.L. Powell, 1837.
26 p. MB; MH-And; NjR;
PCA; RPB. 44064

---- An appeal to the parents
for female education on Christian
principles; with a prospectus
of St. Mary's Hall, Green Bank,
New Jersey. Burlington,
Powell, 1837. 22 p. CtHT;
MH; NjP; PHi; RPB. 44065

---- The Gospel in the Church:
the Sermon before the Annual
Convention of the Diocese of
Massachusetts, in ... Boston.
Burlington, reprinted, Mission-
ary Press, 1837. 20 p. NBuG;
NGH; NNG; PPM. 44066

---- Jesus Christ coming unto

his own: the Rector's Christmas
offering, for MDCCCXXXVII ...
to the parishioners of St. Mary's
church, Burlington ... Burlington, Missionary presss, [1837].
16 p. MHi; MiD; MCh; NGH;
PHi. 44067

Doctrines of baptism & the Lord's
supper in three dissertations by
several authors; and, Reasons
for the necessity of silent waiting
in order to the solemn worship
of God, by Mary Brook. New
York, Yearly meeting of Friends,
1837. 197 p. CtHT; NcGu; OO;
PHC; ViAl. 44068

The doctrines of baptisms, reduced from its ancient and modern corruptions: and restored
to its primitive soundness and
integrity. First printed 1652.
Philadelphia, J. Richards, printer, 1837. 36 p. MWA; NjR;
OClWHi; PSC-Hi. 44069

Doddridge, Philip, 1702-1751.
The family expositor; or, A
paraphrase and version of the
New Testament; with critical
notes, and a practical improvement
to each section. By Philip Doddridge, D.D. Amherst, J. S. and
C. Adams, and L. Boltwood,
1837. 998 p. DLC; LNDil;
NcWC; WBeaHi. 44070

---- The rise and progress of
religion in the soul; illustrated
in a course of serious and practical addresses, suited to persons
of every character and curcum-
stance: with a devout meditation, or prayer, subjoined to
each chapter. By Philip Doddridge, D.D. Baltimore, Armstrong & Berry, 1837. 280 p.
MdBD. 44071

Dods, John Bovee, 1795-1872.

A Sermon delivered in the
Episcopal Church, Gloucester,
Virginia, July 16, 1837. ...
Boston, 1837. 24 p. Vi. 44072

Dodsley, Robert, 1703-1764.
The economy of human life.
Preston, printed by J. Livesey,
1837. 43 p. NIC.   44073

Dolbear, Thomas Pearce.
Chirographic atlas of twenty
four plates to accompany "the
science of practical penmanship"
by Dolbear & Brothers, exhibiting the true position of the
hand and pen. ... second edition. New York, ... 1837.
24 p. KyU.   44074

---- ---- 3 ed. N.Y., Collins
& Keese & Co., 1837. MH.
                          44075
---- ---- 4th ed. New York,
Collins, Keese & co., 1837.
24 plates. MH; MoSU.   44076

---- The Science Of Practical
Penmanship, Deduced From The
Principles Of Physiology And
The Anatomy Of The Hand And
Arm; Containing .... To Which
Is Added A Complete System
Of Pen-making. The Whole
Accompanied By A Chirographic
Atlas Of Twenty-Four Engraved
Plates. By Dolbear & Brothers,
Principles Of The New York
And New Orleans Writing
Academies. Second Edition.
New York, Collins, Keese &
Co., 1837. (25)-118 p.
KyU.   44077

---- ---- Third edition. New
York, Collins, Keese & Co.,
1837. 100 p. CTHWatk; MH;
NBu; NNC; KyLxT.   44078

---- ---- Fourth edition. New
York, Collins, Keese & Co.,

1837. 118, 26 p. MH.   44079

---- ---- Fifth Edition. New
York, Collins, Keese, & Co.,
1837. 120 p. MsNF.   44080

Dolbear and Brothers.
Prospectus of the New-York
and New Orleans writing academ-
ies. n.p., 1837. 26 p. MH.
                          44081
Dole, Benjamin.
An examination of Mr. Ran-
toul's report for abolishing capi-
tal punishment in Massachusetts.
By Benjamin Dole. Boston, printed
for the author, by Fairfield &
Pitman's print, 1837. 72 p. CtY;
ICU; MBC; MWA; RPB.   44082

Domesticus, pseud.
The Doctrine of Incest stated;
with an examination of the question whether a man may marry
his deceased wife's sister, in a
letter to a clergyman of the
Presbyterian Church. By
Domesticus. Second edit. New
York, 1837. PPPrHi.   44083

Donnegan, James, fl. 1841.
A New Greek and English
Lexicon; Principally on the plan
of the Greek and German Lexi-
con of Schneider:----By James
Donnegan, M.D. First Ameri-
can, from the second London
Edition. Revised and enlarged,
by R. B. Patton. Boston, Pub-
lished by Hilliard, Gray and Co.;
New York, G. & C. Carvill &
Co., 1837. 1413 p. InID; MB;
MoSW; OFH; PPL.   44084

---- ---- Philadelphia, Carey,
Lea and Blanchard, 1837.
838 p. DCU; MB; MH; PPL;
PRosC.   44085

Doran, Joseph M.
An account of the proceedings

of the celebration, of St.
Patrick's day. See under title.

Dorchester, Mass.
    Statement of the expenditures
and receipts of the town of
Dorchester, from May 1, 1836
to May 1, 1837. [Boston?
1837]. MB.   44086

Douglass, James Walter.
    Work to do: discourse at
the funeral of Mrs. R. W. Mc-
Iver. Richmond, (Va.), 1837.
16 p. MNtCA; MWA.   44087

Dowling's Charleston Directory,
and Annual Register, for 1837
and 1838...And Embellished
with a Plan of the City of
Charleston. Charleston,...
1837. (2), 3, (1), 19-90, 27,
(1) p. MHi.   44088

Downer, Sarah A.
    The contrast or, Which is
the Christian? A tale. (With
a poem, the gospel jubilee, by
Mr. Z. Porter). Hudson,
[N.Y.], Printed by A. Stoddard, 1837. 24 p. DLC; MH.
                              44089
---- The triumph of truth: A
tale Written for the New York
Christian messenger and Philadelphia universalist. Hudson,
[N.Y.], Printed by A. Stoddard, 1837. 24 p. DLC; MH.
                              44090
Downing, Zek, pseud.
    Political firmament as seen
through Martin Van Buren's
newly invented patent magic
high pressure cabinet spec-
tacles. From a big picter,
painted for the nation..his-
torical painter to Uncle Jack
[pseud. of Seba Smith] and
Jineral Jackson. [New York],
Bisbee, [1837?] Brsde; MB.
                              44091

---- Trying the experiment to
manage the fiscal concerns of
our country, shewing how an old
man may lose his toil and vomit
a message.... [New York],
Bisbee, [1837?] Brsde; MB.
                              44092
Doyle, Edward.
    The improved pocket reckoner,
for timber, plank, boards, saw-
logs, wages, board, and interest. By Edward Doyle. Second
edition. Rochester, Printed and
sold by Hoyt & Porter, 1837.
60 p. NN; NRU.   44093

Drake, Charles D.
    The duties of American citi-
zens. An address delivered before the Franklin Society of St.
Louis, on the occasion of its
second anniversary. January
7th, 1837, ... St. Louis, Printed
by Charles Keemle, 1837. 28 p.
MoHi.   44094

Drake, James.
    Road book of the Grand Junc-
tion Railway. Birmingham, Drake
(1837). 184 p. MB.   44095

Drake, Samuel Gardner, 1798-
1875.
    Biography and history of the
indians of North America. From
its first discovery to the present
time. .... With an account of
the antiquities, manners and
customs, religion and laws.
.... 5th ed. With large additions,
Boston, Antiquarian Institute,
1837. 5 v. in 1. CtMW; CtY;
FOA; NcD; Nh-Hi.   44096

---- ---- 7th ed. with large
additions and corrections. Boston, Antiquarian institute, 1837.
588 p. CtMW; IaU; MiU; PHi;
Wat.   44097

Draper, John William, 1811-1882.

Experiments on solar light.
Phila., 1837. NN.   44098

The Dreamer's Sure Guide, or
the Interpretation of Dreams
faithfully revealed. Numerous
wood blocks, the frontispiece
hand colored. New York, Elton
& Harrison, 1837. 62 p. OCA.
                            44099
Drew, Samuel, 1765-1833.
    Agruments, scriptural and
philosophical, proving the divinity of Christ, and the necessity
of his atonement. By Samuel
Drew. ... New York, T. Mason
and G. Lane, 1837. 28 p.
CBPSR; IEG; NNUT; ODW;
PPL.   44100

---- An essay on the identity
and general resurrection of the
human body: in which the evidences in favour of these important subjects are considered,
in relation both to philosophy
and Scripture. By Samuel
Drew ... Philadelphia, J.
Whetham, 1837. [21]-364 p.
ArBaA; ICP; PWW; RPB;
ViRU.   44101

---- The life of the Rev. Thomas
Coke, LL.D., including in detail his various travels and
extraordinary missionary ex-
ertions ... New York, Mason
and Lane, 1837. [3]-381 p.
KyRe; MnSH; NjMD; OBerB;
ODW.   44102

---- An original essay on the
immateriality and immortality
of the human Soul; founded
solely on physical and rational principles. 5th American from the 6th London
edition...Philadelphia,
Whetham, 1837. 324 p. CtMW;
MBC; OClW; TxH; ViU.   44103

Dryden, John, 1631-1700.
    Mythological fables. Tr. by
John Dryden, and prepared ex-
pressly for the use of youth....
New York, W. E. Dean, 1837.
266 p. CLU; MLow; MPeaI;
NNebg; PPD.   44104

---- The works of John Dryden,
in verse and prose, with a life,
by John Mitford. New York,
Harper & Brothers, 1837-44. 2
v. CtMW; MH; NN; OClW; ViU.
                            44105
Du Buque Lead Mining Company.
    (Description of land and deed
of trust of lands owned by the
Company) (Dubuque ? 1837?)
11 p. IaHi.   44106

Dubois, John, 1764-1842.
    Minutes of a correspondence
between the Right Rev. John
Dubois, and the Trustees of St.
Joseph's Church, relative to the
pastorship thereof. New York,
J. M'Loughlin, printer, 1837.
36 p. DLC; MdBLC; MH.
                            44107
Duke, Edward, 1779-1852.
    Prolusiones historicae; or
Essays, illustrative of the Halle
of John Halle, citizen, and
merchant of Salisbury, in the
reign of Henry VI, and Edward
IV.... By Rev. Edward
Duke ... In two volumes, V. 1.
Salisbury, for the author W. B.
Brodie & Co.; [etc. etc.], 1837.
622 p. CtY; DLC; MiU; PU;
TxU.   44108

Dunbar, John Richard W.
    An introductory lecture, to
the course of surgery, delivered
to the students of Washington
medical college of Baltimore....
Baltimore, John D. Toy, pr.,
1837. 28 p. ICJ; MdHi; MdUM;
PPL.   44109

Duncan, Alexander, 1788-1853.
Remarks of Mr. Duncan, of Ohio, on the resolution offered by Mr. Haynes. Delivered in the House of Representatives, December 18, 1837. Washington, Printed at the Globe office, 1837. 8 p. CSmH; InHi; NNC; PPAmP; ViU. 44110

Dunglison, Robley, 1798-1869.
Address to the medical graduates of Jefferson medical college, March 11, 1837 ... Philadelphia, printed by Adam Waldie, 1837. 24 p. DLC; KyLxT; MnHi; NBuG; OClM. 44111

---- The medical student; or, Aids to the study of medicine. Including a glossary of the terms of the science, and of the mode of prescribing,-- bibliographical notices of medical works; the regulations of different medical colleges of the Union, &c, &c. By Robley Dunglison ... Philadelphia, Carey, Lea & Blanchard, 1837. 323 p. ArL; KyLxT; MoK; PPCP; RNR. 44112

Dunlap, William, 1766-1839.
A history of New York, for schools, By William Dunlap... New York, Collins, Keese, & co., 1837. 2 v. CSmH; Mi; NjR; OCoC; TJoT. 44113

---- Memoirs of a water drinker. By the author of "The history of the rise and progress of the arts of design in the United States:...2d. ed. New York, Saunders and Otley, 1837. 2 v. in 1. CtY; MB; MnU; PHi; OClWHi; WHi. 44114

Dunlap, William C.
The deposite banks, &c. In the House of representatives,

January 3, 1837. (On the resolution proposing an inquiry into the condition of the Executive departments. In the House of representatives, January 3, 1837. (Mr. Dunlap and Mr. Peyton) (Washington? 1837) 8 p. CtY; TxFwTCU. 44115

Dunwody, Samuel.
A sermon upon the subject of slavery. By Samuel Dunwody, minister of the gospel in the Methodist Episcopal Church. Published by request of the South Carolina conference. Columbia, S. Weir, State printers, 1837. 32 p. CtMW; ScSp. 44116

Duparcque, Frederic, 1788-1879.
A treatise on the functional and organic diseases of the uterus. From the French of F. Duparcque.... Translated, with notes, by Joseph Warrington.... Philadelphia, Desilver, Thomas & co., 1837. 455 p. ArU-M; ICJ; LNOP; PPCP; TxU-M. 44117

Dupin, M.
Trial of Jesus. Boston, Little & Brown, 1837. MWiW. 44118

Duponceau, Peter Stephen, 1760-1844.
The history of the silk bill, in a letter from Peter S. Du Ponceau to David B. Warden ... Philadelphia, Printed by A. Waldie, 1837. 12 p. CU; MH; PHi; ScC; WU. 44119

Durant, Charles Ferson, 1805-1873.
Exposition, or a new theory of animal magnetism, with a key to the mysteries: By C. F. Durant... New York, Wiley & Putnam, 1837. 225 p. MB; MH; MWA; PHC; ScU. 44120

Dwight, Maurice William.
The Duties and responsibilities of Christian young men. A discourse, preached in the Reformed Dutch Church of Brooklyn, May 21st, 1837. ... Brooklyn, Alden Spooner & Sons, Printers, Mechanics' Exchange, 1837. 23 p. CSmH; ICU; MB; NjR; NN.   44121

Dwight, Timothy, 1752-1817.
The Genuineness and authenticity of the New Testament. Hartford, P. B. Gleason & Co., 1837. 85 p. Ct; MBC; MWeA.   44122

E

Early Friends and Dr. Ash: or, an exhibition of their principles, in reply to his work on the Christian profession of the Society of Friends." Philadelphia, James Kay, Jun. & Brother, 1837. 40 p. ICN; MH; PHi; PSC-Hi.   44123

East, John.
My Saviour: or Devotional meditations in prose and verse on the names and titles of the Lord Jesus Christ. Boston, Dow, 1837. 273 p. IRA; MB; MdBD; MNS; MWA.   44124

East, Timothy.
The Evangelical rambler; from a series of tracts published in London. Revised by the editors. ... Vol. I. New-York, Published by T. Mason and G. Lane, ... J. Collord, printer, 1837. 13 v. in 4. NNMHi.   44125

East Bridgewater, Mass.
A Statement, of the expenditures of the Town...for 1836-7...April 22, 1837. East

Bridgewater Press - G. H. Brown. Broadside. NN.   44125a

Eastern Railroad Company.
An act to alter the line of the Eastern railroad and an act to aid the construction of the same. Salem, printed at the Gazette office, 1837. DLC.   44126

Eastman, C. C. V.
Funeral disc., R. W. Hart, and farewell address. New York, 1837. CtHT.   44127

---- A sermon delivered in Grace Church, Saybrook, Conn. on Easter morning, 1837, by the Rev. G. C. V. Eastman; ... New York, Printed by Martin, Lambert & Co., 1837. 20 p. Ct; CtHT; MiD-B; MW.   44128

Eastman, Seth, 1808-1875.
Treatise on Topographical Drawing. By S. Eastman, Lieut. U.S. Army. New York, Wiley and Putnam, 1837. 68 p. NcWsS; KHi; MBAt; NhD; PP; ViAl.   44129

Easton, Hosea.
A treatise on the intellectual character, and civil and political condition of the colored people of the U. States; and the prejudice exercised towards them: with a sermon on the duty of the church to them. By Rev. H. Easton ... Boston, Isaac Knapp, 1837. 54, [2] p. CtY; ICU; MWA; NcD; OrP; WHi.   44130

Eaton, John Henry, 1790-1856.
Leben und feldzüge des generals Andreas Jackson, geschichte seines Krieges gegan die Creeks, seines, feldzuges in Suden und seiner demuthigumy der seminolen. Von Johann Heinrich Eaton... Philadelphia, Kiderlen und Stoll-

meyer, [etc, etc], 1837. 419 p.
DLC; NcD; OClWHi.   44131

Eaton, Rebecca.
  A geography of Pennsylvania
for the use of schools and private families ... 2d ed. with
corrections and additions.
Philadelphia, E. C. Biddle,
1837. 282 p. CtY; ICBB;
MB; MWA; PU.   44132

Eberle, John, 1787-1838 .
  A treatise on the diseases
and physical education of children ... 3d ed. Philadelphia,
Grigg & Elliot, 1837. 555 p.
ICJ; MdUM; MeB; MinU; NjR.
                         44133
Eclectic Academy of Music,
Cincinnati.
  Resolutions of the Eclectic
academy of music for the formation of the Eclectic academy's
choir, with the by-laws, and
laws of the orchestra. And a
list of the members' names.
Cincinnati, Printed by James
and Gazlay, 1837. 12 p.
OCHP.   44134

Edes, Peter.
  Diary of Peter Edes, the
oldest printer in the United
States, written during his con-
finement in Boston, by the British, 107 days in the year 1775,
immediately after the Battle of
Bunker Hill. Written by himself. Bangor (Maine) Samuel
Smith, printer, 1837. 24 p.
CtSoP; MBC; MWA; N.   44135

Edgehill School. Princeton,
N.J. [Prospectus] n.p.
[1837]. 5 p. ScU.   44136

Edgeworth, Maria, 1764-1849.
  ... Tales and novels by
Maria Edgeworth ... New York,
Harper and brothers, 1836-1837.

20 v. in 10. fronts. MdBJ.
                         44137
Edmonds, John Worth, 1799-1874.
  Report of the J. W. Edmonds,
U.S. commissioner, upon the dis-
turbance at the Potawatamie payment Sept. 1836. New York, pr.
by Scatcherd & Adams, 1837.
47 p. DLC; InHi; MBC; NHi;
PPL.   44138

---- ---- New York, [Scatherd
& Adams] 1837. 95 p. DLC;
MWiW-C; NHi; NN.   44139

Edmundson, Henry A.
  An oration delivered before
the Phileleutherian society, of
Georgetown College, on the
twenty-second of February, 1837.
By Henry A. Edmundson...
To which are prefixed the re-
marks of Wm. P. Rodgers...
Washington City, 1837. 12 p.
MWH.   44140

Edson, Ambrose.
  Letters to the conscience.
(3rd ed) Hartford, Burgess,
1837. OMC.   44141

Edwards, Samuel L.
  An Address, delivered before
the Alpha Phi Delta and Englas-
sian societies of Geneva college,
August 2, 1837. Geneva, N.Y.,
J. T. Bradt, printer, 1837.
18 p. MH; NGH; NN.   44142

Edwards, Tryon.
  Reasons for thankfulness. A
discourse delivered in the First
Presbyterian church in Rochester,
N.Y. on the day of annual
Thanksgiving, Dec. 15, 1836...
Rochester, Published by the
trustees, Bumphrey, Cook &
Tinkham, printers, 1837. 39 p.
CSmH; GDecCT; MHi; NBuG;
OCHP.   44143

Edwards, Weldon Nathaniel.
Speech on sundry resolutions introduced by him, in the Senate of North Carolina, at the session of 1836-7. [Raleigh, Loring, 1837]. 8 p. NcU.   44144

Eells, Samuel.
Address delivered before the College of Teachers, on the Moral Dignity of the Office of the Professional Teacher. Cincinnati, 1837. 24 p. MB; NBuU; NGH; OCHP.   44145

Egan, Bartholomew.
Address upon the study of the ancient languages, before the Danville Lyceum, April 21, 1837. Danville, 1837. 13 p. MWA.   44146

Egan, Pierce, 1772-1849.
Life in London: or, The day and night scenes of Jerry Hawthorn, esq. and Corinthian Tom ... New Orleans, For sale by W. M'Kean, 1837. 2 v. CSmH; IBloW; MH; NN.   44147

Eight stories for Isabel.
Concord, 1837. 16 p. Nh-Hi.   44148

Elders' journal of the church of Latter Day Saints, v. 1, no. 1. Oct. 1837-Aug. 1838. Kirtland, T. B. Marsh, 1837-1838. 1 v. CtY; ICHi; MiU; OHi; NN.   44149

Electro-magnetism.
History of Davenport's invention of the application of electromagnetism to machinery...and information on electricity by Mrs. Somerville. New York, Carvill, 1837. 94 p. MB; MHi; PP.   44150

Eliot, John.
The life of John Eliot the Apostle of the Indians.... By John Eliot. New York, T. Mason and G. Lane, J. Collard, pr., 1837. 120 p. NjMD.   44151

Eliot, William Greenleaf, 1811-1887.
Discourse preached at the dedication of the First Congregational Church; St. Louis, Mo., October 29th, 1837, ... [St. Louis:] Printed by Chambers, Harris & Knapp, 1837. 11 p. MB; MHi; MiD-B; MBAt.   44152

---- Religious and moral wants of the West. By William G. Eliot. Printed for the American Unitarian association. Boston, James Munroe & co., 1837. 20 p. ICMe; IEG; MeBat; MoHi; OU.   44153

Elkinton, John A.
Monument cemetery of Phila., Late Pere la Chaise, containing several scientific essays on the subject of rural cemeteries, with a lithographic plan. Philadelphia, Rackliff, 1837. 38 p. MdBJ; MdBP; PHi; PPAmP; PU. 44154

Ellen: or Visit of the Rod.... From the London Ed. Revised by the Committee of Publication. Boston, Massachusetts Sabbath School Society, 1837. 71 p. DLC; MNotn.   44155

Elliot, William.
The Washington guide....By William Elliot. Washington City, Published by Franck Taylor, J. Crissy, printer, 1837. 310 p. CSt; GEU; MCon; PU; WHi.   44156

Elliott, Charles, 1792-1869.
Indian missionary reminiscences, principally of the Wyandot nation. In which is exhibited the efficacy of the gospel in elevating ignorant and savage men. By the Rev. Charles Elliott...New York, Pub.

by T. Mason & G. Lane, for
the Sunday-school union of the
Methodist Episcopal church,
1837. [3]-216 p. ICN; MdBE;
NN; OClWHi.   44157

Ellis, Powhatan, ca. 1794-1844.
   Documents relative to the
demand made for his passport,
by the Honorable Powhatan El-
lis, Charge d'Affaires from the
United States of America to the
Mexican Republic. Translated
from the Spanish. New Orleans,
Printed by J. C. Pendergast,
at the Office of the Louisiana
Advertiser, 1837. 44 p.
CSfCW; NN.   44158

Ellis, Sarah (Stickney), 1812-1872.
   Fishers drawing rooms scrap
book with poetical illustrations
by L. E. L. London, Paris &
America. Fisher & Sons & Co.,
1837. "51 p." NHuntL. 44159

---- Home: or, The iron rule.
A domestic story. By Sarah
Stickney.... New York, 1837.
2 v. in 1. CtMW; MBAt. 44160

---- Pretension by Sarah Stickney, author of "Poetry of Life"
would you judge of the lawful-
ness of pleasure," In two volumes. Philadelphia, E. L.
Carey & Hurt, 1837. 2 v. in
1. CtY; KPea; MBL; MsPog;
PPL.   44161

Ellis, William.
   Ellis' Arithmetical Tables,
and mathematical principles.
Philadelphia, 1837. 16 p. PHi.
                               44162
Ellms, Charles.
   Shipwrecks and disasters at
sea, by Charles Ellms. Printed
and published by S. N. Dickin-
son, Boston, 1837. 427 p.
MLen; PPAmP.   44163

Ellsworth, Henry L.
   Statement of the profits in
an investment in farming land
in Illinois. Washington, 1837.
PPL.   44164

Ellsworth Land and Lumber Company.
   Ellsworth Land and Lumber
Company. Ellsworth, Maine
[1837]. 10 [6] p. MHi. 44165

Elton's comic All-my-nack for
1837. New York, R. H. Elton,
1837. 40 p. MsJS; MWA; PHi;
RNHi.   44166

Emerson, Benjamin Dudley.
   Second-class reader. Designed for the use of the middle
class of schools in the United
States. Claremont, N.H., Claremont Manufacturing Co., 1837.
OAsht.   44167

Emerson, Frederick, 1788-1857.
   A key to the North American
arithmetic, part second, for the
use of teachers. By Frederick
Emerson, ... Boston, American
stationers' company; New York,
Collins, Keese & co. ... (and
others), 1837. 54 p. MB; MH;
TxUT.   44168

---- The North American arithmetic. Part second. Uniting
oral and written exercises in corresponding chapters. By Frederick Emerson. Boston, American stationers company, 1837.
191 p. CSt; MH.   44169

---- North American Arith. Pt.
II, III. Bost., American Sta-
tioners' Co., 1837. 2 vols.
MH.   44170

---- The North American arithmetic. Part third for advanced
scholars. By Frederick Emerson

.... Boston, American Stationers' Co., John B. Russell,
1837. 288 p. CSt; ICP; MB;
MH; OO; ViU.   44171

Emerson, Ralph Waldo, 1803-
1882.
An oration, delivered before
the Phi beta kappa society, at
Cambridge, August 31, 1837.
... Published by request. Boston, James Munroe and company,
1837. 26 p. CtMW; ICMe; MWA;
OFM; PU.   44172

Emmons, Francis Whitefield,
1802-1881.
The voice of one crying in
the wilderness; being an essay
to extend the reformation, by
Francis Whitefield Emmons.
Noblesville [Ind.], L. H. Emmons, printer, 1837. [19], 252
p. ICU; IaDmD; OMC; PPM;
RPB.   44173

Emory University.
Annual report of the president. V. 1 - Oxford, Ga.,
1837. LNH.   44174

The englantine; devoted to original and select literature. Boston, 1837. 2 v. MBAt.   44175

Engles, William Morrison, 1797-
1867.
A caution against prevailing
errors: being a conversation
between a presbyterian pastor
and his parishioners, by Wm.
M. Engles. Philadelphia, Presby.
Tract and Sunday-School Society,
1837. 35 p. ICP; InU; NCH;
NjR; PPPrHi.   44176

---- Qualifications and duties
of ruling elders in the Presbyterian church. By Rev. Wm.
M. Engles. Philadelphia, Presbyterian board of publication,

1837. CU; DLC; NcD; PPM;
PPPrHi.   44177

English, Clara.
The affecting history of the
Children in the Wood. ... Sev-
enth series -- No. 8. Concord,
Published by Atwood & Brown,
1837. 16 p. DLC; MeHi; MH.
                       44178
The English annual.... Phila-
delphia, Desilver, Thomas &
co., 1837. 375 p. KyHi; NjR;
OMtV.   44179

Epps, John.
Internal evidence of christianity deduced from phrenology.
By John Epps, M.D. With a
preface and notes, by Joseph A.
Warne, A.M. Boston, Published
by William Peirce, (Sic), 1837.
136 p. ICBB; InCW; MNtCA;
PBa; TKimJ.   44180

Equality; a history of Lithconia,
Philadelphia, Pub. by the Liberal
Union, 1837. PPL; PPL-R.
                       44181
EQUIANO, Olaudah, b. 1745.
EQUIANO, Olaudah, The Life
of, or Gustavus Vassa, the Afri-
can, Written by Himself. Boston,
I. Knapp, 1837. 2 v. in one.
DLC; MB; MWA; OO; PU.
                       44182
Erbaulicher Gebet-Buchlein fur
Kinder. Lancaster, Pa., John
Bar, 1837. PPG.   44183

Eschenburg, Johann Joachim,
1743-1820.
Classical antiquities, being
part of the manual of classical
literature. From the German of
J. J. Eschenburg ... With additions. By N. W. Fiske ... 2d
ed. Philadelphia, E. C. Biddle,
1837. 347 p. ArCH; IaWel;
MiD; NcAS; ViU.   44184

---- Manual of classical literature. From the German of J. J.
Eschenburg, with additions. 2d
ed. By N. W. Fiske. Philadelphia, Edward C. Biddle,
1837. 682 p. CtMW; GHi; LNB;
MiGr; WaPS.   44185

Espy, James Pollard, 1785-1860.
    Hints to observers on mete-
orology. [Philadelphia, 1837].
12 p. CSfA; InU; NhD; PHi.
                              44186
An essay in defence of slave
holding, as existing in the
Southern states of our nation.
By a citizen of New-York.
New-York, W. Osborn, 1837.
32 p. KHi; MH; PU.   44187

An Essay to do Good; or, Relief from the Pressure: Addressed to ... the Wealthy
Classes of New-York. New
York, 1837. 16 p. N.   44188

An essay upon the principles
of political economy: designed
as a manual for practical men.
By an American ... New York,
T. Foster, 1837. 60 p. DLC;
ICU; MB; MH; PU.   44189

Essex Mutual Fire Insurance
Company.
    A list of the members...with
a description of the location of
the property insured. Salem,
1837. 7 p. MH-BA.   44190

Etule, John.
    Treatises on the diseases
and physical education of children, by John Etule?....3d ed.
Philadelphia, Grigg, 1837.
555 p. NcD.   44191

Euler, Leonhard, 1707-1783.
    Letters of Euler on different
subjects in natural philosophy.
Addressed to a German princess.

With notes, and a life Euler, by
David Brewster ... Containing a
glossary of scientific terms with
additional notes, by John Griscom ... New York, Harper &
brothers, 1837. 2 v. FTa; MB;
MH; Mi; NRU.   44192

Euripides.
    The Alcestis of Euripides; with
notes, the use of colleges in the
United States, by T. D. Woolsey,
2d ed. Boston, J. Munroe & co.,
1837. ArL; CtY; KTW; MeBaT;
ViU.   44193

---- Euripides, Alcestis, with
notes by T. D. Woolsey, (gr)
Boston, James Munroe and
Co., 1837. 120 p. MiU; RNR.
                              44194
Eustaphieve, Alexis.
    Homoepathia revealed. A
brief exposition of the whole
system, adapted to general comprehension. With a notice of
Psora and Dr. Duringe's objections. By Alexis Eustaphieve.
New York, G. & C. Carvill &
co., 1837. 77 p. MBM; NNUT;
OO; PPHa; WU-M.   44195

Evangelical Association of North
America.
    Die Geistliche viole, oder:
eine kleine sammlung alter und
neuer geistreicher lieder, zum
gebrauch in den gemeinden der
evangelischen gemeinschaft, und
zur erbauung aller heilsuchenden
seelen ... Sechste auflage. New-
Berlin [Pa.] Gedruckt bey G.
Miller, 1837. 230 p. PPeSchw;
CSmH; PReaAT; ViHarEM.
                              44196
---- Evangelische lieder-sammlung,
genommen aus der lie dersamm-
lung und dem gemeinschaftlichen
gesangbuch, zum bequemeren
gebrauch in den evangelischen
gemeinen. Gettyburg, L. John-

son, 1837. DLC-P4; PSt. 44197

Evangelical Lutheran ministerium
of Pennsylvania and adjacent
states.
    Erbauliche lieder-sammlung
zum Gottesdienstlichen gebrauch
in den Vereinigten evangelisch-
lutherischen gemeinen in Pennsylvanien und den benachbarten
staaten. Gesammelt, eingerichtet,
und zum druck befordert durch
das hiesige Deutsch evangelisch-
lutherische ministerium. Philadelphia, Georg W. Mentz und
sohn, 1837. 512 p. PSt. 44198

Evangelical Lutheran Synod &
Ministerium of North Carolina
and adjacent states.
    Minutes of the Evang. Luth.
Synod and Ministerium, of
N. Carolina and adjacent parts
convened at St. John's Church,
Cabarrus Co., May A.D. 1837.
Salisbury, N.C., Printed at
the Western Carolina Office,
1837. 16 p. ICartC.   44199

Evangelical Lutheran Synod of
Maryland.
    Proceedings of the Evang.
Luth. Synod of Maryland, convened at Emmitsburg, Frederick
Co., on the 15th October, 1837.
Printed by J. W. Woods, Baltimore, 1837. 32 p. IcartC.
                          44200
Evangelical Lutheran Synod of
New York. Convention.
    Proceedings of a convention
of ministers and delegates from
Evangelical Luthern Churches
in the state of New-York. Convened in the chapel, in Fords-
bush, Montgomery County,
May 24, 1837. Albany, Printed
by Hoffman & White, [1837].
24 p. ScCoT.   44201

---- ---- Minutes of the seventh

session of the Hartwick Synod
of the Evangelical Lutheran
Church in the state of New York.
Convened at Cobleskill, Schoharie, Co., Sept. 1837. Albany, Printed by J. Munsell,
1837. 40 p. ScCoT.   44202

---- (Hartwick) Proceedings of
the 6th and 7th sessions of the
Hartwick synod, at West Sand
lake, Rensselace co. Sept. 1836,
and Cobleskill, Schohaine Co.,
Sept. 1837. Troy, N.Y., N. Tuttle, 1836; Albany, J. Munsell,
1837. 56 p.; 40 p. ScCoT; MnMAu.
                          44203
Evangelical Lutheran Synod of
Tennessee.
    Ecclesiastical annals. Report
of the transactions of the Evangelical Lutheran Tennessee Synod,
during their seventeenth session;
held in Coiner's church, Augusta
County, Virginia, from the 11th
to the 14th September, 1837.
Salem, Printed by Blum & son,
1837. 12 p. ScCoT.   44204

Evangelical Lutheran Synod of
West Pennsylvania.
    Proceedings of the thirteenth
session of the Evangelical Lutheran Synod of West-Pennsylvania.
Convened at Blairsville, Indiana
Co. Pa. from Sept. 28th, to
October 4th, A.D. 1837. Gettysburg, Printed by H. C. Nein-
stedt, 1837. 28 p. ScCoT.
                          44205
Evangelische Lieder-Sammlung,
genommen aus der Liedersammlung
und dem Gemeinchristlichen Gesangbuch, zum bequemeren Gebrauch in den evangelischen
Gemeinen. Gettysburg, stereotypirt von L. Johnson, 1837.
588 p. WRich; M.   44206

Evans, Christmas, 1766-1838.
    Sermons on various subjects,

by Rev. Christmas Evans, tr.
from the Welsh by J. Davis.
Beaver, Printed by W. Henry,
1837. 408 p. CSmH; ICU;
MoS; ODW; PPiW.   44207

Evans, James.
The speller and interpreter
in (Chippewa) Indian and English, for the use of The Mission Schools, and such as may
desire to obtain a knowledge of
the OJBWay Tongue by James
Evans. D. Fanshaw, printer,
New York, 1837. 195 p. MBAt;
MHi; CtHWatk; RNHi.   44208

Evans, James Harrington.
The spirit of holiness, by
James Harrington Evans, A.M.,
minister of John-street Chapel.
With an introductory preface,
by Octavius Winslow, Pastor of
the Second Baptist Church,
Brooklyn, N.Y. New-York,
John S. Taylor; Boston, Gould,
Kendall and Lincoln, [1837].
247 p. GDecCT; MeBat; OMC;
ICBB; PCA.   44209

Evans, Joshua.
A journal of the life, travels,
religious exercises and labours
in the work of the ministry, of
Joshua Evans, late of Newton
Township, Gloucester county,
New Jersey. Byberry, Pub.
by John & Isaac Comly, 1837.
212 p. KWiF; MBNEH; Nj;
NNNG; PHC.   44210

Everest, Charles William, 1814-
1877.
Vision of death: a poem....
Hartford, Canfield and Robins,
1837. 16 p. CSmH; IaU; MnU;
NNG; TxU.   44211

Everett, Alexander Hill, 1792-
1847.
An address to the Philermenian

Society of Brown University, on
the moral character of the literature of the last and present century.... Published by request.
Providence, Printed by Knowles,
Vose & Co., 1837. 54 p. MBAt;
MiD-B; OMC; PPM; ScU.   44212

---- The Literary Character of
the Scriptures. An address delivered before the Philorhetorian
and Perthologian Societies of the
Wesleyan University by Alexander Hill Everett. New York,
1837. IEG.   44213

---- The moral character of the
literature of the last and present
century; an address. Providence, 1837. 54 p. NIC.
                        44214
Everett, Edward, 1794-1865.
An address delivered before
the Adelphic Union Society of
William college, on commencement
day, August 16, 1837. By Edward Everett. Boston, printed
by Dutton and Wentworth, 1837.
36 p. KHi; MB; NCH; ScU; Vi.
                        44215
---- An address delivered before the Massachusetts charitable
mechanic association, 20 September,
1837, on occasion of their first
exhibition and fair. By Edward
Everett...Boston, Pub. by Dutton and Wentworth for the Association, 1837. 24 p. CtY; ICJ;
MBAt; NjR; OO; ScU.   44216

---- An address delivered before
the mercantile library association,
on its seventeenth anniversary,
in the masonic temple, Monday
evening, March 20, 1837, by
Isaac C. Pray, Jr. A poem, by
Lovet Stimson, Jr. Together
with the remarks of Hon. Stephen
Fairbanks, and his excellency
Edward Everett on that occasion.
Boston, Weeks, Jordan & Co.,
1837. 37 p. TxU.   44217

---- Address of his excellency
Edward Everett, to the two
branches of the legislature, on
the organization of the government, for the political year commencing January 4, 1837. Boston, Dutton & Wentworth, State
printers, 1837. 19 p. CtHWatk;
MBC; MLow; PPi; PPL.   44218

Everett, Horace.
    Speech of the Hon. Horace
Everett, delivered before the
Whig convention of Windsor
county, May 31, 1837. Pub-
lished at the request of the
Convention. Woodstock, Ver-
mont, Printed by J. B. &
S.L. Chase & co., 1837. 24 p.
LNH; MBAt; MiD-B; WHi. 44219

Everett, L. S.
    An exposure of the principles
of free inquirers. By L. S.
Everett. Boston, B. B. Mussey, 1837. 44 p. NPV.   44220

The Evergreen, revised by the
Committee of publication of the
American S.S. Union. Phila-
delphia, American S.S. Union,
1837. 159 p. CSmH; NNC;
RPB; TxU; WU.   44221

Everybody's Comic Almanack.
New York, Turner & Fisher,
1837. MWA.   44222

Evidence demonstrating the
falsehoods of William L. Stone
concerning the Hotel Dieu nunnery of Montreal. [New York,
1837]. 31 p. CaOTP; MH.
                        44223
Ewing, Thomas, 1789-1871.
    Speech of Mr. Ewing, of
Ohio, on the resolution of Mr.
Benton, to expunge a part of
the Senate journal of 1833-
1834. Delivered in the Senate
... (Washington? 1837) CtY.
                        44224

---- Speech of the Hon. Thomas
Ewing, delivered at a public
festival, given him by the Whigs
of Ross County, O., June 10,
1837. Chillicothe, S. W. Ely,
printer, 1837. 18 p. CSmH;
CU; ICN; MiD-B; MnHi; O.
                        44225
---- Speech...on the resolution
of Mr. Benton to expunge a part
of the senate journal if 1833-
1834, delivered in the senate of
the United States, Jan. 16,
1837. [Washington, 1837.] 7 p.
MH; WHi.   44226

Examination and review of a
pamphlet printed and secretly
circulated by M. E. Gorostiza,
late envoy extraordinary from
Mexico; previous to his departure from the United States
... Washington, Printed by Peter
Force, 1837. 188 p. LNH;
MdBJ; RPB; ScU; TxH.   44227

Exercises in spelling, consisting
of a collection of the most difficult words in use, designed
principally to be written by the
learner. By a teacher. Salem,
Ives & Jewett, 1837. MH;
MPeHi; NNC; TxU-T.   44228

The experience of several eminent Methodist preachers; with
an account of their call to and
success in the ministry, in a
series of letters written by themselves [John Pawson and others]
to the Rev. Johm Wesley. New
York, T. Mason and G. Lane,
for the Methodist Episcopal
church, 1837. 332 p. DLC;
IaU; MH; NcD; TxDaM.   44229

                F

Fairbanks, Stephen.
    An address delivered before

the mercantile library association, on its seventeenth anniversary, in the masonic temple, Monday evening, March 20, 1837, by Isaac C. Pray, Jr. A poem, by Lovet Stimson, Jr. Together with the remarks of Hon. Stephen Fairbanks, and his excellency Edward Everett on that occasion. Boston, Weeks, Jordan & Co., 1837. 37 p. TxU. 44230

Fairchild, Ashbel G.
Memoir of Mrs. Louisa A. Lawrie, of the Northern India Mission. By the Rev. Ashbel G. Fairchild, with an introduction by the Rev. Elisha P. Swift. Second edition, revised and enlarged. Philadelphia, William S. Martien, 1837. 221 p. ArBaA; CSansS; MBC; PPPrHi; ViRut. 44231

Fairfield, N.Y.
College of Physicians and Surgeons of the Western District. Circular and catalogue...1836-37. Albany---E. W. and C. Skinner, 1837. 14 p. NN. 44232
The fairy book; illustrated (with cuts on wood) by J. A. Adams. New York, Harper & brothers, 1837. 301 p. AmSSchU; MH. 44233

Falle, Philip, 1656-1742.
Accounts of Island of Jersey; with Notes and Illus. by Rev. E. Durell. Jersey, Giffard, 1837. 476 p. DLC; MHi; MiU; MNt; PP. 44234

Fallen, Charles.
Blessed are the pure in heart. A sermon preached at the First Congregational Church, in Chambers-Street, on Sunday, February 5th, 1837. By Rev. Charles Fallen. New-York,

Charles S. Francis, 1837. 17 p. MNe. 44235

A Familiar views, of the operation and tendency of usury laws, extracted from the correspondence of a gentleman of New York, with his son; being a reply in part, to the essay of a "Rhode Islander," published in the New York daily express, of Dec. 1836. New York, J. Gray, 1837. 63 p. ArAr; MB; PHi; PPPrHi; ScU. 44236
The Family Herbal and Recipes. Selected mostly from different authors. Containing a minute description of the various medicinal herbs and roots of our country. Also--their peculiar medicinal properties, systematically distinguished and explained. Being mostly arranged in alphabetical order. Hudson, Ohio, James B. Robbins, Printer, 1837. 36 p. 44237

Family temperance agent, containing illustrations of the established principles of the temperance reformation. Boston, 1837. MB; MBMu. 44238

Fanny Forrester. Philadelphia, Thomas Latimer, 1837. 36 p. DLC; MB; NN; ViU. 44239

Farley, Charles A.
... A sermon, delivered Sunday morning, Feb. 26, 1837, before "The First Unitarian Society in Alton," By Charles A. Farley .... Boston, Minot Pratt, Printer, 1837. 19 p. Nh. 44240

---- What is Unitarianism? A sermon, delivered in the Protestant Methodist Church of Alton, Illinois, Sunday Afternoon, Dec. 7th, 1836. By Charles A. Farley. Alton, Illinois, Printed by

Treadway, Parks & Bailey,
1837. 24 p. CSmH; IC; IHi;
MBC; MWA.   44241

Farmer, John, 1789-1838.
Historical sketch of Amherst,
in the county of Hillsborough,
in New Hampshire, from its
first settlement to the year
1837...2d. ed., enl. Concord,
printed by A. M. M'Farland,
1837. 52 p. CtY; ICN; MeHi;
MiD-B; OCHP.   44242

Farmer, John, 1798-1859.
Map of the survey of Michi-
gan by John Farmer. New
York, J. H. Colton, 1837. Mi.
                             44243
Farmer's Almanac. Peekskill,
N.Y., James Baker, 1837.
MWA.   44244

The Farmer's Almanac for the
year of Our Lord and Saviour
1837....By Thomas Spafford....
New York, Sold by N. & J.
White, [1837]. 36 p. PScrHi.
                             44245
Farmer's Almanac for 1838. By
David Young. Vol. 2., No. 20.
New York, N.Y., H. & S. Ray-
nor, [1837]. MWA; NjR. 44246

---- Calculations by John Ward.
Philadelphia, Pa., Published
by M'Carty & Davis, (1837.)
MWA.   44247

Farmer's Almanack. New York,
Doolittle & Vermilye, 1837.
MWA.   44248

The Farmer's almanack, calculated on a new and improved
plan, for the year of our Lord
1837 ... No. 45 ... Established
in 1793 by Robert B. Thomas
... Boston, Carter, Hendee
and co.; [etc.], [1837]. CU;
MBilHi; MNBedf; NjR; RHi.
                             44249

The Farmer's Almanack...For
the year of our Lord, 1838...
By Robert B. Thomas. Boston,
published and sold by Charles
J. Hendee, (1837). 44 p. CoU;
MHa; MS; MWA; PSew.   44250

---- By Thomas Spofford. New
York, N.Y., Robinson Pratt &
Co., [1837]. MWA.   44251

---- Calculations by Zadock
Thompson. Burlington, Vt.,
W. R. & F. C. Vilnas, [1837].
MWA.   44252

---- By Zadock Thompson. Wells
River, (Vt.), [1837]. MDeeP.
                             44253
Farmer's & Mechanic's Almanac
for 1838. Pittsburgh, Pa., R.
Patterson, [1837]. IaHa; MWA.
                             44254
The farmers and mechanics assistant, in writing. deeds,
mortgage, articles of agreement,
notes, receipts, &c. &c. Dayton
O., Published by B. F. Ells,
1837. 39 p. ODa.   44255

Farmer's & Planter's Almanac for
1838. Salem, N.C., [1837].
MWA.   44256

The Farmer's Cabinet and American Herd-book.
Devoted to agriculture, horti-
culture, and rural and domestic
affairs. V 1-12, July 1, 1836-
July 15, 1848. Philadelphia,
Moore & Waterhouse, 1837-48.
12 v. DLC; ICJ; MiU; PPWA;
TxU.   44257

Farmer's Calender. Phila., Pa.
U. Hunt, 1837. MWA.   44258

Farmer's Calendar for 1838. Calculations by Charles F. Egelmann. Baltimore, Md., Cushing
& Sons, [1837]. MWA.   44259

---- Philadelphia, Pa., Grigg
& Elliot, (1837). MWA.   44260

...The Farmer's, Mechanic's,
and Gentleman's Almanack, for
the year of our Lord 1838...
fitted for the latitude and
longitude of Boston, by Nathan
Wild...Keene, N.H., pub. by
John Prentiss, [1837.] [48] p.
MWA; NhHi; WHi.   44261

Farmers', of Dutchess county
almanac for the year 1838....
Poughkeepsie, Potter & Wilson,
n.pr., [1837]. (24) p. NjR.
                            44262
Farmers or Columbia Almanack.
By Tobias Ostrander. Hudson,
N.Y., S. Wescott, 1837. MWA.
                            44263
Farnam, Henry, 1803-1883.
    Mr. Farnham's letter to the
Committee of the City council
of New Haven, in relation to
supplying the City with water
from the Farmington canal.
Printed by order of the common council. New Haven, Palladium office print., 1837.
8 p. Ct; CtY; MB.   44264

Farrar, Eliza Ware (Rotch),
1791-1870.
    Young Lady's friend, by a
lady, improved stereotype.
Boston, American Stationers
Company, 1837. 432 p. DLC;
MBC; OU; PU; RJa.   44265

(Farwell, Wm. and others)
    Letters to the Evangelical
Congreg. Church in Cambridge-
port, under W. A. Stearns.
Boston, 1837. 15 p. MBAt;
MHi.   44266

The Fashionable American letter
writer, or The art of polite
correspondence, ... Brookfield, E. & L. Merriam, 1837.

179 p. CSmH; MH; MWA; TU.
                            44267
---- Newark, N.J., B. Olds,
1837. ViU.   44268

Fayetteville & Western Railroad.
Fayetteville, 1837.
    Charter; passed at the ses-
sion of the general assembly of
1833, and amended session of
1836-7. Fayetteville, Hale,
1837. 13 p. NcU.   44269

The Federalist.
    The Federalist on the new
constitution the year 1788, by
Mr. Hamilton, Mr. Madison, and
Mr. Jay; with an appendix ....
Hallowell, [Me], Glazier, Masters
and Smith, 1837. 500 p. AU;
DLC; MB; MoU; OClW.   44270

Felch, Walton.
    A comprehensive grammar,
presenting some new views of
the structure of language; ...
Boston, Otis, Broaders, and
co., 1837. (17)-122 p. CtY;
MH; MWHi; NNC; TxU-T.
                            44271
Female collegiate institute, Buckingham county, Va.
    Catalogue. Richmond, Va.
[1837?-186?]. Vi.   44272

Female Robinson Crusue: A
Tale of the American Wilderness
... New York, printed by Jared
W. Bell, 1837. 286 p. DLC;
MB; NN; NNS.   44273

Fenderich, Charles.
    Fenderich's Port Folio of liv-
ing American Statesmen. Drawn
and Lithographed by C. F.
Washington, 1837-[47]. 70 p.
DLC.   44274

Fenelon, Francois de Salinac de
Lamothe.
    Aventures de Telemaque.

Philadelphia, 1837. 408 p. MHi.
44275
---- Pious Reflections for Every
Day In The Month. To Which
is prefixed The Life of the
Author, by Francois de Salig-
nac de la Mothe. New York,
1837. IEG.   44276

Fergus, Henry.
Class book of Natural Theology; or the testimony of nature to the being, perfection,
and Government of God. (2nd
Am ed) Boston, Gould, Kendall
& Lincoln, 1837. ArBaA;
InCW; KTW; MB; NBLIHI.
44277

Fergus, T. H.
A Voice from the South. A
poem by T. H. Fergus. ...
Worcester, Published by C.
Harris, 1837. 17 p. MH;
MWborHi.   44278

Ferguson, W.
My early days. Hartford,
1837. MB.   44279

Fessenden, John, 1804-1881.
A sermon preached to the
First Congregational society in
Deerfield, Mass., ... Green-
field, Mass., printed by Phelps
and Ingersoll, 1837. 15 p.
ICN; MDeeP; Nh-Hi; NNG; WHi.
44280

Fessenden, Thomas Green,
1771-1837.
The Modern philosopher; or,
Terrible tractoration! In four
cantos. 4th American ed.
Boston, Samuel Colman, 1837.
264 p. MB; MWA; RPB; TxU;
MBM.   44281

---- Moubray on breeding,
rearing and fattening all kinds
of poultry, cows, swine, and
other domestic animals. Second
American from the sixth London

edition. ... By Thomas G. Fessenden. Boston, Joseph Beck
& Co.; New York, C. G. Thorburn, 1837. 278 p. CtHWatk;
KMK; MWA; Nh; WBeloC.
44282
---- ... The new American
gardener, containing practical
directions on the culture of fruits
and vegetables; including landscape and ornamental gardening,
grapevines, silk, strawberries,
&c. &c. ... 12th ed. Boston,
1837. 306, (1) p. CtY; ICJ;
NhPet; OCN; PFal.   44283

---- Terrible tractoration and
other poems. By Christopher
Caustic. Fourth American edition. To which is prefixed
Caustic's wooden booksellers
and miseries of authorship. Boston, 1837. NNC-Atf.   44284

A few reasons for the repeal of
the eighth section of the medical
laws of this state, which excludes irregular practitioners
from the benefits of law in the
collection of fees, or the passage
of a "public act," giving to
botanic practitioners rights and
privileges in common with their
fellow citizens. Hartford, J. B.
Eldredge, 1837. 7, (1) p.
CtSoP; CtY.   44285

Field, Barnum.
American school geography.
9th ed. Boston, C. J. Hendee,
etc., etc., 1837. MB; MH;
RPB.   44286

Fielding, Henry, 1707-1754.
The history of Amelia...With
illustrations by George Cruikshank...New York, Harper &
brothers, 1837. iv, (5)-524 p.
CtY.   44287

Fields, William.

The literary and miscellaneous scrap book: consisting of tales and anecdotes - biographical, historical, patriotic, moral, religious and sentimental pieces in prose and poetry. Compiled by William Fields, jr. Knoxville, Tenn., Printed and published by William Fields, jr., 1837. 600 p. LNH; TKL-Mc. 44288

Fifty reasons why the Roman catholic religion ought to be preferred to all others. To which are added, three valuable papers. Philadelphia, Eugene Cummiskey, [1837.] 107 p. 44289

Filisola, Vicente.
Evacuation of Texas. Translation of the Representation addressed to the Supreme Government by Gen. Vicente Filisola, in defence of his honor, and explanation of his operations as Commander-in-Chief of the army against Texas. Columbia, Printed by G. & T. H. Borden, public printers, 1837. 68 p. DLC; MBAt; TxWFM; TxU; Vi. 44290

Fillmore, Millard, 1800-1874.
Speech of Mr. Fillmore, of New York, on the bill to suspend the payment of the fourth instalment of the surplus revenue to the states, delivered in the House of Representatives, Sept. 25, 1837. Washington, Gales, 1837. 16 p. CtY; NBu; NNC; PPM. 44291

Finlay, George, 1799-1875.
The Hellenic kingdom and the Greek nation. By George Finlay...With introduction by S. G. Howe...Boston, Marsh Capen, & Lyon; New York, D. Appleton & Co., 1837. 110 p. CtHWatk; IU; MB; MHi; RPB. 44292

Finney, Charles Grandison, 1792-1875.
Lectures to professing Christians, delivered in the city of New York in the years 1836 and 1837. New York, N.Y., John S. Taylor, 1837. 348 p. GDecCT; IEG; MiU; MWA; TJoV. 44293

Fish, Benjamin Franklin.
Greek exercises; containing the substance of the Greek syntax illustrated by passages from the best Greek authors to be cut from the words given in their simplest form. Boston, Hilliard, Gray & co., 1837. 171 p. InCW; KTW; LShC; MH; MoSU. 44294

Fisher, Redwood.
Seventeen numbers, under the signature of Neckar, upon the causes of the present distress of the country. ... New York, Snowden, 1837. 68 p. C; InHi; MdBP; MdHi. 44295

Fisher, William R., d. 1842.
Introductory lecture delivered in the chemical hall of the University of Maryland, October 31, 1837. By William R. Fisher ... Philadelphia, Merrihew & Gunn, 1837. 24 p. CSt-L; MdHi; MH; NBuU-M; NNN. 44296

Fisk, Benjamin Franklin.
Greek exercises; containing the substance of the Greek syntax, illustrated by passages from the best Greek authors, to be written out from the words given in their simplest form. By Benjamin Franklin Fisk.... Stereotype edition. Boston, Hilliard, Gray, and Co., 1837. (1), vii, (1 blank), 171 p. KTW. 44297

Fisk, Charles B.
Report, on the examination of canal routes from the Potomac

River to the city of Baltimore,
especially in relation to the supply of water for their summit
levels by Charles B. Fisk and
George W. Hughes ... to the
governor of Maryland. Annapolis, W. M'Neir, printer, 1837.
DLC; MdHi; NNE; PPL.   44298

Fisk, Theophilus.
    The Banking Bubble Burst;
... Being a history of the
enormous legalized frauds practiced upon the communety by
the present American Banking
System: ... By Theophilus
Fisk. Charleston, S.C., 1837.
85 p. ICN; MBAt; MiU-C; PU;
ScU.   44299

---- Labor the only true source
of wealth... An oration on
banking, education, &c...
also an oration on the freedom
of the press.... Charleston,
S.C., Examiner, 1837. 48 p.
ICJ; MBAt; NcD; NN; TxU.
                        44300
Fisk, Wilbur.
    ... Address to the members
of the Methodist Episcopal
church on the subject of
temperance. New-York, Published for the tract society of
the Methodist Episcopal church
at the conference office, 1837.
16 p. MBC; NNUT.   44301

---- Calvinistic controversy;
embracing a sermon on predestination and election; and
several numbers on the same
subject ... By Rev. Wilbur
Fisk ... New York, L. T.
Mason and G. Lane, 1837.
273 p. CSt; ICU; LNB; NNUT;
ViU.   44302

Fitch, Charles, 1804-1843.
    Slaveholding weighed in the
balance of truth, and its com-

parative guilt illustrated. Ed.
2. Boston, 1837. 32 p. DHU;
MB; MTop; OO; WHi.   44303

Fitz, Daniel.
    A sermon delivered in Essex,
Feb. 11, 1837, at the funeral of
Mrs. Hannah C. Crowell. Bos-
ton, Dutton and Wentworth,
1837. 30 p. CtSoP; MBAt;
MBC; Nh-Hi; RPB.   44304

Fitzball, Edward, 1792-1873.
    False colours; or, The free
trader; a nautical drama, in two
acts... 24 p. New York, Samuel French, [1837]. OCl.
                        44305
Five lessons for young men....
See Southwick, Solomon.

Fletcher, J.
    A phrenological chart, pre-
senting a synopsis of the science of phrenology.... Boston,
1837. 26 p. MHi.   44306

[Fletcher, John].
    An appeal to matter of fact
and common sense; or, A rational demonstration of man's corrupt
and lost estate.... New York,
Published by T. Mason and G.
Lane, for the Methodist Episcopal church, at the conference-
office, J. Collord, printer, 1837.
214, 74 p. TNS.   44307

---- Checks to antinomianism, in
a series of letters to Rev. Mr.
Shirley and Mr. Hill. By Rev.
John Fletcher. In 2 vols. New
York, published by T. Mason
and G. Lane, 1837. 2 v. ArL;
ICU; KyLxT; OBerB; TJal.
                        44308
---- Christian perfection: being
an extract from the Rev. John
Fletcher's treatise on that sub-
ject. To which is added a let-
ter, by Thomas Rutherford. New

York, T. Mason and G. Lane,
1837. 141 p. IEG; MB; NcD;
OO; PPLT.   44309

Fletcher, John William.
  Works. New York, 1837.
2 v. NjNS.   44310

Fletcher, (Richard), 1788-1869.
  Mr. Fletcher's address to his
constituents, relative to the
speech delivered by him in
Faneuil Hall. (Boston, J. H.
Eastburn, 1837.) 15 p. MH;
Nh-Hi; WKenHi.   44311

---- Speech of (Richard Fletcher) to his constituents, delivered in Faneuil Hall. n. pl;
[J. H. Eastburn, pr.], 1837.
16 p. MBAt; MH; MH-BA;
Nh-Hi; NjR.   44312

Fleury, Claude, 1640-1723.
  Manners of the ancient Is-
ralites.... With a short account
of the ancient and modern Sa-
maritans, written originally in
French by Claude Fleury....
The whates merchant from the
principles writters on Jewish
antiquiteis. By Adam Clark
.... From the 2d London ed.
New York (N.Y.), T. Mason
and G. Lane, 1837. 386 p.
GDecCT; KHi; MnSS; OrSaW;
TNS.   44313

Flint, Abel.
  A system of geometry and
trigonometry. Stereo. ed., enl.
with additional tables, by George
Gillet. Hartford, Belknap and
Hamersley, 1837. 160, 112 p.
MA; MH; MiToC; MnU.   44314

Flint, James, 1779-1855.
  A selection of popular sacred
songs, arranged with accomps.
for the Spanish guitar. Boston, Bradlee, 1837. 11 p. MB.
                                    44315

Flint, John.
  First lessons in English grammar, upon a plan inductive and
intellectual; adapted to oral instruction. By John Flint. New-
York, Doolittle & Vermilye, 1837.
125 p. MH; NNC.   44316

Flint, Timothy, 1780-1840.
  Biographical memoir of Daniel
Boone, the first settler of Kentucky: interspersed with incidents in the early annals of the
country, by Timothy Flint. Cincinnati, Conelin, 1837. 252 p.
KyHi; MWA; O.   44317

---- History and geography of
Mississippi valley. Cincinnati,
pr. by Flint, 1837. PHatU.
                                    44318
Florida. (Ter.) Laws Statutes,
etc.
  Acts of the Legislative Council of the Territory of Florida,
passed at the fifteenth session,
commencing January 2d, and ending February the 12th, 1837.
Published by authority. Tallahassee, Fla., William Wilson,
printer, 1837. [2 p.] 3-67 p.
FU-L; InSC; MdBB; Nj; OCLaw.
                                    44319
---- ---- Laws of the U.S. relative to the Territory of Florida,
passed by congress prior to 1838.
By authority. Tallahassee, S. S.
Sibley, 1837. 80 p. FU-L; Ia;
MH; OCLaw.   44320

Flournoy, John Jacobus.
  Facts Important to Know re-
specting the Constitution of The
Federal Government; in a religious
view. Athens, 1837. 8 p. DLC.
                                    44321
[Flournoy, (John James).]
  Expulsion; the Best Earthly
Conservative of Peace in our
Country. Athens, 1837. 19 p.
MH.   44322

Flowers for the nursery...7th
series No. 5. Concord, Published by Atwood & Brown,
1837. 16 p. MH; NNC; RPB.
44323

Follen, Charles.
.... A sermon preached at
the First Congregational church,
by Rev. Charles Follen. New
York, Charles S. Francis,
(James Van Norden, printer),
1837. 17 p. MNe; NjR.   44324

Follen, Charles Theodore Chris-
tian.
A practical grammar of the
German language. By Charles
Follen ... 3d ed. Boston,
Hilliard, Gray and Company,
1837. 283 p. CoU; KWiU;
MdBS; MoSU; OSW.   44325

Folsom, Albert A.
A hint to the ladies. A lec-
ture delivered...August 27,
1837, in the Universalist
Church, in Hingham, Mass.
By Albert A. Folsom, pastor
... Hingham, Jedidiah Farmer,
printer, 1837. 19 p. MMeT-Hi;
PPL.   44326

Fonerden, William Henry.
The institutes of Thomsonism.
By Dr. William Henry Fonerden
... Philadelphia, Printed at the
office of the Botanic sentinel,
1837. [9]-123, [1] p. CSmH;
DNLM; MBCo; PPL; OClWHi.
44327

Ford, Edward E.
A Sermon, containing an
incidental reference to the
Wreck of the Steam Packet
"Home." Preached in St.
Paul's Church, Augusta, Ga.,
on Sunday, October 22d, 1837.
by the Rev. Edward E. Ford,
Rector of St. Paul's Church,
Augusta, Ga. [Published at
the request of the Vestry.]

1837. 15 p. CSmH; NBuDD;
GAuV.   44328

Forsch, Johann August.
Leben, Thaten und Meinungen
Des Ulrich Zwingli, Ersten
Urhebers Der Deutschen Evan-
gelisch Reformirten Kirche.
Von Johann August Forsch....
Chambersburg, Pa., Bei Victor
Scriba, 1837. 156 p. IU;
MoWgT; P; PPG; PPeSchw.
44329
---- Life and opinions of Ulrich
Zwingli, first founder of the
German Evangelical reformed
Church. By John A. Forsch.
Victor Scriba, Chambersburg,
1837. 156 p. NcMHi.   44330

Fort Wayne Company.
Articles of association, and
by-laws of the Fort Wayne Company. August 16, 1837. Detroit, Kingsbury & Dally, 1837.
13 p. MiU-C.   44331

Foster, Benjamin Franklin.
The Clerk's guide, or commercial correspondence; comprising
letters of business, &c. By B. F.
Foster. Boston, published by
Perkins & Marvin; Philadelphia,
Henry Perkins, 1837. 251 p.
MEab; MQ; MWA; NjR; OCY.
44332
---- A concise treatise on commercial book-keeping, elucidating
the principles and practice of
double entry ... 2d ed. Boston, Perkins, and Marvin; Philadelphia, H. Perkins, 1837. 200
p. MH; MiGr; MoS; NCaS; TxU.
44333
---- The counting house manuel;
or the merchant's, bankers, and
tradesman's assistant. Boston,
1837. NN.   44334

---- Education reform. A review
of Wyse on the necessity of a na-

tional system of education, comprising the substance of that work, so far as relates to common school and popular education. By B. F. Foster. New York, Wiley and Putnam, 1837. (5)-108 p. LNH; M; MH; MiU; NBuG. 44335

---- Fosters elementary copy books ... adapted to schools and private instruction. no. 2, 3, 6. Boston, Perkins and Marvin, 1837-1840. 3 nos. ICN; NN. 44336

---- Elementary copy-books... No. 5. Boston, Perkins, & Marvin, etc., etc., 1837. MH. 44337

---- A practical summary of the law and usage of bills of exchange and promissory notes ... Boston, Perkins & Marvin, 1837. 128 p. DAU; MH; MH-BA; NN. 44338

---- Prospectus of the Commercial academy, No. 183 Broadway, New York. Conducted by B. F. Foster...New York, 1837. 11 p. KyLx; MB; MiU-C; NN; WStfSF. 44339

Foster, John W. F.
Lessons on the Lord's prayer in a series of addresses delivered to the South Parish Sunday School. Portsmouth, N.H., 1837. 47 p. MH; Nh-Hi. 44340

The four pistareens; ... Prepared for the American Sunday school union, and revised by the committee of publication. American Sunday-school union. Philadelphia, (1837). 35 p. NNC. 44341

The four seasons; or, Spring, summer, autumn, and winter.

New Haven, S. Babcock, 1837. 16 p. CtY; DLC; MnU; N. 44342

Fowle, William Bentley, 1795-1865.
The Practical French accidence, being a comprehensive grammar of the French language.... Boston, Ide and Dutton, 1837. 286 p. DLC; MBAt; MBC; MH. 44343

---- The primary reader; ... By William Bentley Fowle, ... Boston, Printed for the author, 1837. 160 p. CtHWatk; DLC; MH; NNC. 44344

Fowler, Abijah.
The federal instructor; or, Youth's assistant. Containing the most concise and accurate rules for performing operations in arithmetick.... 3d ed. -- enl. and cor. by the authors. By Abijah & Josiah Fowler,... Published by J. F. & A. Fowler. Printed at the "Knoxville Register" office, by Ramsey & Craighead, 1837. 159, [1] p. DAU; NcAS; TKL-Mc. 44345

Fowler, Orson Squire, 1809-1887.
Phrenology proved, illustrated, and applied, accompanied by a chart embracing an analysis of the primary, mental powers in their various degrees of development....Assisted by Samuel Kirkham. New York, W. H. Colyer, 1837. 7-420 p. A-T; FSa; OO; RPB; ScU. 44346

---- ---- 2nd ed. New York, W. H. Colyer, 1837. 420 p. CtB; GMM; PPAN; WHi. 44347

Fox, Thomas Bayley, 1808-1876.
The ministry of Jesus Christ; compiled and arranged from The four gospels for families and Sunday schools, with poetical illustra-

tions and notes. Boston, Weeks, Jordan and Co., etc., etc., 1837. 2 v. CBPac; IEG; MB; MH; MNBedf. 44348

Fox, William Johnson.
The history of Christ, a testimony that The Father is the only God and sole object of adoration. By W. J. Fox. Printed for the American Unitarian Association. Boston, James Munroe & co., 1837. 16 p. FDeS; ICMe; MB-HP; MeBat; MMeT-Hi. 44349

Foxe, John, 1516-1587.
... Book of martyrs; being a complete history of the lives, sufferings, and deaths of the Christian martyrs, from the commencement of christianity to the latest periods of pagan and Popish persecution. Boston, Rev. and abridged by Henry Wightman. ... Gaylord, 1837. 516 p. CtY; MBAt; MoS; NjP; PPL. 44350

---- The English martyrology .... By John Foxe.... abridged from Foxe by Charlotte Elizabeth (pseud.).... Philadelphia, Presby, bd. of pub., (1837)-1843. 2 v. CSansS; LNB; MiU; NjP; PCC. 44351

France. Commission chargee de l'examen du magnetisme animal.
Animal magnetism. Report of Dr. Franklin and other commissioners, charged by the King of France with the examination of the animal magnetism as practised at Paris. Translated from the French. ... Philadelphia, H. Perkins, 1837. 58 p. CtY; MBC; MiD-B; PP; ScU. 44352

---- ---- ---- 2d ed. Philadelphia, H. Perkins, 1837. 2 p. ℓ., 58 p. CtY; MHi; MiU-C; OC; WHi. 44353

Franckean Evangelic Lutheran Synod.
Journal of the Annual Session of the Franckean Evangelic Lutheran Synod, 1837. Albany, 1837-1908. ICarbC; MH-AH; PPLT. 44354

Franklin, Benjamin, 1706-1790.
Memoirs of Benjamin Franklin written by himself, and continued by his grandson and others....augmented by much matter not contained in any former edition, with a postliminious preface. Philadelphia, McCarty & Davis, 1837. 2 v. CtHT; Ia; NUt; PWW; ScDuE; WyU. 44355

---- The Way to Wealth, or How To Get Rich, by Dr. Franklin. Dayton, Published, Printed and Sold by B. F. Ells. George Conclin, Cinc. J. McMillan, Madison, Ia., 1837. 48 p. ODa. 44356

---- ---- New York, Daniel & Geo. F. Cooledge, 1837. 192 p. CtY; MB; MFran; MSa; PU. 44357

---- ---- Northampton, John Metcalf. ... 1837. 6-27 p. ICBB; MB. 44358

---- The works of Dr. B. Franklin. Consisting of essays, humorous, moral & literary; with his life, written by himself. Exeter, N.H., & J. & B. Williams, 1837. 224 p. CtY; DLC; MdBS; OSW; PPAmP. 44359

Franklin, (Mass.) High School.
Franklin High School. Catalogue of the Instructors and Pupils for the year ending Nov. 21, 1837. Dedham, 1837. 11 p. MH; MHi. 44360

Franklin Almanac for 1838.
Calculations by John Armstrong.
Pittsburgh, Pa., Johnston &
Stockton, [1837]. MWA. 44361

---- Philadelphia, Pa., Mc-
Carty & Davis, [1837]. MWA.
44362
Franklin and Marshall College?
Landcaster, Pa.
Charter of Franklin College.
Published by revolution of the
Board. Passed, 19th October,
A.D. 1837. Lancaster, Bryson
& Forney, Printer, 1837. 8 p.
MiU; PAtM; PHi; PLT; PPPrHi.
44363
The Franklin Farmer, Devoted
To Improvements In The Sci-
ence Of Agriculture, The Prac-
tice Of Husbandry, and The
Mind Morals, and Interests Of
The Cultivators Of The Soil.
"Nothing is beneath the atten-
tion of a great man." Tho. B.
Stevenson, Editor. Frankfort,
Ky., Printed and published by
F. D. Pettit, 1837-8. 416 p.
KyMay. 44364

Franklin Institute. Philadelphia.
For the establishment of a
school of arts. Memorial of the
Franklin Institute of the State
of Pennsylvania, for the promotion of the mechanic arts, to
the legislature of Pennsylvania,
Philadelphia, J. Crissy....
1837. 12 p. PPAmP; PPM.
44365
-- - Report of experiments by
the sub-committee, from the
Committee of the Franklin institute of Pennsylvania, on the
explosions of steam boilers, to
whom was referred the examination of the strength of materials employed in their construction. Philadelphia, 1837.
3-254 p. Ct; DLC; MB; OU;
PPL-R. 44366

---- Report of the Committee of
the Franklin institute of the state
of Pennsylvania, for the promotion of the mechanics arts, on
the explosions of steam boilers,
of experiments made at the request of the Treasury department of the United States. ...
Philadelphia, Merrihew, 1837.
254 p. DLC; MH; NNC; RPB.
44367
The Franklin Magazine Almanac
for 1838. Calculations by John
Armstrong. Pittsburgh, Pa.,
Johnston & Stockton, (1837).
MWA. 44368

Franklin Rail Road Company.
Report of the Chief Engineer,
1836, and Report of president
and managers, January 28, 1837.
Chambersburg, 1837. 8 p.
PHi. 44369

Fraser, Eliza Anne.
Narrative of the Capture,
Sufferings and Miraculous Escape
of Mrs. Eliza Fraser, Wrecked on
an Unknown Island, inhabited
by Savages, ... Mrs. Fraser
was providentially rescued from
her perilous situation ... New
York, Charles S. Webb, 1837.
24 p. DLC; ICN; NN. 44370

Fraser, James Baillie, 1783-1856.
Historical and descriptive account of Persia, from the earliest
ages to the present time. By
James B. Fraser. New York,
Harper, 1837. 345 p. NcU.
44371
Freeman, Frederick, 1799-1883.
A plea for Africa, being
familiar conversations on the subject of slavery and colonization,
[originally published under the
title "Yaradee."] Rev. and enl.
By F. Freeman ... 2d ed. Philadelphia, J. Whetham, 1837. 359
p. CtY; MWA; NcD; OHi; ViU.
44372

---- Yaradee; a plea for Africa, in familiar conversations on the subject of slavery and colonization. 2d. edition. Philadelphia, 1837. RP.   44373

Freeman, George Washington.
The rights and duties of slave-holders. Two discourses, delivered on Sunday, November 27, 1836. In Christ church, Raleigh, North-Carolina. By George W. Freeman, rector of the church. Re-published by permission of the author, for charleston. A.E. Miller, printer to the society, 1837. 40 p. NNG; RPB; ScHi; Tx.   44374

The Freemans', farmers' & gentlemen's almanac for the year 1838....By William B. Leavitt, philom....Claremont, N.H., n. pub. Printed at the Power press office, by N. W. Goddard, (1837). (44) p. MHi; MWA; NjR.   44375

Freemasons. Alabama. Grand Lodge.
Proceedings of a convention of delegates met to form a grand lodge of the state of Alabama, and of the said lodge after its formation. Tuscaloosa, printed by Marmaduke J. Slade, 1837. 28 p. MBFM.
                               44376
---- Connecticut. Grand Lodge.
Proceedings of Grand chapter of the Masonic lodge, in Connecticut; meeting held in 1837. New Haven, (Conn.), Herald Office, 1837. (-1841). IaCrM.   44377

---- Georgia. Grand Lodge.
Proceedings of the Grand lodge of the state of Georgia, at an annual communication held in Milledgeville, on Tues-day, November 7th, A.L. 5837, and continued to Friday, November 10th inclusive. Milledgeville, Printed at the Federal Union office, by Park & Rogers, 1837. 12, 8 p. NNFM.   44378

---- Illinois. Palmyra Lodge.
The By-laws of Palmyra Lodge, No. 18. of Free and Accepted Ancient Masons. Palmyra, Mo., B. F. Hayden, Printer, 1837. 14 p. MoSHi.   44379

---- Kentucky.
Proceedings of the Grand lodge of Kentucky, at a grand annual communication, in the city of Louisville, commencing on the twenty-eighth August, 5837. Frankfort, Ky., Printed by Albert G. Hodges, 1837. 20 p. IaCrM; NNFM.   44380

---- Maine. Grand Lodge.
Grand lodge of the most ancient and honorable fraternity of Free and accepted masons of the state of Maine. ... Augusta, William Hastings, 1837. 12 p. NNFM.   44381

---- Maryland. Grand royal arch chapter.
Proceedings of the G.R.A. chapter of the state of Maryland, at the communications held at the Masonic hall, in the city of Baltimore, for the years 1833 and 1834. Baltimore, printed by Jos. Robinson, 1837. 17 p. MdBP.
                               44382
---- ---- ---- Proceedings of the G.R.A. chapter of the state of Maryland, at the communications held at the Masonic hall, in the city of Baltimore, for the years 1835 and 1836. Baltimore, printed by Jos. Robinson, 1837. 36 p. MdBP.   44383

---- ---- ---- Proceedings of
the G.R.A. chapter of the
state of Maryland, at the communications held at the Masonic hall. in the city of Baltimore, for the year 1837. Baltimore, printed by Jos. Robinson,
1837. 16 p. MdBP.   44384

---- Massachusetts. Grand
Lodge.
Grand lodge ... of free and
accepted masons of Massachu-
setts, ... Boston, press of the
Bunker-Hill Aurora and Boston
Mirror, 1837. 16 p. NNFM.
                                 44385
---- Mississippi.
Extracts from the proceed-
ings of the Grand lodge of the
state of Mississippi, at a grand
annual communication, begun
and held at the Masons hall,
city of Natchez, Monday, 2nd
January, A.D. 1837. Natchez,
Printed at the Free trader
office, 1837. 31 p. MBFM;
MsFM; NNFM.   44386

---- Missouri. Grand Lodge.
Proceedings of the Grand
Lodge of the state of Missouri,
at their grand annual communi-
cation, begun and held in the
city of St. Louis, on the 2nd
October, A.L. 5837, A.D. 1837.
This pamphlet contains but one
sheet. St. Louis, Printed by
Chambers, Harris & Knapp,
1837. 14 p. DSC; IaCrM;
NNFM.   44387

---- New York. Grand Lodge.
The constitutions of the
most ancient and honorable
fraternity of free and accepted
Masons, containing all the particular ordinances and regulations of St. John's Grand lodge,
of the state of New York. Collected, digested and published

under the authority of St. John's
Grand lodge. New York, Charles
N. Baldwin & son, printers,
[1837]. 83 p. NNFM; PPFM.
                                 44388
---- ---- ---- Eulogy on the
M.W. Major General Jacob Mor-
ton, and the M.W. Elisha W.
King, Esquire, ... pronounced
in St. Matthew's Church, New-
York, June 7th, by James Her-
ring, ... New York, Printed by
George F. Nesbitt, 1837. 26 p.
MdHi; NNFM.   44389

---- ---- ---- Extracts from the
proceedings of the Grand lodge
of the....masons....at the quarterly meeting on the 7th of December, A.L. 5836, and at the
quarterly meeting on the 1st of
March, A.L. 5837. New York,
J. M. Marsh, printer, 1837.
12 p. WHi.   44390

---- ---- ---- Proceedings of
the Grand Lodge, of Masonic
lodge, in New York State; meeting held in 1837. New York,
J. M. Marsh, 1837. 15 p.
IaCrM.   44391

---- ---- ---- Proceedings of
the right worshipful Grand lodge
of the state of New York, and
of the right worshipful Grand
Stewards' lodge, from the 12th
of July, A.L. 5837, to the 6th
of September, A.L. 5837, inclusive.... New York, J. M.
Marsh, printer, 1837. 44, 7 p.
NNFM.   44392

---- ---- ---- Statement of
facts....of free and accepted
Masons....New York, n. pub.
printed by Charles N. Baldwin,
[1837]. 36 p. NjR.   44393

---- North Carolina. Grand Lodge.
Proceedings of the Grand lodge

of Ancient York Masons of North
Carolina. A.L. 5836. Raleigh,
Printed by Thomas J. Lemay,
1837. 32 p. NNFM; OCM.
                                    44394
---- Ohio.
Proceedings of the Grand
lodge of the most Ancient and
honorable fraternity of free and
accepted Masons in the state of
Ohio, at the annual grand com-
munication, A.L. 5837. ...
Lancaster, Printed by brother
Geo. Sandesron, (sic) 1837.
21 p. IaCrM; MBFM; NNFM;
OCM.   44395

---- ---- Lafayette Lodge.
The by-laws of Lafayette
lodge, no. 81; adopted March
8, 1837. Cincinnati, [Ohio],
Pugh and Dodd, pr., 1837.
16 p. IaCrM.   44396

---- South Carolina. Grand
Lodge.
Abstract of the proceedings
of the Grand lodge of ancient
Free-Masons of South-Carolina,
during the years 1835 and
1836. Charleston, Printed by
J. S. Burges, 1837. 69 p.
NNFM.   44397

---- Tennessee. Grand royal
arch chapter.
Proceedings of the Grand
royal arch chapter of the state
of Tennessee. October, 1837.
Nashville, S. Nye & co., printers, 1837. 10 p. T.   44398

The free-will Baptist register,
for the year of our Lord 1837.
...Dover, published by the
trustees of the free-will
Baptist connection, 1837.
72 p. MeLewB; MHa; MWA;
NhHi.   44399

French, Jonathan, 1778-1856.

A Sermon delivered in Dover,
N.H. at the reinterment of the
Rev. Joseph W. Clary, Dec. 19,
1835. By Jonathan French....
Dover, N.H., George Wadleigh
....1837. 19 p. IEG; MiD-B;
MnHi; MWA; NjPT.   44400

Frey, Joseph Samuel Christian
Frederick, 1771-1850.
Joseph and Benjamin; A
series of letters on the controversy between Jews and Christians comprising the most important doctrines of the Christian religion. By Joseph Samuel
C. F. Frey.........in two volumes. 5th ed. New York, Published by Peter Hill, 1837. 407
p. ScCoB.   44401

Friedheim, John.
Shamrock quick-step. Bos-
ton, 1837. MB.   44402

Friends, Society of. London.
The Epistle from the Yearly
Meeting of London, 1836. New-
York, Mahlon Day, Printer, 1837.
NNFL.   44403

---- New England Yearly meeting.
Address of the yearly meeting
of Friends for New - England,
held on Rhode - Island, in the
sixth month, 1837... New Bedford, J. C. Parmenter, printer,
1837. 7 p. MH; PHi; RPB;
WHi.   44404

---- New York Yearly meeting.
Address to the citizens of the
United States of America on the
subject of slavery, from the Year-
ly meeting of the religious soci-
ety of Friends, (called Quakers)
held in New-York. New-York,
New-York Yearly meeting of
Friends, 1837. 11 p. CBPac;
MB; MdHi; MWA; OO.   44405

---- ---- (Hicksite).
Memorials concerning deceased Friends...1836. New York, I. T. Hopper, 1837. 42 p. PHC.
44406

---- Philadelphia Yearly Meeting.
An address from the monthly meeting of Friends of Philadelphia to its members.... Philadelphia, n. pub., P. Price & son, printers, 1837. 9 p. NjR.
44407

---- ---- Address of the representatives of the Religious Society of Friends, commonly called Quakers, in Pennsylvania, New Jersey, Delaware, etc. to the citizens of the United States. Philadelphia, Joseph & William Kite, Printers, 1837. 15 p. CtY; MdBJ; MWA; NNUT; WHi.
44408

---- ---- Brief remarks on some of the charges recently made against the early writers of the Society of Friends, by George Richardson. Newcastle, Printed by T. and J. Hodgson. Union Street. Philadelphia, Reprinted, 1837. 36 p. PHC.
44409

---- ---- (Hicksite).
Hicksite Friends' Library, Cherry Street below Fifth St. Phila. Catalogue of books... Philadelphia, 1837. 32 p. PHi.
44410

---- ---- ---- Rules of discipline... Philadelphia, 1837. 12 v. PHC.
44411

---- Scipio quarterly meeting.
Address...on the subject of slavery, to its members. Skaneateles, N.Y., 1837. 12 p. PHC.
44412

Friend's Almanac for 1838. By Joseph Foulke. Philadelphia,

Pa., Elijah Weaver, [1837]. MWA.
44413

Friend's library; comprising journals, doctrinal treatises, and other writings of members of the religious society of Friends; ed. by William Evans and Thomas Evans. Philadelphia, Rakestraw, 1837-50. 14 v. CtHT; ICU; MWA; NcD; PSC-Hi.
44414

Friends Pocket Almanac. Philadelphia, J. E. Chapman, By Joseph Foulke, [1837]. MWA.
44415

Frost, B.
Order of exercises at... ordination.... Concord, (1837). MB.
44416

Frost, John, 1800-1859.
The American speaker; containing numerous rules, observations, and exercises, on pronunciations, pauses, inflections, accent...By John Frost... Philadelphia, E. C. Biddle, 1837. 448 p. KPiT; PEaL; RPB.
44417

---- A history of the U.S.; for the use of schools and academies. By John Frost. New edition with additions and corrections. Philadelphia, E. C. Biddle, 1837. 324 p. A-Ar; KyHi; MH; OCHP; TxU-T.
44418

Frothingham, Nathaniel Langdon, 1793-1870.
The duties of hard times. A sermon, preached to the First church, on Sunday morning, April 23, 1837. Pub. by request. Boston, Munroe & Francis, 1837. 20 p. CBPac; ICMe; MiD-B; MWA; RPB.
44419

Fry, Caroline. See Wilson, Caroline (Fry), 1787-1846.

Full And Correct Account Of
The Supposed Abduction Of
Miss Eliza Allen. Particulars
Of The Trials Of The Sus-
pected Individuals Before Jus-
tice Doty, The Mayor And The
Associate Judges. Cincinnati,
1837. OMC.   44420

Fuller, Andrew, 1754-1815.
   The gospel worthy of all ac-
ceptation; or, The duty of
sinners to believe in Jesus
Christ, by Rev. Andrew Fuller;
abridged by the London religious
tract society. American doctrinal tract society, Boston,
1837. 106 p. CBPSR; ICartC;
MBC; MB-FA; OU.   44421

Fuller, J. G.
   The little casket. N.Y.,
1837. MB.   44422

---- Little Flora. New York,
1837. MB.   44423

Fuller, Jacob.
   Delirium tremens, its causes
and treatment. By Jacob Fuller,
M.D. ... Boston, D. Clapp, Jr.,
1837. MBM; NNN.   44424

Fuller, S.
   Memoir of H. Princhard.
Andover, 1837. MB.   44425

Furman, Garrit, 1782-1848.
   The Naspeth poems. New
York, Conner & Cooke, 1837.
7-128 p. ICU; MB; NBLiHi;
NN; NNQ.   44426

                G

Gale, Leonard Dunnell, 1800-
1883.
   Elements of chemistry. ...
by L. D. Gale, ... New York,
Wiley, Long and Co., 1837.

(9)-294 p. CtY; MNBedF; MWHi;
RPB.   44427

---- Elements of chemistry...
designed for the use of schools
and academies. Second edition.
New-York, Wiley, Long and co.,
1837. 294 p. CtY.   44428

---- Elements of natural philoso-
phy:....Designed for the use of
schools and academies. By
Leonard D. Gale, M.D....New
York, Published by Collins,
Keese, & Co., 1837. 268 p.
CtY; DLC; NjR; OClW; RPB.
                              44429
Gale's North Carolina Almanac
for the year of our Lord 1838.
....Carefully calculated for the
meridian of Raleigh by William
Collom of Philadelphia. Raleigh,
Printed by J. Gales & Son,
[1837]. 36 p. NcD.   44430

The Gallatin Uion--Extra Honors
to the volunteers. Thursday,
the 16th inst. the citizens of
old Sumner turned out amidst
wind, snow and rain, to do hon-
or to the brave Tennessee Volunteers, "whose noble conduct in
the wilds of Florida, has added
new lustre to the bright renown
of their country and their state."
... [ca. Tenn., 1837]. Broadside. NcD.   44431

Gallaudet, Thomas Hopkins, 1787-
1851.
   The Class Book of Natural
Theology, for common schools,
and academies, ... by Rev.
T. H. Gallaudet, late principal
of the American Asylum for the
Deaf and Dumb. Hartford,
Belknap & Hamersley, 1837. 196
p. CtY; IC; MH; OClWHi; PU.
                              44432
---- ---- Ed. 2. Hartford,
Belknap, 1837. 196 p. CtY;
ICN; MH; OClWHi; PU. 44433

---- The history of Josiah, the
young king of Judah. By
Thomas Gallaudet. New York,
American tract society (1837).
108 p. GEU-T; IEG; MA;
MH; NbOM; TJaL.   44434

Galloway, Samuel.
Address on Missionary Character delivered before the Society of inquiry on Missions of
Miami University, December
19th. 1836. By Samuel Galloway. Oxford, Ohio, R. H.
Bishop, Jun., 1837. 32 p.
MWA.   44435

Gallitzin, Demetrius Augustine.
A defence of Catholic principles in a letter to a Protestant
minister, to which is added,
an appeal to the Protestant
public,...3rd ed. corrected
and enlarged with the permission of the author. Baltimore,
Lucas, [1837]. 164 p. MdBS;
MMCHS.   44436

---- ---- Fourth edition...
Baltimore, Lucas bros., [1837?]
7-198 p. DGU; LU; MdHi;
MoSU; NNUT.   44437

Galveston Island in Texas.
City of Galveston, on Galveston island, in Texas: with a
history of the title of the
proprietor, and a brief account
of all its advantages. Accompanied with a plan of the
city and harbor, and a map of
Texas, showing the commercial channels with the interior
through which the city is to de-
rive its extensive trade. New
Orleans, Hotchkiss & co.,
1837. 8 p. DLC.   44438

---- Documents showing the
manner in which the title to the
town site, on Galveston Island

is vested in the trustees.
Printed by Bailie and Gallagher,
1837. 15 p. Tx; TxU.   44439

Gardener, John.
A short treatise on the habits
and character of the Oyster.
Philadelphia, 1837. 14 p. DLC;
PHi.   44440

Gardiner, William, 1770-1853.
Music of Nature: an attempt
to prove that what is pleasing in
the art of singing, etc. is derived from the sounds of the
animated world. By William
Gardiner. Boston, Oliver Ditson
& Co., 1837. 505 p. CtY; ICU;
MB; OCl; PPi; MPeaI.   44441

Gardner, Daniel.
A Treatise on Representative
Government, and its probable
durability: prepared by appointment and read before the Phi
Beta Kappa society of New York,
at Union college, in January,
1837. By Daniel Gardner, esq.,
of the civil class. Troy, published by Elias Gates, 1837. 23
p. CtHT; CtHWatk; MBC; NT.
                               44442

Garland, James, 1791-1885.
Speech of Mr. Garland, of
Virginia, in opposition to the
sub-treasury scheme. Delivered
in the House of representatives,
September 25, 1837. Washington,
1837. 47 p. CtY; GEU; MiU-C;
PPB; Vi.   44443

Garnett, James Mercer, 1770-
1843.
Address to the members of the
Agricultural society of Fredericksburg, on their 20th anniversary.
Virginia Pamphlets. Fredericksburg, Herald office, [1837].
28 p. CSmH; NcD.   44444

Gas Light & Coke Company, Cincinnati.

An Act to incorporate the
Cincinnati Fuel Company passed
March 1837. Cincinnati, 1837.
7 p. OCHP.   44445

Gates, J. C.
   Teacher's Assistance and
Scholar's Guide, being an arrangement of ancient and modern
geography. ... Second edition
revised, etc. Boston, J. Putnam, 1837. N.   44446

Gates, Justin.
   The Thomsonian reflector
and vindicator; being a concise
view of the theory and principles on which is based the
Thomsonian system of medical
practice, it utility and mildness
in removing diseases, and a
contrast of its simplicity ...
Rochester [N.Y.], Printed at
the Herald of truth office ...
1837. [9]-172 p. CSmH; OC.
                              44447
Gates, William, 1788-1868.
   Proceedings of a general
court martial held for the trial
of Maj. Wm. Gates, at Savannah,
for conduct disgraceful, & behavior unworthy of a commanding officer of a military post,
in failing to make sortie after
attack by Indians of inferior
number, at Fort Barnwell Apr.
1836; in failing afterwards to
order out a force to watch or
engage the enemy, or recover
the bodies of Sergeant Holliday
and private Gough. Savannah,
[N.Y.], 1837. DLC; MH-L;
PPB; PPRF.   44448

Gates's Almanac.
   By Tobias Ostrander. Troy,
Elias Gates, 1837. MWA. 44449

Gates' Troy Almanac for 1838.
By C. H. Anthony. Albany,
N.Y., Oliver Steele, [1837].
MWA.   44450

---- Troy, N.Y., N. Tuttle,
(1837). MWA; NT.   44451

Gavin, Anthonio.
   Anti-popery; or, History of
the Popish Church...to which
has been added an account of
the inquisition of Goa and
Macerata. Philadelphia, S. E.
Wallington & co., 1837. 400 p.
GaGTH; NcD; OWoC; PPiW; WU.
                              44452
Gazetteer of the state of Missouri. With a map of the state,
from the office of the surveyor
general.... An appendix containing frontier sketches and illustrations of Indian character.
A frontispiece, engraved on
steel. Compiled by Alphonso
Wetmore, of Missouri. St. Louis,
Mo., Published by C. Keemle,
1837. 382 p. CoD; CoFcS; FSa;
IaHi; NIC.   44453

Gazlay, Theodore, 1815-.
   The musician. A collection
of the most celebrated songs,
duetts, trios, catches, rounds,
and glees. For voices or instruments. Cincinnati, Published by
U. P. James, 1837. 72 p. OCHP.
                              44454
General Association of Massachusetts.
   Minutes of the General Association of Massachusetts. at
their meeting at North Brookfield, June 28, 1837; with the
Narrative of the State of Religion, and the Pastoral Letter.
Boston, Printed by Crocker &
Brewster, 1837. 46 p. A-Ar.
                              44455
The generous planter, and his
carpenter, Ben. Worcester, 1837.
MH; MH-And.   44456

Genesee Wesleyan Seminary.
Lima, N.Y.
   Catalogue of the Officers and

Students of the Genesee Wesleyan Seminary, Lima, N.Y. for the Year, Ending Oct. 5, 1837. Auburn, N.Y., Printed at the office of the Auburn Banner, 1837. 23 p. NLG.
44457

Geneva, N.Y. Charters.
Act of incorporation of the village of Geneva, passed May 6, 1837. Geneva, N.Y., Printed by I. Merrell, 1837. 21 p. NRU.
44458

Geneva Female Seminary. Geneva, N.Y.
Annual circular, report, and catalogue, of the Geneva Female Seminary, under the care of Mrs. Ricord. March, 1837. Mattison & Haskell, Printers, Geneva. [Geneva? 1837?] 19 p. MH.
44459

Geneva Lyceum.
Catalogue of the Geneva Lyceum, 1836 and 1837. [Ira Merrell, Printer, Seneca Street.] [1837?] 12 p. MH.
44460

The Gentleman's magazine. v. 1-7; July 1837 - Dec., 1840. Philadelphia, 1837-40. 7 v. in 6. MiU; NjR; NP; TxU.
44461

George's Creek Coal and Iron Company.
George's creek coal and iron company. 1836. [Baltimore? 1837]. 36 p. CtY; DLC; MdBE; PPAN; PPL.
44462

Georgia. General Assembly, 1836.
Acts of the General assembly of the State of Georgia, passed in Milledgeville, at an annual session in November and December, 1836. Milledgeville, P. L. Robinson - State printer, 1837. 279, 85 p. Ar-Sc; GHi.
44463

---- ---- House of representatives, 1836.
Journal of the House of representatives of the State of Georgia, at an annual session of the General assembly, begun and held at Milledgeville, the seat of government, in November and December, 1836. Milledgeville, P. L. Robinson, 1837. 480 p. G-Ar; GMilvC.
44464

---- ---- Senate, 1836.
Journal of the Senate of the State of Georgia at an annual session of the General assembly, begun and held at Milledgeville, the seat of government, 1836. Milledgeville, P. L. Robinson, 1837. 384 p. GMilvC.
44465

---- ---- ---- Preliminary documents in reference to the survey, location, and construction of the Western and Atlantic rail-road of the state of Georgia. n.p., (1837). MBAt.
44466

---- Laws, statutes, etc.
A digest of the laws of the state of Georgea....with occasional explanatory notes, and connecting references to which is added an appendix....with a copious index, compiled by the appointment and under the authority of the general assembly, by Oliver H. Prince, second edition, Athens, published by the author, 1837. 1046 p. GA; Nb; PU; TMeB.
44467

---- Superior Courts.
Reports of decisions made by the judges of the Superior courts of law and chancery of the state of Georgia. New York, Collins, Keese & co., 1837. 270 p. Ia; Mi-L; Nj; ODaL; Vi-L.
44468

---- University.

Franklin College, Athens, Ga.
Catalogue of the Trustees, Officers, and Graduates of Franklin College, from its Establishment in 1801, to the Annual Commencement in 1836. Athens, 1837.   BrMus.   44469

Gerhard, William Wood, 1809-1872.
Clinical guide, and syllabus of a course of lectures, on clinical medicine and pathology. Philadelphia, Auner, 1837.
37 p. IEN-M; NNNAM; PPPiAM; PPL; RPM.   44470

Gest's anti-masonic almanac for the year of our Lord 1837 ....
Philadelphia, Pr. William R. Boden, 1837. 48 p. IaCrM; MB; MWA.   44471

Getz, George.
A general collection of forms & precedants in conveyancing in which the most abundant examples are introduced, in sufficient variety to enable the scrivener, conveyancer, and man of business, accurately to draw instruments of writing legally and correctly; besides many other forms useful to the farmer, mechanic & trader... 2nd. ed. enl. 7 imp. Reading, Pa., Getz, 1837. 143 p. NNLI; PAtM; PP; PReaHi.   44472

Gholson, [Samuel Jameson].
Speech of Mr. Gholson, of Mississippi, on the motion to arrest Reuben M. Whitney, Esq., of Washington City, for an alleged contempt. Delivered in the House of Representatives of the United States, February 10, 1837. Washington, Printed by Jacob Gideon, Jun. 1837. 22 p. MsJS; OCLaw.   44473

Gibbon, Edward, 1737-1794.
The history of the decline and fall of the Roman empire. By Edward Gibbon, Esq. Fifth American from the last London edition. Complete in four volumes. New York, Published by Harper and Brothers, 1837. 4 v. KyBgB; MAmP; NbOM; RP; ScCoB.   44474

---- The miscellaneous works of Edward Gibbons, newly collected from original sources and including new translations from French texts. New York, F. De Faw & Co., 1837. 443 p. CtY; MB; PPCC; OFM; RNPL.   44475

The gift. A Christmas and New Year's present for 1837. Philadelphia, E. L. Carey and A. Hart, 1837. 325 p. KyOw; MBC; MBMu; MWA; Ia-L-B.   44476

Gilbert, Ann (Taylor), 1782-1866.
Hymns for Infant Minds. By the author of "Original Poems." New York, Mahlon Day, 1837. 128 p. NPalK; NN; NNUT.   44477

Gill, Edward H.
A reply to "a brief analysis of a part of the last annual report of the board of directors and chief engineer of the Sandy and Beaver Canal Company" published by Joshua Malin, [1837]. 16 p. NNC.   44478

[Gill, Thomas] of the Morning Post. Boston.
Selections from the Court Reporters originally published in the Boston Morning Post, from 1834 to 1837, arranged and revised by [Thomas Gill], Reporter for the Post. Boston, Otis, Broaders & Co., 1837. 4-250 p. CtY; MB; Nh-Hi; OrU; WaU.   44479

Gillet, Ransom Hooker, 1800-
1876.
Speech of Mr. Gillet, of New
York, on the bill making appropriations for certain harbors, delivered in the House of representatives, June 24, 1836.
Washington, 1837. 16 p. DLC;
MiGr.   44480

Gillies, John, 1712-1796.
Memoirs of Rev. George
Whitefield. By John Gillies,
D.D. Revised and corrected
with large additions and improvements. To which is appended an extensive collection
of his sermons and other writings. Middletown, Published
by Hunt & Noyes, 1837. 648 p.
CtY; MoSC; NjR; NNUT;
PPPrHi.   44481

Gillmore, Hiram.
Lectures on Christianity:
wherein its necessity, authenticity, and utility, are supported
by evidences.... Cleveland,
Printed by F. B. Penniman,
1837. CSmH; IEG; MoS;
OClWHi; PMA.   44482

Gilman, Caroline H. (1794-1888).
Recollections of a southern
matron. by Caroline H. Gilman.
New York, Harper and brothers,
1837. [9]-272 p. MsCld; NcWfC;
ViHal.   44483

Ginal, Heinrich.
Ueber den Werth der Auf-
klarung. Philadelphia, L. A.
Wollenweber, 1837. PPG. 44484

Girard Almanac for 1838. Philadelphia, Pa., Thomas L. Bonsal,
[1837]. MWA; NjR.   44485

Girard College. Philadelphia.
Report of the Building Committee of the Girard College for

Orphans; with report of the
Architect. Read in the House
of Reps. Jan, 16 1837. Harris-
burg, 1837. 6 p. PHi; PPi.
                                 44486
Girard Life Insurance, Annuity
and Trust Company. See
Girard Trust Corn Exchange
Bank. Philadelphia.

Girard Trust Corn Exchange
Bank. Philadelphia.
(Prospectus) ... Philadelphia,
A Waldie, pr., 1837. 14 p.
MH-BA.   44487

Girault, Arsène Napoléon.
The French guide; or, An
introduction to the study of the
French language. By A. N.
Girault, ... Philadelphia, Henry
Perkins; ... Boston, Perkins
& Marvin, ... 1837. 324 p.
DLC; MH; OO; TBriK; WaPS.
                                 44488
Gird, Henry H.
State exaltation. An address
delivered ... June 13, 1837.
Jackson, La., 1837. 38 p.
Mhi.   44489

The Girl's Manual. .... New
York, D. Appleton & Company.
Philadelphia, George S. Appleton
& Co., [1837?] 288 p. NICLA.
                                 44490
Globe Insurance Life Insurance,
Trust and Annuity Company.
Act of Incorporation, Charter
perpetual. [1837] 8 p. NNC;
PHi.   44491

Gloucester, Mass.
By-laws. Gloucester, 1837.
12 p. S. CtSoP.   44492

---- Fifth Parish Church.
Church-Articles of faith and
covenant, together with rules
and regulations. Adopted by the
Fifth Parish Church in Gloucester,

Massachusetts. Boston, printed by Whipple and Damrill, for the church, 1837. 12 p.   44493

Glover, E.
    Explanation of the Sacraments; and some other practices of the Catholic church. Philadelphia, Eugene Cummiskey, 1837. 192 p. MiDU; MWH; NbOC; OCMtSM.   44494

"Go Ahead!" No. 4. Davy Crockett's 18 almanack, 38 of wild sports in the west, life in the backwoods, sketches of Texas, and rows on the Mississippi. Nashville, Tennessee. Published by the heirs of Col. Crockett, [1837]. 47 p. CSmH; MWA; MWey.   44495

Goddard, Paul Beck, 1811-1866.
    Plates of the cerebro-spinal nerves, with references; for the use of medical students. By Paul B. Goddard ... Philadelphia, J. G. Auner, 1837. [9]-60 p. CSt; MdBJ; NcU; PP; ViU.   44496

Goddard, William Giles, 1794-1846.
    An address to the Phi beta kappa society of Rhode Island, delivered Sept. 7, 1836. Boston, John H. Eastburn, printer, 1837. 30 p. CtY; ICU; MBC; PHi; ScC.   44497

Godwin, William, 1803-1832.
    Transfusion; or, The orphans of Unwalden. By William Godwin, jun. New York, G. Dearborn & co., 1837. 252 p. DLC; MNc; NBuHi; TxU. 44498

Goethe, Johann Wolfgang von, 1749-1832.
    Faust Eine tragedie von Goethe. New York, Zu haben in der verlags handling, 1837. 432 p. CtY; MdBJ; NjP; PP; TNJU.   44499

---- Goetz von Berlichingen, with the iron hand; a drama in 5 acts from the German of Goethe ... Philadelphia, Carey, Lea and Blanchard, 1837. CtHT; MH; PPL-R; PU.   44500

(Göhring, Wilhelm H.)
    Treue wahreit, geschrieben durch einem demuthigen sünder. Durch die hand cires reuenden bussfertigen und nach der grade Gottes ringenden armen sunders ... Lancaster, (Pennsylvania) (n.p.), 1837. (3)-28 p. MiU-C.   44501

Goldsmith, Oliver, 1728-1774.
    The Grecian history from the earliest state to the death of Alexander the Great ... Hartford, Published by Judd, Loomis & co., 1837. 2 v. in 1. 316 p. CtMW; IU; MH; NcAS; PWCHi.   44502

---- ... History of Greece, from the earliest state to the death of Alexander the Great. In three vols. By Goldsmith. New York, Published by T. Mason and G. Lantz, 1837. 3 v. PWaybu.   44503

---- The history of Rome, from the earliest state of the commonwealth to the disolution of the empire, by Oliver Goldsmith. Sanbornton, N.H., Pub. by Charles Lane, 1837. 368 p. CtY; IaHA; LNDil; MDeeP; NhD; NhFr.   44504

---- The miscellaneous works of Oliver Goldsmith, with an account of his life and writings, stereotyped from the Paris edition, edited by Washington Irving. Philadelphia, J. Crissy, 1837. CtY; ICU; KyHi; MLanc; TxD-T.   44505

---- ... Roman history, abridged by himself for the use of schools; 1st ed. divided into sections, for a classbook... Hartford, Judd, 1837. 316 p. CtMW; ICRL; MH; NcAS; OO. 44506

---- The Works ... Collected by James Prior...New York, John W. Lovell Company, [1837.] 4 v. NdU; WBeloC. 44507

Good, John Mason, 1764-1827.
The book of nature. By John Mason Good. Harper's stereotype ed. From the last London ed. To which is now prefixed a sketch of the author's life. Complete in one volume. Hartford, Belknap and Hamersley, 1837. 467 p. GAU; MB; PPLt; NNF; WaU. 44508

---- ---- New York, J. & J. Harper, 1837. (25)-467 p. Ia; GU; MoS; NNN; RLa. 44509

---- ---- 7th ed. Boston, William D. Ticknor, 1837. 224 p. CtHWatk; LNB; MH-Ed; MPlyA. 44510

The Good Boy. Northampton, John Metcalf, 1837. 18 p. NNC; PV. 44511

The good little child's verse book of 1 natural history. New York, Mahlon Day, pub., 1837. 23 p. RPB. 44512

Goodrich, Charles Augustus, 1790-1862.
A History of the Church, from the birth of Christ to the present time; ... History of the Protestant denominations ... an account of the religious cerimonies of all nations.... Brattleboro, Brattleboro Typographic Co., 1837. KPea; MnSH; NhD; PWaybu; VtCas. 44513

---- A History of the United States of America.... By Charles A. Goodrich. ... Boston, American Stationers Co., 1837. 352 p. MNBedf. 44514

---- ---- Hartford, Published by H. F. Sumner & co. Stereotyped by Conner & Cook, New-York, 1837. 540 p. MoS; TCh; TxGeoS; WRichM. 44515

---- Lives of the signers to the Declaration of independence. By the Rev. Charles A. Goodrich. 7th ed. New York, T. Mathew, 1837. 460 p. MiD-B; MWA; RPB; TJoT; ViU. 44516

---- A new family encyclopedia; or, Compendium of universal knowledge.... 7th ed., rev. and imp. By C. A. Goodrich. Hartford, Belknap, 1837. 483 p. NjP; NNC. 44517

---- Outlines of modern geography, on a new plan, carefully adapted to youth. With numerous engravings of cities, manners .... 5th ed. Boston, S. G. Goodrich, 1837. 252 p. MiU-C. 44518

---- Questions on the enlarged and improved edition of Goodrich's school history of the United States... Boston, American Stationers Co., 1837. 87 p. MB; MH. 44519

---- ---- Boston, J. B. Russell, 1837. 87 p. MB; MH; TxU-T. 44520

---- Religious ceremonies and customs; or, The forms of worship practised by the several nations of the world, from the earliest records to the present time. By Charles A. Goodrich. Hartford, Reed and Barber, 1837. 576 p. LNDil; NNiaU; PHi; ScP. 44521

---- The universal traveller: designed to introduce readers at home to an acquaintance with the arts, customs, and manners of the principal modern nations on the globe....3d ed. Hartford, [Connecticut], Canfield & Robins, 1837. 504 p. ICHi; MBC; OOxM; TxGR; WaPS.   44522

Goodrich, Chauncey Allen, 1790-1860.
   Elements of Greek grammar, by Chauncey A. Goodrich, used in Yale college; heretofore published as the grammer of Caspar Frederic Hachenberg ... Hartford, Belknap & Hammersley, 1837. 236 p. CtHT; ICU; MH; OMC; PReaAT.   44523

---- Lessons in greek parsing; or, Outlines of the greek grammar, divided into short portions, and illustrated by appropriate exercises in parsing. By Chauncey A. Goodrich... 2d ed. New Haven, Published by Durrie & Peck, 1837. 138 p. CtY; MH.   44524

---- Lessons in Latin parsing. 3d ed. New Haven, Durrie and Peck, 1837. 214 p. CtHT-W; MH; OSW; WMMU.   44525

Goodrich, Samuel Griswold, 1793-1860.
   The Child's Book of American Geography: Designed as an Easy and Entertaining Work for the Use of Beginners. With Sixty Engravings, and Eighteen Maps, as Follows: [etc.] Second Edition. Boston, James B. Dow, 1837. 64 p. MH; MnU; MWH; NNC; P. 44526

---- The child's botany. 9th ed. Boston, C. J. Hendee,

1837. 103 p. NNU-W.   44527

---- The first book of history; for children and youth. By the author of Peter Parley's tales... Rev. ed. Boston, C. J. Hendee, 1837. 183 p. DLC; MH; MHa; OClWHi; WGr.
                          44528
---- ---- Boston, Jenks & Palmer, (1837?). 183 p. MPeHi.
                          44529
---- Peter Parley's arithmetic ... with numerous engravings. Boston, Charles J. Hendee, 1837. 144 p. DAU.   44530

---- Peter Parley's book of the United States, geographical, political, and historical ... Boston, C. J. Hendee, 1837. 208 p. FSaW; ICBB; MnU; PU-Penn; TNV.   44531

---- Peter Parley's little reader, ... Philadelphia, Published by R. W. Pomeroy, 1837. 143 p. IaU; MH; NNC; NRHi; RPB.
                          44532
---- Peter Parley's method of telling about the geography of the Bible. Boston, American Stationers' Co., 1837. CtY; DLC; MH; NjR.   44533

---- Peter Parley's Method of Telling about Geography to children....New York, F. J. Huntington & Co., 1837. 118 p. MH; MMhHi; NjR.   44534

---- Peter Parley's universal history on the basis of geography; for the use of families. By Samuel G. Goodrich. New York, Horsington, [1837]. MNS; MWbor.   44535

---- ---- 12th edition. By Nathaniel Hawthorne. New York, Mark H. Newman and company;

Cincinnati, W. H. Moore and company; New Orleans, D. Baker and company; Chicago, W. W. Barlow and company; Auburn, J. C. Ivison and company, 1837. 2 vols. in 1. MPiB; OClWHi. 44536

---- The second book of history. Including modern history of Europe, Africa and Asia. Illustrated by engravings and maps. Designed as a sequel to First book of history. Eleventh edition. Boston, Charles J. Hendee; Lancaster, Mass., Manufactured by Oscar C. B. Carter, 1837. 180, 16 p. IaDaP; MH. 44537

---- The story of La Peyrouse. Philadelphia, Desilver, Thomas & co., 1837. 282 p. NjR; TNF. 44538

---- A system of school geography, chiefly derived from Malte-Brun, and arranged according to the inductive plan of instruction. By S. Griswold Goodrich. 12th ed. New-York, F. J. Huntington & co., 1837. 288 p. DLC; InU; MH; MiEM. 44539

---- The third book of history, containing ancient history in connection with ancient geography. Designed as a sequel to the First and Second books of history, by the author of Peter Parley tales. 3d ed. Boston, C. J. Hendee, 1837. MH-Ed. 44540

---- Universal History on the Basis of Geography. Illustrations, maps engravings. Boston, American Stationers Co., John Russell, 1837. [7]-380 p. FTU; IaHA; MFiHi; MH. 44541

---- Universal History on the basis of Geography. For the use of families... 8th ed. New York, Robinson, [1837]. NNC. 44542

Goodsell, Dana.
The Close of the Year. A Sermon delivered in the Third Orthodox Church, in Lowell, Mass. December 25, 1836. By Dana Goodsell. Lowell, Printed at the Messenger Office, 1837. 19 p. CSmH; DLC; MBC; MWA. 44543

Goodwin, Isaac, 1786-1832.
Goodwin's town officer. 4th ed., adapted to the revised statutes, by Benjamin F. Thomas ... Worcester, Dorr, Howland & co., 1837. 365 p. CtY; MB; MeBaHi; MSwan: MWCL. 44544

Goodwise, Timothy.
The Parent's Gift. By Timothy Goodwide. Portland, S. H. Colesworthy, 1837. 64 p. MWA. 44545

Gordon, David.
The wages of sin. A tract ....Albany, printed by Hoffman and White, 1837. 32 p. NjR. 44546

Gordon, Thomas Francis.
A digest of the laws of the United States. Including an abstract of the judicial decisions relating to the constitutional and statutory law. By Thomas F. Gordon. Philadelphia, Printed for the author, 1837. x, [11]-822 p. CLSU; MBC; MdBB; MHi; PWmpDS; TU. 44547

---- ---- [2nd ed.] By Thomas F. Gorden. Philadelphia, Printed for the author, 1837. 822 p. CLSU; PP; PPL. 44548

Gore, Catherine Grace Frances (Moody), 1799-1861.
Memoirs of a Peeress; or, The Days of Fox. Edited by Lady

Charlotte Bury. In 2 Vols.
Philadelphia, E. L. Carey & A.
Hart, 1837. DLC; IaBo; MiU;
NcD; PPA.   44549

Gospel herald. v. 1- Ipswich,
1837?- PCA.   44550

Gottschall, Abraham.
    Wahrer Gerechtigkeit ver-
theidigt oder Ein Beweis, ...
Doylestaun, Pa., Gedruckt und
zu haben in der Druckerei von
J. Jung u. Krapf, 1837. 16 p.
InGo.   44551

Gouge, William M., 1796-1863.
    An inquiry into the expedi-
ency of dispensing with bank
agency and bank paper in the
fiscal concerns of the United
States. By William M. Gouge
....Philadelphia, Printed by
William Stavely, 1837. 56 p.
IU; MdBJ; NjP; ScU; WHi.
                             44552
Gould, William.
    Memoir of Susanna T. Pierce,
who died in Freetown, Mass.
Sept. 24th, 1836. aged 7 years
and 10 months. By Rev. William Gould, Fairhaven ... Boston, Massachusetts Sabbath
School Society. Depository,
1837. 72 p. DLC; MBNEH.
                             44553
Governor Dummer Academy.
South Byfield, Mass.
    An account of Dummer Acad-
emy, together with a statement
of the alterations and improvements, about to be made. Boston, 1837. 12 p. MBAt; MBC;
MH; MHi.   44554

Gow, Niel.
    A practical treatise on the
law of partnership, with an appendix of precedents. By Niel
Gow ... 3d. Amer. from the
last London ed.; with consider-

able alterations and additions,
notes and references to Amer.
decisions, by Edward D. In-
graham. Philadelphia, Robert
H. Small, 1837. 500 p. ICLaw;
KyLxT; Me-LR; NIC; OCY.
                             44555
Gowen, James.
    Democratic address respect-
ing... Philadelphia, 1837. PPL.
                             44556
Graham, Sylvester, 1794-1851.
    A Lecture to young men, on
Chastity .... By Sylvester
Graham .... Light & Stearns,
Crocker & Brewster, Boston,
1837.... 206 p. CtMW; IaBo;
MeBat; MWA; OO.   44557

---- ---- 3rd ed. Boston, Light,
1837. 246 p. MBBC; MNF; OO.
                             44558
---- A treatise on bread, and
breadmaking. By Sylvester
Graham. Boston, Light &
Stearns, 1837. 131 p. CtMW;
IEN-M; MBC; MiD; MPeHi.
                             44559
The Graham journal of health
and longevity. Devoted to the
practical illustration of the sci-
ence of human life, as taught
by Sylvester Graham and others.
David Cambell ed. v. 1-3; April
1837-Dec. 1837. Boston and
New York, 1837-1839. AAP;
KyU; MB; MnU; OO; WU-A.
                             44560
Granger, Arthur.
    The Apostle Paul's opinion
of slavery and emancipation; a
sermon preached to the congre-
gational church and society in
Meridian, at the request of several respectable anti-abolitionists
... Middletown, printed by
Charles H. Pelton, 1837. 27 p.
TNF.   44561

Granger, Ralph.
    Introductory lecture, delivered

at the Willoughby medical college of the Willoughby university of Lake Erie, 1837-8, ... Painesville [O.], Printed by Howe & Jaques, 1837. 16 p. CSmH; DNLM; MB; NBuU-M; OClWHi.   44562

Grant, Innes.
The Comparative value of Greek and Hebrew poetry in a course of liberal study. An inaugural address by Innes Grant. Whitesboro, 1837. 14 p. MAnP; MiU-C.   44563

[Grant, James]
The great metropolis, by the author of "Random recollections of the lords and commons." New York, Saunders & Otley, 1837. 2 v. in 1. MdBP; ScU.
44564
---- ---- [1st Amer. ed.] New York, T. Foster, 1837. 329 p. CtMW; DLC; FU; NNUT; PPAmP.
44565
---- ---- ... 2d ed. New York, Saunders and Otley, 1837. CSt; IU; NNG; OClW; PU.
44566
---- ---- 3rd ed. New York, London, Saunders and Otley, 1837. 2 v. in 1. GU; MB; RPB; ViU.   44567

---- ---- 4th ed. New York, Saunders and Otley, 1837. 2 v. in 1. CtMW; NN; NT; RPAt.
44568
Granville, Ohio. Congregational church.
Articles of faith, and form of covenant, of the Congregational church of Granville, Ohio. Columbus, Printed by Cutler and Pilsbury, 1837. 8 p. OClWHi.   44569

Gratiot, Charles.
Protection of Western Frontiers.

Washington, D.C., 1837. map. O. MnHi.   44570

Graves, William.
Examination of Dr. William Graves before the Lowell court, from Sept. 25th-Sept 29 1837, for the murder of Mary Anne Wilson, of Greenfield, N.H. by attempting to produce an abortion. [Lowell, the court, 1837] 36 p. Mh-M; NN; PP.
44571
Graves, William Jordon, 1805-1848.
Speech against the bill to postpone the fourth instalment of the deposites with the states; in the House of Representatives, Sept. 28, 1837. Washington, 1837. KyRE; MBAt.   44572

Gray, Asa, 1810-1888.
Melanthacearum Ameircae septintrionalis revisio. Novi-Eboraci, Scott, 1837. MH; PPAmP.
44573
---- Remarks on the structure & affinities of the order Ceratophyllaceae. From v. 4 of Annals of the Lyceum of Nat. Hist. New York, 1837. 22 p. C-S; CtY; MBHo.   44574

Great Western Almanac for 1838. Philadelphia, Pa., Jos. McDowell, (1837). MWA.   44575

Green, Ashbel.
The Saviour's last command; or, what is implied in preaching the gospel, ... a discourse delivered Dec. 4, 1836, to the people of the fifth Presbyterian church, Philadelphia. Philadelphia, W. S. Martien, 1837. 42 p. CSansS; ICP; NNMr; PPPrHi.   44576

Green, Eriah, 1795-1874.
The basis of a sound reputa-

tion. A valedictory address to
the Senior class of the Oneida
institute delivered Sept. 13,
1837. By Beriah Green. Published by request of the Senior
class. Whitesboro, Press of
the friend of man, 1837. MH-
And; OClWHi; OMC.   44577

---- The martyr. A discourse,
in commemoration of the mar-
tyrdom of the Rev. Elijah P.
Lovejoy,... By Beriah Green
... (New York), The American
Anti-slavery society, 1837.
18 p. DLC; MH-AH; NNUT.
                          44578
Green, E. Brewster.
   The child of passion. a
poem. Middletown, E. Hunt
and co., 1837. 40 p. DLC;
NBuG; NjP; PPM; ViU.   44579

Green, Jacob.
   Chemical diagrams; or, Concise views of many interesting
changes produced by chemical
affinity. By Jacob Green.
Philadelphia, Dobson, 1837.
(5)-90 p. NjP; NNNAM; NNC;
PPAmP.   44580

Green, James D.
   An Address, delivered at
the Anniversary Celebration of
The Birth of Spurzheim, and
The Organization of The Bos-
ton Phrenological Society, De-
cember 30, 1836. By James D.
Green. Boston, Marsh, Capen
& Lyon, 1837. 27 p. CTHWatk;
ICMe; MBC; MH; MiD-B.   44581

---- Virtue Not Happiness, for
End of Man's Creation. By
James D. Green. Boston,
James Munroe & Co., 1837.
20 p. ICMe; MB-HP; MeB;
MCon; MMeT-Hi.   44582

Green, Richard W.

An arithmetical guide, in
which the principles of numbers
are inductively explained...2nd
ed. Philadelphia, Henry Perkins,
1837. 288 p. CtY; MH; OClWHi.
                          44583
---- The little reckoner or inductive exercises in mental
arithmetic...7th ed. Philadelphia,
H. Perkins; Boston, Perkins
and Marvin, 1837. 108 p. DLC.
                          44584
---- ---- Ninth edition, corrected
and improved. Philadelphia,
Henry Perkins, (1837). 108 p.
NNC.   44585

Green, Samuel, d. 1859.
   The practical accountant, or,
Farmer's and Mechanick's best
method of book-keeping. [Itica]
N.Y., [1837]. MH.   44586

[Greene, Asa], 1788-1837.
   A glance at New York: embracing the city government,
theatres, hotels, churches, mobs,
monopolies, learned professions
newspapers, rogues, dandies,
fires and firemen, water and
other liquids, &c., &c. ... New-
York, A. Greene, 1837. 262 p.
Ct; ICN; MH; OCl; PHi. 44587

Greene, B. H.
   Sunday school class-book.
Boston, 1837. MB.   44588

(Greene, George Washington),
1811-1883.
   The life and voyages of Ver-
razzano ... Cambridge, (Mass.),
Folsom, Wells, and Thurston,
1837. 21 p. MeHi; MH; Nh-Hi;
RHi.   44589

Greenleaf, Benjamin, 1786-1864.
   A key to The national arithmetic, exhibiting the operation
of the more difficult questions
in that work ... By Benjamin

Greenleaf ... Boston, R. S.
Davis [etc.], 1837. 110 p.
DLC; MH; MiU.   44590

---- The National Arithmetic
on the inductive system...book-
keeping and forming a complete
mercantile arithmetic...By Benjamin Greenleaf, A.M., Boston,
published by Robert S. Davis
and Gould, Kendall, and
Lincoln, 1837. 314 p. CtMW;
MHaHi.   44591

Greenleaf, Jeremiah, 1791-1864.
   Grammar simplified; or, an
ocular analysis of the English
language. By J. Greenleaf.
Twentieth edition; corrected,
enlarged, and improved by the
author. Stereotyped by James
Conner, New-York. New York,
Published by Robinson, Pratt &
co., 1837. 50 p. MH; NNC.
                                 44592
[Greenleaf, Simon], 1783-1853.
   The right of the eastern
diocese to elect an assistant
bishop....Cambridge, Folsom,
Wells, and Thurston, 1837.
26 p. IEG; MHi; MiD-B; Nh;
NNG.   44593

Greenwood, Francis William
Pitt, 1797-1843.
   A Collection of psalms and
hymns for Christian worship.
Twentieth ed. Boston, 1837.
MB; MBC; MH-AH; MNoanNP.
                                 44594
---- ---- Twenty-third edition.
Boston, 1837. (2), 608 p.
MHi; OO.   44595

---- A sermon preached at the
ordination of the Rev. John T.
Sargent as Minister at large
in Boston on the evening of
Oct. 29, 1837...Boston, Weeks,
Jordan and company, 1837.
32 p. MWA; NH-Hi; NNG;

OClWHi; WHi.   44596

Gregory, John, of Woburn, Mass.
   The Bramble. To which is
added a letter to Rev. Thomas
Whittemore, an answer to the hoe,
a sermon on temperance in all
things, delivered at Woburn,
Stoneham, and New Rowley,
2d ed. Methuen, S. J. Varney,
Printer, 1837. 114 p. DLC;
ICN; MB; NN.   44597

Gregory, Olinthus Gilbert, 1774-
1841.
   Memoirs and private corres-
pondence of the Rev. Robert
Hall, of Bristol, England. 1st
American edition. Philadelphia,
Published by Charles Bell, 1837.
2 (3) 234 p. CtHC; NcDaD.
                                 44598
Gregory, T. H.
   Original miscellaneous poetry.
Albany, 1837. MB.   44599

Gresley, Richard Newcombe.
   A treatise on the law of evi-
dence in the Courts of Equity.
By Richard Newcome Gresley,
Esq., barrister at law. Phila-
delphia, P. H. Nicklin & T.
Johnson, 1837. [1]-564 p. DLC;
LU; PP; RPL; Sc-SC; WU-L.
                                 44600
Grew, Harriet Catharine.
   Memorials of A Young Christian.
Merriheu and Gunn, Printers.
Philadelphia, 1837. 106 p. MH;
MHi; MWA; PHi.   44601

Grierson, Miss.
   Pierre and his family: or A
story of the Waldenses. By the
author of "Lily Douglas." Revised by the editors. New York,
Published by T. Mason and G.
Lane, 1837. 192 p. OBerB.
                                 44602
Griffith, Robert Eglesfeld, 1798-
1850.

Lecture introductory to the course on pathology and practice of medicine, in the University of Virginia, for the session of 1837-8. By R. Eglesfeld Griffith, M.D. Published by members of the class. Charlottesville, James Alexander, printer, 1837. 16 p. KyLxT; NcU; TxU; Vi. 44603

Grigg, Jacob, d. 1836.
The Doctrine of Predestination examined in a sermon, delivered at Mangohick Church, King William County, Va., on Lord's Day, Oct. 9, 1814, at the annual meeting of the Baptist Dover Assoc. By Jacob Grigg. Richmond, Religious Herald, 1837. 34 p. DLC; MB; NcWfC; Vi. 44604

Grimshaw, William, 1782-1852.
The history of France from the foundation of the monarchy to the death of Louis XVI. Philadelphia, 1837. 302 p. IaMpI; MWA; ScDuE. 44605

Griswold, Alexander Viets.
A discourse on worshipping God in Spirit and in truth. By A. V. Griswold, Bishop of the Eastern Diocese, Boston, Protestant Episcopal Press. Torrey & Blair, Printers, 1837. 16 p. MBD; MiD-B; NNG; PCA; RPB. 44606

Groesbeck, Herman J.
Address delivered at the second anniversary celebration of the Alpha Delta Phi Society of Miami University Aug. 10, 1837. By Herman J. Groesbeck. Cincinnati...R.P. Brooks & co., printers, 1837. 24 p. CSmH; ICU; MHi; NBuU; OHi. 44607

Groves, John.
A Greek and English Dictionary, Comprising all the words in the Writings of the most popular Greek Authors; with the difficult inflections in them and in the Septuogint and New Testament: .... By The Rev. John Groves. With corrections and additional Matter, by the American Editor. Boston, Hilliard, Gray and Company, 1837. MsJMC; PU; ScNc; TNP. 44608

Grund, Francis Joseph, 1805-1863.
The Americans, in their moral, social and political relations ... Boston, Marsh, Capen and Lyon, 1837. 9-423 p. CoU; ICBB; LU; TxD-W; ViU. 44609

---- Elements of natural philosophy, with questions for review; for the use of schools. 5th ed. Boston, C. J. Hendee, 1837. MH. 44610

The Guardian. Philadelphia, Desilver, 1837. 244 p. CoU; I; NNC; RPB; ViU. 44611

Guenebault, J. H.
Natural history of the negro race. Extracted from the French. By J. H. Guenebault ... Charleston, S.C., D. I. Dowling, 1837. 162 p. GEU; MHi; NcD; PPPrHi; ScC. 44612

A guide to the lions of Philadelphia; comprising a description of the places of amusement, exhibitions, public buildings, public squares, &c. in the city ... Philadelphia, T. T. Ash and co., 1837. [9]-96 p. DLC; MH; NN; PPL; ViU. 44613

Gummere, John, 1784-1845.
Complete key to Gummere's

surveying. See Alsop, Samuel, 1813-1888.

---- An elementary treatise on astronomy. In two parts. The first containing, a clear and compendious view of the theory; the second, a number of practical problems. To which are added, solar, lunar, and other astronomical tables. By John Gummere ... 2d ed., enl. and improved. Philadelphia, Kimber & Sharpless, 1837. [9]-373, 104 p. CtMW; PAtM; RP; TNP; Wv.   44614

---- Mathematical tables; difference of latitude and departure; logarithms, from 1 to 10.000; and artificial sines, tangents, and secants. Stereotype edition, carefully revised and corrected. Philadelphia, Pub. by Kinber and Sharpless, 1837. 152 p. plates. PPi.
44615

---- A treatise on surveying, containing the theory and practice: to which is prefixed a perspicuous system of plane trigonometry. The whole clearly demonstrated and illustrated by a large number of appropriate examples, particularly adapted to the use of schools. By John Gummere ... 8th ed., improved. Philadelphia, Kimber & Sharpless, 1837. 7-216, 152 p. DLC; PPi; PPL; TBriK; ViU.   44616

Gummere, Samuel R., 1789-1866.
Elementary exercises in geography for the use of the schools. 9th ed. corrected and improved. Philadelphia, Kinber & Sharpless, 1837. 180 p. In; MnDu; PSC-Hi; Vi.   44617

---- The progressive spelling-book, in two parts; containing a great variety of useful exercises in spelling, pronunciation, and derivation; including extensive tables of words deduced from their Greek and Latin roots. The second part arranged on the basis of Butter's etymological spelling-book, by Samuel R. Gummere. Philadelphia, Kimber & Sharpless, 1837. 216 p. PHi; PLFM; PSH-Hi; PU.   44618

Gunn, [John C.]
Gunn's Domestic Medicine, or Poorman's friend, in the hours of Affliction, pain and sickness... Seventh edition. Madisonville, Ten., S. M. Johnston, publisher, 1837. [1], 18-635 p. NcAS; NcD.   44619

---- ---- Ninth edition. Xenia, Ohio, Published by J. Peary, J. H. Purdy, printer, 1837. ICACS; InMuB; OClWHi; OCo; OU.   44620

Gurney, Joseph John, 1788-1847.
A letter to a friend on the authority, purpose, and effects of Christianity, and especially on the doctrine of redemption... Cincinnati, O. Reprinted by Pugh and Dodd, 1837. 35 p. OClWHi; WHi.   44621

---- Sermon and prayer...delivered at Arch Street meeting, on the evening of First-day, 8th month 27th, 1837...Philadelphia, Kay & brother, 1837. 16 p. MH; PHC; PHi; PSC-Hi; WHi.   44622

Gurney, Marie (Rowe), 1802-1868.
Rhymes for my children. By a mother.... Boston, S. Colman, 1837. 108 p. DLC; ICU; MB; NN; RPB.   44623

H

Hagerstown Town and Country
Almanack for 1838. By John
F. Egelmann. Hagerstown, Md.,
J. Gruber, [1837]. MWA. 44624

Hagner, Thomas Holme.
   An address delivered in the
Senate Chamber of Maryland,
before "The Association of the
Theta Delta Phi" of St. John's
College, 4th July, 1837. By
Thomas Holme Hagner....
Annapolis, Printed by J.
Hughes, 1837. 32 p. CtY;
MH; NjP; NNC; ScU.   44625

Haines, John Thomas, 1799?-
1843.
   ...The French spy; or,
The siege of Constantina; a
military drama, in three acts
... New York, Samuel French,
[1837?] 24 p. C; LNH; OCl.
                            44626
Haiti (Republic) Laws, statutes.
   The rural code of Haiti,
literally translated from a publication by the government
press, together with letters
from that country concerning
its present condition. By a
southern planter, Granville,
Middletown, N. J., George H.
Evans, 1837. 46 p. KHi;
MHi; MWA.   44627

Hale, Benjamin, 1797-1863.
   An inaugural address, de-
livered in the chapel of Geneva
College, December 21, 1836.
Geneva, N.Y., printed by J. J.
Mattison, 1837. 31 p. CSmH;
MBAt; NGH; OCHP; RPB. 44628

---- ---- 2d ed. Albany,
Printed by J. Munsell, 1837.
32 p. CtY; MH; NNC; OWoC.
                            44629
Hale, Matthew.

The great audit or good
steward: ... Newport, R.I.,
James Atkinson, printer, 1837.
16 p. RP.   44630

Hale, Salma, 1787-1866.
   History of the United States
from their first settlement as
colonies to the close of the war
with Great Britain in 1815 to
which are added questions
adapted to the use of schools.
Cooperstown, H. & E. Phinney,
1837. 298, 24 p. Ct; MH;
NIP; NP; ViU.   44631

Hale, Sarah Josepha [Buell],
1788-1879.
   Flora's interpreter. 6th ed.
Boston. Mussey, 1837. 254 p.
CoD; IU-P; NPla.   44632

---- The ladies' wreath; a selection from the female poetic
writers of England and America.
With original notices and notes:
prepared especially for young
ladies. A gift-book for all seasons. By Mrs. Hale ... Boston,
Marsh, Capen & Lyon; New York,
D. Appleton & co., 1837. [3]-
408 p. C-S; KyLx; MWA; OO;
TxU.   44633

[Haliburton, Thomas Chandler],
1796-1865.
   The clockmaker; or, The sayings and doings of Samuel Slick,
of Slickville. Philadelphia, Carey,
Lea, and Blanchard, 1837. 218 p.
"First American ed." Also published under titles: Sam Slick,
the clockmaker; and Judge Hali-
burton's Yankee stories.
CaNSWA; CtY; IU; MH.   44634

---- ---- 2d ed. Philadelphia,
Carey, Lea, and Blanchard,
1837. 8, [13]-218 p. ArMor;
CSmH; ICU; MH; PU.   44635

Hall, Edward Brooks.
Hymns for social worship and private devotion. Providence, 1837. 148 p. MB; MH-AH; RPB. 44636

Hall, Francis Russel, 1788-1866.
The errors and history of the Apocrypha, ... Part I-Errors. 3d ed., ... Cambr., 1837. CtY. 44637

Hall, Frederick, 1780-1843.
Notes on a tour in France, Italy, and Elba, with a notice of its mines of iron. By Prof. F. Hall. [New Haven? 1837]. 12 p. DLC. 44638

Hall, James, 1793-1868. Notes on Western States.... See his statistics of the West.

---- Statistics of the West, at the close of the year 1836. By James Hall. Cincinnati, J. A. James & co., 1837. 13-284 p. IaDaP; LN; MnU; PRAt; TxU. 44639

Hall, John, 1783-1847.
Reader's guide. 3d edition. Hartford, Canfield & Robins, etc., etc., 1837. CtHWatK; MH; NjR. 44640

Hall, Louisa Jane (Park), 1802-1892.
Miriam. A dramatic poem. By Mrs. Louisa Jane (Park) Hall. Boston, Hilliard, Gray & co., (Freeman & Bolles, printers.) 1837. 124 p. CtY; LNH; MB; MWA; NjR. 44641

Hall, Samuel Carter, 1800-1889.
The book of gems: the poets and artists of Great Britain. Edited by S. C. Hall. London, Saunders and Otley; Philadelphia, Thomas Wardle,

1837. 304 p. F; FSar. 44642

Hall, Sarah [Ewing], 1761-1830.
Conversations on the Bible between a mother and her children. 5th edition. By Mrs. Sarah Hall. Philadelphia, Hall, 1837. DLC; MH-AH; NjP; OO; PP. 44643

Hallam, Henry, 1777-1859.
View of the state of Europe during the middle ages, by Henry Hallam.... From the sixth London edition, complete in one volume. New York, published by Harper & brothers, 1837. 568 p. KyLo; MdBP; MiD-B; RPB; TxH. 44644

Hallick, Fitz-Greene, 1790-1867.
Fanny. [Verse. Anon.] New York, 1837. MB. 44645

Hallock, William Allen, 1794-1880.
Memoir of Harland Page; or, The power of prayer and personal effort for the souls of individuals. By William A. Hallock. New York, American Tract society, [1837]? [3]-230 p. LNB; PWmpDS. 44646

Halsted, William, d. 1878.
Speech of the Hon. William Halsted, on the bill to authorize the postponement of the payment of the fourth instalment. Delivered in the House of representatives U.S., September 23, 1837. Washington, 1837. 11 p. CtY; MiD-B. 44647

Hamer, Thomas Lyon, 1800-1846.
Speech of Mr. Hamer, of Ohio. (In the House of representatives, March 2, 1837. On the bill making appropriations for the civil and diplomatic expenses of the government for the year 1837). (Washington, 1837.) 8 p. MiU-C; OClWHi; TxU. 44648

---- Speech, on the bill to postpone the fourth instalment of
deposite with the States: delivered in the House of representatives of the U.S., Sept.
25, 1837. Wash., 1837. 16 p.
CtY; MdHi; MnSM; RPB;
TxDaM.   44649

---- Speech...on the resolution of Mr. Wise proposing an
inquiry into the condition of
the executives departments.
Delivered in the house of representatives, Jan. 5, 1837. Washington, Printed at the Globe
office, 1837. 15 p. CtY; NjR;
OClWHi; WHi.   44650

Hamilton, Frank Hastings.
Introductory address, and
catalogue of students attending
the annual course of lectures, on
anatomy and surgery, delivered
by F. H. Hamilton, M.D. Au-
burn, Published by the class,
January, 1837. 16 p. DSG;
MH-M; MBCo; NNNAM; OC.
                         44651
Hamilton, James, d. 1839.
Practical Observations on
Various Subjects Relating to
Midwifery. By James Hamilton,
M.D., F.R.S.E., ... Philadel-
phia, Published by A. Waldie,
1837. (6), 102 p. CtY; ICU;
MeB; PPA; ViU.   44652

Hamilton, William.
A descriptive geography, of
Europe; comprising a description
of that country ... Arranged for
the use of Mr. & Mrs. Hamilton's seminary for young ladies,
Baltimore. ... Baltimore, Printed
by John D. Toy, 1837. 331 p.
MdBP; MdHi; MdW.   44653

Hamilton College.
Catalogue Senatus Academici,
et eorum qui munera et officia

academica gesserunt, quique
aliquo gradu exornati fuerunt,
in Collegio Hamiltoniensi, comitatus Oneidensis, in republica
Neo-Eboracensi. Uticae. Typis
Bennett et Bright, [1837].
16 p. CSmH; N.   44654

Hamilton County, Ohio. Demo-
cratic Citizens.
Resolutions of a number of
Democratic Citizens of Hamilton
County, Ohio, approving the
measures proposed by the execu-
tive, etc. October 10, 1837.
Laid on the table and ordered
to be printed, Blair & Rives,
printers, [1837?] 5 p. Sc.
                         44655
Hammeken, George Louis.
Brief remarks on Dr. Chan-
ning's letter to Hon. Henry
Clay.... Boston, n. pub.,
Marden & Kimball, printers,
1837. 21 p. CtHT; MBAt;
MdBD; RPB; TxU.   44656

Hamon, Andre Jean Marie, 1795-
1874.
The Spirit of St. Francis De
Sales. Translated from the
French of Bishop Camus Fortiter
Et Suavater. New York, P.
O'Shea, 1837. (1) 2-372 p.
KyOwSF.   44657

Hancock. pseud.
Essays on Texas, by Han-
cock. New York, Printed by
Thomas W. McGowran, 1837.
20 p. CU; DLC; NHi; ScU;
TxU.   44658

Handel and Haydn Society. Boston.
Boston Handel and Haydn Society Collection of Church Music,
etc. 17th edition with additions
and improvements. Boston,
Wilkins, 1837. ICN; NcD;
NHerCHi.   44659

Hanging Rock and Lawrence Furnace Railroad Company.

Report of the engineer to the president of the Hanging Rock and Lawrence furnace railroad company; to which is added a letter to R. Hamilton, esq., on the resistance of curves and proposing a remedy. Cincinnati, Printed by R. P. Brooks, 1837. 16, [2] p. CtY; DLC; MH-BA; OClWHi. 44660

Hannah Swanton, the Casco captive; or, The Catholic religion in Canada, and its influence on the Indians of Maine. Written for the Massachusetts Sabbath school society, and rev. by the Committee of publication. Boston, Massachusetts Sabbath school society, 1837. 63 p. CtY. 44661

Hannegan, Edward A. -1859.

Speech ... on the resolution of Mr. Wise proposing an inquiry into the condition of the executive departments; delivered in the House of representatives, Jan. 5, 1837. Washington, printed at the Globe office, 1837. 6 p. InU; TxU; WHi. 44662

Hannett, John, 1803-1893.

Bookbinders school of design, as applied to the combination of tools in the art of finishing. By John Andrews Arnett [pseud.] ... New-York, H. Jackson, [etc., etc.], 1837. MiU. 44663

Hanover College, Hanover, Ind.

Catalogue. 1836-7. South Hanover, 1837. 16 p. CtY; DLC; In; InHC. 44664

Hanscom, William C.

An expose of falsehood and slander, in an appeal to the public ... By Wm. C. Hanscom. ...Concord, printed at the Star & Universalist office, 1837. 12, 2, 60, 4 p. MH; MMeT. 44665

Harbor Island bar, entrance into Core Sound, N.C. Surveyed 1837. No. 1. Washington, Map. PPL-R. 44666

Hare, Edward, 1774-1818.

The principal doctrines of Christianity defended against the errors of Socinianism: being an answer to the Rev. John Grundy's lectures. By Edward Hare. New-York, Pub. by T. Mason and G. Lane, for the Methodist Episcopal church, 1837. 396 p. CLSU; DLC; IaMpI; OO; TCHu. 44667

Hare, Robert, 1781-1858.

Suggestions respecting the reformation of the banking system. By R. Hare, M.D. Philadelphia, J. C. Clark, 1837. 29 p. CLU; MdBJ; MWA; OCHP; ScC. 44668

Harkey, Simeon Walcher, 1811-1889.

True greatness, an address delivered before the Phanakosmian Society of Pennsylvania College...By Rev. S. W. Harkey. Gettysburg, Pa., Robert W. Middleton, 1837. 15 p. MdBP; ScCoT. 44669

Harlan, James, 1800-1863.

Remarks of Mr. Harlan, of Kentucky, on the Mississippi contested election. Delivered in the House of representatives, September 26, 1837. Washington, 1837. 8 p. CtY; DLC. 44670

Harlan, Richard, 1796-1843.

On the affiliation of the natural and physical sciences: being the introduction to "Medical and

physical researches." By R.
Harlan ... Philadelphia, 1837.
31 p. DLC; MH-Z.   44671

Harmonist: being a collection
of tunes from the most approved
authors: adapted to every variety of metre in the Methodist
hymn-book.... New ed., in
patent notes-rev. and greatly
enl. Wm. C. Brown & others,
comp. New York, Published by
T. Mason & G. Lane, for the
Methodist Episcopal church, at
the conference office.... James
Collord, printer, 1837. 384 p.
DLC; IEG; NBu; OClWHi; WHi.
                          44672
Harney, John H.
    Party Spirit: An Address
before The Society of Alumni of
Hanover College, at their Second Anniversary, Sept. 27,
1837. By John H. Harney,
A.M. South Hanover, Ind.
Published for the Society,
Printed by James Morrow, 1837.
13 p. CSmH; In: MWA; OCHP;
PPPRHi.   44673

Harrington, Henry F, 1835.
    Marian. A play, in five
acts. By the author of Ber-
narde del Carpio," and "Francisco, the avenger." N.p.
[1837?] 38 p. MB.   44674

Harrington, John.
    Letter to the Rev. John Har-
rington in reply to his Sermon
on Baptism. Charleston, W.
Riley, 1837. [3]-32 p. LNB.
                          44675
Harris, Isaac, comp.
    General business directory
of the cities of Pittsburgh &
Alleghany, with the environs.
1837, 1839, 1841, 1844, 1847.
Pittsburgh, Pa., Published by
Isaac Harris, (1837-47). MH;
NBu: OClWHi; PPi; PSeW. 44676

---- Harris' Pittsburgh business
directory.... See Harris's General
business directory of the cities of
Pittsburgh and Allegheny.

Harris, John, 1802-1856.
    The great teacher: charac-
teristics of Our Lord's ministry:
by the Rev. John Harris, with
an introductory essay, by He-
man Humphrey, D.D....Third
edition. Amherst, J. S. & C.
Adams, 1837. 444 p. CU; ICU;
MoSpD; NNUT.   44677

---- Mammom: or, Covetousness
the Sin of the Christian Church.
By Rev. John Harris. Boston,
Gould, Kendall & Lincoln, 1837.
261 p. MChiA.   44678

---- ---- New York, American
tract society, [1837]. 291 p.
CtHT; IAIS; OMC; TxAuPT;
ViU.   44679

---- ---- Second American, from
the tenth London edition. Boston, Gould, Kendall & Lincoln,
... 1837. 261 p. ArCH; GDecCT;
ICBB; TNB; ViRut.   44680

---- ---- Third American from
the twentieth London edition.
Boston, Gould, Kindall and
Lincoln, 1837. 261 p. ICU;
MeBat: NjMD; PCA; TxH.
                          44681
---- Zebulon; or, The moral
claims of seamen stated and en-
forced. By Rev. John Harris.
Boston, Gould, Kendall and
Lincoln, 1837. (2) 20-115 p.
CU; GDecCT; MH; MPiB; PPiW;
RNHi.   44682

Harris, Thomas, 1784-1861.
    The life and services of Com-
modore William Bainbridge, United
States navy. By Thomas Harris
... Philadelphia, Carey, Lea &

Blanchard, 1837. [17]-254 p.
Ct; LU; NcD; ScCC; WaU.
44683

Harrisburg, Portsmouth, Mount
Joy & Lancaster R. R. Company.
Reports. Philadelphia, 1837- .
PHi. 44684

Harrison, John Pollard.
An address, delivered at the
twelfth anniversary celebration
of the Union literary society of
Miami university, August 8th,
1837. Oxford, Ohio, Bishop,
1837. 21 p. ICU; MoKU; NN;
OClWHi; PPiU. 44685

---- Oration guidance of a
sound philosophical spirit in
concerning the investigations
of medical science. ... by
John P. Harrison, M.D., ...
Cincinnati, Published by Truman and Smith. Printed by
A. Pugh, 1837. 22 p. IEN-M;
MBAt; NNNAM; PU. 44686

Hartford, Conn. Phoenix Bank.
Report of a committee ap-
pointed to inquire into the condition and management of the
bank. Hartford, 1837. 8 p.
MBC. 44687

---- Public High School.
Catalogue of the trustees,
instructors, and pupils of the
Hartford, Grammar School.
October, 1837. Hartford,
Printed by Case, Tiffany and
Company, 1837. 12 p. CTHWatk.
44688

Hartwick synod of the Evangelical Lutheran church in the
state of New York.
The Augsburg confession,
with explanatory notes and observations, by a committee of
the Hartwick synod of the
Evangelical Lutheran church in
the state of New-York. Troy,

N.Y., Tuttle, Belcher & Burton,
printers, 1837. 30 p. DLC; N;
RPB. 44689

Harvard University.
Catalogue. Cambridge, Folsom, Wells, and Thurston,
Printers to the University, 1837.
38 p. MS. 44690

---- A catalogue of officers and
students of Harvard University
for the academical year 1837-38.
Printed by Folsom, Wells &
Thurston, Cambridge, 1837.
38 p. MeAug; MiU-C. 44691

---- ... Order of performances
for exhibition, Tuesday, October
17, 1837. Cambridge, Folsom,
Wells, and Thurston, printers
to the university, 1837. 3 p.
MdBJ. 44692

---- Orders and regulations of
the faculty of Harvard university. Cambridge, Folsom, Wells,
and Thurston, Printers, 1837.
13, [1] p. MHC; MiU-C.
44693
---- Statutes and laws of Harvard university relative to under-
graduates. Boston, Folsom,
Wells, and Thurston, printers,
1837. 42 p. MH; NNUT.
44694
---- Class of 1837.
Valedictory Exercises of the
senior class of 1837. Tuesday,
July 18th, 1837. BdSe. MHi.
44695
---- Pierian Sodality.
Report made at a meeting of
the honorary and immediate members of the Pierian Sodality, in
Harvard University, Cambridge,
August 30th, 1837, with a record
of the meeting. Cambridge, 1837.
16 p. MHi. 44696

Harvey, Joseph, 1787-1873.

An examination of the Pelagian and Armenian theory of moral agency as recently advocated by Dr. Beecher in his "Views in theology." Hartford, Case, Tiffany & co., 1837. 223 p. RPB. 44697

---- ---- New York, Ezra Collier, 1837. 223 p. CtHT; ICP; NbOP; OClW; PPPrHi. 44698

Haskins, William L.
Considerations on the project and institution of a guarantee company, on a new plan; with some general views on credit, confidence, and currency. New York, Felt, 1837. 48 p. DLC; MB; MH-BA; PU. 44699

Hastings, Thomas, 1784-1872.
Christian psalmist; or, Watts' psalms and hymns; with copious selections from other sources, the whole carefully rev. and arr. ... by Th. Hastings and Wm. Patton, New York, Collier, 1837. 626 p. NcSalL; RPB. 44700

---- The Manhattan collection of psalm and hymn tunes and anthems. .... New York, E. Collier and Gould & Newman, 1837. 352 p. IEG; MB; MeHi; MiU; MPiB. 44701

---- Spiritual songs, for social worship: Adapted to the use of families and private circles in seasons of revival, to missionary meetings, to the monthly concert, and other occasions of special interest. Words and music arranged by Thomas Hastings, of New-York, and Lowell Mason, of Boston. Fifth edition. Utica, Gardiner Tracy; New-York, Robinson, Pratt & Co., F. J. Huntington & Co., Leavitt, Lord & Co., and E.

Collier, 1837. 328 p. DLC; IaDa; MBC; NUt; OCoC. 44702

Hatfield, Edwin Francis, 1807-1883.
What teachers ought to be. A sermon addressed to the general association of Sunday school teachers in New York. Nov. 13, 1836. New York, John Gray, pr. 1837. 14 p. CtY; IaGG; MB; PPAmS; PPPrHi. 44703

Havana Journal. Printed Havana (Montour Falls) 39 binders covering period, 1837-42. 1849-51. 1853-55. 1857-93. Papers from 1849-1919 include Havana Republican. Free Press and Havana Journal in binder. Montour Falls, 1837-1919. NMonto. 44704

Haven, Samuel Foster, 1806-1881.
An historical address delivered before the citizens of the town of Dedham, on the twenty-first of September, 1836, being the second centennial anniversary of the incorporation of the town. By Samuel F. Haven. Dedham, Printed by H. Mann, 1837. 79 p. ICN; MH; MiD; PPAmP; RHi. 44705

Haverhill Academy, Mass.
A Catalogue of the Officers and Students of Haverhill Academy. for the year ending November, 1837. Concord, Printed by Asa Mc Farland, 1837. 9 p. NGH. 44706

Hawes, Joel, 1789-1867.
Discourse at the dedication of the North Congregational church, New Bedford, Dec. 22, 1836. Boston, Leavett, Lord & Co., 1837. 33 p. ICN; MBC; RPB. 44707

---- A discourse, Dec. 20, 1836, at the installation of John Storrs in Holliston, Mass. Boston, Leavett, Lord & Co., 1837. 34 p. Ct; MBNEH; MeBat; MWA; RPB. 44708

---- Lectures to young men, on the formation of character, &c. .... 11th ed. Hartford, Belknap and Hamersly, 1837. 172 p. NbCrD; OMC. 44709

Hawes, Noyes Payson.
The United States spelling book, and English orthoepist, ... by Noyes P. Hawes. Belfast, [Me.], published by John Dorr, 1837. 232 p. NNC. 44710

Hawks, Francis Lister.
History of the United States #11 or Uncle Philip's Conservation with children about New York. New York, Harper & Brothers, 1837. 2 v. xi & 13-204. 196(10) p. NICLA. 44711

---- Poems, hitherto uncollected. By Francis Lister Hawks. New York, Privately printed by Charles L. Morean, 1837. 27 p. NcU. 44712

Hawley, Silas.
Sermon on God's method of drawing sinners to Christ... Cazenovia, [N.Y.] 1837. CSmH; RPB. 44713

Hawthorne, Nathaniel, 1804-1864.
Twice-told tales.... Boston, American stationers co., 1837. 334 p. CtY; DLC; MH; NN; PU. 44714

---- ---- New York, Thomas Y. Crowell and co., 1837. 534 p. FAp; IC. 44715

Haydn, Joseph, 1732-1809.
Westborough. Mighty-God, Eternal Father.... Boston, 1837. 11 p. MB. 44716

---- The words of the creation. An Oratorio. By Joseph Haydn. As performed by the Baltimore musical association. 1837. Baltimore, J. W. Woods, 1837. MdHi; NNUT; PPL. 44717

Hayes, Alexander, 1793- .
The Annual Address Delivered before the Belles-Lettres and Union Philosophical Societies of Dickinson College, Carlisle Pa., July 19, 1837. By the Hon. A.L. Hayes. Published at the request of both Societies, Washington, Printed by Gales and Seaton, 1837. DLC; KyLx; MHi; NCH; PPL. 44718

Hayne (Arthur P.).
A Brief Sketch of the Life and Military Services of Arthur P. Hayne, of Charleston, South Carolina. Philadelphia, Printed by T. K. & P. G. Collins, 1837. 16 p. ICN; MB; MHi; PPAmP; Sc. 44719

Haynes, Charles Eaton, 1784-1841.
Remarks of Mr. Haynes of Georgia, on the bill imposing additional duties, as depositories in certain cases, on public officers. Delivered in the House of Representatives, October 12, 1837. [Washington, 1837]. 8 p. CtY; DLC; NNC; ViW. 44720

Hayward, George.
A discourse on some of the diseases of the knee-joints; delivered before the Massachusetts Medical Society, at their annual meeting, May 31, 1837. Boston, Whipple, 1837. 28 p. DS-G; NNNAM; OC; RPB. 44721

Hazen, Edward.
Das deutsche sinnbildliche
A B C buechlein; oder, Erstes
buch fuer kinder. Philadelphia,
Walker, 1837. 35 p. PU. 44722

---- The panorama of profes-
sions and trades; on every
Mans book. By Edward Hazen,
.... Philadelphia, Published by
Uriah Hunt, 1837. [13]-320 p.
ICJ; KyLOS; MH; NjR; OClWHi.
44723
Hazen, Nathan W.
An address before the Essex
Agricultural Society, at Danvers,
September 28, 1836, at their an-
nual Cattle Show. By Nathan
W. Hazen. Published by order
of the Society. Salem, Printed
at the Gazette Office, 1837.
(3)-23 p. MB; MWA.   44723a

Heath, William, 1795-1840.
Pickwickian illustrations.
New York, Published by Thomas
McClean, 1837. 20 etchings.
MoSW.   44724

Heaven: or, conversations be-
tween a mother and her child
in relation to the world of glory.
Boston, Mass., Sabbath School
Society, 1837. 68 p. MNF.
44725
Hecker, Justus Friedrick Karl,
1795-1850.
The black death ... trans-
lated by B. G. Babington.
Philadelphia, Pa., 1837. MdBM.
44726
---- The dancing mania.
Translated by B. G. Babing-
ton. Philadelphia, Pa., 1837.
MdBM.   44727

---- The epidemic of the middle
ages: from the German of
J. F. C. Hecker ... trans. by
B. G. Babington. Philadelphia,
Haswell, Barrington, and Has-

well, 1837. 2 v. in 1. CSt-L;
ICU; MiU; NjR; P.   44728

Hedding, Elijah, 1780-1852.
The substance of an address,
delivered to the Oneida annual
conference...August 31; and to
the Genesee conference, September 21, 1837...By Elijah Hedding...To which is annexed,
Thoughts on evil speaking, by
the same: together with a Report on slavery, adopted by the
Genesee conference at its late
session. Auburn, N.Y., Printed
at the office of Auburn banner,
1837. 28 p. CSmH; DeWi; MoS;
N.   44729

Hedge, Levi, 1766-1844.
Elements of logick; or, a sum-
mary of the general principles
and different modes of reasoning.
By Levi Hedge...Boston, Hilliard,
Gray and Co., 1837. 178 p.
MeB.   44730

Hegenberg, F. A.
Lehrbuch der zahlen arith-
metik buchstaben rechnenkunst
und algebra. New ed. Balti-
more, Scheld, 1837. 2 v. PU.
44731
Hegewisch, Dietrich Hermann,
1746-1812.
Introduction to historical
chronology, by D. H. Hegewisch
... Tr. from the German, by
James Marsh. Burlington [Vt.],
C. Goodrich, 1837. 144 p.
CtMW; IaGG; NNUT; OClW; WU.
44732
Heidelberg Catechism.
The Heidelberg Catechism.
Translated from German. Cham-
bersburg, Pa., Printed by Henry
Ruby, 1837. 72 p. P; PLERC-Hi;
PPeSchw.   44733

---- The Heidelberg catechism,
or method of instruction in the

Christian religion. Tr. from
the German. Philadelphia,
Mentz, 1837. PPPrHi.   44734

---- Der Heidelberger Kate-
chismus, sammt auszügen aus
der Kircehn-ordnung....Der
Deutsch Reformirten Kirche
....Chambersburg, Pa., Verlag von John Smith....1837.
92 p. PRHi.   44735

Heine, Heinrich, 1797-1865.
Das Buch der Lieder. xiv,
186 p. New York, E. Steiger
& co., [1837]. OCl.   44736

Heistand, Henry.
Travels in Germany, Prussia,
and Switzerland. By Rev. Henry Heistand ... Edited by a
minister of the gospel in New
York. New York, J. S. Taylor,
1837. 199 p. ICBB; ICP; LNB;
RPAt; ViAl.   44737

Helfenstein, J. C. Alburtus.
A collection of choice sermons,
by the Rev. J. C. Alburtus
Helfenstein. Translated from
the German by I. Daniel Rapp.
Carlisle, Published by Rev.
Charles Helfenstein, George
Fleming, Printer, 1837. 261 p.
PPLT.   44738

Hemans, Felicia Dorothea
Browne, 1793-1835.
The Poetical works of Mrs.
Hemans. Philadelphia, Thomas
T. Ash and company, 1837.
2 v. FSar; MH; NcAs; PSeW;
ScU.   44739

Hendee, Charles J.
The first book of history;
for children and youth. With
60 engravings and 16 maps.
Boston, [1837]. 181 p. NBuHi.
      44740
Henke, Heinrich Philipp Konrad,

1752-1809.
Handbuch Allgemeinen Seo-
chichts. Philadelphia, bei Rider-
len und Stollmeyer, 1837. (9)
3-606 p. KyDC.   44741

Henry, Caleb Sprague, 1804-1884.
A compendium of Christian
antiquities: being a brief view
of the orders, rites, laws and
customs of the ancient church
in the early ages. By the Rev.
C. S. Henry, A.M. Philadelphia,
Joseph Whetham, 1837. 332 p.
CtHC; LNB; MBC; NjR; PU;
ScCC.   44742

---- A discourse before the Phi
Sigma Nu Society of the Univer-
sity of Vermont. 2nd Ed. New
York, Published by George W.
Holley, Burlington, N.J., Printed
by J. L. Powell, 1837. 44 p.
MBC; NjR; PPL.   44743

---- The importance of exalting
the intellectual spirit of the nation; and need of a learned
class; a discourse pronounced
before the Phi Sigma Nu society
of the university of Vermont,
Aug. 3, 1836.... Ed. 2. New
York, George W. Holley, 1837.
44 p. CTHWatk; MBAt; MHi;
NN; WHi.   44744

Henry, George.
Nu-gu-mo-nun O-je-boa an-oad
ge-e-se-iiu-ne-gu-noo-du-be-iing
uoo Muun-gou-duuz [George Hen-
ry] gu-ea Moo-ge-gee-seg [James
Evans] ge-ge-noo-ii-muu-ga-oe-
ne-ne-oug. New York, printed
by D. Fanshaw, 1837. DLC;
CaOTP; MBAt; NBu; NN.
      44745
(Henshaw, David), 1791-1852.
Remarks upon the rights &
powers of corporations and of the
rights, powers, & duties of the
legislature toward them. Embrac-

ing a review of the opinion of
the Supreme Court of the United
States, in the case of Dartmouth
College...1819. By a citizen
of Boston. Boston, Beals &
Greene, 1837. 31 p. InHi;
MH; PPL; ScU; WU.   44746

Henslow, John Stevens.
  A reformer's duty. An ad-
dress to the reformers of the
town of Cambridge. By the
Rev. J. S. Henslow, ...
Cambridge, Printed by Metcalf
& Palmer, 1837. 27 p. ICJ.
                             44747
Herald and Star, The. Semi-
weekly ... (Boston) Harring-
ton & co., 1837. 1 v. MB.
                             41748

Herald of truth. Devoted to
the incalculations and defence
of universal and impartial
grace ... V. 1-4; April 27,
1834-December 29, 1837. Geneva, N.Y. [I. Prescott, etc.],
1834-1836; Rochester [etc.],
G. Sanderson, 1837. DLC; MH-
AH; NN.   44749

Herbert, George.
  The temple and the country
parson; with his life abridged
from Isaac Walton. By George
Herbert. Boston, David H.
Ela, 1837. MA; MH; MWfo; NN.
                             44750
The Heretic detector. A month-
ly publication ... conducted by
Arthur Crihfield. Middleburgh,
Logan co., O., 1837-1841. 5 v.
No more published. OClWHi.
                             44751
Herg, Henri.
  Night at sea. (Song with
pianoforte acc.) Phila., Fiot
Meignen & Co., (1837). 3 p.
MB.   44752

Hering, Constantin, 1800-1880.

Homopathischer hausarzt f
d deutschen burger der vereinig-
ten staaten nach den desten
aderlandischen werken. Phila-
delphia, I. G. Wesselhoeft, 1837.
DLC; DSG; PPeSchW; PPHa.
                             44753
Herring, James.
  Eulogy on M. W. Major-general
Jacob Morton and M. W. Elisha
W. King, esquire, past grand
masters, pronounced in St.
Mathew's church, New York,
June 7th, 1837 ... By James
Herring, grand secretary. New-
York, Printed by George F. Nes-
bitt, 1837. 26 p. NNFM; PPFM.
                             44754
Herring, James, 1794-1867.
  The National portrait gallery
of distinguished Americans. Con-
ducted by James B. Longacre
and James Herring. Philadelphia,
J. B. Longacre, [etc.], 1837-
1846. 4 v. DLC; MWA; PPL-R;
ViU.   44755

Hersey, John, 1786-1862.
  The importance of small things;
or, A plain course of self-examination to which is added, Signs
of the times. Baltimore, Armstrong & Berry, 1837. [9]-299
p. MdHi.   44756

[Hewson, John], b. 1768?
  An oration, pronounced on
the twenty-fifth of December,
1835, on the character, nature
and attributes of Jesus Christ,
in the Second Baptist meeting
house of Philadelphia, by an
orthodox believer in divine revelation ... 4th ed., embellished
with nine plates. Baltimore,
Printed by Bull & Tuttle, 1837.
72 p. DLC; NN; PPPrHi.
                             44757
Heyrick, Elizabeth.
  ... Immediate, not gradual
abolition, by Elizabeth Heyrick ...

Philadelphia, Published by the Philadelphia A.S. society, Merrihew and Gunn, printers, 1837. 35 p. Ct; DLC; MdBJ; NN-Sc. 44758

Hickok, John Hoyt, 1792-1841.
Evangelical musick; or, the sacred minstrel and sacred harp united. By J. H. Hickok and Geo. Fleming. Philadelphia, Pa., Published by J. Whetham. C. Dingley, 1837. 312 p. PPLT; PWW. 44759

Hiestand, Henry, b. 1788.
Travels in Germany, Prussia and Switzerland. By Rev. Henry Hiestand. Including some account of his early life, conversion, and ministerial labours in the United States. Edited by a minister of the gospel in New-York. New York, J. S. Taylor, 1837. 199 p. CtY; LNH; MeBaT; NBuG; ViU.
44760

Higham, Robert.
Auburn and Rochester rail road. Report, made Oct. 3, 1837, to the directors of the Auburn and Rochester railroad company. By Robert Higham, engineer, &c. Canandaigua, Printed by D.C.M. Rupp, 1837. 1 p. ℓ., 8 p. CSmH; DLC; DBRE; NNE; NRU. 44761

[Hildreth, Richard], 1807-1865.
Brief remarks on Miss Catherine E. Beecher's essay on slavery and abolitionism. By the author of Archy Moore. Boston, Isaac Knapp, 1837. 28 p. MB; MBC; MH; OClWHi; PHi. 44762

---- The history of banks: to which is added, a demonstration of the advantages and necessity of free competition in the business of banking. Boston, Hilliard, Gray & company, 1837. (5)-142 p. ICU; LNH; MiD-B; MnHi; OO; RHi. 44763

[Hildreth, Samuel Prescott, 1783-1863].
Miscellaneous observations made during a tour in May, 1835 to the falls of the Cuyahoga, near Lake Erie: extracted from the diary of a naturalist. From the American Journal of Science, v. 3, 1837. N. Haven, 1837. 84 p. MH; WHi. 44764

Hill, Isaac, 1788-1851.
Message of Isaac Hill, Governor of New Hampshire to both Houses of the legislature. June session....Concord, n. pub. Cyrus Barton, pr., 1837. 22 p. NjR. 44765

Hilliard, Francis, 1808?-1878.
A digest of Pickering's reports, volumes viii-xiv inclusive, by Francis Hilliard. Boston, Otis, Broaders & Co., 1837. 1, [2], vii, 350 p. DLC; MH; MHi; NhD. 44766

Hilliard, Gray & Company.
A select Catalogue of Books. Hilliard, Gray, & Co. Boston, 1837. 96 p. MB; MHi. 44767

Hinton, Isaac Taylor.
A discourse delivered in the Baptist Church, Chicago, November 26, 1837. By Isaac Taylor Hinton. Occasioned by the murder of the Rev. E. P. Lovejoy. Chicago, Published by B. H. Clift, 1837. 14 p. MH-And; MiD-B; MoSM. 44768

An historical account of the circumnavigation of the globe and of the progress of discovery in the Pacific ocean. New York,

Harper and Brothers, 1837.
366 p. FTU; LNH; MB; NbOM;
WaU.   44769

The History of Edwin Forrest,
the celebrated American
tragedian, from his childhood
to his present elevated station
as a performer. Written by an
individual who has known him
from his boyhood. New York,
printed and published for the
author, 1837. 24 p. MB; MH.
                                44770
History of Haman and Mordecai.
Compiled by a friend to youth,
for their entertainment and instruction. New York, M. Day,
1837. 46 p. DLC.   44771

The History of Insects. Concord, John F. Brown, 1837.
15 p. DLC; MH; RPB.   44772

The history of insects, and
God made everything that
creepeth upon the earth....
Portland, Bailey & Noyes,
[1837?] 15, (1) p. MeHi.
                                44773
The history of Rome. Philadelphia, Carey, Lea & Blanchard,
1837. 496 p. CtY; IaK; MH;
PPA; ViU.   44774

History of the Federal and Democratic parties in the United
States, from their origin to the
present time .... by a citizen
of Wayne county, Indiana.
Richmond, published for the
Richmond democratic association,
1837. 56 p. CSmH; In; NcU;
ScU; WHi.   44775

History of the wanderings of
Tom Starboard. New-York,
Mahlon Day, 1837. 79 p. CtY;
MH.   44776

Hitchcock, Edward, 1793-1864.

An argument for early temperance; addressed to the youth of
the United States. By Edward
Hitchcock, professor of chemistry and natural hsitory in Amherst College... Boston, published by Whipple and Damrell.
New York, Scofield and Voorhies,
1837. 89 p. CtHC; DLC; MBC;
MDeeP; PPPrHi.   44777

Hiwassee Rail Road Company.
   Charter, together with the
by laws, adapted by the directory
for the government of the Hiwassee Railroad Company... Athens,
Tennessee Journal Office, 1837.
13 p. NN.   44778

---- 1st quarterly report of the
President to the directory; and
the report of the Engineer in
chief; also an address of the
Board of directors to the stock-
holders, and to the citizens of
East Tenn. Athens, 1837.
MBAT; WU.   44779

---- Memorial of ... to the general assembly of Tennessee.
October 2, 1837, to which is
appended the report of the engineer, in chief. Nashville, S.
Nye and Co., 1837. DLC; MBAt;
NN.   44780

Hoare, Charles James, 1781-1865.
   A charge delivered to the
clergy of the Archdeaconry of
Winchester, in April, 1837.
...Winchester, Jacob & Johnson,
1837. 31 p. CtY; IEG; MnU.
                                44781
Hoare, Clement.
   A practical treatise on the cul-
tivation of the grape vine on open
walls. By Clement Hoare; 1st
Amer. ed. Boston, William D.
Ticknor, 1837. 137 p. MBAt;
MNBedf; MWA; NjR; PU. 44782

Hoban, James.

Speech of James Hoban...
one of the counsel of John
Williams, Oculist, before the
circuit court of the District of
Columbia, for the County of
Washington, on Thursday, the
fifth day of Jan. 1837. Washington, Published at the request of the bar, 1837. 16 p.
MBAt; MH-L; MWA; MWH; PPB;
ScU.   44783

Hobart, John Henry, 1775-1830.

A Companion for the Altar;
or, week's preparation for the
Holy Communion: consisting of
a Short Explanation of the
Lord's Supper, and Meditation
and Prayers, proper to be used
before and during the receiving
of the Holy Communion; according to the form prescribed by
the Protestant Episcopal Church
in the United States of America. By John Henry Hobart,
D.D., Bishop of the Protestant
Episcopal Church in the State
of New York. Stereotyped by
A. Chandler, New York, Swords,
Stanford & Co., 1837. 244 p.
ScCMu.   44784

---- The Churchman, the principles of the church-man stated
and explained in distinction
from the corruptions of the
church of Rome, and from the
errors of certain Protestant
sects ... New York, 1837.
15 p. CtHT; IES; MBC; NN;
WNaE.   44785

---- The high churchman vin-
dicated: in a fourth charge to
the clergy of the protestant
Episcopal church in the state
of New York, on Tuesday,
Oct. 17, 1826. New York,
Published, by the Protestant
Episcopal Tract Society, 1837.

12 p. CtHC; CtHT; NN; VtU;
WHi.   44786

Hobart College. Geneva, N.Y.

Course of study &c. This
course of study being, in some
respects, different from that
heretofore followed, is adopted
in full with the freshman class;
with the others, as far as practicable. Ira Merrell, Pr inter,
Seneca Street, Geneva, [1837.]
15 p. CtY; DLC; MiU-C; MWA;
N.   44787

Der Hochdeutsche Amerikansiche
Calender auf das Jahr 1838.
Philadelphia, Gedruckt und zu
haben bey Wm. W. Kalker, Phila-
delphia, 1837. 34 p. PReaHi.
                                        44788
Hoch-Deutsche Germantaun Calen-
der for 1838. By Carl F. Egel-
mann. Philadelphia, Pa., Wm.
W. Walker, [1837]. MWA.
                                        44789
Hocking Valley Canal Company.

Rules and specifications relating to the construction of
the Hocking Valley canal, and
estimating of work performed
thereon. Athens, O., A. Van
Vorhes, printer, 1837. 23 p.
CSmH; DLC; OClWHi; OHi.
                                        44790
Hodges, Rufus.

Record of the families in New
England of the name of Hodges
... Cincinnati, Published by Rufus
Hodges, 1837. 22 p. DLC;
MWA; NBLIHI; OClWHi; WHi.
                                        44791
[Hoffman, Charles Fenno], 1806-
1884, ed.

The New-York book of poetry
... New-York, G. Dearborn,
1837. 253 p. Added t.-p.,
engraved, with vignette. "By
natives of the state of New York."
CtMW; IEG; McU; PWW; RPA.
                                        44792

Hoffman, David.
Introductory lectures, and syllabus of a course of lectures. Baltimore, John D. Toy, 1837. DLC; MdBB. 44793

---- Miscellaneous thoughts on men, manners, and things; by Anthony Grumbler ... Baltimore, Coale & co., 1837. [9]-374 p. DLC; MB; MdBE; MiD; OMC. 44794

[Holbrook, Josiah], 1788-1854.
A Familiar treatise on the fine arts, embracing painting, sculpture, and music; with sketches of the lives of the most celebrated masters. 2d ed. Boston, J. B. Dow, 1837. MH. 44795

Holdick, Joseph, 1804-1893.
Questions on the Historical part of the Old Testament for the use of Bible Classes by Rev. J. Holdich, A.M. New York, T. Mason & G. Lane, 1837. 194 p. KyBvU. 44796

Holding, Archibald, Tomlinson, 1787-1837.
Confession of Adam Jones [alias of A. T. Holding] who was executed for the murder of William S. Thomas, a money dealer and broker, in the city of Louisville. Louisville, Ky., D. Holcomb, printer, 1837. 36 p. DLC; MWA. 44797

Holiday present.
Being a variety of stories for children... Newark, N.J., Olds., 1837. 127 p. MB. 44798

Holland, Henry, 1788-1873.
Medical notes & reflections. Philadelphia, 1837. PhGenlHos. 44799

Holley, Myron, 1779-1841.
Address delivered before the Rochester Anti-slavery Society, on the 19th January, and again, by request of several citizens, at the Court House, in Rochester, on the 5th February, 1837. By Myron Holly. Rochester, Hoyt and Porter, 1837. 22 p. CtHT; MH; NIC; NNG; NRHi. 44800

Holliston Academy. Holliston, Mass.
A catalogue of the instructors and students of the Holliston Manual Labor School. Fall, Winter and Spring Terms. 1836-7. Dedham, Printed by Herman Mann, 1837. 12 p. MWHi. 44801

Holman, James T.
Form Book, adapted to the use of lawyers, clerks, sheriffs, justices of the peace, constables and private citizens, with a memorandum of the principal English statutes in force and use in the state of Tennessee. By James T. Holman, attorney at Law, and Preston Hay, Esq. Nashville, S. Nye & co. printers, 1837. 255 p. MH-L; T; TN. 44802

Holmes, Abiel, 1763-1837.
Indian copy of the Hebrew Pentateuch. Boston, 1837. MB. 44803

Holt, Edwin.
Anecdotes of Christian missions: compiled, at the request of the Executive committee of the Southern board of foreign missions, by the Rev. Edwin Holt. Boston, Crocker & Brewster, 1837. 282 p. CtY; GDecCT; MH; NBLIHI; OO. 44804

---- Spiritual nature of Christ's kingdom. A sermon preached at the installation of the Rev. Andrew Rankin, over the Congregational Society in South-Berwick, Me. March 1, 1837. By Edwin

Holt, pastor of the North Church in Portsmouth. Portsmouth, Printed by C. W. Brewster, 1837. 23 p. CSmH; MBC; MMet-Hi; Nh. 44805

Homerus.
The Iliad of Homer, from the text of Wolf, with English notes and Flaxman's designs. Edited by C. C. Felton. Boston, Hilliard, Gray and co., 1837. 476 p. CtY; GHi; MoSW; NhD; PU. 44806

Hood, W.
Map illustrating the plan of the defences of the Western and North-west frontier as proposed by J. R. Poinsett. Dec. 30, 1837. Washington, [1837]. 1 p. PHi. 44807

Hook, Theodore Edward, 1788-1841.
Cousin William, and the man of many Friends. N(ew) Y(ork), 1837. MH. 44808

---- The humorist. Ed. by Theodore Hook. Philadelphia, E. L. Carey & A. Hart, 1837. (7)-193 p. CtY; IEG; MH; NcD; RWe. 44809

---- Jack Brag. By the author of "Sayings and doings" ... Philadelphia, Carey, Lea, and Blanchard, 1837. 2 v. in 1. MiDSH; NN; NNC; PHi; TxFTC. 44810

Hooker, Edward William, 1794-1875.
Love to the doctrines of the Bible an essential element of Christian character, by Rev. Edward W. Hooker. Philadelphia, Presbyterian Tract and Sunday School Society, 1837. 18 p. ICP; ICU; NjPT; OCHP; PPPrHi. 44811

Hopkins, John Henry, 1792-1868.
The Church of Rome, in her primitive purity, compared with the Church of Rome, at the present day... By John Henry Hopkins. Burlington, Vernon Harrington, 1837. 406 p. CtHC; KTW; PPP; TxHR; VtB. 44812

Hopkins, Mark, 1802-1887.
A discourse occasioned by the death of the Rev. Edward Dorr Griffin...November 26, 1837 in the chapel of Williams College...Troy, N.Y., Tuttle, Belcher & Burton, printers, 1837. CtHC; ICT; MiGr; PHi; RPB. 44813

---- Influence of the Gospel in liberalizing the mind. An address .... before the Porter rhetorical society of the Theological seminary....By Mark Hopkins, D.D.....Andover, Gould and Newman, n.pr., 1837. 19 p. CtY; MBC; MH; NjR; RPB. 44814

---- Troy, N.Y., n. pub., N. Tuttle, printer, 1837. 19 p. CtHC; MH-And; MHi; NCH; NjR; ScU. 44815

Hopkins, William R.
Report on the new town at the foot of Lake Huran. Geneva, N.Y., 1837. 19 p. MiGr; N. 44816

Hopkinson, Joseph, 1770-1842.
In the case of Robert Morris, a bankrupt. [Feb. 3d., 1837. Philadelphia? J. and W. Kile, printers, 1837] 20 p. NIC. 44817

Hopper, Isaac Tatem, 1771-1852.
Narrative of the life of Thomas Cooper. 4th ed. N.Y., published by Isaac T. Hooper, 1837. 35 p. CSfCP; DHU; MCR; MBC; MH. 44818

Hoppus, John.

The continent in 1835, sketches in Belgium, Germany, Switzerland, Savoy, and France. By John Hoppus. New York, Theodore Foster, 1837. 340 p. DLC; MH; NNUT; RPAt; TxU.   44819

Horn, Charles Edward, 1786-1849.
They say thou has forsaken me! .... Rosy .... New York, Dubois and Bacon, 1837. MB.
44820

Horne, Thomas Hartwell, 1780-1862.
Compendious introd. to the study of the Bible: being an analysis of "an introd. to the critical study of knowledge of the Holy Scriptures" in four Vols. by the Same author. New York, T. Mason & G. Lane, 1837. 391 p. GAuP; ILM; KWiU; PPC; ScC.   44821

Hornyold, John Joseph, 1706-1778.
The real principle of Catholics, or, A catechism of general instruction for grown persons: explaining the principle points of the doctrine and ceremonies of the Catholic Church, by the Right Rev. Dr. Hornihold. Philadelphia, Eugene Cummiskey, 1837. 329 p. IaDuC; MdBS; ScClip; WStfSF.
44822

Horse-racing, and christian principle and duty, incompatible. Charleston, 1837. 23 p. DLC; MH.   44823

Horticultural society of Maryland.
Constitution and by-laws of the Horticultural society of Maryland. Baltimore, Printed by Joseph Robinson, 1837. 28 p. MdHi.   44824

Horton, George Moses, 1798?-ca. 1880.
Hope of liberty; or, poems by a slave. 2d. ed. Phila., 1837. 21 p. NcU; OO.   44825

The hours of childhood: a poem ... New York, Printed by J. F. Trow, 1837. 24 p. DLC; RPB.
44826
The house keeper's book...with a complete collection of receipts for economical domestic cookery ...the whole carefully prepared for the use of American housekeepers by a lady. Philadelphia, Marshall, 1837. 217 p. DLC; NN; PP.   44827

Howard, Edward, d. 1841. Midshipman's expedients.... See under title.

---- The old commodore. By the author of "Rattlin the reefer," &c.... In two volumes.... Philadelphia, Carey, Lea & Blanchard, 1837. 2 v. CtHT; MBL; OrP; RPB; TNP.   44828

---- Rattlin, The Reefer. Edited by The Author of "Peter Simple." (Captain Marryatt.) "All hands reef topsails-Away, Aloft!" In 2 Volumes. .... Second edition. Philadelphia, Carey, Lea & Blanchard, 1837. ArBaA; Cu; MWA; ViU; WU.
44829
Howard, H. R.
History and adventure in capturing and exposing the great "Western Land Pirate," and his gang; also the trials, confessions, and execution of a number of Murrell's associates... New York, Harper and brothers, 1837. CU.   44830

---- The history of Virgil A. Stewart, and his adventure in

capturing and exposing the great "western land pirate" and his gang, in connexion with the evidence; also of the trials, confessions, and execution of a number of Murrell's associates in the state of Mississippi during the summer of 1835, and the execution of five professional gamblers, by the citizens of Vicksburg, on the 6th July, 1835 ... Comp. by H. R. Howard. New-York, Harper & brothers, 1837. [7]-273 p. CU.   44831

Howard, John R.
An Anniversary Address on Female Education. Delivered in Paris, Tenn., at the first annual examination of the pupils of the Henry Academy, under the management of Mr. Thos. Johnson, on 30th. June. By John R. Howard. Paris, Tennessee, Printed by Gates & McCowat, 1837. [2], [3]-15, [1] p. MBAt; MH; T.   44832

Howe, Samuel Gridley, 1801-1876.
Atlas of the United States printed for the use of the blind, at the expense of John C. Gray, under the direction of Samuel G. Howe, at the New England institution for the education of the blind. Boston, 1837. MWatP; NN; O.
44833
---- A discourse on the social relations of man; delivered before the Boston Phrenological society, at the close of their course of lectures. By S. G. Howe. Published at the society's request. Boston, Marsh, Capen & Lyon, 1837. 40 p. DLC; KyLoF; MBAt; NNUT; RPB.   44834

Howell, John, 1788-1863.
The Life and adventures of Alexander Selkirk, the real Robinson Crusoe; a narrative founded on facts. New-York, M. Day, 1837. 64 p. CtY; DLC; MH.   44835

Howitt, Mary (Botham), 1799-1888.
Wood leighton; or a year in the country ... in three volumes. Philadelphia, Carey, Lea and Blanchard, 1837. 3 v. CtY; InU; LNH; MBL; NNS.   44836

Howitt, William, 1792-1879.
George Fox and his first disciples: or the Society of Friends as it was, and as it is. By William Howitt. Philadelphia, Merrihew and Gunn, Printers, 1837. 38 p. ICMe; MWA; MWHi; PPM.   44837

Hubbard, Henry, 1784-1857.
Speech of Mr. Hubbard, of New Hampshire, on the resolution of Mr. Ewing for rescinding the Treasury order. Delivered in the Senate December, 1836. Washington, 1837. 15 p. CtY; IU; MH; TxU; WHi.   44838

---- Speech of Mr. Hubbard, on the bill imposing additional duties, as depositories in certain cases, on public officers. Delivered in Senate U.S. September, 28, 1837. Washington, 1837. 14 p. CtY; IU; NjR; NNC; PPM.   44839

Hudson, Charles, 1795-1881.
Questions on select portions of scripture, designed for the higher classes in Sabbath schools, ... 4th ed. Boston, B. B. Mussey and Abel Tompkins, 1837. 182 p. ICRL; M; MH; MH-And; WHi.   44840

Hudson, John, 1800-1891.
The peaceful end of the
Christian. A sermon delivered
in Lebanon, Ohio, Oct. 22nd
1836, occasioned by the death
of Mrs. Amanda Crane...
Dayton, O., B. F. Ells, 1837.
16 p. DLC; NjPT; OClWHi;
PPPrHi. 44841

Hudson and Boston Rail-Road
Company.
Report of the Directors...
1837. Hudson, P. Dean Car-
rique, Printer, 1837. 30 p.
DLC; NN (TPS). 44842

Hübner, Johann, 1668-1731.
Huebner's Bible narratives,
from the Old and New Testaments. Philadelphia, Published
by George W. Mentz & Son,
1837. 468 p. CtHWatK; MoKBC;
NcWsM; PAle. 44843

---- (Hübner's) Biblische his-
torien aus dem Alten und Neuen
Testamente. Fur die jugend
und volks-schulen nach der
anforderung unserer zeit
auss neue bearbeitet. Mit
leicht fasslichen fragen unter
dem texte, einer kurzen
geschichte der Christlichen
religion, nebst 52 holzschnitten.
Philadelphia, G. W. Mentz und
sohn, 1837. [9]-490 p. MnU.
44844

Hughes, George Wurtz, 1806-
1870.
Extracts from reports of an
examination of the coal measures
belonging to the Maryland mining
company, in Alleghany county;
and of a survey for a railroad
from the mines... Washington,
Gales & Seaton, 1837. 33 p.
DLC; MdHi; MH-BA; NcD;
OClWHi. 44845

---- Report on a survey of Jackson City, D.C. With a plan for
its improvement. By George W.
Hughes... Brooklyn, Printed
by F. G. Fish, 1837. 15 p.
NH; DLC. 44846

---- Report on the location and
survey of the Potomac and Annapolis Canal by George W.
Hughes, U.S. Civil Engineer
to the Governor of Maryland.
Annapolis, William M'Neir, 1837.
42 p. DLC; MB; MdHi; PPM.
44847

Hughes, Henry.
A Treatise on Hydrophobia,
(Taken from the Manuscript of
a Late Eminent Physician.) ...
by Henry Hughes, H. M. ...
New York, Geo. Dearborn &
Co., 1837. 30 p. CtY-M; DLC;
MBAt; MWA; NNNAM. 44848

Huidekoper, Harm Jan, 1776-1854.
Calling things by their right
names: a brief reply to an
article under that title in the
Southern Watchman of May 19,
1837. By a Unitarian layman.
Charleston, Walker and James,
1837. 12 p. MB; NcD. 44849

Hull, Amos G., b. 1775.
A brief account of the application and uses of the utero-
abdominal supporter, a new instrument ... invented by the
late A. G. Hull, M.D. ... Sixth
edition. New York, D. Murphy,
printer, 1837. 13 p. DNLM;
MBCo; MH-M; NNNAM; PPHa.
44850

Hume, David, 1711-1776.
The history of England, from
the invasion of Julius Caesar,
to the revolution in 1688 ...
Philadelphia, M'Carty & Davis,
1837. 4 v. CtHT; GAuW; PP;
ScU; WaPS. 44851

---- Hume and Smollet's celebrated history of England from its first settlement to the year 1760...and a continuation from that period to the coronation of George IV. July 19, 1821, embracing a period of nearly 2000 years... New York, Robinson, Pratt and Co., 1837. 496 p. ViU.   44852

[Hunt, Freeman], 1804-1858.
    Letters about the Hudson river. And its vicinity. Written in 1835-1837 ... 3d ed., with additions ... New York, F. Hunt and company, 1837. [11]252 p. DLC; ICU; MnHi; MWA; WHi.   44853

Hunter, Henry, 1741-1802.
    Sacred biography: or, the History of the patriarchs to which is added the history of Deborah, Ruth & Hannah... being a course of lectures delivered at the Scots church by Henry Hunter...Philadelphia, M. E. Cross, 1837. 596 p. KSalW; MiU; MnHi; NcGI; PP.
                                  44854
Hunter, John H.
    A sermon delivered....on resigning his pastoral charge. By Rev. John Hunter. Springfield, (N. pub.; n. pr.), 1837. 19 p. DLC; MBAt; MBC; NjPT.
                                  44855
Hunter, Robert Mercer Taliaferro, 1809-1887.
    Remarks of ... of Va. on the bill imposing additional duties, as depositories in certain cases, on public officers. In the House, Oct. 10, 1837. [Washington, 1837]. 8 p. DLC; NcD; NNC; ViU; ViW.   44856

Hunter, W. Ed.
    The Sabbath School Assistant. By William Hunter, editor....

Pittsburgh, Published by William Hunter, D. N. White, Printer, 1837. PPi.   44857

Huron, Michigan. Sketch of Huron. N.Y., 1837. 32 p. MWA.   44858

Hutchin's improved almanac, for the year of our Lord 1837, being the first after bissextile, and until the fourth of July, the 61st year of the independence of the United States, calculated for the horizon and meridian of New York, in equal or clock time.... Newark, Benjamin Olds, pr., (1837). (36) p. NjMoW.   44859

Hutchins' improved almanac, for 1838....By David Young, philom. New Brunswick, N.J., Terhune & Letson, n.pr., [1837]. 35 p. MWA; NjR.   44860

---- New York, N.Y., A. & S. Raynor, [1837]. MWA.   44861

---- New York, Robinson, Pratt & co., n. pr., [1837]. (36) p. NjR.   44862

Hutchings' Imroved Almanack for 1838. By David Young. New York, N.Y., A. & S. Raynor, [1837]. Imprint varies. MWA.
                                  44863
Hutchings' Improved Farmer's and Mechanic's Almanac for 1838. New York, N.Y., Turner & Fisher, [1837]. DLC; MWA.
                                  44864
Hutton, Joseph.
    Omniscience the Attribute of the Father Only. 4th ed. 1st Series. No. 4. Printed for the American Unitarian Association. Boston, James Munroe & Co., 1837. 36 p. CtHC; ICMe; MMeT; NjR; OO.   44865

I

I can do without it: a tale for
Sunday School scholars. New
York, published by T. Mason
& G. Lane, ... J. Collord,
printer, 1837. 16 p. DLC;
NNMuCN.   44866

Ide, Jacob.
The office of the Christian
ministry, a sermon at the
ordination of Charles T. Torrey,
as pastor of the Richmond St.
Congregational Church, March
22, 1837. Providence, John E.
Brown, 1837. 31 p. CtHC;
DLC; MBC; MWA; RPB.   44867

---- A sermon preached in Med-
way February 26, 1837, occa-
sioned by the death of Mr.
George Nourse, ... who died
Feb. 23, 1837, aged 24 years.
By Jacob Ide, ... Boston,
Printed by S. N. Dickinson...
1837. 3-24 p. IEG; MBAt;
MBC; MBNEH; MiD-B.   44868

Illinois. Auditor and treasurer.
Reports of the auditor and
treasurer. Made in compliance
with a resolution of the house
of representatives of the state
of Illinois, at its special session,
begun and held in Vandalia,
July 10, 1837. Vandalia, (Ill.),
William Walters, public printer,
1837. 19 p. IHi; ICHi; IG.
                    44869
---- Auditor of Public Accounts.
Biennial report. Illinois
Reports to General Assembly,
1837. WHi.   44870

---- Auditors Office.
Statement showing the number
of acres of land subject to taxation in his state for 1836, and
the amount of taxes payable upon
said land, etc. Vandalia, 1837.

7 p. MB; WHi.   44871

---- Board of Commissioner of
Public Works.
An abstract of the proceed-
ings of the Board of Commis-
sioners of Public Works of the
State of Illinois. December
session, A.D. 1837. Vandalia,
Ill., by William Walters, 1837.
(III), 76 p. DLC; DNA; OCHP;
P.   44872

---- Canal Commissioners (1836-
1917)
Annual report of the Board
of Commissioners of the Illinois
and Michigan Canal for 1836.
Vandalia, W. Walters for T.
Sawyer, 1837. 83 p. ICJ; MiU.
                        44873
---- General Assembly.
... Memorial of the legislature
of Illinois, in favor of removing
the restrictions against the taxation of land for five years after
sale. January 23, 1837. Referred to the Committee on public
lands, and ordered to be printed.
Washington, Gales and Seaton,
[1837]. 3 p. IHi.   44874

---- ---- House of Representatives.
Journal of the house of representatives of the tenth General
Assembly of the state of Illinois,
at a special session of the General Assembly, begun and held
in the town of Vandalia, July 10,
1837. Vandalia, Ill., William
Walters, public printer, 1837.
182 p. ICJ; ICN.   44875

---- ---- ---- Journal ... at
their ... session, begun and
held ... December 5, 1836 [-
March 4, 1839]. Vandalia, Ill.,
Printed by William Walters, 1836-
38. 2 v. CSmH.   44876

---- ---- ---- Committee on internal improvements.
... Mr. Smith, of Wabash, from the committee on internal improvements, made the following report.... [Springfield, 1837.] 15 p. IC.   44877

---- ---- ---- ---- Report of the committee on internal improvements. Vandalia, S. T. Sawyer, public printer, 1837. 16 p. IC; IHi.   44878

---- ---- ---- Committee on roads and canals.
...Report ... Vandalia, Printed by W. Walters for S. T. Sawyer, 1837. 38 p. OClWHi.
                                       44879
---- ---- Joint Select committee upon the State Bank of Illinois.
Report of the joint select committee upon the state bank of Illinois. Vandalia, By Wm. Walters, agent for S. T. Sawyer, public printer, 1837. 48 p. IHi; MiD-B.   44880

---- ---- Senate.
Journal of the Senate of the tenth general assembly of the State of Illinois, at a special session, begun and held in Vandalia, July 10, 1837. Vandalia, Ill., Printed by William Walters, public printer, 1837. ICJ; IGK; ILM.   44881

---- ---- ---- Journal of the Senate of the ... General Assembly of the State of Illinois. Springfield, 1837. ICU; IU; MiU.   44882

---- ---- ---- Committee on Canals and Canal Lands.
... Report of the Committee on Canals and Canal Lands [in re message of Governor transmitting Annual report of Canal

Commissioners and on report of House Committee on Roads and Canals on various matters submitted to them for consideration]. Vandalia, By W. Walter, agent for S. T. Sawyer, public printer, 1837. 42 p. ICJ; IHi.   44883

---- Governor 1834-1838. (Joseph Duncan)
Governor's message. Register --extra. Vandalia, July 11, 1837. [Vandalia, Illinois State Register office, 1837.] Broadside. IHi.
                                       44884
---- ---- Message of the governor of the state of Illinois, with accompanying documents transmitted to the general assembly, at a special session, begun and held at Vandalia, July 10, 1837. Vandalia, Ill., William Walters, public printer, 1837. 33 p. I-Ar.   44885

---- Laws, statutes, etc.
An act to establish and maintain a general system of internal improvements, ... passed at a general assembly ..., begun and held at Vandalia on the 5th of December, 1836. Vandalia, Printed by William Walters, public printer, 1837. 28 p. IHi.
                                       44886
---- ---- Incorporation laws of the State of Illinois; passed at a session of the General Assembly, begun and held at Vandalia the 6th day of December, 1836. Published in pursuance of law. Vandalia, (Ill.), William Walters, Public Printer, 1837. 344, xxi p. DLC; ICN; MH-L; OClWHi; WHi.
                                       44887
---- ---- Laws of the State of Illinois passed by the Tenth General Assembly at their First Session ... William Walters, Public Printer, Vandalia, 1837. 366 p. Nv.   44888

---- ---- Laws....tenth General assembly, at their special
session....1837....Vandalia,
Ill., William Walters, public
printer, 1837. 125, vi p.
Ar-SC; IHi; MdBB; NNLI;
RPL; Wa-L.   44889

Illinois Anti-Slavery Convention.
Alton observer. Extra.
Proceedings of the Ill. anti-
slavery convention. Held at
Upper Alton on the twenty-
sixth, twenty-seventh, and
twenty-eighth October, 1837.
36 p. CLSR.   44890

Illinois College. Jacksonville,
Ill.
Catalogue of the Officers
and Students of Illinois College, 1836-7. Jacksonville,
1837. 24 p. ICJ; IHi; IU;
MHi.   44891

---- Laws of Illinois College in
Jacksonville, Illinois, enacted
by the trustees. Jacksonville,
printed by E. T. and C.
Goudy, 1837. 22 p. IHi. 44892

Illinois in 1837; a sketch descriptive of the situation,
boundaries, face of the country,
prominent districts, prairies,
rivers, minerals, animals, agricultural productions, public
lands, plans of internal improvement, manufactures etc., of the
state of Illinois....By the Honorable H. L. Ellsworth....Phila-
delphia, S. A. Mitchell, 1837.
143 p. ICHi; NNUT; OCY;
PAit; RPB.   44893

Imitatio Christi.
The imitation of Christ. In
three books. By Thomas A'
Kempis. Rendered into the
English from the Latin by John
Payne...With an introductory

essay by Thomas Chalmers....
Boston, Gould, Kendall and
Lincoln, 1837. 228 p. CtY;
ICP.   44894

Immigrants Friend Society.
Proceedings of the second annual meeting...for the valley of
the Mississippi, held May 23,
1837, in the Second Presbyterian
Church, Cincinnati, Ohio. (Cincinnati), Johnson, (1837). IHi;
OCHP; OOxM; PPPrHi; WHi.
                      44895
Important Decision regarding the
Observations of the Sabbath.
Report of the case of D. Innes,
Barber..., Dundee, against his
apprentice, W. Phillips... [Dun-
dee, N.Y.?], 1837. 24 p. CtY.
                      44896
Impositions and frauds, in Phila.,
by a Citizen of Philadelphia,
formerly Lord B...of England,
now living incog. Philadelphia,
1837. 24 p. DLC; PHi. 44897

--- Improved New-England primer:
or an easy and pleasant guide
for the instruction of children.
Concord, 1837. 46 p. Nh-Hi.
                      44898
Indian Anecdotes. (Concord),
Rufus Merrill, (1837). 192 p.
MWA.   44899

Indian anecdotes and barbarities,
being a description of their customs and deeds of cruelty, with
an account of the captivity, sufferings and heroic conduct of
many who have fallen into their
hands...All illustrating the general traits of Indian character.
Barre, Mass., n.p., 1837. 40 p.
ICN; MB; MWA; NjP; WHi.
                      44900
Indiana. Fund Commissioners.
Report of the Canal Fund
Commissioners [relating to the
Wabash and Erie Canal fund, etc.

Jan. 11, 1837.] [Indianapolis, 1837] 7 p. InU; WHi.   44901

---- General Assembly. House.

Journal of the House of Representatives of the state of Indiana; being the twenty-second session of the General Assembly, commenced at Indianapolis on Monday, the fifth day of December, 1837. Indianapolis, Bolton and Livingston, 1837. 814 p. IN-SC; LU.   44902

---- ---- Senate.

Journal of the Senate of the State of Indiana during the 22nd session (continued to the 31st, inclusive) of the General Assembly..at Indianapolis ..1837 (to 1846, inclusive). 10 v. Indianapolis, 1837-46. LU; BrMus.   44903

---- Governor's Message.

Governor's Message, delivered to both Houses of the General Assembly of the State of Indiana, ... 1837. Indianapolis, Printed by Douglass and Noel, 1837. 7 p. WHi.   44904

---- Laws, statutes, etc.

Laws of a general nature passed and published at the twenty-first session of the General Assembly of the state of Indiana, held at Indianapolis, on the first Monday in December, one thousand eight hundred and thirty-six. By authority. Indianapolis, Printed by Douglass and Noel, 1837. 118 p. IaU-L; MdBB; NNLI; RPL; Wa-L.   44905

---- ---- Laws of a local nature, passed and published at the twenty first session of the General Assembly of the state of Indiana; held at Indianapolis; on

the first Monday in December, one thousand eight hundred and thirty six. By authority. Indianapolis, Bolton and Livingston, printers, 1837. 460 p. Wa-L.   44906

---- State Bank.

By-laws, rules & regulations for the government of.... Indianapolis, Douglas & Mel, 1837. 15 p. In.   44907

---- State Board of Internal Improvement.

Report, .. [relating to loans; report of the principal engineer relating to roads and railways, etc.] [Indianapolis, 1837]. WHi.   44908

---- University.

Catalogue .... Bloomington, Ind., Deal 1837. 12 p. InU.   44909

Indiana Mutual Fire Insurance Co.

Act of incorporation and by-laws of the ... Indianapolis, Bolton & Langston, 1837. 16 p. MH-BA.   44910

Infant Sabbath school questions. (By P. H. B.) Boston, Mass. S.S. Soc., 1837. 72 p. AmSSchU; DLC; MBC; MH; MiGr.   44911

Infant school primer and arithmetical tables in verse, with a simple catechism for infant schools... New York, M. Day, 1837. MH.   44912

Ingalls, William, 1769-1851.

On scarlatina in a letter addressed to his son in which is contained cases of anginasine efflorescentia.... by William Ingalls, M.D. ... Boston, Otis Broaders & Co., 1837. 39 p. DLC; DNLM; MB; OO.   44913

Ingersoll, Charles Jared, 1782-1862.

Pennsylvania Convention.
Minority report on currency
and corporations. Read May
23rd, 1837, with speech on
impeachments and of the convention, May 24, 1837. Harrisburg, 1837. 17 p. PHi.
                               44914
Ingersoll, George Goldthwait,
1796-1863.
   Address delivered before the
literary societies of the University of Vermont, Aug. 2, 1837.
Burlington, Hiram Johnson &
company, University Press, 1837.
46 p. CSmH; ICN; MH; RPB;
VtU.   44915

Ingersoll, Joseph Reed, 1786-
1868.
   An Address delivered before
the Phi Beta Kappa Society,
Alpha of Maine, in Bowdoin
College, Brunswick, September
7, 1837. By Joseph R. Ingersoll. Brunswick, Printed for
the Society, 1837. 40 p. DLC;
MeB; MH; RPB; TNP.   44916

---- Speech of Mr. Ingersoll,
on the Judiciary delivered in the
Convention of Pennsylvania,
November 1, 1837. Harris-
burg, Printed by Packer, Barrett, and Parke, 1837. 26 p.
CU; DLC; PHi; PPL; ScU.
                               44917
An inquiry into the condition
and prospects of the African
race in the United States, and
the means of bettering its for-
tune. By an American. Philadelphia, 1837. PPL-R.   44918

An inquiry into the Spirit of
Truth; being some serious considerations on the physical,
physiological, and moral evidences of the natural immortality of man's present physical
existence. With an appendix,

entitled Religion as it is. New-
York, 1837. 38 p. MdBD.
                               44919
The inspiration of the Bible. By
a Correspondent in the far west.
Boston, 1837. MH; MH-AH.
                               44920
Institution of Civil engineers.
   Transactions of the institution
of Civil Engineers. Vol. I. London, 1836. Re-Printed in numbers, et the office of the Railroad journal, New-York by D. K.
Minor, and George C. Shaeffer,
1837. 42 p. ScU.   44921

Interesting miscellany, selected
from various sources, in three
volumes ... J. Collord, Printer,
1837. [6]-143 p. ViRU.
                               44922
Ipswich Female Seminary.
   Catalogue of the officers and
members of the officers Seminary
for female teachers, at Ipswitch,
Massachusetts, for the year ending April, 1837. Salem, (Mass.),
Palfrey & Chapman, 1837.
16 p. DLC; IaHi; ICU; MBC;
OClWHi.   44923

... The irish peasant; or, the
history of Peter Lacy, and his
wife Susan. Philadelphia, Baptist General Tract Society,
[1837?] DLC; ScGF.   44924

Irving, Christopher, d. 1836.
   A Catechism of Mythology;
being a compendious history of
the Heathen Gods, Goddesses,
and Heroes. Designed chiefly
as an introduction to the study
of the ancient classics. With
engraved illustrations. By C.
Irving, LL.D. Holyrood-House,
Southampton. adapted to the
use of schools in the United
States. Fifth American edition,
revised and corrected. New
York, Published by Collins, Keese

& co., 1837. 84 p. MdHi;
NjR. 44925

---- A catechism of practical
chemistry. .... By C. Irving.
First American edition; revised
and corrected by John Griscom.
New York, Published by Collins,
Keese & Company, 1837. 83 p.
CtY; DSG; NcWsS; NN. 44926

Irving, John Treat.
The Hawk chief: a tale of
the Indian country. By John
T. Irving, jr. In two volumes.
Vol. I. Philadelphia, Carey,
Lea and Blanchard, 1837. 2 v.
ICN; LNH; NNS; PPL; RPB.
44927

Irving, Washington, 1783-1859.
The Adventures of Captain
Bonneville, U.S.A., in the
Rocky Mountains and the Far
West. Digested from his jour-
nal and illustrated from various
other sources by W. Irving.
With the rare large folding
maps. Philadelphia, 1837.
496 p. AU; CoU; MtU; PMA;
ViU. 44928

---- Astoria; or, Anecdotes of
an enterprise beyond the Rocky
mountains. Rev. ed. Knickerbocker ed. pl. D. Philadelphia,
Lippincott, 1837. In. 44929

---- The beauties of Washington Irving ... Philadelphia,
Carey, Lea & Blanchard, 1837.
viii, (9)-270 p. NNUT; RJPHL;
PHi; WGr. 44930

---- A chronicle of the conquest of Granada. .... Philadelphia, Carey, Lea and
Blanchard, 1837. 2 v. KyDC;
MBAt; OCY; OHi; OSW. 44931

---- A History of New York,
from the Beginning of the

World to the End of the Dutch
Dynasty ... By Diedrich Knicker-
bocker (pseud.) ... Philadelphia,
Carey, Lea & Blanchard, 1837.
2 v. DLC; OCl; OClW; PU;
ViRVal. 44932

---- History of the life and
voyages of Christopher Columbus. ... A new ed. rev. and
cor. by the author. In 2 vols.
Philadelphia, Carey, Lea, &
Blanchard, 1837. 2 v. IU;
MdBE; NjP; PU; ScU. 44933

---- The Rocky Mountains; or,
Scenes, incidents and adven-
tures in the far West; digested
from the journal of Captain B.L.E.
Bonneville, of the Army of the
United States ... by Washington
Irving ... Philadelphia, Carey,
Lea, and Blanchard, 1837. 2 v.
DeWi; IaDmD; LNH; PPA; WyU.
44934

---- A series of tales and
sketches of the Moors and Spaniards. New ed. Philadelphia,
1837. 2 v. OCY. 44935

---- The sketch-book of Geof-
frey Crayon, gent. (pseud.)...
A new ed. Philadelphia, Carey,
Lea, & Blanchard, 1837. 2 v.
CSmH; MB; NN; OCl; PU.
44936

---- Tales of a Traveller ...
By Geoffrey Crayon, Gent.
(pseud.) ... Philadelphia, Carey,
Lea & Blanchard, 1837. 2 v.
DLC; KyDC; MBAt; NcD; OCY.
44937

---- [The works of W. Irving.]
Philadelphia, Carey, Lea, and
Blanchard, 1837. 11 v. DLC;
ScU. 44938

Ives, Elan, 1802-1864.
The American infant school
singing book, designed as the
first book for the study of mu-

sic. By E. Ives, Jr. New
York, F. J. Huntington and
co., 1837. 108 p. MnSM.
                           44939

Ives, Eli, 1779-1861.
    Extracts from an address
delivered by Prof. Eli Ives, before the New Haven horticultural society, at their annual
meeting in October, 1837.
(New Haven) Published by the
Society, (1837). 16 p. CtY;
MB; MBAt; NN.   44940

                    J

Jack and the beanstalk. A
new version. Boston, T. H.
Carter, 1837. 3 pt. in 1 v.
MH.   44941

Jackson, Andrew, 1767-1845.
    An extract from his farewell
address in 1837. n.p., [1837].
1 p. MH.   44942

---- The farewell address of
Andrew Jackson; and the
inaugural of Martin Van Buren,
president of the U.S. Published and delivered on the
fourth of March, 1837. Raleigh,
N.C., T. Loring, 1837. 36 p.
DLC; NcD.   44943

---- Farewell address .. to the
people of the United States...
Harrisburg, S. D. Patterson,
1837. 16 p. DLC; MiU-C;
NN.   44944

---- ---- Printed in pursuance
of a resolution of the House
of Representatives, adopted on
the 6th March, 1837. Harrisburg, Samuel Patterson, 1837.
16 p. CSmH; ICN; MiU-C;
NBuG; PPL.   44945

---- ---- Patterson, N.J., A

Mead, 1837. Broadside. NN;
ViU.   44946

---- ---- Washington, Blair and
Rives, 1837. 23 p. DLC.
                       44947
---- ... Gen. Jackson's response
to Judge White's testimony.
[Lexington, Ky.? 1837]. 28 p.
InU.   44948

---- Messages with a short sketch
of his life. See U.S. President,
1829-1837 (Jackson).

Jackson, Charles Thomas.
    First report on the geology
of the state of Maine. See
Maine. Geological Survey (1836-
1839).

Jackson, Daniel, b. 1790.
    Alonzo and Melissa: or, The
unfeeling father. An American
tale ... Portland [S. H. Coles-
worthy], 1837. 141 p. CtY;
ViU.   44949

Jackson, John.
    Address on "Divine spiritual
worship." Philadelphia, 1837.
PSC-Hi.   41950

Jackson, John, 1809-1855.
    An address to the members
of the monthly meetings, constituting Concord quarterly meeting
of Friends. Philadelphia, n.pub.
Printed by Thomas B. Town, 1837.
10 p. NjR; PSC-Hi.   44951

Jacobs, Bela, 1786-1836.
    Memoir of Rev. Bela Jacobs,
A.M. compiled chiefly from his
letters and journals by his daugh-
ter, with a sketch of his charac-
ter ... Boston, Gould, Kendall
& Lincoln, 1837. 305 p. MB;
MBC; OClWHi; PHi; ViRU.
                       44952
Jacobs, Friederich, 1764-1847.

The Greek Reader, By Frederic Jacobs, with Improvements, additional notes, and corrections. By David Patterson, A.M., Tenth New York, from the ninth German Edition, Corrected and Improved with numerous notes, additions, and alterations, Not in any former Edition. By Patricks S. Casserly, T.C.D. New York, W. E. Dean, 1837. 214 p. KyBvU; MB; MH; NCH; ViU.   44953

---- The Greek reader, with an enlarged and complete lexicon. From the 12th German ed. Boston, Hilliard, Gray and Co., 1837. 516 p. IaPeC; MH; MoU.   44954

Jagger, William.
    Address to mechanics and laborers of New York. n.p., 1837. MBAt.   44955

---- An address to the people of New York in reference to the cause of the great change of business in this city, and remedy. 2nd ed. New York & Printed for the author, 1837. CtY.   44956

---- Address to the people of Suffolk Co., N.Y. .... N.Y., Craighead & Allee, 1837. 8 p. DLC; NSm.   44957

---- Letter to the people of Suffolk Co., N.Y., June 27, Sept. 4, and Dec. 20. New York, 1837. DLC; MBAt; NSm.   44958

---- To the people of the United States. [Washington, 1837.] 7 p. ScU.   44959

(James, George Payne Rainsford), 1801?-1860.

Attila; a romance. By the author of "The Gipsy," "One in a Thousand," &c. New-York, Harper & Brothers, 1837. 2 v. CtHC; CtY; MBL; MH; NbU; OCl.
                                        44960
---- The gipsy; a tale. By the author of "Richelieu"....New York, Published by Harper & brothers, 1837. 2 v. CtMW; ICarlB; MoSW; PLFM.   44961

No entry   44962

---- ... The history of Charlemagne. By G. P. R. James ... (Harper's stereotype ed.) New York, J. & J. Harper & brothers, 1837. (11)-408 p. IaDuC; IEG; Mh-And; NUtHi; TxGR.   44963

---- Lives of Cardinal de Retz. Jean Baktiste Colbert. John DeWitt and the Marquis de Lauvois. Philadelphia, Carey, Lea & Blanchard, 1837. 2 v. CtY; LNH; PPA; RNR; TNP.   44964

---- Mary of Burgundy; or, the revolt of Ghent. By the author of "Philip Augustus"....New York, Published by Harper & Brothers, 1837. 2 v. IaFair; MH; MoSW; PU; TNP.   44965

James, John H.
    An address, delivered before the Springfield high school, by John H. James, Esq. With a catalogue of the officers and pupils, and a report of the institution, for the second year. September, 1837. Cincinnati, Pugh & Dodd, printers, 1837. 16 p. MHi; OS; TNP.   44966

James, T. D.
    Five good reasons for not play-

ing marbles. Philadelphia, 1837.
4 p. PHi.   44967

Jameson, Anna Brownell
(Murphy), 1794-1860.
 Characteristics of women,
moral, poetical and historical.
... New York, Saunders and
Otley, 1837. 382 p. CPet;
CtHT; DLC; MH; NPV.   44968

---- Memoirs of celebrated fe-
male sovereigns. By Mrs.
Jameson. New York, Harper
and bros., 1837. 2 v.
ArBaA; FTU; MH; PMA; PPL.
                            44969
---- Shakespeare's heroines;
characteristics of women, mor-
al, poetical, and historical.
By Mrs. Anna Jameson. New
York, Saunders and Otley,
1837. 382 p. GMM; InCW;
NhPet; RP; TNP.   44970

Jamieson, Alexander.
 A grammar of logic and intellectual philosophy on didactic
principles; for the use of colleges, schools and private instruction... 6th ed. stereotyped. New Haven, A. H.
Maltby, etc...1837. 304 p.
KyLoP; MPiB; OO; PCA; RPB.
                            44971
---- #1. A grammar of rhetoric
and polite literature: Comprehending the principles of language and style the elements of
taste and criticism; with rules
for the study of composition
and eloquence: Illustrated by
appropriate examples, selected
chiefly from the British classics,
for the use of schools, or private instruction. By Alexander,
Jamieson, L.L.D. Seventeenth
edition. Stereotyped. New
Haven, Connecticut, A. H.
Maltby, 1837. 306 p. CtW;
MB; MH; NcCJ; OOxM.   44972

---- Mechanics for practical men.
By Alex. Jamieson ... Treatises
on the composition and resolution
of forces; the centre of gravity;
and the mechanical powers ...
London, Paris, and New York,
Fisher, son and co., [1837?].
[9]-132. viii, [9]-130, vi, [9]-
238 p. OO.   44973

Jamison, Robert W.
 To the people of Arkansas.
Little Rock? 1837. 6 p. 44974

Janes, Edmund Storer.
 The Opportunity of Doing
Good Unto All Men, 4th Annual
Sermon, preached before the
Supts. and Teachers of the Phila-
delphia Sunday School Union,
1837. Philadelphia, T. K. &
P. G. Collins, 1837. 36 p.
IEG; MBNMHi; NNMHi.   44975

Janeway, Jacob Jones, 1774-1858.
 The scriptural doctrine of the
atonement illustrated and defended...Philadelphia, Presbyterian tract and Sunday school
society, 1837. 24 p. IaDuU;
ICP; MeBat; NjPT; PPPrHi.
                            44976
Jarvis, Samuel Farmar, 1786-1851.
 Christian unity necessary for
the conversion of the world: a
sermon .... in St. Thomas church,
New York .... By Samuel Farmar
Jarvis .... New York, n. pub.,
printed by William Osborn, 1837.
50 p. CtY; ICP; MWA; NjR;
PPL.   44977

Jay, William, 1769-1858.
 Morning exercises for the
closet: for every day in the
year. Baltimore, Plaskitt, 1837.
2 v. in 1. GEU-T; InU; TxU-L.
                            44978
---- Standard Works of the Rev.
William Jay of Argyle Chapel
Bath comprising all his works

known in this country and also several which have not heretofore been presented to the American Public. From a copy furnished by the Author to the Publisher. Baltimore, Published by Plasket & Fite, 1837. 3 v. NcElon. 44979

Jay, William, 1789-1858.
An Inquiry into the character and tendency of the American colonization, and American anti-slavery societies ... Fourth edition, New York, R. G. Williams, 1837. 206 p. CtY; KyU; ICU; MeBat; MWA. 44980

Jefferson, Thomas, 1743-1826.
A manual of Parliamentary practice, composed originally for the use of the Senate of the United States. By Thomas Jefferson.... To which are added the rules and orders of both Houses of Congress. Philadelphia, Hogan and Thompson, 1837. 192 p. DLC; IaB; MBBC; PU; RPA. 44981

Jefferson County, N.Y.-Citizens.
Memorial of sundry citizens of the County of Jefferson, composing the Dexter Company, relative to injuries which they will sustain by diverting the waters of the Black River to supply the Black River Canal and Erie Canal feeder. In Assembly, March 1, 1837. [Albany, 1837]. 3 p. WHi. 44982

Jefferson Medical College, Philadelphia.
Annual announcement of lectures, etc. in Jefferson medical college.... Philadelphia, Printed by A. Waldie, 1837. 1837. 16 p. CtY; DLC; MBC; OC. 44983

Jelleff, Joseph.
Jelleff & Hull's patent pocket interest tables, at 7 per cent. New stereotype edition. Carefully revised and corrected. Cooperstown, Printed and sold by H. & E. Phinney, 1837. MH-BA; NN. 44984

Jennifer, Daniel, d. 1855.
Speech...on the bill for the admission of Michigan into the union, delivered in the House of representatives, Jan. 25, 1837. Washington, printed by Gales and Seaton, 1837. 16 p. Md; WHi. 44985

Jenkins, Warren.
The Ohio gazetteer and travellers' guide; containing a description of the several towns, townships and counties....together with an appendix, or general register.... By Warren Jenkins. Columbus, Isaac N. Whiting, 1837. 546 p. CoD; IaHi; MB; OHi; RPB. 44986

Jennings' landscape annual; or, Tourist in Spain, 1837. New York, 1837. CtSoP. 44987

Jeremy Bentham and the Usury Law. From the New-York Daily Express. Albany, Hoffman & White, 1837. 32 p. CtY; MB; NBuU; NN. 44988

Jeter, Jeremiah Bell, 1802-1880.
A memoir of Abner W. Clopton, A.M., pastor of Baptist churches in Charlotte county, Virginia. By Jeremiah B. Jeter. Richmond, Va., Yale & Wyatt, 1837. 283 p. GMM; NcU; PCC; ViU; WHi. 44989

Jewell; or, Token of Friendship. 1837. New York, 1837. 246 p. NIC. 44990

The Jewish intelligencer. A
monthly publication. V.1-
June 1836- New York, 1837-
DLC; IaU; MBC; NN; OCH.
44991

Jews. Liturgy and Ritual.
Hagadah seder Hagadah shal
Pesah.
Service for the two first
nights of the Passover in He-
brew and English, according
to the custom of the German &
Spanish Jews. Translated into
English by the late David Levi.
... 1st American ed. New
York, S. H. Jackson, 5597
[1837]. 86 p. OO.   44992

Joe Anderson and old Jim Bay-
ley. Boston, Cassady and
March, 1837. 16 p. MBAt;
MH; NNC.   44993

Johnson, Elizabeth.
Exercises for private devotion. Boston, Simpkins, 1837.
130 p. ICMe; MB; MH; MWA.
44994

Johnson, Hezekiah.
The unity and purity of the
morality contained in the two
testaments. By Hezekiah Johnson, a minister of the Gospel...
Circleville, Ohio, Printed at
the religious telescope office,
1837. 57 p. ICN; OClWHi.
44995

Johnson, James, 1777-1845.
The economy of health; or,
The stream of human life, from
the cradle to the grave. With
reflections, moral, physical, and
philosophical, on the septen-
nial phases of human existence.
By James Johnson ... New-
York, Harper & brothers, 1837.
[13]-283 p. CSt-L; KyLx;
MBL; NhPet; OO.   44996

Johnson, Neville.
Bible quadrupeds: ....

Philadelphia, Barrington & Haswell, (1837). 276 p. Mi-Mus.
44997

Johnson, Samuel, 1709-1784.
The beauties of Samuel Johnson, consisting of maxims and
observations, moral critical,
and miscellaneous, to which is
prefixed a sketch of his life.
Boston, Joseph Dowe, 1837.
285 p. M Belm.   44998

---- Rasselas; a tale... Bestuce
Porter, 1837. 124 p. MB;
OClW.   44999

---- Select thoughts of Dr. Samuel Johnson, consisting of maxims and observations, moral,
critical, and miscellaneous, to
which is prefixed a sketch of
his life, sixth American, from
the fifth London edition. Boston,
published by Joseph Dowe, 1837.
285 p. MB; PPL; RBa; TxU.
45000

---- The works of Samuel Johnson, LL.D. with an essay on
his life and genius, by Arthur
Murphy, esq. 1st complete American ed... New York, G. Dearborn, 1837. 2 v. KyBgW;
KyLoP; MH; NIC; PSG.   45001

(Johnson, W. O.)
... The omnibus. A laugh-
able farce, in one act ...
Philadelphia, F. Turner, New-
York, Turner & Fisher (1837?)
CtY.   45002

Johnson, Walter R[ogers], 1794-
1852.
... Experiments on the adhe-
sion of iron spikes of various
forms, when driven into different species of timber. By Walter
R. Johnson ... [New Haven,
1837]. 12 p. DLC; PPAN.
45003

---- Report of experiments by

the sub-committee, from the committee of the Franklin institute of Pennsylvania, on the explosions of steam boilers, to whom was referred the examination of the strength of materials employed in their construction. By Walter Rogers Johnson and Benjamin Reeves. (Philadelphia, 1837?) MH.
45004

Johnson, William Cost, 1806-1860.
Speech of William Cost Johnson, of Md., on the subtreasury bill, entitled A bill imposing additional duties, as depositaries, in certain cases, on public officers, delivered in the House of representatives, October 12, 1837. Washington, Printed at the National register office, [1837]. 22 p. IaHi; LNT; MdBE; NjR; PPL.   45005

Johnson's Almanac for 1838. Philadelphia, Pa., Willard Johnson, [1837]. MWA.   45006

Johnston, David Clugpoole, 1797-1865.
Illustrations of the Adventures & Achievements of Unrenowned Don Quixote.... Boston? 1837? Broadside. MB; MH.   45007

Johnston, James Harvey, d. 1876.
"The love of Money, the Root of all evil." A discourse. ... Madison, 1837. 8 p. OCHP.
45008

Johnstone, James, 1754-1783.
A therapeutic arrangement and syllabus of materia medica. By James Johnstone, M.D.... Philadelphia, Haswell, Barrington, and Haswell, 1837. 71 p. CtY; ICU-R; MdBJ; NjR; PU.   45009

Jones, Charles Colcock, 1804-1863.

Address to the senior class in the theological seminary of the synod of South Carolina and Georgia, on the evening of the anniversary, Columbia, July 10th, 1837.... Savannah, Thomas Purse & co., 1837. 18 p. DCL; MBC; NjPT; PPPrHi; WHi.
45010

---- Catechism of scripture doctrine and practice: For families and Sabbath schools. Designed, also, for the oral instruction of colored persons. By Charles C. Jones. Second edition. Savannah, T. Purse & co., 1837. (1)-257, (1) p. G; Gu-De; NjP; TNF; TxU.   45011

Jones, Edmond.
Fellow-Citizens, A long, laborious, and greatly excited General Assembly is now drawing to a close. Letter to citizens of Raleigh from Edmund Jones discussing about the finances of the country. Raleigh, Jan. 20, 1837. NcU.   45012

Jones, Henry.
Principles of interpreting the prophecies; briefly illustrated and applied with notes. By Henry Jones... Andover and New York, published by Gould & Newman, 1837. [13]-150 p. GDecCT; ICP; MBC; PPM; VtU.
45013

Jones, Jacob.
... The gladiator. A play, in five acts. Familiarized by the popular tragedy of that name by Doctor Bird. Written by Jacob Jones... Correctly printed from the most approved acting copy ... as now performed in the London and American theatres. Embellished with a fine wood engraving. Philadelphia, New-York, Turner & Fisher (etc.), (1837). 2 p. ℓ., (7)-66 p.

CtY; DFo; MH; PPL; PU-F.
                            45014
Jones, John Winston, 1791-1848.
    Speech of Mr. Jones, of
Virginia, on the bill to postpone
the fourth instalment of deposite
with the States: delivered in
the House of representatives of
the United States September 20,
1837. Washington, 1837. 15 p.
CtY; InHi; MdBJ; MnSM; Vi.
                            45015
Jones, Samuel.
    Rule of faith. chiefly an
epitome of the Right Rev. Dr.
Milner's end of religious controversy. By Rev. Samuel
Jones....First American edition.
Boston, P. Mooney, 1837.
140 p. MBrigStJ; MoSU. 45016

Jones, William, 1762-1846.
    History of the Christian
church....with an account of
the Waldenses and Albigenses.
5th edition. 2 volumes in one.
Dover, Trustees, Freewill Baptist Convention Publishers,
1837. 2 v. in 1. 453 p.
MeLewB; Nh; OClW; PP; RWe.
                            45017
Joseph; or, sketches of scripture history illustrating the
life and character of Joseph,
the son of Jacob, and first
ruler of Israel. New York, T.
Mason and G. Lane, 1837.
NPV.   45018

Josephus, Flavius.
    The works of Flavius
Josephus....Tr. by William
Whiston....Complete in 1 vol.
....Cincinnati, E. Morgan and
son, 1837. 648 p. CtY; KyLxT;
MWH; OU; TxAbM.   45019

Joslin, B[enjamin] F[ranklin],
1796-1861.
    ... Observations on the tails
of Halley's comet, as they ap-

peared at Union college, Schenec-
tady, N.Y., in October, 1835.
By Prof. B. F. Joslin. [New
Haven, 1837]. 24 p. DLC;
NNN.   45020

---- Physiological explanation of
the beauty of form. By B. F.
Joslin, M.D. ... Albany, E. W.
and C. Skinner, 1837. 30 p.
DLC; IaU; MBAt; Nh; PPPM.
                            45021
Josse, Augustin C.
    A grammar of the Spanish
language, with practical exercises. ... By M. Josse. Revised, amended, improved and
enlarged by F. Sales, A.M.,
... Eighth American edition. ...
First part. Boston, Perkins
and Marvin; Charles C. Little
& co., James Munroe & co., and
S. Burdett, 1837. 468 p. DLC;
MH; NjP; NNC; OO.   45022

Josse, Augustin Louis, 1763-1841.
    A grammar of the Spanish lan-
guage with practical exercises.
8th American ed. Boston, Perkins and Marvin, 1837. DLC;
MB; MH; Nh; NjP.   45023

A Journal of an excursion to the
Franconia Mountains: by a corps
of cadets of the Norwich university, under Capt. Alden Par-
tridge, July, 1837. [Northfield,
Vt., 1837]. 14 p. DLC.
                            45024
Journeymen House Carpenter's
Association of the City and
County of Phila.
    Constitution and By Laws of
the Journeymen House Carpenters'
Association of the City and County of Phila. Philadelphia, 1837.
12 p. Phi.   45025

Journeys into the moon, several
planets and the sun. History
of a female somnambulist, of Weil-

heim on the Teck, in the kingdom of Wuertemberg, in the years 1832 and 1833. A book in which all persons will find important disclosures, concerning their fate hereafter. Tr. ... from the original, in German, which was published by a daily eye-witness, and friend of truth ... Philadelphia, Printed for Vollmer and Haggenmacher, 1837. 2 p. *l.*, 203 p. DLC; ICBB; MiPon; MnU; RPB.
45026

Joynes, John G.
An address to the members of the Legislature of Virginia, and to the citizens of Acomack and Northampton Counties, Va. In reference to certain slanders, and the course pursued by the members of the legislature from the counties of Acomack and Northampton, in the election of Brigadier General of the 21st. brigade Virginia militia, by John G. Joynes. Printed for the publisher, 1837. 17 p. MdBLC.   45027

Judson, Andrew Thompson, 1784-1853.
Address delivered at South Coventry, Conn., at the request of the Hale Monument Association, November 25, 1836. Norwich, 1837. 23 p. Ct; ICN; MB; MWA; NNC.
45028

Judson, Ann (Hasseltine), 1789-1826.
Sketches of the lives of distinguished females. Written for girls ... by an American Lady. New York, 1837. ICBB; RPB.   45029

Junius.
Letters by the same writer under other signatures to which are added his confidential correspondence with Mr. Wilkes and his private letters addressed to Mr. H. S. Woodfall. 1st edition. Published by Walker, Philadelphia, Pa., 1837. MdHi; NcDaD.
45030

Juvenalis, Decimus Junius.
Juvenal. Tr. by Charles Badham. New ed. With an appendix containing imitations of the third and tenth satires. By Dr. Samuel Johnson. To which are added the satires of Persius. New York, Harper & brothers, 1837. 227, xv-58 p. AzU; CU; LU; NjP; PPL.   45031

The Juvenile primer and child's own progressive guide to learning, carefully arranged on a new simple, and interesting principle. Baltimore, Bayly & Burns, 1837. 24 p. DLC; MH.
45032

Juvenile Stories, for little readers. Mt Hani, S. Babcock, 1837. 16 p. CtY; DLC; ICU; NN.   45033

Juvenile stories, for the instruction of children. Concord, 1837. MBAt.   45034

K

Karthaus, Peter Arnold.
... A Statement of various commercial transactions, by Peter Arnold Karthaus, Illustrated by a faithful narrative of sundry events, which occurred since the embargo was raised in 1809, and war declared against Great Britain by the United States of America to defend her commerce and independence against her encroachments. [Baltimore, Printed by J. T. Hanzsche, 1837] 12 p. MBAt; ScU.   45035

Kearny, Stephen Watts, 1794-
1848.
   Carbine manual; or, rules
for the exercise and
manoeuvres for the U.S.
dragoons. Washington, War
Dept., 1837. 28 p. NWM.
                          45036
Keble, John, 1792-1866.
   The Christian year.
Thoughts in verse for the
Sundays and holidays through-
out the year. By the Rev.
John Keble. New York, Hurst
& Co., 1837. [9]-288 p.
LNB; NBuU.   45037

Keightley, Thomas, 1789-1872.
   The mythology of ancient
Greece and Italy: for the use
of schools. By Thomas Keightley ... 1st American ed., enl.
and improved. New York, D.
Appleton & co., 1837. [13]-
232 p. DLC; MB; MdToH;
NNUT; PJa.   45038

Kelsey, Francis.
   A practical treatise on the
description, cultivation and
management of honey bees. By
Francis Kelsey.... New York,
1837. 24 p. MWA; TxU. 45039

Kemble, Frances Anne, 1809-
1893.
   The star of Seville, a drama.
In five acts. N.Y., Saudners
and Otley, 1837. 130 p. DLC;
IU; OU; PU; TNV.   45040

Kemble and Wetmore's map of
the State of Missouri, with the
latest additions and surveys
from the office of the surveyor
general. (New York, Kemble
and Wetmore, 1837.) MoKCM.
                          45041
Kendall, John, 1726-1815.
   A catechism explanatory of
some of the principles and pre-

cepts of the Christian religion.
Designed for the instruction of
the youthful members of the Society of Friends... 3d ed...
New York, D. & G. F. Colledge,
1837. 128 p. DLC; MWA; PHC;
PPL; RPB.   45042

Kennebec Locks and Canals Company.
   Report of Col. William Boardman ... Engineer of the Kennebec Locks and Canals Company.
November 1, 1837. Augusta,
Printed by Luther Severance,
1837. (3), 4-11, (1) p. MeU;
MWo.   45043

Kennicott, E. D.
   Zethe and other poems.
Rochester, Published by Pratt
& Nichols, L. Tucker, Printer,
1837. 63 p. NBuG; NN; VtU;
WU.   45044

Kenrick, Francis Patrick, 1796-
1863.
   Twenty-eight letters written
to the most Rev. Samuel Eccles-
ton directed to vindicate the
primacy of the Apostolic See.
[Philadelphia, n.p., 1837]. 359
p. WMMU.   45045

Kensington and Penn-Township
Railroad Co.
   Report of the managers of
the Kensington and Penntown-
ship rail-road company, to the
stock-holders at their annual
meeting, held January 9th, 1837.
Philadelphia, Joseph & William
Kite, printers, 1837. 9 p.
DBRE; MiU-T; MWA; NbO; PPF.
                          45046
Kent, James, 1763-1847.
   Opinion of Chancellor Kent
on the usury laws. Albany,
Printed by J. Munsell, 1837.
12 p. CtY; NjR; NN.   45047

Kentucky. Board of Internal Improvements.
Report of the Board of Internal Improvement (1837). 174 p. MHi; PPAmP.							45048

---- House. Journal.
Journal of the House of Representatives of the Commonwealth of Kentucky, begun and held in the town of Frankfort, on Monday the fourth day of December, in the year of our Lord, 1837, and of the Commonwealth the Forty-Sixth. Frankfort, A. G. Hodges, Public printer, 1837. (Pagination varies) KyBgW; KyU-L; KyU.							45049

---- Jefferson Circuit Court.
Rules of the Jefferson Circuit Court; and the Act regulating the Terms...Louisville, 1837. 8 p. MHi.							45050

---- Laws, statutes, etc.
Acts of the General Assembly of the Commonwealth of Kentucky. December session, 1836. James Clark, Governor. Published by authority. Frankfort, A. G. Hodges state printer, 1837. 376 p. A-SC; KyHi; Nj; OrSC; Wa-L.							45051

---- ---- Militia Law of Kentucky. An act to amend the Militia law; approved February 9, 1837. Frankfort, Ky., A. C. Hodges, printer to the state, 1837. 57 p. KyU; MiU-L; NcD.							45052

---- University.
Catalogue of the officers and students,...1836-7. Georgetown, Ky., College Press, 1837. 15 p. KyLx; MH.							45053

Kenyon college, Gambier, O.

Library.
Catalogue of books belonging to the library of the theological seminary of the diocese of Ohio, Kenyon college and the preparatory schools. MDCCCXXXVII. Gambier, G. W. Myers, printer, 1837. 76 p. CSansS; DLC; OCHP; PPAmP.							45054

Kerr, John.
Rip Van Winkle; or, The demons of the Catskill mountains!!! A national drama, in two acts, by John Kerr, author of the "Wandering boys" "Anaconda" ...&c. Printed from the acting copy... Philadephia, Published by R. H. Lenfestey, (1837). 76 p. NNC.							45055

Key to The Shorter Catechism. New York, Trow, 1837. OMC.							45056

Kiener, Louis Charles, 1799-1881.
General species and iconography of recent shells, comprising the Massena museum... Translated from the French by D. Humphreys Storer. Boston, William D. Ticknor, 1837. 6 parts in 1. CtY; DSI; MBM; MeB; MHi.							45057

King, Alonzo, 1796-1835.
Facts not fiction; in a series of letters addressed to his children...Revised by the Committee of Publication. Boston, New England Sabbath School Union, 1837. (10)-106 p. DLC; MPeHi.							45058

---- Memoir of George Dana Boardman, late Missionary to Burmah. Containing much intelligence relative to the Burmah Mission. By Alonzo King, ---- [Quotation] With an introductory essay, new and improved stereotype edition. Boston, Gould, Kendall & Lincoln, 1837. 319 p. MsSC.							45059

---- The ruined family in a letter from a father to his children. Boston, 1837. DLC.
45060
King, David.
Cholera infantum, its causes
and treatment. By David King,
Jr. M.D. ... Boston, D. Clapp,
Jr., office of the medical and
surgical journal, 1837. 22 p.
MB; MdBM; NNN; RNR; RPB.
45061
---- Purpura haemorrhagica,
its causes and treatment. By
David King, Jr. M.D. ... Boston, D. Clapp, Jr., office of
the medical and surgical journal, 1837. 38 p. DSG; MBAt;
RNR; RPB.   45062

King, John Pendleton, 1799-
1888.
Speech...delivered in the
United States senate, Sept.
23, 1837, upon the Subtreasury
bill. n.p., [1837]. 24 p.
CtY; MH; WHi.   45063

---- Speech of Mr. King, of
Georgia, on the Bill Imposing
Additional Duties, as Depositories, in certain cases, on
Public Officers. Delivered in
the Senate of the U.S., Sept.
23, 1837. Washington, Printed
by Gales and Seaton, 1837.
15 p. MBAt; NNC; OClWHi;
PPPAmP; WHi.   45064

---- Speech on the land bill,
delivered in the Senate of the
United States on the 31st of
January 1837. [Washington?
1837]. 15 p. DLC; MH. 45065

King, S. W.
Songs of Zion. Being a
new selection of hymns, ... By
Dr. S. W. King. New Ipswich,
N.H., Published by S. Wilson
King, 1837. 186, (6) p. DLC;

MDeeP; MWHi; Nh; WHi. 45066

King, Thomas Butler, 1804-1864.
Speech...on the land bill,
delivered in the senate of the
United States on the 31st January, 1837. [Washington city,
1837]. 15 p. MBAt; MH; NcD;
TxU; WHi.   45067

Kingsley, George, 1811-1884.
The social choir. Designed
for a class book, or a domestic
circle...arranged as solo's,
duets, trios, and quartettes,
with an accompaniment for the
piano forte. 6th ed. Boston,
Crocker and Brewster, 1837.
3 v. CoU; ICN; MB; NcD; NNUT.
95068
Kinnost, Alex.
Circular Addressed to the
First New Jerusalem Society,
Cincinnati, O., May 17, 1837.
OCHP.   45069

Kippis, Andrew, 1725-1795.
A narrative of the voyages
round the world, performed by
Captain James Cook, with an
account of his life during the
previous and intervening periods.
By A. Kippis, D.D.F.R.S. and
S.A. In two vols. Cincinnati,
Published by U. P. James, 1837.
2 v. CtY.   45070

Kirby, William, 1759-1850.
On the power, wisdom and
goodness of God, as manifested
in the creation of animals, and
in their history, habits and in-
stincts. By the Rev. William
Kirby...2d American ed. Philadelphia, Carey, Lea & Blanchard,
1837. 519 p. CtY; ICT; MH;
PPiW; ViW.   45071

Kirk, Edward Norris.
A Valedictory Sermon, de-
livered at the Fourth Presby-

terian Church in the City of
Albany, April 2, 1837. By the
Rev. E. N. Kirk. Albany,
Packard & Van Benthuysen,
Printers, 1837. 38 p. CSansS;
MBC; MWA; NjR; RPB. 45072

Kirkham, Samuel.
English grammar in familiar
lectures: embracing a new
systematic order of parsing, a
new system of punctuation,
exercises in false syntax, and
a system of philosophical grammar to which are added, A
compendium, an appendix, and
a key to the exercises: designed for the use of schools
and private learners. By
Samuel Kirkham ... 43d ed.,
enl. and improved. Rochester,
N.Y., W. Alling & co., 1837.
228 p. NHem; NRU; PLFM;
WU. 45073

---- ---- 105th ed. Baltimore,
Plaskitt, Fite & co., 1837.
228? p. ICN; MH; NjR; OClWHi.
45074
---- An essay on elocution,
designed for the use of schools
and private learners by Samuel
Kirkham, third edition, enlarged and improved stereotyped
by F. F. Ripley. New York,
published by Robinson, Pratt
and co., 1837. 357 p. CtHC;
GU; MoS; NCaS; NK. 45075

Kissam, Richard S.
Young mother's guide and
nurse's manual; containing advice on the management of infants ... 2nd. ed. Hartford,
Belknap, 1837. 152 p.
CtHWatk; LNT-M. 45076

Eine kleine Lieder-Sammlung
zum allgemeinen Gebrauch des
wahren Gottesdienstes, fur die
Gemeinde Gottes. Pub. Gustav

Peters, Harrisburg, Pa., 1837.
214 p. NK; PHi; ViHarEM.
45077
(Knapp, John Leonard), 1767-
1845.
The journal of a naturalist.
Philadelphia, G. W. Donohue,
1837. MeSaco; MH; NhLeb.
45078
Knapp, Samuel Lorenzo.
Advice in the pursuits of
literature, containing historical,
biographical and critical remarks.
By Samuel L. Knapp ... Middletown, N.J., Evans, 1837. 296
p. CtHT; KyHop; NhD; NjP;
RPB. 45079

Knickerbocker, Diedrich. See
Irving, Washington.

Knickerbocker Almanac for 1838.
By David Young. New York,
N.Y., (1837).
CtY; DLC; MWA; NBuG; NNC.
45080
Knight, A. F.
Sutton's Quick Step. ... com-
posed by Walch. ...Boston,
Parker & Ditson, 1837. (2) p.
MHi. 45081

Knowles, James Davis, 1798-1838.
Memoir of Mrs. Ann H. Judson;
incl. A history of the Amer.
baptist mission in the Burman
empire. 8th ed. Boston, 1837.
395 p. MW. 45082

Knowles, James Sheridan, 1784-
1862.
The daughter. A play in five
acts. By James Sheridan Knowles
... New-York, G. Dearborn &
co., 1837. 107 p. CtY; MH;
MoSC; MWo; RPB. 45083

---- ---- New York, printed by
Scatcherd & Adams, 1837. 107
p. CtHT-W; MB; MH; NCH.
45084

---- The love-chase; a comedy in five acts, by James Sheridan Knowles, as played at the Park theatre... New York, Samuel French, publisher, 1837. (2)-67 p. NBuG; NNC.
45085

---- Select Works of, consisting of His Most Popular Tales and Dramas, with an original notice of His Life and Writings. N.Y., George Dearborn & Co., 1837. 2 v. in 1. NBLIHI; NNS; PPM.
45086

---- The Wrecker's daughter. A play in five acts. By James Sheridan Knowles, ... New York, P. Menard, 1837. 60 p. InU; MB; MH; MMal; OC.   45087

Knowlton, Miner.
Military pyrotechny for the use of the cadets at the United States Military academy West Point. Lithographed by Geo. Aspinwall, West Point, 1837. 40 p. CtY; DLC; ICJ.   45088

Knox, John, 1790-1858.
Comfort in sorrow; a discourse occasioned by the death of Mrs. Marianne F. M'Elroy ....delivered on Sabbath.... Nov. 27, 1837. By John Knox. New York, (n. pub. n. pr.), 1837. 11 p. DLC; NjPT; NN; PPPrHi.   45089

Koch, Christophe Guillaume.
History of the Revolutions in Europe, from the subversion of the Roman Empire in the West, to the Congress of Vienna. From the French of Christopher William Koch. With a continuation to the year 1815, by M. Schoell. Revised and corrected by J. G. Cogswell. With a sketch of the late revolutions in France, Belgium, Poland, and Greece. Embellished with engravings. In two volumes. Middletown, published by Hunt & Noyes, 1837. 2 v. CoCra; InBra; KyU; MiD-B.
45090

Kock, Charles Paul de, 1794-1871.
The good fellow, by Paul de Kock ... Translated from the French, by a Philadelphian ... Philadelphia, E. L. Carey & A. Hart, 1837. 2 v. CSt; CtWatk; PPAmP; TNP; WU.   45091

Kollock, Shepard Kosciuszko.
The doctrine of the perseverance of the saints, illustrated, proved and applied. By Rev. Shepard K. Kollock. Philadelphia, Presbyterian tract and Sunday school society, 1837. 20 p. MiU; NcU; NcOahMI; OCHP; PPPrHi.   45092

[Kraitsir, Charles V], 1804-1860.
The Poles in the United States of America, preceded by the earliest history of the Slavonians, and by the history of Poland. Philadelphia, Kiderlen and Stollmeyer, 1837. 196 p. ICHi; MiU; NbU; PPL; RPB.
45093

Kuhn, William.
Speech pronounced by William Kuhn, of Philadelphia, on the occasion of his graduation at Mount St. Mary's College, Emmittsburg, June 29th, 1837. Baltimore, Murphy & Spalding, Printers, 1837. 24 p. MdBLC; PHi; PPL.   45094

L

Lacey, William Brittingham, 1781-1866.
An illustration of the principles of elocution; designed for

the use of schools, academies, and colleges. 3rd ed., improved and corrected. ... D.D. ... Pittsburgh, pub. by Patterson, Forrester & Co., and by Patterson, Ingram & Co., 1837. [12]-300 p. CSt; MdW; MsAb; OSW.   45095

---- System of moral philosophy; or, Christian ethics designed for the use of parents in their domestic instruction, advanced courses in Sunday Schools and literary institutes. Pittsburgh, Patterson, Forrester & Co. (etc.), 1837. 312 p. PPi.
45096
---- ---- Second edition. By Rev. William B. Lacey, D.D. ... Pittsburgh, (Pa.), Published by Patterson, Ingram and Co., 1837. 312 p. DLC; ICU; LNT; MdBS; MoK.   45097

Lacroix, Silvestre Francois, 1765-1843.
An elementary treatise on plane and spherical trigonometry,...Tr. from the French for the use of the students of the university of Cambridge, New-England. 4th ed. Boston, Hilliard Gray and co., 1837. Ct; MS; NIC; NRU; OO; PPF.   45098

---- Elements of algebra tr. from the French ... by John Farrar. ed. 5. Bost. Hilliard, 1837. 298 p. DGU; MoS; NcU; NJP; OO.   45099

Ladies' garland, devoted to literature instruction, amusement, female biography, etc. Philadelphia, Moore, Waterhouse and Libby, n.pr., 1837. CoU; InU; NjR; NBU; RPB.   45100

The lady's annual register and

housewife's memorandum-book, for 1838. Boston, T. H. Carter; Philadelphia, H. Perkins, (1837). 140 p. DLC; MWA; NNNAM; TxU; ViU; WU. 45101

The lady's cabinet album. N.Y., E. Sands, 1837. xii, 348 p. DLC; IaU; NBuG.   45102

Lafayette, Marie Joseph Paul Yves Roch Gilbert du Motier, marquis de, 1757-1834.
Memoirs, correspondence and manuscripts of General Lafayette. Published by his family. Vol. I. New York, Saunders and Otley, 1837. 552 p. ("Only vol. I was issued.") CtY; LU; MiD-B; PPi; Sc.   45103

Lamb, Charles, 1775-1834.
The life and letters of Charles Lamb. By Thomas Noon Talfourd one of his executors. Philadelphia, Willis P. Hazard, 1837. KyDC; MMe; NjP; PRosC.
45104
---- Tales from Shakspeare: designed as an introduction to the reading of Shakspeare... Third American from the tenth London edition. Baltimore, Bayly & Burns, 1837. [9]-366 p. CtY; MdHi; NjP.   45105

---- The works of Charles Lamb ... A new edition. New York, A. C. Armstrong, [pref. 1837]. 5 v. in 3. IDecJ; KOtU; MiGr; MoClay; OLak.   45106

Lamb, M. T.
Golden Bible; or, The Book of Mormon. Is it from God? N.Y., Ward, 1837. 14-344 p. OO.   45107

Lambard, William.
Report of the committee of the council on the petitions for

the pardon of...with accompanying papers. Augusta, 1837.
20 p. PHi; PPL.   45108

Lamson, David R.
  Earthly and Heavenly Wis-
dom. A Discourse.... By
David R. Lamson. Boston,
Published by Isaac Knapp, 1837.
22 p. ICMe.   45109

Land wirth schaftlicher Calen
der. Lancaster, Pa. Benjamin Bofinger, 1837. MWA.
                              45110
Lander, Richard Lemon, 1804-
1834.
  Journal of an expedition to
explore the course and termination of the Niger, with a narrative of a voyage down that
river to its termination. By
Richard and John Lander.
New York, Harper and bros.,
1837. 2 v. FTU; NNMr;
PMA; PReaHi; ScChP.   45111

Landon, Letitia Elizabeth, afterwards Mrs. George McLean,
1802-1838.
  Traits and trials of early
life. By L. E. L. ... Philadelphia, E. L. Carey & A.
Hart, 1837. [11]-240 p.
DLC; TNP.   45112

Lane, Benjamin Ingersol, 1797-
1875.
  Decision of character. An
address delivered before the
Franklin club, of Rensselaer-
ville, on the evening of the
27th of Nov. 1836. By Rev.
Benjamin I. Lane. Albany,
Printed by J. Munsell, 1837.
15 p. DLC.   45113

Lane Theological Seminary.
Cincinnati, Ohio.
  Catalogue of the Officers and
Students of Lane Theological

Seminary. Cincinnati, Ohio,
1836-7. Cincinnati, Kendall &
Henry, printers, 1837. [4],
[5]-7, [1] p. CSmH; MBC;
MHi; MWA.   45114

Der lange verborgene Schatz und
Haus freund. Skippackville, Pa.,
A. Puewelle, 1837. PPeSchw.
                              45115
Langley, J.
  Catalogues of the Chatham
Circulating library.... New
York, L. Buckingham, 1837.
155 p. DLC.   45116

(Lansing, Abraham).
  Brief remarks in reply to an
article in the Boston Morning
Post, of March 11, 1837, purporting to give an account of
the proceedings of the Democratic
legislative conventions recently
held in Boston, touching the
nomination of a candidate for the
Boston collectorship. By one of
the people. Boston, 1837. 16
p. MH.   45117

Latham, Peter Mere, 1789-1875.
  Lectures on subjects connected with clinical medicine...
Philadelphia, Haswell, Barrington, and Haswell, 1837. (9)-
154 p. KyLxT; MdBJ; NjR; OC;
RPM.   45118

The Laurel: a gift for all seasons. Being a collection of
poems. By American authors.
Baltimore, Bayly & Burns, 1837.
252 p. CtY; ICN; MB; RPB;
VtMidbC.   45119

Laurel Hill cemetery, Philadelphia.
  Regulations of the Laurel Hill
cemetery, on the river Schuylkill,
near Philadelphia. Incorporated
by the legislature of Pennsylvania.
[Philadelphia, A. Waldie, pr.],
1837. 16 p. DLC; MH; NN;
PPAmP.   45120

Law, William, 1686-1761.
An extract from Mr. Law's
Serious Call to a Holy Life.
By the Rev. John Wesley, A.M.,
Late fellow of Lincoln College.
New York, Published by T.
Mason & G. Love, 1837. [2],
307 p. CoDI; InLW; MShi;
NcD.   45121

Lawrence, Abbott, 1792-1855.
Letter of the Hon. Abbott
Lawrence, to a Committee of
the Citizens of Boston, on the
Subject of the Currency &c.
Boston, John H. Eastburn,
Printer, 1837. 12 p. ICJ;
MH; Mos; MWA; PHi.   45122

Lawrence, John, 1753-1839.
Moubray on breeding, rear-
ing and fattening all kinds of
poultry, cows, swine, and oth-
er domestic animals; 2d.
American [ed.] Boston, Joseph
Breck, 1837. 278 p. DNAL;
MB; MWA; NN.   45123

Lawrence, Levin.
The pioneer: or a treatise
upon the subject of money.
By Levin Lawrence. ... Baltimore, printed for the publisher,
1837. 44 p. DLC; MB; MdHi.
                              45124
Lawton, Carr.
Elements of knowledge...
for use of schools, etc. Providence, H. H. Brown, 1837.
36 p. DLC.   45125

Lazarus, E.
The human trinity. N.
York, 1837. MB.   45126

Leake, John G.
The last will, and testa-
mental of J. G. Leake; act of
incorporation of the Leake and
Watts Orphan House, in the
city of New York....(etc.)

(By John G. Leake). New York,
(n.pub., n.pr.), 1837. 20 p.
NjPT.   45127

Leavitt, Joshua, 1794-1873.
The Christian lyre; a collection of hymns and tunes adopted
for social worship, prayer meetings, and revivals of religion.
18th ed. rev. New York,
Leavitt, Lord; Boston, Crocker
and Brewster, 1837. 106 p.
ICN; MH-AH; ViU.   45128

---- ... Easy lessons in reading.
For the use of the younger
classes in common schools. Keene,
N.H., J. Prentiss, 1837. 156 p.
NjP.   45129

---- Visions of heavenly glory.
The substance of an address delivered...Dec. 15, 1836, at the
funeral of Rev. John R. Mc-
Dowell. New York, Benedict,
1837. 24 p. CBPSR; MBAt;
MWA; NcD; PPPrHi.   45130

Lecture delivered before the
Ogdensburgh lyceum, on the
political rights of women. December, 1837. Ogdensburgh,
N.Y., (1837?). 35 p. IU.
                              45131
Lee, Edwin.
Observations on the principal
medical institutions and practice
of France, Italy and Germany;
with notices of the universities
and cases from hospital practice, to which is added an appendix on animal magnetism and
homoeopathy. Philadelphia, Haswell, Barrington & Haswell, 1837.
102 p. CtY; KyLo; MB; NjR;
PP.   45132

[Lee, Hannah Farnham (Sawyer)],
1780-1865.
The contrast; or, Mosed of
education. [A novel.] Boston,

Whipple and Damrell; New York,
Scofield & Voorhies, 1837.
116 p. CSmH; DLC; MB; MWA;
OClW.   45133

---- Elinor Fulton. By the
author of Three Experiments of
Living....first edition. Boston,
Published by Whipple & Damrell
....1837. 144 p. MB; MBAt;
MoSMa; RBr.   45134

---- ---- 7th ed. Boston,
Whipple & Damrell, 1837. 144 p.
CTY.   45135

---- ---- 7th ed. Boston,
Whipple & Damrell; New York,
S. Colman, 1837. (9)-144 p.
CtY.   45136

---- ---- 9th ed. Boston,
Whipple & Damrell; New York,
S. Colman, 1837. viii, (9)-
144 p. CtHC; DLC; MWA;
RPB.   45137

---- ---- Eleventh edition.
Boston, published by Whipple
& Damrell; New York, Samuel
Colman, 1837. 144 p. ABBS;
DLC; MB.   45138

---- The experiments of living:
... tenth edition. Boston, Published by William S. Dumrell,
... 1837. 68 p. ArLSJ; ICN;
MB-FA; MLy; NNS.   45139

---- Fourth experiment...living
without means. Boston, 1837.
MB.   45140

---- ---- 2nd ed. Boston,
Broaders and Co., 1837.
68 p. MB.   45141

---- ---- Third edition. Boston, Otis, Broaders & Company.
... 1837. 68 p. DLC; NjP;
NNS.   45142

---- ---- 6th ed. Boston, Otis,
Broaders and Company, 1837.
68 p. ICU; NN.   45143

---- ---- 8th ed. Boston, Otis,
Broaders & Company, 1837.
68 p. MB; MH; MWA.   45144

---- ---- 10th ed. Boston, Otis,
Broaders & Company, 1837.
68 p. CTY.   45145

---- ---- 13th ed. Boston, Otis,
Broaders and Company, 1837.
68 p. MBAt.   45146

---- The Harcourts; illustrating
the benefit of retrenchment and
reform, by a lady. Part III.
Stories from real life. New York,
S. Colman; Boston, Weeks, Jordan, 1837. 144 p. CU; KEmt;
MBL; MdBD.   45147

---- ---- Part 3. Second Edi-
tion ... (anon.). New York, S.
Colman, 1837. 144 p. CtY; MB;
MWA.   45148

---- ---- 3d ed. New York, S.
Colman; Boston, Weeks, Jordan
& co., 1837. 144 p. DLC; NjP.
                             45149
---- ---- 4th ed. New-York, S.
Colman; Boston, Weeks, Jordan
& Co., 1837. 144 p. ViU.
                             45150
---- Living on other people's
means; or The history of Simon
Silver. Boston, Weeks, Jordan
& Co., 1837. 72 p. DLC; MB;
MH-BA; MWA.   45151

---- ---- 3rd ed. Boston, Weeks,
Jordan and Co., 1837. 72 p.
MH-BA.   45152

---- Rich Enough, A Tale of
the Times...(anon.). Boston,
Whipple & Damrell, 1837. 72 p.
CtY; ICBB; IUC; MBAt; MWA.
                             45153

---- ---- Boston, Whipple and
Damrell; New York, S. Colman,
1837. 72 p. CtY; ICN; MB;
NN; ViU.   45154

---- Three Experiments of
Living: Living within the
Means; Living Up to the Means;
Living beyond the Means ...
(anon.). Boston, William S.
Damrell, 1837. 143 p. CU;
DLC; MB; MPiB; RPB.   45155

---- ---- Boston, published by
William S. Damrell and Benj. H.
Greene, 1837. 10, 143 p.
DLC; MiU-C; MH; NN; WU.
                            45156
---- ---- 2d ed. Boston,
W. S. Damrell, 1837. 143 p.
CtY; DLC; MBAt; MWA; NN.
                            45157
---- ---- Seventh Edition.
Boston, Published by William
S. Damrell, And Samuel Col-
man, 1837. [13]-143 p. CtHC;
CtY; ViRut; ViU.   45157a

---- ---- 10th ed. Boston,
William S. Damrell, 1837. 143 p.
MHi; NNS.   45158

---- ---- 15th ed. Boston,
William S. Damrell, 1837. 143 p.
DLC; IEG; KyHop; OClWHi;
RPB.   45159

---- ---- 20th ed. Boston,
Whipple & Damrell, 1837. 143 p.
CtY; MB; ViU.   45160

Lee, John.
    Proportional formulae, bi-
complex and tri-complex; or,
A system algebraically, derived
from the nature of proportionals,
for the facilitation of that process in arithmetic commonly called
the rule of three ... Cambridge,
Metcalf, Torry, and Ballou, 1837.
23 p. CtY; M.   45161

Lee, Jonathan.
    The labors of a pastor de-
feated and his hopes disappointed.
An address designed to be presented to a mutual council, called
for the dismission of a pastor
from his charge. Middlebury,
(Vt.), pr. by Elam R. Jewett,
1837. 23 p. CtHWatk; MBAt;
MH; MWA; VtMidSM.   45162

Lee, N. K. M.
    The cook's own book and house-
keeper's register, comprehending
all valuable receipts for cooking
meat, fish, and fowl...by a Boston housekeeper, ... Boston,
Munroe & Francis...1837. 300,
37 p. CtHWatk; DLC; NNNAM.
                            45163
Lee, Richard Henry, 1794-1865.
    An address, delivered at the
dedication of the new hall of the
Washington literary society of
Washington college, September
1st, 1837. By Richard Henry
Lee ... Washington, Pa., Printed
by John Grayson, 1837. 13 p.
CSmH; InU; PWW.   45164

Leeser, Isaac, 1806-1868.
    Discourses, argumentative and
devotional, on the subject of the
Jewish religion, delivered at the
Synagogue Mikveh Israel, in
Philadelphia, in the years 5590-
5597. Philadelphia, 1837. 2 v.
in 1. ICU; MoU; OCH; PPA;
PPDrop.   45165

---- ---- Philadelphia, Sherman,
1837-41. 3 v. in 2. CtY; ICU;
MdW; NNC; PU.   45166

---- Form of prayers according
to the custom of the Spanish and
Portuguese Jews. Philadelphia,
Haswell, 1837-38. 6 v. GratzC;
MdBJ; NN; PPAmP; PU; UofPLea.
                            45167
Legare, Hugh Swinton, 1797-1843.

Speech of Mr. H. S. Legare, of South Carolina, on the bill imposing additional duties as depositaries in certain cases, on public officers. Delivered in the House of representatives, U.S. October, 1837. Washington, 1837. 32 p. CtY; MWA; NNC; PHi; RPB; ScCC. 45168

---- ---- 3d ed. Washington, 1837. CtHWatk; ICN; MHi. 45169

Legare, John D.
Grey Sulphur Springs. Account of the medical properties of the Grey Sulphur Springs, Virginia. Second edition, with a statement of the cases of 1835 and 1836. Charleston, Miller, 1837. 24 p. DNLM; MB; MH-M; NNNAM; ViU. 45170

Legendre, Adrien Marie, 1752-1833.
Elements of geometry and trigonometry. Translated... by David Brewster...revised... by Charles Davies... New York, A. S. Barnes and Co., Cincinnati, Rickey, Mallory and Webb, 1837. GAuY; MiU; PPAN. 45171

---- ---- Tr. from the French, ... New York, Wiley & Long; Collins, Keese & Co.; Philadelphia, Desilver, Thomas & Co., 1837. 297, 62 p. MiU. 45172

Legrand, Baptiste Alexis Victor.
Summary description of the lighthouses and watch, lights lighted on the coast of France, to the 1st of August 1837... tr. by L. Pleasonton. Washington, Davis, 1837. 45 p. DLC; PPAmP. 45173

Lehigh Coal & Navigation Company.

History, charter, acts, mortgages, leases, &c. Philadelphia, n.pr., 1837-1874. 10 v. P. 45174

---- Report of the board of managers of the Lehigh Coal and Navigation Company, to the stockholders. January 9, 1837. Philadelphia, Printed by James Kay, Jun. & Brother, 1837. (V) 16 p. NcWsM; P. 45175

Leib, James Ronaldson.
Thoughts on the elective Franchise. Philadelphia, 1837. 20 p. PHi. 45176

Lempriere, John, 1765?-1824.
... Bibliotheca classics; or, A dictionary of all the principal names and terms relating to the geography, topography, history, literature and mythology of antiquity and of the ancients with a chronological table. Rev. and cor. ... by Lorenzo L. Da Ponte and John D. Ogilby. 10th American ed. ... N.Y., Dean, 1837. 800 p. CtHT; CU; IU; Md; MH; OCir. 45177

---- Classical dictionary for schools and academies containing every name and all that is either important or useful in the original work. Boston, American Stationer's Co., 1837. MH. 45178

Leominster, (Mass.).
The Report of a committee chosen by the inhabitants of Leominster, to take into consideration the subject matter of the future relief and support of their paupers. Courier Press, J. Garfield, Printer, 1837. 7 p. ICN; MLeo. 45179

Leonard, Levi Washburn.
The literary and scientific class book, embracing the leading

facts and principles of science [etc.]. Selected from John Platt's Literary and Scientific class book, and from various other sources and adopted to the wants and conditions of youth in the United States. Keene, N.H., J. Prentiss, 1837. MH; Nh. 45180

Leslie, Charles, 1650-1722.
Leslie's method with deists: wherein the truth of the Christian religion is demonstrated: in a letter to a friend. New York, Published by T. Mason and G. Lane, J. Collord, printer, 1837. 32 p. Ct; TNS.
45181
---- A Short and easy method with the Jews. Hartford, P. B. Gleason & Co., 1837. 32 p. Ct; MBC. 45182

Leslie, Eliza, 1787-1858.
Pencil sketches; or, Outlines of character and manners, by Miss Leslie ... 3d series. Phil., Carey, 1837. 4-283 p. CtHT; MBL; NBuG; RPA. 45183

---- Seventy-five receipts for pastry, cakes, and sweetmeats. Boston, Munroe & Francis, 1837. 37 p. NNNAM. 45184

---- The violet: a Christmas and New Year's gift. See under title.

Lessons for good children, in easy rhyme. New Haven, S. Babcock, 1837. 16 p. CtY; ICU. 45185

Lessons for Lent; or, Instructions for every day in the year, on the two sacraments of penance and the blessed Eucharist. Philadelphia, Eugene Cummiskey, 1837. 144 p. IaDaSA; IaDuMtC; MdBLC; MdW; PLatS. 45186

Letters about the Hudson River and its vicinity. See Hunt, Freeman.

Letters on the church by an Episcopalian. New York, Harper & brothers, 1837. 180 p. GDecCT. 45187

Letters on the origin and progress of the New Haven theology. See Tyler, Bennet.

Letters on the Pennsylvania system of solitary imprisonment.... 2d. ed. Philadelphia, n. pub. John C. Clark, pr., 1837. 31 p. NjR; PPAmP; ScC. 45188

Letters to the Honourable Levi Woodbury, secretary of the treasury of the United States. New York, E. B. Clayton, printer and stationer, 1837. 24 p. ICN; MdHi; MH; MiU; WHi.
45189
Leverett, Frederick Percival, 1803-1836.
A new and copious lexicon of the Latin language; compiled chiefly from the "Magnum Totius Latinitatis Lexicon: of Facciolati and Forcellini, and the German works of Scheller and Luenemann.; edited, by F. P. Leverett. Boston, J. H. Wilkins and R. B. Carter, and C. C. Little and James Brown, 1837. 2 v. in 1. IU; MH; NjP; NN; WAsN.
45190
Levizac, Jean Pons Victor Legcutz de, 1775-1813.
A theoretical and practical grammar of the French tongue. 15th Amer. ed. New York, 1837. KyBgW; MB; MH. 45191

Levy, Morris.
Map of Steuben county, New

York... Philadelphia, 1837.
PPL.   45192

Lewis, S. J.
Showing the manner in which
they do things...Presbyterian
Ch. Morris-Town, the Author,
1837. 28 p. MB.   45193

Lewis, William Henry.
Sermon before the annual
convention of the Protestant
Episcopal Church, New Bedford,
Sept. 27, 1837. Boston, Torrey
& Blair, 1837. 21 p. MeBat;
MWA; NcD; PPL; RPB.   45194

Lewis County Anti-Slavery
Society.
Sketch of proceedings...in
the village of Lowville, January
10, 1837. Watertown, Pr. by
Knowlton & Rice for the Com-
mittee of Publication, 1837.
NN.   45195

L'Homond, Charles Francois,
1727-1794.
Elements of French grammar:
by M. L'Homond, ... translated
from the French, with additional
notes, for the use of schools.
By H. W. Longfellow, ...
Fourth edition. Hallowell,
Glazier, Masters & Smith, 1837.
MB; MH; NN; PPT.   45196

---- French exercises; selected
chiefly from Wanostrocht and
adapted to L'Homond's Elements
of French grammar. 4th ed.
Hallowell, Glazier, Masters and
Smith, 1837. (2), (5)-97 p.
MWH.   45197

The library of health, and
teacher on the human constitution. See The teacher of
health and the laws of the human constitution, 1835.

Lieber, Francis, 1800-1872.
Political hermeneutics; or On
political interpretation and con-
struction; and also on precedents.
Boston, C. C. Little and J.
Brown, 1837. 78 p. DLC; PPL;
ScU.   45198

The life of Benjamin Franklin.
Illus. by tales, sketches, and
anecdotes. Adapted to the use
of schools with engravings.
Philadelphia, Desilver, Thomas
and Co., 1837. 180 p. IEG;
InU; LNT; PPAmP; RHi. 45199

The life of Christopher Columbus, illustrated by tales,
sketches, and anecdotes.
Adapted to the use of schools.
With engravings. Philadelphia,
Desilver, Thomas & Co., 1837.
187 p. NN; OCh; ViU.   45200

No entry   45201

The life of Fredrich Schiller.
See Carlyle, Thomas.

The life of King Hezekiah. Boston, Massachusetts Sabbath School
Union, 1837. 51 p. DLC.
                             45202
The life of George Washington,
illustrated by tales, sketches
and anecdates. Adapted to the
use of schools. With engravings.
Philadelphia, Desilver, Thomas
and co., 1837. 178 p. CSmH;
DLC; FS; MWA; PHi.   45203

Life of George Washington. See
also Weems, Mason Locke.

The life of Philip Melanchton.
Printed for the blind under the
direction of S. Howe at the ex-
pense of the American Sunday
School Union. Boston, 1837.
CtY; MB.   45204

The Lilly. A Holiday Present.
New York, E. Sands, 1837.
232 p. MdCatS; MiU.   45205

Lincoln, Allen.
The Student's Account Book.
By Allen Lincoln. Boston,
Whipple & Damrell; New York,
Scofield and Voorhies, 1837.
208 p. DLC.   45206

Lincoln, Almira. See Phelps,
Almira (Hart) Lincoln.

Lincoln, Ensign, 1799-1832.
Sabbath school classbook,
comprising copius exercises on
the sacred scriptures. Boston,
1837. 123 p. NHC-S.   45207

Lincoln, Levi, jr., 1782-1868.
Speech...in the House of
Representatives of the U.S.
Feb. 7, 1837 on the resolution
to censure the Hon. John Q.
Adams, for inquiring of speaker, whether a paper, purporting
to come from slaves, came within the resolution laying on the
table all petitions relating to
slavery. Wash. Gales, 1837.
9 p. CtMW; ICMe; MiD-B;
NcD; WHi.   45208

Lincoln, Luther Barker, 1802-
1855.
An address delivered at
Deerfield before the Society of
Adelphi, on the evening of
January 1, 1837. Greenfield,
Mass., C. J. J. Ingersoll,
printer, 1837. 26 p. CSmH;
MDeeP; MHi; MWA; PHi.   45209

Lincoln, Robert W.
Lives of the presidents of
the United States;...By Robert W.
Lincoln. Embellished with a portrait of each of the presidents
and forty-five engravings. New
York, W. W. Reed, 1837. 508 p.

Ct; MC; NIC; PP.   45210

Lincoln, Sumner.
The glory of the man. A
sermon, by Rev. Sumner Lincoln.
Gardner, Mass. Delivered January 1, 1837. Published by the
Gardner female moral reform society. Boston, Isaac Knapp,
1837. 15 p. MBC; MiD-B;
NNUT.   45211

Lincoln, (William), 1801-1843.
An Address ... before the
Massachusetts Horticultural So-
ciety ... September 20, 1837.
... Boston, Dutton and Went-
worth, Printers, 1837. 56 p.
DLC; MH; MToP; MWA; PPL.
                         45212
---- Circular, dated Worcester,
May 20, 1837, regarding the
publication of the Journals of
the Provincial Congress of
Massachusetts. [Worcester?
1837?] MHi.   45213

---- (Circular sent to towns and
cities of Massachusetts requesting
material to aid in the publication
of the Journals of the Provincial
Congress, etc.) by William
Lincoln. (Worcester, 1837).
(2) p. M.   45214

---- History of Worcester, Massachusetts, from its earliest settlement to September, 1836:
With various notices relating to
the history of Worcester county
...Worcester, M.D. Phillips and
co., 1837. 383 p. CoD; ICU;
MBBC; NhD; PHi.   45215

Lindsley, Philip.
A lecture on popular educa-
tion. By Philip Lindsley, D.D.
President of the University of
Nashville. Nashville, S. Nye
& Co.--Printers, 1837. [3]-38,
[1] p. DLC; MH; PPPrHi; T.
                         45216

---- Speech in behalf of the university of Nashville, delivered on the day of the anniversary commencement, October 4, 1837. By Philip Lindsley. Nashville, S. Nye and co., printers, 1837. 38 p. DLC; MH; PPPrHi; ScU; TxU.   45217

Linsley, James H.
Select hymns, adapted to the devotional exercises of the Baptist denomination by James H. Linsley and Gustavus F. Davis. Second edition. Hartford, Canfield and Robins, 1837. 407 p. OCl.   45218

Lionel Wakefield. See Massie, W.

Lispenard, Alice, d. 1836.
Testimony taken in the matter of proving the last will and testament of Alice Lispenard ... before James Campbell ... surrogate of the city and county of New York. New-York, W. Applegate, printer, 1837. 354 p. CU; Cu-Law.   45219

Liston, Robert, 1794-1847.
Elements of Surgery. By Robert Liston, Fellow of the Royal Colleges of Surgeons in London and Edinburgh, Senior Surgeon to The Royal Dispensary For The City and County of Edinburgh, Lecturer on Surgery, Etc. Etc., Philadelphia, E. L. Carey and A. Hart, 1837. 540 p. Ia; LNT-M; NhD; OClW; ViU.
                                45220
---- ---- Philadelphia, Haswell, Barrington, and Haswell, 1837. 540 p. ArU-M; KyLo; MdBJ; PPA; OC.   45221

Littell, Squire, 1803-1886.
A manual of the diseases of the eye. By S. Littell, Jr., M.D. one of the surgeons of the Wills hospital for the blind and lame, fellow of the College of physicians of Philadelphia, etc. etc. Philadelphia, Published by John S. Littell, 1837. 255 p. IaGG; MdBJ; NcU; PPiU; TCh.
                                45222
Little, Brown & Company. Boston.
A Catalogue of Law Books. Boston, 1837. 8, 70, (1) p. MHi.   45223

Little Frank's Almanack, to show little boys and girls their play days. Concord, John F. Brown, 1837. 7, [7] p., 1 ℓ. DLC.
                                45224
Little Harry and the Apples. Northampton, J. Metcalf, 1837. 18 p. ICU.   45225

The Little lamb; or Virtue's reward. (anon.). Boston, Mass. S. S. Society, 1837. 92 p. DLC.
                                45226
Little lessons for little learners. New Haven, S. Babcock, 1837. 16 p. DLC.   45227

Little rhymes for little readers. Northampton, J. Metcalf, 1837. 18 p. ICU.   45228

Little Sally of the Sabbath-School. (Seventh Series-No. 11.) Concord, Published by Atwood & Brown, 1837. 16 p. MH.
                                45229
Livermore, Abiel Abbot.
A discourse delivered at Walpole, Oct. 31, 1837, before the "Sunday School Association in connection with the Cheshire Pastoral Association," By Abiel A. Livermore....Keene, John Prentiss, 1837. 12 p. ICMe; MB; MBAt; MH-AH; NjR.
                                45230

---- A discourse delivered on Thanksgiving day, Dec. 7, 1837, in the Unitarian church, Keene, N.H. By A. A. Livermore. ... Keene, John Prentiss, 1837. 19 p. MBAU; MBAt; MH-AH; Nh; RPB.   45231

The lives and bloody exploits of the most noted pirates,... including correct accounts of the late piracies, committed in the West Indias, and the expedition of Commodore Porter; also, those committed on the Brig Mexican, who were executed at Boston in 1835. Hartford, Con., published by Ezra Strong, 1837. 208 p. MBevHi; MMel; NN; RHi.   45232

....Lives of the apostles and early martyrs of the church. [Designed for Sunday readings.] By the author of "The trial of skill." New-York, Published by Harper & brothers, 1837. 204 p. TNP.   45233

Living on other people's means. See [Lee, Hannah Farnham (Sawyer)].

Livius, Titus.
   Titi Livii Patavini Historiarum Liber primus et selecta quaedam capita, Curavit motulisque instruxit Carolus Folsom. Bostoniae, Sumptibus Hilliard, Gray, et soc., 1837. 287 p. OCl; OO.   45234

Lloyd, William Freeman, 1791-1853.
   Sketch of the life of Robert Raikes, esq., and of the history of Sunday Schools, by W. F. Lloyd. New York, T. Mason & G. Lane, J. Collord, printer, 1837. [9]-125 p. CSansS; NNMHi.   45235

Lockhart, John Gibson, 1794-1854.
   ... The history of Napoleon Buonaparte. By J. G. Lockhart, esq. With copper-plate engravings ... New York, Harper & Brothers, 1837. 2 v. CU; FTU; LNH; Mok; PMA.   45236
---- Memoirs of the life of Sir Walter Scott, bart. Boston, Otis, Broaders and Company, 1837. 4 v. MH.   45237

---- ---- Boston, Otis, Broaders, and Company, 1837. 7 v. CtMW; MB; OCX; RPA; VtU.   45238

---- ---- New York, W. Lewer, 1837. (Foster's cabinet miscellany). CtY; InGrD; NN; MBC; MLen.   45239

---- ---- Philadelphia, Carey, Lea, and Blanchard, 1837. 2 v. CSmH; DLC; MoKU; OU; PU.   45240
---- ---- (volumes 1-4 - Boston, Otis, Broaders, and Co.) Philadelphia, Carey, Lea, & Blanchard, 1837-1838. 7 v. CtY; CU; MB; MH; OO.   45241

Lockwood, Rufus A, 1811-1857.
   Speech of R. A. Lockwood, esq., delivered in defence of J. H. W. Frank, at the October term of the Tippecanoe Circuit court, 1837. Indianapolis, Bolton and Livingston, 1837. 76 p. CSmH; DLC; InLW; MH-L; NN.   45242

Long, J.
   The nightingale arranged as a rondo for the piano forte, by J. Long. N.Y., First & Hall, 1837. 3 p. WHi.   45243

Long, Stephen Harriman, 1784-1864.
   Report on a reconnoissance &

survey of the Western & Atlantic Rail Road of the State of Georgia. Milledgeville, Printed at the Federal Union Office, by Park & Rogers, 1837. 51 p. ViU.   45244

---- Report on a reconnoissance for a rail road from Portland to Bangor, by order of the Board of Internal Improvements for the State of Maine. Augusta [Maine], Smith & Robinson, 1837. 31 p. DBRE; MH-BA; MiU-T; NN.   45245

---- Report on the preliminary survey of the Belfast Quebec Rail Road, 1836. By S. H. Long ... Augusta, Smith & Robinson, printers, 1837. 30 p. DBRE; MeHi; MeU; NN.   45246

---- Supplement: Explanatory of certain improvements in the construction of wooden, or frame bridges, patented by Lt. Col. S. H. Long, in 1837. Concord, N.H., John F. Brown, 1837. 72 p. DLC; Nh.   45247

The Long Island Railroad Company.
    Report of special committee to inspect the books and transactions of the Long Island railroad company. And their opinion upon the condition and future prospects of the company's concerns. New-York, Printed by J. Booth & Son, 1837. 14 p. DLC; NBuG; NN; NRU.   45248

---- To the stockholders of the L.-I.R.R. Co. [N.Y., 1837.] 12 p. NN.   45249

Longden, Henry, 1754-1812.

The life of Henry Longden, minister of the gospel, compiled from his memoirs, diary, letters, and other authentic documents .... New York, Mason and G. Lane; J. Collord, printer, 1837. 207 p. ArPb; ICU; MnSH; NjPass; PPiW.   45250

Longworth's American almanac, New York register and city directory, for the sixty-second year of American independence. New York, Thomas Longworth, 1837. 708, 13-36 p. NjHo; NjR; NNA; NNIA; NNS. 45251

Loomis' No. 4 Pittsburgh Almanac,....for the year of our Lord 1838:....Calculated by Sanford C. Hill....Pittsburgh, Published and Sold by Luke Loomis, [1837.] 36 p. MWA; PWCHi.
                          45252
Lord, John Chase, 1805-1877.
    Signs of the times. A sermon, delivered at the Pearl street church, and at the First Presbyterian church, on Sabbath, November 26, 1837. By John D. Lord, A.M. Buffalo, N.Y., Press of Oliver G. Steele, 1837. 18 p. CSmH; MBAt; MH-And; NN; OO.   45253

Lords prayer. Remarks on the Lord's prayer. By an Anastasian Boston, 1837. ICMe; MA.
                          45254
Lord's supper: in three dissertations. By several authors. New York, New-York Yearly Meeting of Friends, 1837. 197 p. ICU.   45255

Lothrop, Samuel Kirkland, 1804-1886.
    Why should we Labor to Extend our Faith? By S. K. Lothrop. 1st series, No. 115. Boston, James Munroe & Co.,

1837. 12 p. CBPac; ICMe;
MeB; MH-And; RHi. 45256

Loubat, Alphonse.
The American Vine--dresser's
guide. N.Y., 1837. MnHi.
45257

Louisa Railroad Company.
The president and directors
of the Louisa Railroad Company
respectfully request your attendance at the opening of the
Louisa Railroad on the 20th in-
stant. Taylorsville, Dec. 15,
1837. [n.p., 1837] Broadside.
ViU. 45258

---- Report of the surveys for
the Louisa railroad, charter of
the company and proceedings
of the stockholders at their
annual meetings. Richmond,
printed by T. W. White, 1836.
30 p. CSt. 45259

Louisiana. General assembly.
Joint committee of finance.
Report of the committee on
the banking situation of the
monied institutions of New Orleans, Submitted to the legislature, Feb. 1837. New Orleans,
1837. 23 p. MH. 45260

---- ---- Joint committee on
the affairs of the Citizen's
bank of Louisiana.
Report of the members of
the committee named on the
part of the Senate to compose
the joint committee, and relative
to certain measures proposed by
the Committee of the House of
representatives for 1836. Submitted to the legislature, Jan.
1841-New Orleans, G. Hewes,
1837. 8 p. MH. 45261

---- Laws, statutes, etc.
Acts passed at the first session of the thirteenth legislature

of the State of Louisiana, began
and held in the City of New Orleans, the second day, of January, 1837. Published by authority. New Orleans, Jerome Bayon,
1837. In-SC; LNBA; MdBB;
NNLI; Wa-L. 45262

Louisville, Ky. Medical Institute.
Circular address of the president and faculty of the Louisville Medical Institute. Louisville, Ky., Prentice and Weissinger, 1837. 10 p. Ky; MB;
OC. 45263

Louisville, Cincinnati & Charles-
ton R.R. Company.
Annual report of the presi-
dent and directors of the Louis-
ville, Cincinnati & Charleston
Rail-road Company. Charleston,
A. E. Miller, 1837- . No. 1- .
DLC; NNE; TxU. 45264

---- Proceedings of the stockholders of the Louisville, Cincinnati and Charleston Railroad
company, at their first meeting,
held in Knoxville, on the 9th
January, 1837. Knoxville,
Printed at the Knoxville Register office, by Ramsey and Craighead, 1837. 20 p. DLC; NN;
TxU; WM; WU. 45265

---- Proceedings of the stockholders of the Louisville, Cincinnati and Charleston Rail Road
Company, at their second meeting,
held at Flat Rock, North Carolina,
on the 16th of October, 1837,
with the first annual report of
the president and directors, the
report of the chief and associate
engineers, and the bylaws.
Charleston, E. A. Miller, 1837.
67 p. WU; WM. 45266

Lovejoy, Joseph Cammet.
Memoir of the Rev. E. P.

Lovejoy; who was murdered in defence of the liberty of the press, at Alton, Ill., Nov. 7, 1837. New York, 1837. 380 p. RHi. 45267

Lover, Samuel.
Rory O'More: a national romance. By Samuel Lover, Esq. In 2 vols. Philadelphia, Carey Lea & Blanchard, 1837. 2 v. MBAt; MBL; PFal. 45268

(Lowell, James Russell), 1819-1891.
(Uncollected poems and prose sketches contributed to Harvardiana vol. 4, nos. 1, 2, 5, 6, 10, by James Russell Lowell, one of the editors, while a student at Harvard.) Cambridge, J. Owen, 1837-38. 5 pts. (in 1.) MH. 45269

Lowell, Mass.
Address of ... Mayor of ... Lowell, to the City on Council, ... April 3, 1837. [Lowell,] Huntress-Printer, [1837.] 8 p. MB. 45270

---- The charter of the city of Lowell, and the rules and orders of the city council. Published by order of the government. Leonard Huntress, printers, (Lowell, April), 1837. 471 p. MB; MLow; MLowCH. 45271

---- First annual report of the receipts and expenditures of the city of Lowell. February, 1837. Lowell, printed by Dearborn & Bellows, 1837. 650 p. MLow. 45271a

---- Map Auditors Rep. Lowell, 1837-1894. 9 & Covs. MB. 45272
---- Second Baptist Church.
Facts relative to the Second

Baptist meeting house in Lowell ... Lowell,? 1837. ICN; MHi. 45273
---- ---- A Summary declaration of the faith and practise ... Lowell, 1837. 23 p. MBC. 45274
The Lowell directory ... Boston, Mass., Sampson & Murdoch company, 1837. 1 v. DLC; ICN. 45275
Lowell Sabbath School Union.
First Annual Report ... of the Lowell Sabbath School Union ... Lowell, Leonard Huntress, Printer, 1837. 45276

Lumpkin, Joseph Henry, 1799-1867.
Address delivered before Hopewell Presbytery, the board of trustees of Oglethorpe University, and a large concourse of the ladies and gentlemen at the Methodist Church in the city of Milledgeville...[Milledgeville], 1837. 24 p. GU-De. 45277

[Lundy, Benjamin], 1789-1839.
The war in Texas; a review of facts and circumstances showing that this is a crusade against Mexico, set on foot and supported by slave holders, land speculators, etc., in order to reestablish, extend and perpetuate the system of slavery and slave trade. 2d ed., rev. and enl. By a citizen of the United States. Philadelphia, Printed for the publishers by Merrihew and Gunn, 1837. 64 p. CSt; MHi; PHC; RPB; TxU. 45278
Lunt, William Parsons, 1805-1857.
The Manager and the Star. A discourse preached Christmas Day, December 25th, 1836, in the First Congregational Church in Quincy, by William P. Lunt. Quincy, Printed by Green & Os-

borne, 1837. 12 p. ICMe;
ICN; MBAU; MBC; NN.   45279

---- Psyche. A Poem. (Be-
fore the Phi Beta Kappa Society Alpha of Massachusetts,
in Cambridge, 1837.) 15 p.
MHi.   45280

Luther, Martin, 1483-1546.
[De Servo Arbitrio. Eng]
The bondage of the will, written
in answer to the Diatribe of
Erasmus on freewill. By Mar-
tin Luther. Translated from the
latin by the Rev. Henry Cole,
of Clark-Hall, Cambridge.
Baltimore, printed by John F.
Toy, 1837. 431 p. MdBS;
MPiB; NjNbS.   45281

---- A commentary upon the
epistle of Paul to the Galatians.
By Martin Luther. To which
is prefixed an account of the
life of the author.... [Hart-
ford], Published by Solmon S.
Miles, 1837. 528 p. GEU;
NcD; TChFPr.   45282

---- Der Kleine Catechismus des
seligen D. Martin Luthers...
Philadelphia, G. W. Mentz und
Sohn, 1837. PPeSchw.   45283

The Lutheran pulpit, and month-
ly religious magazine. V. 1-2;
Jan. 1837-Dec. 1838. Albany,
N.Y., J. Munsell, pr., 1837-
1838. 2 v. CBPL; IaDuW;
MH-AH; NAl; PPLT.   45284

Luzerne County.
Memorial of citizens of Luzerne County, relative to "An
act requesting lateral railroads." Read in Convention,
November 6, 1837. Harrisburg,
Printed by Thompson & Clark,
1837. 6 p. PPM.   45285

Lyell, Charles, 1795-1875.
Principles of geology: being
an inquiry how far the former
changes of the earth's surface
are referable to causes now in
operation. By Charles Lyell,
Esq., F.R.S.... In two volumes. First American, from the
fifth & last London edition.
Philadelphia, James Kay, Jr. &
Brother, 1837. 2 v. ArBaA;
CoU; LNL; MdBJ; OUrC; ViU;
WU.   45286

Lyford, William Gilman, 1784-
1852.
The western address directory:
containing the cards of merchants,
manufacturers, and other business men, ... of those cities,
and towns in the Mississippi Valley ... added a list of steam-
boats on the western waters...
Baltimore, Printed by J. Robinson, 1837. 468 p. ICHi; KyU;
MHi; PSeW; WHi.   45287

(Lykins, Johnston), 1800?-1876.
Wa fa fe wa gry sy Laekens
wa kaxa peo. Shawanoe Mission,
J. G. Pratt, printer, 1837.
24 p. KHi.   45288

Lynn, Mass., First Church of
Christ.
Articles of faith and the
covenant of the church, adopted
Jan. 1837. Lynn, Record Press,
J. B. Tolman, printer, 1837.
16 p. MBC; MH; MH-And; MHi;
NjR.   45289

Lyon, Mary, 1780-1817.
Memoirs of Miss Mary Lyon,
of New Haven, Conn., New
Haven, Maltby, 1837. 250 p.
CPBac; CtY; MBNEH; MWA; PU.
                        45290

Lytton, Edward George Earl
Lytton Bullwer, 1803-1873.
Athens, its rise and fall, with

views of the literature, philoso-
phy, and social life of the
Athenian people, by Edward
Lytton Bulwer... New York,
Harper and brothers, 1837.
2 v. GHi; IaDu; MB; ScCC;
WvU.   45291

---- Devereux. A tale by the
author of Pelham. ... In two
vols. ... Boston, Charles Gaylord, 1837. 2 v. LNH; OClW;
ViU.   45292

---- The disowned. By the
author of "Pelham," and
"Devereux." ... Boston,
Charles Gaylord, 1837. 2 v.
OCel; OClW; NcSalL; TxDaM.
                            45293

---- The duchess De la Valliere;
a play in five acts. By the
author of "Eugene Aram," &c.
Baltimore, J. Robinson, 1837.
96 p. MH.   45294

---- ---- 2nd ed. New York,
Saunders and Otley, Ann Street,
and Conduit Street, London,
1837. 4-131 p. CU; InU; IU;
MiU; PU.   45295

---- Ernest Maltravers. By
the author of "Eugene Aram,"
"Pelham," "Rienze" ... New
York, Harper & bros., 1837.
2 v. CSt; MdBP; NcD; PU;
ViU.   45296

---- Falkland, by the Author
of "Pelham," "Paul Clifford,"
etc. Boston, Charles Gaylord,
1837. MB.   45297

---- The last days of Pompeii
.... Boston, C. Gaylord,
1837. 2 v. ViU.   45298

---- Paul Clifford. By the author of "Pelham," "The disowned" etc... Boston, C.

Gaylord, 1837. 2 v. ICU; PPL;
PU.   45299

---- Pelham Novels:....By Edward Lytton Bulwer, Esq., M.P.
In two volumes. Boston, published by Charles Gaylord, 1837.
2 v. in 1. MeU; MH; MsJMC;
NBuU; ViU.   45300

---- The pilgrims of the Rhine.
By the author of "Pelham" ....
Boston, Published by Charles
Gaylord, 1837. 234 p. MeBa;
MLei.   45301

M

MacCabe, Julius P. Bolivar.
   A directory of the cities of
Cleveland & Ohio, for the years
1837-38: comprising historical
and descriptive sketches of each
place ... By Julius P. Bolivar
MacCabe. Cleveland, Sanford
& Lott, printers, 1837. 3 p.
l., [9]-142 p. DLC; ICHi;
MiD-B; OO; WHi.   45302

---- Directory of the City of
Detroit. With its environs, and
register of Michigan, for the
year 1837. Containing an epito-
mised history of Detroit; an alphabetical list of its citizens; a
classification of professions and
principal trades in the city;
every information relative to
officers of the municipal government, to public offices and officers, to churches, associations
and institutions, to shipping,
steam boats, stages, &c. - Also,
a list of the officers of the United
States' Government; the names
of the Governor, and members
of the legislature of Michigan,
and county officers of the State,
&c. &c. &c. By Julius P. Bolivar MacCabe. Detroit. Printed

by William Harsha, 1837. 44,
114 p. DLC; Mi; MiD-B; MiU;
OCHP.   45303

MacCallan, George.
The sacred melodist: a collection of hymns and tunes
suitable for family and social
worship. Boston, Kidder &
Wright, 1837. 35 p. MB. 45304

M'Clintock, Thomas.
Observations on the articles
published in the Episcopal re-
corder, over the signature of
"A member of the Society of
Friends," By Thomas M'Clintock.
New York, Published by Isaac
T. Hopper, 1837. 70 p. MH;
NcD; PPFr; PSC-Hi.   45305

McClung, John Alexander, 1804-
1859.
Sketches of western adventure:
containing an account of the most
interesting incidents connected
with the settlement of the West,
from 1755 to 1794,: with an appendix, Rev. and cor. ... By
John A. M'Clung. Cincinnati,
J. A. James & Co., 1837. 315 p.
NN; OCHP; OClWHi.   45306

M'Conaughy, David, 1775-1852.
Address, delivered at the
dedication of the hall of the
Union Literary Society of Wash-
ington, College, July 21, 1837.
Pittsburgh, 1837. CtY; InU.
                            45307
McCoy, Isaac, 1784-1846.
... Periodical account of
Baptist mission within the In-
dian territory, for the year
ending, December 31, 1836...
n.p., 1837. Published by
Isaac McCoy. 52 p. CSmH;
MiD-B; MiU-C.   45308

---- Plat of Cherokee land,
indian territory surveyed in

1837. PPAmP.   45309

Mc'Dowell, John, 1780-1863.
A sermon preached at Newark,
N.J., Sept. 13, 1837, before
the American Board of Commissioners for Foreign Missions, at
their twenty-eighth annual meeting. Boston, Crocker & Brewster, 1837. 24 p. IaGG; KyLo;
MBC; NCH; PHi.   45310

Mace, Fayette.
Familiar dialogues on Shakerism; in which the principles of
the United Society are illustrated
and defended...Portland, Charles
Day & Co., 1837. 120 p. ICT;
McU; NNUT; OClWHi; WHi.
                            45311
McElroy's Philadelphia city directory for 1837-1867. [v. 1]-
30. Philadelphia, A. McElroy &
co., 1837-67. 30 v. DLC; KHi;
MH; OCl; PHi.   45312

McEwen, William, 1734-1762.
Grace and truth; or, The
Glory of fulness of the Redeemer
displayed in an attempt to ex-
plain ... the Old Testament ...
By William McEwen ... Philadelphia, William S. Martien, [1837].
(13)-359 p.   45313

McGill, Walter Marshall.
The western world: a poem,
founded on the facts recorded
of the Revolutionary War; consisting of several books, in one
volume. Together with a description of American scenery,
&c. By Walter Marshall McGill.
Printed by F. A. Parham Maryville, Tenn., 1837. 381 p.
DLC; MBAt; OClW; T.   45314

M'Gready, James.
The Posthumous works of the
reverend and pious James M'-
Gready, late minister of the gospel

in Henderson, Ky. ... Edited
by the Reverend James Smith.
Two volumes in one. Nash-
ville, Ten., Printed and published at J. Smith's steam
press, 1837. xiv, 511 p.
CSansS; LNB; NcAS; PPPrHi;
TxDaM.   45315

McGuffey, William Holmes, 1800-
1873.
    The eclectic first-fourth
reader: consisting of progressive lessons in reading and
spelling... By W. H. M'Guffey...
Cincinnati, Truman and Smith,
[1837]. OC.   45316

---- The Electric Primer: of
Young Children etc. (Cincinnati, 1837.) OClWHi.   45317

---- The eclectic third reader;
containing selections in prose
and poetry, from the best
American and English writers.
With plain rules for reading,
and directions for avoiding
common errors. By William H.
M'Guffey, president of Cincinnati college--late professor in
Miami university, Oxford. Cincinnati, Published by Truman
and Smith, 1837. 165 [8] p.
OCHP; WRHist.   45318

---- McGuffey's New Fifth
Eclectic Reader: Selected and
Original Exercises for Schools.
By Wm. M. McGuffey, LL.D.
Electrotype Edition. Wilson,
Hinkle & Co., Cincinnati, New
York, 1837. WvEj.b.   45319

McIlvaine, Charles Pettit.
    Baccalaureate discourse, de-
livered in Rosse chapel, Gambier ... Sunday Sept. 6, 1837,
by the Right Rev. Charles P.
McIlvaine ... Gambier, G. W.
Myers, 1837. 16 p. IES; MB;

MdBD; NNG; OClWHi.   45320

McJimsey, Wm.
    The Memory of the Sabbath;
A Poem. Baltimore, Machett &
Neilson, (1837). 96 p. KyLoP;
MdHi; MH; NjPT; PPPrHi.
                         45321
McKeen, Silas.
    God Our Only Hope. Dis-
course on the Condition and
Prospects of our Country; de-
livered in Belfast, Maine, on
Fast Day, April 20, 1837. Bel-
fast, F. P. Ingalls, (1837). 29
p. MeB.   45322

McKenney, Frederic.
    A complete key to the teach-
ers' assistant; or system of practical arithmetic. Compiled by F.
McKenney. 4th ed. Philadelphia,
Published by McCarty & Davis,
1837. 252 p. CSmH; InU; MB;
OOxM; PLor; ViW.   45323

M'Kenney, Thomas Loraine, 1785-
1859.
    History of the Indian tribes
of North America, with biographical sketches and anecdotes
of the principal chiefs...by T. L.
M'Kenney...and James Hall...
Philadelphia, Edward C. Biddle,
1837-44. 3 v. CtSoP; ICU;
OCA; OkU; OO; T.   45324

Mackenzie, Henry, 1745-1831.
    The miscellaneous works of
Henry Mackenzie ... Complete
in one volume. New York, Harper
& brothers, 1837. 512 p. CtMW;
KyU; MH; NUt; WLac.   45325

MacKeon, John, 1808-1883.
    Report ... protectors to
American seamen. Wash., 1837.
16 p. MB.   45326

---- Speech of Mr. M'Keon, of
New York, on the resolution of

Mr. Wise, proposing an inquiry into the condition of the
Executive departments. Delivered in the House of representatives, January 17, 1837.
Washington, Blair and Rives,
printers, 1837. 8 p. MB;
MiU-C; WHi.   45327

Mackintosh, John, d. 1837.
Principles of pathology, and
practice of physic. By John
Mackintosh ... 2nd American
from the 4th London edition,
with notes and additions, by
Samuel George Morton ...
Philadelphia, E. C. Biddle,
1837. 2 v. CtMW; MnU;
NbOM; OCo; TxGre.   45328

McLean, Allen.
A Thanksgiving sermon on
practical agriculture, preached
at Simsbury, Nov. 24, 1836,
the day of the anniversary
Thanksgiving. Hartford, 1837.
16 p. MBC; OClWHi;
WU-A.   45329

MacLure, William, 1763-1840.
Opinions on various subjects,
dedicated to the industrious
producers. .... New Harmony,
Ind., 1837. 556 p. IaDuU;
LNH; MH; PPL; OMC.   45330

McNaughton, James.
Address delivered before
the Medical society of the state
of New York, February 8,
1837, by James McNaughton,
M.D. ... Albany, E. W. and
C. Skinner, 1837. 40 p. DSG;
MB; NNNAM; PPL-R.   45331

---- Address delivered before
the New York State agricultural
society, at the capitol in Albany,
February 10, 1837. By James
McNaughton, M.D. Albany,
Packard and Van Benthuysen,

1837. NN; OCGHM; P; PU.
                          45332
McNemar, Richard, 1770-1839.
...A friendly letter to Alexander Mitchell. A solitary
Christian of Eaton, Ohio in
answer to his "religious circular" lately presented to the
public, dated June 1837. Written
at his request; and for the better information of ___ others,
on some important parts of his
said letter. Union Village, 1837.
10, [4] p. OClWHi.   45333

---- The Kentucky revival, or
A short history of the late extraordinary out-pouring of the spirit of God, in the western states
of America agreeably to, Scripture-
promises and prophecies concerning the latter day, with a brief
account of the entrance and progress of what the world call
Shakerism, among the subjects
of the late revival in Ohio and
Kentucky. Presented to the true
Zion-traveller, as a memorial of
the wilderness journey. By
Richard M'Nemar ... 3rd edition.
Printed, 1807: Albany, Re-printed,
1808; Union village, 1837. [9]-
119 p. DLC; KyRE; OClWHi.
                          45334
McRae, John J.
An address delivered before
the Graduates of the Erodelphian
Society... Oxford, O. R. H.
bishop, Jun, 1837. 15 p. PPiXT.
                          45335
McVickar, John, 1787-1868.
Alumni anniversary of Colum-
bia college, New-York. Address
delivered in the College chapel,
4th October, 1837. By John
McVickar ... New-York, G. &
G. Carvill & co., 1837. 40 p.
DLC; MH; NNC; PU; ScU.
                          45336

No entry   45337

---- First lessons in political
economy, for the use of
primary and common schools.
By John McVickar. Albany,
"Common School Depository"
from the Steam presses of
Packard & Von Benthuysen,
1837. 115 p. CtHWatk; NCas;
ScCliTO.   45338

---- ---- Geneva, J. & J. N.
Bogert, 1837. 126 p. DLC.
                           45339
The Madisonian, Washington,
D.C. Aug. 16, 1837-June 29,
1845. (In 1841 called the Daily
Madisonian) DLC; MLow; NSyU.
                           45340
Magie, David, 1795-1865.
The ministry magnified, a
sermon, preached at the instal-
lation of Rev. C. Hoover, as
pastor of the Central Presby.
church, Newark, N.J., Newark,
N.J., Central presby. church,
1837. 24 p. CSmH; DLC; MB;
NCH; PPPrHi.   45341

Magrath, Andrew Gordon, 1813-
1893.
An address delivered in the
Cathedral of St. Finbar, before
the Hibernian Society, and the
Irish volunteers, on the 17th
March, 1837. By A. G. Ma-
grath......Charleston, S.C.
Printed by Thomas J. Eccles,
1837. 36 p. ScU.   45342

Mahan, Dennis Hart, 1802-1871.
An elementary course of civil
engineering, for the use of the
cadets of the United States'
Military academy. By D. H.
Mahan ... New York, Wiley and
Putnam, 1837. 1 ℓ., 310 p.

DLC; IU; NcU; RPA; WaU.
                           45343
Maine.
Rules for the government of
the Executive Department for
1837, 73, 74. Augusta, 1837-
1874. MB.   45344

---- Adjutant General of Militia.
Report of the Adjutant General of the Militia of Maine, Dec.
31, 1836. Published agreeably
to Resolve of Mar. 22, 1836.
Augusta, (Me.), Smith & Robinson, printers to the state, 1837.
13, 2 p. IaHi; MeHi.   45345

---- Board of Internal Affairs.
Report on a reconnoissance
for a railroad from Portland to
Bangor, by order of the Board
of Internal Improvements for the
State of Maine. By Lt. Col.
S. H. Long, of the U.S. Topo-
graphical Engineers. Augusta,
Smith & Robinson, Printers to
the State, 1837. 32 p. MeHi.
                           45346
---- Geological Survey.
First Report on the Geology
of the Public Lands in the State
of Maine. By Charles T. Jack-
son, M.D. Boston, Dutton and
Wentworth, Printers, 1837. 93
p. CtHT; MBAt; MdBP; MeB;
MHi.   45347

---- ---- First, second, and
third reports on the geology of
the state of Maine, [with] catalogue of geological specimens in
the state cabinet. Augusta,
1837-39. 3 v. DLC; MB; MdBP;
NIC; OrCS.   45348

---- Governor, 1834-1838 (Robert
P. Dunlap)
Communication from his excellency, Robert P. Dunlap, governor of the state of Maine, to the
governor of Maryland. Annapolis,

William M'Neir, printer, 1837.
7 p. MdHi.   45349

---- ---- Message of Governor
Dunlap, to both branches of
the Legislature of the State of
Maine, January, 1837. Augusta,
Smith & Robinson, printers to
the State, 1837. 19 p. MBAt;
MeB; MeHi; MeLR.   45350

---- Laws, statutes, etc.
Private and special acts of
the state of Maine, passed by the
seventeenth Legislature, January
session, 1837. Published agreeably to the resolve of June 28,
1820. Augusta, Smith & Robinson, printers to the state,
1837. 332-509, 13 p. A-SC;
CSfLaw; MeLR; MeU; Wa-L.
                         45351
---- ---- Public acts of the
state of Maine, passed by the
Seventeenth Legislature, January session, 1837. Published
agreeably to the resolve of June
28, 1820. Augusta, (Maine),
Smith & Robinson, Printers to
the State, 1837. (2), 6 p.
A-SC; MeU; Nj; T; Wa-L. 45352

---- ---- Resolves of the Sixteenth Legislature of the State
of Maine....Smith & Robinson,
State Printers, Augusta, 1837.
96 p. Nv.   45353

---- ---- Resolves of the seventeenth legislature of the state of
Maine, passed at the session
which commenced on the fourth
day of January, and ended on
the thirtieth day of March, in
the year of our Lord one thousand eight hundred and thirty-
seven. Published agreeably
to the Resolve of June 28, 1820.
Augusta, Smith & Robinson,
printers to the state, 1837.
135-231 p. A-SC; IaU-L; MeB;

MeU; NNLI.   45354

---- Legislature.
Rules for the Government of
the Executive Department of
Maine, for 1837. Augusta,
Smith & Robinson, Printers,
1837-1874. 2 v. MB; MeHi.
                         45355
---- ---- Committee of the
Council of the Petitions for Pardon.
Report of the Committee of
the Council of the Petitions for
the pardon of William Lambard,
with accompanying papers....
Augusta, Smith & Robinson,
printers to the State, 1837.
20 p. MeB; MeHi; MeLR; MeU.
                         45356
---- ---- Committee on the North-
east Boundry.
Report presented by Mr.
Holmes, of Alfred, in the Hs.
of Reps., Feb. 2, 1837, on the
North Eastern boundary. Augusta, Smith and Robinson, [1837].
22 p. CaNSWA; DLC; MBAt;
MeHi.   45357

---- ---- House. 1837.
Rules and orders of the House
of Representatives of the State
of Maine. 1837. Augusta, Smith
& Robinson, 1837. 36 p. MeB;
MeHi; MeLR; MeU.   45358

---- ---- Senate. 1837.
Rules and orders to be observed in the Senate of the
State of Maine, during the current political year, 1837. Augusta, Smith & Robinson, printers, 1837. 36 p. MeB; MeHi;
MeLR.   45359

---- Secretary of State.
Abstract from the returns of
the directors of the several incorporated banks in Maine, as
they existed on the Saturday

preceding the first Monday of
June 1837. Augusta, Printers
to the State, 1837. IaHi; MC.
45360

---- State Treasurer.
Report of the Treasurer of
the State, on the finances....
Augusta, (Maine), Smith &
Robinson, printer to the state,
1837. 20, (5) p. IaHi.   45361

---- Supreme Judicial Court.
Reports of cases argued
and determined in the Supreme
judicial court of the state
of Maine. By John Fairfield
....Vol. III. Hallowell, Glazier,
Masters and Smith, 1837.
540 p. FDeS; LU-L; Me-LR;
ODaL; ViL.   45362

The Maine farmer and journal
of the useful arts; devoted to
agriculture, mechanics and
general news. Conducted by
E. Holmes. Vol. 5. Published
by William Noyes, Hallowell,
Maine, 1837. 416 p. NNNBG.
45363
Maine Farmers' Almanack for
1838. By Daniel Robinson.
Hallowell, Me., Glazier, Masters & Smith; Augusta, R. D.
Rice, (1837). MWA.   45364

---- Hallowell, Me., Glazier,
Masters & Smith; Portland,
William Hyde, (1837). MWA.
45365
Maine Mining Company.
List of Mines and Minerals
.... Boston, Beals & Greene,
printers, 1837. 15 p. MH-BA.
45366
Maine monthly magazine. Ed.
by Chas. Gilman. July 1836-
June 1837. Bangor, Duren &
Thatcher; Portland, E. Stephens,
1837. Vol. 1, vi, 568 p.
DLC; LNH; MB; MiD-B; RPB.
45367

Maine register for 1837, ... Hallowell, Glazier, Masters & Smith,
1837. 196 p. MeAu; MeBa; MeHi;
NBLiHi.   45368

Maine Wesleyan Seminary and Female College. Kent Hills.
Catalogue ... of the Maine Wesleyan Seminary, Kents Hill, ...
Augusta, Luther Severance, printer, 1837. 14 p. MeHi.   45369

Mair, John, 1702-or 3-1769.
Mair's introduction to Latin Syntax, from the Edinburgh stereotype edition, revised and corrected by A. R. Carson, by David
Patterson, A.M....New York,
Collins, Keese, & Co., 1837. [4],
248, [4] p. NNC.   45370

Malibran, Maria Felicita Garcia.
The celebrated Tyrolienne of
Madame Malibran. With variations
for the piano forte by Ch. Chaulieu.
Philadelphia, Fiot, Meignen & co.,
(1837). 9 p. MB.   45371

Mallery, Samuel Sawyer.
Memoir of Joanna Woodberry
Reddington, by Samuel S. Mal-
lery.... Boston, New England
Sabbath School Union. Depository,
1837. 92 p. DLC; MBNEH; MWA;
OrCS; WaU.   45372

Mallory, [Francis].
Remarks of Mr. Mallory, of Vir-
ginia, on a motion to refer the
President's message and accompany-
ing documents to the Committee of
the whole on the state of the union.
Delivered in the House of Repre-
sentatives, December 21, 1837.
Washington, Printed by Gales and
Seaton, 1837. 8 p. DLC; Vi.
45373
Malte-Brun, Conrad, 1775-1826.
A New general Atlas,... of the
Globe, ... corrected to the present
time. Drawn and engraved,...

by M. Malte-Brun. Philadelphia,
published by Grigg & Elliot,
1837. 90 p. DLC; MNBedf.
                    45374
Manayunk Athenaeum and Library Co.
    Articles of Association and
catalogue of the books. Philadelphia, 1837. 48 p. PHi.
                    45375
Mandeville, Henry.
    An essay on the interpreta-
tion of Romans, Chap. vii. 14-
25; with a general survey of
chapters iii-viii, followed by
a brief commentary, in which
the principles of the essay are
applied. Utica, (N.Y.), Bennet & Bright, 1837. 208 p.
CtHC; NRCR.   45376

Manly, Basil.
    Mercy and Judgment. A
discourse, containing some frag-
ments of the history of the
Baptist Church in Charleston,
S.C. Delivered by request of
the corporation of said church,
Sept. 23 and 30, A.D. 1832.
By Basil Manly, Pastor. Charleston, Knowles Vose and Co., 1837.
80 p. AB; ICU; MBAt; RPB.
                    45377
Mansfield abolition, double mob
riot. Canton, Mass., Gazette
Press, 1837. 8 p. NN.   45378

Manual of American principles.
Common era, 1837, of the nation,
61. Independence, liberty, jus-
tice: from the three, shall pro-
ceed happiness. Francis Wright
Darusmont, editor. Philadelphia;
New York; Boston; Cincinnati,
July 1837. MHi; NNC; PHi;
PReaHi.   45379

A manual of politeness, comprising the principles of eti-
quette and rules of behavior
in genteel society, for persons

of both sexes. Philadelphia,
W. Marshall & co., 1837. 7-287,
[1] p. CSt; DLC; MB; MNe;
MWA.   45380

Manual of private prayer; or,
closet devotions.... by the fathers of the reformation in England.
Charleston, A. E. Miller, n.pr.,
1837. 38 p. NjR.   45381

A map of North and South
Carolina. Accurately copied
from the old maps of James Cook.
Published in 1771, and of Henry
Mouzon, in 1775. Scale: 69.5
mi. to a degree. [N.Y.], Harper
& Brothers, 1837. 17 x 21.75 in.
ScU.   45382

Map of Penna. Philadelphia,
1837. PPL.   45383

Map of the States of Louisiana,
Mississippi and Alabama. Phila-
delphia, Published by S. Augus-
tus Mitchell, 1837. MsU.
                45384
Map of the village of Auburn,
[Auburn] Published by Hagaman
& Markham, 1837. NN. 45385

Marblehead, Mass. First Church
of Christ.
    The first Church of Christ in
Marblehead. Salem, Observer
Press, 1837. 11 p. MMhHi.
                45386
Marcellus, pseud. Letter to the
Hon. Daniel Webster.... See
Webster, Noah, 1758-1843.

Marcellus, Uyl.
    Letter on the political affairs
of the U.S. Philadelphia, 1837.
PPL.   45387

[Marcet, Jane (Hallimand)], 1769-
1858.
    Conversations on natural
philosophy, in which the elements

of that science are familiarly
explained, and adapted to the
comprehension of young pupils.
Illustrated with plates. By the
author of Conversations on chemistry, and Conversations on political economy. Improved by
appropriate questions, for the
examination of scholars; also illustrative notes, and a dictionary of philosophical terms. By
Rev. J.L. Blake,... Boston
stereotype edition. Boston,
Gould, Kendall & Lincoln,...
1837. 276 p. IGK; MB; MBAt;
TBrik; TNP.   45388

---- Conversations on vegetable
physiology; comprehending the
elements of botany, with their
application to agriculture. By
the author of "Conversations on
Chemistry," and "Natural
Philosophy"....By Rev. J. L.
Blake, A.M. Seventh American
edition, with engravings. Philadelphia, E. L. Carey & A. Hart
....1837. 372 p. MB; MH;
MoSU; PU.   45389

Marcus, Moses.
A valedictory address to the
members of his congregation,
delivered on Tuesday evening,
February 21, 1837, at the par-
sonage house. By the Rev.
Moses Marcus, ... New York,
Protestant Episcopal press, print.,
[1837]. 37 p. MB; MH; NNQ.
                           45390
Marietta, Ohio.
The Act of incorporation and
ordinances and regulations of
the Town of Marietta, Washing-
ton County, Ohio. Marietta,
Printed by C. Emerson & Co.,
1837. 23 p. CSmH; MH; MH-L.
                           45391
Marks, A. W.
Address Delivered before the
Philological Institute. On The

evening of its Tenth Anniversary.
By A. W. Marks, Esq. Published
by order of the Institute. Pittsburgh, Printed by D. N. White,
1837. 28 p. KyU; NjR. 45392

Marks, Elias, 1790-1886.
Hints on female education.
Columbia, S.C., I. C. Morgan,
1837. 41 p. MH.   45393

Marlborough, Massachusetts.
Congregational Church.
The Confession of faith,
covenant and articles of the Union
Congregational Church in Marlborough, Mass. .... Boston,
Printed by Perkins & Marvin,
1837. 23 p. MBNEH; Nh.
                           45394
Marlow, Nicholas.
An oration, delivered before
the Hibernian society, of the
city of Savannah, in the church
of St. John the Baptist, on the
festival of St. Patrick, March
17th, 1837.... Savannah, Williams, 1837. 28 p. GHi; NcD.
                           45395
Marryat, Frederick, 1792-1848.
The dog fiend.-The privateers-
man Snarleyyow; by Captain Marryat. Boston, Little, Brown &
co., (1837). (1)-2-421 p. MBev.
                           45396
---- Frank Mildmay, or, The
Naval Officer, by Captain Marryatt. Complete in two vols.
Vol. II. Sandbornton, N.H.,
Published by Charles Lane, 1837.
2 v. NIDHi; NNU-M; NSsA;
ViU.   45397

---- ... Japhet in search of his
father... Sanborton, N.H.
(Lane's uniform edition). Charles
Lane, 1837. 2 v. KyU; NIDHi;
NSsA.   45398

---- ... The king's own; By
Captain Marryat ... New York,

Dearborn, 1837. 243 p. CtHT.
45399

---- Mr. Midshipman easy.
Lane's uniform ed. Sanbornton,
N.H, C. Lane, 1837. 2 v.
DLC.   45400

---- The naval officer ... N.Y.,
Dearborn, 1837. 219 p. CtHT.
45401

---- Newton Forster; or the
merchant service. Marryat,
Frederick, 1843. Sanbornton,
N.H., C. Lane, 1837. 2 v.
DLC; Nh-Hi.   45402

---- Marryatt's [sic] novels...
Sandbornton, N.H., C. Lane,
1837-1838. CtY.   45403

---- The pacha of many tales...
New York, Dearborn, 1837.
208 p. MB; OClWHi.   45404

---- ---- Sanborton, N.H....
Charles Lane, 1837. 2 v. MB;
NSsA; TNP; WaU.   45405

---- Peter Simple; or the ad-
ventures of a midshipman. ...
Sandbornton, N.H., Published
by Charles Lane, 1837. 2 v.
CSmH; MBAt; MsColS; NSsA;
WaU.   45406

---- The Pirate, and The Three
Cutters. By Captain Marryatt.
Complete in one volume. Sandbornton, N.H. (sic) Published
by Charles Lane. Stereotyped
by Allison and Porter, 1837.
276 p. NIDHi; OO.   45407

---- Snarleyyow; or, The dog
fiend. An historical novel. By
Captain F. Marryat ... Philadelphia, Carey and A. Hart,
1837. 2 v. MCli; MH; PLFM;
NN; RPB.   45408

---- Stories of the sea. D.

New York, 1837. 232 p. VtU.
45409
Marryat's Comic Naval Almanac.
New York, 1837. MWA.
45410
Marsh, Christopher Columbus.
Lecture on the study of book-
keeping, with the balance sheet,
being an easy introduction to
double entry book-keeping.
3 ed. New York, C. Shepard,
1837. 38 p. RPB.   45411

Marsh, John.
An epitome of general ecclesiastical history, from the earliest
period to the present time, with
an appendix giving a condensed
history of the Jews from the
destruction of Jerusalem to the
present day ... by John Marsh
... Fifth edition. New York,
Tilden and co., 1837. 4 p. l.
(13)-450 p. CtMMHi; InCW;
NcSaIL; NNUT.   45412

Marsh-Caldwell, Anne (Caldwell),
1791-1874.
Two old men's tales. New
York, George Dearborn and co.,
1837. 124 p. FTU.   45413

Marshall, Elihu F.
Marshall's spelling book of
the English language, ... By
Elihu F. Marshall. First revised edition. Concord, N.H.,
Published by Oliver L. Sanborne,
1837. 156 p. MeHi.   45414

Marshall, John.
Practical observations on diseases of the heart, lungs,
stomach, liver, etc., etc., occasioned by spinal irritation: and
on the nervous system in general,
as a source of organic disease.
By John Marshall. Philadelphia,
Haswell, Barrington and Haswell,
1837. 110 p. CSt-L; ICJ;
MdBJ; NhD; PPA.   45415

Marshall, John J.
Public school writing book.
In three numbers. No. 1...
Framingham, Boynton and
Marshall, 1837. 1 no. MWA;
NN.   45416

---- ---- No. 2 ... Hartford,
Cranfield, and Robins, 1837.
14 ℓ. NNC.   45416a

---- ---- No. 3 ... Hartford,
Cranfield and Robins, 1837.
14 ℓ. NNC.   45417

Marshall, Samuel V.
The Influence of letters on
the human condition. An ad-
dress, delivered before the
Louisville Mechanics' Institute,
... Feb. 11, 1837. Louisville,
Parrott, Wampler & Co.,
Printers, 1837. 44 p. PPPrHi;
TxU.   45418

Martineau, Harriet, 1802-1876.
Society in America. By Har-
riet Martineau. New York,
Saunders and Otley, 1837. 2 v.
CtMW; IaHi; Nh-Hi; PPM; ScC.
                                 45419
---- ---- 2d edition. New York,
Saunders and Otley, 1837. 2 v.
IaOskW; LNT; MHa; NJost; TxU.
                                 45420
---- ---- Third Edition. New
York, Saunders and Otley,
1837. 2 v. IEG; KyU; MPiB;
MdHi; OrPD.   45421

---- ---- 4th edition. New
York, Saunders & Otley, 1837.
2 v. CoCs; IaCec; MnU; OUrC;
ScU.   45422

---- Views on Slavery and Emancipation. "from Society In America" New York, Piercy & Reed,
1837. 79 p. MBAt; MHa;
NbCrD; OMC; OO.   45423

Martyn, Francis.
Homilies, on the book of Tobias; or, A familiar explication
of the practical duties of domestic
life. By the Rev. Francis Martyn. Baltimore, Published by
Fielding Lucas, Jr., 1837.
264 p. MoCgSV.   45424

Maryland. Canal commissioners.
Report of the engineer and
map. Baltimore, 1837. PPL.
                                 45425
---- Commissioners of the Eastern
Shore.
Report of the commissioners
of the Eastern Shore rail road,
to the governor of Maryland.
Annapolis, William M'Neir, print-
er, 1837. 46, [1] p. DLC;
MdHi.   45426

---- General Assembly.
An abstract of the report of
the colleges, academies and schools,
in the different counties in this
state, made at December session,
1837. Annapolis, Printed by
Jeremiah Hughes, 1837. 5 p.
MdHi.   45427

---- ---- Journal of proceedings
of The Committee of the Whole
House upon the bill reported by
Mr. Ford, Chairman of the Com-
mittee on the Constitution, en-
titled, an act to alter and amend
The Constitution and Form of
Government, of the state of
Maryland. Annapolis, Printed
by Jeremiah Hughes, 1837. 12 p.
MdHi.   45428

---- ---- Report of the committee
on claims, on account of the
treasurer of the W. shore. December session, 1836. Annapolis,
Jeremiah Hughes, printer, 1837.
15 p. MdHi.   45429

---- ---- Committee on Education.

Report of the minority of the committee on education, relative to establishing a general system of education. Annapolis, Printed by Jeremiah Hughes, 1837. 10 p. MdHi.
45430

---- ---- Committee to examine awards under indemnity law.
Report of the Com. to examine the awards under the indemnity law. Annapolis, Jeremiah Hughes, 1837. MdHi; PPL.
45431

---- ---- House.
Rules and orders for the regulation and government of the House of delegates, of the state of Maryland, at December session, eighteen hundred and thirty seven. Annapolis, Printed by Jeremiah Hughes, 1837. 10 p. MdHi.
45432

---- ---- ---- Committee on Agriculture.
Report of the committee on agriculture, respecting The Growth of the Mulberry and Sugar Beet. Annapolis, Jeremiah Hughes, printer, 1837. 7 p. MdHi; MH.
45433

---- ---- ---- Committee on Education.
Report of the Committee on education, relative to establishing a general system of education. Annapolis, Printed by Jeremiah Hughes, 1837. [3] p. MdHi.
45434

---- ---- ---- Committee on grievances and courts of justice.
Report of the Committee on grievances and courts of justice on the Bill to settle and adjust the western boundary line of the state of Maryland. Annapolis, Jeremiah Hughes, printer, 1837. 5 p. MdHi.
45435

---- ---- ---- ---- Report of the committee on grievances and courts of justice, relative to the attendance of judges. Annapolis, Printed by Jeremiah Hughes, 1837. 14 p. MdHi.
45436

---- ---- ---- ---- Report of the committee on grievances and courts of justice, relative to the memorial of Margaret Moore, and others, against Ewing, and wife. Annapolis, Jeremiah Hughes, printer, 1837. 7 p. MdHi.
45437

---- ---- ---- ---- ... Reports of the majority and minority of the Committee on grievances and courts of justice on the memorial of James Clarke, of Anne Arundel county. Annapolis, J. Hughes, 1837. 7 p. MdBE; MdHi.
45438

---- ---- ---- Committee on Lotteries.
Report of the committee on lotteries, on the memorial, praying the grant of a lottery, For the purpose of building a State Armory, Public Drill Rooms, & Town Hall in the city of Baltimore. Annapolis, Printed by Jeremiah Hughes, 1837. 4 p. MdHi.
45439

---- ---- ---- Committee on Ways & Means.
Report of the Committee of Ways and Means, relative to the surplus revenue. Annapolis, Printed by Jeremiah Hughes, 1837. 6 p. MdHi.
45440

---- ---- ---- ---- Report of the committee on ways and means, to the House of delegates. Annapolis, Jeremiah Hughes, printer, 1837. 18 p. MdHi.
45441

---- ---- ---- Joint Committee ... on St. John's College.

On the part of the Senate.
Chas. Sterett Ridgely, Chair'n,
On the part of the House of
Delegates. Report of the joint
committee, appointed to investigate and report to the general
assembly, The Proceedings of
the Visiters [sic] and Governors
of St. John's College. Annapolis,
Jeremiah Hughes, printer, 1837.
6 p. MdHi.   45442

---- ---- Joint Committee on
the Library.
Mr. Culbreth, Chairman.
Report of the joint committee
on the Library. Annapolis,
Printed by Jeremiah Hughes,
1837. 11 p. MdHi.   45443

---- ---- Joint committee to
investigate the affairs of the
penitentiary.
The Maryland penitentiary,
containing The proceedings of
the joint committee of both
Houses of the General assembly,
during the year 1837; their report to the legislature of 1837-
8; the proceedings of the legislature thereon, and the project of the law relating to the
penitentiary, proposed by said
committee. Annapolis, Printed
by Jeremiah Hughes, [1837?]
364 p. ScU.   45444

---- ---- Select Committee appointed to inquiry into the
expediency of making it a crime
to conspire against the constitution.
Report of the select committee appointed to inquiry into
the expediency of reporting a
bill making it High Crime and
Misdemeanor for Citizens to
conspire against the constitution
of the state. Annapolis,
printed by Jeremiah Hughes,
1837. 7 p. MdHi.   45445

---- ---- Select Committee on
... Penitentiary.
Report of the minority of the
select committee, to whom was
referred sundry memorials from
citizens of the city of Baltimore,
respecting The Maryland Penitentiary. Annapolis, Printed
by Jeremiah Hughes, 1837. 10
p. MdHi.   45446

---- ---- Select Committee on
Retrenchment.
Report of the select commit-
tee on retrenchment. Annapolis,
Jeremiah Hughes, printer, 1837.
6 p. MdHi.   45447

---- ---- Select Committee on
the Real Estate Banks.
Report of the select committee
on the Real Estate bank of the
state of Maryland. Annapolis,
Jeremiah Hughes, printer, 1837.
15 p. MdHi.   45448

---- ---- Select Committee Relative to Public Printing.
Report of the majority of the
select committee relative to the
public printing. Annapolis,
Printed by Jeremiah Hughes,
1837. 6 p. MdHi.   45449

---- ---- ---- Mr. Culbreth,
Report of the minority of the
select committee relative to the
public printing. Annapolis,
Printed by Jeremiah Hughes,
1837. 9 p. MdHi.   45450

---- ---- Senate.
Journal of proceedings of the
Senate of Maryland, at the December session, 1836. [Dec.
26th, 1836 to March 22d, 1837]
... Annapolis, William M'Neir,
... 1836, [i.e. 1837]. 350, 23,
3, 83 p. MdHi.   45451

---- ---- ---- Committee on Banks.

Statements showing the condition of certain banks in Maryland. [Annapolis, 1837]. 9 p.
WHi.   45452

---- Geologist.
Annual report. Annapolis,
1837-1840. 4 v. CSmH; DLC;
ICJ; PPAN; WaS.   45453

---- Governor.
Annual message from the
executive, to the Legislature
of Maryland, December Session,
1837. Annapolis, Jeremiah
Hughes, printer, 1837. 17 p.
MdHi; WHi.   45454

---- ---- Communication from
the Executive in relation to the
demand made by the (Executive
of Pennsylvania) for the delivery of Nathan S. Bemis and
others. [Annapolis, 1837].
42 p. MH.   45455

---- ---- Communication from
the Governor of Maryland, enclosing a communication from
the Governor of Georgia. Annapolis, Jeremiah Hughes,
printer, 1837. [11], [3]-7 p.
MdHi.   45456

---- Laws, statutes, etc.
Bill entitled, "An act to
incorporate the bank of the
state of Maryland." Baltimore,
Printed by Lucas & Deaver,
1837. 16 p. WHi.   45457

---- ---- Laws made and passed
by the General Assembly, of
the state of Maryland, at a
session begun and held at Annapolis, on Monday the 26th day
of December, 1836. Published
by authority. Annapolis, (Md.),
Printed by Jeremiah Hughes,
1837. 478 p. IaU-L; Mi-L;
MdBB; Nj; R.   45458

---- Penitentiary, Baltimore.
Reply of the directors to the
charges against the Penitentiary.
Baltimore, Printed by J. W.
Woods, 1837. 18 p. MdHi.
                             45459
---- State library, Annapolis.
Catalogue of the library of
the state of Maryland. D. Ridge-
ly, librarian. December, 1837.
Annapolis, Printed by J. Hughes,
1837. v, [7]-132 p. MdBE;
MdBP; MH.   45460

---- Treasurer of the Western
Shore.
(D.) Communication of the
treasurer of the W. shore, in
obedience to an order of the
House of delegates, relative to
indemnity. Annapolis, Jeremiah
Hughes, printer, 1837. 4 p.
MdHi.   45461

---- ---- Report of the treasurer
of the W. shore, in obedience to
an order of the House of delegates of 25th January, 1837.
Annapolis, Jeremiah Hughes,
printer, 1837. 39 p. MdHi;
MiD-B.   45462

---- University.
Memorial of the Trustees of
the University of Maryland, to
the Legislature of Maryland.
Baltimore, Printed by Sands &
Neilson, 1837. 13 p. MdBS-P.
                             45463
Maryland Academy of Science
and Literature, Baltimore.
Transactions of the Maryland
Academy of science and literature.
Vol. I. Published by the Acad-
emy. Baltimore, Printed by John
D. Toy, 1837. [17]-190 p. DLC;
ICJ; MWA; TxU; WU.   45464

Maryland Canal Co. President.
Communication from William
Krebs, Esq. President of the

Maryland Canal Company, to
the Governor of Maryland.
Annapolis, William M'Neir, printer, 1837. 5 p. MdHi.   45465/66

Maryland in Liberia.
    Constitution and laws of
Maryland in Liberia; with an
appendix of precedents. Pub-
lished by authority of the
Maryland State Colonization
Society. Baltimore, John D.
Toy, printer, 1837. 1-168 p.
KyLoP; MBC; MH-L; MdToH;
NcU.   45467

Maryland pocket annual. An-
napolis, Hughes, 1837. MNS.
                              45468
Mason, Erskine.
    The Inconsistencies of
Christian professors. A ser-
mon, preached in the Bleeker-
Street Church, N.Y., Nov.
12th, 1837, by Erskine Mason.
New-York, E. French, 1837.
32 p. MBC; MeBat; MiD-B;
MNe; PPPrHi.   45469

Mason, James Murray.
    Speech Mr. James M. Mason,
of Virginia, on the bill imposing
additional duties as depositaries
in certain cases, on public officers, delivered in the House of
representatives, U.S., October
11, 1837. Washington, Printed
at the Madisonian office, 1837.
15 p. NNC; PPM.   45470

Mason, Lowell, 1792-1872.
    Choir: or Union collection
of music. 7th ed. Boston,
J. E. Wilkins and R. B.
Carter, 1837. 357 p. CtHWatk;
DLC; MB; RPB.   45471

---- Church psalmody: a collection of psalms and hymns
adapted to public worship.
Selected from Dr. Watts and

other authors. Boston, Perkins
and Marvin, 1837. [37]-576 p.
CtY-D; MH-AH.   45472

---- The Juvenile Singing School
by Lowell Mason, and T. J.
Webb, professors in the Boston
Academy of music. Boston,
J. H. Wilkins, R. B. Carter,
1837. 128 p. ICU; MB; MH;
MHaHi; NNC; NNUT.   45473

---- Manual of christian psalmody:
a collection of psalms and hymns,
for public worship. Boston,
published by William D. Ticknor
and Perkins & Marvin...1837.
(37)-588 p.   MB; MDeeP; MLaw;
PCA.   45474

---- Manual of the Boston Academy of Music for instruction in
the elements of vocal music, on
the system of Pestalozel. By
Lowell Mason, Professor in the
academy. Second edition. Boston, J. H. Wilkins & R. B.
Carter, 1837. 252 p. CtHWatk;
MdW; MLanc; PPL.   45475

---- Occasional psalm and hymn
tunes; selected and original,
designed as supplementary to
the several collections of church
music in common use. Boston,
J. H. Wilkins and R. B. Carter,
1837. 96 p. CLU; DLC; OrP.
                            45476
---- The Sabbath school harp:
being a selection of tunes and
hymns adapted to the wants of
Sabbath schools...2d edition.
Boston, Massachusetts Sabbath
School Society, 1837. 96 p.
MB; MH; NjPT; NNUT; PPPrHi.
                            45477
---- The sacred harp; or,
Eclectic harmony: a new collec-
tion of church music...by Lowell
Mason, and by Timothy B. Mason;
stereotype ed. Cincinnati, Tru-

man, 1837. 357, (3) p. CtMW;
WBeloC.   45478

Mason, Monck, 1803-1889.
    Account of the late aero-
nautical expedition from London to Weilburg accomplished
by Robert Holland, esq.,
Monck Mason, esq., and Charles
Green, aeronaut ... New York,
Foster, 1837. 35 p. CtHt;
CtMW; MBAt; MdBP; WUE.
                             45479
Mason, Timothy Battelle, 1801-
1861.
    Mason's young minstrel; a
new collection of juvenile songs,
with appropriate music. Boston, American stationers' company, 1837. 60 p. ICN; NNUT;
OClWHi; PPiU; RPB.   45480

Massachusetts. Adjutant General.
    Directions for keeping the
roll books of standing companies
.... [Boston,] 1837. Broadside. MB.   45481

---- Commissioners appointed
to consider & report upon the
practicability & expediency of
reducing to a written & systematic code the common law of
Massachusetts.
    Report...made to His excel-
lency the governor, January 1837.
Boston, Dutton, 1837. 46 p. Ct;
CtHWatk; IaU-L; MH-L; WaU.
                             45482
---- Commissioners for the survey of Boston Harbor.
    ...Report of the Commis-
sioners for the survey of Boston Harbor. (Boston? 1837?)
26 p. DLC; MB; MBAt; MH;
NNC.   45483

---- Commissioner on the Geological, Mineralogical, Botanical
and Zoological Survey.
    Circular containing questions

... Amherst, 1837. 7 p. MB.
                             45484
---- General Court.
    Memorial of the directors of
the American Institute of Instruction, 1837. 18 p. MBC.
                             45485
---- ---- Report and bill relating to Chelsea Bank. Boston,
1837. 13 p. MBC.   45486

---- ---- Report and bills relating to the abolition of capital
punishment. [Boston, 1837].
35 p. M.   45487

---- ---- Report and bill to aid
the construction of the Norwich
and Worcester railroad. Boston,
1837. 15 p. M; MW.   45488

---- ---- Report on sundry
petitions for the establishment
of houses of industry...Boston,
1837. 12 p. MB.   45489

---- ---- Resolutions relating to
the abolition of slavery. Boston,
1837. MB.   45490

---- ---- Committee: Geological
survey.
    ... Report, etc. [of special
committee] relating to the geological survey of the state.
[Boston, 1837]. 16 p. M.
                             45491
---- ---- Committee on mercantile affairs and insurance.
    An act to preserve the harbor
of Boston. [Boston, 1837]. 10
p. MH-BA.   45492

---- ---- Committee on Railways
and Canals.
    ... Annual reports of the rail-
road corporations in the state of
Massachusetts...(1836-1856)
Boston, Dutton and Wentworth,
state printers (etc., 1837)-56.
21 v. CU; IaHi; MdBJ; MH;
Mtl; NjP.   45493

---- ---- ---- Report and Bill
Respecting the Boston and
Lowell rail-road Corporation.
[Boston, 1837] 28 p. [Senate.
[Doc] no. 83]. CtY.   45494

---- ---- House.
Report and resolves relating
to slavery in the District of
Columbia. [Boston], 1837.
8 p. DHU; MH; NIC.   45495

---- ---- ---- Report on the
laws relating to the public
health. Boston, 1837. 12 p.
MBM.   45496

---- ---- ---- Rules & orders
to be observed by the house of
representatives of the commonwealth of Massachusetts for the
year 1837. Boston, Dutton &
Wentworth, state printers, 1837.
(3) 4-47 p. MH-AH; MWHi;
MWo.   45497

---- ---- ---- Committee on
Capital Punishment.
Report and bills relating to
the abolition of capital punishment. (Signed by Robert Rantoul, Jr. and 2 others, committee) (B.1837). 34+ p. ICJ;
MBAt; MH; WHi.   45498

---- ---- ---- ---- ... Reports on the abolition of Capital
punishment. Reprinted by
order of the House of Representatives, from the legislative documents of 1835 and 1836. Boston, Dutton and Wentworth,
1837. 136 p. DLC; ICJ; MB;
MW; N.   45499

---- ---- ---- Committee on
petition of Francis Jackson and
others.
... The committee to whom
was referred the petition of
Francis Jackson and others of

Boston ... with 64 other petitions...on the subject of slavery.
[Boston, 1837]. 8 p. MB.
                           45500

---- ---- ---- Committee on
testimony and witness.
... Petition etc., relating to
the testimony of witnesses.
[Boston, 1837]. 15 p. DLC;
NIC.   45501

---- ---- ---- Committee of the
judiciary.
Report on the trial by jury,
in question of personal freedom.
[Boston? 1837]. 38 p. MH-L;
NIC; TNF.   45502

---- ---- ---- Joint committee
on mercantile affairs and insurance on Boston Harbor.
Report of Joint committee on
Mercantile affairs and insurance
on Boston Harbor. 1837. MCM.
                           45503

---- ---- ---- Special committee
(on a geological survey).
... Report, etc. (of special
committee) relating to the geological survey of the state. (Boston, 1837). 16 p. Ct; DGS.
                           45504

---- ---- Joint Committee on
Insurance affairs.
Report and bill to cause the
several insurance companies to
make annual returns. [Boston,
1837[. 19 p. DLC.   45505

---- ---- Joint committee on
public charitable institutions.
... Report, etc., relating to
the state lunatic hospital. [Bos-
ton, 1837]. 10 p. DLC.
                           45506

---- ---- Joint Committee on the
Kilby Bank, Boston.
... Report of the committee
on the Kilby Bank. [Boston,
1837]. 8 p. MB.   45506a

---- ---- Joint Special Committee on Congress of Nations.
Report and resolves in relation to a congress of nations. April 4, 1837. [Boston, 1837.] 18 p. CtHT; ICN; MH; NNC; WHi.   45507

---- ---- Joint special committee on the Norwich and Worcester railroad.
Report and bill to aid the construction of the Norwich and Worcester railroad. [Boston? 1837]. 15 p. CSt.   45508

---- ---- Joint Special Committee to examine the Nahant Bank.
Report on the Nahant Bank. [Boston, 1837]. 20 p. NIC.
45509

---- ---- (1837)-Senate.
(Amendments to the resolves relating to slavery. Boston, 1837.) 2 p. MH.   45510

---- ---- ---- Documents relating to the Mass. Charitable Eye and Ear Infirmary... [Boston, 1837.] 27 p. DSG.
45511

---- ---- ---- Letters on the geological survey of Massachusetts. Senate. ... No. 9. Boston, 1837. 7 p. M; MSaP.
45512

---- ---- ---- Report in the Massachusetts Senate on the Petition of the Trustees of Amherst College, (Boston, 1837). 16, (1) p. IU; MHi.   45513

---- ---- ---- Rules and Orders, Senate, Mass. Boston, Dutton & Wentworth, State Printers, 1837. 43 p. MWHi.   45514

---- ---- ---- Comm. on capital punishment.
Report on Expediency of abolishing Capital Punishment.

(Signed by Charles Hudson, chairman.) [Boston, 1837]. 39 p. DSG; MH.   45515

---- Geological Survey.
Circular containing questions about the economic geology of Massachusetts. [Amherst, 1837] 7 p. MB.   45516

---- Governor, 1836-1840 (Edward Everett).
... Address of His Excellency, Edward Everett, to the two branches of the Legislature, on the organization of the government, for the political year commencing Jan. 4, 1837. Bost., Dutton & Wentworth, state ptrs., 1837. 20 p. MH; MHi; MiD-B.
45517

---- ---- By His Excellency Edward Everett ... a proclamation for a day of public fasting, humiliation and prayer. n.p., 1837. Broadside. M; MB; MBC.
45518

---- Insane hospital. Worcester.
Reports and other documents relating to the State lunatic hospital at Worcester, Mass. Printed by order of the Senate. Boston, Dutton and Wentworth, printers to the state, 1837. (7)-200 p. ICJ; MH; NNN; RPB; TNV.   45519

---- Laws, statutes, etc.
An act concerning railroad corporations. [Boston, Dutton and Wentworth, 1837.] NN.
45520

---- ---- ... An act concerning the deposits of the surplus revenue. Boston, 1837. 12 p. DLC.   45521

---- ---- Act to alter the Line of the Eastern Rail Road and an Act to aid the Construction of the same. Salem, 1837. 12 p. CSt; DLC.   45522

---- ---- An act to preserve
the harbor of Boston. Boston,
1837. 10 p. MB.   45523

---- ---- ... Bills respecting
Eastern railroad co., ...
(Boston, 1837.) 1 pam. DLC.
45524
---- ---- Extracts from the Revised statutes...[Lowell], Lowell
journal press, 1837. 17 p. DLC.
45525
---- ---- Report and bill concerning licensed houses and
the sale of intoxicating liquors.
[Boston, 1837.] DSG; MBC.
28 p.   45526

---- Overseers of the Poor.
Abstract of the returns of
the overseers of the poor.
Boston, 1837. PPL.   45527

---- Prisons.
Abstract of returns of keep-
ers and inspectors of jails and
houses of correction. [Boston,
1837]. 12 p. CtHWatk.   45528

---- Secretary of commonwealth.
Abstract of the average bank
returns, 1837-9. Boston,
1837-9. Nh.   45529

---- Treasurer and receiver-
general.
An account of the state of
the Treasury. 1837-1848. MH.
45530
Massachusetts Charitable
Mechanic Association.
First exhibition and fair of
the Massachusetts charitable
mechanic association, at Fanenil
and Quincy halls, in the city
of Boston, Sept. 18, 1837.
Bost., Dutton & Wentworth,
1837. 104 p. CBPac; MBB;
NbHi; PPM; WaPS.   45531

---- Report of the special com-

mittee of the Massachusetts
Charitable Mechanic Association,
on the subject of an annual fair
... Boston, printed by Homer &
Palmer and J. T. Adams, 1837.
(2)-7 (1) p. MWA; NNC.
45532
The Massachusetts Family Al-
manac, or the Merchants' &
Farmers' Calender,...1837;...
Boston, Pub. by...Allen & Com-
pany,...(1837.) (34) p. MB;
MiD-B; MiU.   45533

Massachusetts General Hospital.
Acts, resolves By-laws, and
Rules and regulations. Boston,
Press of James Loring, 1837.
(2) p. DLC; IcHi; KyLoJM;
MHi.   45534

---- By-laws, rules and regulations.... Boston, 1837. MB.
45535
Massachusetts Medical Society.
Acts of incorporation and by-
laws and orders of the Massachusetts medical society. Boston,
Press of John Putnam, 1837.
(21)-88 p. NNNAM.   45536

---- Amendments of the by-laws
of the Massachusetts Medical
Society with a corrected list of
fellows, June, 1837. Boston,
Putnam, 1837. 32 p. DNLM;
DSG; MB; MBC; MH-M.   45537

Massachusetts Mining Company.
Correspondence relating to
the Operations of the Massachusetts Mining Company, (1837).
6 p. MHi.   45538

The Massachusetts register, and
Business Directory, also city offi-
cers in Boston, and other useful
information. Boston, James
Loring, 1837. 252 p. MeBa;
MeHi; MoSpD; MTop.   45539

[Massie, W.]
Lionel Wakefield, by the au-
thor of "Sydenham." Phila-
delphia, Carey, Lea and
Blanchard, 1837. 2 v. MBL;
OSW; WU.   45540

Mathematical problems & examples, arranged according to
subjects fr. senate-house examination papers, 1821 to 1836
inclusive with appendix cont.
senate-house questions for
1837... Cambridge, [Mass.],
1837. 365 p. DLC; MB; NN;
OO.   45541

Mathews, (Charles James).
Why did you die? ... N.Y.,
Happy Hours Co., [1837?]
CSmH; NN.   45542

Matthews, Lyman, 1801-1866.
Memoir of the Life and Char-
acter of Ebenezer Porter, D.D.,
late President of the Theological
Seminary, Andover. By Lyman
Matthews, Pastor of the South
Church Braintree, Mass.
Boston, Published by Perkins
& Marvin; Philadelphia, Henry
Perkins, 1837. ArBaA; KWiU;
MB; NjMD; RPB.   45543

Mattison, Seth.
Substance of a discourse, oc-
casioned by the death of the
Rev. Joseph Tomkinson; de-
livered before the Genesee an-
nual conference, at Lockport,
October 20, 1835. By Seth
Mattison. Published by request
of the conference ... Geneva,
N.Y., Printed by Ira Merrill,
1837. 34 p. MBAt; MoS;
NNMHi.   45544

Maury, Jean Siffrein, 1746-1817.
The principles of eloquence,
adapted to the pulpit and the
bar. By the Abbe Maury.

Translated from the French, with
additional notes by John Neal
Lake. New York; Mason & Lane,
1837. 266 p. MH-L; NcA-S;
ODW; PAtM.   45545

Maxwell, Darcy Brisbane, 1742-
1810.
The life of Darcy, Lady Maxwell, of Pollock, late of Edinburgh, compiled from her volumi-
nous diary and correspondence,
and from other authentic documents, by the Rev. John Lancaster. New York, Mason, 1837.
IaMp; MdBE; MoK; RPB. 45546

Maxwell, William Hamilton.
The Bivanac; or, Stories of
the Peninsular war. By W. H.
Maxwell, author of "stories of
Waterloo," etc.... Philadelphia,
E. L. Carey and A. Hart, 1837.
2 v. GAuY; LMO; MBL; MVh;
NN.   45547

May, Samuel Joseph.
A sermon preached at Hing-
ham, March 19, 1837; being the
Sunday after the death of Mrs.
Cecilia Brooks. By Samuel J.
May, minister of the second par-
ish in Scituate, Mass. printed
by request - not published.
Hingham, Press of J. Farmer,
1837. 31 p. CtY; DLC; InID;
MWA; PPL.   45548

---- These bad times the product
of bad morals. A sermon preached
to the Second Church in Scituate,
Mass. May 21, 1837. By Samuel
J. May. Published by request.
Boston, Printed by Isaac Knapp,
1837. 20, 1 p. ICMc; MB;
MiD-B; MWA; NjPT.   45549

Mayhew, Edward, 1813-1868.
Make your wills! A farce in
one act, by E. Mayhew and G.
Smith...New York, Samuel French,

(1837). 29 p. IaU; IEdS;
ViU.   45550

Mayo, Robert, 1784-1864.
A Chapter of sketches on
finance; with an appendix,...
By Robert Mayo, M.D....Pub-
lished by F. Lucas, Jr., Balti-
more; Frank Taylor, Washing-
ton; R. J. Smith, Richmond;
Carey, Hart & Co., Desilver,
Thomas & Co. and James Kay,
Jr. & Brother, Philadelphia;
G. & C. Carvill & Co. and
Collins, Keese & Co., New York;
Hilliard, Gray & Co., Boston,
1837. xxxi, [1]-115 p. CtY;
DLC; MsJs; NIC; PHi; PU.
                            45551
---- The misrepresentations of
"a member of the Hickory club
..." 2d ed. Wash., G. Ander-
son, 1837. 36 p. MiD-B;
MdHi; Nh.   45552

---- A reply to the sketches
of an eight years' resident in
the city of Washington, by Dr.
R. Mayo, author of Thesis,
&c. &c. By a member of the
Hickory club. Washington,
1837. 14, 4 p. DLC; MdHi.
                            45553
Meadows, F. C.
A new French and English
pronouncing dictionary on the
basis of Nugent's, with many
new words in general use,
in two parts; I French and
English II English and French;
to which are prefixed principles
of French pronounciation, and
an abridged grammar. 4th
American ed. by George Folson.
New York, George Dearborn
and co., 1837. 356 p. InRchE;
NSyHi.   45554

Mechanic's Almanac ... for
1837. Hartford, Canfield &
Robbins, 1837. MWA.   45555

Mechanics' Institute of the City
of N.Y. 3d annual fair. N.Y.,
1837. MB.   45556

The mechanics receipt book: a
selection of interesting experiments, which may be performed
easily, safely, and at little expense. Improved ed. Worcester,
Benjamin Martin, 1837. 106 p.
MBoy; MH-BA.   45557

Mechanics' Society. Buffalo,
N.Y.
The act of incorporation and
by-laws of the Mechanics' Soci-
ety of Buffalo. Passed April,
1836. Buffalo, press of Oliver
G. Steele, 1837. 12 p. NBuHi.
                            45558
Medfield, Mass. Evangelical
Church.
The Articles of faith and
covenant...Boston, 1837. 8 p.
MBC.   45559

Medical Society of the county of
Kings. Brooklyn.
Statutes regulating the prac-
tice of physic and surgery, in
the State of New-York: and the
By-Laws of the Medical Society,
of the County of Kings. Re-
vised and adopted January 9,
1837. Published by order of the
Society. Brooklyn, Printed for
the Society, by Alden Spooner
& Sons, Mechanics Exchange, 10
Front Street, 1837. 50 p. DLC;
DNLM; NBLiHi.   45560

Medway, Mass. First Congregational Church.
Confession of Faith and Covenant of the First Congregational
Church in Medway. Organized
in 1724. Boston, ... 1837. 12
p. ICN; MBC; MHi.   45561

Meek, Alexander Beaufort.
An oration delivered before

the society of the alumni of the University of Alabama, December 17, 1836. Tuscaloose, Slade, 1837. 13 p. A-Ar; NcD. 45562

Mellen, Grenville.
A book of the United States: a view of the republic generally of the individual states; with a condensed history of the land, the biography of about three hundred of the leading men, and a description of the principlal cities and towns. Hartford, H. F. Summers, 1837. InU; KyDc; MBBCC; NSy; VtWmt. 45563

Memes, John Smythe.
... Memoirs of the Empress Josephine. By John S. Memes ... New York, Harper & brothers, 1837. 396 p. FTU; IE; MH; Nh-Hi; WvW. 45564

Memminger, Charles Gustavus.
Speech of Mr. Memminger, Commissioner from South Carolina, before the Senate of North Carolina, on the bill to confer banking privileges on the stock holders of the Charleston and Cincinnati railroad co. delivered Jan. 2, 1837. Raleigh, Gales, 1837. 14 p. NcU. 45565

Memoir of Martha C. Thomas, late of Baltimore, Maryland. Second edition. Philadelphia, Printed by Joseph Rakestraw, 1837. [9]-46 p. DLC; MdHi; MH; PHi; WHi. 45566

Men of different countries. Cooperstown, H. and E. Phinney, 1837. 31 p. NBu; NBuG. 45567

Mennonites.
The confession of faith, of the Christians known by the name of Mennonites, in thirty-three articles; with a short extract from their catechism. Translated from the German, and accompanied with notes. To which is added an introduction. ... Winchester, Printed by Robinson & Hollis, 1837. 461 p. ArCH; IEG; MWA; NN; PPLT; ViU. 45568

Mercer, Charles Fenton, 1778-1858.
Speech on the bill to suspend the payment of the 4th instalment of the surplus...Washington, Gales, 1837. 33 p. PPAmP; PPM; PHi. 45569

Mercer, Jesse, 1769-1841.
Review of a report by a Committee appointed to reply to reasons assigned by certain Churches for seceding from the Flint River Association. Washington, Ga., 1837. 34 p. NHC-S. 45570

Merchants' Bank of Baltimore.
Charter and by-laws of the Merchants' bank of Baltimore. Baltimore, Printed by John D. Toy, 1837. 23 p. MdHi. 45571

Meredith, Thomas.
Address delivered before the literary societies at the Wake Forest Institute, North Carolina, Nov. 24th 1836. By Thomas Meredith. Newbern, Recorder Office, 1837. 14 p. NcU; NcWfC; OClWHi; PSC-Hi. 45572

(Merriam, George), 1803-1880.
The intelligent reader: designed as a sequel to the child's guide. Springfield, G. and C. Merriam, 1837. MH; MShi. 45573

Merrill, Josiah G.
Sermons for Children. By Josiah G. Merrill. ... Portland, Merrill & Byram, 1837. 104 p. InCW; MeB. 45574

Merril, Rufus.
A Collection of Indian Anecdotes. Concord, N.H., 1837.
190 p. ICN; NN.   45575

Methodist Almanac for 1838.
Calculated to the Horizon and
Meridian of Boston. Lat. 42°
20' N. Long. 71° 4 W. By
David Young, Philom. New
York, J. Collord, 1837.
MBNMHi; MWA; NoiR; TxGeoS.
                          45576
Methodist Episcopal Church.
Conferences. Illinois.
Minutes of the 14th Illinois
Annual Conference ... Jackson-
ville, Sept. 27, 1837. Jackson-
ville, Brooks, Curran and Day,
1837. 8 p. IHi.   45577

---- ---- Ohio.
Minutes of the Annual Conference of the Methodist Episcopal Church, for the year 1837.
Cincinnati, Published by J. F.
Wright and L. Swormstedt for
the Methodist Episcopal Church
at the Western Book Concern,
R. P. Thompson, Printer, 1837.
86 p. Wv.   45578

---- Cumberland, R.I.
Statement of Facts In Rela-
tion to the difficulties in the
Methodist Episcopal Church,
Cumberland, R.I. Pawtucket,
Printed by R. Sherman, Paw-
tucket, Mass., 1837. 40 p.
RHi.   45579

Methodist Protestant church.
Constitution and discipline of
the Methodist Protestant church.
2d ed. Baltimore, Methodist
Protestant church, 1837. 177 p.
DLC; GDecCT; IEG; MdBAHi;
MoFayC; NcD.   45580

---- Hymn book of the Methodist
Protestant Church. Compiled by

authority of the General conference. Baltimore, published by
the book company of the Methodist Protestant church, 1837.
648 p. NNUT.   45581

The Metropolitan Catholic almanac, and Laity's directory,
for the year of Our Lord 1838.
Baltimore, Fielding Lucas, Jr.,
[1837]. [3]-162 p. WStfSF.
                          45582
Meucci, G.
Description of Signor Riboni's
painting of the Massacre of Wyoming. Philadelphia, Waldie,
1837. 8 p. PPAmP.   45583

Miami Exporting Company. Judiciary committee.
Report, in House of Representatives, Jan. 9, 1837. n.p.,
1837. 8 p. OHi.   45584

Miami university, Oxford, O.
The twelfth annual catalogue of
the officers and students ...
July, 1837. Oxford, Printed by
R. H. Bishop, jun., 1837. 12 p.
CSmH.   45585

Michigan. Bank Commissioner.
The first annual report of
the bank commissioner of the
State of Michigan: Made to the
legislature, January 5, 1837.
Detroit, John S. Bagg, printer
to the legislature, 1837. 11 p.
Mi; MiD-B; Mi-L; MiGr; WHi.
                          45586
---- Governor (Stevens T. Ma-
son).
Governor's message and ac-
companying documents; delivered
to the legislature of Michigan,
June 12, 1837. By authority.
Detroit, John S. Bagg, State
printer, 1837. 24 p. Mi; MiD;
MiD-B; MiU.   45587

---- ---- Message of the Governor

of the State of Michigan, to
both houses of the legislature,
delivered on the second day of
January, 1837. Detroit, By
John S. Bagg, printer to the
legislature, [1837]. 24 p.
CSmH; MiD-B; MiGr; MiU-C.
                                45588
---- Laws, statutes, etc.
Act establishing the
Farmers' and mechanics' Bank
of Michigan. Passed November
5, 1837. Detroit, Bagg,
Bames and Co., 1837.
MiD-B.   45589

---- ---- An act to provide for
taking the census. Be it enacted by the Senate and House
of Representatives of the State
of Michigan...[Detroit, 1837].
MiD-B.   45590

---- ---- Acts of the legislature of the state of Michigan,
passed at the annual session of
1837. By authority. Detroit,
John S. Bagg, state printer,
1837. (3), 4-354 p. Ar-Sc;
ICHi; MiD-B; OCLaw; Wa-L.
                                45591
---- ---- Laws in relation to
banking institutions, passed at
the session of 1837. Detroit,
John S. Bagg, 1837. 24 p.
MiD-B; MiGr; NcD; NGH. 45592

---- ---- Laws in relation to internal improvement in the state
of Michigan, passed at the
session of 1837. [n.p.], 1837.
16 p. MB; MiD; NcD; NN.
                                45593
---- ---- Legislative manual of
the senate and house of representatives of the State of Michigan, for 1837. By authority.
Detroit, John S. Bagg, printer
to the legislature, 1837. 102 p.
DLC; MiD-B; Mi-Hi; MiPh;
MiU-Hi.   45594

---- ---- House.
Journal of the house of representatives of the State of Michigan, 1837. By authority. Detroit, John S. Bagg, State
printer, 1837. 629 p. CtMW;
ICU; MiGr; PP; WHi.   45595

---- ---- ---- Journal of the
house of representatives of the
State of Michigan; adjourned
session. 1837. By authority.
Detroit, John S. Bagg, State
printer, 1837. 187, 50 p.
CtMW; ICHi; MiD-B; PP; WHi.
                                45596
---- ---- ---- Committee on Internal Improvements.
Report of the committee on
internal improvements; made to
the house of representatives of
the State of Michigan, January
24, 1837. Detroit, John S.
Bagg, printer to the legislature,
1837. 17 p. M; MiD; NGH;
PHi; WHi.   45597

---- ---- Senate.
Executive journal of the senate
of the State of Michigan, for
1835-6; and first and special
sessions, in 1837. By authority.
Detroit, John S. Bagg, State
printer, 1837. 84 p. ICHi;
MiGr; Mi-L; NHi; WHi.   45598

---- ---- ---- Journal of the
senate of the state of Michigan,
at the adjourned session of the
legislature, in the year 1837.
By authority. Detroit, John S.
Bagg, State printer, 1837. 279
p. ICHi; MiD; MiPh; MnU; WHi.
                                45599
---- ---- ---- Journal of the
senate of the State of Michigan,
at the first and special sessions
of the legislature, in the year
1837. By authority. Detroit,
John S. Bagg, State printer,
1837. 529, 192 p. ICU; IU;
MiD-B; MiU; NHi.   45600

---- ---- ---- State of Michigan. No. 15. Special session.
In senate, December 21, 1837.
Amendments reported by the
committee on finance to title
5, part 1st. [Detroit, 1837?].
4 p. MiD-B.   45601

---- ---- ---- Select Committee
on Imprisonment for Debt.
Report of the select committee of the senate, on imprisonment for debt. Detroit, John S.
Bagg, printer to the legislature,
1837. 10 p. Mi-Hi.   45602

---- Militia. First Brigade.
Brigade orders. Head-
quarters, first brigade, M.M.
Detroit, April 13, 1837....
[Detroit, 1837]. Broadside.
MiD-B.   45603

---- Superintendent of Public
Instruction (John D. Pierce).
Report of the superintendent
of public instruction of the
State of Michigan; made to the
legislature, January 5, 1837.
Detroit, John S. Bagg, printer
to the legislature, 1837. 60 p.
MdBJ; MiD-B; MiGr; MnU;
ScU; WHi.   45604

---- University. Board of Regents.
Code of laws for the government of the branches of the
University of Michigan. Adopted
by the board of regents of the
university. Printed by order
of the board. Detroit, Kingsbury and Dally, printers,
1837. 18 p. MiD-B; MiU.
                                45605
---- ---- ---- Journal of the
proceedings of the board of
regents, of the University of
Michigan, at Ann Arbor.
Printed by Kingsbury & Burnham, Office of the Morning

Post. Detroit, 1837. 25 p.
MH; MWA; MiGr; PHi; PU.
                                45606
Middlebrook's Almanac for 1838.
By Elijah Middlebrook. Bridge-
port, Josiah B. Baldwin, (1837).
MWA; NCH.   45607

---- New Haven, Conn., Durrie
& Peck, (1837). MWA.   45608

Middlebury College, Middlebury,
Vt.
Catalogue of library of philo-
mathesian society, 1837. Middle-
bury, 1837. 16 p. NAlbi; WHi.
                                45609
---- Catalogue of the Officers
and Students of Middlesbury
College, October, 1837. Mid-
dlesbury, Office of the Peoples'
Press, 1837. 16 p. MH; NAlbi;
WHi.   45610

Middlesex Mechanic Association.
Lowell, Mass.
Constitution and by-laws,
instituted, October, 1825. Lowell,
Dearborn and Bellows, printers,
1837. 30 p. MB; MH-BA.
                                45611
Midshipman's expedients. By
the author of "Rattlin the reefer;"
and other tales, by celebrated
writers....Philadelphia, Carey
Lea and Blanchard, 1837. 2 v.
in 1. CtY; ICBB; NjR; NN;
WU.   45612

Midway, Mass. First Congregational Church.
Confession of faith ... Boston,
D. H. Ela, 1837. 12 p. ICN.
                                45613
Mifflin, Samuel W.
Methods of location; or, Modes
of describing and adjusting railway curves and tangents as
practised by engineers of Pennsylvania, rev. and extended by
Samuel W. Mifflin ... Philadelphia,

E. C. Biddle, 1837. 41 p.
CSt; ICJ; OCy; PHi; RPA.
45614

Milburn, William Henry.
The rifle, axe and saddle-
bags and other lectures. By
William Henry Milburn. With
introduction by Rev. J. Mc-
Clintock, D.D. New York,
Derry & Jackson, George Russell & Co., Printer, 1837.
309 p. PLT.   45615

Miles, Stephen.
A correspondence in which
the positive certainty of punishment for sin is ... proved ...
by a Universalist clergyman.
While on the other hand,
there is an entire failure on the
part of a Presbyterian minister
in proof of the least possibil-
ity of escape from a just retri-
bution ... By Rev. Stephen
Miles....J. Taylor Bradt,
printer, Geneva, N.Y., 1837.
36 p. MMet-Hi.   45616

Millard, David, 1794-1873.
Hymns and spiritual songs
for the use of christians. Supplementary to D. Willard and J.
Badger's collection, published
by the Christian gen. book
association. Exeter, N.H.,
Published by M. Femald and E.
Shaw, 1837. 64 p. CSmH.
45617
---- Hymns and spiritual songs
original and selected. For the
use of Christians. By D. Millard & J. Badger. ... Fourth
edition. Union Mills, N.Y.,
Published by the Christian Gen.
Book Association. Printed at
the Office of the Ch. Palladium,
1837. 464 p. CtY-D.   45618

---- The true Messiah, in
Scripture light; or the Unity
of God, and proper worship of
Jesus Christ, affirmed and de-
fended. Second edition, with
additions and improvements.
By David Millard....Union Mills,
N.Y., Published by the Christian
General (sic) Book Association,
Printed at the office of the
Christian Palladium, 1837. 256
p. ICMe; MH; MoSpD; PPiPT.
45619
---- ---- 2nd ed. Union Mills,
N.Y., 1837. CSmH; MH-AH;
PPiPT.   45620

Miller, Adam.
A new and easy spelling and
reading book in German and
English; designed as a help to
the Study of both language.
Cincinnati, 1837. 125 p.
45621

Miller, J. R.
The history of Great Britain,
from the death of George II, to
the coronation of George IV....
By J. R. Miller. Philadelphia,
M'Carty and Davis, 1837. 724 p.
CtHT; IA; IaScT; LNDil; NGcA.
45622

Miller, Samuel, 1769-1850.
Infant baptism scriptural and
reasonable: and baptism by
sprinkling or affusion, the most
suitable and edifying mode.
Philadelphia, Wm. Martien, 1837.
122 p. IEG; MBC; NbOP; NjP;
PPPrHi.   45623

---- Lives of Jonathan Edwards
and David Brainerd. Boston,
Hilliard, Gray, 1837. 373 p.
CSfP; MeB; NNS; PMA; CBPac.
45624
---- Presbyterianism, the truly
primitive and apostical constitution of the Church of Christ.
By Samuel Miller, D.D. Philadelphia, Printed and for sale by
Wm. S. Martin for the Presbyterian Tract and Sunday School
Society, 1837. (5)-98 p. KyLoS.
45625

Miller's Planter's and Merchants Almanac. 2nd ed. Charleston, S.C., H. E. Miller, [1837]. MWA.   45626

Miller's Planters' & Merchants' Almanac for 1838. 3rd ed. Charleston, S.C., A. E. Miller, [1837]. MWA.   45627

[Mills, Robert], 1781-1855.
Design no. 1 for a marine hospital on the western waters to accommodate 100 patients (Mills, Robert). Design no. 1 for a marine hospital ... Washington, D.C., (1837?) DLC; MH.   45628

---- Design no. 2 for a marine hospital on the western front to accommodate 50 patients. (Mills, Robert). Design no. 2 for a marine hospital, Wash., D.C.?, (1837?) DLC; MH.
                                   45629
Milman, Henry Hart, 1791-1868.
The history of the Jews. From the earliest period to the present time. By Rev. H. H. Milman. With maps and engravings ... New York, Harper & Brothers, 1837. 3 v. FTU; LNF; MsSC; ScCliP; TxDaTS.
                                   45630
Miltitz, Carl Borromaeus von, 1780-1845.
The game of life; or, The chess-players, a drawing by Moritz Retzsch, explained, according to hints from himself, with additional remarks on the allegory, re-pub. for the Warren street chapel. Boston, Weeks, Jordan and co., 1837. 4 p. MB; MH; NjR; NWM; OCl.
                                   45631
Milton, [Charles William].
A narrative of the gracious dealings of God in the conversion of William Mooney Fitz-

gerald and John Clark, executed Dec. 18, 1789...Newburyport, [Mass.], W. & J. Gilman, 1837. MB; MH; MNe; RPB.   45632

Milton, Mass. First Congregational Church.
The order of services for the installation of Rev. Joseph Angier as pastor of the Church on Sept. 13, 1837. Boston, Torrey & Blair, 1837. 4 p. MH.   45633

Mine Hill and Schuylkill Haven R.R. Co.
Reports. 1836- Philadelphia, 1837- PHi.   45634

Miner, Thomas, 1777-1841.
An address to the annual convention of the Medical society of Connecticut, convened at Hartford, May 10, 1837...New Haven, Printed by B. L. Hamlen, 1837. 12 p. Ct; CtHT-W; CtSoP; MB; NNNAM.   45635

Mines, John.
The infant: a poem in four books: by the Rev. John Miner. To which are added miscellaneous poems by the same author.... New York, J. S. Taylor, 1837. [15]-266 p. MdBP; MdHi; NcD; PPL-R; RPB.   45636

Miniature Almanack. Concord, Jno. F. Brown, 1837. MWA.
                                   45637
Miniature Almanack, for 1838. Exeter, N.H., E. Fellowes, (1837). MWA.   45638

Miniature Almanack and Pocket Memoranda for...1838...Concord, Roby, Kimball & Merrill, [1837]. 16 ℓ. MWA.   45639

---- Exeter, Published by Oliver Smith, [1837]. 16 ℓ. MWA; NhHi.   45640

Mississippi. Laws, statutes, etc.

Laws of the State of Mississippi, passed at a called session of the Legislature, held in the City of Jackson in April and May, 1837. Printed by G. R. Fall, 1837. MdBB; Mi-L; Ms; OCLaw; Or-SC.   45641

---- ---- Laws of the State of Mississippi passed at an adjourned session of the Legislature, held in the city of Jackson in January, 1837. Jackson, printed by G. R. & J. S. Fall, 1837. [2 p.] 8-62 p. Index 2-4 p. C-L; Ms; MdBB; NNLl; OCLaw; WaU-L.   45642

---- Legislature.

Resolutions of the Legislature of Mississippi relative to the Franking privilege. Executive department, Jackson, July 10, 1837. [i] p. MdHi.   45643

---- ---- House.

Journal of the House of Representatives of the State of Mississippi, at an adjourned meeting thereof, held in the town of Jackson. Printed by order of the House of Representatives. Jackson, Printed by G. R. & J. S. Fall, 1837. Ms; MsWJ; WHi.   45644

---- ---- Senate.

Journal of the Senate of the state of Mississippi, at an adjourned meeting thereof, held in the town of Jackson. Printed by order of the Senate. Jackson, Printed by G. R. & J. S. Fall, 1837. Ms; MsJs; WHi.   45645

Mississippi. Eine geographisch-statistisch-topographische Skizze für Einwanderer und Freunde der Lander- und Volkskunde. 4. Buch Moses, Kap. 13. B. 19. 20.21. Baltimore, Md., Verlag von C. Scheld und Co., 1837. 24 p. MdBSHG; PU.   45646

Missouri. House of Representatives.

Journal of the House of Representatives, of the State of Missouri, at the first session of the ninth General Assembly, begun and held at the city of Jefferson, on the twenty-first day of November, in the year of our Lord, one thousand eight hundred and thirty-six. Bowling Green, Printed at the Office of the Salt River Journal, 1837. 474 p. DLC; Mo; MoHi; WHi.   45647

---- Laws, statutes, etc.

An act to regulate, govern and discipline the Militia of the State of Missouri, passed at the First Session of the Ninth General Assembly, begun and held at the City of Jefferson, on Monday, the twenty-first day of November, in the year of our Lord, one thousand eight hundred and thirty-six. Printed by Chambers, Harris and Knapp. Missouri Republican Office, St. Louis, 1837. 42 p. MoS.
                           45648
---- ---- Laws of the State of Missouri, Passed at the First Session of the Ninth General Assembly, begun and held at the City of Jefferson, on Monday, the twenty-first day of November, in the year of our lord one thousand eight hundred and thirty six. City of Jefferson, Printed by Calvin Gunn, Jeffersonial Office, 1837. 334, [1] p. I; ICLaw; Mo; MoHi; MsS. 45649

---- Senate.

Journal of the Senate, of the

State of Missouri, at the first session of the ninth General Assembly, begun and held at the city of Jefferson, on the twenty-first day of November, in the year of our Lord one thousand eight hundred and thirty-six. Bowling-Green, Printed at the Office of the Salt River Journal, 1837. 340, xiii p. Mo; MoHi; WHi.
45650

Missouri Iron Company, Missouri City, Mo.

Prospectus of the Missouri Iron Company and Missouri and Iron Mountain cities, together with a map of the state of Missouri and plans of the cities. Boston, Marden & Kimball, 1837. 40 p. ICJ; MBC; MH; MoHi; NNC.   45651

---- ---- Hartford, Printed by P. Canfield, 1837. 40 p. OClWHi; PPAmP; WHi.   45652

---- Prospectus of the Missouri Iron Company. With act of incorporation. Philadelphia, 1837. 36 p. DLC; IU; MH-BA; MoSW; TxU.   45653

Mitchel, Ormsby MacKnight, 1809-1862.

Survey of the Little Miami Railroad. Report and estimates made by the Board of Directors ....Cincinnati, Pugh and Dodd, 1837. 16 p. DBRE; MH. 45654

Mitchell, Isaac.

The Asylum; or, Alonzo and Melissa. An American Tale, Founded on Fact ... Portland, 1837. 141 p. MWA.   45655

Mitchell, John, 1794-1870.

A sermon preached before the First church and the Edwards church, Northampton, on the late Fast, Sept. 1, 1837. By John Mitchell, pastor of the Edwards church. Published by request. Northampton, printed by W. A. Hawley, 1837. 4-30 p. CtHC; ICU; MiD-B; MPiB; WHi.
45656

Mitchell, Samuel Augustus, 1792-1868.

An accompaniment to Mitchell's map of the world, on Mercator's projection; containing an index to the various countries, cities, towns, islands, etc. represented on the map.... Philadelphia, Hinman & Dutton, 1837. 11-572 p. LNH; OClWHi; PP; RP; TNP.   45657

---- Map of the state of New York, compiled from the latest authorities. Philadelphia, 1837. ICN; PHi.   45658

---- Map of the states of Ohio, Indiana & Illinois with the settled part of Michigan. Philadelphia, 1837. IaU; OC; OO; PHi.   45659

---- Map of The World. By Mitchell. Also a general description of the Five Great Division of the Globe. Philadelphia, Pa., Hinman & Dutton, Publisher, 1837. 572 p. DLC; NcNb.
45660

---- Mitchell's traveller's guide through the United States, containing the principal cities, towns, &c., alphabetically arranged; together with the stage, steam-boat, canal, and railroad routes, with the distances, in miles, from place to place. Illustrated by an accurate map of the United States. Philadelphia, Mitchell & Hinman, 1837. 78 p. CtY; DLC; IU; VtU.   45661

---- Mitchell's Travellers Guide

to the United States. A map
of roads, steam boat and canal
routes, etc., by J. H. Young,
Philadelphia. Published by S.
Augustus Mitchell, 1837. CtY;
IU; WvU. 45662

Mitchell, Thomas Duché, 1791-
1865.
A Cursory View of the History of Chemical Science, and
Some of its more Important
Uses to the Physician: being
an Introductory, to the Course
of Lectures, for the Session
1837-8. Lexington, Finnell &
Zimmerman, Printers, 1837.
22 p. DNLM; KyLxT; KU;
OCHP. 45663

Miville, De Chene, J. G. F.
Summary of a new French
grammar raisonnee; containing
the rules of correct pronunciation
for the use of colleges and
schools. Boston, American
stationers Company, John B.
Russell. Lowell, Daniel Bixby,
L. Huntress, printer, 1837.
(6), 5-92 p. InCW; MH; MPiB.
45664

Molony, Cornelius.
Masterpiece on wool, silk
and cotton dyeing: containing
his best receipts, without the
least reserve; according to his
practice in Great Britain and
America. Lowell, [Mass.],
Dearborn and Bellows, 1837.
DLC; DSI; MB. 45665

Monk, Maria, d. ca. 1850.
Further disclosures by Maria
Monk, concerning the Hotel
Dieu, nunnery of Montreal:
also, her visit to Nuns' Island
... Preceded by a reply to the
Priests' book, by the Rev. J. J.
Slocum. New York, Published
for Maria Monk, and sold by
Leavitt, Lord, & co.; Boston,

Crocker & Brewster; (etc., etc.),
1837. 194 p. DLC; GDecCT;
KyLoS; MBC; WHi. 45666

Monroe Railroad and Banking
Company.
Charter of the Monroe railroad and Banking Company, comprising the several acts relating
thereto, together with the act
chartering the main line of said
road to the Tennessee line.
Macon, S. Rose and Company,
pr., 1837. 21 p. DBRE.
45667
---- Report and estimate of the
engineer to the president, directors, and stock-holders met
in Convention Aug. 1837. Macon, 1837. PPFrankI. 45668

Montagu, Lady Mary (Pierrepont)
Wortley, 1689-1762.
The letters and works of Lady
Mary Wortley Montagu. Edited
by her great grandson, Lord
Whorncliffe. Philadelphia, Carey,
Lea and Blanchard, 1837. 2 v.
CtHT; GU; MdBJ; OCl; PPA.
45669
Montgomery, George W.
The First and second creations.
A sermon. By Rev. G. W. Mont-
gomery. Rochester, printed at
the Office of the Herald of
Truth, 1837. 12 p. MMeT-Hi.
45670
---- A Reply to the main argu-
ments of Rev. L. Beecher, D.D.
By Geo. W. Montgomery ... Au-
burn, Allen & Lounsbury, print-
ers, 1837. 24 p. MMeT; MMeT-
Hi. 45671

Montgomery, Henry.
The importance and method of
early religious education. By
Rev. Henry Montgomery, of Ire-
land. 2nd ed. ... 1st Series.
No. 40. Boston, James Munroe
... (I. R. Butts, printer), 1837.

48 p. IaPeC; ICMe; MB-HP;
MMeT-Hi.   45672

Moore, Ely, 1798-1861.
Speech of Mr. Moore, of New
York, on the bill imposing addi-
tional duties as depositories in
certain cases on public officers,
delivered in the House of
Representatives October 13,
1837. Washington, Blair and
Rives, 1837. 30 p. MdHi;
MiD-B; MsJS; PPPrHi; Tx.
                              45673
Moore, Henry, 1751-1844.
The life of Mrs. Mary
Fletcher,....compiled from her
journal and other authentic
documents, by Henry Moore.
New York, Published by T.
Mason and G. Lane, for the
Methodist Episcopal church,
1837. 398 p. DLC; InGr;
KyU; MTr; NjPT.   45674

Moore, Henry Eaton, 1803-1841.
The Northern Harp; a new
collection of church music...
harmonized expressly for this
work, with a figured bass...
Concord, 1837. CtY; MoSpD;
Nh; Nh-Hi.   45675

Moore, Joshua.
Sermon on the Preaching of
the gospel at Rome, delivered at
the F Street church, Washington
City, on Sabbath morning,
February 19, 1837, by Joshua
Moore, V.D.M. Washington,
Jacob Gideon, Jr., printer,
1837. 14 p. ScU.   45676

Moore, Margaret. defendant.
Memorial to the General Assembly of Maryland, of the defendants in the case of Ewing
and wife vs. Moore, et al. decided in the Court of appeals at
June term, 1836. Baltimore,
Lucas & Deaver, 1837. 90 p.
MdBE; MdHi.   45677

Moore, Thomas, 1779-1852.
Lalla Rookh, with select notes
By Thomas Moore, Esq. A new
edition. Exeter, J. and B.
Williams, 1837. 184 p. KyHi;
MBBC; MHaHi; PHi; PMA.
                              45678
---- The poetical works of
Thomas Moore. Complete in one
volume. A biographical and
critical sketch by T. W. Lake.
Philadelphia, Desilver, Thomas
and Co., 1837. 419 p. IaOskJF;
MoSW; NTSJ; OCan.   45679

The moral almanac, for the year
1838....by William Collom.
Philadelphia, Tract assoc. of
Friends; J. Rakestraw, pr.,
(1837). (34) p. MWA; NjR;
PPF.   45680

Moravian Church.
A brotherly agreement,
adopted by the congregation of
Bethabara, Bethania, Friedland...
in North Carolina, as revised
after the synod of the United
Brethren's Church in the year
of our Lord, 1836. Salem, Blum
and son, 1837. NcU.   45681

More, Hannah, 1745-1833.
Book of private devotion ...
with an introductory essay on
prayer, chiefly from the writings
of Hannah More. Rev. and enl.
N.Y., Leavitt, Lord and Co.,
1837. CtHC; MB; OO.   45682

---- The works of Hannah More.
First complete American ed...
New York, Harper & Bros., 1837.
2 v. in 1. ILM; MiU-C; MNS;
PLFM; TxU.   45683

Morgridge, Charles.
Appendix to the "True be-
liever's defence;" or a reply to
"The true faith vindicated," a
Work purporting to have been

written by Phineas Crandall, Pastor of the Second Methodist Episcopal Church in New Bedford, by Rev. Chas. Morgridge, the author of the defence. New-Bedford, (Mass.), Printed by J. C. Parmenter, for William Howe, 1837. 60 p. MBC; MNBedf; TxDaM.   45684

---- The True believer's defence, against charges preferred by Trinitarians, for not believing in the divinity of Christ ... Boston, Benjamin H. Greene, 1837. 168 p. MBAU; MBC; MH; Nh; PCA.   45685

[Morier, James Justinian].
Abel Allmutt. A novel. By the author of "Hajji Baba," "Zorab," &c.... In two volumes.... Philadelphia, E. L. Carey & A. Hart, 1837. 2 v. ICBB; NjR; MB; RPB; TNP.
45686

Morison, John, 1791-1859.
Counsels to young men on modern infidelity and the evidence of Christianity...New York, Publ., by the Amer., tract Soc., 1837. 201 p. MB; MiU; NBuG.   45687

[Morison, Nathaniel Holmes], 1815-1890.
Song for the Sophomore class of 1837. [n.p., 1837?] 1 leaf fold. MdBJ.   45688

The morning ride.... New Haven, S. Babcock, 1837. 16 p. TxD-T.   45689

Morrill, Henry E.
An address, delivered in the Methodist Episcopal church, Natchez, at the formation of the "Natchez temperance society," on Sabbath evening, March 5, 1837: (and subsequently, by

request, at Vicksburg, Miss.,) by Henry E. Morrill Published by the Natchex temperance society. Natchez [Miss.], Printed at the office of the Cold water man, 1837. 24 p. CSmH.
45690

Morris canal and banking Company.
Report. New York, 1837. PPL.   45691

Morrison, John.
Counsels to the young. Norwich, 1837. CtHWatk.
45692

Morse, Samuel Finley Breese.
Confessions of a French Catholic priest. To which are added warnings to the people of the United States. By the same author. Ed. by Samuel F. B. Morse, A. M. New York, Van Nostrand, 1837. 255 p. CtHWatk; GDecCT; MBBC; OWoC; PPLT.   45693

Morton, Samuel George, 1799-1851.
Illustrations of plumonary consumption; its anatomical characters, causes, symptoms and treatment. To which are added some remarks on the climate of the United States, the West Indies, &c. ... 2. ed. Philadelphia, E. C. Biddle, 1837. 349 p. CSt; ICJ; NjR; RPM; WNAM.   45694

Mosheim, John Laurence.
An Ecclesiastical History;
ancient and modern. By the
Late Learned John Laurence
Mosheim, D.D. Translated
from the original Latin, by
Archibald MacLaine, D.D. A
new edition, in two volumes,
continued to the year 1826.
By Charles Coote, LL.D.
Baltimore, Plaskitt, Fite & Co.,
1837. 2 v. MdBE; OBerB;
OkEnS; WBeloC.   45695

Mott, Abigail (Field), 1766-
1851.
Biographical sketches and
interesting anecdotes of persons of color. To which is
added, a selection of pieces in
poetry. Comp. by A. Mott...
2d ed. much enl. New-York,
M. Day, 1837. 260 p. ICN;
LNH; MdHi; MH; OClWHi. 45696

Moubray, Bannington.
On breeding, rearing and
fattening all kinds of poultry,
cows and swine. ... Boston,
Breck, 1837. 278 p. InLPU;
MB; MdBLC.   45697

Mount Auburn Cemetery. Cambridge, Mass.
Catalogue of lots from which
proprietors may make selections. Boston, 1837. 7 p.
MBC.   45698

Mount Holyoke College, South
Hadley, Mass.
First annual catalogue of the
officers and members of the
Mount Holyoke Female Seminary,
South Hadley, Mass. 1837-8.
12 p. CtHC; CtHWatk; MH;
MWF.   45699

----General view of the principles
and design of the Mount Holyoke
female seminary. Pub. by direction of the Trustees. Boston,
Printed by Perkins & Marvin,
1837. 22 p. DLC; MBC; MH;
MiU; Nh.   45700

---- ---- [South Hadley? Mass.,
1837]. 18 p. CtY; DHEW; NH.
                         45701
Mt. Pleasant Military Academy.
Ossining, N.Y.
Annual catalogue. Mt. Pleas-
ant, 1837. MB.   45702

The Mountain bugle. [Song, T.
accomp.] arranged for the Spanish guitar by J. B. L'Hulier.
Philadelphia, Willig, 1837. (2) p.
MB.   45703

Mudge, Enoch.
A Temperance address, in
Poetry, delivered before the
Seaman, at the Bethel, July 16,
1837. By Rev. Enoch Mudge,
... New Bedford, Printed by
J. C. Parmenter, 1837. 12 p.
MB; MBNMHi; MBC; Nh. 45704

Muller, John von, 1752-1809.
Universal history, translated
from the German of John von
Muller. In four volumes....
Published by authority of the
Boston society for the diffusion
of useful knowledge. Boston,
American stationers company,
J. B. Russell, 1837. 4 v. LNB;
MdW; MiU; ScNC; TNP. 45705

Munroe, James, and Co.'s.
Select catalogue of books for
1837. Published annually. Boston, 1837. 92 p. MH-And;
RPB.   45706

Murray, Andrew.
Holy in Christ. Thoughts on
the calling of God's children to
be Holy as he is Holy. New
York, Revell, 1837. 302 p.
PAnL.   45707

Murray, Hugh, 1779-1846.
   The encyclopedia of geography; comprising a complete description of the earth, physical, statistical, civil, and political.... By Hugh Murray, F.R. S.E.... Revised, with additions, by Thomas G. Bradford. Philadelphia, Carey, Lea and Blanchard, 1837. 3 v. ICU; MB; PAtM; ViU; WHi.
45708

Murray, John, 1741-1815.
   The life of Rev. John Murray, late minister of the reconciliation, and senior pastor of the Universalists, congregated in Boston ... 6th ed. ... Boston, Marsh, Capen & Lyon, 1837. 324 p. MiD-B.   45709

Murray, Lindley, 1745-1826.
   English exercises, adapted to Murray's English Grammar... New York, 1837. PPM.   45710

---- Murray's English exercises, consisting of exercises in parsing; instances of false orthogography; violation of the rules of syntax; defects in punctuation.... Adapted to the use of schools:... By Israel Alger, jun., A.M. Boston, Published by Robert S. Davis,... 1837. 252 p. MH; TMeG.   45711

---- ... English grammar adapted to the different classes of learners...Newark, N.J., Benjamin Olds, 1837. CSmH.
45712

---- The English reader; or, pieces in prose and poetry, selected from the best writers. With a few preliminary observations on the principles of good reading. Bridgeport, Conn., J. B. Baldwin, 1837. 263 p. MoU.   45713

---- ---- Cincinnati, Published by J. W. Ely, at Franklin Book-Store, Lower Market-street, 1837. 204 p. IaBl, KHi.   45714

---- ---- Concord, N.H., Atwood and Brown, 1837. MH.   45715

---- ---- Cooperstown, E. Phinney, 1837. 252 p. CSmH; ICU; MH; NN; PSC-Hi.   45716

---- ---- Hamilton, [N.Y.], Butler Maynard, 1837. CSmH.
45717
---- ---- Newark, N.J., printed & published by Benjamin Olds, 1837. 252 p. CtY; ICU; MB; NjR.   45718

---- Introduction to the English reader; or, a selection of pieces in prose and poetry....By Lindley Murray. Philadelphia, A. I. Dickinson, 1837. 166 p. NcD; NNT-C.   45719

---- ---- Philadelphia, Thomas Sutton, 1837. 166 p. ICBB; PReaAT.   45720

---- Sentiments of several eminent persons on the tendency of dramatic entertainments, and other amusements; with a few reflections on the same subject subjoined. New York, Redfield and Lindsay, 1837. MH. 45721

---- Murray's system of English grammar. Improved by E. Pond. 16th ed. Worcester, (1837). MB.   45722

---- ---- New ed. with the parts of speech illustrated by engravings. Worcester, Dorr, Howland, & Co., 1837. 70 p. CLSU; MH.   45723

Murray, Nicholas.

Address to the teachers and scholars of the Winchester Sunday Schools, on the Fourth of July, 1837. By Nicholas Murray, Esq. Superintendent of the Presbyterian Sunday School. Winchester, Wm. Towers, 1837. 16 p. ViU.   45724

Muse, Joseph E.
    An address....Before the Dorchester agricultural society, and a large assemblage of the citizens of Dorchester...At the fourth exhibition and fair, held in Cambridge.... By Joseph E. Muse.... Baltimore, n. pub., Printed by John D. Toy, 1837. 29 p. MdHi; NjR; PPL; PPM.   45725

Museum der deutschen klassiker ...hrsg. von Wilhelm Radde. N.Y. (W. Radde), 1837-41. v. 1-2, 4-5. CtMW.   45726

Mussey, Reuben Dimond, 1750-1866.
    Prize essay on ardent spirits, and its substitutes as a means of invigorating health... By Reuben D. Mussey, M.D. ...Washington, Published by Duff Green, 1837. 64 p. MBAt; MHi; NNNAM; NSyU; ScU.
                                45727
Muzzey, Artemas B., 1802-1892.
    A Sermon preached before the Ancient and Honorable Artillery Company, on their CXCIXth anniversary, June 5, 1837. By Rev. Artemas B. Muzzey, of Cambridge-Port. Boston, Marden & Crawford, printers, 1837. 32 p. ICMe; MBAt; MH-And; MNe; MWA.   45728

My Daughter's Manual, comprising a summary view of female studies, accomplishments, and principles of conduct.

New York, D. Appleton & Co., 1837. 288 p. CtY; MH; NNC; OCHP; VcU.   45729

My Happy Home, Or The Benefits of Religious Training: A Sabbath-School Teacher's Gift To Young Friends. [3 line quotation] "And what doth the Lord require of thee, but to do justly, and to love mercy, and to walk humbly with thy God?" Micah VI, 8. Philadelphia, George and Byington. William Stavely, 1837. 144 pp. ICBB.
                                45730
My son's manual, comprising a summary view of the studies, accomplishments, and principles of conduct, best suited for promoting respectability and success in life. New York, D. Appleton & Co., 1837. 281 p. CtHWatk; LNH; MB; MdBLC; OCHP.
                                45731
Myers, Peter D.
    Representation of the heart of man in its depraved state by nature....by Peter D. Myers. New York, J. H. Minuse, 1837. 72 p. NRivHi.   45732

Mythological fables. Translated by Dryden, Pope, Congreve, Addison and Others. Prepared expressly for the Use of Youth. In one volume. N.Y., W. E. Dean, 1837. MB; MeBaT; MiGr; NbO; PAtM.   45733

─── N ───

Nance, C. W.
    A Counter Report on the Central Railroad, by C. W. Nance, Assistant Civil Engineer. Upon the Report of A. M. Lea, Chief Engineer of Tennessee. [Printed by Order of the House of Representatives.] Nashville, S. Nye

& Co., Printers to the State, 1837. 12 p. T; THi.   45734

---- Report of Examinations and Surveys, Made at Randolph, Fulton, Mouth of Coal Creek, and Ashport. By C. W. Nance, Assistant Civil Engineer. Nashville, S. Nye & Co., Printers to the State, 1837. 63-81 p. DLC; NN; T; TKL-Mc; TNV.   45735

Napoleon: his army and his generals; their unexampled military career, with a sketch of the French Revolution. By an American. New York, Leavitt & Allen, 1837. x, [1]-422 p. FTa; LNH.   45735a

Nares, Edward, 1762-1841.
    Thinks- I- to-myself: a serio- ludicro, tragico-comico tale; written by Thinks- I-to-myself, Who? Two volumes in one. Boston, George Clark; stereotyped by Allison & Foster, 1837. 237 p. MB; NjR.   45736

A narrative of the Life and Sufferings of Mrs. Jane Johns, who was barbarously wounded and scalped by Seminole Indians, in East Florida...Published exclusively for her benefit. Baltimore, Printed by Jas. Lucas & E. K. Deaver, 1837. 56 p. DLC; PPL; ScU.   45737

---- Charleston, Printed by Burke and Giles, 1837. 29 p. ICN; MH; WHi.   45738

A narrative of the singular sufferings of John Fillmore and others, on board the noted pirate vessel commanded by Captain Phillips: ...Aurora, (New York), Printed by A. M. Clapp, 1837. (13) p. IU; MH; NNC; RPB; TxU.   45739

Nashua [N.H.] High School.
    Catalogue of the instructors and students for the year ending November, 1837, '39. Nashua, 1837-39. Nh-Hi.   45740

Nashua & Lowell Railroad Corporation.
    (Annual report, 1st. 1836/37). (Boston, 1837). DLC; ICJ; MB; MiVt; NN.   45741

Nashville, Tenn. Ordinances, etc.
    Laws of the Corporation of Nashville, to which are Prefixed the Laws of North Carolina and Tennessee relating to the town of Nashville. Published by authority. Nashville, Printed by Wm. E. Matthews, 1837. 95 p. NN; T; TKL-Mc; TxD-T.
                                   45742
Natchez, Miss. Ordinances, etc.
    An ordinance, to define and regulate the harbor of the city of Natchez. Natchez, Daily courier, city print, 1837. 14 p. CSmH.   45742a

The National Comic Almanac for the year 1838, calculated for each state in the Union; with humorous stories and anecdotes. Massachusetts? published by an association of Gentlemen, [1837]. [36] p. illus. ICU; MHi; MWA; RNHi.   45743

National convention of businessmen. Philadelphia, 1837.
    Address of the National Convention of Business Men ... Philadelphia, ... Nov. 15, 1837. ... Philadelphia, 1837. 6 p. DLC; MB; MBAt.   45744

---- Proceedings of the National convention of business men which assembled at Philadelphia, on Wednesday, November 15,

1837. Philadelphia, By order of the Convention, 1837. 16 p. CtHWatk; DLC; ICU; MH-BA; OKU; OO.   45745

The natural history of insects. Harper's stereotype ed. New York, Harper and bros., 1837. 292 p. FTa; IdU; IU; MH-Z; NJNbS; PPF.   45746

The Natural History of The Seasons, Or Youth's Year Book: Containing Also A Number Of Historical And Interesting Facts For Each Month, arranged In Chronological Order. Enlarged And Corrected From A London Edition. New York, Mahlon Day, Publisher, 1837. DLC; MPlyA.   45747

Naylor, Charles, 1806-1872. Speech on the bill imposing additional duties as depositories, in certain cases on public officers; delivered in the House of Representatives. United States, October 13, 1837. n.p., (1837). 24 p. ICU; LNT; OCHP; PHi.   45748

Neal, Daniel, 1678-1743. History of the puritans, or protestant nonconformists: From the Reformation in 1517 to the Revolution in 1688; comprising an account of their principles; their sufferings and the lives and characters of their most considerable divines. New ed. Philadelphia, Whetham, 1837. 3 v. InDanN.   45749

Neal, (John), 1793-1876. Banks and Banking. A Letter to the Bank-Directors of Portland, ... Portland, [Me.], 1837. 8 p. MH; MH-BA. 45750

Neal, Joseph Clay, 1807-1847.

Charcoal sketches; or Scenes in a metropolis. Philadelphia, Getz, Buck & Co., [1837]. 222 p. illus. DeU; IP; NjP.   45750a

[Neale, William Johnson], 1812-1893. Gentleman Jack. A naval story. By the author of "Cavendish" ... Philadelphia, E. L. Carey & A. Hart, 1837. 2 v. DLC; GU; MBL; NPV.   45751

Needham, John Rainsford. The pleasures of poverty. A poem, adapted to the present hard times, and intended to console the unfortunate. New York, 1837. 12 p. RPB.   45752
---- ---- 2 ed. New York, Pub. for the proprietor ... 1837. 12 p. TxU.   45753

---- ---- Third Edition. New-York, For the Proprietor, 1837. 12 p. MB; NjR.   45754

Needham, M. Manufacture of iron; reprinted from the Library of useful knowledge. Philadelphia, Rogers, 1837. 114 p. IU; MB; PU; StTeachC.   45755

Needham's pocket library, and miniature magazine. (New York.) Vol. I, no. 1 (Nov. 10, 1837). MH.   45756

The Negro Pew. See Newcomb, Harvey.

Neill, William. The great salvation and the sin and danger of neglecting it. Philadelphia, Martien, 1837. MH-AH; PPPrHi.   45757

Nelson, David, 1793-1844. The cause and cure of infidelity: with an account of the author's conversion. By the Rev. David Nelson, of Quincy, Illinois; late of Marion county, Missouri. New-York, Published by John S. Taylor, Brick church chapel, 1837. 348 p. GDecCT; MH; NCH; NNUT; TNP.   45758

Nelson, John, 1786-1871.
The work of the ministry. A sermon delivered before the Pastoral association of Massachusetts, in the Park street church, Boston, May 30, 1837. By Rev. John Nelson, Leicester. Boston, Printed by Crocker & Brewster, 1837. 24 p. CtHC; ICN; MeBat; NjR; RPB.   45759

Nelson, Sydney.
The deep, deep ocean [Song for Bar Accomp. for pianoforte], New York, Riley, (1837). 3 p. MB.   45760

A Net for the Fishers of men; the same which Christ gave to His Apostles, wherein the points controverted betwixt Catholics and sectaries are briefly vindicated, by way of delemma ... Philadelphia, E. Cummiskey, 1837. 36 p. DLC; IaDuMtC; MBBC; MdBS; NRSB.   45761

Neue Americanische Landwirthschafts Calender, 1838. Von Carl Friedrich Egelmann. Reading, Pa., Johann Ritter und Comp., [1837]. MWA.   45762

Neuer Calender für die Bauern und Handwerker, 1838. Von Carl F. Egelmann. Philadelphia, Pa., George W. Mentz, [1837]. MWA.   45763

Neuer Calender für Nord-Amerika, 1838. Von Carl F.

Egelmann. Philadelphia, Pa., George W. Mentz und Sohn, [1837]. MWA.   45764

Neuer Gemeinnütziger Pennsylvanischer Calender, 1838. Lancaster, Pa., Johann Bär, [1837]. MWA.   45765

Neukomm, Sigismond Ritter von, 1778-1858.
Hymns of the night, a sacred work, words by William Ball. From the London copy. Boston, printed by the Handel and Haydn society, 1837. DLC; MB; MBNEC; MLanc; OOC.   45766

Neuman, Henry.
Dictionary of the Spanish and English languages. In two volumes. Vol. 1. Spanish and English. Boston, Hilliard, Gray & Co., 1837. 723 p. ArBaA; KyU.   45767

Never despair: a tale of the emigrants. Founded on fact. New York, Scofield & Voorhies; Boston, Whipple & Damrell, 1837. [9]-104 p. MH; NNM; OClWHi; RPB.   45768

Nevin, John Williamson.
Personal holiness. A lecture .... in the western theological seminary, by Rev. John W. Nevin. Pittsburgh, n. pub., William Allinder, printer, 1837. 16 p. MeBat: NjR; OClW; PLFM.
                                    45769

Nevins, William.
Practical Thoughts By Rev. William Nevins, D.D. Published by the American Tract Society. New York, 1837. 216 p. ICartC.
                                    45770
---- Select remains of the Rev. William Nevins, D.D., with a memoir. Third edition, revised and corrected. New York, Pub-

lished by John S. Taylor,
1837. 398 p. IaMp; GMM;
MoWgT; NcMHi; PLT; RPB.
45771

---- Sermons by the late Rev.
William Nevins, D.D. New York,
published by John S. Taylor,
1837. 8, 12-428 p. CBPSR;
GDeecT; KyLoP; MH-And;
TxAuPT.   45772

The new American speaker
comprising elegant selections
in eloquence and poetry...
Cincinnati, E. Morgan & Son,
1837. 250 p. OCHP; OClWHi.
45773

New and alluring source of
enterprise in the treasures of
the sea, and the means of
gathering them. [anon] New
York, I. Narine, 1837. 26 p.
DLC.   45774

New Bedford, Mass.
    List of voters, in the town
of New-Bedford, qualified to
vote for town and state officers,
and representatives to Congress.
Revised by the selectmen.
J. C. Parmenter...Printer,
1837. (24) p. MNBedf. 45775

---- Fire Department.
    Law Establishing the New-
Bedford Fire Department, ...
1837. New Bedford, J. C. Parmenter, Printer, 1837. 11 p.
45776

---- Lyceum.
    General directions for collect-
ing and preserving articles in
various departments of Natural
history: Respectfully submitted
by the Lyceum, New-Bedford,
Mass. to the attention of
traveling sea-faring Men. New-
Bedford, printed by J. C.
Parmenter, 1837. 8 p. MB;
MNBedf.   45777

---- Rural Cemetery.
    Constitution of the New-
Bedford Rural Cemetery, incorporated April 12, 1837.
New-Bedford, (Mass.), Printed
by J. C. Parmenter, 1837. 12
p. MNBedf.   45778

---- Mass. School Committee.
    The New-Bedford School Com-
mittee Present To The Town
Their Annual Report. New Bedford, (Mass.), J. C. Parmenter,
Printer, (1837)? 8 p. MNBedf.
45779
New-Bedford and Fairhaven sig-
nal book. New Bedford, (Mass.),
published by Charles Taber.
J. C. Parmenter, printer, 1837.
(57) p. MNBedf.   45780

New Castle and Frenchtown turnpike and Railroad Company.
    Acts of incorporation of the
New Castle and Frenchtown turnpike & rail road company, passed
by the Legislature of Maryland
and Delaware. Also, the articles
of union between the turnpike
and rail road companies. Philadelphia, Printed by John C.
Clark, 1837. 40 p. DLC; MdHi.
45781
The New England Almanack,
and Farmers' Friend....1838....
Nathan Daboll. New-London,
published by Samuel Green; E.
Williams, printer, [1837]. 32 p.
PHi; RWc; WHi.   45782

New England Almanack for 1838.
By Nathan Daboll. New London,
Conn., Samuel Green, [1837].
MWA.   45783

New England anti-slavery convention. 4th, Boston, 1837.
    Proceedings of the fourth
New-England anti-slavery convention, held in Boston, May 30,
31, and June 1 and 2, 1837.

Boston, Printed by I. Knapp,
1837. 124 p. DLC; MdBJ;
MeB; MHi; TxU.   45784

New England Christian Academy.
Address of the trustees of
the New-England Christian
Academy, to the friends and
patrons of the institution; together with the rules and regulations, course of instruction,
charter of the institution, &c.
Boston, B. True, 1837. 12 p.
MH; Nh.   45785

New England Farmer's Almanac,
1838. Truman W. Abell.
Claremont, N.H., Claremont
Bookstore, (1837). 24 ℓ.
MWA; NhHi; WHi.   45786

---- ... by Truman W. Abell.
1838....Windsor, Vt., Published
by N. C. Goddard....[1837].
(48) p. MeHi; MWA.   45787

The New-England farmer's and
scholar's almanack, on an im-
proved plan; for the year of our
Lord 1838....By Dudley Leavitt
....Number XLII. Concord, N.H.,
Published by Marsh, Capen, and
Lyon, (1837). MHa; MiD-B;
MWA; NjR; WHi.   45788

The New England Primer; and
easy and pleasant guide to the
art of reading. Adorned with
cuts. To which is added the
Cathecism. Boston, Congregational Publishing Society, Congregational House, 1837. (2), 1-
64 p. NWattJHi.   45789

New England Sabbath School
Union.
Catalogue of Sabbath School
and Miscellaneous Books. Pub-
lished and for sale at the Deposi-
tory of the New England S. S.
Union. Boston, 1837-8. 18 p.
MHi.   45790

A new English-German and
German-English dictionary; containing all the words in general
use, designating the various parts
of speech in both languages with
the genders and plurals of the
German nouns. Compiled from
the dictionaries of Lloyd,
Nohden, Flugel, and Sporschil.
In two volumes. vol. I. English
and German. Philadelphia, Published by George W. Mentz and
Son, 1837. 1175 p. MdBD; MH;
NCaS; ODaGSG.   45791

New experiments. Means without
living. Boston, Weeks, Jordon
& Co., 1837. xi, (13)-72 p.
CLU; DLC; ICN; MH-BA; ViU.
45792

A new financial project; together
with some remarks upon the currency and credit system of the
United States. New York, G. &
C. Carvill & co., 1837. 29 p.
IU; MdHi; NNC; ScU; WHi.
45793

New Hampshire. General Court.
Act relating to banks and
banking, and to establish bank
commissioners for the state of
New Hampshire. New Hampshire
(?), [1837]. 13 p. Nh-Hi.
45794

---- Laws, Statutes, etc.
Laws of the State of New
Hampshire; passed June session,
1837. Published by authority.
Concord, Cyrus Barton, State
printer, 1837. Ar-SC; Ky; Mo;
NNLI; R.   45795

---- ---- Laws of the State of
New Hampshire; passed November
session, 1836. Concord, Pub-
lished by Cyrus Barton, for the
State, 1837. In-SC; MdBB; Mo;
NNLI; T.   45796

---- State Norman School.
Plymouth, N.H. Teachers'

Seminary. Catalogue....(1837).
Andover, 1837. 24 p. MHi.
                               45797
The New Hampshire annual
register and United States
calendar. (For the year 1837).
By John Farmer. Concord,
Marsh, Capen and Lyon (pub-
lishers); William White, printer,
1837. 142 p. KWiU; MiD-B;
MnHi; Nh-Hi.   45798

New Hampton, N.H. Academical
& theological institution.
   Catalogue of the officers
and students...for the year ending November 1, 1837. Concord,
C. Young printer, 1837. 24 p.
MiD-B.   45799

New Haven (Colony).
   Records of the colony and
plantation of New Haven 1638-
65. with notes and an appendix.
Case. Hartford, 1837-58. 2 v.
O.   45800

New Haven. City Bank.
   Answer of the board of directors of the city bank, of
New Haven, by their agents,
to the report of the committee
of investigation, made to the general assembly May session. Hartford, 1837. 21 p. Ct; MB; MH-
BA.   45801

---- Committee of the City bank.
   Report of the special commit-
tee concerning the City bank of
New Haven. Hartford, n. pub.,
Russell & Jones, printers,
1837. 26 p. CtSoP; MiD-B;
NjR; WHi.   45802

---- Connecticut, Free Congre-
gational Church.
   Manual of the Free Congre-
gational Church of New Haven,
September, 1837. New Haven,
Hitchcock & Stafford, 1837.

[16] p. WBeloC.   45803

New Haven County Horticultural
Society.
   By-Laws of the Horticultural
Society of New Haven. [n.p.,
1837]. 4 p. CtY.   45804

New Haven county medical association, New Haven.
   A report of the New Haven
county medical society, on the
expediency of repealing that
section of the medical laws of
this state, which excludes irregular practitioners from the
benefits of law in the collection
of fees. New Haven, Printed by
B. L. Hamlen, 1837. 16 p.
Ct; MB; MBM; PPL; PU. 45805

New Haven verd-antique marble
co.
   Plan, by-laws, &c.&c.&c. of
the New Haven verd-antique
marble company. New Haven,
Hitchcock & Stafford, 1837.
11 p. Ct; CtY.   45806

New Jersey. Laws, statutes,
etc.
   Acts of the sixty-first General assembly of the state of
New Jersey. At a session begun at Trenton, on the twenty-
fifth day of October, eighteen
hundred and thirty-six: being
the first sitting. Trenton,
Printed for the state, 1837.
492 (1) p. Ar-SC; In-SC; MHi;
NjR; T.   45807

---- Legislature. General Assembly. Committee on condition
of the New Jersey Railroad and
Transportation Company.
   Report of the committee of
the legislature, appointed to examine into the condition, affairs,
revenues, and future prospects,
of the New Jersey Rail and trans-

portation company. Trenton, Joseph Justice and son, 1837. 19 p. CSmH.   45808

---- ---- ---- Committee on petition of William M'Elroy.

Report of the Committee of the House of assembly on petition of William M'Elroy, of the county of Warren. Trenton, Joseph Justice & son, printers, 1837. 7 p. NjR.   45809

---- ---- ---- Committee on the Embarrassment of the Country.

Report of the minority of the Committee of the House of assembly, on the embarrassments of the country. Trenton, James T. Shermen, 1837. 9 p. CSmH; InHi; NjR; PHi; RPB.
45810

---- ---- ---- Committee on the Railroad at Trenton.

Report of the minority of the Committee of inquiry, relative to the railroad at Trenton, etc. Trenton, J. Justice and son, 1837. 43 p. DBRE; NN.
45811

---- ---- ---- Joint Committee on the State Prison Accounts.

Report of the Joint Committee of the Two Houses on the State Prison Accounts, read Nov. 9, 1837. Trenton, 1837. 27 p. MB; MH-L.   45812

---- ---- House of representatives. Committee.

Report of the majority of the committee of the House of assembly, to inquire by whom and by what authority a railroad from the Delaware bridge to the line of the Delaware and Raritan canal, which is to be continued, as is said, to New Brunswick, has been constructed, etc....Trenton, n. pub., n. pr., 1837. 10 p.   45813

---- ---- Joint committee on New Jersey railroad transportation co.

Report of the committee appointed to examine into the condition of affairs, revenue and future prospects. Trenton, Joseph Justice & son, 1837. 19 p. DBRE; Nj; NNC; NNE.   45814

---- ---- Senate.

Minutes of the proceedings of the Legislative council of the state of New Jersey, sitting as a high court of impeachment, at the city of Trenton, in the year ... one thousand eight hundred and thirty-seven ... [Woodbury, N.J.], 1837. 17 p. DLC.
45815

New Jersey Harbor Company.

An act to incorporate the New Jersey harbor company .... 1837. New York, F. Price, 1837. 7 p. MiD-B; Nj. 45816

The New Jersey register, for the year eighteen hundred and thirty-seven; being the first year of publication. By Joseph C. Potts. Trenton, W. D'Hart, 1837. 260, 40, (2) p. CtY; DLC; MH; MiD-B; NjP; PHi.
45817

New Orleans. Board of Fire Commissioners.

Annual report. New Orleans, 1837- . PU.   45818

---- Chamber of commerce.

An address to the Legislature of Louisiana, showing the importance of the credit system, on the prosperity of the United States, ... By the New-Orleans Chamber of commerce. December, 1837. New-Orleans, Printed by Benjamin Levy, 1837. 38 p. CSmH.   45819

---- ---- Decision of the New-

Orleans chamber of commerce from January the 1st 1836, to January the 1st. 1837. New-Orleans, Johns, 1837. 51 p. NNC; TxHUT. 45820

---- ---- Documents relating to the improvement of the navigation of the Mississippi River. New Orleans, 1837. 82 p. ICHi; LU; MB; MH-Z; PPAmP. 45821

---- Commercial library society. Proceedings at the annual meeting, of the New-Orleans commercial library society. December 6th, 1837. New-Orleans, 1837. 25 p. DLC; OCH. 45822

New Orleans and Carrollton Railroad Company. Charter of the New Orleans and Carrollton Railroad Company. Approved, February 9th, 1833. New Orleans, E. Johns & Co., 1837. [1]-12 p. AU; DBRE; NcD; NN; ViU. 45823

The New Orleans guide; or, General directory for 1837, embracing the three municipalities, and containing the names, professions and residences of all the heads of families and business men. New Orleans, Gaux & Maynier, 1837. AU. 45824

New Rochelle. Order of the celebration of the Fourth of July, at New Rochelle... n.t.-p. (New Rochelle, 1837.) 1 broadside. NN. 45825

A new system of paper money, by a citizen of Boston. Boston, I. R. Butts, 1837. 20 p. DLC; MH-BA; Mos; NjR; PU. 45826

New Theatre, Philadelphia.

(Report of a committee of the stockholders in the New theatre of the city of Philadelphia, submitting new rules, regulations and by-laws for the association. Philadelphia, 1837). 12 p. MH. 45827

New York (City). Forsyth St. German Reformed Ch. The case of the Forsyth St. Ch. N.Y. as presented in the proceedings of the Phila. Classes of the Ger. Reformed Ch. of N.A...1837. With the documents in the case. New York, Order of Classes, 1837. PPPrHi. 45828

---- General Theological Seminary of the Protestant Episcopal Church in the United States. Catalogue of officers and students of the general theological seminary of the protestant episcopal church in the United States, located in the city of New-York. 1836-7. To which is added a catalogue of the alumni. New-York, Protestant Episcopal Press, print., 1837. 20 p. InID; MH. 45829

---- ---- Publication of the associate alumni of the General Theological Seminary of the Protestant Episcopal Church in the United States, for the year of Our Lord MDCCCXXXVII. being the sermon and essay delivered at the annual meeting in June. New York, Protestant Episcopal Press, Pront., 1837. 48 p. CtHT; NGH. 45830

---- Mayor, 1834-1837 (Cornelius W. Lawrence). Messages delivered to the common Council during the mayorality of C. W. Lawrence, from May 1834-May 1837. New York, printed by order of the Common Council, [1837?]. 85, 114, 108, 118 p. N; NN. 45831

---- Mayor. 1837-1839 (Aaron Clark).

Message from his honor the Mayor, Aaron Clark, May 22, 1837. Document no. 2. Published by order of the common council. [New York], T. Snowden, 1837. 15 p. ViW. 45832

---- St. George's church.

Report of the Board of directors of the association of St. George's church, New-York, for the promotion of Christianity, presented at the annual meeting of the association, on the evening of the Epiphany, January 6th, 1837. New-York, Printed by G. F. Bunce, 1837. 23 p. NNG. 45833

---- St. Joseph's Church.

Minutes ... trustees ... New York, 1837. 26 p. DLC. 45834

New York (City) Democratic Republican Meeting, 1838.

Proceedings and address of democratic republicans, opposed to the sub-treasury and special deposit schemes. New York, 1837. J. Booth and son, 1837. 30 p. DLC; MBC; MH; MHi; MH-BA. 45835

New York (City) Mercantile Library Association.

Systematic catalogue of books in the collection of the Mercantile Library Association of the City of New York: with a general index, and one of dramatic pieces; together with an appendix; containing the constitution, and the rules and regulations of the Association. Library in Clinton Hall. New York, Printed by Harper & Brothers ....1837. DLC; MdBE; MoSM; NBu; NjR. 45836

---- ---- New-York, printed by Harper & Brothers, 1837(-38). xi, 312, 54, (2) p. DLC; MB; MdBP; NBu; NN. 45837

---- ---- New York, Printed by Harper brothers, 1837 [-40]. 312, 2 ℓ. [271]-385 p. DLC; MB; NBu; NN. 45838

New-York (City) National Academy of Design.

National academy of design. Catalogue of the twelfth annual exhibition, 1837.... New-York, Printed by Edwin B. Clayton, near Pearl, [1837]. 20 p. ScU. 45839

New York (city) Union Theological Seminary.

Plan of the New York theological seminary, founded on the 18th of January A.D. 1836. New York, Printed by William Osborn, 1837. 18 p. MdBD; NNG; NNUT; OO; WHi. 45840

New York (State).

Commissioners appointed to Digest and Report a Judicial and Equity system for the State of N.Y. Report. Albany, 1837. MB. 45841

---- Adjutant-general's office.

General order, regulating the uniform of the militia of the state of New-York. Adjutant-general's office, Albany, June 1, 1837. Albany, Printed by Croswell, Van Benthuysen and Burt, 1837. 15, [1] p. DLC; PPL. 45842

---- Agricultural Convention. 1837.

Resolutions of the State agricultural convention for aid in the cause of agriculture. In Assembly, Feb. 15, 1837. [Albany, 1837]. 3 p. WHi. 45842a

---- Allegany County, N.Y.-
Citizens.

Petition of citizens of the
county of Allegany, praying for
an investigation into the mal-
practices of the banks of this
state, and remonstrating against
the charter of any bank to be
located in said county. In
Assembly, Feb. 7, 1837. [Al-
bany, 1837]. WHi.   45843

---- ---- Proceedings of a public meeting of the inhabitants of
seven towns in the counties of
Allegany and Cattaraugus, addressed to the Legislature upon
the subject of banking. In Assembly, Feb. 27, 1837. [Albany,
1837]. 3 p. WHi.   45844

---- Attorney General.

Report of the Attorney general on the bill entitled "An
act in relation to limited partner-
ships, and to authorize assign-
able interests therein," referred
to him by the legislature. In
Assembly, April 18, 1837. [Al-
bany, 1837]. 7 p. WHi. 45845

---- ---- ... Report of the
attorney-general on the bill
entitled "An act to authorize
associations for the purpose of
banking"...[Albany? 1837].   9
p. MP-BA; WHi.   45846

---- ---- Report of the Attorney
General, on sundry petitions for
the formation of a new county
[from the counties of Madison,
Chenango and Otsego], referred
to him by the Assembly. In
Assembly, Feb. 7, 1837. [Al-
bany, 1837]. 4 p. WHi. 45847

---- Canal Commissioners.

Minutes of the Canal board
in the case of the petition of
James Quige and Gloudy Hamilton, [for an extra allowance on
their contract to construct section 51, south division, Chenango
canal]. In Assembly, March 21,
1837. [Albany 21, 1837]. WHi.
          45848

---- ---- Report of the Canal
board in relation to a weigh-
lock at Oswego, [in the Oswego
canal]. In Assembly, March 10,
1837. [Albany, 1837]. 4 p.
WHi.   45849

---- ---- Report of the Canal
board, in relation to the estimated and actual cost of canals
that are finished, and the estimated cost of those unfinished,
&c. In Assembly, Feb. 23,
1837. [Albany, 1837]. 11 p.
WHi.   45850

---- ---- Report of the Canal
board on the claim of Jacob
Trumpbour, [for surveying and
mapping the Erie and Champlain
canals]. In Assembly, Feb. 23,
1837. [Albany, 1837]. 5 p.
WHi.   45851

---- ---- Report of the Canal
board on the petition of Arnold
Mason and Frederick Pratt for
relief, [relating to contracts
for locks on the Chenango canal].
In Assembly, March 6, 1837.
[Albany, 1837]. 2 p. WHi.
          45852

---- ---- Report of the Canal
board on the petition of John E.
Hinman and Henry W. Schroeppel,
[relating to lands overflowed by
the erection of a dam in the Oswego river, for the Oswego
Canal]. In Assembly, Feb. 23,
1837. [Albany, 1837]. 3 p.
WHi.   45853

---- ---- Report of the Canal
board on the reference from the
Assembly of the petition of B. W.

Babcock for extra compensation
for the construction of Lock no.
9, on the Chenango canal. In
Assembly, Feb. 24, 1837. [Al-
bany, 1837]. 5 p. WHi. 45854

---- ---- Report of the Canal
commissioners, in answer to a
resolution of the Assembly of
31st. January last, relative
to the construction of the
Chenango canal. In Assembly,
Feb. 28, 1837. [Albany,
1837]. 4 p. WHi.   45855

---- ---- Report of the Canal
commissioners in relation to the
improvement of the Cayuga in-
let, the Seneca river, and the
Oneida and Seneca rivers. Under three acts of the legislature. In Assembly, Jan. 30,
1837. [Albany, 1837]. 5 p.
WHi.   45856

---- ---- Report of the Canal
commissioners on a resolution
of the Assembly, and on a petition of inhabitants of Liverpool,
in relation to the use of water
from the Oswego canal to pro-
pel a pump to raise salt water.
In Assembly, Jan. 31, 1837.
[Albany, 1837]. 5 p. WHi.
                           45857
---- ---- Report of the Canal
commissioners, on petitions in
relation to towing-path bridge
in Cayuga and Seneca canal.
In Assembly, March 20, 1837.
[Albany, 1837]. 2 p. WHi.
                           45858
---- ---- Report of the Canal
commissioners on the petition of
Barker and Stroud, and Gilbert
and Sprague. In Assembly,
Jan. 19, 1837. [Albany, 1837].
3 p. WHi.   45859

---- ---- Report of the Canal
commissioners on the petition of

Catharine Fridley, [for damages
in the construction of the
Chemung canal]. In Assembly,
Feb. 1, 1837. [Albany, 1837].
3 p. WHi.   45860

---- ---- Report of the Canal
commissioners on the petition of
John C. Wanmaker [relating to
the Chemung canal]. In Assembly, March 1, 1837. [Al-
bany, 1837]. 3 p. WHi. 45861

---- ---- Report of the Canal
commissioners on the petition of
John Gregg, [relating to the
Chemung canal]. In Assembly,
Jan. 27, 1837. [Albany, 1837].
2 p. WHi.   45862

---- ---- Report of the Canal
commissioners, on the petition
of John N. DeGraf, [relating to
a bridge over the Erie canal].
In Assembly, Feb. 21, 1837.
[Albany, 1837]. 3 p. WHi.
                           45863
---- ---- Report of the Canal
commissioners, on the petition
of Peter B. Ten Brook, [for
damages from flooding of
Chemung canal]. In Assembly,
March 1, 1837. [Albany, 1837].
3 p. WHi.   45864

---- ---- Report of the Canal
commissioners on the petition of
Peter Bargy, Jr., [relating to
services as contractor on the
Chenango canal]. In Assembly,
April 8, 1837. [Albany, 1837].
36 p. WHi.   45865

---- ---- Report of the Canal
commissioners on the petition of
sundry inhabitants of Sherburne,
asking to be exonerated from
their liabilities to the state, [in
relation to the Chenango canal].
In Assembly, March 2, 1837.
[Albany, 1837]. 3 p. WHi.
                           45866

---- ---- Report of the canal commission on the petition of the Cohoes Company. April 6, 1837. [Albany? N.Y., 1837]. 6 p. ViU. 45867

---- ---- Report of the Canal commissioners on the petition of Q. Planton, [for an appropriation for building a canal steam-boat for the navigation of the Erie Canal]. In Assembly, Feb. 1, 1837. [Albany, 1837]. 2 p. WHi. 45868

---- ---- Report of the Canal commissioners on the petition of William Newton, asking an extra allowance for the construction of Section 4 of the southern division of the Chenango canal. In Assembly, March 8, 1837. [Albany, 1837]. 2 p. WHi. 45869

---- ---- Report of the Canal commissioners on petitions in relation to the upper level of the Crooked Lake canal. In Assembly, Feb. 28, 1837. [Albany, 1837]. 5 p. WHi. 45870

---- Commissioners of the Canal Fund.

Forms and instructions, etc. in relation to the accounts of collectors of tolls on the New-York State canals, ... 1837. Albany, Printed by Croswell, Van Benthuysen and Burt, [1837]. 38 p. NNE; PPL. 45871

---- Committee of the New York Hospital.

Report of the Building committee of the New-York hospital, to inquire into the expediency of erecting a new building. New-York, Mahlon Day, 1837. 10, (1) p. NNNAM. 45872

---- Comptroller.

Communication from the Comptroller respecting the revised statutes. [Albany, 1837]. 5 p. WHi. 45873

---- ---- Report of the Comptroller on the bill respecting the state dredging machine. In Assembly, Feb. 11, 1837. [Albany, 1837]. 2 p. WHi. 45874

----. Court of Chauncery.

Reports of Chancery cases, decided in the first circuit of the State of New York. .... By Charles Edwards. Published by Gould, Banks & Co., 1837-51. 4 v. Ar-SC; MsU; PU-L. 45875

---- ---- Rules and orders of the court of chancery of the state of New-York ... With precedents ... and notes ... Albany, Published by Wm. & A. Gould & co., New York, 1837. (25)-191 p. CU-AL; DLC; MnU-L; NN; NNLI. 45876

---- Department of Public Instruction.

Decisions of the superintendent of common schools...selected... by John A. Dix...with laws relating to common schools and the forms and regulations prescribed for their government. Albany, Croswell, 1837. InU; KyLo; MoS; NUt; WHi. 45877

---- Governor.

... Message from the Governor [W. L. Marcy] Jan. 3, 1837 [with accompanying documents on Indian treaties]. In Assembly Jan. 3, 1837. Albany, 1837. 29 p. WHi. 45878

---- Land Office Commissioners.

Report of the Commissioners of the Land office, on the peti-

tion of Christian J. Burchle,
[relating to lands in West Os-
wego]. In Assembly, March 3,
1837. [Albany, 1837]. 3 p.
WHi.   45879

---- ---- Report of the Commissioners of the land office
on the petition of John J.
Campbell, [relating to lands
in Oneida county]. In Assembly,
Feb. 11, 1837. [Albany, 1837].
3 p. WHi.   45880

---- ---- Board of Commissioners
of the Canal Office.
Report of the Commissioners
of the land office on the petition
of the trustees of the First
Presbyterian society of Lewis-
ton. In Assembly, March 3,
1837. [Albany, 1837]. 2 p.
WHi.   45881

---- ---- Report of the Commissioners of the land office on the
petition of the trustees of the
village of Oswego, relative to
the cemetery in East Oswego.
In Assembly, March 13, 1837.
[Albany, 1837]. 2 p. WHi.
                              45882
---- ---- Report of the Commissioners of the land office on the
petition of Z. P. Gillet [relating
to the title to land in the town
of Junius, originally granted to
Capt. John Otoawighton, an Indian, for military services in
the revolutionary war]. In
Assembly, April 28, 1837. [Al-
bany, 1837]. 2 p. WHi. 45883

---- ---- Report of the Commissioners of the land office relative to the cemetery ground in
East Oswego, in compliance with
the resolution of the Assembly
of March 17, 1837. In Assembly,
April 4, 1837. [Albany, 1837].
2 p. WHi.   45884

----. Laws, statutes,
etc.
An act to authorize associa-
tions for the purpose of banking.
[Albany? 1837]. 12 p. MH-BA.
                              45885
---- ---- Laws of the state of
New-York, passed at the Six-
tieth session of the Legislature,
begun and held at the city of
Albany, the third day of Janu-
ary, 1837. Albany, Printed by
E. Croswell, printer to the state,
1837. 620 p. Ar-SC; IaU;
NNLI; TxU-L; Wa-L.   45886

---- Legislative Assembly.
Journal of the assembly of
the state of New York, at their
sixtieth session, begun and held
at the capitol, in the city of
Albany, on the third day of
January, 1837. Albany, Printed
by E. Croswell, 1837. 1351 p.
NNLI; NPot.   45887

---- ---- Amendment to the constitution, [relating to the court
of Chancery, circuit and county
courts etc.], offered by Mr.
Patterson. In Assembly, Jan.
10, 1837. [Albany, 1837]. 3 p.
WHi.   45888

---- ---- ---- Memorial of the
directors of the Sackett's Harbor bank against the repeal of
its charter. In Assembly, March
30, 1837. [With accompanying
documents]. [Albany, 1837].
10 + 12 p. WHi.   45889

---- ---- ---- Memorial of the
majority of the Commissioners
appointed to distribute the increased capital of the Jefferson
county bank. In Assembly, May
9, 1837. [Albany, 1837]. 24 p.
WHi.   45890

---- ---- ---- Memorial of the

majority of the Commissioners
appointed to distribute the increased capital of the Jefferson county bank, with accompanying documents, [relating
to the hearings before the
legislative committee of in-
quiry]. In Assembly, April
3, 1837. [Albany, 1837].
18 p. WHi.   45891

---- ---- ---- Preamble and
resolution offered by Mr. C. E.
Shepard, [on the retirement
of President Jackson from public life]. In Assembly, Jan.
30, 1837. [Albany, 1837].
1 p. WHi.   45892

---- ---- ---- Report ... on
a communication from the governor in relation to the geological
survey of the state, and the
reports of the persons engaged
in the execution thereof.
March 23, 1837. [Albany,
1837]. 3 p. NN.   45893

---- ---- ---- Resolution proposing an amendment to the
constitution [relating to the
courts of the state]. Offered
by Mr. Bradish. In Assembly,
Feb. 20, 1837. [Albany, 1837].
2 p. WHi.   45894

---- ---- ---- Committee on
Albany Basin.
Report of the Select committee on the petition of the corporation of Albany for an amendment
of the law relative to the navigation of the Albany basin. In
Assembly, April 7, 1837. [Al-
bany, 1837]. 2 p. WHi. 45895

---- ---- ---- Committee on
Albany Exchange.
Report of the Select committee on the petition of several
citizens of Albany for incorporat-

ing the Albany exchange company. In Assembly, Jan. 17,
1837. [Albany, 1837]. 2 p.
WHi.   45896

---- ---- ---- Committee on
Banks.
Report of the Select committee on the investigation of the
banks of the state, relative to
the increased capital of the Jefferson county bank, passed May
19th, 1836. In Assembly, April
11, 1837. [Albany, 1837]. 51 p.
WHi.   45897

---- ---- ---- Committee on
Bridge in Erie.
Report of the Select commit-
tee on the petition of sundry
inhabitants of the county of
Erie, relative to money raised
in said county to build a bridge.
In Assembly, Feb. 16, 1837.
[Albany, 1837]. 2 p. WHi.
                         45898
---- ---- ---- Committee on
Canals & Internal Improvements.
Report of the Committee on
canals and internal improvements
on a resolution of the Assembly
of the 10th February, 1837.
[Albany, 1837]. 9 p. WHi.
                         45899
---- ---- ---- ---- Report of
the Committee on canals and internal improvements on petitions
for the survey of a canal from
Socnadaga river to the Erie
canal. In Assembly, Feb. 10,
1837. [Albany, 1837]. 4 p.
WHi.   45900

---- ---- ---- ---- Report of
the Committee on canals and internal improvements, on the
memorial of John I. Degraff,
W. L. Crossett and E. M. Townsend, [praying for a law authorizing the Canal commissioners to
pay claims for extra expense in

erecting bridges across any of the canals in the state]. In Assembly, March 6, 1837. [Albany, 1837]. 2 p. WHi. 45901

---- ---- ---- ---- Report of the Committee on canals and internal improvements on the petition of Peter Bargy, Jr., [for additional compensation for construction work on the northern division of the Chanango canal]. In Assembly, April 26, 1837. [Albany, 1837]. 27 p. WHi. 45902

---- ---- ---- ---- Report of the majority of the committee on canals and internal improvements, on petitions of inhabitants of Catskill, &c. for the survey of a canal route from the Schoharie creek at its junction with the Erie canal to the village of Catskill.] In Assembly, April 4, 1837. [Albany, 1837]. 6 p. WHi. 45903

---- ---- ---- Committee on Catskill Dry Dock Co.
Report of the Select committee on the petition of Evan Griffith and others, [for the incorporation of the Catskill dry dock company]. In Assembly, Jan. 20, 1837. [Albany, 1837]. 2 p. WHi. 45904

---- ---- ---- Com. on Cayuga, Seneca, Eric Canals.
Report of the Select committee on the memorial of Jacob Trumpbour [praying for re-numeration for surveys of the Cayuga, Seneca, Erie, and other canals]. In Assembly, Jan. 19, 1837. [Albany, 1837]. 4 p. WHi. 45905

---- ---- ---- Com. on Checks Circulated as Bank Notes.

Report of the Select committee to which was referred the resolution of the 17th. January last [relating to the issue of checks circulated as bank notes by the Sackett's Harbor bank and other banks]. In Assembly, March 20, 1837. [Albany, 1837]. 37 + 5 p. WHi. 45906

---- ---- ---- Committee on Chemung County Buildings.
Report of the majority of the Select committee on the petitions and remonstrances of inhabitants of the county of Chemung, [relative to the removal of the county buildings]. In Assembly, March 16, 1837. [Albany, 1837]. 1 p. WHi. 45907

---- ---- ---- Committee on Chenango Canal.
Report of the Select committee on the petition of E. M. Townsend and others, [contractors for the construction of the Chenango canal.] In Assembly, Feb. 23, 1837. [Albany, 1837]. 4 p. WHi. 45908

---- ---- ---- Committee on Chenango Canal Contracts.
Report of the Select committee on the petition of William L. Crossett, Amos Story and Moses Cole, and the report of the Canal commissioners on the same subject, [relating to contracts on the Chenango canal.] In Assembly, May 2, 1837. [Albany, 1837]. 100 p. WHi. 45909

---- ---- ---- Com. on Chenango County Court House.
Report of the majority of the Select committee on the subject of the Chenango county court house, and the removal of the public buildings. In Assembly, Jan. 5, 1837. [Albany, 1837]. 7 p. WHi. 45910

---- ---- ---- Committee on
Claims.

Report of the Committee on
claims, on the petition of
Adonijah Carter [for injuries
sustained in the discharge of
militia duty]. In Assembly,
March 20, 1837. [Albany,
1837]. 2 p. WHi.   45911

---- ---- ---- ---- Report of
the Committee on claims on the
petition of Dan Chapman, [for
services rendered in the revolutionary war]. In Assembly,
March 2, 1837. [Albany, 1837].
2 p. WHi.   45912

---- ---- ---- ---- Report of
the Committee on claims, on the
petition of Daniel Hadcock, [re-
lating to Indian lands in
Cazenovia, Chenango county].
In Assembly, Feb. 17, 1837.
[Albany, 1837]. 3 p. WHi.
                         45913
---- ---- ---- ---- Report of
the Committee on claims, on
the petition of David Fitzgerald,
[praying to be indemnified
against a judgement obtained
against him by William Young for
obstructing the waters of Mud
Creek while repairing the Erie
Canal aqueduct across said
creek in 1830]. In Assembly,
Feb. 2, 1837. [Albany, 1837].
4 p. WHi.   45914

---- ---- ---- ---- Report of
the Committee on claims on the
petitions of David Harris, Jonathan Tamblin and others, [re-
lating to contracts on the
Chenango canal]. In Assembly,
March 10, 1837. [Albany,
1837]. 2 p. WHi.   45915

---- ---- ---- ---- Report of
the Committee on claims, on the
petition of Nathan Underwood,

[relating to lands in Freemason's
Patent, Herhimer county]. In
Assembly, Feb. 25, 1837. [Al-
bany, 1837]. 3 p. WHi.
                         45916
---- ---- ---- ---- Report of
the Committee on claims on the
petition of Peter B. Ten Brook,
[for injury by water from the
Chemung canal]. In Assembly,
March 13, 1837. [Albany, 1837].
2 p. WHi.   45917

---- ---- ---- ---- Report of
the Committee on claims, on the
petition of William C. West and
others, [relating to contracts
for constructing a road from
Cedar Point to Newcomb in Essex
county]. In Assembly, Feb. 20,
1837. [Albany, 1837]. 3 p.
WHi.   45918

---- ---- ---- Committee on Colleges, Academies, etc.

Report of a majority of the
committee on colleges, academies
and common schools on the bill
entitle "An act to improve common school education." In Assembly, March 7, 1837. [Albany,
1837]. 4 p. (N.Y. Legisl. docs.
1837, v. 3. Assemb. docs. no.
222). Same. Report of the
minority. 5 p. WHi.   45919

---- ---- ---- ---- Report of
the Committee on colleges,
academies and common schools,
on a communication from the
Governor in relation to the Geological survey of the state, and
the reports of the persons engaged in the execution of the
same. In Assembly, March 23,
1837. [Albany, 1837]. 3 p.
WHi.   45920

---- ---- ---- Committee on Dam
in the Hudson River.

Report of the Select commit-

tee on the petition of inhabitants
of Fort Edward, Washington
county, relative to a dam in the
Hudson River. In Assembly,
Feb. 15, 1837. [Albany, 1837].
2 p. WHi.   45921

---- ---- ---- Committee on
Dispensary.
Report of the Select committee
on the memorial of the mayor,
aldermen, and commonalty of
the city of New York relative
to a piece of ground in the
sixth ward of said city [to be
conveyed to the New York dis-
pensary]. In Assembly,
March 20, 1837. [Albany,
1837]. 2 p. WHi.   45922

---- ---- ---- Committee on
Excise Laws.
Report of the Select committee on a petition to amend the
excise laws. In Assembly, Jan.
17, 1837. [Albany, 1837]. 2
p. WHi.   45923

---- ---- ---- ---- Report of
the Select committee on the
memorial of the common council
of the city of Hudson, and a
petition from the citizens in relation to the excise law. In Assembly, April 22, 1837. [Al-
bany, 1837]. 2 p. WHi. 45924

---- ---- ---- Committee on
Game Preservation.
Report of the Select Committee on the petition of sundry
inhabitants of the counties of
Queens, Kings, Richmond,
Westchester and New York, for
an amendment of the act for
the preservation of game in
those counties. In Assembly,
Feb. 25, 1837. [Albany, 1837].
2 p. WHi.   45925

---- ---- ---- Committee on

Grievances.
Report of the Committee on
grievances on the petition of
John I. Cambell, [relating to
land in the Fish Creek reservation, Oneida county]. In Assembly, Feb. 21, 1837. [Albany,
1837]. 3 p. WHi.   45926

---- ---- ---- ---- Report of
the Committee on grievances on
the petition of Westlake and Mc-
Connell, [for an extra allowance
for work done on the Chemung
canal]. In Assembly, Jan. 24,
1837. [Albany, 1837]. 5 p.
WHi.   45927

---- ---- ---- ---- Report of
the Committee on grievances on
the resolution of the town of
Manheim, in the county of
Herkimer, [to support its own
poor and retain the excise money
collected in the town for that
purpose]. In Assembly, March
30, 1837. [Albany, 1837]. 2 p.
WHi.   45928

---- ---- ---- Committee on
Hamilton College.
Memorial of C. O. Shepard
relative to a late memorial of the
faculty of Hamilton college [on
a student petition relating to
abolition societies]. In Assembly,
April 29, 1837. [Albany, 1837].
5 p. WHi.   45929

---- ---- ---- Committee on
Hawking & Peddling.
Report of the Select committee on the petition of Lewis
Benedict and others, citizens of
Albany, [relating to the prohi-
bition of hawking and peddling
in the city of Albany]. In Assembly, March 23, 1837. [Al-
bany, 1837]. 2 p. WHi.
                         45930
---- ---- ---- Committee on Hol-

land Purchase.

Report of the minority of
the select committee on the
petition of inhabitants residing
on the Holland Purchase. In
Assembly, April 10, 1837.
[Albany, 1837]. 27 p. WHi.
                                    45931

---- ---- ---- Committee on
Hudson & Berkshire R.R.

Report of the Select committee on the petition of inhabitants
of the city of Hudson, [for
authority to borrow money to
be applied to the subscription of
stock in the Hudson and Berkshire railroad company]. In
Assembly, March 25, 1837.
[Albany, 1837]. 2 p. WHi.
                                    45932

---- ---- ---- Committee on
Hudson, N.Y. Loan.

Report of the Select committee on the memorial of the corporation of the city of Hudson,
for authority to raise money by
loan on the credit of the city.
In Assembly, Feb. 23, 1837.
[Albany, 1837]. 2 p. WHi.
                                    45933

---- ---- ---- Committee on
Jurors Compensation.

Report of the Select committee on the petition of sundry
citizens of New York praying for
the passage of a law granting
additional compensation to jurors.
In Assembly, March 13, 1837.
[Albany, 1837]. 3 p. WHi.
                                    45934

---- ---- ---- Committee on
Land in Bethlehem.

Report of the Select committee on the petition of William
Russell, [for compensation for
a defective title to a lot of land
in Bethlehem, [Albany county].
In Assembly, Feb. 15, 1837.
[Albany, 1837]. 2 p. WHi.
                                    45935

---- ---- ---- Committee on

Lands in Hamilton & Herkimer
Counties.

Report of the Select committee on the petition of Jeremiah
Drake and others, for the purchase of certain lands [in Hamilton and Herkimer counties]. In
Assembly, April 7, 1837. [Al-
bany, 1837]. 5 p. WHi. 45936

---- ---- ---- Committee on Little Falls, N.Y. School District.

Report of the Select committee
on the petition of school district
no. 1, in the town of Little
Falls, Herkimer County, [for a
loan from the state etc.]. In
Assembly, Feb. 2, 1837. [Al-
bany, 1837]. 2 p. WHi. 45937

---- ---- ---- Committee on Medical Societies & Colleges.

Report of the minority of the
Committee on medical colleges
and societies, against the incorporation of a medical college in
Albany. In Assembly, Feb. 17,
1837. [Albany, 1837]. 4 p.
WHi.   45938

---- ---- ---- Committee on
Militia & Public Defense.

Report of the Committee on
the military and the public defense on a preamble and resolution offered by Mr. Willis, [re-
lating to the exemption of all
persons under 21 from military
duty]. In Assembly, April 11,
1837. [Albany, 1837]. 2 p.
WHi.   45939

---- ---- ---- Com. on Montgomery County Buildings.

Report of the Select committee on the resolutions of the
Board of supervisors of Montgomery county, relative to the
new county buildings. In Assembly, Jan. 19, 1837. [Albany,
1837]. 2 p. WHi.   45940

---- ---- ---- Committee on Morgan Property.

Report of the Select committee on the petition of Southmayd Stillman, [asking that some public officer be appointed to take charge of the property of Jonathan Morgan, supposed to be deceased]. In Assembly, April 27, 1837. [Albany, 1837]. 2 p. WHi.   45941

---- ---- ---- Com. on New York & Brooklyn Coal Co.

Report of the Select committee on the petition of the New York and Brooklyn coal company. In Assembly, Feb. 18, 1837. [Albany, 1837]. 6 p. WHi.   45942

---- ---- ---- Committee on Oneida County Courts.

Report of the Select committee on the bill from the Senate entitled "An act relative to the county courts and jails in Oneida county," In Assembly, April 29, 1837. [Albany, 1837]. 8 p. WHi.   45943

---- ---- ---- Committee on Paper Money.

Report of the Committee to inquire and report what, if any, measures should be taken at the present session to reduce the amount of paper money in circulation. In Assembly, April 14, 1837. [Albany, 1837]. 28 p. WHi.   45944

---- ---- ---- Committee on Poor of Warren County.

Report of the Select committee on the petition of the supervisors and superintendents of the poor of the county of Warren. In Assembly, Jan. 17, 1837. [Albany, 1837]. 2 p. WHi.   45945

---- ---- ---- Committee on Post Notes.

Report of the majority of the Committee on the petitions of the citizens of Albany and Troy relative to the issuing of post notes. In Assembly, April 25, 1837. [Albany, 1837]. 7 p. WHi.   45946

---- ---- ---- Committee on Prisons.

Report of the minority of the committee on state prisons, [relating to convict labor]. In Assembly, Feb. 17, 1837. [Albany, 1837]. 5 p. WHi. 45947

---- ---- ---- Committee on Revised Statutes.

Report of the Select committee on the bill to furnish the Revised statutes [containing laws passed from 1828-1836]. In Assembly, Jan. 31, 1837. [Albany, 1837]. 2 p. WHi. 45948

---- ---- ---- Committee on Roads & Bridges.

Report of the Committee on roads and bridges on the petition of inhabitants of Richmond County. In Assembly, Feb. 6, 1837. [Albany, 1837]. 2 p. WHi.   45949

---- ---- ---- Committee on Seneca River.

Report of the Select committee on the bill to amend the act to improve the Seneca river, &c. In Assembly, April 15, 1837. [Albany, 1837]. 7 p. WHi.   45950

---- ---- ---- Committee on Trade & Manufactures.

Report of the Committee on trade and manufactures, on a resolution referred to them, relative to the propriety and expediency of prohibiting the distillation of grain into alcohol.

In Assembly, Feb. 25, 1837.
[Albany, 1837]. 3 p. WHi.
                                45951
---- ---- ---- Committee on
Turnpike Roads.

Report of the Select committee
on the memorial of the corporation of the City of New York,
relative to the alteration of
turnpike roads. In Assembly,
Feb. 20, 1837. [Albany, 1837].
2 p. WHi.   45952

---- ---- ---- Committee on
Two Thirds Bills.

Report of the Committee on
two-third bills, on the bill "relating to licensing retailers of
ardent spirits in the county of
Monroe." In Assembly, April
22, 1837. [Albany, 1837].
5 p. WHi.   45953

---- ---- ---- Committee on
Ways & Means.

Report of the Committee on
ways and means on the bill entitled "An act authorizing the
sale of certain buildings in the
village of Johnstown, heretofore
known as the court-house, jail
and clerks office, of the county
of Montgomery, and for other
purposes." In Assembly, Jan.
23, 1837. 3 p. WHi.   45954

---- ---- ---- ---- Report of
the Committee of ways and means
on the bill from the Senate, entitled "An act amending the
Revised statutes in relation to
insurances made on property in
this state against losses by
fire, in foreign countries, and
by individuals and associations,
unauthorized by law." In Assembly, Feb. 20, 1837. [Al-
bany, 1837]. 3 p. WHi. 45955

---- ---- ---- ---- Report of the
Committee on ways and means on

the bill levying a tax on banks,
for the more speedy enlargement
of the Erie canal. In Assembly,
May 4, 1837. [Albany, 1837].
42 p. WHi.   45956

---- ---- ---- ---- Report of
the Committee of ways and means
on the petition of Thomas Maxwell, treasurer of the county of
Chemung, for a loan to build a
county poor-house. In Assembly,
Feb. 13, 1837. [Albany, 1837].
1 p. WHi.   45957

---- ---- ---- Select committee
on the petition of Inhabitants
residing on the Holland Purchase.

Report of the majority....
[Albany, 1837?] 34 p. NBu;
NRU; WHi.   45958

---- ---- Joint Committee on
so much of the governors message as relates to the investment and distribution of surplus
revenue.

Report. [1837] 15 p. MB;
WHi.   45959

---- ---- Senate.

Journal of the senate of the
state of New York at their sixtieth session, begun and held at
the capitol, in the city of Albany,
on the third day of January,
1837. Albany, printed by E.
Craswell, printer to the state,
1837. (1)-563 p. NNLI; NHerCHi.
                        45960
---- ---- ---- Committee on
Banks & Insurance Companies.

Report of the Committee on
banks and insurance companies,
on so much of the Governor's
message as relates to banks, and
a resolution of the Senate in relation to the Safety fund system.
In Senate, Feb. 25, 1837. [Al-
bany, 1837]. 15 p. WHi.
                        45961

No entry   45962

---- ---- ---- Committee on
Oneida Bank.

Report of the majority of the
Select committee on the petitions
of sundry persons, asking for
a repeal of the charter of the
Oneida bank. In Senate, April
1, 1837. [Albany, 1837].
120 p. WHi.   45963

---- ---- ---- Committee on
Railroads.

Report of the committee on
railroads, on the petition of the
president, directors and company
of the Canajoharie & Catskill
Railroad company in senate April
3, 1837. 5 p. MH-BA.   45964

---- ---- ---- Select Committee
on Private Banking.

Report of the Select committee consisting of one senator
from each senate district on
sundry petitions for the passage
of a law creating a general system of private banking. In
Senate, Mar. 18, 1837. [Al-
bany, 1837]. 24 p. WHi.
                            45965

---- ---- ---- Select Committee
to investigate the banks.

Report of the select committee appointed to investigate the
banks, May 11, 1837. N.p.
[1837]. 55 p. InU; M; WHi.
                            45966

---- Measurer-General of Grain

in New York City.

Report of the Measurer-
general of grain of the city of
New York in answer to a resolution of the Assembly. In Assembly, March 7, 1837. [Albany,
1837]. 3 p. WHi.   45967

---- Natural History Survey.

Communication from the governor, transmitting several reports
relative to the Geological survey
of the state....Albany, 1837-41.
CU; NNC; PPAmP; PPL; TxU.
                            45968

---- Oneida County-Citizens.

Memorial of sundry inhabitants
of Oneida county against the
enlargement of the Erie canal,
and for the construction of a
ship canal from Oswego to Utica.
In Assembly, Feb. 7, 1837.
[Albany, 1837]. 9 p. WHi.
                            45969

---- Secretary of State.

Communication from the Secretary of state, transmitting a
list of inspectors of provisions,
produce and merchandise. In
Assembly, March 8, 1837. [Al-
bany, 1837]. 10 p. WHi.
                            45970

---- ---- Report of the Secretary
of State relative to pardons, in
obedience to a resolution. Transmitted to the legislature. Albany, C. Van Benthuysen, 1837.
54 p. CU.   45971

---- State Hall.

Report of the trustees of the
state hall. In senate Feb. 11,
1837. Albany, 1837. 2 p. WHi.
                            45972

---- Supreme court.

Reports of cases argued and
determined in the supreme court,
and in the court for the trial of
impeachments, and the correction
of errors, of the State of New
York. By Esek Cowen....New

York, Gould, Banks & co.;
Albany, Wm. & A. Gould & co.,
1837-1847. 9 v. DLC.   45973

---- ---- Reports of cases argued and determined in the Supreme court of the judicature,
and in the court for the trial of
impeachments, and the correction
of errors, of the state of New
York. [1828-1841]. By John
L. Wendell...Albany, Gould,
Banks and Co.; New York,
Banks, Gould and Company,
1837-1854. 26 v. HBCC;
LNL-L; OCIW.   45974

---- ---- ---- Albany, Gould,
Banks and company; [etc.,
etc], 1837-1855. 26 v. ICU;
MdBB; NN.   45975

---- ---- Rules and orders of
the Supreme court of the state
of New York; revised and established by the court, pursuant
to the directions of the revised
statutes, and adapted to the
provisions thereof, in the January term, 1837. Albany, William
& A. Gould & co., 1837. 9-43,
(4) p. Ky; NNLI; NNC-L; W.
                        45976
----. University. College
of Physicians and Sur-
geons.
  Catalogue of the officers and
students of the College of Physicians and Surgeons of the city
of New York, for 1836-7. New
York, Printed by W. E. Dean,
1837. 8 p. NNC.   45977

New York Academy of Sciences.
  Charter, Constitution, and
By-Laws of the Lyceum of
Natural History in the City of
New York. New York, W. S.
Dorr, 1837. 28 p. DLC; MB;
MWA; NNC; PU.   45978

New York and Boston Illinois
Land Company.
  Annual report to the board of
trustees...1837. New York,
Stationers' hall press, 1837.
MH.   45979

New York and Erie Railroad
Company.
  Memorial of the N.Y. and
Erie Railroad Company, to the
Legislature of the State of New
York. New York, G. P. Scott
and Co., printers, 1837. 20 p.
CSt; DBRE; DLC; MB; MH-BA;
NN.   45980

New-York and Erie railroad con-
vention, Elmira, N.Y., 1837.
  Address of the New-York and
Erie railroad convention, to the
people of the state of New-York.
Auburn, Oliphant & Skinner,
printers, 1837. 30 p. CSmH;
CSt; MWA; NBu; NNE.   45981

New York and Harlem Railroad
Company.
  Report of the President...
on the affairs of the company.
New York, Childs and Devoe,
printer, 1837. 40 p. MH-BA.
                        45982
New York and Phipsburg Granite
Co.
  Charter and By-Laws....New
York, E. B. Clayton, 1837. 11
p. MH-BA.   45983

The New York annual register
for 1837; containing an almanac,
civil and judicial list, with political, statistical, and other information, respecting the state
of New York and the United
States. 8th year of publication.
New York, Published by G. and
C. Carvill and Co., 1837. 528
p. IaWas; MiD; NNNG.   45984

The New-York book of poetry.

See Hoffman, Charles Fenno, 1806-1884.

No entry   45985

New York City Portage Canal & Manufacturing Co. Charter Circular & Map. New York, 1837. OCHP.   45986

New York Committee of Vigilance.
    The first annual report of the New York Committee of Vigilance, for the year 1837, together with important facts relative to their proceedings... Published by direction of the Committee...New York, Piercy & Reed, printers, 1837. 83, (1) p. ICN; MB; OO; RP; ScU.   45987

---- ---- Report. 1st. 1837. New York, 1837- . OU. 45988

The New York cries in rhyme. New York, 1837. MB.   45989

New York daily news. v. 1-Jan. 5, 1837- . New York, 1837-38. CU.   45990

New York Institute for the Education of the Blind.
    ...Annual report of the managers...to the legislature of the state... New York, M. Day, 1837- . InHi; PHC; PPCP; PPL; PP.   45991

New York Life Insurance and Trust Company.
    In chancery, before the chancellor in the matter of the New York life insurance and trust co. answer and report, 1836. New York, Van Norden, 1837. 69 p. PPAmP.   45992

The New York primer; or, Second book. New York, S. S. &

W. Wood, [1837]. 33 p. DLC; MBC; MH; N; NN.   45993

New York, Providence and Boston Railroad.
    Acts of the legislatures of Rhode Island and Connecticut, relating to the New York, Providence and Bost. R.R. company and the New York and Stonington R.R. company...New York, James Van Norden, 1837. 39 p. CtSoP; DBRE; Nb; RPB. 45994

The New York review. v.1-10; Mar. 1837-Apr. 1842. New York, G. Dearborn & co. [etc.] 1837-42. 10 v. CSt; LNH; NcD; PU; ScU.   45995

New York state pocket almanac, for 1838: being the second after bissextile or leap year. ... Auburn, Published and sold ... by Oliphant & Skinner. Oliphant & Skinner, printers, [1837?]. [24] p. N.   45996

Newbury, Mass. Ordinances.
    Report of the town officers. Newburyport, Mass., [1837-1876]. 23 v. M.   45997

Newburyport Herald. Newburyport, published by J. B. Morss and W. H. Brewster, 1837-1841. MAm.   45998

Newcastle and Carlisle Railway Company.
    The managing committee's report to the directors ... Newcastle, J. Hernaman, 1837. 6 p. MH-BA.   45999

Newcastle [Del.] County School Convention.
    Proceedings of the New Castle County school convention. Wilmington, 1837. PPL. 46000

Newcomb, Butler.

The vision of Butler New-
comb 7 July, 1908, with a
sketch of his life. 2nd ed.
Bridgeton, N.J., 1837. 26 p.
RPB.   46001

Newcomb, Harvey, 1803-1863.

The attributes of God; being
a series of Sabbath evenings
conversations designed to illustrate the character of God. By
Harvey Newcomb. written for
the Massachusetts Sabbath
school society, and revised by
the committee of publication.
Boston, Massachusetts Sabbath
School Society, 1837. 151 p.
NNC.   46002

---- First question book. Boston, Mass., S.S. Society, 1837.
AmSSchU; DLC; MB; MBC; MH.
                            46003
---- ---- 4th ed. Boston, Mass.
Sabbath school society, 1837.
110 p. MBevHi; MH; MH-AH.
                            46004
---- The "negro pew": being
an inquiry concerning the
propriety of distinctions in the
house of God, on account of
color. Boston, I. Knapp, 1837.
[7]-108 p. ICU; MnHi; OCHP;
RP; VtBt.   46005

[Newman, John Henry].

Make ventures for Christ's
sake. A sermon ... 1st American ed. New York, Doolittle
& Vermilye, 1837. 12 p. NNG.
                            46006
Newman, Phebe.

A brief narrative of recent
occurrences in the Church and
at a meeting of the ecclesiastical council at Parker River
Village Newbury (Mass.).
Printed only for private circulation. Newburyport, W. & J.
Gilman Printer, 1837. 16 p.

MB; MBC; MHi; MNe; PPPrHi.
                            46007
News and Courier. Amesbury,
published by J. Caldwell and
T. J. Whittem. C. E. Potter,
ed. 1837 (-38). MAm.   46008

Newton Theological Institution.
Newton Center, Mass.

Catalogue of the officers and
students of the Newton Theological Institution. 1836-37. Boston,
Gould, Kendall & Lincoln. Power
Press of Wm. S. Damrell, 1837.
11 p. MBC; MH; PCA.   46009

Niagara and Detroit Rivers Rail
Road Company.

Report of the engineer upon
the preliminary surveys for the
Niagara & Detroit Rivers Rail
Road, with a map, profile, and
a plan of construction. May,
1837. [Detroit, 1837]. 58 p.
CSmH; DBRE; ICU; MiD-B.
                            46010
Nicholson, Peter, 1765-1844.

Carpenter's new guide: being
a complete book of lines for carpentry & joinery...the whole
founded on true geometric principles. Ed. 12. Philadelphia,
Grigg and Elliot, 1837. AU;
OCIW; OClCS.   46011

---- The student's instructor in
drawing and working the five
orders of architecture. Fully
explaing [!] the best methods
for striking regular and quirked
mouldings...The 6th edition -
considerabey [!] augmented and
improved. New York, Office of
the Railroad Journal, 1837. 47
p. IEG; MH-FA; NcU; NNC;
PPFrankI.   46012

(Nicklin, Philip Holbrook), 1786-
1842.

Letters descriptive of the Virginia springs; the roads leading

thereto, and the doings there-
at. Collected, cor., annotated,
and ed. by Peregrine Prolix
(pseud.)...2nd ed. ... containing eight more letters.
Philadelphia, H. S. Tanner,
1837. 248 p. LNH; MH; OFH;
PWW; TxD-W.   46013

Niles, John Milton, 1787-1856.
   History of South America
and Mexico; comprising their
discovery, geography, politics,
commerce and resolutions. By
Hon. John M. Niles....To
which is annexed, a geographical and historical view of
Texas, with a detailed account
of the Texcan revolution and
war. By Hon. L. T. Pease
....Hartford, H. Huntington,
print., 1837. 2 v. in 1. IaU;
MB; MdBE; NcAS; RPB. 46014

---- Speech of Mr. Niles, of
Connecticut, on the bill imposing
additional duties, as depositories
in certain cases, on public officers. Delivered in Senate U.S.
September 20, 1837. Washington, 1837. 13 p. DLC; NNC;
ViW.   46015

---- Speech of Mr. Niles of
Connecticut, on the resolution
of Mr. Ewing, on recinding the
Treasury order; delivered in
the Senate, December, 1836.
Washington, Blair, 1837. 12 p.
CtSoP; MnSM; NNC; OCHp.
                      46016
Niles, Mark Antony Haskell.
   A sermon, delivered at New-
buryport, on the 26th of Febru-
ary, 1837, before the church
and congregation under the
pastoral care of Rev. Charles
W. Milton. By M. A. H. Niles
... Newburyport, printed by
W. & J. Gilman, 1837. 16 p.
CU; MeBat; NjR; PPPrHi. 46017

Nisbet, Eugenius Aristides, 1803-
1871.
   Address delivered before the
Gwinnett manual labor institute,
at its examination, on Friday,
June 20th, 1837. Athens, 1837.
19 p. A-Ar; NcD.   46018

Noah, Mordecai, Manuel.
   Discourse on the evidence of
the American Indians being the
descendants of the lost tribes
of Israel....New York, J. Van
Norden, 1837. 40 p. MHi; NNC;
PPAN; RPJCB; ScU.   46019

Norfolk County Temperance Convention.
   The subscribers having been
appointed a Committee by the
Norfolk County Temperance Convention assembled at Dedham on
the 26th ult to see that the laws
regulating licensed hours be duly
observed in the town of Weymouth, Quincy, Braintree and
Cohasset. ... Weymouth, Oct. 19,
1837. Broadside. MWeyHi.
                      46020
... Norris' Dover directory....
By D. L. Norris. [1837, 1843,
1846, 1848. Dover (N.H.)].
E. Wadleigh, 1837-1848. 4 v.
DLC; NhD.   46021

North American Calendar, or the
Columbian Almanac for 1838.
Wilmington, Del., P. B. Porter,
[1837]. DLC; MWA.   46022

North American Lumber Company.
   Articles of Association of the
North American Lumber Company:
the report of the Commissioners,
with Maps, and statements of
property, &c. &c. November 22d,
1837. New York, 1837. 31 p.
MH-BA; MHi.   46023

---- Extensive sale of Standing
Timber and Real Estate, To be

held at the Village of Lower
Stillwater, Maine, ... Septem-
ber 8, 1837. Broadside. MHi.
                              46024
North Carolina. Board of in-
ternal improvement.
    Reports of The Board of
Internal Improvements, Cape-
Fear Navigation Company, and
Trustees of the University,
1837. Raleigh, Thomas Loring,
Printer, 1837. 8 p. NcU.
                              46025
---- Board of Literature.
    Extracts from "Reports on
public improvements" in the state
of North Carolina. Raleigh, Pr.
by Thomas J. Lemay, 1837.
36 p. Di-GS; IU; MB; NcU;
NN.   46026

---- General Assembly.
    Journals of the Senate and
House of Commons, of the General Assembly of the State of
North Carolina, at its session
in 1836-37. Raleigh, Printed
by J. Gales and Son, Office of
the Raleigh Register, 1837.
513 p. Nc; NcW.   46027

---- Laws, Statutes, etc.
    Act concerning the militia
of North Carolina; published by
the Adjutant-General of the
State, by order of the General
Assembly of 1836-37. Raleigh,
Lemay, 1837. 36 p. MH-L;
NcU; OCLaw.   46028

---- ---- Acts passed by the
General Assembly of the State of
North Carolina, at the session of
1835. Raleigh, (N.C.), Philo
White, Printer to the State,
1836. 132, (4) p. Ar-Sc; C;
IU; MB; MdBB; NjU; OrSC.
                              46029
---- ---- Laws of the state of
North Carolina, passed by the
General assembly, at the session

of 1836-37. Raleigh, Thomas J.
Lemay, printer, 1837. 344, 20,
(1) p. Ar-SC; IaU-L; MdBB;
Nj; W.   46030

---- ---- The revised statutes
of the state of North Carolina,
passed by the General assembly
at the session of 1836-7...by
James Iredell & Wm. H. Battle,
in 2 Vols. Turner and Hughes,
Raleigh, North Carolina, 1837.
Nv; OCLaw; TxU; WaU; WHi.
                              46031
---- Supreme Court.
    Reports of cases at law, ar-
gued and determined in the Supreme Court of North Carolina.
Vol. 1. 1837. Raleigh, North
Carolina, Turner, & Hughes,
1837. 634 p. Mi-L; NCH; OClW;
ViU; Wy.   46032

---- University.
    Catalogue ... October 1, 1837.
Raleigh, Pr. by J. Gales and
Son, Office of the Raleigh Register, 1837. 14 p. NN; MHi.
                              46033
North Coventry, Conn. Congre-
gational church.
    Historical notice of the Con-
gregational church in North
Coventry, Conn. with the ar-
ticles of faith, covenant, & a
catalogue of members. Hartford,
Case, Tiffany & Co., 1837.
16 p. Ct; CtHC; MBC; PPPrHi.
                              46034
North Kingstown, R.I.
    By-laws of the town of North
Kingstown relative to roads and
highways: passed at a town
meeting holden Aug. 29, 1837.
Newport, 1837. 10 p. RHi;
RNHi; RP.   46035

Northern banner devoted to
temperance and education. V. 1.
no. 1-4. Concord, 1837. Nh-Hi.
                              46036

Norton, Andrews, 1786-1853.
   The evidences of the genuine-
ness of the gospels, by Andrews
Norton. Boston, John B. Rus-
sell, 1837. 3 v. ICU; MB;
MiDU; OkU; RNR.   46037

Norwich and Worcester railroad
company.
   ... Memorial of the Norwich
and Worcester railroad company.
[Worcester? 1837]. 11 p. CSt;
DLC.   46038

---- Norwich and Worcester
Rail Road. [Norwich? 1837?]
8 p. IU; NN.   46039

---- (Report of the directors
of the Norwich and Worcester
rail-road company) to the senate
and house of representatives of
the commonwealth of Massachusetts in general court assembled,
Jan., 1837. (B. 1837). 16 p.
MH.   46040

Norwich university, Northfield,
Vermont.
   A catalogue of the officers
and students, of Norwich uni-
versity, for the academic year,
1836-7. Montpelier, Wm. Clark,
1837. 15 p. MdBD; MiU-C.
                           46041
Notes on the Northern Part of
Ohio. Cuyahoga Falls, James
Lowry, Printer, 1837. 22 p.
CtHT-W; DLC; OHi; PHi; WHi.
                           46042
(Nott, Eliphalet), 1773-1866.
   Tribute to the memory of
Mrs. Mary L. Sprague, wife of
W. B. Sprague... Albany,
Packard and Van Benthuysen,
printers, 1837. CtHC; ICN;
MH-AH; NNUT; WHi.   46043

Nott, Paul.
   Incidents of travel. New
York, Harper & Bros., Pub.,

1837. 312 p. IaPeC.   46044

Nourse, James, 1805-1854.
   Views of Colonization. By
Rev. James Nourse. Philadel-
phia, Merrihew and Gunn, 1837.
MH; MH-And; OO; PPL; PSC-Hi.
                           46045

O

Obert, Peter G.
   Obert's system of nature;
or, Infidelity exposed being a
philosophical explanation of the
existence of the two first principles, called God and nature, as
well as the manner in which all
things grow out of the same.
By Peter G. Obert. New York,
Printed by Joseph M. Marsh,
1837. [9]-148 p. CtY; NjR.
                           46046
Obstacles and objections to the
cause of permanent and universal
peace considered by a layman.
Boston, American peace societies,
1837. CtHC; DLC; MeBat: PHi;
PPPrHi.   46047

O'Callaghan, Jeremiah.
   The creation and offspring of
the Protestant church, also the
vagaries and heresies of John
Henry Hopkins and other false
teachers, by Jeremiah O'Callaghan. Burlington, printed for
the author, 1837. iv, 328 p.
ArLSJ; CSansS; MBBCHS; MWH;
PScrM; VtB; VtU; WHi; BrMus.
                           46048
Ogden, N.Y., Presbyterian
Church.
   Manual of the Presbyterian
church in Ogden, containing notices of its history, a list of its
members, its important resolutions and its articles of faith
and covenant. ... Rochester,
Luther Tucker, printer, 1837.

32 p. NN; NRHi; NRU; WHi.
46049

Ohio. Board of Public Works.

First annual report of the Board of Public Works to the thirty-fifth general assembly of the State of Ohio. Columbus, James B. Gardiner, Printer to the State, 1837. 27 p. OCl; P.
46050

---- General assembly.

Report of John L. Riddell, M.D. one of the special committee appointed by the last legislature to report on the method of obtaining a complete geological survey of the state. [Columbus, 1837]. 34 p. DLC; MdBJ; OU; PPL; WU-G.
46051

---- ---- House.

Journal of The House of Representatives, of The State of Ohio; Being The First Session of The Thirty-Fifth General Assembly, Begun and Held In The City of Columbus, Monday, December 5, 1836. And In The Thirty-Fifth Year of Said State. Columbus, James B. Gardiner, Printer To The State, 1837. 984 p. O; O-LR.
46052

---- ---- Select Committee.

Counter report of the select committee to whom were referred so much of the Governor's message as relates to the surplus revenue, accompanied with a bill. Presented by Mr. Glover. Columbus, James B. Gardiner, Printer to the State, 1837. 27 p. P.
46053

---- ---- Senate.

Journal....Columbus, Ohio, State printer, 1837. WaPS.
46054

---- ---- ---- Committee on finance, etc.

Report on surplus revenue of the United States to which is entitled, with a bill on the subject. Cols. State, 1837. 26 p. OHi.
46055

---- Governor (Joseph Vance), 1836-1838.

Message of the Governor of Ohio, to the thirty-sixth General assembly, begun and held in the city of Columbus, Monday, December 4, 1837. Columbus, Samuel Medary, 1837. 22 p. MiU-C; OCHP.
46056

---- ---- Special message from Governor Vance relative to the Wabash and Erie Canal lands [to the House of Representatives]. Columbus, O.? 1837? 35 p. OCl.
46057

---- Laws, statutes, etc.

An act prescribing the duty of supervisors, and relating to roads and highways. Printed by authority. Columbus, J.B. Gardiner, 1837. 12 p. DLC.
46058

---- ---- An act to authorize a loan of credit by the state of Ohio, to rail road companies; and to authorize subscriptions by the state, to the capital stock of turnpike, canal, and slack-water navigation companies. Printed by authority. Columbus, James B. Gardiner, printer to the state, 1837. 10 p. MB; OCHP; PPL.
46059

---- ---- An act to incorporate the borough of Conneaut. Conneaut. Charles A. Randall & co., printers, 1837. 7 p. OClWHi.
46060

---- ---- An act to organize and discipline the militia of Ohio; passed at the thirty-fifth General assembly. Printed by authority. Columbus, S. R. Dolbee, printer to the state, 1837. [3]-56 p. MB; MiU-L; OClWHi. 46061

---- ---- An act to provide for a geological survey of the state of Ohio, and for other purposes; passed at the thirty-fifth general assembly. Columbus, 1837. 4 p. WU. 46062

---- ---- Acts for the protection of the Ohio canals; and regulating the navigation and collection of tolls on the same. Columbus, Medary & Bros., 1837. 35 (1) p. OCoSo. 46063

---- ---- Acts of a general nature, passed at the first session of the thirty-fifth General assembly of the state of Ohio; begun and held in the city of Columbus, December 5th 1836, and in the thirty-fifth year of said state .... Columbus, S. R. Dolbee, 1837. 144 p. IaU-L; In-SC; MdBB; Nj; W. 46064

---- ---- Acts of a local nature, passed at the first session of the thirty-fifth General assembly of the state of Ohio; begun and held in the city of Columbus, December 5th, 1836, and in the thirty-fifth year of said state. IaU-L; In-SC; Nj; NNLI. 46065

---- ---- Index to all the laws and resolutions of the state of Ohio...to the year 1835-6 inclusive...Columbus, Samuel Medary, 1837. 123 p. IaHi; In-SC; MiD-B; OHi; WHi. 46066

---- State Library. Catalogue of the State Library of Ohio. December, 1837. Published by authority Zechariah Mills, Librarian.

Columbus, Samuel Medary, Printer to the State, 1837. 42 + 5 + 6 + 5 p. O. 46067

Ohio and Indianapolis Railroad Company. An act to incorporate the Ohio & Indpls. railroad company. Jeffersonville, Ia., Robert R. Lindsay, printer, 1837. 34 p. In. 46068

Ohio Anti-Slavery society. Report of the second anniversary of the Ohio anti-slavery society, held at Mount Pleasant, Jefferson county, Ohio, on the twenty-seventh of April, 1837. Cincinnati, Pub. by the anti-slavery society, 1837. 67 p. KyU; OCoY; OO; TxH; TNF; WHi. 46069

Ohio City. First Presbyterian church. The history, confession, and covenant of the First Presbyterian church of Ohio city: with the names of its members. January, 1837. Ohio city, Timothy H. Smead, 1837. 29 p. OClWHi; OO. 46070

Ohio Railroad Company. Report of the engineer, to the directors of the Ohio rail road company, March 20, 1837. Painesville, Printed by Howe & James, 1837. 16 p. DBRE; NjP; NN; OClWHi; PPL. 46071

The Ohio Statesman. July 26, 1837. S. Medary and Brothers. Prop. Vol. I. Columbus, Ohio, 1837. OYO. 46072

Oldbuck, A., pseud. A legend of Boston, (Eng.). Boston, 1837. MB. 46073

Olds, Chauncey Newell.

An address on the nature and cultivation of a missionary spirit, delivered before the Society of inquiry on missions of Miami university, Sunday evening, February 26th. 1837. Oxford, O., Bishop, 1837. 22 p. ICU; MWA; OClWHi; OMC; PPPrHi.
46074

Olmstead, Denison.
A compendium of natural philosophy; adapted to the use of the general reader, and of schools and academies. By Denison Olmstead, A.M., professor of natural philosophy at Yale college. Charleston, Published by S. Babcock & Co., 1837. 359 p. CtHT-C; IaHi; MH; NNC; OO.   46075

---- Observations on the meteoric shower of November, 1837. By Denison Olmstead, professor of astronomy and natural philosophy at Yale College. New Haven, printed by B. L. Hamlen, 1837. 16 p. TxH.   46076

---- Outlines of lectures on meteorology, delivered at Yale College...New Haven, L. Hamlen, 1837. 16 p. CSmH; CtY; DAS.   46077

Olney, Jesse, 1798-1872.
History of the United States, on a new plan; adapted to the capacity of youth. To which is added,... New Haven, Durrie & Peck, 1837. 288 p. CtHT-W; ICU; MH; PHi; ScMar.   46078

---- National preceptor: or, Selections in prose and poetry ...6th ed. Hartford, 1837. 336 p. Ct; CtHWatk; MWiW.
46079

---- A new and improved school atlas, to accompany the Practical system of modern geogra-

phy, By J. Olney ... New York, Robinson, Pratt & co., 1837. IU; MH; MiU-C; PHC; RPB.
46080

---- Practical system of modern geography; or a view of the present state of the world ... 24th ed. N.Y., Robinson, Pratt and company, 1837. 228 p. MB; MnHi; NBuG.   46081

---- ---- New York, Robinson, Pratt and company, 1837. 288 p. CtY; ICU; MB; MnHi; Nh.
46082

On the rights and powers of corporations; a notice of the pamphlet by a citizen of Boston, by his fellow citizen. Boston, 1837. 17 p. IU; MH-BA; NNC; OCLaw.   46083

Onderdonk, Benjamin Tredwell.
A pastoral letter to the children belonging to the schools in union with the New York protestant Episcopal Sunday School Society; presented to them at the 20th anniversary of the society, March 30, 1837. New York Protestant Episcopal Sunday school Union, [1837?] 15 p. NJQ; Nh.   46084

Oneida Almanac for 1838. Utica, N.Y., Gardiner Tracy, (1837). MWA; NRU; NUtHi.   46085

Oneida conference seminary.
Catalogue of the officers and students of the Oneida conference seminary, Cazenovia, New-York, 1836-7. Cazenovia, J. W. Fairchild & son, printers, 1837. 16 p. N.   46086

Oneida institute, Whitesboro, N.Y.
Catalogue of the trustees, faculty and students of the Oneida institute, Whitesboro, 1837. 15 p. MiU-C; NUt; OClWHi.   36087

Ontario county, N.Y. Electors.
Reasons for rejoicing at the
result of the late election in the
state of New-York: At a meeting of the electors of Ontario
county, held at Canandaigua,
Nov. 21. [Canandaigua? 1837?]
8 p. McM.   46088

Ontario county anti-slavery
society.
Gerritt Smith, Esq. will
address the people on the subject of slavery, at the Brick
Church in this village on Friday
and Saturday of this week at
2 o'clock.... A county anti-
slavery society will be formed
during the continuance of the
meeting.... Rev. Orange Scott,
and George Storrs, the two
Methodist ministers who took
such a bold and uncompromising
stand against Southern slave-
holders in the General Conference at Cincinnati in 1836, will
also attend, and address the
meeting. Canandaigua, Sept.
12, 1837. Broadside. NCanHi.
                             46089
Opie, Amelia (Alderson).
Illustrations of lying, in all
its branches. From 2d. London
ed. Hartford, Conn., Andrus,
Judd and Franklin, 1837. 283 p.
MB; MH; MNan; OMC; PPiW.
                             46090
Opinions of Sprague and Hallitt
with the report of the town's
committee on the surplus
revenue disposition. Weymouth,
published by order of the town
1837. 16 p. MWeyHi.   46091

The Order of Services at the
Installation of Rev. Joseph
Angier, as Pastor of the First
Congregational Parish in Milton,
on Wednesday, Sept. 13, 1837.
Boston, Torrey & Blair, Print-
ers, 1837. 4 p. MH.   46092

The oriental annual. Lives of
Moghul emperors. Philadelphia,
Desilver, Thomas & Co., 1837.
x, [1]-240 p. LNL.   46093

Osage Mining and Smelting Com-
pany.
(Reports)... Baltimore,
Woods, Print., 1837. 20 p.
MH-BA; PPL.   46094

Osbourn, James.
Contemplations on Aaron the
high priest, and his illustrious
successor the Son of God; in a
series of letters to C. B. Has-
sell, esq. By James Osbourn,
minister of the gospel in the city
of Baltimore. Baltimore, Printed
by John D. Toy, 1837. 93 p.
MdHi.   46095

Otey, James Hervey, 1800-1863.
The Dity of Ministers of the
Gospel, to their people, con-
sidered in their Civil Relations:
Set Forth in a primary charge
to the Clergy of the Diocese of
Tennessee. By Rt. Rev. James
H. Otey, D.D. Bishop of said
Diocese. Delivered in Christ
Church, in the City of Nashville,
during the session of the Con-
vention, on Thursday October
11th, 1837. Printed by order
of the Convention. Nashville,
S. Nye & Co. Printers, 1837.
27, [1] p. CSmH; LU; MBDiL;
MHi; MnHi; NN; T.   46096

Overbrook School for the Blind.
Constitution, character and
by-laws, and documents relating
to the ... Institution ... at Philadelphia. [Philadelphia], C. Ser-
man prtr., 1837. 32 p. M; OO;
ScC.   46097

Oxenford, John, 1812-1877.
A quiet day. A farce, in one
act, by John Oxenford, esq. ...

as performed at the Royal Olympic theatre: London, W. Strange; New York and Philadelphia, Turner and Fisher, 1837. 2 p l., [7]-28 p. CSt; OC; ViU. 46098

Oxford, Massachusetts. First Church.

The confession of faith and covenant of the first church in Oxford, Mass. With a catalogue of surviving members, to which are prefixed some historical sketches of said church. 1837. Worcester, Printed by Henry J. Howland, 1837. 15 p. MB; MBC; MWHi. 46099

[Owen, Robert Dale], 1801-1877.

Pocahontas: a historical drama, in five acts; with an introductory essay and notes. By a citizen of the West. New-York, G. Dearborn, 1837. 240 p. ICN; MoK; OFH; PU; RPB. 46100

P

(Pacificus) pseud. Maseres, Francis, 1713-1824.

What will Congress do? Philadelphia, Printed by L. R. Bailey, 1837. 14 p. MB; MH-BA; NN. 46101

Packard, A(lpheus) S(pring).

An address delivered at the dedication of the Teachers' Seminary, at Gorham, Maine, September 13, 1837. Portland, A. Shirley, 1837. 24 p. MBC; MeB; MH; MH-And; NNC. 46102

Packard, Frederick Adolphus, 1794-1867.

The Union Bible dictionary. Prepared for the American Sunday-School Union, and revised by the committee of publication.

Philadelphia, American Sunday-School Union, 1837. 648 p. IaJ; KPea; LNB; MeBa; TNP. 46103

Packard, Levi, 1793-1857.

False reasoning upon the ways of God tested. A sermon preached at Spencer, Mass., Lord's Day. August 6, 1837. Brookfield, (Mass.), E. and L. Merriam, pr., 1837. 24 p. CtY; IaGG. 46104

Packard, Theophilus, 1802-1855.

Thanksgiving sermon, Shelburne, Dec. 1, 1836. Greenfield, 1837. MBC; MDeeP; N. 46105

Paine, Robert.

Baccalaureate Address, Delivered at the Annual Commencement of Lagrange College, June 8th, 1837; By Robert Paine, A.M. President of the College. Published at the Office of the Southwestern Christian Advocate, Nashville, Ten., 1837. 19 p. KyLx; MBC; MH; T. 46106

Paine, Thomas, 1737-1809.

The age of reason: being an investigation of true and fabulous theology.....Boston, 1837. 207 p. ICT. 46107

---- The political writings of Thomas Paine, Secretary to the Committee of Foreign affairs in the American revolution. To which is prefixed a brief sketch of the author's life....Middletown, N.J., Granville, 1837. 2 v. CLSU; MB; NjP; PHi; TxHR. 46108

Paley, William, 1743-1805.

Natural theology; or, Evidence of the existence and attributes of the Deity, collected from the appearances of nature. Illustrated by the plates and by a selection from the notes of James

Paxton, with additional notes,
original and selected, for this
edition, and a vocabulary of
scientific terms. Stereotype
edition. Boston, Gould, Kendall
& Lincoln, 1837. 344 p. GMM;
NN; ODaB.   46109

---- The Principles of Moral
and Political Philosophy. By
William Paley, D.D. Two volumes in one. Vol. I, with
additions and improvements.
New York, Published by Collins,
Keese and Co., 1837. 2 v. in
1. ArLSJ; CtHT; FMU; TU;
ViL.   46110

Palmer, John.
    Awful Shipwreck. An Af-
fecting Narrative of The Un-
paralled Sufferings of The Crew
of the Ship Francis Spaight,
which foundered on her passage
from St. John's, N.B. to Limer-
ick, in November last. ...
Communicated for the Press, by
John Palmer, one of the survivors. Boston, Published by
G. C. Perry, 1837. 24 p.
CU; DLC; IEG; MB; Nh.   46111

Palmer, Ray, 1808-1887.
    The spirit's life; a poem; de-
livered before the Literary
fraternity, Waterville college,
and the Porter rhetorical society, Theological seminary, Andover, at their anniversaries,
August and September, 1837.
By Rev. Ray Palmer. Boston,
Whipple and Damrell, 1837.
16 p. CtHWatk; MeBat; MH;
RHi; RPB.   46112

Pardoe, Julia, 1806-1862.
    The City of the Sultan; and
domestic manners of the Turks,
in 1836. By Miss Pardoe. ...
In two volumes. Philadelphia,
Carey, Lea, & Blanchard, 1837.

InNd; MeBa; OCY; PPA; RPA.
                     46113
Park, Harrison G.
    ... A sermon occasioned by
the death of the Rev. George
Cowles and Mrs. Elizabeth R.
Cowles; preached in Danvers
... By Harrison G. Park, ...
Salem, Printed by Wm. Ives &
Co., Observer Office, 1837.
40 p. MBevHi; MH-And; MPeHi;
Nh; PHi.   46114

Parke, Benjamin.
    ... A complete digest of the
laws of Pennsylvania.... Philadelphia, Kay, 1837. v. 2, 984 p.
Mi-L.   46115

Parker, Joel.
    Moral tendencies of our pres-
ent pecuniary distress; a discourse delivered May 14th, 1837.
New Orleans, printed at the Observer Office, 1837. 15 p.
MBC; MH; MH-And: OClWHi.
                     46116
Parker, John R.
    ... The semaphoric telegraph
... [Boston? 1837] [4] p. MnU.
                     46117
Parker, Richard Green, 1798-
1869.
    The Boston school compendium
of natural and experimental
philosophy, embracing the elementary principles of mechanics,
pneumatics, hydraulics...with a
description of the steam and loco-
motive engines. By R. G. Parker...Boston, Marsh, Capen &
Lyon, 1837. 23 p. DLC; MB;
MBAt; MH.   46118

---- Progressive exercises in
English composition. 12th stereo-
type edition. Boston, Robert S.
Davis, etc., 1837. MDeeP; MH;
NcGU; PPStCh.   46119

---- Progressive exercises in

English grammar. Part I and
II. By R. G. Parker and
Charles Fox. 4th edition. Boston, Crocker & Brewster, etc.,
etc., 1837. MH; PPM.   46120

---- ---- ... 5th ed. Boston,
Crocker and Brewster; New
York, Leavitt, Lord & co.,
1837. MH; TxU-T.   46121

Parker, S. E.
Logic, or the art of reasoning
simplified.... By S. E. Parker.
Philadelphia, Robert Davis;
Boston, Jas. B. Dow, 1837.
323 p. CtSoP; NjP; OCY; PPP;
TxShA.   46122

Parker, Wooster.
A discourse delivered in
Orono, Maine, ... November
30th, 1837. By Wooster Park-
er, ... Bangor, Printed by
Charles Cobb, 1837. 22 p.
MBC; MeBat.   46123

Parkman, Francis, 1788-1852.
The spirit of the Christian
ministry. A sermon delivered at
the ordination of the Rev. John
Parkman, to the pastoral care
of the Third Congregational
church in Greenfield Oct. XI,
MDCCCXXXVII. ... Boston,
Samuel N. Dickinson, 1837.
30 p. CtSoP; ICMe; MBC;
OClWHi; PPAmP.   46124

Parnassian wreath: consisting
of choice selections from the
most eminent ancient and modern
poets. New York, Liddle,
1837. CtHWatK; MA.   46125

Parr, S. S.
The Reviewer Reviewed; Or,
An Expose Of The Late Billings-
gate Production Of Mr. "William
Sims" M'Atee Elder, Against The
Rev. N. L. Rice, His Counsel,

And Part Of The Jury. By
James Cain, Of Bloomfield, Ky.
Bardstown,....D. D. Jones....
1837. 24 p. KyLoF; RPB.
       46126
Parsons, John Usher, 1761-1838.
The analytical spelling book.
[2d ed.] Portland, William Hyde,
1837. 163 p. OCl.   46127

---- ---- ... Sixth edition.
Portland, William Hyde, 1837.
179, (1) p. MeHi; NNC. 46128

---- ---- 7th ed. Boston, W.
Pierce, 1837. 180 p. MH; Mi;
OClWHi.   46129

---- The analytical system of
teaching orthography. Boston,
Whipple & Damrell, 1837. MB;
MeHi; MH; OClW.   46130

---- Analytical vocabulary, or
analytical system of teaching orthography, in which the spelling,
meaning, and construction of
80000 words are taught from
8000 roots. 2nd ed. Framingham, Boynton and Marshall,
1837. MH.   46131

---- ---- 3 ed. Cambridge,
Metcalf, Torry, and Ballou,
1837. 1-176 p. CtHWatk; RPB.
       46132
---- The Biblical analysis; or,
A topical arrangement of the in-
structions of the Holy Scriptures
.... Compiled by J. U. Parsons.
Boston, Whipple & Damrell, 1837.
[17]-311 p. InUpT; MoSpD;
NbOM; WHi.   46133

---- The Nazarite; or the letter
and spirit of the Bible, on the
use of wine. By an abstinence
man. Boston, Whipple and Damrell, 1837. 36 p. DLC; MBC;
MH; NN.   46134

---- The Reign of Public Opinion; or, the Achievements of the popular will triumphing over law; being the substance of a discourse delivered on the day of annual fast, 1837, in Bowdoin Street Church, Boston. Boston, 1837. 60 p. DLC; MB; NcD; NPV.   46135

Parsons, Lemuel H.

An inquiry into the kind and extent of education, demanded by the ordinary circumstances, duties, and wants of life: being an address delivered at the organization of the Newtown lyceum. By Lemuel H. Parsons ... Doylestown, Pa., Kelly & Larga, printers, 1837. 19 p. CtY; DHEW; MH; OClWHi; PU.   46137

Pastoral and circular letters of the General assembly of 1837. Philadelphia, printed by L. R. Bailey, 1837. 14 p. NjR; OOxM; VtMidbC.   46138

Patrick, Mrs. M. A.

The Mourner's Gift. Edited By Mrs. M. A. Patrick. New York, Van Nostrand & Dwight, 1837. 192 p. CtY; DLC; KyBC; MWA; NNUT; RPB.   46139

Pattengill, J. S.

How shall the ministry be proved? A sermon at the institution of Phineas Robinson, Jefferson, N.Y., Oct. 29, 1836. Walton, Berray & Pine, 1837. 16 p. RPB.   46140

[Paulding, James Kirke], 1778-1860.

The Dutchman's fireside.... By the author of "Letters from the South" ... 5th ed. New York, Harper & bros., 1837. 2 v. in 1. CtNb; DLC; KyLo; MWA; TxDaM.   46141

Paxton, James, 1786-1860.

An introduction to the study of human anatomy. By J. Paxton ... 3d Amer. ed., with additions. By Winslow Lewis, jr. ... Boston, W. D. Ticknor, 1837. 2 v. ICJ; MBC; MdBJ; NNN; PPCP.   46142

Peabody, Andrew Preston.

Discourse at the installation of Linus H. Shaw, over the First Congregational church at Townsend, Mass., Dec. 21, 1836. Boston, J. N. Bang, 1837. 15 p. ICMe; MiD-B; Nh-Hi; OClWHi; RPB.   46143

---- Views of duty adapted to the times. A sermon preached at Portsmouth, May 14, 1837. By Andrew P. Peabody, Pastor of the South Church and Parish. Portsmouth, J. W. Foster, J. F. Shores and Son, 1837. 16 p. ICMe; MB; MPiB; MMeT-Hi; PPPrHi.   46144

Peabody, Ephrain.

Charges against Unitarianism. Printed for the American Unitarian Association. 1st. series No. 123. Boston, James Munroe & co., October, 1837. 12 p. ICMe; ICT; MBC; MeBat; MPeHi; Nh-Hi.   46145

---- "Come over and help us." A letter to Rev. Geo. Putnam. By E. Peabody. 1st Series. Boston, James Munroe & Company, 1837. 42 p. ICMe; MeB; MH; MMeT-Hi; NH-Hi.   46146

The Pearl; or Affections gift; a Christmas and New Years present. Philadelphia, Thomas T. Ash, [1837]. 224 p. WU.
46147

Pearson, Henry Bromfield.

The Little Orator for boys and

girls. Part 1. By a teacher
of reading at the West Chester
Academy, A. Bolmar's. West
Chester, 1837. 108 p. CSmH;
MB; PHi; PPL.   46148

Pearson, Hugh Nicholas, 1767-
1856.
   Memoirs of the life and writ-
ings of the Rev. Cladius Buchanan, D.D., late Vice - provost
of the College of Fort William
in Bengal, by the Rev. Hugh
Pearson, D.D., dean of Salis-
bury with notes relative to the
present state of religion in
India; and an introduction, by
Caspar Morris, M.D., (Greek
quotation). Philadelphia,
George & Byington, and Wm.
Stavely; New York, Swords,
Stanford & Co., 1837. 422 p.
ICP; KyDC; OrPD; PWW; TxU.
                          46149
Peck, John, 1735-1812.
   A descant on the Universal
plan, or Universal salvation, il-
lustrated, by John Peck, with
Rev. L. Haynes's sermon,
printed for the publisher.
Lowell, 1837. 24 p. MH; MLow;
RPB.   46150

Peck, John, 1780-1849.
   An historical sketch of the
Baptist missionary convention of
the state of New York; embracing a narrative of the origin and
progress of the Baptist denomination in central and western New
York. By John Peck and John
Lawton. Utica, printed by Bennett & Bright, 1837. 255 p.
CtMW; ICU; LNH; PHi; WHi.
                          46151
Peck, John Mason, 1789-1858.
   A Gazetteer of Illinois, in
three parts: containing a general view of the State, a general
view of each County, and a particular description of each town,

etc. By John Mason Peck. 2nd
edition, entirely revised, corrected and enlarged. Philadelphia, Grigg and Elliott, 1837.
328 p. CU; IaD; InHi; MBBC;
Mok; PPM.   46152

---- A new guide for emigrants
to the West containing sketches
of Michigan, Ohio, Indiana,
Illinois, Missouri, Arkansas,
with the territory of Wisconsin
and the adjacent parts. By
J. M. Peck ... 2d ed. Boston,
Gould, Kendall & Lincoln, 1837.
881 p. MH; NBU; OU; TxDaM;
WaU.   46153

A peep at the various nations
of the world, with a concise
description of the inhabitants.
Seventh series. No. 6. Concord, Published by Atwood &
Brown, 1837. 16 p. MH; MiHi;
Nh-Hi.   46154

Peirce, Benjamin.
   An elementary treatise on algebra; to which are added ex-
ponential equations and logarithms by Benjamin Peirce, A.M.,
university professor of mathematics and natural philosophy in
Harvard university. Boston,
James Munroe and company, 1837.
276 p. CSt; MB; MH; NNC;
RPB.   46155

---- An elementary treatise on
plane and solid geometry. By
Benjamin Peirce.... Boston,
James Munroe and company,
1837. 159 p. CSt; KHi; MBC;
MH; Nh; TxU-T.   46156

[Peirce, Oliver Beale.]
   Common school grammar in
miniature. [Utica, William Williams, 1837.] Broadside. MnU.
                          46157

---- Grammatical instructor; or,
Common school grammar, a new
and practical system of English
grammar ... 3d ed., Rev.,
enl. and improved. Utica,
William Williams, 1837. 370 p.
MH; MiU; MnU; N; NUtHi. 46158

Peixotto, Daniel Levy Maduro,
1800-1843.
Introductory lecture de-
livered at the Willoughby Medical College of the Willoughby
university of Lake Erie, 1836-
'37. Clevel'd, Canfield, 1837.
30 p. DLC; DNLM; OCHP;
OClW-H; OHi.   46159

Pellew, George, 1793-1866.
A sermon, preached in the
parish church of St. Dionis,
Fenchurch Street, on Sunday,
February 5, 1837, in behalf of
the Melropolis churches' fund.
Norwich, 1837. 24 p. WHi.
                           46160
Pendleton, James M., 1811-1891.
A sermon on the death of
Rev. William Warder, delivered
in the Baptist Meeting House
in Russellville, Ky. September
11th, 1836, by Rev. James
M. Pendleton. Published at the
request of Mrs. Warder. Hop-
kinsville, Gazette Office, 1837.
15 p. MoSM.   46161

Pengilly, R.
... The Scripture guide to
baptism: containing a faithful
citation of all the passages of
the New Testament which relate
to this ordinance .... By R.
Pengilly .... Philadelphia,
Baptist general tract society,
1837. 91 p. LNB; MdBD;
NjR; PPL; ViRU.   46162

Penn, William, 1644-1718.
Advice of William Penn to his
children...by William Penn....
New York, Samuel S. & William

Wood, 1837. 12 p. TxHuT.
                           46163
---- A letter from William Penn
to his wife and children; written
a little before his first voyage
to America. Salem, N.J., 1837.
CSmH; CtY; HSMontgCo; PSC-
Hi; PNortHi.   46164

Pennsylvania. Auditor-General's
office.
Report of the Auditor-General,
in relation to the circulation of
paper currency, under the denomination of five dollars. Read
in the House of Representatives,
March 13, 1838. Harrisburg,
Packer, Barrett and Parke,
1837. 28 p. DLC; OSW; P.
                           46165
---- Board of Canal commissioners.
Communication from the Canal
commissioners, transmitting the
report of B. Aycrigg, principal
engineer, on the proposed connection of the West Branch improvements with the Allegheny
River. Read in Senate, March 1,
1837. Harrisburg, Emmanuel
Guyer, printer, 1837. 56 p.
NbO; NNC.   46166

---- ---- Final report and estimates of the survey of a canal
route between the west bank
improvements and the town of
Franklin. Harrisburg, 1837. 54
p. ICJ; PHi.   46167

---- ---- Message from the governor, transmitting a communication
from the board of canal commissioners, with a report and estimate for avoiding the inclined
planes at Philadelphia, a report
of the survey of the Western
Philadelphia railroad, and the
estimate of cost... Harrisburg,
S. D. Patterson, 1837. 19 p.
DBRE.   46168

---- ---- Pennsylvania canal
regulations and rates of toll,
as established by the Board
of Canal Commissioners, and
put in force on the first day
of April, 1837: Together with
the acts for the protection of
the canal. Harrisburg,
Printed by Theo. Penn, 1837.
(V), 46 p. P.   46169

---- ---- Report. Harris-
burg, printed by Packer,
Barrett and Parke, 1837-[57].
5 v. M.   46170

---- ---- Report of the Canal
Commissioners. Read in The
House of Representatives, December 9, 1836. Harrisburg,
printed by Samuel D. Patterson, 1836-7. (3)-141 p.
MiD-B; NNE.   46171

---- ---- Report of the Canal
Commissioners, with the ac-
companying documents. Read
in the House of Representatives,
Dec. 7, 1837. Harrisburg,
printed by Packer, Barrett and
Parke, 1837. (4)-151 p.
MiD-B.   46172

---- ---- Report ... relative to
the Pennsylvania canals, and
railroads, read in Senate, December 9, 1837. Harrisburg,
Emanuel Guyer, printer, 1837.
45 p. RPB.   46173

---- ---- Reports of surveys,
by Chas. T. Whippo and Chas.
De Hass ... for a railroad from
New Castle to Freeport: from
Laughlinstown to Pittsburg...
Harrisburg, E. Guyer, 1837.
40 p. DLC; PBL.   46174

---- Constitutional Convention,
1837-1838.
    Convention director, contain-

ing the rules and orders of the
Convention....at Harrisburg,
Pennsylvania, May 2, 1837....
Harrisburg, Printed by Thompson
& Clark, 1837. 32 p. NIC;
NjR; PPL; PPM.   46175

---- ---- Journal of the Convention of the state of Pennsylvania,
to propose amendments to the
constitution, commenced and
held at the State capital in Harrisburg, on the second day of
May, 1837. Harrisburg, Printed
by Thompson & Clark, 1837-38.
2 v. CtHT; Ia; MH; PPi; RPL;
TxU.   46176

---- ---- Minority report of a
special committee, on the subjects
of the currency and corporations,
made by Mr. Ingersoll, Chairman:
read May 23, 1837: together
with the speech of Mr. Ingersoll,
on the subjects of impeachment
life offices and the powers of
the convention, made May 24,
1837. Harrisburg, Keystone
Office, 1837. (3)-17 p. MiD-B;
PHi; PPM; MH-BA.   46177

---- ---- Minutes of the committee of the whole of the convention of the state of Pennsylvania
to propose amendments to the
constitution, commenced and held
at the State Capitol in Harrisburg, on the second day of May,
1837. Harrisburg, printed by
Thompson & Clark, 1837. 289 p.
DLC; Ia; MH; NjR; PP.   46178

---- ---- Proceedings and debates of the Convention of the
commonwealth of Pennsylvania,
to propose amendment to the constitution, commenced ... at Harrisburg, on the second day of
May, 1837. Reported by John
Agg: stenographer to the convention; Assisted by Messrs.

Kingman, Drake, and M'Kinley
... Harrisburg, Printed by
Packer, Barrett, and Parke,
1837-38. 14 v. CtMW; IaU;
NBuU; NhD; OSW.   46179

---- ---- [Tagebuch] der convention von dem Staat Pennsylvanien, un verbesserungen
vorzuschlagen zu der constitution, angefangen und gehalten
im Staate Capitol zu Harrisburg,
am zweyten May 1837. Harrisburg, Gedruckt bey Joseph
Ehrenfried, 1837. v. MH-L;
PMA.   46180

---- ---- Verhandlungen und de-
batten der convention der Republic Pennsylvanien um berbes-
serungen zu der constitution
vorzuschlagen, angefangen zu
Harrisburg, Mai 2, 1837.
Berichtet von John Agg,
schnellschreiber, mit beihülfe
der Herren Wheeler, Kingman,
Drake, und M'Kinley. Harrisburg, G. Guyer, [1837-1839?].
v. DLC; MiD-B; PHi; PMA;
PP.   46181

---- Gen. Assem. Committee on
revenue bills.
Report...relative to repealing
the tax on dealers in foreign
merchandise; March 1, 1837.
Harrisburg, 1837. 7 p. PHi.
                          46182
---- ---- House.
Journal of the 47th House of
Representatives of the Commonwealth of Pennsylvania, commenced at Harrisburg, Tuesday,
the 6th of December, 1836....
Vol. I, Dec. 6, 1836 - April 4,
1837. Harrisburg, Printed by
Samuel D. Patterson, 1837.
1107, 71 p. PWmpDS.   46183

---- ---- ---- Committee appointed for the purpose of ascertaining the propriety of providing education for the deaf
and dumb.
Report of the committee appointed for the purpose of ascertaining the propriety of providing by law for the education
of all children born within this
commonwealth deaf & dumb;
read in the House...Feb. 2,
1837. Harrisburg, Patterson,
1837. 8 p. NjR; PPAmP; PP.
                          46184
---- ---- ---- Committee appointed to inquire into the best
mode of extending the Benefits
of Instruction to the Blind of
this Commonwealth.
Report of The Committee appointed to inquire into the best
mode of extending the Benefits
of Instruction to the Blind of
this Commonwealth. Mr. Johnston, Chairman. Read in The
House of Representatives, February 28, 1837. Harrisburg, printed
by Samuel D. Patterson, 1837.
(2)-4 p. MiD-B; PPPlB. 46185

---- ---- ---- Committee of Ways
and Means.
Report of the Committee Of
Ways And Means, upon that part
of the Governor's Message which
relates to the Surplus Revenue,
The State Debt, &c. Mr. Johnston, Chairman. Read in The
House of Representatives, January 10, 1837. Harrisburg,
Printed by Samuel D. Patterson,
1837. [3]-12 p. MiD-B. 46186

---- ---- ---- Committee to Visit
the Eastern Penitentiary and
House of Refuge in the County
of Philadelphia.
Report of the Committee appointed to visit and inquire into
the condition and circumstances
of the Eastern penitentiary and
the House of refuge, in the

county of Philadelphia, and the Moyamensing prison... Read in the House of representatives, February 14, 1837. Harrisburg, S. D. Patterson, 1837. 10 p. CU; MH-L; NN; PPAmP. 46187

---- ---- ---- Select Committee Relative to making free certain bridges over the River Schuylkill.
Report. Read into the House of Representatives, March 24, 1837. Harrisburg, S. D. Patterson, 1837. 7 p. NIC. 46188

---- ---- ---- Select Committee relative to Canals & Railways.
Report of the Select Committee relative to the Canals and Railways, together with the testimony taken in relation thereto. Mr. Hill, chairman. Read in the House of Representatives, March 27, 1837. Harrisburg, printed by Samuel D. Patterson, 1837. (4)-180 p. MiD-B; PPAmP. 46189

---- ---- Senate.
Journal of the Senate of Pennsylvania, session 1836-37. Vol. I. Dec. 6, 1836 to April 4, 1837. Harrisburg, Emanuel Guyer, Printer, 1837. 821, 49 p. PWmpDS. 46190

---- ---- ---- Report of the minority of the committee on the judiciary system, on the resolution to inquire into the expediency of providing by law to supply an alledged vacancy in the convention to alter & reform the state constitution, occasioned by the death of Dan Caldwell of the district composed of the counties of Union, Mifflin and Juniata, and to fill vacancies which may hereafter happen in such convention be-

fore the assembling of the same. Mr. Penrose, Chairman. Harrisburg, Emanuel Guyer, 1837. 13 p. MB; PHi; PPAmP. 46191

---- ---- ---- Committee to visit the Eastern Penitentiary and House of Refuge in the County of Philadelphia.
Report of the committee appointed to visit the Eastern State Penitentiary and House of Refuge in the County of Philadelphia...Mr. Read, chairman. Read in Senate, February 14, 1837. Harrisburg, E. Guyer, 1837. 7 p. CU; DNLM; NN; PPM. 46192

---- ---- ---- Select Committee Relative to Making Free Certain Bridges over the River Schuylkill.
Reports of the Select Committees of the Senate and House of Representatives of the State of Pennsylvania, relative to making free certain bridges over the River Schuylkill. Dr. Burden, chairman, Senate, Mr. Trego, chairman, House of Representatives. Read in the Senate, March 30, 1837. Read in the House of Representatives, March 24, 1837. Philadelphia, Printed by L. R. Bailey, 1837. 14 p. N. 46193

---- Governor.
Communication from The Governor, accompanied with a Communication From The Board of Canal Commissioners, transmitting the reports of Charles T. Whippo and Charles DeHass, Principal Engineers for a Rail Road from New Castle to Freeport, From Laughlintown to Pittsburg, from Lewistown to Hollidaysburg, and to avoid the inclined plane over The Allegheny Mountain to Pittsburg. Read in The House of

Representatives, January 20, 1837. Harrisburg, printed by Samuel D. Patterson, 1837. (4)-40 p. MiD-B; PPAmP.
46194

---- ---- Message from the Governor transmitting a communication from the president & managers of the...co. relative to avoiding the Schuylkill inclined planes of the Philadelphia & Columbia railroad, read in the House of Representatives, Mar. 4, 1837. Harrisburg, Patterson, 1837. 7 p. PPAmP; PHi.
46195

---- ---- Message of the Governor, read in the House of Representatives, of the Commonwealth of Pennsylvania, December 6, 1837. Harrisburg, Printed at the office of the Reporter, 1837. (3)-28 p. MiD-B.
46196

---- Laws, statutes, etc.
An act to consolidate and amend the several acts of assembly....Harrisburg, E. Guyer, Printer, 1837. 32 p. PPi-Hi.
46197

---- ---- 2d ed. Harrisburg, Guyer, 1837. 32 p. CtY; DLC; PPAmP.
46198

---- ---- Acts of the General Assembly of Pennsylvania concerning the Lehigh Coal and Navigation Company, together with the by-laws. Philadelphia, James Kay, Jun. and Brother, 1837. 79 p. NIC; NN; PBL.
46199

---- ---- A Digest of the revised code and Acts, forming a complete Digest of the Laws of Pennsylvania, to the present time. Philadelphia, James Kay Jun., & Brother, 122 Chestnut Street, Harrisburg; Packer, Barrett & Parke, Pittsburgh;

John I. Kay & Co., 1837. 984 p. In-SC.
46200

---- ---- Eine Akte zur Vereinigung und Abänderung der unterschiendlichen akten, betreffend ein allgemeines Unterrichts system durch Volksschulen, gebilligt den 13ten Juny, 1836...Harrisburg, Gedruckt bey J. Enrenfried, 1837. 42 p. DLC-P4.
46201

---- ---- Laws of the General assembly of the commonwealth of Pennsylvania, passed at the session of 1836-1837, in the sixty-first year of independence. Harrisburg, Printed by Theo Fenn, 1837. 412, 36 p. CU; IaU-L; MdBB; PAtM; PMA; Nj.
46202

---- Secretary of the Commonwealth.
Letter from the Secretary of the Commonwealth accompanied with a statement of number of institutions for banking incorporated by the Legislature of Pa., since 1776. Harrisburg, Printed by Thompson & Clark, 1837. PPi.
46203

---- ---- Report of the secretary of the commonwealth and auditory general, showing the name, official station, time of appointment ... Harrisburg, Thompson & Clarke, 1837. 11 p. OClWHi.
46204

---- ---- Report of the secretary of the commonwealth showing the number of persons executed and the number of pardons and remissions during the term of office of each Governor, since the adoption of the present constitution. Harrisburg, Thompson & Clark, 1837. 91 p. OClWHi.
46205

---- Treasury dept.

Report of the state treasurer, showing the expenditures, income, debts, and property of the commonwealth ... Harrisburg, Thompson & Clark, 1837. 11 p. OClWHi.   46206

---- University.

Trustees, Officers and Students in the collegiate department of the University of Pennsylvania. Philadelphia, 1837. 15 p. DLC; MHi.   46207

Pennsylvania & New Jersey Almanac for 1838. Philadelphia, Pa., Thomas L. Bonsal, [1837]. MWA.   46208

Pennsylvania and Ohio Canal Company.

Pennsylvania and Ohio canal company's charter. An act to incorporate the Pennsylvania and Ohio canal company. (Columbus, O., 1837?) 16 p. OClWHi.   46209

Pennsylvania Company for Insurances on lives & granting annuities. Philadelphia.

Circular, Mar. 13, 1837, Philadelphia, 1837. 2 p. PHi.
                               46210

---- Proposals...Incorporated March 10, 1812, with a perpetual charter. Philadelphia, printed by James Kay, Jun. & Bro., 1837. 16 p. MH-BA; OClWHi; PPAmP; PU.   46211

Pennsylvania Hospital.

The charter, laws, and rules of the Pennsylvania hospital. Phila., 1837. 31 p. WHi.   46212

---- Library.

Catalogue of the medical library. Philadelphia, Kite,

1837. 426 p. PP; PPL-R; PhGen Hos; PPCP.   46213

Pennsylvania Horticultural Society.

Programmes; or, lists of premiums & other titles. Philadelphia, 1837. PHi; PPAmP; PU.
                               46214

---- Report of the Tenth Exhibition of the Pennsylvania Horticultural Society. To which is added a List of Premiums awarded in ... 1837. Philadelphia, 1837. 16 p. PPAmP.
                               46215

Pennsylvania State Antislavery Society.

Address to the coloured people of the state of Pennsylvania. Merrihew and Gunn, 1837. 7 p. DLC; MiD-B; OClWHi; PHC; PHi.   46216

---- Proceedings of the Pennsylvania convention, assembled to organize a state anti-slavery society,...Philadelphia, Printed by Merrihew and Gunn, 1837. 97 p. MB; MH; OClWHi; PHi; TNF.   46217

---- Reports. 1st-. Philadelphia, 1837-. NNC; OU; PSt.
                               46218

Pennsylvania State Temperance Society.

Memorial of the Board of Managers of the Pennsylvania State Temperance Society, to the Convention for revising the constitution of the state of Pennsylvania. Philadelphia, Brown and Singnet, printers, 1837. 29 p. MB; MiU; NNUT; PHi; PU.
                               46219

Pennsylvania Temperance Almanac for 1838. Philadelphia, Pa., Penn. State Temperance Society, [1837]. MWA.   46220

Pennybacker, Isaac Samuels.
Speech of Mr. Pennybacker,
in the House of representatives
of the United States, September,
1837, on the Mississippi election. Washington, Blair and
Rives, 1837. 8 p. NNC; PPM.
46221

Penobscot Medical & Surgical
Association.
Constitution, By-laws &
Regulations of the Penobscot
Medical & Surgical Association.
Bangor, L. L. Smith, Printer,
1837. 12 p. IEN-M.   46222

People's Almanac for 1838.
(Vol. 1, no. 5.) Boston, Mass.,
S. N. Dickinson, [1837]. ICHi;
MWA.   46223

---- New-York, N.Y., Sold by
D. Felt & Co., [1837]. MWA.
46224
---- Philadelphia, Pa., Grigg
& Elliot, [1837]. MWA.   46225

A perfect description of Virginia...(Washington, P. Force,
1837). 18 p. DLC; KyU; MB;
NN; OCl.   46226

Perils of the sea; being authentic narratives of remarkable and
affecting disaster upon the deep
with illustrations of the power
and goodness of God in wonderful
preservations. New-York, Harper
& brothers, 1837. 205 p. TNP.
46227
Perkins, Aaron.
The doctrine of future punishment. Utica, Bennett &
Bright, 1837. 19 p. ICU;
NHC-S; NN.   46228

Perkins, Samuel.
The world as it is: Containing a view of the present condition of its principal nations....
with numerous engravings. By

Samuel Perkins. 2nd edition.
[New Haven], T. Belknap, 1837.
(13)-457 p. DLC; MoHi; CSMH;
NcU; TxU.   46229

Perrin, (J.)ean Baptiste, 1786.
A selection of one hundred
Perrin's fables, accompanied
with a key. A new edition.
Philadelphia, Carey, Lea, &
Blanchard, 1837. 1, 181 p.
MH; NRU.   46230

Perry, G. B.
The saints gain in glory. A
sermon delivered at the interment
of Mrs. Sarah C. Moseley. At
Canton, Illinois, October 30,
1837. By the Rev. G. B. Perry
... Canton, Illinois, Printed by
P. Stone, 1837. 28 p. OCHP;
DLC; N.   46231

Persiani, Giuseppe, 1799-1869.
Grand march in the opera
Danao. Philadelphia, Fiot,
Meignen & Co., (1837). 2 p.
MB.   46232

Persius, Flaccus Aulus.
Persius. Translated by The
Rt. Hon. Sir. W. Drummond,
Fellow of the Royal Societies of
London and Edinburgh. New-
York, Harper and Brothers,
1837. (17)-58 p. Ct; IaDmD;
MeBaT; NNS; PPL.   46233

A personal narrative of events
by sea and land, from the year
1800 to 1815, including the ex-
peditions to Ferrol and Egypt,
battle of Trafalgar, etc. By a
captain of the navy. Portsmouth,
printed by W. Harrison, 1837.
MH; PHi.   46234

Peter, Robert, M.D. & C., 1805-
1894.
Art. VII. - A Summary of
Meteorological Observations, made

during the latter six months of
the year 1836, in the City of
Lexington, Ky. By Robert
Peter, M.D. & C. (Reported
to the College of Physicians and
Surgeons), 1837. 17 p. CtY;
DAS; DNLM; KyU; MB.   46235

Peter Parley's almanac, 1837
....Boston, Otis, Broaders &
Co., (Tuttle, Weeks, & Den-
nett, printers), 1837. 74 p.
MMhHi.   46236

Peter Parley's almanac, for old
and young. Boston, printed
by Tuttle, Weeks and Dennert,
1837. 80 p. MBMu; MFai;
MHi.   46237

---- New York, Freeman, Heart
& Co., 1837. MWA.   46238

Petersburg female seminary.
Petersburg, Va.
    Annual catalogue, 1st
(1837/38). MH.   46239

Peterson, Henry.
    An address delivered before
the Junior anti-slavery society
of the city and county of Philadelphia, Dec. 23, 1836. Philadelphia, 1837. 12 p. MBAt;
PHC; WHi.   46240

[Peyton, Bailie].
    Speech relative to an examina-
tion of the deposite [sic] banks,
etc., in the house of representatives, Jan. 3, 1837. [Washing-
ton, 1837.] 5 p. WHi.   46241

Phelps, Almira [Hart] Lincoln,
1793-1884.
    Botany for beginners: an
introduction to Mrs. Lincoln's
lectures on botany.....By Mrs.
Phelps. Third edition. New
York, Published by F. J. Huntington & Co., 1837. 216 p.

MoSpD; MSaP; OO; TNP. 46242

---- Familiar lectures on botany,
practical, elementary and physiological; ... By Mrs. Almira H.
Lincoln....5th ed., rev. and
enl....New York, F. J. Huntington & co., 1837. 9-246, 186 p.
A-GS; MAm; MB; MH; Nh.
                              46243
---- Familiar lectures on natural philosophy, for the use
of schools. Mrs. A. H. Lincoln
Phelps, author of familiar lectures on botany, chemistry,
and geology for beginners, female student....New York, Published by F. J. Huntington and
Co., 1837. 280 p. CtMW; IaDaM;
IEG; MH; MikT.   46244

Phelps, Dudley.
    An Address, delivered Janu-
ary 24, 1830 in the Second
Baptist Meeting house in Haver-
hill preparatory to the organiza-
tion of the East Haverhill
Temperance Society. Haver-
hill, [1837?]. (1), 23 p. MHi.
                              46245
Phi Beta Kappa. New York
Alpha, Union university.
    Catalogue. 1837. Schenectady,
(etc.), 1837. MH; MWA; NN.
                              46246
Philadelphia, Bank Laws.
    An act to re-charter certain
banks. To which are added,
The by-laws of the Schuylkill
Bank in the City of Phila.
Philadelphia, R. P. DeSilver,
1837. 40 p. MiD-B.   46247

---- Citizens.
    Proceedings of a town meet-
ing of the citizens of the city
and county of Philadelphia, without distinction of party, held at
the county court room on Wednesday evening, December 6, 1837
to hear the report of their dele-

gates to the National Convention
of businessmen. Philadelphia,
John Wilbank, 1837. 16 p. PSt.
46248

---- City Commissioners.
Quarterly Reports, 1837-.
Philadelphia, 1837-. PHi;
PPAmP.   46249

---- Common Council. Journal.
Philadelphia, 1837-79. 17 v.
NIC.   46250

---- ---- Committee on legacies
& trusts.
Annual report made in Common council to which is appended a statement of all the
devises & bequests, & grants
made to the corporation of the
city of Philadelphia...[Phila-
delphia?] 1837-. PP; PPL-R;
PPAmP.   46251

---- ---- ---- Report of the
Committee, made in Common
Council, April 27, 1837. Mr.
Thomason, chairman. Phila-
delphia, printed by L. R.
Bailey, 1837. 28 p. MB; MH;
MiD-B; PPL-R.   46252

---- ---- Special report...on
the Boudinot lands...(&) on
the fire and hose establishments
...made in Common Council, the
14th & 28th of September,
1837... Phila., 1837. 16 p.
CtHWatk; MiD-B; PHi; PPL-R.
46253

---- County prison.
Answers to Questions sub-
mitted to the Inspectors of
the Philadelphia County Prison,
by the committee of the House
of Representatives. Philadelphia, 1837. 7 p. PHi.
46254

---- ---- Board of inspectors.
Report of the inspectors of
the Philadelphia County Prison

in relation to queries pronounced
by the committee of the House of
Representatives. Read in the
House, March 10, 1837. Harrisburg, Samuel Patterson, 1837.
10 p. CSmH.   46255

---- Fire Dept.
Oration on Centennial anniversary of organization of the
Fire Dept. of Phila. Philadelphia, 1837. 16 p. PHi. 46256

---- High School for Young
Ladies.
Half-sheet Periodical. Philadelphia, 1837. 18 p. PHC; PHi.
46257

---- Horticultural Society.
Report 18th Exhibition Sept.
1837. Philadelphia, 1837. OCHP.
46258

---- Library Company. Loganian
Library.
Catalogue of the books belonging to the Loganian library:
to which is prefixed a short account of the institution, with
the Law for Annexing the said
library to that belonging to
"The Library Company of Philadelphia," and the rules regulating
the manner of Conducting the
same. Philadelphia, C. Sherman
and Co., Printers, 1837.
450 p. CtMW; ICJ; MH; NBu;
PHi; MdBJ.   46259

---- Monument Cemetery.
Articles of association. Phila-
delphia, Thompson, 1837. 20 p.
MB; PPAmP; PPL; PPM. 46260

---- New Theatre.
Report of a committee of stockholders in the new theatre of
the city of Philadelphia, submitting new rules, regulations
and by-laws for the association.
[Philadelphia, 1837]. 12 p.
MH.   46261

---- Ordinances.

Ordinance to secure the un-
interrupted navigation of the
River Delaware, by the use of
a steam Ice Boat, and the by-
laws of the board of trustees.
Philadelphia, 1837. 10, 6 p.
PHi; PPL-R.   46262

---- Stock Exchange.

Rules and regulations of the
Philadelphia stock and exchange
board. [Philadelphia], C. A.
Elliott, printer, 1837. 8 p.
MH-BA.   46263

---- Third Presbyterian Church.

An historical sketch of the
Pine Street or Third Presbyterian Church...Philadelphia,
1837. PPL.   46264

---- United Brethren's Church.

Principles and discipline of
the United Brethren's Church
at Philadelphia, with an extract
of the twenty-one articles of
the Augustan or Augsburg Confession. Published by order of
the committee of the Church,
and sanctioned by the provincial helper's conferences for
Pennsylvania, and the adjacent
States. Philadelphia, Printed
by John Young, Black Horse
Alley, 1837. 19 p. PNazMHi.
                               46265
---- Watering Committee, 1836.

Annual Report of the Watering Committee, for the year
1836, to The Select and Common
Councils of The City of Philadelphia: to which are prefixed,
The Report for the year 1822,
and An extract from The Report
for 1823. Philadelphia, Printed
by L. R. Bailey, 1837. 56 p.
MH-BA; MHi; NBu; NRom.
                               46266
Philadelphia Almanac for 1838.
Calculations by William Collom.

Philadelphia, Pa., Uriah Hunt,
[1837]. MdHi; MWA.   46267

Philadelphia Association for the
Moral and mental improvement of
the people of color.

Minutes of proceedings at
the Council of the Philadelphia
association for the Moral and
Mental improvement of the people
of color. June 5th-9th, 1837.
Philadelphia, Merrihew and Gunn,
printers, 1837. 16 p. DHU; MB.
                               46268
Philadelphia Bar Association.

Catalogue of the books.
Philadelphia, 1837. 32 p. PHi.
                               46269
Philadelphia Ice Company.

Charter, April 4, 1837. With
by-laws, May 16, 1837. Philadelphia, 1837. 12 p. PHi; PPL-
R.   46270

Philadelphia Medical Society.

Report on the radical cure
of hernia. By the committee of
the Philadelphia medical society.
[Philadelphia, n. pub., 1837?]
48 p. MnHi; PU.   46271

No entry   46272

Philip, Robert, 1791-1858.

Devotional guides. By Rev.
Robert Philip,....with an intro-
ductory essay by Rev. Albert
Barnes. New York, D. Apple-
ton & Co., 1837. 2 v. ICP;
MBC; NbCrD; NNUT; ScCliTO;
MoSpD.   46273

---- The life and times of George
Whitefield, M.A. By Robert
Philip. New York, D. Appleton
& Co., 1837. 554 p. IU; MNS;
OM; PLT; PReaAT.   46274

---- The Lydias; or, the develop-
ment of female character. By
Robert Philip,....Second edition.
New York, D. Appleton & Co.,
1837 (-1841.) CtHC; MB; MH;
MiD; MoSpD. 46275

---- Manly piety, in its spirit.
By the Rev. Robert Philip...
With an introduction by Rev.
Albert Barnes. Philadelphia,
Presbyterian Committee, [1837?]
215 p. MiU; NBuG. 46276

---- The Marthas; or, The vari-
eties of female piety. 5th ed.
New York, D. Appleton, 1837.
251 p. MFiHi; MiD; MWA. 46277

---- The Marys; or, the beauty
of female holiness. 7 ed. New
York, 1837. DLC; MB; MiD.
46278
Phillips, John.
A report on the probability
of the occurrence of coal and
other minerals in the vicinity
of Lancaster. Lancaster, 1837.
PPAN. 46279

Phillips, Willard, 1784-1873.
The inventor's guide; comprising the rules, forms, and
proceedings for securing patent
rights, by Willard Phillips.
Boston, S. Colman; New York,
Collins, Keese, & Co., 1837.
9-368 p. ICBB; Me; NjR;
NNC; RP. 46280

---- The law of patents for inventions; with remedies and
legal proceedings in relation to
patent rights. Boston, American stationers company; New
York, Gould, Banks, and company, 1837. 540 p. CoU;
MH-L; MnU; NcD; PPB. 46281

Phillips, William, 1796-1836.
Campbellism exposed; or,

Strictures on the peculiar tenets
of Alexander Campbell. By Rev.
William Phillips ... to which is
prefixed a memoir of the author.
Cincinnati, J. F. Wright and L.
Swormstedt for the Methodist
Episcopal church, 1837. 267 p.
CSmH; IaAt; KSalW; NbOM;
TxU. 46282

Phillips Exeter Academy.
F.S.T. Catalogue of the
golden branch of Phillips Exeter
Academy. Boston, 1837. 12 p.
MH; NNC; OClWHi. 46283

The philosophy of animal magnetism: together with the system of manipulating adapted to
produce ecstasy and somnambu-
lism--the effects and the rationale.
By a gentleman of Philadelphia
....Philadelphia, Merrihew &
Gunn, 1837. 84 p. ICN; MH;
PHi; PPA; RPB. 46284

[Philp, Robert Kemp], 1819-1882.
Inquire within for anything
you want to know; or, Over
three-thousand seven hundred
facts worth knowing. ... New
York, Garrett, Dick & Fitzgerald,
1837. 434 p. WKenHi. 46285

Phinneys' Calendar, or Western
Almanac,... 1838.... By George
R. Perkins,... Cooperstown,
N.Y., Printed by H. & E. Phin-
ney, and sold by them whole-
sale and retail at their Book-
Store....[1837]. 36 p. DLC;
MWA; NN; WHi. 46286

Phipps, Joseph, 1708-1787.
A dissertation on the nature
and effect of christian baptism.
New York, 1837. 44 p. CtHT;
MBC; PHC. 46287

The pic nic and other papers.
The pic nic of Josephus, revised

and conected by Mum, the grand
musical soiree...Utica, [1837].
MH; NIC.   46288

Pickens, F[rancis] W[ilkinson],
1805-1869.
   Remarks of the Hon. F. W.
Pickens, on the separation of
the government from all banks.
Delivered in the House of representatives, Oct. 10, 1837. Washington, printed at the Globe office, 1837. 13 p. CU; MdHi;
MWA; PPM; ScU.   46289

---- Remarks on the subject of
the right of slaves to petition
congress, in the house of
representatives, Feb. 11, 1837.
Washington, 1837. 8 p. WHi.
                            46290
---- Speech on the resolution
proposing an inquiry into the
condition of the executive departments, in the house of
representatives, Jan. 3, 1837.
Washington, 1837. 12 p. WHi.
                            46291
Picket, Albert, 1770-1850.
   Pickets Class book No. 1.
New juvenile spelling book and
rudimental reader... Cincinnati,
Barnes and Carpenter, 1837. 168
p. OHi.   46292

---- Picket's Class-book, No. 2.
The New Juvenile Reader: ... 192
pp. Cincinnati, C. P. Barnes,
etc., 1837. CinPL; ICU; OC.
                            46293
---- Introduction to Picket's
Expositor; containing exercises
in English etymology....Being
the sequel to the author's
spelling book; and Part I-of
the New Juvenile instructor.
By A. Picket, and John W.
Picket, A.M. authors of the
American school class books....
Cincinnati, (Ohio), C. P.
Barnes, and C. Cropper,

1837. 216 p. IaHi; OC. 46294

---- The principles of English
grammar. By A. Picket, ...
and John W. Picket, A.M. ...
Cincinnati, Published by C. P.
Barnes;- and C. Cropper.
Stereotyped by J. A. James
and co., 1837. 213, (3) p.
DLC; NNC; OCHP; WU.   46295

Picnics; or, Legends, Tales,
and Stories of Ireland. ...
Philadelphia, E. L. Carey & A.
Hart, 1837. 9-186 p. NcU.
                            46296
Pictures and stories for children.
Boston, T. H. Carter, 1837.
12 pt. (in 1 v.). MH; PWcS.
                            46297
Pictures of animals. Northampton,
[Mass.], J. Metcalf, 1837. 18
p. IU.   46298

Pictures of the Kings of England,
... Boston, Munroe and Francis;
C. S. Francis, New York, 1837.
18 p. MB; MHa.   46299

Pierce, John, 1773-1849.
   Reminiscences of forty years,
delivered, 19 March, 1837, the
Lord's day after the completion
of forty years from his settlement in the ministry, in Brookline. By John Pierce ... Boston, Minot Pratt, printer, 1837.
35 p. CtSoP; ICN; MBr; MWA;
NNUT.   46300

Pierce, Willard, 1790-1860.
   Sermon ... mutual duties of
parents & children. Boston,
Perkins and Marvin, 1837. MB;
RPB.   46301

Pierpoint, John, 1785-1866.
   The "address to the people"
delivered at the installation of
H. A. Miles as pastor of the
South Congregational society,

Lowell, 14 Dec. 1836. Lowell, Norton's book and job printing office, 1837. 8 p. ICMe; MB; MeLewB; MiD-B; MWA. 46302

---- Angelic ministrations; sermon, Hollis street church, Boston, April 16, 1837. Boston, Weeks & Jordan & company, 1837. 17 p. InHi; MB; MWA; PU; RPB. 46303

---- ... A Discourse ... By John Pierpont. Boston, Tuttle, Weeks & Dennett, 1837. 30 p. MBBC. 46304

---- Introduction to the National reader. ... By John Pierpont. Compiler of the American first class book and the national reader, twenty-seventh edition. Boston, Published by Charles Bowen, 1837. 168 p. CtHWatk; MBarn; MH; MWC; NhD; NHem. 46305

---- Moral resurrection. A sermon preached at the ordination of the Rev. Oliver C. Everett, Northfield, Mass., Mar. 8, 1837. Boston, James Munroe & Co., 1837. 31 p. CtHC; ICMe; MH-And; MWiW; RPB. 46306

---- New heavens and a new earth. A discourse preached in Hollis street church, Jan. 1, 1837. Boston, Tuttle, Weeks and Dennett, 1837. 18 p. CtHC; ICN; MH-And; MWA; RPB. 46307

---- ... A sermon preached in Hollis Street Church, in Boston, Sunday, April 16, 1837, The spire of the church having been struck by lightning, on Saturday 8th of the month. By John Pierpont, Minister of that church. Published at the request of the proprietors. Boston, Weeks, Jordan & Co., 1837. 17 p. MBC; MiD-B. 46308

---- "The things that make for peace." A sermon preached in Hollis Street church. Sunday, 3rd. December, 1837. By John Pierpont. Boston, printed by Isaac Knapp, 1837. 15 p. CtHC; MBAt; MHi; MiD-B; MMeT. 46309

Pike, John Gregory, 1784-1854.
Guide for young disciples. New York, American Tract Soc., 1837. 465 p. IaPeC. 46310

Pike, Robert, Jr.
Intellectual chronology: in two parts, for schools and private learners. By Technica Memoria, [pseud.]. Montrose, Pa., Printed at the "Spectator" Office, 1837. 75 p. CtY; DLC; PScrHi. 46311

Pike, Stephen.
The teachers' assistant, or a system of practical arithmetic, wherein the several rules of that useful science are illustrated by a variety of examples...Philadelphia, M'Carty and Davis, 1837. 198 p. PPRF. 46312

Pinckney, Henry Laurens, 1794-1863.
An Oration on the Pleasures and Advantages of knowledges, and the Necessity of moral, as well as Mental Cultivation, to Individual Excellence and National Prosperity; delivered Before the Literary Societies of the University of Georgia, August 3d, 1837, By Henry L. Pinckney, of South Carolina, a member of the Phi Kappa Society. Athens, Printed at the office of the Southern Whig, 1837. 22 p. GMW; Gu-De; MH; ScU. 46313

---- Speech of Mr. Pinckney,
of South Carolina, delivered in
the House of representatives,
Feb. 21, 1837. On a proposition submitted by him to establish a navy yard and dry
dock at Charleston harbor,
South Carolina. (Washington,
D.C., 1837.) 8 p. DLC; MH;
ScC; ScU.   46314

---- Speech of the Hon. H. L.
Pinckney, of South Carolina,
on the Resolutions relating to
the Hon. John Quincy Adams,
of Massachusetts, Delivered in
the House of representatives,
February 6, 1837. Washington,
Printed by Gales and Seaton,
1837. 12 p. MH; ScU.   46315

Pindarus.
    Pindar, translated by the
Rev. C. A. Wheelwright, and
Anacreon, translated by
Thomas Bourne. [New York],
Harper & bros., [1837]. 2 v.
in 1. CSansS; GDecCT; MB;
NbOM; ViU.   46316

Pirates own book; authentic
narratives of the lives, exploits, and executions of the
most celebrated sea robbers.
With historical sketches of the
Jossamee, Spanish, Ladrone,
West India, Malay and Al-
gerine pirates. Portland, Sanborn & Carter; Philadelphia,
Thomas, Cowperthwait & co.,
[1837]. 432 p. CSf; MB;
MoK; OC; WHi.   46317

Pisani, Marianna.
    Vandeleur; or, Animal mag-
netism. A novel.... In two
volumes.... Philadelphia, Carey,
Lea and Blanchard, 1837. 2 v.
CSmH; DLC; MnH; TNP.   46318

Pise, Charles Constantine,

1802-1866.
    Address delivered before The
Philodemic Society of Georgetown
College, July 25, 1837, By
Charles Constantine Pise, D.D.
Washington, printed by Jacob
Gideon, Jr., 1837. 19 p. DLC;
MdHi; ScU.   46319

Pitkin, John Budd, 1802-1835.
    Sermons by Rev. J. B. Pit-
kin ... With a memoir of the
author, by Rev. S. G. Bulfinch.
Boston, David Reed, 1837. 352
p. MdW; MH-And; MMeT-Hi;
MNF; ViRut.   46320

Pitman, Johm.
    Discourse delivered at Provi-
dence August 5, 1836 ... being
the second centennial anniversary
of the settlement of Providence.
Providence, 1837. 72 p. NNC.
                         46321
Pittsburgh, Pa. Ordinances, etc.
    Ordinances passed by the Se-
lect and Common Councils since
the 29th day of April 1833,
with acts of assembly and judicial decisions relating thereto up
to the 1st of Jan., 1837.
[Pittsburgh], 1837. MH-L.
                         46322
Pittsburgh views; 26 illustrations
of early Pittsburgh, 1837-82, collected from various sources,
1837-82. Pittsburgh, [1837?].
PPi.   46323

Pittsfield, Mass. Berkshire
Medical Institution.
    Catalogue of the trustees,
overseers, faculty and students
of the Berkshire medical insti-
tution, ... Pittsfield, Mass. ...
Albany, Printed by Packard and
Van Benthuysen, 1837. 16 p.
CtY; NNN.   46324

Pixis, Johann Peter, 1788-1874.
    The Swiss bride ... National

air, with variations for the voice. Philadelphia, Fiot, Meignen & Co., (1837). 11 p. MB. 46325

Planché, James Robinson, 1796-1880.
Lavater the physiognomist. Boston, 1837. MB. 46326

[Plantagenet, Beauchamp].
A description of the province of New Albion and [a] direction for adventurers with small stock to get two for one, and good land freely ... Printed in the year 1648. [Washington, P. Force, 1837]. 35 p. CSt; IU; MnHi; RPB; TxU. 46327

Platts, John, 1775-1837.
(The) world's encyclopedia of wonders & curiosities of nature & art, science & Literature ... New ed. N.Y., Anderson, 1837. MH; NSyU; OCl. 46328

Playfair, John, 1748-1819.
... Elements of geometry, containing the first six books of Euclid. ... By John Playfair, F.R.S. ... From the last London ed., enl. New York, W. E. Dean, printer & publisher, 1837. 318 p. MH; MPeal; OAU; OWoc. 46329

A plea for voluntary societies, and a defence of the decisions of the General assembly of 1836, against the strictures of the Princeton reviewers and others. By a member of the assembly. New York, John S. Taylor, 1837. 187 p. CtHC; GDecCT; IEG; MiU; RPB. 46330

Pleasonton, Stephen.
Summary description of the light houses and watch lights, lighted on the coasts of France ...1837. Washington, 1837. PPAN. 46331

Plumbe, Samuel.
A practical treatise on the diseases of the skin, arranged with a view to their constitutional causes and local characters ... by Samuel Plumbe ... From the last London ed., rev., cor., considerably enl. ... Philadelphia, Haswell, Barrington, and Haswell, 1837. 396 p. CU; LNOP; MWHi; PPCP; TNP. 46332

Plumer, William Swan, 1802-1880.
Theatrical entertainments; a premium tract. Philadelphia, Baptist General Tract Society, [1837?] 28 p. CSmH; MiU; NcD; WU. 46333

Plutarch
Plutarch's lives, translated from the original Greek; with notes critical and historical, and a life of Plutarch. By John Langhorne, D.D., and William Langhorne, A.M. New York, Harper & Brothers, publishers, 1837. 748 p. MsOk; OO; ViU. 46334

Pocket letter writer... Ed. 2. Tr. Providence, 1837. 255 p. OHi. 46335

Pocock, Isaac, 1782-1835.
The omnibus, a laughable farce in one act. Philadelphia, etc., F. Turner, (1837?). 24 p. CtHWatk: mH. 46336

Political Portraits with Pen and Pencil of Thomas Hart Benton. Washington, D.C., Langtree & O'Sullivan, 1837. 8 p. NSyHi. 46337

Pollok, Robert, 1798-1827.
The course of time. A poem. By Robert Pollok, A.M. With a memoir of the author, by William Livingston Prall, Esq..... Philadelphia, James Kay, Jun. & Brother....1837. 256 p. IEG; MoSpD. 46338

Pond, Enoch, 1791-1881.
The Church. By Enoch Pond, D.D. ... Boston, Published by Whipple & Damrell, No. 9 Cornhill. New York; Scofield & Voorhies; Boston, William S. Damrell, printer, 1837. 9-126 p. CtHC; MBC; MH; MeBaT; MH-And. 46339

---- Probation. By Enoch Pond, D.D., Professor in the Theological Seminary, Bangor. Bangor, Duren and Thatcher; S. S. Smith, printer, 1837. 13-137 p. ICP; MeBat; MPiB; MWiW; OO. 46340

Poole, John, 1786?-1872.
Paul Pry's delicate attentions and other tales ... Philadelphia, Carey, 1837. 192 p. MiU; NSyHi; OClW; OrU. 46341

The poor law bill explained.... Wakefield, William Bittleston, printer, 1837. 8 p. M. 46342

Poor Richard's New Farmer's Almanack, ... 1838 .... Concord, N.H., Published by Roby, Kimball & Merrill, [1837]. 24 ℓ. MeHi; MWA; Nh-Hi; NjR; RPB. 46343

Poor Wills almanac, for the year, 1838, the second after bissextile or leap year. Carefully calculated for the latitude and meridian of Philadelphia, by William Collom. Philadelphia, Published by Joseph M'Dowell, [1837]. MWA; PPM. 46344

Pope, Alexander, 1688-1744.
Essay on man, in four epistles to H. St. John, Lord Bolingbroke. Ithaca, Mack, Andrus and Woodruff, 1837. 70 p. CtSoP; MshM; NIC; NN. 46345
---- ---- Portland, [Me.], W.

Hyde, 1837. 72 p. CSmH; MB; MH; MnU; PPL. 46346

---- ---- Watertown, N.Y., Printed and published by Knowlton & Rice, 1837. (1)10-47 p. CtY; KU; NN; NWattJHi. 46347

---- ---- Worcester, Published by Henry J. Howland. Dorr, Howland and Co., 1837. 48 p. MB; MWA; RBr. 46348

Popery as it now is, especially in America, two hundred important facts... 6th ed... New York, 1837. 32 p. Ct. 46349

Pope's journey to Heaven...a poem. Philadelphia, 1837. PPL. 46350

Poppo, (Ernst Friedrich), 1794-1866.
Poppo's Prolegomena on the peculiarities of Thucydidean phraseology, translated, abridged, and criticized by George Burges ... who has subjoined an appendix postscript and supplements on the merits of the mss., the use of the scholia, the value of Valla's version and the inveterate corruptions of the text. Cambridge? Printed by and for J. Hall; (etc., etc., 1837). MBBC; MH. 46351

Portage Canal & Manufacturing Company.
An act to incorporate the Portage canal & manufacturing company Passed the twenty-seventh day of February, 1837. [1837?] 9 p. OClWHi. 46352

---- Charter of the Portage canal and manufacturing company, with the official circular of the commissioners, and other papers relating thereto. New-York, Piekcy & Read, 1837. 36 p. MH-BA; NCH; NN; OClWHi; OHi. 46353

Porter, Anna Maria, 1780-1832.
The Hungarian brothers.
... Exeter, N.H., Vol. I: Pub-
lished by J. C. Gerrish, 1832;
Vol. II: Published by J. & B.
Williams, 1837. 2 v. CSmH.
46354
Porter, Benjamin F.
Substance of the remarks of
Benjamin F. Porter, on the bill
for the better regulation of
trade, in the city of Mobile.
Delivered in the House of representatives of Alabama. Tuscaloosa, Slade and Handley,
printers, 1837. 32 p. TxU.
46355
Porter, Ebenezer, 1772-1834.
The rhetorical reader. 21st
edition. Andover, Gould and
Newman, etc., etc., 1837. MH.
46356
---- ---- ... Ed. 23. An-
dover, Mass., Gould & Newman, 1837. 304 p. MHa. 46357

---- ---- 24th edition. Andover,
Gould and Newman, etc., etc.,
1837. MB; MH.   46358

---- ---- 27th ed. Andover,
Gould and Newman, etc., etc.,
1837. MH; MShr.   46359

---- ---- 28th edition. Andover,
Gould and Newman, etc., etc.,
1837. MH.   46360

---- ---- 29th ed. with an appendix. Andover, Gould & Newman, 1837. (13), 304 p. MBE.
46361
Porter, James Madison.
Speech ... in the convention
of Pennsylvania on the subject
of the right to annul charters
of incorporation, delivered Nov.
20, 1837. Philadelphia, Peter
Hay and company, printers,
1837. 59 p. MBAt; MnHi;
OClWHi; PPM; WHi.   46362

Porter, Jane, 1776-1850.
The Scottish chiefs: a ro-
mance. By Miss Jane Porter.
Hartford, Conn., Andrees, Judd,
& Franklin, 1837. 719 p.
46363
---- Thaddeus of Warsaw. In
two vols. By Miss Porter....
Exeter, Published by J. & B.
Williams, 1837. 2 v. NbHM;
OCM.   46364

---- ---- ... Sandborton, N.H.,
C. Lane, 1837-1838. 2 v. CtY;
WU.   46365

Porteus, Beilby, 1731-1808.
A summary of the principal
evidences for the truth and divine origin of the Christian
revelation.....By Beilby Porteus,
D.D. Bishop of London. With
notes and questions, by Robert
Emory. New York, Published by
T. Mason and G. Lane, 1837.
94 p.   46366

---- ---- Norwich, T. Robinson,
1837. 120 p. CtHC; InCW;
OMC; OO.   46367

Portland, Me. Directories.
The Portland Directory, containing the names of the inhabitants....Portland, A. Shirley,
printer, 1837. 105 p. MBNEH;
MeHi.   46368

---- Free Street Baptist Church.
Declaration of Faith, ... Free
Street Baptist Church, Portland.
... Portland, Printed by Charles
Day and Co., 1837. 16 p.
MeHi.   46369

Portland Sacred Music Society.
Act of incorporation and by-
laws of the Portland sacred music society. Formed May, 1836.
... Portland, Printed at the Orion
office, 1837. 14 p. MeBa; MeHi.
46370

Portland transcript; ... v. 1-62,
1837-1899. Portland, Gould &
Elwell [etc.], 1837-1899. 62 v.
TxU.   46371

A portrait of the character and
conduct of Aaron Dow, and Nathaniel S. Magoon.... Boston,
n. pub., n. pr., 1837. 8 p.
NjR.   46372

Portraits of the Principal Reformers. New York, O. Wells,
1837. ICMe.   46373

Portsmouth (N.H.) Male High
School.
   Catalogue of the officers and
students for the fall term 1837.
Portsmouth, 1837. Nh-Hi.
                              46374
(Potter, Elisha Reynolds), 1811-
1882.
   Brief account of emissions
of paper money made by the
Colony of Rhode Island. Provi-
dence, Published by John E.
Brown, 1837. 48 p. CtSoP;
ICU; MB; PPL; RNR.   46375

Potter, Horatio, 1802-1887.
   The importance of liberal
tastes & good intellectual habits
as a provision for pure &
permanent enjoyment; being an
introductory lecture, delivered
on the 5th December, 1837, before the Young men's association of Troy...Troy, N.Y.,
Tuttle, Belcher & Burton, 1837.
29 p. CtHT; MH; MWeA; NBu.
                              46376
---- Intellectual liberty; or,
truth to maintained by reason,
not by physical power: a discourse ... by the Rev. Horatio Potter ... Albany, Packard
and Van Benthuysen, 1837.
16 p. CtHC; MBAt; NBuDD;
NjR; PPPrHi.   46377

Potter, O. W.
   Memoir of A. M. Slade, embracing a journal. Written by
herself; and other circumstances
of her life taken from the notes
and lips of her friends. Fall
River, W. Canfield, 1837. 14 p.
MH.   46378

---- ---- 2nd ed. William Canfield, Printer, Fall River, Sept.
1837. 14 p. MB; MH; MWA;
MTaHi; NNC.   46379

Poughkeepsie Almanac for 1838.
Poughkeepsie, N.Y., Potter and
Wilson, (1837). MWA.   46380

No entry   46381

Poyen Saint Sauveur, Charles.
   A letter to Col. Wm. L. Stone
of New York, on the facts re-
lated in his letter to Dr. Brigham,
and a plain refutation of Durant's
exposition of animal magnetism,
&c. By Charles Poyen. With
remarks on the manner in which
the claims of animal magnetism
should be met and discussed.
By a member of the Massachusetts
bench. Boston, Weeks, Jordan
and company; New York, C.
Shepard, 1837. 72 p. CtY-M;
ICN; MH; PHi; WHi.   46382

---- Progress of animal magnetism
in New England; being a collection of experiments, ... pre-
ceeded by a dissertation on the
proofs of animal magnetism.

Boston, Weeks, Jordan & co.,
1837. 212 p. MBAt; MH; NH;
NIC; NNQ.   46383

A practical plan for a national
& state currency. Oct. 1837.
New York, printed by Spinning
and Hodges, (1837). 8 p. DLC;
MH-BA; PU.   46384

Pratt, Luther.
    Exposition of the constitution
of the United States...Albany,
at "Common School Depository,"
1837. MH; MH-L.   46385

Pratt, Parley Parker, 1807-1867.
    A voice of warning and in-
struction to all people, containing a declaration of the faith
and doctrine of the church of
the Latter Day Saints, commonly called Mormons...N.Y.,
Printed by W. Sandford, 1837.
216 p. CtHWatk; ICJ; NPStA;
OClWHi; WHi.   46386

Pray, Isaac Clarke, 1813-1869.
    An Address delivered before
the Mercantile Library Association on its seventeenth Anniversary, in the.... By Isaac
C. Pray, Jr., a Poem, by Lovet
Stimson, Jr.... Boston,
Printed for the Association,
1837. 37 p. DLC; ICMe; MH;
TxU; WHi.   46387

---- Poems: by Isaac C. Pray,
Jr. Boston, Weeks, Jordan and
Co., 1837. (3)-42 p. MB;
MWH; NNC; NRU.   46388

Prentiss, Sergeant Smith.
    Speech of S. S. Prentiss,
in the House of Representatives
of the state of Mississippi on
Mr. Bingaman's resolution in-
viting the delegates from the
new counties to take their seats.
Vicksburg, printed at the Sen-

tinel and Expositor Office, 1837.
16 p. MH.   46389

Presbyterian church. U.S.A.
    The constitution of the Pres-
byterian church, in the U.S.A.:
containing the confession of faith,
the catechisms [!] and the directory for the worship of God.
Together with the plan of Government and Discipline ... Philadelphia, Alex. Towar, [etc.],
1837. 466 p. CSmH; ICN;
OClW; OrU; PPPrHi.   46390

---- The form of government,
the discipline, and the directory
for worship, of the Presbyterian
church in the United States of
America. Philadelphia, Alexander Towar, 1837. GDecCt;
PPPrHi.   46391

---- Board of education.
    Annual report of the board of
education of the general assembly
of the Presbyterian Church, in
the United States presented May,
1837. Philadelphia, published
for the Board, 1837. 15 p.
ICJ; MB; OMC; ViW; WU.
                                   46392
---- Convention. Auburn, N.Y.,
1837.
    Minutes of the...held August
17, 1837, to deliberate upon the
doings of the last General Assembly in relation to the Synod
of Western Reserve, Utica,
Geneva & Genesee & the third
presbytery of Phila. Auburn,
Oliphant, 1837. 36 p. MB;
NAut; OCHP; PPPrHi; PHi.
                                   46393
---- ---- Pittsburgh, 1835.
    Minutes of the Philadelphia
convention of ministers and ruling
elders in the Presbyterian Church
in the United States called by
the minority of the General Assembly of 1836, May 11, 1837.

Philadelphia, Pub. for the convention, 1837. 31 p. IEG; NbOP; NN; TxHuT; ViRut.
46394

---- General Assembly.
Original draft of a pastoral address from the eastern subordinate synod of the reformed presbyterian church. N.Y., 1837. 32 p. NNC.   46395

---- ---- Pastoral and circular letters of the General assembly of 1837. Philadelphia, n. pub. Printed by L. R. Bailey, 1837. 14 p. NjR; PHi; PPPrHi; TxU.
46396

---- ---- A plea for voluntary societies, and a defence of the decisions of the general assembly of 1836, against the strictures of the Princeton reviewers and others. New York, J. S. Taylor, 1837. 187 p. MBC; RPB.   46397

---- ---- Remarks on the act of the General assembly of 1837, declaring four synods to be "neither in form nor in fact, an integral portion of the Presbyterian church of these United States: ... by a Presbyterian of Virginia. Richmond, N. MacFarlane, 1837. 40 p. IEG; MBC; NcD; PPPrHi. 46398

---- ---- A review of the proceedings of the General assembly of the Presbyterian church in the United States. n.p., n. pub., n. pr., 1837. 40 p. CSansS; NjR.   46399

---- Presbyteries. Oneida.
Confession of faith and covenant, adopted by the Presbytery of Oneida, February, 1831.... Utica, R. Northway, Jr., 1837. 12 p. MBAt; MWA.
46400

---- Synods. New Jersey.
Minutes of the Synod of New Jersey, for the year ending October, 1837. Newark, Published by order of the Synod under the direction of the stated clerk. Printed by Aaron Guest, 1837. 28 p. MBC.   46401

---- ---- Philadelphia.
Declaration of the Sabbath. [Philadelphia? 1837?] 4 p. IU.
46402
Prescott, William Hickling, 1796-1859.
Prescott's Ferdinand and Isabella. By William H. Prescott. In two volumes. New York, John B. Alden, publisher, 1837-1838. MRoxSPP.   46403

A Present from New York! Containing many pictures worth seeing, and some things worth remembering. New York, M. Day, 1837. 23 p. MB. 46404

Pressly, John Taylor, 1795-1870.
An address to the students of the theological seminary of the associate reformed synod of the west, at the opening of the session, December 4, 1837... Pittsburgh, William Allinder, 1837. 15 p. ICHi; OClWHi; PPPrHi.   46405

---- ---- 2nd ed. Pittsburgh, Printed by William Allinder, 1837. 16 p. ICHi; ICP; NbOP; NjR.
46406
The Pressure and its causes; being the old fashioned notions of an old fashioned man. Boston, Otis, Broaders & Co., 1837. 69 p. M; MH; OCHP; WHi.   46407

---- 2d ed. Boston, Otis, Broaders & company, 1837. 69 p. M; MH; MHi.   46408

Preston, Jonas.
The accounts of Jane Preston, John R. Thomas & Eli K. Price. Executor of Jonas Preston and Trustees under the last will and testament of Dr. Jonas Preston. Also resolutions adapted by the Board of The Preston Retreat. Philadelphia, 1837. 20 p. PHi.
46409

Preston, Lyman, b. 1795.
The book-keeper's diploma: or, A full and lucid treatise on the equation of payments. By Lyman Preston... New York, Stereo. by Francis F. Ripley, 1837. 32 p. DLC; IU; MH: NNC; VtMidSM.   46410

---- Preston's complete time table: showing the number of days from any date in any given months to any date in any other month; embracing upwards of 130 thousand combinations of dates ... New York, R. and R. S. Woods, 1837. (24) p. NCaS; RP; VtU.   46411

---- Cubical estimates of boxes, bales, and casks, adapted to the use of merchants and carriers, [1837?] MH.   46412

---- Preston's table's of interest at six per cent ... New York, R. and G. S. Wood, 1837. 220 p. CtY; NcU; RP.
46413
---- Preston's treatise on bookkeeping; or arbitrary rules made plain: in two parts, adapted to the use of academies and common schools, with varied examples accompanied with detailed explanations, by Lyman Preston. New York, Robinson, Pratt and company, 1837. 2 v. in 1. 168 p. MH; MoSU; OclW; RP.   46414

Preston, William Campbell, 1794-1860.
Speech of Mr. Preston, of South Carolina, on the bill to provide for the collection and safe keeping of the public revenue. In the United States Senate, September 29, 1837. Columbia, S.C., Telescope print, 1837. 19 p. ScU.   46415

---- Speech on the resolution of Mr. Benton to expunge a part of the journal of the senate of the session of 1833-34, delivered in the senate of the United States, Jan. 13, 1837. Washington, Duff Green, 1837. 8 p. DLC; MBAt; WHi.   46416

Preston Retreat. Philadelphia.
Charter ... with rules and regulations adapted for the government of the same together with an extract from the will of Dr. Jonas Preston ... [Philadelphia? 1837?] 3 p. DL; PHi; PPL.   46417

Price, Ebenezer.
A funeral discourse, delivered December 27, 1836, at the interment of the Rev. Samuel Wood, D.D., pastor of the First Congregational Church in Boscawen. By Ebenezer Price, ... Concord, Printed by David Kimball, 1837. 24 p. CtSoP; MHi; MiD-B; OMC; RHi.   46418

[Price, Eli Kirk], 1797-1884.
The address delivered at the laying of the corner-stone of the Preston retreat, July 17, 1837. Philadelphia, J. Richards, 1837. 12 p. DLC; MdBJ; MdBJ-W; NN; PPL-R.   46419

Price, Jacob F.
Both sides; or, Falsehood detected & exposed, being an ex-

posure of Elder Wm. Hunter's
conduct...during the debate
between Mr. Stiles and Mr.
Johnson... Frankfort, Ky.,
Hodges, 1837. PPPrHi.   46420

Prichard, James Cowles, 1786-
1848.
    A treatise on insanity and
other disorders affecting the
mind. By James Cowles
Prichard ... Philadelphia, Haswell, Barrington, and Haswell,
1837. 337 p. CSt-L; Nh;
PPA; ScCMe; ViW.   46421

Priest, Josiah, 1788-1851.
    American antiquities and
discoveries in the west ... 5th
ed. Albany, Hoffman and
White, 1837. 400 p. IEG; KU;
NN.   46422

Priest, Josiah, 1788-1851.
    The Anti-universalist; pr,
history of the fallen angels of
the scriptures; proofs of the
being of satan and of evil spirits.... In two parts. Albany,
printed by J. Mansell, 1837. 2
v. in 1. GAGTh; MH; MMeT;
PU; TxHR.   46423

Priest, Josiah, 1788-1851.
    Stories of early settlers in
the wilderness, embracing the
life of Mrs. Priest, late of Otsego county, N.Y., with various and interesting accounts of
others, the first raftsmen of the
Susquehannah, a short account
of Brant, the British Indian
chief and of the massacre of
Wyoming. Albany, 1837. 40
p. CSmH; CtHWatk; ICN; NCH;
WHi.   46424

The Primary Reader: Being
Easy Lessons For Young Chil-
dren. By The Compiler Of The
"Western Primer," & "Elementary

Reader." Cincinnati, Burgess &
Crane, 1837. 144 p. KyBC.
                           46425
Prime, Nathaniel S.
    Charge to Rev. Samuel Irena-
eus Prime .... at his installation
as pastor of the First Presby-
terian church of Matteawan, N.Y.
... By Nathaniel S. Prime....
Newburgh, n. pub., printed by
J. D. Spalding, 1837. 22 p.
ICP; MBC; MHi; NjR; PPPrHi.
                           46426
Prime, William Cowper.
    Tent life in the Holy Land.
By Wm. C. Prime. New York,
New York, Harper, 1837. 498
p. OOxW.   46427

Prince George's County Agricul-
tural Society. Proceedings...
Upper Marlbro, 1837. PPL.
                           46428
Princeton University. American
Whig society.
    Catalogue of the honorary
and graduate members of the
American Whig society instituted
in the college of New Jersey.
Princeton, John Bogart, 1837.
16 p. NN; NjR.   46429

---- Cliosophic society.
    Catalogue of the Cliosophic
society instituted in the college
of New Jersey. New York,
William Osborn, 1837. 29 p.
NjR; NNC; PPL.   46430

Prindle's almanac, for the year
of our Lord 1838: ... Calculated for the meridian of New
Haven, ... By Charles Prindle,
successor to Andrew Beers.
New Haven, ... (1837). (28) p.
CtW; MWA.   46431

Prior, James, 1790?-1869.
    The life of Oliver Goldsmith,
from a variety of original sources.
Philadelphia, E. L. Carey & A.

Hart, 1837. 17-550 p. IaDuU;
MB; PPA; RNR; WaU. 46432

Proceedings of convention for
the promotion of common school
education, with the formation
of a society for furthering the
interests of common schools, and
as address, delivered at the annual meeting of the society, by
Hon. C. Barland, Jr.
Charles U. Cushman, Printer,
Newburgh, 1837. 23 p. N.
46433

Proceedings of the convention,
upon the subject of an immediate enlargement of the Erie
canal; held at the court-house
in Rochester, on the 18th
and 29th days of January,
1837. Buffalo, Charles Foxon,
printer, 1837. 28 p. NUtHi.
46434

The progressive reader or juvenile monitor. ... Stereotyped
by Fisk & Chase, Concord,
N.H. Montpelier, Vt., Published by George W. Hill, 1837.
216 p. MH; Nh-Hi; NNC. 46435

Prolix, Peregrine. See Nicklin,
Philip Holbrook.

Protection Insurance Company.
Instructions and explanations
for the use and direction of the
agents of the Protection Insurance Company. Hartford, Hudson and Skinner, Printers, 1837.
28 p. ScHi. 46436

---- New book of instruction
for the use and direction of the
agents of the Protection insurance company in the western
states. Cincinnati, N. S. Johnson, printer, 1837. 44 p. OCHP.
46437

Protestant Episcopal church in
the U.S.A.
Journal of the proceedings
of the sixth annual convention
of the Protestant Episcopal
church, in the Diocese of Alabama, held in Greensborough,
on Saturday, June 10th, 1837.
Mobile, Morning Chronicle, 1837.
14 p. AU; MBD. 46438

---- Board of missions.
Proceedings of the Board ...
at their 2nd annual meeting held
in the city of Baltimore ... with
the reports of the ... committees and the accounts of ...
treasurers. New York, W. Osborn, printer, 1837. 130 p.
CtHT; MHi; MnHi; NBuDD;
TSewU. 46439

---- Book of common prayer.
Book of common prayer, and
administration of the sacraments
and other rites and ceremonies
of the church, according to the
use of the Protestant Episcopal
church in the United States of
America; together with the Psal-
ter or Psalms of David. Philadelphia, Desilver, 1837. 531,
248 p. CtHT. 46440

---- ---- ---- Philadelphia, Female Protestant Episcopal prayer-
book society of Pennsylvania,
1837. 531, 248 p. CtY-D;
MBD; MiU-C; MnHi; NHem.
46441

---- ---- ---- Philadelphia, W.
Marshall and co., 1837. 283 p.
IEG; WMMt. 46442

---- ---- Oneida.
A prayer book, in the lan-
guage of the six nations of In-
dians containing the morning
and evening service by Rev.
Solomon Davis of the Protestant
Episcopal Church: ... New
York, Swords Stanford & Co.,
D. Fanshaw, printer, 1837.
168 p. CtSoP; IaB; MWA; NSy;
PPP; WHi. 46443

---- Catechism.

A catechism, to be used by the teachers in the religious instruction of persons of colour ... Selected from a little catechism prepared in England ... Prepared ... under the direction of the bishop. Charleston, A. F. Miller, 1837. 106 p. CU; DLC; MBD; MiU-C; NcD; ScU.   46444

---- Chicago (Diocese).

Journal of the Third Annual Convention of the Protestant Episcopal Church, in the Diocese of Illinois, held in Springfield, May 15th and 16th, 1837. Peoria, S. H. Davis, Printer, 1837. 16 p. CSmH; MBD; NBuDD; NN; IHi.   46445

---- Connecticut (Diocese).

Journal Of The Proceedings Of The Annual Convention Of The Protestant Episcopal Church, In The Diocese of Connecticut Held In Trinity Church And St. Paul's Chapel, New Haven, June 13th and 14th 1837. New Haven, Printed By Hitchcock & Stafford, 1837. 56 p. CtHC; MBD; MiD-B.
                                   46446

---- Convention.

Journal of the Proceedings of the Annual Convention of the Protestant Episcopal Church, Grace Church, New Bedford. Boston, James B. Dow, 1837. 20 p. MBD.   46447

---- Delaware Diocese.

Journal of the Proceedings of the Forty-Seventh Annual Convention, of the Protestant Episcopal Church of the Diocese of Delaware, 1837. Wilmington, Printed by R. & J. B. Porter, 1837. 8 + 16 p. MBD; MoWgT; RPB.   46448

---- Eastern Diocese.

Journal of the proceedings of the annual convention...in the eastern diocese...Boston, James B. Dow, 1837. 20 p. MiD-B; RPB.   46449

---- Georgia Diocese.

Journal of the proceedings of the 15th annual convention ... together with the Constitution and Canons of said church. Savannah, W. T. Williams, 1837. 23 p. RPB.   46450

---- Hymnal.

Hymns of the Protestant Episcopal church in the United States of America. Set forth in general convention of said church, in the year of our Lord, 1739, 1808, and 1826. Standard stereotyped ed. New York, Swords, Stanford & company, 1837. 132 p. NbOP.   46451

---- Kentucky (Diocese).

Journal of the Proceedings of the Ninth Convention of the Protestant Episcopal Church in the Diocese of Kentucky. Lexington, Ky., Printers, J. C. Noble & Co., 1837. 98 + 2 p. IHi; MBD; MiD-B.   46452

---- Kentucky Theological Seminary.

Charter. Regulations, Course of Study, etc. of the Theological Seminary of the Protestant Episcopal Church in the State of Kentucky. Lexington, Ky., Intelligencer Print, 1837. 9 p. MBD; MdBD; MH; MHi; MoWgT.

---- Maryland (Diocese).

Journal of a Convention of the Protestant Episcopal Church of Maryland, Held in Saint Paul's Church, Baltimore, Printers, Jas. Lucas & E. K. Deaver, 1837. 56 p. MBD.   46454

---- Massachusetts Diocese.
Considerations of the Eastern
diocese. By a presbyter of
the diocese of Mass. Boston,
Dutton and Wentworth, printers,
1837. 35 p. MBD; MiD-B.
46455

---- ---- Journal of the Pro-
ceedings of the Forty-Seventh
Annual Convention of the
Protestant Episcopal Church
in the Commonwealth of Massa-
chusetts...With an Appendix.
Boston, Protestant Episcopal
Press. Torrey & Blair, Print-
ers, 1837. 59 p. MBD; MiD-
MCh.   46456

---- Mississippi (Diocese).
Journal of the proceedings
of the annual convention of the
Protestant Episcopal church in
the state of Mississippi: held
in Trinity church, Natchez,
Wednesday, May 3, 1837. New
York, printed at Protestant
Episcopal press, 1837. 11 p.
LU; MiD-B; NBuDD.   46457

---- New Hampshire (Diocese).
Journal of the Proceedings
of the Thirty-Seventh Convention of the Protestant Episcopal
Church in the State of New-
Hampshire, 1837. Concord,
N.H., Printed by Asa McFar-
land, 1837. 9 p. MBD; MiD-B.
46458

---- New Jersey (Diocese).
An appendix containing the
constitution and canons of the
Protestant Episcopal church in
the United States of America;
the constitution and canons of
the diocese of New Jersey.
Burlington, Missionary press,
1837. 71 p. MiD-MCh; NBuDD;
NjR.   46459

---- New York (Diocese).
Journal of The Proceedings of
the Fifty-Second Convention of
the Protestant Episcopal Church
in the State of New-York A.D.
1837. Printed at the Protestant
Episcopal Press, New York, 1837.
131 + 32 p. MBD; NBuDD;
NGH; RPB.   46460

---- Ohio (Diocese).
A form of prayer and thanks-
giving, set forth and appointed
to be read in the Episcopal
churches in the diocese of Ohio.
... Gambier [Ohio], George W.
Myers, printer, 1837. 4 p.
CSmH.   46461

---- ---- Journal of the proceed-
ings of the twentieth annual con-
vention...in Trinity Church,
Columbus, on Thursday the 14th,
Friday the 15th, and Saturday
the 16th days of September,
A.D. 1837. Gambier, Acland
Press. - George W. Myers, Pr.,
1837. 68 p. MBD; MiU-B;
NBuDD; NN; OMC.   46462

---- Pennsylvania (Diocese).
Journal of the Proceedings of
the Fifty-Third Convention of the
Protestant Episcopal Church in
the State of Pennsylvania Held
in St. Andrew's Church, in the
City of Philadelphia. On Tuesday, May 16, Wednesday May 17,
and Thursday, May 18, 1837.
Philadelphia, Published by Order
of the Convention, Jesper Harding,
Printer, 1837. 93 p. MiD-MCh;
NBuDD; RPB.   46463

---- Rhode Island (Diocese).
Journal of the Proceedings of
the forty-seventh Annual Convention of the Protestant Episcopal Church of the State of Rhode
Island, held in St. Mark's Church,
Warren, on Tuesday, June 13,
and Wednesday, June 14, A.D.
1837. Providence, H. H. Brown,

1837. 32 p. NBuDD; RWe.
46464
---- South Carolina (Diocese).
Journal of the Proceedings
of the 48th Annual Convention
of the Protestant Episcopal
Church in the Diocese of South
Carolina. Charleston, Printed
by A. E. Miller, 1837. 39 p.
MBD; NN.   46465

---- Tennessee (Diocese).
Journal of the Proceedings of
the Ninth Annual Convention of
the Clergy and Laity of the
Protestant Episcopal Church, in
the diocese of Tennessee: Held
in Christ Church, Nashville,
on the 11th, 12th, 13th, 14th,
& 16th days of October, 1837.
Nashville, S. Nye & Co.,
Printers, 1837. 44 p. ICN;
MBD; MnHi; NN.   46466

---- Vermont (Diocese).
Journal of the Proceedings of
the Forty-Seventh Annual Con-
vention, of the Protestant Epis-
copal Church in the Diocese of
Vermont; ... Burlington, Hiram
Johnson & Co., 1837. 52 p.
ICN; ICW; MBD; MiD-B; NBuDD.
46467
---- Virginia (Diocese).
Journal of the Convention of
the Protestant Episcopal Church
of the Diocese of Virginia which
Assembled in the Town of
Petersburg, May 17th, 1837.
Richmond, Va., Printed by
B. R. Wren, Southern Church-
man Office, 1837. 48 p. MBC;
MBD; MiD-B; NBuDD; NcU.
46468
Providence, R.I.
A list of persons assessed
in the City Tax of forty-five
thousand dollars, ordered by
the City Council, June, 1837.
With the amount of valuation
and tax of each. Providence,

Published by H. H. Brown, 1837.
52 p. RHi.   46469

---- Athenaeum.
Annual reports ... Providence,
1837-1938. 97 v. WHi. 46470

---- ---- Catalogue of the
Athenaeum Library; with an appendix containing the library
regulations and a list of the
officers and proprietors. Providence, Knowles, Vose and Company, 1837. 116 p. CU-S;
DLC; MH-L; RPA; WHi. 46471

---- Central Baptist Church.
Sketch ... with a list of members. Providence, H. H. Brown,
printer, 1837. 36 p. RPB;
RHi.   46472

---- City Council.
Reports upon the expediency
of a new organization of The
Public Schools, presented to the
City Council of Providence, by
their Committee appointed Sep-
tember 25, 1837. Providence,
Printed by E. A. Marshall, 1837.
15, (1) p. MH; RHi; RPB.
46473
---- High Street Congregational
church.
Confession of faith and cove-
nant. Providence, B. Cranston
& Company, 1837. 16 p. RPB.
46474
---- Pine Street Second Baptist
Church.
A Sketch of the Pine-Street
(2d) Baptist Church, in Provi-
dence, with a List of Members.
Providence, H. H. Brown,
Printer, 1837. 36 p. RHi.
46475
---- Warren St. Chapel.
Report ... 1837. In envelope.
RHi.   46476

Providence Female Benevolent

Society.

Report and Proposal from a Committee of the Providence Female Benevolent Society, to the Public, on the subject of Female Wages. Providence, 1837. 24 p. MH-BA; MiD-B; RPB.   46477

Public ledger (Philadelphia).
Addresses of the carriers of the public ledger. New York, 1837- . PPL; MB; RPB.
46478
The public schools, public blessings. ... New-York, M. Day, printer, 1837. 35, (1) p. CtHC.   46479

Pulsifer, David, 1802-1894.
Inscriptions from the burying grounds in Salem, Massachusetts. Boston, James Loring, 1837. 28 p. CtSoP; ICN; MBAt; MLy; RPB.   46480

Purdy, Lucius M.
The missionary argument: an address... Richmond, Ptd. by B. R. Wren, 1837. 12 p. MiD-B.   46481

Purdy, Welch, Macomber & Company.
Their magnificent collection of zoological & ornithological subjects from the zoological institute, New York...a delineated description & history of the beasts & birds contained therein... New York, Bell, 1837. 32 p. PPAmP.   46482

Purry, Jean Pierre, fl. 1718-1731.
A Description of the Province of South Carolina, drawn up at Charles Town, in September 1731. Translated from Mr. Purry's Original Treatise, in French, and published in The Gentlemen's Magazine, for August, September, and October, 1732. Printed by Peter Force, 1837. 15 p. CoU; GU; NcU; PPL; TxWB.   46483

Put off and put on, or the Vile and beautiful apparel. By Simon. Written for the Massachusetts Sabbath school society and revised by the committee of publication. Boston, Massachusetts Sabbath School Society, 1837. ICBB.   46484

Putnam, Samuel.
The introduction to the analytical reader; ... By Samuel Putnam, stereotype edition. Portland, William Hyde, 1837. 144 p. NNC.   46485

---- Sequel to the analytical reader: ... By Samuel Putnam. Portland, Published by William Hyde, 1837. 300 p. MeHi.
46486
Pym, William Wollaston.
Word of warning in the last days.... Philadelphia, E. G. Dorsey, printer, 1837. 49 p. CtMW; NjR; PPL.   46487

Q

Questions, adapted to Paley's moral and political philosophy. By a citizen of Massachusetts .... New York, Published by Collins, Keese & co., 1837. 42 p. MoSpD.   46488

Quincy, Mass.
Rules and Regulations of the School Committee of the Town of Quincy, With extracts from the Laws of The Commonwealth Relating to the Public Schools. Quincy, Printed by John A. Green, 1837. ICMe.   46489

R

Rafinesque, Constantine Samuel, 1783-1840.

First scientific circular for 1837 to the governors, Lieut'ts governors and speakers of the legislatures of all the states and territories in the United States. Philadelphia, 1837. N; WU.   46490

---- Safe banking, including the principles of wealth: being an enquiry into the principles and practice of safe and unsafe banks, or monied institutions etc.... Philadelphia, Divitial institution of North America, and 6 per cent savings bank, 1837. 136, [2] p. DLC; LNH; MH; PU; WHi.   46491

Raleigh and Gaston Railroad Co.
First Annual Report of the Raleigh and Gaston Rail-road Company. February 6, 1837. Raleigh [N.C.], Printed by J. Gales and son, Office of the Raleigh Register, 1837. 11 p. NcU.   46492

Rambach, Johann Jakob, 1693-1735.
Betrachtungen uber das ganze Leiden Christi...nach der harmonischen beschreibung der vier Evang. ... als anhang ist beigefugt Betrachtungen der sieben letzten worte des gekreuzigten Jesu. Philadelphia, Schelly, 1837. 1059 p. MH; PPLT; PPeSchw; ViHarEM.   46493

Ramberg, Andreas Jakob, 1767-1821. See Romberg, Andreas Jakob, 1767-1821.

No entry   46494

Randolph Academy.
Catalogue of the officers and students of Randolph Academy, from Aug. 1, 1836, to Aug. 1, 1837. Dedham, printed by Herman Mann, 1837. 8 p. MBNEH.   46495

Rankin, John, 1793-1886.
Letters on American slavery, addressed to Mr. Thomas Rankin, merchant at Middlebrook, Augusta Co., Va. By John Rankin ... 2d ed. Newburyport, C. Whipple, 1837. [5]-118 p. NB; OO; PPL.   46496

Rantoul, Robert, 1805-1852.
An Oration delivered before the Democratic Citizens of County of Worcester. Worcester, July 4, 1837. Worcester, Published by Mirick & Bartlett, Printers, 1837. 6-72 p. MH; MiD-B; NN; PPL; RPB.   46497

---- ---- Second edition. Worcester, Published by Mirick & Bartlett, 1837. 35 p. CtSoP; MeB; MnHi; MWA; PHi.   46498

Rapp, Adam William.
Testimonials and certificates of scientific penmanship as taught by Adam William Rapp. Princeton, 1837. 12 p. PHi.   46499

A rare opportunity for investment. 200 quarter sections of land, for sale, on the Maxwell Grant...New York, W. Applegate, printer, 1837. 8 p. MH-BA.   46500

Rathbun, Benjamin.
In chancery, before the chancellor. Hiram Pratt, Joseph Clary and Lewis F. Allen, complainants, vs. Benjamin Rathbun and his creditors, defendants. Buffalo, 1837. [99] p. NBuHi.   46501

Ravels.
Pantomime of the magic pills.
New York, 1837. PPL.   46502

Ray, Isaac, 1807-1881.
A Treatise on the Medical
Jurisprudence of Insanity. By
I. Ray, M.D. Boston, Charles
C. Little and James Brown,
1837. 480 p. MeB.   46503

Ray, Joseph, 1807-1855.
Ray's eclectic arithmetic, on
the inductive and analytic
methods of instruction. Designed for common schools and
academies. By Joseph Ray...
Stereotype ed. Cincinnati,
Truman and Smith, 1837. 9-
239 p. DLC; NjR; OHi.   46504

Raymond, F. L.
The lancer's quick step re-
spectfully dedicated to General
Davis, and the officers and
members of the National lancers.
As performed by J. Bartlett's
Brass Band, Aug. 30th 1837.
Boston, published by H. Pren-
tiss, 1837. 2 p. MB; MBNEC.
                        46505
Read, Almon H.
Speech delivered in the con-
vention to amend the Constitution
of Pennsylvania. 1837. Harris-
burg, Printed by William D.
Boas, 1837. PPi.   46506

---- Speech on the individual liability of stockholders for the
debts of Banking Institutions,
delivered in the Convention of
Pennsylvania, Nov. 16 and 17,
1837. Philadelphia, 1837. 16
p. PHi.   46507

Read, Daniel.
The inaugural address of
Daniel Read. A.K. professor of
languages, in the Ohio University, delivered at the commence-

ment, Sept. 1836. Athens, I.
Maxon, 1837. 15 p. OClWHi.
                        46508
[Reade, Thomas Shaw Bancroft].
Christian retirement; or,
Spiritual exercises of the heart,
by the author of "Christian ex-
perience, as displayed in the
life & writings of St. Paul."
2d American from the 8th Lon-
don ed. New York, John S.
Taylor, 1837. 476 p. CtHC;
LU; MB; MeBat; RRu.   46509

The Reading Rail-road; its advantages for the cheap transportation of coal as compared
with the Schurykill Navigation
and Lehigh Canal. Nos. I to
VIII. By X. Philadelphia, 1837.
43 p. WU.   46510

Rector, N.D.
A short account of the life,
experience, call to the ministry,
and exclusion of N. D. Rector.
To which is added, some proceedings of the benevolent associations of the day, from their
own records. .... Boston,
(Erie co.). Published by the
author. Day, Stagg & Cadwal-
lader, prs. Buffalo, 1837. 67
p. NBu.   46511

Red Book. State of New-York.
1837. Albany, Printed by Croswell, Van Benthuysen and Burt,
1837. 1-259, (1). NNS; NUtHi;
NSchHi.   46512

Red Hook Building Company.
Prospectus and articles of
association. New York, T.
Snowden, 1837. 40 p. MH;
MH-BA; NNC.   46513

Redfield, William Charles, 1789-
1857.
Some account of two visits to
the Mountains in Essex County,

N.Y., in 1836 and 1837; with a sketch of the Northern Sources of the Hudson. New York, 1837. 23 p. PHi. 46514

[Reed, Anna C].
Vie de George Washington. Pris de l'anglais, et dédié á la jeunesse américaine, por A. N. Girault...6. ed. Philadelphia, H. Perkins; Boston, Perkins and Marvin, 1837. 321 p. CSmH; DGU; DLC; NN; Vi. 46515

Reed, Caleb.
Address delivered before the Boston Society of the New Jerusalem, July 4, 1837. By Caleb Reed. Boston, Otis Clapp, 1837. 11 p. MB; PBa; OUrC. 46516

Reed, Thomas C., d. 1883.
A discourse on the character of the late Chester Averill, A.M.,....delivered at the request of the faculty of said college, on the evening of July 16, 1837. By the Rev. Thomas C. Reed....Schenectady (New York), printed by S. S. Riggs, 1837. 78 p. CtHT; IaU; MBC; NCH; RNR. 46517

Reese, [David Meredith], 1801-1861.
A letter from Dr. [David Meredith] Reese to Amariah Brigham, New York, Howe & Bales, 1837. 30 p. DLC; MdUM. 46518

---- Strictures on Health; or Temperance in all things: being an appeal to all who value health and long life. Second edition, with additions. New York, Mason and Lane, 1837. 142 p. CtY-M. 46519

Reflections on the Nature and dignity of the enterprise for establishing Universal and permanent peace considered. Boston, 1837. 76 p. KyDC; MeB. 46520

Reflections on the system of the Union Benevolence Association, stating its beneficent effects on the manners, habits, conduct and comforts of the poor.... By a citizen of Philadelphia. Second edition, considerably improved. Philadelphia, Printed by William F. Geddes, October 12, 1837. 12 p. PPM. 46521

Reformed Church in America.
The acts and proceedings of the Reformed Dutch Church in North America, New York: June, 1837. New York, Merecein & Post's Press. (sic), 1837. 93 p. IaPeC. 46522

---- The psalm and hymns, with a catechism, confession of faith and liturgy, of the Reformed Dutch Church in North America, selected at the request of the General Synod. 4th ed. New York, W. A. Mercein, 1837. 330 p., 11, 77 p. NN. 46523

---- General Synod. Sabbath School Union.
The spelling book of the general synod's sabbath school union, of the Reformed Protestant Dutch Church in the United States of America. New York, Board of managers, [1837?]. 104 p. NN. 46524

Reformed Church in the U.S.
Verhandlungen der Synode der Hochdeutschen Reformirten Kirche in den Vereinigten Staaten von Nord Amerika. Gehalten zu Sunbury, Pa., von 23sten bis zum 30sten September, 1837. Chambersburg, Gedruckt bei Victor Scriba, 1837. 47, [1] p. MoWgT; PLERCHi. 46525

The Religious magazine, and family miscellany. [E. A. Andrews, ed. Boston,] 1837-. Vol. 1-. CoCsC; CtHT; MHi; MPLyA; OClWHi.   46526

The religious souvenir for 1837. New York, Hall & Voorhies, 1837. CSansS; KU; PHi; RPB; TxHR.   46527

Remarks On The Act Of The General Assembly Of 1837. Submitted For The Consideration Of Southern Presbyterians By A Presbyterian Of Virginia. Richmond, Wm. Macfarlane, Printer, 1837. 40 p. CSmH; DLC; NcD; TxU; ViRut.   46528

Remarks on the Lord's Prayer. By an anastasian. Boston, Hilliard, Gray and Company, 1837. 92 p. ICMe; MA; MBC; MBrZ; RPB.   46529

Remarks on the township system. Philadelphia, J. Crissy, Printer, 1837. 12 p. OClWHi; PPM.   46530

Remington, Stephen, 1803-1869.
    Anti-universalism; or, Universalism shown to be unscriptural, in a course of lectures delivered in the Methodist Episcopal church in Willet street, New York ... Published by the request of the trustees of said church and the young men of the congregation. N.Y., Harper, 1837. 142 p. CtMW; GEU; NIC.   46531

Rencher, Abraham.
    To the people of the tenth Congressional district of North Carolina. Washington, no pub., 1837. 8 p. NcU.   46532

Rennie, James, 1787-1867.

Alphabet of Botony.....by Arabella Clark, New York, Mahlon Day. Charleston, B. B. Hussey, 1837. 151 p. ScCliTO.   46533

Reply to a discourse delivered at the Methodist chapel, in Nantucket, by the Rev. S. Hull, of Falmouth, on Sabbath evening, Dec. 10, 1836. By a Universalist. Nantucket, Printed by Silas W. Wilder, 1837. 28 p. CtY; MB; NNUT.   46534

The Restorationist. Volume I. Paul Dean, Resident Editor. Charles Hudson, William Morse, Adin Ballou, Edwin M. Stone, Corresponding Editors. Boston, 1837. DLC; ICN; MB; MBAt; MH.   46535

Retreat gazette, Hartford, (Conn.) v. 1, no. 1. August, 1837. 2 p. CtHT-W.   46536

A Review of Mr. (John) Mitchell's Sermon preached at the late Fast (Sept. 1, 1837). By one of his Parishioners. Northampton, Mass., Gazette Office, 1837. 32 p. CtHC; MDeeP; MH; MH-AH; OMC.   46537

Reynolds, Alexander G.
    Introductory lecture for the students of Union Academy. Bedford N.Y., J. Narine, 1837. 21 p. MB.   46538

Reynolds, Jeremiah N., 1799-1858.
    Exploring Expedition. Correspondence between J. N. Reynolds and the Hon. Mahlon Dickerson ... touching the South Sea Surveying and Exploring Expedition ... 1837-38. New York, 1837-1838. 151 p. MB; MBAt; N; RPB; ScU.   46539

Rhett, Edmund.
A discourse delivered before
the citizens of Beaufort at the
request of the Beaufort volun-
teer artillery on the 4th of
July, A.D., 1837, by Edmund
Rhett. Published by request.
Charleston, Printed by Edward
C. Councell, 1837. [3], 23 p.
MBAt.   46540

Rhett, Robert Barnwell, 1800-
1876.
Speech of R. Barnwell Rhett,
on the bill authorizing an issue
of treasury notes: delivered in
the House of Representatives,
September 29, 1837. Washington, Blair and Rives, 1837. 14
p. CtY; DLC; NNC; ViU.
                            46541
Rhode Island. Governor.
Gov. Fenner's letter to Capt.
Robinson Potter, relating to the
candidacy for Congress of Dutel
J. Pearce, dated July 24, 1837.
[Providence, 1837.] NN. 46542

---- Supreme Judicial Court.
Opinion of the judges of the
Supreme Court, acting as
referees in cases William Allen
and others, owners of mills on
the Blackstone River, vs. the
Blackstone Canal Company.
(Providence? 1837?). 14 p.
DLC; MH-L; RHi; RPB.   46543

---- ---- Rules of the Supreme
Judicial Court of the State of
Rhode Island and Providence
Plantations; regulating practice
both in law and in equity,
adopted May, 1837. Providence,
Printed by Knowles, Vose &
Company, 1837. 24 p. RPB.
                            46544
The Rhode Island Almanac, for
the year 1838; ... Providence,
Published by H. H. Brown,
[1837]. 24 p. MWA; RNHi;
RPE; WHi.   46545

Rice, Nathan Lewis, 1807-1877.
An account of the law-suit instituted by Rev. G. A. M.
Elder...against Rev. N. L.
Rice...for a pretended libel on
the character of Rev. David Du-
parque, a Roman priest. Together with some remarks on
celibacy and nunneries, by Rev.
N. L. Rice...Louisville, Ky.,
D. Holcomb & Co., printers,
1837. 192 p. DLC; ICU; KyDC;
MnSM; PPiW.   46546

Richards, G.
Disc. introd. to his pastorate.
Boston, 1837. MB.   46547

Richards, William.
A plain statement of facts....
By W. Richards. Richmond,
Mass., 1837. 36 p. USlC.
                            46548
Richardson, Charles, 1775-1865.
A new dictionary.... Lon-
don, W. Pickering; New York,
W. Jackson, 1837-39. 2 v.
ICU.   46549

Richardson, James, 1771-1858.
An address delivered before
the members of the Norfolk bar.
At their request. February 25,
1837. By James Richardson...
Boston, Toney & Bair, printers,
1837. 24 p. ICMe; MBAt; MWA;
NCH; RPB.   46550

Richardson, James P.
The public worship of God; a
sermon delivered in Harrison,
December 29, 1836 at the dedica-
tion of the Congregational Meet-
ing House in that place. By
James P. Richardson....Portland,
Merrill & Byram, 1837. 23 p.
MeHi; RPB.   46551

Richardson, William, d. 1842.
A scriptural inquiry respecting
the obligation of ritual observances

under the Christian dispensation. Newcastle, printed at
the Courant Office, by J.
Blackwell and Co., 1837. 32 p.
ICN; MH; NN; PHC.   46552

Richmond, Legh, 1772-1827.
Beauties of the Rev. Legh
Richmond. Selections from his
writings.... New-York, 1837.
127 p. MB.   46553

Richmond, Va. Ordinances.
An Ordinance, reducing into one the several ordinances
concerning Fires, Fire Companies and the Fire Department, Jan. 23, 1837. Richmond, 1837. 8 + 7 + 8 p.
PHi.   46554

The Richmond County Mirror:
a weekly paper printed on
Staten Island, devoted to sci-
ence, literature, & news...
New Brighton, July 1837.
Volume I. - Number I. NN.
                         46555
Richmond Trading and Manu-
facturing Company.
Charter of....incorporated
March 3, 1837. Richmond,
1837. 8 p. In.   46556

Ridgely, Richard H.
An Oration delivered on the
4th of July, 1837, at Lewis's
Ferry, ... Lexington, Intelligencer Print, 1837. 14 p.
                         46557
---- An oration on the birthday
of George Washington, delivered
in Nicholasville, Kentucky, by
Richard H. Ridgely. Lexington,
Kentucky, Intelligencer Print,
1837. 16 p. MoS.   46558

[Riley, James, 1777-1840].
The story of Captain Riley,
and his adventures in Africa.
With engravings. Philadelphia,

Desilver, Thomas & Co., 1837.
[v]-vi, [9]-240 p. front.
ViSwc.   46559

Ripley, George, 1802-1880.
The temptations of the times:
a discourse delivered in the Congregational church in Purchase
Street...May 4, 1837. Boston,
1837. 17 p. DLC; MBC; MHi;
NNG; RPB; WHi.   46560

[Ritchie, Mrs. Anna Cora (Og-
den) Mowatt], 1819-1870.
Reviewers reviewed ...
New York, printed for the au-
thor, 1837. [19]-72 p. DLC;
MB; MH; NBuG; TxU.   46561

Ritner, Joseph, 1780-1869.
George Washington. Ueber
seine Freimaurerei. Brief an
eine auserlesene Committee vom
Hause der Repraesentaten. Al-
lentown, Pa., G. A. Sage, 1837.
PPG.   46562

---- Governor Ritner's vindication of General Washington and
veto message. Gettysburg,
Pa., R. W. Middleton, 1837.
30 p. DLC; MH.   46563

---- Vindication of General
Washington from the stigma of
adherence to secret societies.
By Joseph Ritner, governor of...
Pennsylvania. Communicated by
request of the House of representatives, to that body, on the
8th of March, 1837, with the Proceedings which took place in its
reception. Harrisburg, T. Fenn,
1837. 26 p. DLC; ICN; MH; PP;
ViU.   46564

---- ---- Philadelphia, 1837.
16 p. CSmH; MiU-C; PPAmP;
PPL.   46565

Riverview academy, Poughkeepsie, N.Y.

Catalogue ... 1837, 1856.
Poughkeepsie, N.Y., 1837-56.
2 v. CSmH.   46566

Rives, William Cabell, 1793-1868.
Speech of Mr. Rives, of Virginia, in support of the bill introduced by him designating the
funds receivable in payment of
the public revenue, and in opposition to the sub-treasury
scheme. Delivered in the Senate
of the U.S. Sept. 19, 1837.
Washington, Printed at the
Madisonian office, 1837. 32 p.
DLC; InHi; MiD-B; NNUT;
ScCC.   46567

---- Speech of Mr. Rives of
Virginia, on the currency of
the United States, and the col-
lection of the public revenue.
Delivered in the Senate U.S.
January 10, 1837. Washington,
Printed at the Globe office,
1837. 20 p. DLC; MBAt;
MWA; NjR; WHi.   46568

Rob Roy [stud horse]. April,
1837. Joseph Duncan. E. T.
& C. Goudy, printers. [Jack-
sonville, 1837.] Broadside.
IaDaM.   46569

Robbins, Asher, 1757-1845.
Speech of Mr. Robbins, on
the joint resolution reported by
the library committee, to purchase the copyright of Madison's
manuscript works, ... Delivered in the Senate....Febru-
ary 18, 1837. Washington,
Printed by Gales and Seaton,
1837. 7 p. CtHWatk; NjR;
RHi; RPB.   46570

Robbins, Chandler.
A pebble against the tide.
A sermon, preached to The Second Church, on Sunday, November 6, 1836, by its minister,

Chandler Robbins. Published
by request. Second edition.
Boston, S. G. Simpkins, 1837.
16 p. ICMe; MHi; MiD-B; MWA;
NNG.   46571

Robbins, Royal, 1787-1861.
Outlines of ancient and modern
history on a new plan. Embracing biographical notices of illustrious persons and general views
of the geography, population,
politics....of ancient and modern
nations. Accompanied by a
series of questions, and illustrated with engravings. By
Reverend Royal Robbins. 6th.
revised edition. Hartford,
Belknap and Hamersley, 1837.
2 v. in 1. MB; MH; MoS; ViW.
                             46572
---- ---- 7th rev. ed. ... Hartford, Belknap and Hamersley,
1837. 2 v. in 1. ICartC;
NBuU; NcCQ; OClWHi.   46573

---- The World displayed in its
history and geography; embracing
a history of the world, from the
creation to the present day.
With general views of the politics,
religion, military and naval affairs, arts, literature, manners,
customs, and society, of ancient
as well as modern nations. By
the Rev. Royal Robbins. New
York, H. Savage, 1837. 432,
[60] p. MWA.   46574

Robbins, Thomas, 1777-1856.
A sermon preached at Matta-
poisett Village, Rochester, at
the funeral of the Rev. Lemuel
Le Baron. By Thomas Robbins.
New-Bedford, Printed by J. C.
Parmenter, 1837. 20 p. MPlyP;
MWA; MWiW; NnU; RPB. 46575

Roberts, Edmund, 1784-1836.
Embassy to the Eastern courts
of Cochin, China, Siam and Mus-

cat; in the U.S. Sloop-of-War, Peacock, David Geisinger, Commander, during the years 1832-3-4. By Edmund Roberts. New York, Harper & Brothers, 1837. 432 p. DLC; IaPeC; MH; NNA; RP. 46576

Roberts (Robert).
Desertation on the plagues of Chester in the sixteenth, seventeenth and nineteenth centuries. Chester, F. P. Evans, 1837. 33 p. DSA.
46577

Roberts, William, 1767-1849.
Memoirs of the life and correspondence of Mrs. Hannah More. New York, Harper and Brothers, 1837. 2 v. GEU; MH; RRu; ViU; WBeloC. 46578

Robertson, John, 1787-1873.
Speech of Mr. Robertson, on the bill imposing additional duties, as depositories in certain cases, on public officers, delivered in the House of representatives, October 11, 1837. Washington, Printed at the Globe office, 1837. 7 p. Ct; DLC; PHi; RP; WHi. 46579

---- Speech on Mr. Wise's resolution of inquiry into the condition of the executive departments delivered in the House of Representatives, Jan. 4 and 5, 1837. Washington, 1837. RP.
46580
---- Speech on the proposition to censure Mr. Adams delivered in the House of representatives, Feb. 7, 1837. [Washington, 1837]. 3 p. WHi. 46581

Robertson, William, 1721-1793.
... The history of the discovery and settlement of America, by William Robertson...By John Frost, A.M. Complete in one volume. New York, Harper & brothers, 1837. 570 p. CSmH; DeWi; Ia; NcRA; TxU. 46582

Robinson, James.
A compend of book-keeping by single entry;... Stereotype edition, with improvements. By James Robinson,... Boston, Charles Stimpson, (1837). 5, (26) p. MB; MH; MHi; NNC.
46583

Robinson, Richard P.
A letter from Richard P. Robinson; as connected with the murder of Ellen Jewett, sent in a letter to his friend, Thomas Armstrong, with a defence of the jury.... New York, n. pub., n. pr., 1837. 16 p. Ct; MH-L; NIC-L; NjR. 46584

Robinson, Sarah (Harwood), 1775-1854.
Genealogical history of the families of Robinsons, Saffords, Harwoods, and Clarke. By Sarah Robinson. Bennington, Vt., 1837. (5)-96 p. ICN; IaHa; MiD-B; MWA; VtU. 46585

Rochester, New York. Rochester High School.
Catalogue of the officers and members of the Rochester high school for the year ending April, 1837. Rochester, Luther Tucker, printer, 1837. 12 p. MH.
46586
---- Canal convention, 1837.
Proceedings of the convention, upon the subject of an immediate enlargement of the Erie canal; held at the court-house in Rochester, on the 18th and 19th days of January, 1837. Buffalo, Charles Faxon, printer, 1837. 28 p. NBu. 46587

Rogers, Ammi, 1770-1852.
Memoir of the Rev. Ammi

Rogers, A.M. a clergyman of
the Episcopal church,...falsely
accused and imprisoned in Norwich jail, for two years,...
Also, a concise view of the
authority, doctrine, and worship,
in the protestant Episcopal
church, and a very valuable
index to the Holy Bible, composed, compiled, and written by
the said Ammi Rogers...Ed. 7.
Johnstown, N.Y., 1837. 264 p.
CSmH; MB; MH; MWA; WHi.
                                    46588
Rogers, George.
    Address on our destiny.
N.Y., (1837). MBAt.   46589

---- The Pro and Con of Universalism...By George Rogers.
In 3 vols. Vol. 1. Cincinnati,
pr. by R. P. Brooks & Co.,
1837. 192 p. KyBgW; MMeT-
Hi.   46590

Rogers, Henry Darwin, 1808-
1866.
    On the geology of the ancient
secondary basis of the United
States. [Philadelphia, 1837].
74 ℓ. RPB.   46591

Rogers, Hester Ann, 1756-1794.
    Account of the experience of
Hester Ann Rogers; and her
funeral sermon, by Rev. T.
Coke, LL.D., to which is added
her Spiritual letters .... New
York, T. Mason and G. Lane,
for the Methodist Episcopal
church, 1837. 290 p. DLC;
MB; MiU; MnSM; OO; TxGR.
                                    46592
Rogers, William H.
    Address delivered before the
Athenaean & Delta Phi soc. of
Newark college, Del. Sept. 7,
1837. Philadelphia, Walker,
1837. 42 p. DeWi; PPL. 46593

Roget, F.

Outlines of physiology. With
an appendix on phrenology.
1st. American edition. Philadelphia, Lea and Blanchard, 1837.
3, 516 p. LNOP.   46594

Rollin, Charles, 1661-1741.
    The ancient history of the
Egyptians, Carthaginians, Assyri-
ans, Babylonians, Medes and
Persians, Grecians, and Mace-
donians; by Charles Rollin ...
Translated from the French, To
which is prefixed, a life of the
author, by the Rev. R. Lyman
... From the 15th London ed.,
rev. and cor... Hartford, Judd,
Loomis & co., 1837. 8 v. Ct;
FCl; MsB; OCU; WKenHi. 46595

---- ---- Hartford, Con., Judd,
Loomis and Co., 1837-1839. 6
v. NN; OCU.   46596

---- ---- New York, Published
by Long, 1837. 8 v. GAM-R;
IaMc; OBerB; OCX; ViU. 46597

Romberg, Andreas Jakob, 1767-
1821.
    The song of the bell, trans-
lated from the German of Schiller,
for the Boston Academy of Music, by S. A. Eliot. Boston,
Kidder & Wright, 1837. 70 p.
MH; MiD; CtY.   46598

Root, David, 1790-1873.
    A memorial to the martyred
Lovejoy... A discourse delivered
in Dover, N.H. n.p. [1837].
16 p. CtHWatk; ICN; Nh-Hi;
RPB; WHi.   46599

Rose, Israel G.
    A funeral sermon delivered at
Chesterfield, January, 1, 1837,
in view of the death of Francis
Clapp. By Israel G. Rose.
Northampton, printed by John
Metcalf, 1837. 20 p. MBC; MHi;
MNF; NRU.   46600

Rose, William Stewart, 1775-1843.
Rhymes by William Stewart
Rose ... Brighton (Creasy and
Baker, printers), 1837. (2),
104, (1) p. CtY; DLC; MH;
NNUT.   46601

Ross, John, 1790-1866?
Letter from John Ross, the
principal chief of the Cherokee
nation, to a gentleman of Phila-
delphia (i.e. Job R. Tyson).
(Philadelphia, 1837). 40 p.
MBC; MH; PHi; PPPAmP; T.
                         46602
Rossini, Gioacchino Antonio,
1792-1868.
The Alpine flower girl. A
celebrated Tyrolienne (with
pianoforte accompaniment).
Philadelphia, Fiot Meignen &
Co., (1837). 3 p. MB.   46603

---- The fireman's call ...
Music from the opera of the
Maid of Judah (with pianoforte
accomp.). Boston, Keith,
1837. 4 p. MB.   46604

Rowson, Susanna [Haswell],
1762-1824.
Charlotte Temple, A tale of
truth... Cincinnati, V. P.
James, 1837. 139 p. CtY;
MWA.   46605

---- ---- Hartford, Judd, Loomis & Co., 1837. 138 p. NN;
RPB.   46606

---- ---- Philadelphia, A. I.
Dickinson, 1837. 143 p. CtY;
IU; OU; PU; ViU.   46607

Roy, William L.
A complete Hebrew and English critical and pronouncing
dictionary, on a new and improved plan, containing all the
words in the Holy Bible, both
Hebrew and Chaldel... New

York, Collins, Keese & co.,
1837. 9-740 p. GAGT; IEG;
KyDC; MBr; OClW.   46608

---- ---- 2nd ed. New York,
Collins, Keese and Company,
1837. 832 p. NB; PBa. 46609

Rudd, George R.
A Thanksgiving Discourse,
delivered in Fredonia, N.Y.
Nov. 30, 1837. By George R.
Rudd, Minister of the First
Presbyterian Church in Fredonia.
Fredonia, Printed by H. C.
Frisbee, 1837. 15 p. MC;
NBu.   46610

Rudd, John Churchill, 1779-1848.
The Bible and its companion:
sermon in Manlius to the Bible
and Common Prayer Book Society,
July 12, 1837. Utica, Hobart
press, R. Beresford, printer,
1837. 12 p. PHi; RPB. 46611

Ruffner, Henry.
Inaugural address, by Henry
Ruffner, president of Washington college, Va. delivered on
the twenty-second of February,
1837... Lexington, C. C. Baldwin, 1837. 23, (1) p. CSmH;
MH; NNUT.   46612

Rupp, Israel Daniel, 1803-1878.
The geographical catechism of
Pennsylvania and the Western
states; designed as a guide and
pocket companion, for travellers
and emigrants, to Pa., Ohio, Indiana, Ill., Mich., and Missouri
... Philadelphia, Bonsal & Desilver; New York, Lord & co.
[etc etc], 1837. 384 p. DLC;
OClWHi; OSW; PHi; WHi. 46613

Rushville, Ill.
An ordinance, to amend and
reduce into one, the several
ordinances heretofore adopted by

the president and trustees, of
the town of Rushville. Rushville,
Printed by J. B. Fulks, 1837.
21 p. NN.   46614

Rusling, Joseph, 1788-1839.
   Devotional Exercises; and
Miscellaneous Poems. By...J.
Rusling, Minister of the Gospel
in the M.E. Church. Second
Edition, Enlarged. Philadelphia,
1837. 252 p. NNMHi; NNUT;
OCoC.   46615

---- ---- 3rd ed. Philadelphia,
1837. 252 p. CCSC; NNUT.
                             46616
---- Hymns composed for the
use of Sunday schools and
youthful Christians. By Joseph
Rusling, ... Philadelphia, 1837.
136 p. DLC; NNMHi; NNUT.
                             46617
Russell, Henry, 1812-1900.
   Come brothers arouse. A
song [Bar.] & chorus from the
opera of the Bride's band. [Ac-
comp. for pianoforte.] New
York, Hewitt & Co., 1837.
6 p. MB.   46618

---- ---- third ed. New York,
Hewitt and Jaques, 1837. 6 p.
NN; ViU.   46619

---- The friar of the olden
time. A ballad [Bar.] supposed
to have been written in the
12th century. The symphonies
& accompaniments [for pianoforte]
composed by Henry Russell. New
York, Hewitt & Co., 1837. 6
p. MB.   46620

---- My heart's in the High-
lands. [Song, Bar. Accomp.
for pianoforte.] New York,
Hewitt & Co., 1837. 7 p.
MB.   46621

---- ---- Philadelphia, Nunns,

[1837]. 5 p. MB; NbHi; ViU.
                             46622
---- The old English gentleman.
A ballad. Composed by Henry
Russell. Boston, Published by
Oliver Ditson, 1837. 4 p. KU.
                             46623
---- Some love to roam O'er the
dark sea foam. The poetry by
Charles Mackay. Philadelphia,
Osbourn, 1837. PPL.   46624

---- A song of the oak. The
brave old oak. Part of the symphonies & accompaniments composed by Henry Russell. [Words
by H. F. Chorley.] New York,
Hewitt & Co., 1837. 6 p. MB.
                             46625

---- Woodman, spare that tree,
words by George P. Morris, esq.,
music by Henry Russell. New
York, Firth & Hall, 1837. 6 p.
WHi.   46626

---- ---- New York, S. J. Gordon, 1837. 6 p. MB; MChiA;
WHi.   46627

---- ---- 13th edition. New
York, Firth & Hall, 1837. 5 p.
KU; ViU.   46628

Russell, John.
   History of France, from the
earliest times to the present day
.... By John Russell, A.M....
Philadelphia, Hogan and Thomp-
son, 1837. 234 p. DLC; ICU;
OrPD; TNT; WHi; WyU. 46629

---- A History of the United
States of America, from the
period of the discovery to the
present time: Arranged for the
use of schools ... Philadelphia,
Hogan & Thompson, (1837).
256 p. DLC; ICHi; MB; PHi.
                             46630
Russell, L. B.

Plan and profile of a survey for an aqueduct from Long Pond in Natich to Boston. Boston, City documents, 1837. DLC; MB.   46631

Russell, Michael, 1781-1848.
History and present condition of the Barbary States. New York, Published by Harper & Brothers, 1837. 343 p. CU; FTa; OO PEaL; PMA; TxGR.   46632

---- Nubia and Abyssinia: comprehending their civil History antiquities, arts, Religion, Literature and natural history. By the Rev. Michael Russell, L.L.D. New York, Published by Harper & Brothers, 1837. 331 p. InNd; Me; MH; NcHil; TxGR.   46633

---- ... Palestine; or, The Holy Land. From the earliest period to the present time. By ... Michael Russell ... New York, Harper & brothers, 1837. (9)-330 p. FTU; MH; MoK; MoSpD; NNUT.   46634

Russell, William C.
Farewell address, as rector of St. Andrew's Wilmington, Del. April 9, 1837. Philadelphia, 1837. 12 p. PHi.   46635

S

Sabbath school results. By the secretary of the Massachusetts Sabbath school society. Written for the Massachusetts Sabbath school society, and revised by the Committee of publication. Boston, Massachusetts Sabbath school society, 1837. (21)-304 p. DLC; GMilvC; NbCrD; OWoC.   46636

The Sailor's Temperance Almanac, for the year of our Lord 1837. Adopted to all parts of the United States and Canada. Prepared and published under the direction of the executive committee of the New York State Temperance Society. Albany, from the steam presses of Packard and Van Benthuysen, 1837. [24] p. MWA; NT.   46637
St. Andrews' Society of Philadelphia.
Charter, with A List of Members' Names. Philadelphia, Pa., Bain & Orr, 1837. 24 p. IaHA; PHi; PPL.   46638

Saint-Ceran, Tullius, 1800-1855.
Rien-ou Moi. De M. Tullius St. Ceran.... Nlle-Orleans, De Guston Erusle, 1837. xi, [12]-194 p. CtY; MB; NBuG; RPB; WU.   46639

St. John, James Augustus, 1801-1875.
Lives of celebrated travelers. New York, Harper & Bros., 1837. 3 v. CtB; MH; Mi; NGlo: PMA.   46640
St. Louis, Board of Aldermen, Mayor's Petition.
Petition of the Mayor and Aldermen of the City of St. Louis, praying the rejection of any claim to land within the limits of the common of that city; February 13, 1837....Washington, D.C., np., 1837. 2 p. MoHi. 46641

---- Chamber of Commerce.
An act to incorporate the St. Louis Chamber of Commerce. St. Louis? 1837. 1 leaf. MoS.   46642
---- Gas-Light Company.
An act to incorporate the St. Louis Gas-Light Company, approved 4th of February, 1837,

to which is prefixed the contract with the City of St. Louis, and other papers, relative to the transactions of the St. Louis Gas-Work Company. Published by the Company, MDCCCXXXVII. [St. Louis, 1837.] 38 p. MoS.   46643

St. Louis and Belleview Mineral Rail-Road.
An Act to incorporate the St. Louis and Belleview Mineral Rail-Road Company. Approved, January 25, 1837. St. Louis, Printed by Charles Keemle, 1837. 14 p. MoS.
46644

Salem, Mass. City Council.
Rules and orders of the common council with the city charter, and city ordinances, etc. Salem, Register office, 1837. 58 p. M; MB.   46645

---- East India marine society.
Supplement to the catalogue of the articles in the museum, journals, &c. of the East India marine society of Salem. Salem [Mass.] Printed for the Society by William Ives & co., 1837. 24 p. CSmH; MB; MHi; MSa.
46646

---- First Baptist Church.
Summary declaration of the faith and practice of the first Baptist Church of Christ...together with its covenant....
Salem, Palfray and Chapman, 1837. 20 p. NRAB.   46647

---- Light Infantry Company.
Constitution of the Salem light infantry company: with a list of the members from its organization, formed May 1805. Salem, William Ives and co., printers, 1837. 20 p. DLC; MHi; NjR.   46648

---- Ordinances.
An Act to empower the inhabitants of the town of Salem to choose a Board of Health, and for removing and preventing nuisances in said town. (1837). 23 p. MHi.   46649

Salem Directory.
The Salem Directory, and city register, containing names of the inhabitants, their occupations, places of business...with lists of city officers, banks... Salem, Published by Henry Whipple, 1837-. IaHi; KHi; OClWHi; PHi; T.   46650

Sallustius Crispus, C.
The history of the conspiracy of Catinline and the Judgurthine war. By C. Crispus Salluslius. Translated by William Rose, A.M. Philadelphia, Thomas Wardle, 1837. 66 p. DLC; NcU; OO; PMA; VtU.   46651

---- ... Sallust. Translated by William Rose ... With improvements and notes. New York, Harper & brothers, 1837. [9]-242 p. MdBJ; NjR; NNYMCA-Ed.
46652
---- Sallust's Jugurthine war and Conspiracy of Catiline with an English commentary, and geographical and historical indexes. By C. Anthon ... 6th ed., cor. enl. New York, Harper & brothers, 1837. 332 p. IU; NN; OCl; PLFM; TxU.   46653

Sanderson, George.
The Mirror of Partialism, being a collection of cases of Insanity & Suicide, produced by a belief in the doctrine of Endless Misery. Rochester, N.Y., Published at the office of the Herald of Truth, 1837. (1), 8-48 p. MMeT.   46654

[Sandwich Islands' mission].
Results of missionary labor
at the Sandwich Islands. Bos-
ton, 1837. DLC.   46655

Sanford, John.
A sermon preached at the
funeral of Capt. Levi Crowell
...Published by request. Boston, 1837. 19 p. DLC; MHi.
                                   46656
Sandford, Peter P.
Christian Baptism. A dis-
course on Acts 11: 38, 39. In
which an attempt is made to investigate the nature and per-
petuity, the subjects and the
mode, of Christian Baptism.
3rd edition, enlarged. New
York, 1837. 32 p. MBNMHi;
MaS; Nh; NHCS; NNUT.   46657

---- The Christian sabbath;
or, The universal and perpetual
obligation of the Sabbath, and
the divine authority of its
change from the seventh to the
first day of the week, under
the Christian dispensation;
being a discourse on Matthew
XII: 8. Third edition, revised
by the author. New York, published by T. Mason and G.
Lane, 1837. 24 p. CtMW;
IEG: Nh; TxH.   46658

[Santangelo, O de A].
To the Honorable John Forsyth, secretary of State of
the United States of America.
[New-Orleans, April 29, 1837.]
36 p. TxWFM.   46659

Sargent, John H.
Plan for establishing...a
general print mint at Washington
for the emission of paper money
to the amount perhaps of two
hundred millions.... Charlestown, 1837. 15 p. DLC; ICU;
MBAt.   46660

Sargent, Lucius Manlius, 1786?-
1867.
Fritz Hazell. Founded on
fact. Eighth ed. Boston, Whipple and Damrell, 1837. ICN;
TxU.   46661

---- ---- Eighth edition. Boston, Published by Whipple and
Damrell; New York, Scofield
and Voorhies, 1837. [7]-98 p.
TxU.   46662

---- Der goldne ring meiner
mutter; eine wahre geschichte.
Uebersetzt aus dem englischen
von der zwei und zwanzigsten
aufl (by Hermann Bokum). Boston, Hilliard, Gray, und die
Gesellschaft; New-York, Scofield
und Voorhies, 1837. 24 p. MH.
                                   46663
---- ... Groggy Harbor, or a
smooth stone from the brook and
a shepherd's sling Ninth Ed.
Boston, Published by Whipple
and Damrell; New York, Scofield
and Voorhies, 1837. 76 p.
MBAt; TxU.   46664

---- I am afraid there is a God.
Boston, 1837. CtY; TxU.
                                   46665
---- An Irish heart. 7th ed.
Bound with: Well enough for
the vulgar. 7th Ed. Boston,
Whipple and Damrell, 1837.
158 p. CtY; IU; PV; TxU.
                                   46666
---- ... Kitty Grafton. Founded
on fact. Boston, Pub. by Whip-
ple and Damrell; New York,
Scofield and Voorhies, 1837.
[15]-130 p. MWA; NjR; NN;
TxU.   46667

---- ... My mother's gold ring.
Founded on fact. One hundred
& eleventh edition. Boston, Pub.
by Whipple and Damrell, 1837.
[5]-24 p. CtY; TxU.   46668

---- Nancy Le Baron. Founded
on Fact (anon.). Boston, William S. Damrell, 1837. 89 p.
CtY; CU; MNS; MWA.   46669

---- ---- 5th ed. Boston, Pub.
by Whipple and Damrell, 1837.
(7)-89 p. ICBB; MB; MMedHi;
TxU.   46670

---- Ode for the opening of the
Marlboro Hotel in Boston as a
temperance house (4 July 1837)
by L. M. Sargent, Esq.,
[1837?] Bdse. MHi.   46671

---- Right opposite. 8th ed.
Boston, Whipple and Damrell,
1837. vi, [7]-64 p. TxU.
                            46672
---- A sectarian thing. By
(Lucius M. Sargent.) Boston,
Whipple and Damrell, 1837.
48 p. NjP.   46673

---- ... Seed time and harvest.
... 9th ed Boston, Pub. by
Whipple and Damrell, 1837.
24 p. TxU.   46674

---- The temperance tales.
Boston, Whipple and Damrell,
1837-1838. 5 v. CtY; IU;
RPB; TxU.   46675

---- ... Too fast and too far;
or the cooper and the currier
founded on fact. Boston, Pub.
by Whipple & Damrell, 1837.
[5]-34 p. CtY; CU; TxU. 46676

---- Well enough for the vulgar.
Founded on fact. Sixth Ed.
No author shown. Boston,
Published by William S. Dam-
rell, 1837. 99 p. ICMe. 46677

---- ---- 7th ed. Boston, Pub.
by Whipple and Damrell, 1837.
[5]-99 p. CtY; TxU.   46678

---- ... What a curse? or Johnny
Hodges, the blacksmith. ... 6th
ed. Boston, Pub. by Whipple
& Damrell, 1837. vi, [7]-32 p.
TxU.   46679

---- ... Wild Dick and good little Robin. 24th ed. Boston,
Whipple and Damrell; New York,
Scofield and Voorhies, 1837.
41 p. CtY; MnU; TxU. 46680

---- ... A word in season, or
the sailor's widow. ... 9th ed.
Boston, Pub. by Whipple and
Damrell, 1837. iv, [5]-36 p.
CtY; MHoly; TxU.   46681

Sarlandière, J[ean Baptiste],
1787-1838.
    Systematized anatomy, or hu-
man organography, in synoptical
tables, with numerous plates ...
By the Chev.r J. Sarlandière
... Tr. from the French by W.
C. Roberts ... 2d ed. improved
and cor. New York, J. S.
Rohrer and G. Hills, 1837. 2 p.
CU-M; NjP; P; PPHa.   46682

Saunders, John Simcoe.
    The law of pleading and evi-
dence in civil actions, arranged
alphabetically; with practical
forms; and the pleading and evidence to support them. By
John Simcoe Saunders, Esq.
Third American edition.... Philadelphia, Robert H. Small, 1837-
/1844/. 2 v. KyLxT; MiDU-L;
NcD; OClW; TMeB.   46683

Savannah & Memphis R.R.
    Its local advantages & impor-
tance as...link...line from St.
Louis to Savannah. N.Y.,
(1837?). MB.   46684

Savile, Jeremy.
    Here's a health to all good
lasses [Glee, A. T. B.]. Boston,

Ditson, [1837]. 6 p. MB.
46685
Sawyer, Leicester Ambrose,
1807-1898.
An appeal in favor of good
works; a farewell sermon delivered to the church of Christ
in the United society New Haven,
December 3, 1837. New Haven,
1837. 24 p. Ct; CtHC; CtHT;
MB; WHi. 46686

---- Dissertation on servitude;
embracing an examination of the
scripture doctrines on the subject and an inquiry into the
character and relations of
slavery. New Haven, Durrie,
1837. 108 p. IaU; MBAt;
PHi; OClW; TNF. 46687

Sawyer, T. J.
The Penalty of sin; a sermon
...in reply to a sermon against
Universalism...by Rev. Edwin
F. Hatfield. By T. J. Sawyer
...New York, Universalist Union
Press...1837. 24 p. MMeT-Hi.
46688
Sayers, Edward.
A Manual on the Culture of
the Grape with a dissertation on
the Growth and Management of
Fruit Trees adapted to the
Northern States. Newark, 1837.
48 p. DLC; MBHo; MH. 46689

Scenes in Spain. By A. Slidell
Mackenzie. New-York, printed
by Scatcherd & Adams, for
George Dearborn, 1837. 334 p.
46690. AU; DLC; InUpT;
MNBedf; MoS; OrU. 46690

Schabaelje, Jan Philipsen, 1585?-
1656.
The pilgrim soul; or dialogues
between the pilgrim soul, and
Adam, Noah.... 2nd ed. Pittsburgh, Published by John Wilson,
1837. 312 p. MA; MH; PPiHi.
46691

Schatz und Haus-Freund, Lange
verborgene, von I. S?--------s.
Skippacksville, Pa., 1837. 123
p. PHi. 46692

Schauffler, William Gottlieb,
1798-1883.
Meditations on the last days
of Christ, consisting of ten
sermons, preached at Constan-
tinople and Odessa. By William
G. Schauffler....Boston, Published by William Pierce, 1837.
380 p. CtHC; InCW; MPiB; OO;
PPW. 46693

Schenck, Robert Cumming, 1809-
1890.
Address delivered before the
Society of alumni of Miami uni-
versity, at their anniversary
meeting. September 27, 1836.
Dayton, Comlys, Ohio, 1837.
ICU; OCHP; OClWHi; PPPrHi;
WHi. 46694

Schiller, Johann Christoph
Friedrich von, 1759-1805.
Song of the bell. Trans-
lated for the Boston Academy of
Music. By S. A. Eliot. Boston,
Perkins & Marvin, 1837. 16 p.
DLC; IU; MB; MeB; NNC; RPB.
46695
---- Wallenstein's camp. Tr.
from the German of Schiller by
George Moir. With a memoir of
Albert Wallenstein, by G. Wallis
Haven. Boston, J. Munroe and
company, 1837. (7)-142 p.
CSmH; ICU; MHi; MiD; RPB.
46696
Schlosser, Friedrich Christoph.
The history of Rome, by
Friedrich Christoph Schlosser.
Philadelphia, Carey, Lea &
Blanchard, 1837. 496 p. CSr;
IaFairP; NNebg. 46697

Schneider, Benjamin, 1807-1877.
Letters from Asia Minor. By

Rev. Benjamin Schneider. Phila-
delphia, American Sunday
School Union, [1837]. 45 p.
CtHC; DLC; FU; ICBB.   46698

The scholars manual: containing
the Declaration of Independence,
....with questions for the use
of schools. By a teacher.
New York, Published by Samuel
S. and William Wood, 1837.
108 p. IaHi; MoS; NCH; NGlf;
OrSaw.   46699

Scholfield, Cidney.
    Memorial concerning Cidney
Scholfield. n.p., [1837?]. 4
p. OClWHi.   46700

The School of good manners.
... Boston, Massachusetts Sabbath school society, 1837. x,
(11)-62 p. DLC; MH.   46701

Science made easy: being a
familiar introduction to the
principles of chemistry, mechanics, hydrostatics and pneumatics. Philadelphia, Carey,
Lea & Blanchard, 1837. MdW;
NNS; PHatU; PPL; PU.   46702

Scientific and literary journal,
for the diffusion of useful knowledge. Boston, Light and
Stearns, 1837. 288 p. DLC;
ICJ; MH; MnU; PPFrankI. 46703

Scituate, R.I. First Congregational Church.
    The Confession of Faith and
Covenant ... Providence, 1837.
16 p. MBC; MHi.   46704

Scott, James.
    Questions on the doctrine of
life for the New Jerusalem by
James Scott. Boston, published
by Otis Clapp, 1837. 17 p.
MCMC.   46705

Scott, John Welwood.
    An historical sketch of the
Pine Street, or Third Presby-
terian Church in the city of
Philadelphia. Philadelphia,
Lydia R. Bailey, 1837. 86 p.
DLC; Ia; LNH; MnHi; PPL.
                       46706
Scott, Julia H. (Kinney), 1809-
1842.
    The blind widow, and her
family. Hudson, [Pa?], A. Stod-
dard, 1837. 24 p. DLC; MH.
                       46707
---- ... The sacrifice; a clergy-
man's story, by Julia H. Kinney.
Hudson, [Pa?], A. Stoddard,
1837. 24 p. DLC; MH. 46708

Scott, Michael, 1789-1835.
    The cruise of the Midge. By
the author of "Tom Cringle's
Log." New York, G. Dearborn
and Company, 1837. 318 p.
MiU.   46709

---- Tom Cringle's log. By
Michael Scott. New York, Dearborn, 1837. MNS.   46710

Scott, Walter, 1771-1832.
    The lady of the lake. A
poem. In six cantos. By Sir
Walter Scott. Ithaca, Mack,
Andrus, & Woodruff, 1837. 273
p. CtY; N; NIDHi; NIC; OO.
                       46711
---- ---- New York, Wiley and
Putnam, 1837. 414 p. LNT;
MH; PCA.   46712

---- The poetical works of Sir
Walter Scott. With a sketch of
his life, by J. W. Lake. Complete in one volume. Philadelphia, J. Crissy, Desilver, Thomas
and co., 1837. [1]-443 p. IEG;
MB; NcU; WPta.   46713

---- Tales of A grand father,
first series being stories taken

from Scottish History. Exeter,
N.H., J & B Williams, 1837. 2
v. ViU; WvU.   46714

---- Tales of my landlord. 1st
series. Black Dwarf. Old Mortal-
ity. Parkers edition in 2 vol.
Boston, Pub. by Sam. H.
Parker, for Desilver, Thomas
& Co., Philadelphia, 1836. 2
v. in 1. MEr; MH; MWbri.
                            46715
Scott, Winfield, 1786-1866.
   ...Proceedings of the mili-
tary court of inquiry, in the
case of Major General Scott and
Major General Gaines...[Wash-
ington? 1837]. 734 p. CSt;
MBAt; MdBE; NWM.   46716

Scott and Perkins, firm,
tailors, New York.
   The tailors masterpiece,
being the tailor's complete guide
for instruction in the whole art
of measuring and cutting, according to the variety of fashion
and form. 7th ed. New York,
C. Vinten, 1837. NN.   46717

Scribe, Augustin Eugene, 1791-
1861.
   La sommambule; a ballet and
pantomine in three acts by
W. M. Scribe and Aumer.
New York, printed by T.
Snowden, 1837. MH.   46718

Scripture questions on the gos-
pels and acts, for the use of
schools or private instruction
....Philadelphia, Printed by
William Brown, 1837. 233 p.
KWiF; NcD; PPF; PPWe.   46719

A Scripture Text-book: comprising a concise view of the
evidences and design of Divine
Revelation, of the leading
events and doctrines of the
Bible, and of the consistency

and harmony of its parts ...
By a Teacher. New-York, Wiley
and Putnam, 1837. MNtCA;
MoSpD.   46720

Seabury, Samuel.
   Tribute to the memory of
Frederick Augustus Muhlenberg,
M.D. by the Rev. Dr. Seabury.
Boston, Marden & Kimball,
Printers, 1837. "27 p." DLC;
NNNAM; NNUT; NSmb.   46721

Seamen's Widow and Orphan As-
sociation, Salem.
   Seamen's Widow and Orphan
Association, Salem. Salem,
Printed at the Gazette Office,
1837. 8 p. DLC; MB.   46722

Search, John.
   What? and who says it? an
exposition of the statement that
the Established Church "de-
stroys more souls than it saves."
Worcester, 1837. 66 p. MBC.
                            46723
Sears, Barnas.
   Memoir of Rev. Bela Jacobs,
A.M. comp. chiefly from his letters and journals, by his daughter; with a sketch of his character. By Barnas Sears. Boston,
Gould, Kendall & Lincoln, 1837.
305 p. NjMD.   46724

Second New Jerusalem Society.
Cincinnati.
   Documents of the Second New
Jerusalem Society of Cincinnati
1837. Printed by Kendall and
Henry, 1837. 16 p. MCNC;
OUrC; PBa.   46725

Sedgwick, Catherine Maria, 1789-
1867.
   Home; by the author of "Redwood," ... Boston, James Munree
and co., 1837. 158 p. MBAt;
TxD-T.   46726

---- ---- 12th ed. Boston,
James Munroe and Company,
1837. 158 p. MB; MBAt;
MWalp; NN; TxD-T.   46727

---- Live and let live; or,
Domestic service illustrated.
By the author of "Hope Leslie,"
"The Linwoods" ... New York,
Harper & brothers, 1837. (9)-
216 p. In; MPiB; MWA; RLa;
WHi.   46728

---- A love token for children.
Designed for sunday-school libraries. By the author of
"The Linwoods," "Live and
let live," "Poor rich man," &c.,
&c. (C. M. Sedgwick) (1 line
quotation) New York, Harper &
Brothers, 1837. 142 p. NcD;
NN.   46729

---- The poor rich man, and
The rich poor man. By the
author of "Hope Leslie," "The
Linwoods," &c. New-York,
Harper & Brothers, 1837.
186 p. CSmH; MB; MnU; MWA;
PAtM.   46730

Seekonk Branch Railroad Company.
  First report of the directors
... to the Legislature. [Bos-
ton, Dutton and Wentworth,
1837]. 3 p. DLC; MB; MBAt;
NN.   46731

Segar, Joseph E., 1804-1885.
  Speech on the motion of Mr.
Chapman of Monroe, to instruct
the senators and request the
representatives in Congress from
the state of Virginia to vote for
the immediate recognition of
Texas. Delivered in the House
of Delegates of Virginia, February 23, 1837. Richmond,
Printed by Shepherd & Colin,
1837. 26 p. CSmH; CU-B; TxU;
Vi.   46732

Selections from female poets. A
present for ladies. Boston, S.
Coleman, 1837. [9]-192 p. CtY;
DLC; MB; MNan: WBeloC. 46733

Senneff, George.
  The Bible advocate, or, An
answer to Elias Hicks' blasphemies
and others. Second edition.
Philadelphia, 1837. PPL-R.
                           46734
Sergeant, John.
  Speech of the Hon. Mr.
Sergeant, of Pennsylvania on
the resolution reported from the
committee of ways and means,
... Published from the notes of
the reporter, revised and corrected by the author. Washington, 1837. 16 p. DLC; MH;
MiD-B; NNC; PPM.   46735

Seventeen numbers under the
signature of Neckar.... See
Fisher, R.

Sevier, Ambrose Hundley, 1801-
1848.
  Remarks on the army bill,
in the senate, Feb. 16, 1837.
[Wash., 1837.] 4 p. WHi.
                           46736
Sewall, Thomas, 1786-1845.
  An examination of phrenology;
in two lectures, delivered to the
students of the Columbian college,
District of Columbia, February,
1837. By Thomas Sewall ...
Washington city, B. Homans,
printer, 1837. 70 p. MH-And;
NBMS; OU; PHC; ScNC. 46737

---- Memoir of Dr. Godman:
being an introductory lecture,
delivered November 1, 1830, by
Thomas Sewall, M.D. ... New
York, Published for the Tract
society of the M. E. church, J.
Collord, pr., 1837. 24 p. DSG;
MdBP; MdHi.   46738

Sewalls' Falls Bridge Proprietors.
Act of incorporation and by-laws. Concord, 1837. 11 p.
Nh-Hi.   46739

Seward, William Henry, 1801-1872.
Discourse on education, delivered at Westfield, July 26, 1837. By Wm. H. Seward. Albany, n. pub. Printed by Hoffman & White, 1837. 26 p. DLC; ICU; MiD-B; NjR; ScU.
                                     46740

Seymour, Jonathan.
Questions for the examination of scholars in Tytler's elements of general history, by an experienced teacher. Concord, New Hampshire, John F. Brown, 1837. 44 p. MH; MoKCM.
                                     46741

Sganzin Joseph Mathieu, 1750-1837.
An elementary course of civil engineering; translated from the French. 3d. ed., with notes and applications adapted to the United States. Boston, Hilliard, Gray & Co., 1837. 232 p. CtHT; InCW; OO; PPA; TNV.   46742

Shakespeare, William, 1564-1616.
Dramatic works and poems; with notes, ... and introductory remarks to each play, by S. W. Singer, and a life of the poet, by Charles Symmons. New York, Harper, 1837. 2 v. AMob; ArL; ViRU.   46743

---- The dramatic works of William Shakespeare, accurately printed from the text of the corrected copy left by the late George Stevens, Esq. In two volumes. Hartford, Andrus, Judd & Franklin, 1837. 2 v. Ct; MB; OC; RPB; ViU.   46744

---- ---- Philadelphia, McCarty & Davis, 1837. 2 v. NbOC; WGr.   46745

---- The dramatic works of William Shakespeare; with a life of the poet, and notes, original and selected. In 7 volumes. Boston, Hilliard, Gray, and Company, 1837. 7 v. LNB; MiDU; PU; TNP; ViU.   46746

Sharp & Richard Scrafton.
Old friend ... 1837.   46747

Shelley, Mary Wollstonecraft (Godwin).
Falkner. A novel. By the author of "Frankenstein," "The last man"... Complete in one volume. New York, Harper & brothers, 1837. (5)-321 p. NBLiHi; NRMA; OkU; RPA.
                                     46748

---- ---- New York, Saunders, 1837. 2 v. PU.   46749

(Shelton, Frederick William), 1814-1881.
The Trollopiad; or, Travelling gentlemen in America. A satire by Nil Admirari, Esq ... New York, C. Shepard, Providence, Shepard, Tingley & co., 1837. 151 p. MB; MiD-B; OClW; PU; WHi.   46750

Miss Sheldon's School.
Catalogue of the names of the pupils belonging to Miss Sheldon's school, during the year ending August 17, 1837; two terms of which the institution was in Schenectady, and the third in Utica. Utica, Printed by Bennett & Bright, 1837. 21 p. NUt.
                                     46751

Shepard, Charles Upham.
A report on geological survey of Connecticut. See Connecticut Geological Survey.

Sherwood, Adiel, 1791-1879.

A Gazetteer of the state of Georgia; embracing a particular description of the Counties, towns, villages, rivers, etc. By Adiel Sherwood. Third edition greatly enlarged and improved. Washington City, Force, 1837. 344 p. GHi; MH; NcD; PHi; WHi.   46752

Sherwood, Henry Hall.

Electro-galvanic symptoms, and electro-magnetic remedies, in chronic diseases of the class hypertrophy, or chronic enlargements of the organs and limbs, including all the forms of scrofula, with illustrative diagrams and cases. By H. H. Sherwood, M.D. Third edition, revised and enlarged. New-York, Printed by J. W. Bell, 1837. 88 p. MH-M; MWA; NNNAM; PPL.   46753

---- New or electric symptoms of chronic diseases; or, chronic tubercula of the organs and limbs, by which they may be easily and invariably distinguished by any person of common education and capacity, and their natural or electric remedies...2nd. edition. Cincinnati, Surguy, 1837. 70 p. PPCP.
                                   46754
Sherwood, Mary Martha (Butt), 1775-1851.

The Butterfly. Berwick, T. Melrose, 1837. MB.   46755

---- History of the Fairchild Family. New York, Harper & Bros., Pub., 1837. 387 p. IaPeC.   46756

---- The Lady of the Manor: Being a series of Conversations on the subject of confermation. Intended for the use of the middle and higher ranks of young females. By Mrs. Sherwood, ... In four volumes. New York, published by Harper & Brothers, 1837. 4 v. ILM; LNMas; NcU.   46757

---- The violet leaf by Mrs. Sherwood. Newark, N.J., Benjamin Olds, 1837. 58 p. MNF.
                                   46758
Short stories concerning the faithful dog.... Auburn, Published by Oliphant & Skinner, 1837. 16 p. MWA.   46759

Sibbald, Charles F[raser].

Documents in evidence of a claim submitted by Charles F. Sibbald, of Philadelphia, to the honorable the Senate and House of representatives of the United States of America. [Philadelphia], 1837. 44 p. OCl; OClWHi; WHi.
                                   46760
---- Evidence taken by authority of the honorable, the secretary of the Treasury, under a report of the Committee of claims, and a resolution concurred in by the House of representatives of the United States of America, in the case indemnity of Charles F. Sibbald, of Philadelphia. Together with the official orders and documents in relation to the same, obtained from the executive departments at Washington. Philadelphia, Printed by J. Richards, 1837. 54 p. DLC; NIC; OO.   46761

(Sigourney, Charles).

To the stockholders of the Phoenix bank, Hartford, Conn. (Hartford, 1837). n. imp. 15 p. MiD-B.   46762

Sigourney, Lydia Howard (Huntley), 1791-1865.

Ginzerdorff, and other poems.

By Mrs. L. H. Sigourney.
Second edition... Printed by
West & Throw. New York,
Published by Leavitt, Lord and
Co.; Boston, Crocker and
Brewster, 1837. 300 p. MeBa.
46763
---- The girls reading book in
prose and poetry, for schools.
By Mrs. L. H. Sigourney,
Fifth edition. New York, Pub-
lished by Turner & Hayden;
Raleigh, N.C., Henry D. Turn-
er, 1837. 243 p.   46764

---- Letters to young ladies.
By Mrs. L. H. Sigourney ...
3d ed. New-York, Harper &
brothers, 1837. 259 p. IaMuC;
NBP; NNQ; NNMer; ScDuE.
46765
---- ---- Fourth edition. New
York, Harper & Brothers, 1837.
259 p. CtSoP; ICU; NB;
NCats; NRSB.   46766

---- Zinzendorff, and other
poems ... (2d ed.) Leavitt,
Lord and co.; Boston, Crocker
and Brewster, 1837. 300 p.
MB; MnU; OC; SdMit; WHi.
46767
Silver, Samuel.
Remarks for the serious con-
sideration of members of Indiana
Yearly Meeting. Richmond,
Ind., 1837. PSC-Hi.   46768

Silvestre De Sacy, Antoine
Isaac, 1758-1838.
Principles of general grammar,
adapted to the capacity of youth,
and proper to serve as an intro-
duction to the study of languages.
Translated and fitted for Ameri-
can use by D. Fosdick, Jr.
2d American, from the 5th
French ed. Andover, etc.,
Gould & Newman, 1837. CoU;
MDeeP; MH; NCH; VtU. 46769

Sim, Thomas Jun.
Lectures on phrenology, or
the physiology of the brain.
... by Thomas Sim. ... Cincinnati, Published by Burnet &
Sim, 1837. 4 p. OC.   46770

Simms, Frederick Walter, 1803-
1865.
A treatise on the principles
and practice of leveling; showing
its application to purposes of
civil engineering particularly in
the construction of roads. with
Mr. Tilford's rules for the same
.... By Frederick W. Simms....
to which have been added tables
for calculating earth-work....
Baltimore, Fielding Lucas, jr.
(John D. Toy, pr.), 1837. 121,
32 p. IaAS; MBAt; NjR; PU;
ViU.   46771

Simms, William Gilmore, 1806-
1870.
Damsel of Darien. New York,
Harper, 1837. 2 v. ScU.
46772
---- Guy Rivers: A Tale of
Georgia ... (anon.). 3d ed.
New York, Harper & Brothers,
1837. 2 v.   46773

---- Martin Faber, the story of
a criminal; and other tales. By
the author of "The yemassee,"
"Guy Rivers," "Mellichampe,"
&c. In two volumes. New-
York, Published by Harper &
brothers, 1837. 242 p. GAuY;
MH; NjP; PU; ScC.   46774

Sinclair, Catherine, 1800-1864.
Modern society; or, The march
of intellect. The conclusion of
modern accomplishments. By
Miss Catherine Sinclair...New
York, R. Carter, 1837. [9]-
441 p. CtHT; MdBG; NjP; OTifH.
46775
The singer's own book. 4th ed.

Woodstock, Vt., Haskell &
Palmer, 1837. 184 p. MH;
RPB.   46776

The sisters: or a history of
the Stanley family written for
the Massachusetts Sabbath
school society, and revised by
the committee of publication,
Boston (Christopher C. Dean),
1837. 46 p. DLC; MWal. 46777

Sketches and eccentricities of
Col. David Crockett, of West
Tennessee ... 10th ed. New
York, Harper & brothers, 1837.
[9]-209 p. DLC; LN; MH; NNC;
OClWHi.   46778

Sketches of the Indian war in
Florida, embracing a minute account of the principal cruel
and horrible Indian massacres,
together with the providential
and miraculous preservation of
the life of Mrs. Simmons, who
has been twice taken by the
Indian. ... N.Y., 1837.
23 p. NN; PPRF; WHi.   46779

Skinner, Otis A.
    Easy lessons designed for
the use of small children in
Sabbath schools. Boston, 1837.
18 p. DLC; PHi.   46780

Skinner, Thomas, 1800?-1843.
    Adventures during a journey
over land to India, by way of
Egypt, Syria and the holy
land. By Major Skinner, Author
of "Excursions in India." First
American edition. Philadelphia,
A. Waldie; Boston, Weeks, Jordan & Co., 1837. 359 p. MeU;
NCH; PHi; PU; RLa.   46781

Slacum, William A.
    Memorial, 1837. Washington,
Pub. by Govt., 1837. 31 p.
CSmH; ICN; OrHi; Wa; WaU.
                                46782

Slade, William, 1786-1859.
    Speech of Mr. Slade, of Ver-
mont, on the abolition of slavery
and the slave trade in the District of Columbia, delivered in
the House of representatives of
the U.S. December 20, 1837.
To which is added the intended
conclusion of the speech, sur-
pressed by resolution of the
House. [Washington, 1837?].
24 p. ICU; LNT; NBu; OO;
RPB.   46783

Slavery rhymes, addressed to
the friends of liberty throughout
the United States. By a looker
on. New York, John S. Taylor,
1837. 84 p. MB; OClWHi; OO;
PU.   46784

Sleigh, William Willcocks, b. 1796.
    The Christian's defensive dic-
tionary. Being an alphabetical
refutation on the general objec-
tions to the Bible... By W. W.
Sleigh. Philadelphia, Edward
C. Biddle, 1837. 437 p. ArCH;
GDecCT; KyDC; PPiW; WHi.
                                46785
No entry   46786

---- Exposure of Maria Monk's
pretended abduction and convey-
ance to the Catholic Asylum,
Philadelphia, August 15, 1837.
Philadelphia, T. K. & P. G. Col-
lina, 1837. 36 p. CaOTU; DLC;
NN; PPL-R; PHi.   46787

---- Libel on W. W. Sleigh.
Commonwealth versus Thomas
Clark. Philadelphia, 1837. 57
p. PHi.   46788

No entry   46789

(Smedley, Edward), 1789-1836.
    ... Sketches from Venetian
history ... New York, Harper &

brothers, 1837. 2 v. C-S;
FTa; MH; PLFM; TxDaM. 46790

Smiley, Thomas Tucker, d. 1879.
A complete key to Smiley's
new federal calculator, or
scholar's assistant. By Thomas
T. Smiley. Philadelphia, Published by Grigg and Elliott,
1837. 177 p. PLor.   46791

---- An easy introduction to the
study of geography, on an improved plan... 25th edition.
improved. Philadelphia, Griggs
and Ellis, 1837. 252 p. PPM.
                            46792
---- ---- 35th ed. improved.
Philadelphia, Grigg and Elliot,
1837. 252 p. MiU-C.   46793

---- The new federal calculator,
or scholar's assistant: containing the most concise and accurate rules for performing the
operations in common arithmetic;
together with numerous examples
under each of the rules, varied
so as to make them conformable
to almost every kind of business,
for the use of schools and counting houses... Philadelphia,
Published and for sale by Grigg
and Elliott, 1837. 180 p., [8]
p. MoS.   46794

---- Scripture geography; or,
A companion to the Bible, being
a geographical and historical
account of the places mentioned
in the Holy Scriptures. Philadelphia, Colling, 1837. 288 p.
InR; MdW; NcMfC; ODaB; PPM.
                            46795
Smith, Asa Dodge.
Dancing as an amusement for
christians; a sermon delivered
in the Brainerd Presbyterian
Church, New York. New York,
1837. 27 p. Nh-Hi.   46796

Smith, Benjamin Bosworth, 1794-
1884.
An address delivered on the
occasion of the 3rd commencement, October 26, 1836, of the
Theological seminary of the
Protestant Episcopal church in
the diocese of Kentucky. Lexington, Ky., 1837. 16 p. MBD;
MdBD; MH; MH-And.   46797

Smith, Charles Adam, 1809-1879.
The catechumen's guide, prepared with special reference to
the wants of the Evangelical
Lutheran church in the United
States. By Charles A. Smith.
Albany, Joel Munsell, Printer,
1837. 312 p. NAl; OSW; PPLT.
                            46798
Smith, Daniel B., 1792-1883.
Inquiry into nature and functions of the moral sense; address
to senior class of Haverford
school, twelfth of ninth month,
1837. Philadelphia, Joseph Rakestraw, printer, 1837. 24 p.
MH; PHC; RPB; WHi.   46799

---- Lectures on domestic duties.
By Daniel D. Smith ... Portland,
S. H. Colesworthy, 1837. 160 p.
DLC; MeHi; MH; MMeT-Hi.
                            46800
---- The principles of chemistry
...by Daniel B. Smith, 2nd ed.
rev... Philadelphia, Dobson,
1837. 213 p. PHC; PPCP.
                            46801
Smith, Delazon, 1816-1860.
A history of Oberlin, or New
lights of the West. Embracing
the conduct and character of the
officers and students of the institution; together with the
colonists, from the founding of
the institution. Delazon Smith
... Cleveland, S. Underhill &
son, printers, 1837. 82 p.
ICRL; MB; NcU; OU; PPPrHi.
                            46802

Smith, Elias, 1769-1846.
The American physician and family assistant in five parts. 4th ed. Boston, 1837. 306 p. MB; MBM; NhD; Nh-Hi; NNNAM.
46803

Smith, Ethan, 1762-1849.
Key to the Revelation. In 38 lectures, taking the whole book in course. 2d ed. Boston, Whipple & Damrell, 1837. 396 p. CBPSR; ICN; MeBaT; NhD; OO.
46804

Smith, (Francis Osmond Jonathan, 1806-1876.
Letters from Mr. Smith, Member of Congress from Maine, in vindication of his Vote against the Sub-Treasury Bill. [Portland, 1837.] 16 p. MBAt; MeHi.
46805

Smith, Gerrit, 1797-1874.
Letter of Gerrit Smith to Rev. James Smylie, of the state of Mississippi. New York, R. G. Williams for the American anti-slavery society, 1837. 66 p. CtMW; IU; NNUT; TxH; WHi.
46806

---- Letter to Edward C. Delavan on temperance. Whitesboro, 1837. Press of the Friend of Man, 1837? 18 p. CtY-D; DHU; MBC; NN; WHi.
46807

---- Letter to Hon. Gulian C. Verplanck. (Dated Dec. 12, 1837) [Whitesboro?, Press of the Friend of Man, 1837]. 18 p. MiU-C; NIC; NN.
46808

Smith, Henry.
The church harmony. Containing a selection of approved psalm and hymn tunes, set pieces, and anthems adapted to the divine worship of the various religious denominations, and a concise introduction to music.

With additions and improvements. By Henry Smith. Chambersburg, Pa., 1837. 296 p. MoWgT; PReaHi; PRHi.
46809

Smith, Horatio, 1779-1849.
Brambletye house, or Cavaliers and roundheads. By Horatio Smith, New York, Dearbon, 1837. 296 p. MB; MH; MNS.
46810

---- Tor Hill. By Horace Smith .... New York, George Dearborn & Co., publishers, 1837. 267 p. MeB; MWA; WaPS.
46811

Smith, Jerome Van Crowninshield, 1800-1879.
The class book of anatomy, explanatory of the first principles of human organization, as the basis of physical education. 3d ed. Boston, R. S. Davis, 1837. CU; MB; MBC; MH; NN.
46812

Smith, John, 1580-1631.
A description of New England; or The observations, and discoveries by Captain John Smith (admirable of that Country) ... in the year of our Lord 1614; with the successe of sixe ships, that went the next yeare 1615... London, Printed by H. Lownes, for R. Clerke, 1616. [Washington, P. Force, 1837]. 6 p. 1, 34, [2] p. CtHT; CU; MdBP; ViU; WHi.
46813

---- New Englands trials... ... Written by Captain John Smith, sometimes gouernour of Virginia, and admirall of New-England. The 2d ed. London, Printed by W. Jones, 1622. [Washington, P. Force, 1837.] 23 p. AzU; CtHT; MH; NjP; WHi.
46814

Smith, John Augustine, 1782-1865.
On the sense of touch, or,

Physiology and philosophy opposed to materialism and athe-
ism. Being an introductory
discourse, delivered on the 6th
day of November, 1837, on the
opening of the new college on
Crosby street. New York,
W. E. Dean, 1837. 7-62 p.
MH-And; NNNAM; NNC; WHi;
Wu.   46815

Smith, John Cross, 1803-1878.
The unpardonable sin. A
sermon, delivered on Sabbath
afternoon, July 23, 1837, in
Georgetown, D.C. by John C.
Smith ... Washington, J.
Gideon, jr., 1837. 18 p.
OClWHi; PCA; PPPrHi; ScU;
ViU.   46816

[Smith, John Jay], 1798-1881.
Celebrated trials of all countries and remarkable cases of
criminal jurisprudence. Selected
by a member of the Philadelphia
bar ... Philadelphia, E. L.
Carey & A. Hart, 1837. 5-
596 p. IaU-L; NNebg; MB;
PP; WU.   46817

---- Notes for a history of the
Library Co. of Philadelphia.
Philadelphia, 1837. 8 p. DLC;
PHi; PPL; PPLT.   46818

Smith, John William, 1809-1845.
A compendium of mercantile
law. By John William Smith ...
Philadelphia, J. S. Littell, [etc.,
etc], 1837. [3]-320 p. CU;
GU-M; MiD-B; PP; RPL.   46819

Smith, Joseph, 1796-1868.
An inaugural address, de-
livered by the Rev. Joseph
Smith, A.M. upon his entrance
on the office of president of
Franklin college, New Athens,
Ohio, June 1837. Pittsburgh,
William Allinder, 1837. 12 p.
IaMP; OClWHi.   46820

Smith, Marcus A.
The Boston Speaker, being
a collection of pieces in prose,
poetry, and dialogue. By
Marcus A. Smith. Stereotype ed.
Boston, published by Joseph
Dowe, 1837. 216 p. MH; MWfo.
                             46821
---- Epitome of systematic theology... 2d ed. rev. and cor.
Watertown, Hunt, 1837. 292 p.
IEG; MBC; MH-AH; NCH; NCaS.
                             46822
Smith, Oliver Hampton, 1794-
1859.
Speech of Mr. Smith, of Indiana, on the sub-treasury system, delivered in the Senate of
the United States, September 21,
1837. Washington, Gales, 1837.
13 p. In; MBAt; MH; NNC; PPL.
                             46823
Smith, Prudence.
Modern American cookery:
containing directions for making
soups, roasting, boiling, baking,
dressing vegetables, poultry etc.,
with a list of family medical recipes and a valuable miscellany.
By Miss Prudence Smith. New
York, Harper & Bros., 1837.
222 p. DLC.   46824

Smith, Richard Penn, 1799-1834.
Col. Crockett's Esploits and
adventures in Texas ..... Written by himself. The narrative
brought down from the death of
Col. Crockett to the battle of
San Jacinto, by an Eye-witness.
6th ed. Philadelphia, T. K. &
P. G. Collins, 1837. 216 p.
DeWi; MeB; NcD; OCHP; ViRU.
                             46825
Smith, Roswell Chamberlain,
1797-1875.
Smith's Atlas for schools,
academies and families; an atlas
to accompany the productive
geography... Philadelphia, W.
Marshall and Co., [1837?]. MH.
                             46826

---- English grammar on the productive system, a method of instruction recently adopted in Germany and Switzerland, designed for schools and academies. Edition 2. Philadelphia, Marshall, [etc.], 1837. 192 p. MB; MWHi; OO; PU.   46827

---- Smith's geography. Geography on the productive system; ... By Roswell C. Smith, ... Philadelphia, W. Marshall & co.; Hartford, D. Burgess & co. ... 1837. 274 p. front. CtY; MeAu; MH; NhD; NNC.   46828

---- Practical and mental arithmetic, on a new plan: [i]n which mental arithmetic is combined with the use of the slate; 61st ed., rev. and enl. with exercises for the slate. To which is added a practical system of bookkeeping, by Roswell C. Smith. Cincinnati, Burgess and Crane, 1837. 284 p. MoU.   46829

---- ---- New York, R. Lockwood, 1837. MH.   46830

---- ---- Philadelphia, William Marshall & Co., 1837. 282 p. CtHWatk; ICU; KyBgW; PPM; WHi.   46831

Smith, Sarah Pogson.
    Zerah, the believing Jew; published in aid of laying the cornerstone of Jesus' church, a Protestant church in the valley of the Mississippi.... New York, n. pub., printed by the N.Y. Protestant Episcopal press, 1837. 286 p. MLow; NjR; PPDrop.   46832

Smith, Thomas, 1775 or 6-1830.
    The origin and history of missions ... comp. from authentic documents; forming a complete missionary repository ... By the Rev. John O. Choules ... and the Rev. Thomas Smith ... 4th ed., continued to the present time ... Boston, Gould, Kendall and Lincoln [etc.], 1837. 2 v. CU; KKcBT; MeAu; MH; OMC.   46833

Smith, Worthington, 1795-1856.
    A sermon delivered at the dedication of the Washington Street Church, in Beverly, March 29, 1837. By Worthington Smith, ... Salem, Palfray and Chapman, printers, 1837. 20 p. CBPSR; MBev; MeBat; MWA; RPB.   46834

Smollett, Tobias George, 1721-1771.
    The history of England from the revolution in 1688 to the death of George the second, designed as a continuation of Hume. by T. Smollett, M.D. Philadelphia, published by M'Carty & Davis, 1837. [6], 967 [6] p. CtHT; Ia; KM; MoSM.   46835

Smyser, Daniel M.
    Address delivered before the Philomathaean Society of Pennsylvania College on the 17th of February, 1837. Gettysburg, Printed by H. C. Neinstedt, 1837. 16 p. InU; OSW; PHi; PLT.   46836

Smyth, Thomas, 1808-1873.
    The history of the Second Presbyterian church, Charleston, S.C. Two discourses, delivered in the Second Presbyterian church, on the occasion of its 26th anniversary, April 3d, 1837. By the Rev. Thomas Smyth, pastor. Charleston, S.C., 1837. GDecCT.   46837

---- Oration, delivered on the
48th anniversary of the orphan
house, in Charleston, S.C.
By the Rev. Thomas Smyth.
Charleston, J.S. Burges, 1837.
v. p. GDecCT; MBC; MiD-B;
PPL; ScC.   46838

---- The Voice of God in calam-
ity: or, Reflections on the loss
of the steam-boat Home, October 9, 1837. A sermon: delivered in the Second Presbyterian church, Charleston. On
Sabbath morning, October 22,
1837: by the Rev. Thomas
Smyth, pastor, 2th ed. Charleston, Jenkins and Hussey, 1837.
DLC; GU; NcU; PHi; PPPrHi.
                             46839
---- ---- 4th ed. Charlestown,
Jankins & Hussey, 1837. 32 p.
MH; MiD-B; NjR; PPPrHi; TxU.
                             46840
Snelling, William Joseph, 1804-
1848.
    Rat-trap, The; or cogitations
of a convict in the House of
Correction...[1st ed.]. Boston,
G. N. Thompson, Weeks, Jordan
and Co., 1837. DLC; MBAt;
MH-L; MiU-C.   46841

---- ---- 2nd ed. Boston,
G. N. Thomson, Weeks, Jordan
and Co., 1837. DLC; MB; MH;
NjP.   46842

Snowden, Edgar.
    An address delivered before
the Enosinian Society of the
Columbian College, D.C., July
4, 1837, by Edgar Snowden.
Published by request of the
Society. Washington, printed
by Peter Force, 1837. 23 p.
MBC; NCH; OClWHi; PPL; ScU.
                             46843
Society for inquiry of the Hamil-
ton Literary and Theological
Institution.

    Annual report of the Society
for inquiry of the Hamilton Lit-
erary & Theological Institution,
March 1837. Utica, Printed by
Bennett & Bright, 1837. 20 p.
PScrHi.   46844

Songs of Zion, being a choice
collection of hymns selected from
different denominations for the
use of pious christians. Con-
cord, 1837. 189 p. Nh-Hi.
                             46845
Sophocles.
    The Aias of Sophocles ....
with notes and a critique on the
subject of the play by I. W.
Stuart.... N.Y., Gould and
Newman, 1837. 222 p. WaU.
                             46846
---- The Electra of Sophocles,
with notes, for the use of colleges in the United States. By
T. D. Woolsey ... Boston, J.
Munroe and co., 1837. 134 p.
CtHT; KWiU; MeB; PU; ViU.
                             46847
---- The Oedipus Tyrannus of
Sophocles, with notes and a
critique on the subject of the
play. By I. W. Stuart, Pro-
fessor of Greek and Roman Lit-
erature in the college of South
Carolina. New York, Gould and
Newman, 1837. 3-222 p. CtMW;
IAIA; NcD; MH-AH; RWe.
                             46848
---- Tragedies: literally, trans-
lated into English prose, with
notes; 3d ed. New York, Wm.
Jackson, 1837. 307 p. KyDC;
MH; MnS; MoKiW; ScCC. 46849

South Brooklyn Building Associa-
tion.
    Articles of Agreement of the
South Brooklyn Building Associa-
tion. New York, Printed by
J. M. Elliott, 1837. (4), 3-17 p.
NHi; NN.   46850

South Carolina, Constitutional
Court.

Reports of Judicial decisions
in the Constitutional Court of
South Carolina, held at
Charleston and Columbia, in
1817, 1818. A new edition.
Two volumes in one Vol. I.
By John Hill, Charleston, W.
Riely, 1837. 2 v. in 1. CLCL;
F-SC; KyU-L; MdBB; TxU-L.
46851

---- Laws, statutes, etc.

Acts and resolutions of the
General assembly of the state
of South Carolina, passed in
December, 1836. Columbia,
S. Weir, 1837. IaU-L; In-SC;
Nj; R; Sc.   46852

---- ---- Statutes at large of
South Carolina. Edited under
authority of the legislature.
Columbia, A. S. Johnston, 1837.
10 v. CLSU.   46853

---- Medical College. Charleston.

Annual announcement of the
trustees & faculty of the Medical College of S.C., for the
session of 1837-38. Charleston,
Burges, 1837. 16 p. NcD; NN.
46854
---- ---- Catalogue of the
Trustees, Faculty, and Students,
1836-1837. Charleston, J. S.
Burges, 1837. 8 p. CSmH;
DLC; MHi; NcD; ScU.   46855

South Cove Corporation.

Report of the Board of directors of the South cove corporation, to stockholders ....
By Edward H. Robbins, Nathaniel
Curtis and Edward D. Clark.
Boston, n. pub., Printed by
Crocker and Brewster, 1837.
14 p. M; NjR.   46856

South Hanover College.

... Memorial of the corporation
of South Hanover College, Indiana praying the donation of a
tract of land in aid of that institution. December 19, 1837.
[at foot of sheet:] Blair & Rives,
printers. [Washington, 1837.]
NN.   46857

Southard, Samuel Lewis, 1787-
1842.

An address delivered before
the American Whig and Cliosophic societies of the College of
New Jersey, September 26, 1837.
By Samuel L. Southard, LL.D.
Princeton, Printed by R. E.
Hornor, 1837. 50 p. CSmH;
InU; MB; NNUT; PU.   46858

---- ... Speech of Mr. Southard
... on the specie circular. Thursday, December 29, 1836. Washington, 1837. 2 p. DLC.
46859
Southern Literary Messenger,
Richmond.

Prospectus ... Richmond,
Va., 1837. NjP.   46860

Southey, Robert, 1774-1843.

Poetical works, by Robert
Southey. New York, Crowell,
[1837]. 592 p. CoCsC; InNd;
KWi; NjN; OM.   46861

Southwark Fire Insurance Co.
Phila.

Act of Incorporation with By-
Laws, July 1837. Philadelphia,
1837. PHi.   46862

[Southwick, Solomon], 1773-1839.

Five lessons for young men.
By a man of sixty. Albany, Alfred Southwick, 1837. [7]-196
p. CSt; ICP; LNB; MH; NN.
46863
Sparks, Jared, 1789-1866.

Life of George Washington....
Boston, American Stationery co.,

1837. LNH; MDeeP; MH; MS.
46864

---- Lives of Sir William Phips,
Israel Putnam, Lucretia Maria
Davidson, & David Rittenhouse.
Boston, Hilliard, Gray & co.;
London, R. J. Kennett, 1837.
398 p. (v. 7 of Library of
American biography). CtHT;
MB; MdToH; NNS; PPPrHi.
46865

Sparrow, Patrick J.
The Sabbath: a sermon
preached Sept. 11, 1836, in
the Sixth Pres. Ch., Phila.
Philadelphia, Martien, 1837.
MdBP; PHi; PPPrHi. 46866

Spear, William Wallace.
Ministerial devotedness. A
sermon occasioned by the death,
of the Rev. Daniel Cobia ...
By William W. Spear ...
Charleston, A. E. Miller, 1837.
18 (1) p. MH-AH; NNG; RPB.
46867

Specimens of American eloquence,
consisting of choice selections
from the productions of the
most distinguished American
orators. Middletown, E. Hunt
and Co., 1837. 383 p. CtY;
IU; PHi; OCHP; TU. 46868

Speeches in Congress on the Mississippi election, the bill to postpone the 4th instalment under the
deposit act, the issuing of
treasury notes, the message, &c.
Washington, 1837. PPL. 46869

Speeches of Messrs. Buchanan
and Benton, on the bill to ad-
mit the state of Michigan into
the Union ... Senate ... Jan.
3, 1837. Washington, D.C.,
1837. 14 p. ICU; MiD-B;
OClWHi; PPM; WHi. 46870

Sprague, Hosea, 1779-1843.
Sprague's Register of the

Weather, in Hingham, Massachusetts, on the plain, one mile
from the Sea. Printed at Hingham, 1837. 32, (14) p. MB;
MDeeP; MH; MWA. 46871

Sprague, William Buell, 1795-
1876.
Contrast between true and
false religion. New York, Daniel
Appleton, 1837. CtHC. 46872

---- Lectures illustrating the contrast between true Christianity
and various other systems. By
William B. Sprague.... New-
York, Daniel Appleton & co....,
1837. 386 p. CSansS; ICP;
KyLoP; NjP; RPB. 46873

---- A Sermon addressed to
the Second Presbyterian Congregation in Albany, April 23,
1837, the sabbath after the interment of Mrs. Ruth Savage:
wife of the Hon. John Savage,
late Chief Justice of the State
of New-York. Albany, Packard
& Van Benthuysen, printers,
1837. MB; NjR; NN; PPL; WHi.
46874

---- A Sermon, delivered March
22, 1837 at the ordination and
installation of the Rev. Montgomery T. Goodale. Albany,
printed by Packard & Van
Benthuysen, 1837. 12 p. I;
MBC; PHi; NN; RPB. 46875

---- Tower of Babel; a sermon
addressed to the Second Presbyterian congregation in Albany,
May 11th, 1837. Albany, Packard, 1837. 26 p. MBC; NCH;
NjR; NN; PPPrHi. 46876

Spring, Caleb.
Death and Heaven. A sermon
preached at Newark, at the in-

terment of the Rev. Edward D. Griffin, D.D. on the 10th of Nov. 1837. New York, 1837. 40 p. MHi. 46877

Spring, Gardiner, 1785-1873.
Address before the Mercantile Library Association of the city of New York... New York, Published by John S. Taylor, 1837. 39 p. CtY; NBu; PPAmP; RPB; WHi. 46878

The Standard of Christian Benevolence and Self-Denial. The Last Supper. "(2 lines)." Boston, George P. Oakes, 1837. (3), 4-16 p. DLC; MMeT. 46879

Stanhope, Philip Henry, 1805-1875.
The life of Belisarius. Philadelphia, Published by G. W. Donohue, 1837. 306 p. DSU; MWA; PPF. 46880

Stanley, Jesse, Comp.
Conversations as between parents and children. Designed for instruction of youth. 3rd ed. Richmond, Iowa, pub. by ..., 1837. [5]-131 p. OSW; TKL-Mc. 46881

(Stansbury, Joseph).
The town meeting, a Tory squib, from the copy found among the papers of the late Edward Duffield, of Moreland. Philadelphia, (printed by E. D. Ingraham), 1837. 8 p. MH. 46882

Stanton, Benjamin F.
Salvation by Grace or; Justification by Faith in the imputed Righteousness of Christ alone. A sermon delivered at Hanover Church, Prince Edward, Va. Jan. 15, 1837 by Benjamin F. Stanton, Pastor, designed as "A Word in Season."

(Published by request). Richmond, Printed by the Franklin Press, 1837. [3], 23 p. NcMHi. 46883

Stanton, Henry Brewster, 1805-1887.
Remarks of Henry B. Stanton, in the representatives' hall on the 23rd and 24th of February, before the Committee of the House of representatives, of Massachusetts, to whom was referred sundry memorials on the subject of slavery. Boston, I. Knapp, 1837. 84 p. CtHC; ICU; MH; MiD-B; NNUT. 46884

---- ---- 2d ed. Boston, I. Knapp, 1837. [3]-90 p. MH; OClWHi; PHi; TxU; WHi. 46885

---- ---- 5th ed. Boston, Published by Isaac Knapp, 1837. 90 p. MH; MHi; MnHi; NNCoCi. 46886

Starck, Johann Friedrich, 1680-1756.
Daily handbook for good and evil days...with a daily prayerbook. Philadelphia, Mentz, 1837. 534 + 104 p. OHi. 46887

---- Tägliches Handbuch in Guten und Bösen Tagen. Enthaltend Aufmunterungen, Gebete und Lieder....von M. Johann Jacob Starck,....Mit fünf Holzschnitten. Philadelphia, Herausgegeben von Georg W. Mentz und Sohn....1837. 536, (104) p. PReaHi; PSt. 46888

Starkie, Thomas.
A practical treatise on the law of evidence and digest of proofs in civil and criminal proceedings. Sixth edition from a New England edition. In two volumes. Philadelphia, P. H. Nicklin and T. Johnson, 1837. 2 v. CLSU; InCW; IaDmD-L; NbCrD; PU; TU. 46889

Starling, Thomas.

A new geographical and historical index, exhibiting at one view all that is interesting in geography and history in the Holy Scriptures, and forming a complete Bible gazetteer. Compiled and arranged under the inspection of Thomas Starling. Published by the Brattleboro Typographic Company (Incorporated, October 26, 1836.). Brattleboro, Vt., 1837. 46 p. KWiU.   46890

State Bank of Indiana.

By-laws, rules and regulations for the government of the state bank of Indiana and branches. Revised May, 1837. Indianapolis, Douglas and Noel, 1837. 15 p. In.   46891

Statements in relation to the proceedings of Friends in England in aid of the efforts for the abolition of slavery. n.p., (1837?). 8 p. MH; MiU-C.   46892

Stearns, Isaac.

Right and wrong, in Mansfield, Massachusetts or, an account of the pro-slavery mob of October 10th, 1836: when an anti-slavery lecturer (Charles C. Burleigh) was silenced by the beat of drums, etc...Pawtucket, R. Sherman, printer, 1837. 61 p. DLC; MWA; NcU; NIC; RHi.   46893

Stearns, (J. Milton).

The unhappy life of Stephen Frothingham, designed for Sabbath Schools. Norwich (U.S.), 1837. 65 p. AmSSchU.   46894

Stearns, Jonathon French, 1808-

Female influence, and the true Christian mode of its' exercise. A discourse delivered in the First Presbyterian church in Newburyport, July 30, 1837. Newburyport, John G. Tilton, 1837. 24 p. CU; MWA; NjR; OClWHi; RPB.   46895

Stebbins, Sumner.

Address in refutation of the Thomsonian system of medical practice, delivered in the lecture room of the Chester Co. cabinet of natural science, West Chester, Pa. on Dec. 31, 1836. West Chester, n. pub., 1837. 47 p. MdBM; WU-M.   46896

Steele's Albany almanac, for the year 1838 .... Albany, n. pub. Printed by Packard and Van Benthuysen, (1837). (38), 44 p. MWA; NjR.   46897

Steele's Western Guide Book, and Emigrant's Directory; containing different routes through the states of New-York, Ohio, Indiana, Illinois, Michigan, Wisconsin Territory, &c. with short descriptions of the Climate, Soil, Productions, Prospects, &c. Ninth edition. Greatly improved and enlarged. Buffalo, Published by Oliver G. Steele, 1837. 108 p. ICHi; IU. 46898

Stephani, Heinrich, 1761-1850.

Handfibel zum lesenlernen nach der lautirmethode. Ed. 53. Zum ersten male für die deutschen schulen Nord-Amerika's zum druck befördert. Philadelphia, Wesselhoeft, 1837. 58 p. DLC; PU.   46899

Stephen, Henry John, 1787-1864.

A treatise on the principles of pleading in civil actions: comprising a summary view of the whole proceedings in a suit at law. By Henry John Stephen ... From the 3d. and last London

ed. ... The 3d Amer. ed. ...
Philadelphia, Robert H. Small,
1837. 453 p. CLSU; MdBB;
MoU; TMeB; ViU. 46900

Stephen, James, Fitzjames.
Liberty, equality, fraternity.
By James Fitzjames Stephen.
New York, Holt, (1837). 350 p.
PLFM. 46901

Stephens, Daniel.
A sermon, preached at the
ordination of Prof. A. Stephens
& the Rev. Mr. Forbes, at Nash-
ville, during the session of the
Episcopal convention, on the 15th
October, 1837. By Rev. Daniel
Stephens, D.D. rector of St.
James' parish, Bolivar, Tenn.
(Published at the special request
of the lay members of the con-
vention). Nashville, S. Nye &
Co., Printers, 1837. 28 p.
NNG; T; TNL. 46902

[Stephens, John Lloyd], 1805-
1852.
Incidents of travel in Egypt,
Arabia Petraea and the Holy
Land. By an American [pseud.]
With a map and engravings.
New York, Harper & brothers,
1837. 2 v. GHi; MB; NNS;
PHi; TU. 46903

---- ---- 2nd ed. N.Y., Harper
& Bros., 1837. 2 v. IaMP;
KWiU; MB; MBBC; NNUT. 46904

---- 10th ed. New York, Harper
& brothers, 1837. 2 v. DNC;
MB; MeB; MH; OKentU. 46905

---- ---- 11th ed. New York,
Harper & bros., 1837. V. 2.
ICMS; NNZi. 46906

Stephens, Joseph, of Philadelphia?
Great worshop; or, The way
to amass wealth and be happy:
connected with the way to keep

and appropriate it, both in a
temporal and moral sense. Philadelphia, printed for the author,
1837. 214 p. NNC; PPM; PU.
46907
Steubenville Female Seminary.
Catalogue and Outline of the
Steubenville Female Seminary,
1837. N.p., 1837. 16 p. MHi.
46908
Stevens, Alex(ander) H(odgdon).
A clinical lecture on the
primary treatment of injuries,
delivered at the New-York hospital, Nov. 22, 1837. By Alex
H. Stevens ... New York, Adlard & Saunders, 1837. 34 p.
MBAt; MH-M; NNNAM; NNC; OC.
46909
Stevens, George A.
An address delivered before
the Hawes juvenile association
for the suppression of profanity,
at the public annual exhibition
of the male department of the
Hawes school, Wednesday, August
23, 1837. By George A. Stevens.
With the constitution of the
H.J.A. and a list of the members annexed.... Boston, Weeks,
Jordan and Co., 1837. 11 p.
MiD-B. 46910

Stewart, Dugald, 1753-1828.
Elements of the Philosophy of
the Human Mind By Dugald Stewart in two volumes. Boston,
James Munroe and Company,
1837. 2 v. OWoC. 46911

[Stewart, John], 1749-1822.
The moral state of nations,
or travels over the most interesting parts of the globe to dis-
cover the source of moral motion,
communicated to lead mankind
through the conviction of the
sense of intellectual existences
and an enlightened state of nature ... In the year of man's
retrospective knowledge, by as-

tronomical calculations 5000
[Year of the comon era, 1790]
Granville, Middletown, N.J.
Reprinted by G. H. Evans,
1837. 122 p. NcD; NT.   46912

Stiles, Joseph Clay.
    A sermon on Predestination,
preached in Milledgeville, August,
1826. By Joseph C. Stiles.
Second Edition. Frankfort, Ky.,
A. C. Hodges, printer, 1837.
83 p. ICU; PPPrHi.   46913

Stimpson's Boston directory,
containing the names of inhabitants, their occupations, places
of business and dwelling houses,
and the city register with lists
of streets...and other information. Boston, Charles Stimpson, Jr., 1837. 14, 314 p.
MBCH; MCanHi; MLy; WHi.
    46914

Stirling, Edward, 1807-1894.
    Bachelor's buttons: a farce
in one act... 18 p. London,
New York, Samuel French, [1837].
OCl.   46915

Stoddard's Diary, or the Columbia Almanack for 1838. Hudson, N.Y., Ashbel Stoddard,
[1837]. MWA.   46916

Stokes, William, 1804-1878.
    Lectures on the theory and
practice of physic. 1st. Amer.
ed. Philadelphia, A. Waldie,
1837. 407 p. DNLM; ICU;
MB; OrU-M; PP.   46917

---- ... A treatise on the
diagnosis and treatment of dis-
eases of the chest. Part I.
Diseases of the lung and windpipe.
By William Stokes...Philadelphia,
A. Waldie, 1837. 360 p. CoCsC;
ICU; MB; MdBM; PU.   46918

Stone, Alvan, 1807-1833.

    Memoir of Alvan Stone, of
Goshen, Mass. By David Wright.
Boston, Gould, Kendall and
Lincoln; Hartford, Canfield and
Robbins; Northampton, J. H.
Butler; Northampton, printed
by John Metcalf, 1837. 256 p.
IAIS; MoSM; Nh; PCA; WHi.
    46919

Stone, Edwin Martin, 1805-1883.
    Coll. of hymns for Sabbath
schools. Boston, 1837. MB.
    46920

---- A sermon. The Forbear-
ance of Christ, an example for
Christians. Boston, 1837. 16
p. RHi.   46921

Stone, John.
    The Contrast, or The Evan-
gelical and Cractarian Systems,
compared in their Structure and
Tendencies. By the Rev. John
Stone, D.D. Rector of St. Paul's
Church, Brookline. New York,
Protestant Episcopal Society for
the Promotion of Evangelical
Knowledge. Lester Place, 1837.
240 p. NSchU.   46922

Stone, John Seeley, 1795-1882.
    The preaching of the word.
A sermon delivered at the institution of the Rev. Charles Mason
into the rectorship of St. Peter's
church, Salem, May 31, 1837
..... Salem, Wm. Ives & co.,
1837. 23 [1] p. CtSoP; MBC;
NNG; RPB; VtU.   46923

Stone, Thomas Treadwell, 1801-
1895.
    A sermon delivered in North
Yarmouth, June 28, 1837, before the Maine Missionary Society,
at its thirtieth anniversary.
By Thomas T. Stone, pastor of
the Congregational Church in
East Machias, Portland, Merrill
and Byram, 1837. 39 p. ICU;
MBC; MeB; MeHi; NjR.   46924

Stone, William L[eete], 1792-
1844.
Letter to Dr. A. Brigham on
animal magnetism, being an account of a remarkable interview
between the author and Miss
Loraina Brackett, while in a
state of somnambulism. By
William L. Stone ... New York,
George Dearborn and company,
[Scatcherd and Adams, printers,]
1837. 66 p. ICJ; MdBD;
MnHi; PPHa; ViU.   46925

---- ---- 2d. ed., with additions. New-York, G. Dearborn
& co., 1837. 75 p. ICU; MH;
NNP; ScU; WHi.   46926

---- ---- 3rd edition, with
additions. New-York, George
Dearborn & Co., 1837. 76 p.
MH; MiD-B.   46927

---- ---- Ed. 4, with additions.
New York, Dearborn, 1837.
76 p. IEN-M; MH; NCH;
NjP; OO.   46928

---- The Witches: A Tale of
New England ... (anon.).
Bath (N.Y.), R. L. Underhill,
1837. 72 p. CSmH; DLC;
MH; MWA.   46929

Stoneroad, Joel.
Christ the glorious builder
of the spiritual temple: a sermon...delivered...21st September, at the laying of the
corner-stone of the new Presbyterian church, Robbstown,
Pa. Pittsburgh, Pa., 1837.
10 p. [pamphlet]. PPPrHi;
WHi.   46930

Stories from real-life. New
York, S. Coleman; Boston,
Weeks, Jordan and Co., 1837.
DLC; MB.   46931

Stories illustrating four of the
Commandments. Boston, 1837.
MB.   46932

Stout, Arthur B.
A thesis on the cataract,
with some remarks on the eye.
By Arthur B. Stout. ... April,
1837. New York, Published by
Henderson Greene, 1837. 56 p.
CSt; MB; NNNAM; NNC; PPCP;
RNR.   46933

Stow, Baron, 1801-1869.
A brief narrative of the Dan-
ish mission on the coast of
Coromandel. Boston, 1837.
1 v. CtY; DLC.   46934

---- Voluntary associations--their
use and abuse. A discourse de-
livered in the meeting house of
the Second Baptist Society, in
Baldwin place, Thanksgiving-Day,
November 30, 1837. By Baron
Stow. Boston, Gould, Kendall
& Lincoln, 1837. 23 p. ICMe;
MBC; MiD-B; PCA; PPPrHi;
RPB.   46935

Stowe, Calvin Ellis, 1802-1886.
Queries on education. [Cin-
cinnati, Printed by Kendall and
Henry, 1837.] 7 p. OClWHi;
OO.   46936

---- Report on elementary public
instruction in Europe, made to
the thirty-sixth General assembly
of the state of Ohio, December
29, 1837. By C. E. Stowe.
Columbus, S. Medary, printer to
the state, 1837. 57 p. CSmH;
DLC; NcD; OClW; PPPrHi.
                            46937
Strafford Co., Conference, N.H.
Anniversaries of Strafford
County. ... Holden at Sandbornton, N.H., June, 1837. Gilmanton, 1837. CSmH.   46938

Strange, Robert, 1796-1854.
An address delivered before the two literary societies of the University of North Carolina by Hon. Robert Strange, June, 1837. Raleigh, Gales and son, 1837. 46 p. CSmH; MWA; NcD; PPL; ScU.   46939

---- Speech on the bill imposing additional duties on certain officers, as depositories in certain cases; Senate, September 21, 1837. (1837). 16 p. CtSoP; InHi; MH; NNC; RPB.
46940

Stranger's guide through New York City. New York, 1837. PPL.   46941

Streeter, Sebastian.
The new hymn book, designed for Universalist Societies. Compiled from approved authors, with variations and additions. By Sebastian and Russell Streeter. Seventeenth edition. Boston, Thomas Whittemore, P. Price, N.Y. and Haskell & Palmer, Woodstock, Vt., 1837. 408 p. IGK; MdBD; PPPrHi.   46942

---- ---- Eighteenth Edition. By the Publishers, Thomas Whittimore, Boston; P. Price, New York and Haskell & Palmer; Woodstock, Vt., 1837. 416 p. NSon.   46943

---- ---- 19th Ed. Boston, Thomas Whittemore, 1837. [4], 410 p. IEG; IGK.   46944

Strictures on "a letter to the Hon. Henry Clay on the annexation of Texas to the United States, by William E. Channing," by a friend to Texas. [Hoboken, September 15, 1837.] 24 p. CtY; DLC; MBAt; NjR; TxWFM.
46945

Strong, Jedediah.
Treatise on the growing of the silk worm. By Jedediah Strong of Germantown. Philadelphia, 1837. 16 p. PHi; PPL-R.   46946

Strong, Titus, 1787-1855.
Address before two engine companies in Greenfield at their anniversary, Jan. 4, 1837. Greenfield, 1837. MDeeP. 46947

---- The Deerfield captive; an Indian story, being a narrative of facts for the instruction of the young. 3d ed. Greenfield, Mass., A. Phelps, 1837. 67 p. IEN; MDeeP; MNF; NN; MHi.
46948

Stuart, John, d. 1838.
A sketch of the Cherokee and Choctaw Indians. By John Stuart, Captain. United States Army, Choctaw Nation. Little Rock, Printed by Woodruff & Pew, 1837. 42 p. DGU; GU; RPB.   46949

Stuyvesant Institute of the City of New York.
Charter and by-laws. New York, J. Narine, 1837. DLC; MH; OCHP.   46950

Suddards, William, 1805.
The British Pulpit: consisting of discourses By the most emminent living divines in England, Scotland, and Ireland....By the Rev. W. Suddards....Third edition. Philadelphia, Grigg & Elliott; DeSilver, Thomas & Co.; New York, Leavitt, Lord & Co.; D. Appleton & Co.; Boston, Crocker & Brewster, 1837. 503 p. CtMW; KSalW; MdBD; MsU.
46951

Sugden, Edward Burtenshaw, 1st baron St. Leonards, 1781-1875.
A practical treatise of powers.

By the right honorable Sir
Edward Sugden. From the
sixth London edition. Philadelphia, John S. Little, 1837.
2 v. KyLxT; NcD; PP; RPL;
WaU.   46952

.... Sukey Soap Suds: Hail
Columbia: Yankee volunteer....
Bay of Biscay, Ohio. Philadelphia, 1837. 8 p. NjP.
                              46953
Sullivan, William.
    Political class book; intended
to instruct the higher classes in
schools in the origin, nature,
and use of political power...
New edition. Boston, Hendee,
1837. 157 p. IaGG; LNL;
MHans; PPAmP; TxElp.   46954

---- Sea life; or, what may or
may not be done, and what
ought to be done by ship-
owners, ship-masters, mates
and seamen. By William Sullivan. Boston, published by
James B. Dow, 1837. 96 p.
CSmH; MB; MH; MNBedf; RHi.
                              46955
Summary description of the light
houses on the coasts of France
... Washington, 1837. PPL.
                              46956
Summerville, William, 1800-
1878.
    A treatise on psalmody, ad-
dressed to the worshippers of
God. Containing the work of
the Rev. Wm. Summerville...
Pittsburgh, printed for the pub-
lisher, 1837. DLC; NNUT.
                              46957
The sunday scholar's own book.
Philadelphia, 1837. MB.   46958

Sunday School and youth's Library. I can do without it...
New York, 1837. DLC.   46959

Sunderland, LaRoy, 1802-1885.

Anti-slavery manual, contain-
ing a collection of facts and argu-
ments on American slavery. By
LaRoy Sunderland. New York,
Piercy & Reed, 1837. 162 p.
CtMW; MeHi; MH; MnU; TxU.
                              46960
---- ---- 2d. ed., improved.
New York, S. W. Benedict, 1837.
142 p. MB; MH-And; Nh-Hi;
PHC; WHi.   46961

---- ---- 3d ed., improved.
New York, 1837. 155 p. NIC.
                              46962
A superintendent's offering ....
memoir of two schools in the Ma-
son Street Sabbath School, Bos-
ton .... by the superintendent.
Boston, Massachusetts Sabbath
School Society, 1837. 63, 8 p.
DLC; IaHi; MH; MH-AH. 46963

Swaim, William.
    Coleccion de casas en ilustra-
cione de la propiedades restaura-
tivas i sanativas de la panacea
de Swaim, en varias enfermedades.
Filadelfia, 1837. 124 p. DNLM; MB.
                              46964
Swan, Joseph Rockwell, 1802-
1884.
    A treatise on the law relating
to the powers and duties of justices of the peace, and constables, in the state of Ohio,
with practical forms, &c. &c.
Columbus, Published by Isaac
N. Whiting, 1837. 582 p. IU;
OCHP; OClWHi; OU; WHi. 46965

Swan, William Draper, 1809-1864.
    Questions adapted to Emerson's
N.A. arithmetic. pt. 3. Bost,
1837. MB.   46966

Swendenborg, Emanuel, 1688-1772.
    Concerning Heaven and its
wonders and concerning Hill;
from things heard and seen from
the Latin of Emanuel Swendenborg:

Boston, for Boston New Church printing society, 1837. 396 p. CtHT; IEG; MB; OUrC; RNHS.
46967

---- Heavenly arcana, which are in the Sacred Scripture, laid open. Originally published in Latin, at London, 1749-1756. Boston, 1837-47. 12 v. CtMW; MCNC; MH-And; MiU; PPL-R.
46968

Sweetser, William, 1797-1875.

A treatise on digestion, and the disorders incident to it which are comprehended under the term dyspepsia. ... By William Sweetser, M.D. ... Boston, Published by T. H. Carter, 1837. 359 p. IU-M; MH-And; PPCP; VtU; WU-M.
46969

Swift, Mary A.

First lessons about natural philosophy, for children. Part first. By Miss Mary A. Swift, principal of the Litchfield female seminary. Stereotype edition. Hartford, Belknap and Hamersley, 1837. 2 p. 1. (7)-107 p. CtHWatk; CtNwchA.
46970

---- First lessons about natural philosophy. Part II. Hartford, Belknap & Hammersley, 1837. 176 p. CtHWatk; MH; MPlyA; PHi.
46971

Sword's pocket almanack, Churchman's calendar, and ecclesiastical register for the year of our Lord, 1838.... New York, Swords, Stanford and co., 1837. NNS.
46972

Syme, James, 1799-1870.

On diseases of the rectum. Philadelphia, A. Waldie, 1837. [1]-42 p. LNT-M.
46973

---- The Principles of surgery. 2nd edition. Philadelphia, Carey & Lea, 1837. 375 p. CtY; MH-M; PPC; WU-M.
46974

Symington, William, 1795-1862.

The nature, extent and results of the atonement. By Rev. William Symington. Philadelphia, Presbyterian Tract and Sunday School Society, William S. Martian, printer, 1837. 88 p. ArBaA; KyDC; MeBat; PPM.
46975

---- The necessity of atonement. By The Rev. William Symington. Philadelphia, Presbyterian Board of Publication, (1837?). 48 p. CU; GDecCT; MBC; PPM; TxShA.
46976

---- On the intercession of Jesus Christ. Philadelphia, Presbyterian Board of Publication, [1837]. 40 p. CU; DLC; ICP; NcD; PPPrHi.
46977

Synod of the Reformed Presbyterian Church of North America.

(The) Reformed Presbyterian and covenanter. v. 1-26, March 1837-1862; combined ser., v. 1-33, 1863-1895. Newburgh, N.Y., 1837-1848. Pittsburgh, 1854-1895. 59 v. OO.
46978

T

T. D. James Academy, Philadelphia, Pa.

The monthly record of lessons and conduct of the pupils of T. D. James's Academy; together with various original pieces, in prose and verse.... Philadelphia, n. pub. (Joseph & William Kite, printers), 1837-8. 136 p. NjR; PHi.
46979

Talbott, John L.

The Western practical arithmetic, wherein the rules are il-

lustrated ... Cincinnati, E.
Morgan and son, 1837. 182, 7,
5 p. OClWHi.   46980

Talfourd, Thomas Noon, 1795-
1854.
  Ion; a tragedy in five aots.
New York, G. Dearborn & Co.,
1837. "American ed." MH;
MB; MWA; Nh.   46981

---- ---- 2nd ed. New York,
George Dearborn & Co., 1837.
110 p. CLU; IU; MB; MdBD;
MWA.   46982

---- ---- 3rd ed. New York,
G. Dearborn & Co., 1837. 109p.
CL; InGrD; MWA; NcU; NhD.
                               46983
---- ---- 4th ed. New York,
George Dearborn & co., 1837.
109 p. GDecCT; IU; PP; WHi;
WU.   46984

Taliaferro, John.
  Circular to his constituents.
Washington, 1837. PPL. 46985

Tallmadge, D(aniel) B., 1793-
1847.
  Opinion ... of the 6th of
June 1837, in relation to the
entering upon lands, &c., for
temporary purposes, in the
construction of the Croton
aqueduct ... also his supplementary opinion of the 13th of
February 1837 ... N.Y., 1837.
16 p. NNC; NNE.   46986

Tallmadge, Frederick A.
  Speech on the bill to regulate the deposites of the public
money, in senate June 17,
1836. N.Y., 1837. 26 p. Whi.
                               46987
Tallmadge, James, 1778-1853.
  Address delivered May 20,
1837, in the chapel of the University of the City of New York,

on occasion of the dedication of
the building to the purposes of
science, literature, and religion,
by the Hon. James Tallmadge,
esq., president of the council.
New York, Printed by D. Fanshaw, 1837. 23 p. ICP; MiU;
NCH; NNC; PPL.   46988

Tallmadge, Nathaniel Pitcher,
1795-1864.
  Speech of Mr. Tallmadge, of
New York, on the bill imposing
additional duties in certain cases
on public officers. Delivered
in the Senate of the U.S. September 22, 1837. Washington,
Printed at the Madisonian office,
1837. 19 p. MiD-B; MWA;
NNC; RPB; Tx.   46989

Tanner, Henry Schenck, 1786-
1858.
  The American traveller; or,
Guide through the United States.
Containing brief notices of the
several states, cities, principal
towns, canals and rail roads, &c.
... Philadelphia, The author,
1837. (5)-144 p. DLC; DIC;
InU; MH; PPL.   46990

---- ---- Third edition. By
H. S. Tanner. Philadelphia,
Published by the author, 1837.
144 p. InU; MsLE; NBP; Tx;
WvA.   46991

---- Map of the canals, railroads of Pennsylvania; New Jersey the adjoining states. Philadelphia, Tanner, 1837. NN;
PPAmP.   46992

Tappan, Benjamin, 1788-1863.
  Why is my Liberty judged of
another man's conscience? A
sermon, delivered in Augusta,
March 12, 1837. By Benjamin
Tappan, D.D. Augusta, Smith
& Robinson, Printers, 1837.

17 p. CtHT; MeHi; MH-And;
NN; RPB. 46993

Tarascon, Louis Anastasius.
Louis Anastasius Tarascon, to
his fellow citizens of the United
States of America; and, through
their medium, to all his other
fellow human beings on earth;
not any where else. New York,
Published by H. D. Robinson,
n. pr., 1837. 82 p. MdBP;
NjR. 46994

The tattler, with notes, and a
general index....complete in one
volume. Philadelphia, Desilver,
Thomas and co., 1837. 7-244 p.
IaCrC; NNebg; OCX; RPB.
46995

Taunton, Mass. Spring Street
Church.
The confession of faith and
covenant... Taunton, 1837.
12 p. MBC; NN. 46996

Taylor, Ann, 1757-1830.
The wife at home;....By
Mrs. Taylor. Boston, Published
by James Loring, 1837. 216 p.
MoSpD; NNU-W. 46997

Taylor, C. B.
A universal history of the
United States of America, embracing the whole period, from
the earliest discoveries, down
to the present time. Giving a
description of the western country ... By C. B. Taylor. New-
York, E. Strong, 1837. 540,
vi p. DLC; IaB; IEN-M; MH;
NNC. 46998

Taylor, Emily, 1795-1872.
The boy and the birds. With
designs by Thomas Landseer.
Boston, Otis Broaders and Co.,
1837. 130 p. MB; MBAt; MH;
MWA; NN. 46999

Taylor, Isaac, 1759-1829.
The mine; or, sketches of the
mines of different countries, the
modes of working them, and their
various productions... New
York, T. Mason & G. Lane,
1837. PPL-R. 47000

---- The Ship, or Sketches of
the vessels of various countries
with the manner of building and
navigating them. By the Rev.
Isaac Taylor.... Philadelphia,
Desilver, Thomas & Company,
1837. 224 p. MeB. 47001

---- Youth's own book. Character essential to success in life.
By Isaac Taylor....2d ed.
Hartford, Canfield & Robins,
1837. 132 p. ICU. 47002

Taylor, James Barnett, 1804-1871.
Biography of Elder Lott Cary,
late missionary to Africa. ...
With an Appendix...by J. H. B.
Latrobe, Baltimore, Armstrong &
Berry, 1837. [9]-108 p. DLC;
MdHi; MH; ViRU. 47003

---- Lives of Virginia Baptist
ministers. By James B. Taylor
... Richmond, Yale & Wyatt;
Baltimore, Armstrong & Berry;
[etc., etc.], 1837. [9]-444 p.
LNB; NcD; PCC; ScNC; ViR.
47004

(Taylor, Jane), 1783-1824.
Rhymes for the nursery....
New York, George A. & J. Curtis,
(1837). 112 p. MH; NN; OHi;
PHi; RPB. 47005

Taylor, John Orville.
The farmer's school book,
prepared and published by J.
Orville Taylor ... Albany, "Common school depository," 1837.
238 p. MAA; MeU; MH; NIC;
PU. 47006

---- ---- Auburn, Published by
Ivison & Terry, S. W. Benedict,
print., 1837. 236 p. NCH;
NjR.   47007

---- ---- Ithaca, printed and
published by Mack, Andrus &
Woodruff, 1837. 236 p. NIC;
NjR.   47008

---- ---- Rochester, William
Alling, 1837. 236 p. TxD-T.
                                47009
Taylor, William Cooke, 1800-
1849.
   History of Ireland, from the
Anglo-Norman invasion till the
union of the country with Great
Britain. By W. C. Taylor...
With additions, by William
Sampson... New York, Harper
& brothers, 1837. 2 v. FTU;
MBBC; MH; Nh-Hi; OHi.   47010

Teachem, Mrs.
   The Infant's School Reader.
Concord, N.H., C. S. Sanborn,
1837. MWbor.   47011

The Teacher; a supplement to
the elementary spelling book.
New Haven, 1837. 156 p. NIC.
                                47012
A teacher's offering; or, letters
addressed to the members of a
Sabbath school class. By the
wife of a Clergyman. Boston,
Massachusetts Sabbath School
society, 1837. 102, (6) p.
NNT-C; VtMidSM.   47013

Telegraph and Texas Register.
Houston.
   Telegraph---Since the paper
of this week went to press,
much important intelligence has
been received, which we hasten
to lay before our readers in the
form of an extra... [Houston,
1837]. Broadside. TxGr.
                                47014

Teller, C. W.
   Directions for the correct
measurement and cutting of
garments on the most approved
principles. New York, 1837.
12 p. DLC.   47015

The Temperance Almanac....
1838....astronomical calculations
by David Young, prep. & pub.
under the direction of the Executive Committee of the New York
State Temperance Society....
Albany, from the Steam Press of
Packard and Van Benthuysen,
[1837]. 48 p. MBevHi; MiD-B;
MWA; NN; WHi.   47016

Temperance Convention of Northern Kentucky. Maysville, 1837.
   The minutes of a temperance
convention of Northern Kentucky
held in Maysville on the 28th and
29th of November, 1837. Maysville, Ky., L. Collins, 1837.
16 p. KyLoU; PPPrHi; TxHuT.
                                47017
The Temperance text-book; a
collection of facts and interesting
anecdotes illustrating the evils of
intoxicating drinks. 3d ed.
Philadelphia, E. L. Carey and A.
Hart, 1837. 161 p. MB; MH;
MWA; NBMS.   47018

Tennant, Abel.
   The Vegetable materia medica
and practice of medicine, ... containing in detail his practical
kowledge of American remedies
in curing diseases, Stafford.
D. D. Wait, Printer, Batavia,
N.Y., 1837. 448 p. KyBC; NN;
NRMA.   47019

Tennessee. Chief engineer.
   Report of the chief engineer
of the state of Tennessee on the
surveys and examinations for
the Central railroad, and for the
Central turnpike. Under an act

... passed October 25th, 1836. Nashville, S. Nye & co., printers to the state, 1837. 60 p. CSt; DLC; NN; T; TKL.   47020

---- ---- ---- Nashville, S. Nye & co., printers, 1837. 81 p. DLC; NN; T; TKL-Mc.
47021
---- Department of Public Instruction.
Report of the superintendent of Public instruction to the General assembly of the state of Tennessee. Printed by order of the Senate. Nashville, S. Nye & co., printers to the state, 1837. 14 p. T.   47022

---- General Assembly. Board of Internal Improvement for East Tennessee.
Report of the Board of internal improvement for East Tennessee, to the General assembly of the State of Tennessee. Nashville, Printed at the South western Christian advocate office, 1837. 6 p. T; TN.   47023

---- ---- Joint select committee on a system of education.
Report to the legislature of Tennessee, of the Joint committee of both Houses, on the subject of a system of education, embracing common schools, academies and colleges. [Printed by order of the General assembly] Nashville, S. Nye & co. printers to the state, 1837. T.   47024

---- ---- Joint Select Committee on Banks.
Report of the Joint Select Committee on banks. Printed by order of the General Assembly. Nashville, S. Nye and Co., printers to the State, 1837. 55 p. MB; MH-BA; T; THi.   47025

---- ---- Senate.
Journal of the Senate, of the state of Tennessee, at the Twenty-second General assembly, held at Nashville. F. K. Zollicoffer, Ramsey & Craighead, and S. Nye & co. printers to the state. Columbia, Tenn., Printed by F. K. Zollicoffer, 1837. 628 p. NN; T; TMeC.
47026

---- Governor, 1835-1839 (Cannon).
Republican banner--extra. Governor's message to the Twenty-second General assembly of the state of Tennessee. October, 1837. Nashville, S. Nye & co. printers, Republican banner office, [1837]. 16 p. T.   47027

---- State penitentiary. Nashville, 1837-1897. 37 v. in 26. DLC; MB; NcD; PP; T.   47028

---- Treasury. Comptroller of the Treasury.
Report of the Comptroller of the state of Tennessee. Printed by order of the General assembly. Nashville, S. Nye & co., printers to the state, 1837. 12 p. T.   47029

Termo, M. B.
Schlussel Zur Botanik, nach Linné's system in Klassen und ordnungen. Baltimore, Md., 1837. 133 p. NNBG; OCLloyd.
47030
Texas (Republic).
Declaration of independence made at Washington, on the second of March, 1836, and the Constitution of the republic of Texas, adopted by the convention, March 17, 1836. Columbia, Printed by G. & T. H. Borden, public printers, 1837. 7, [3]-19 p. NHi; TxU; TxWFM.
47031

---- Texas documents. Columbia, Tex., 1837. DLC.   47032

---- Congress. House.
Journal of the House of representatives of the Republic of Texas ... [Houston, Tex? etc.], [1837?-41]. CU-B. 47033

---- ---- ---- Standing rules for conducting business in the House of Representatives; and the Constitution of the Republic of Texas. Columbia, Printed by G. & T. H. Borden, public printers, 1837. 30 p. CtY; Tx; TxU.   47034

---- ---- Joint Committee on Finance.
Report of the Committee on Finance, October 18, 1837. Printed by order of Congress. Houston, Printed at the Office of the Telegraph, 1837. 8 p. TxU.   47035

---- ---- Senate.
A bill to be entitled an act to amend the act incorporating the "Texas Railroad Navigation and Banking Company." Printed by order of the Senate. Houston, Printed at the office of the Telegraph, 1837. 8 p. Tx; TxWFM.   47036

---- ---- ---. Committee on Public Lands.
Report of the Committee to whom was referred so much of the President's message, as relates to the Land Bill. Houston, Printed by Borden & Moore, 1837. 8 p. CtY; TxH; TxU; TxWFM.   47037

---- Currency.
The Treasurer of the Republic of Texas will pay to or order Ten Dollars, in twelve months

from date, with interest at ten per cent. per annum, in accordance with an act of Congress passed June 9, 1837. City of Houston, 1837. Broadside. TxU.   47038

---- Customs collector, Velasco.
Tariff of duties on importation. Jeremiah Brown, collector. July 10, 1837. Broadside, TxU.
47039

---- Land scrip.
Republic of Texas. [Blank] Acres. Know all men to whom these presents shall come: That [Blank] having served faithfully and honorably for the term of [Blank] months from the [Blank] day of [Blank] until the [Blank] day of [Blank] and being honorably discharged from the [Blank] is entitled to [Blank] Acres Bounty Land, for which this is his Certificate. And the said [Blank] is entitled to hold said Land, or to sell, alienate, convey and donate the same and exercise all rights of ownership over it. This Certificate will be transferable by endorsement, with a deed before any competent authority, with witnesses to the same. In Testimony Whereof, I have hereunto set my hand, at this day of 1837. McKean, Printer, New Orleans, [1837]. Broadside. TxU.   47040

---- Laws, statutes, etc.
An act creating a general postoffice, and passed Dec. 20, 1836. Columbia, T. H. Borden, 1837. 18 p. NN; TxU. 47041

---- ---- ... An act entitled "An act to reduce into one act, and to amend the several acts relating to the establishment of a General Land Office." Passed December 1837. Printed by order of Cong ress [!] Houston, Printed

at the office of the Telegraph,
1837. 16 p. CtY; NHi; NN.
47042

---- ---- A bill relating to
finance and for establishing a
circulating medium. [Houston?,
1837?]. 3 p. TxU; TxWFM.
47043

---- ---- ... A Bill to be entitled an Act to amend the act
incorporating the "Texas Rail-
Road Navigation and Banking
Company," Printed by order of
the Senate. Houston, Printed by
order of the Senate. Houston,
Printed at the office of the Telegraph, 1837. 8 p. Tx.   47044

---- ---- Collection of legisla-
tive enactments relative to land
titles in Texas. Houston,
Printed and for sale by Cruger
& Moore, 1837. 24 p. CtY;
NHi; NN.   47045

---- ---- Laws of the Republic
of Texas, in two volumes.
Printed by order of the Secretary of State. Volume 1. Houston, Printed at the Office of the
Telegraph, 1837. 163 p. CtY;
NN; NNB; TxU.   47046

---- ---- Translation of laws
(1821-29), orders, and contracts on colonization. 1821 to
1829. Columbia, 1837. OCLaw.
47047

---- President. 1836-1838.
(Houston).
By the President of the Re-
public of Texas. A proclamation.
[Houston, 1837]. Br. TxU.
47048

---- ---- ... Message of the
President, to both houses of
Congress. Delivered, Nov. 21,
1837. [Houston, Printed at the
Telegraph Office, 1837]. 8 p.
DNA; TxU; TxWFM.   47049

---- ---- Message of the President to both houses of Congress.
Received September 28, 1837.
[Houston, 1837]. 3 p. TxU.
47050

---- ---- President Houston's
speech, to the Senate and House
of Representatives of the Republic of Texas. (Printed by
order of the House of Representatives.) [Houston, 1837].
8 p. TxU; TxWFM.   47051

---- Treasury dept.
Report of Secretary of Treasury. Houston, 1837. DLC.
47052

Texian loan contractors.
Memorial of the Texian loan
contractors to the Congress of
Texas. New-Orleans, Printed by
William McKean, 1837. 14 p.
TxWFM.   47053

Thacher, Peter Oxenbridge.
Two charges to the grand
jury of the county of Suffolk
for the Commonwealth of Massachusetts at the opening of the
Municipal Court of the city of
Boston, on Dec. 5th, 1836, and
March 13th, 1837. Boston, Dutton and Wentworth, 1837. 31 p.
DLC; IaDa; MH; MHi; WHi.
47054

Thatcher, Benjamin Bussey, 1809-
1840.
Indian biography: or, An
historical account of those individuals who have been distinguished among the North American natives as orators, warriors,
statesmen etc... By B. B.
Thatcher, Esq. New York, J. &
J. Harper, 1837. 2 v. FTU;
MH; MiD; PMA; ScCliP.   47055

Thayer, Caroline Matilda, d. 1844.
Religion recommended to youth,
in a series of letters addressed
to a young lady. To which are

added, poems on various occasions. By Caroline Matilda
Thayer. New-York, published
by T. Mason and G. Lane, for
the Methodist Episcopal Church,
at the Conference Office, 1837.
157 p. CtY-D; IEG; OBerB;
PPL.   47056

Thayer, John, 1758-1815.
    The Conversion of the Rever-
end John Thayer, of Boston ...
Philadelphia, E. Cummiskey,
1837. 140, 84 p. DLC; MdBS.
                             47057
Thelwall, Algernon Sydney,
1795-1865.
    Thoughts In Affliction By
The Rev. A. S. Thelwall, A.M.
of Trinity College, Cambridge.
First American Edition Revised
And Enlarged. To Which Is
Added Bereaved Parents Con-
soled; By John Thornton.
Also, Sacred Poetry; Carefully
Selected By A Clergyman.
New York, Daniel Appleton &
Co., 1837. 320 p. ICBB.
                             47058
Theological Seminary of the
Protestant-Episcopal Church in
Kentucky. Charter, Regula-
tions, Course of Study....
Another Edition. Lexington,
Ky., 1837. 16 p. MH.   47059

Theophilanthropos (pseud.).
    An Impartial, Critical, and
Scriptural Investigation of the
Biblical Views of Universalism
and Destructionism: And after
a careful examination of all those
passages in the New Testament
in which the word Hell is used,
this proven that there are but
two passages which have any
reference to the literal grave.
By Theophilanthropos. Richmond, Printed by James C.
Walker, 1837. (5), 6-46 p.
MMeT.   47060

Thomas, R.
    An authentic account of the
most remarkable events; containing the lives of the most noted
pirates and piracies, remarkable
shipwrecks, fires, famines, etc.
in the world. By R. Thomas.
New York, Published by Ezra
Strong, 1837. 2 v. DLC;
MBAt; PAtM.   47061

---- Glory of America; compromising memoirs of the lives and
glorious exploits of some of the
distinguished officers engaged
in the late war with Great Britain.
New York, Strong, 1837. CSmH;
MB; NNC; OClW; VtVe.   47062

---- Interesting and authentic
narratives of the most remarkable shipwrecks, fires, etc., in
most parts of the world. Hartford, E. Strong, 1837. CSmH;
ICN; MH; MsaP; NUtHi.   47063

---- ---- New York, E. Strong,
1837. CSmH; ICN; MH.   47064

Thomas Benton (alias Uncas),
will stand the ensuing season at
the stable of the undersigned, in
Little Rock... [Little Rock,
1837]. Broadside. Dated:
Little Rock, March 24th, 1837.
                             47065
Thompson, Edward.
    An address delivered before
the Total Abstinence Temperance
Society, of the City of Detroit
by the Rev. Edward Thompson,
February 23, 1837. Published
by the society. Detroit, Printed
by William Harsha, 1837. 22 p.
IEG; MiGr; ODW; OO.   47066

Thompson, George, 1804-1878.
    Letters and addresses by
George Thompson during his mis-
sion in the United States, from
October 1st, 1834 to Nov. 27,

1835. Boston, Isaac Knapp, 1837. 126 p. ICMe; MdBJ; NhD; RHi; TxHuT. 47067

---- Thompson in Africa, or an account of the Missionary Labors, Sufferings, travels and observations, By George Thompson in Western Africa, at the Mendi Mission Eighth Thousand. Dayton, Ohio, Printed for the author, 1837. 362 p. OWoC. 47068

Thompson, M. A.
Life of Anna Maria Taigi. New York, Pustet Co., 1837. 414 p. KyLoSH. 47069

Thompson, Otis.
Address before the Bristol Co. Agric. Soc. Taunton, 1837. MBAt. 47070

Thompson, Waddy, 1798-1868.
Speech of the Hon. Mr. Thompson, of South Carolina, on the bill to postpone the payment to the states of the fourth instalment of the surplus revenue, delivered in the House of representatives, September 23, 1837. Washington, Gales, 1837. 12 p. A-Ar; CU; MiU-C; NNC; PPM; ScHi; WHi. 47071

---- Speech ... on the right of slaves to petition. House of Representatives, Tuesday February 7, 1837. [n.p., 1837]. 8 p. CU. 47072

Thomson, James, 1700-1748.
The seasons, by James Thompson(!), to which is prefixed the life of the author by P. Murdock. Hartford, Andrus, 1837. 192 p. CtMW; NbHC; NcGU. 47073

Thomson, Katherine (Byerley),

1792-1862.
Memoirs of the life of Sir Walter Raleigh with some account of the period in which he lived. Philadelphia, G. W. Donohue, 1837. 287 p. PHi; PU. 47074

Thomson, Samuel.
Letter addressed to Dr. R. K. Frost. Boston, 1837. 3 p. OCLloyd. 47075

Thomsonian Almanac for 1838. Cal. by William Collom. Philadelphia, Pa., [1837]. MWA. 47076

Thorburn, Grant.
Catalogue of double dahlias. (New York, 1837.) Broadside. MH. 47077

Thornton, Henry, 1760-1815.
Family Prayers: to which is added a Family Commentary upon the Sermon on the Mount. By the late Henry Thornton, Esq., M.P. 3rd. American Edition. Edited by the Rev. Manton Eastburn, D.D., Rector of the Church of the Ascension, New York. New York, Swords, Stanfield & Co., 1837. 168, 160 p. CtHC; ICMe; KyBC; MiHi; OrPD. 47078

Thornton, Thomas C., 1794-1860.
Theological colloquies; or, A compendium of Christian Divinity,...Founded on scripture and reason.... By Thomas C. Thornton, Baltimore, Lewis & Coleman, 1837. (1), 14-723 p. IEG; MdBP; PPLT; TxDa; ViW. 47079

Thorp, John.
Letters of the late John Thorp, of Manchester, a minister of the gospel in the Society of Friends to which is prefixed a memoir of the life of the writer; reprinted from the 2nd ed. Philadelphia,

Friends' book store, 1837. 196 p. PHC. 47080

Thoughts on life and death. With other pieces. By an old lady. Utica, Hobart Press, 1837. 12 p. MB. 47081

Thoughts on the causes of the present distresses, in a letter addressed to the citizens of the United States....Albany, Printed for the author, at the Elm Tree Press, 1837. 32 p. MH; N; NjR; P. 47082

Three experiments in drinking, or Three eras in the life of an inebriate. Boston, Otis, Broaders & Co., etc., 1837. 72 p. CU; KEmT; MH; MiU; NNC. 47083

---- Boston, Otis, Broaders, Cassady and March, 1837. 72 p. CtY. 47084

"Three things have mighty sway with Men, The Sword, the Sceptre, and the Pen! And he who can the least of those command, In the first rank of Fame is sure to stand." Mr. Foster. Newport, James Atkinson, Printer, October 27, 1837. Broadside. RNHi. 47085

Ticknor, Caleb Bingham, 1804-1840.
The Philosophy of Living; or The way to enjoy life and its comforts. By Caleb Ticknor, A.M., M.D. New York, Harper & Bros., 1837. 336 p. DLC; MH; MoK; PMA; ScClip. 47086

Tinelli, Lewis.
Hints on the cultivation of the mulberry; with some general observations on the production of silk. By Lewis Tinelli, ... New York, Printed by William J. Spence, 1837. 54 p. MB; MCM; NN; PPAmP; ScU. 47087

Tissot, P.
The Real Presence. By P. Tissot. New York, P. O'Shea, 1837. IES. 47088

Title papers of the Clamorgan Grant, of 536,904 arpens of alluvial lands in Missouri and Arkansas. New York, T. Snowden, 1837. [2]-24 p. ICN; LNH; MoSM; NN. 47089

To Aaron Clark, Mayor of the City of New York:--[New-York, 1837?] 16 p. CtY; MB; NN; NNC. 47090

To G. W. Toland, Esq. One of the representatives of the city of Philadelphia in Congress. Dear Sir,-I beg leave to submit to you some reasons which have occurred to me, as justifying the course pursued by our banks in not contracting our currency and ruining their otherwise solvent debtors, in order to imitate the New York banks in their involuntary resumption of specie payments. With great esteem I am, Yours sincerely, Robert Hare.... [ca. Penn., 1837?]. Broadside. NcD. 47091

To pastors and churches throughout the country. Union of ministerial and Christian effort for the salvation of sinners. [New York, 1837]. 4 p. DLC; NN. 47092

To the independent voters of Middlesex County. n.p., (1837?) 12 p. MH. 47093

To the patrons of the Cleveland Gazette, January 1, 1837. OClWHi. 47094

To the people of the United
States. Vague ... New York,
Oct. 25, 1837. 23 p. P. 47095

Todd, John, 1800-1873.
Todd's complete works: con-
taining Sunday school teacher,
Student's manual, ... Lectures
to children, and index rerum.
New ed. London, New York,
Ward, Lock & co., (1837?).
MiU; MSbri.   47096

---- Index rerum; or, Index of
subjects, intended as a manual,
to aid the student and the professional man, in preparing
himself for usefulness. By Rev.
John Todd. Northampton,
J. H. Butler; New York,
Leavitt, Lord & Co...., 1837.
[3]-8 p. LNH; MH.   47097

---- ---- 3d ed. Northampton,
J. H. Butler, etc., etc., 1837.
246 p. MdBMAS; MH.   47098

---- Lectures to children,
familiarly illustrating important
truth. Northampton, 1837.
PPL-R.   47099

---- Principles and results of
Congregationalism. A sermon
delivered at the dedication of
the house of worship erected by
the First Congregational Church
in Philadelphia, November 11,
1837. By Rev. John Todd...
Philadelphia, William Marshall &
co., 1837. 64 p. CtHC; MBC;
MHi; N; PHi; TChU.   47100

---- The Sabbath school teacher: designed to aid in elevating and perfecting the Sabbath school system. By Rev.
John Todd ... Northampton,
J. H. Butler; Philadelphia, W.
Marshall & co.; [etc., etc.],
1837. 15-432 p. CBPac; InCW;
PHi; NbOM; TxDaM.   47101

---- Student's Manual designed
by specific directions to aid in
forming and strengthening the
intellectual and Moral character
and habits of the student. By
Rev. John Todd. 6th ed.
Northampton, J. H. Butler, 1837.
392 p. MH; NbOM.   47102

---- ---- 7th ed., Northampton,
Published by J. H. Butler, 1837.
392 (8) p. MFiHi; MiKT; NcGU;
NvU.   47103

The token and Atlantic souvenir;
a Christmas and New Year's
present. Edited by S. G. Goodrich. Boston, published by
Charles Bowen, 1837. 9-348 p.
CtMW; MeU; MH; TJoV; WaSp.
                      47104

Tommy True, the industrious
scholar and Little Agnes. New
Haven, S. Babcock, Church St.,
1837. 16 p. MHolliHi.   47105

Tompkins County, N.Y.
Loan Office. (Drafts and
certificates showing moneys
loaned by the Commissioners
for loaning certain moneys of
the United States, of the County
of Tompkins, 1837. NIC. 47106

Tonawanda Railroad Company.
Report upon the Tonawanda
rail-road company, exhibiting its
present situation and future prospects. By a committee. Rochester, Printed by William Alling &
co., 1837. 17 p. NNE; NRHi.
                      47107

Tooley, Henry.
An address delivered to the
Masonic Fraternity in the Meth-
odist meetinghouse, in the city
of Natchez, on the festival of
St. John, the Baptist, being the
24th June, 1837. By Henry
Tooley, K.T. & C. Natchez,
Printed at the Daily Courier Office,

1837. 8 p. IaCrM; MsFM.
47108

Toomer, Joshua W.
An oration, delivered at the celebration of the first centennial anniversary of the South-Carolina society, in Charleston, on the twenty-eighth day of March, Anno Domini, 1837.... Charleston, Printed by A. E. Miller, 1837. 94 p. MH; PPM; ScU; ScCC; TxU; WHi.   47109

Tooth, Mary.
Memoirs of Miss Sarah Jenkins, by Miss Tooth. New York, Mason, 1837. 80 p. NcD.
47110

Torrey, Henry Warren, 1814-1893.
An English Latin lexicon, prepared to accompany Leveretts Latin English lexicon. Boston, J. H. Wilkins and R. B. Carter and Charles C. Little & Co., 1837. 318 p. CtMW; LNB; MeBat; OO; PCC.   47111

Town, Salem, 1779-1864.
Town's spelling book, in which children, from the alphabet, are taught the formation, spelling and meaning of words at the same time. ... Also, an easy-introduction to Town's Analysis. Albany, J. O. Taylor, 1837. (13)-96 p. DLC; MWelC; NCH.   47112

The town and Country almanac for....1838. Carefully calculated....by Charles F. Egelmann. Baltimore, Pub. by James Lovegrove....[1837]. [19] p. MWA; PPM.   47113

The Town of Huron at the foot of Lake Huron, St. Clair Co., Michigan. Circular addressed to Capitalists and those who design removing to the West. Published by the Proprietors.

New York, E. D. Clayton, Printer, 1837. 32 p. MiGr; NjR; MiPh; OFH; WHi.   47114

Towndraw, Thomas, 1810-1898.
A complete guide to the art of writing shorthand: being an entirely new and comprehensive system of representing the elementary sounds of the Eng. language in steno. characters. ... By T. Towndraw ... Boston, Perkins & Marvin, 1837. 120 p. DLC; ICU; MH; MiDT; NjR.
47115

Townsend, Thompson.
Mary's dream; or, Far far at sea! A melodrama, in three acts.... London, New York, Samuel French, [1837?]. 35 p. OCl.   47116

Trajetta, Philip, 1777-1854.
Six sacred hymns. Philadelphia, 1837. PPL.   47117

Trask, George, 1796-1875.
A farewell discourse, preached on the first sabbath in May, 1836, by Rev. George Trask, to his late charge in Framingham. Boston, Published by Whipple & Damrell, 1837. 29 p. ICN; MBC; MiD-B; MWA.   47118

Tredgold, Thomas, 1788-1829.
Elementary principles of carpentry; a treatise on the pressure and equilibrium of timber framing; ... By Thomas Tredgold.... 1st American from the 2d London ed.; cor. and considerably enl. Philadelphia, E. L. Carey and A. Hart, 1837. 280 p. A-CS; IaB; MPiB; NNC; ViU.   47119

Trimble, Isaac Ridgeway, 1802-1888.
Report of the engineer appointed by the commissioners of

the mayor and City council of
Baltimore, on the subject of
the Maryland canal. By Isaac
R. Trimble. Baltimore, Lucas
& Deaver, pr., 1837. 27 p.
MB; MdBP; MH; NIC; NjP. 47120

Trimmer, Sarah Kirby, 1740?-1810.
   The ladder to learning; a collection of fables, arranged pro-
gressively in words of one,
two and three syllables, edited
and improved by Mrs. Trimmer.
2d Amer., from the 13th London
ed. Boston, Otis, Broaders &
Co., etc., 1837. MH.   47121

Troubat, Francis Joseph, 1802-
1868.
   Practice in civil actions and
proceedings in the Supreme
Court of Penna. in the Dist.
Court and Court of Common
Pleas for the City and County
of Phila. and in the Courts of
the U.S. by F. J. Troubat and
W. W. Haly. Philadelphia,
R. H. Small, 1837. 2 v. DLC;
MBS; NNC-L; PU-L; WaU. 47122

Trow, John Fowler, 1810-1886.
   Alton trials: of Winthrop S.
Gilman, who was indicted with
Enoch Long, Amos B. Roff,
[etc.] for the crime of riot,
... 7th of November, 1837 ...
Written out from notes of the
trial ... by a member of the
bar of the Alton municipal court.
Also, the trial of John Solomon,
Levi, Palmer [etc.] indicted ...
for the riot commited ... 7th of
November, 1837 ... Written from
notes taken at the trial by
William S. Lincoln ... N. Y.,
Trow, 1837. 158 p. CBPSR.
                          47123
Truman, George, 1798-1877.
   Friends belonging to Salem
Quarterly Meeting. Philadelphia,
1837. PSC-Hi.   47124

No entry   47125

Tucker, George, 1775-1861.
   The laws of wages, profits
and rent, investigated By George
Tucker. ... Philadelphia, E. L.
Carey & A. Hart, 1837. 189 p.
CU; KyU; MdBE; OCY; ViU.
                          47126
---- The life of Thomas Jeffer-
son, third president of the United
States. With parts of his corres-
pondence never before published,
and notices of his opinions on
questions of civil government,
national policy, and constitution-
al law. By George Tucker...
Philadelphia, Carey, Lea &
Blanchard, 1837. 2 v. CtB;
IaHi; PU; ScDuE; WvU. 47127

Tucker, Levi, 1804-1853.
   Lectures on the dangerous
tendency of modern infidelity
delivered to young men, is the
First Baptist church in the city
of Cleveland, Ohio... Cleveland, F. B. Penniman, 1837.
189 p. DLC; IaDmD; IEG; MiU;
OClWHi.   47128

Tucker, Waldo.
   The mechanics assistant;
being a selection of valuable receipts, from the best authors
and practical artists in Europe
and America. Windsor, Vt.,
1837. 176 p. MWA; NTiHi; Vt;
VtU.   47129

Tuckerman, Henry Theodore,
1813-1871.
   The Italian Sketch Book. By
Henry T. Tuckerman. ... Second

Edition Enlarged. Boston,
Light & Stearns, 1837. 272 p.
CSmH; MB; NjHo; OO; RNR.
47130

Tuckerman, Joseph, 1778-1840.
A letter respecting Santa
Cruz as a winter residence for
invalids; addressed to Dr. John
C. Warren, of Boston, Mass.
By Joseph Tuckerman. Boston,
D. Clapp, Jr., 1837. 27 p.
CBPac; MB; NN; MWA; WHi.
47131

Tuke, Henry.
The principles of religion,
as professed by the society of
Christians, usually called
Quakers. New York, Mahlon
Day, printer, 1837. (13)-
148 p. IaMp; IEG; KWiF;
NjN; RLa.
47132

Turnbull, Robert.
The theatre, in its influence
upon literature, morals, and
religion. ... Hartford, Canfield
and Robins, 1837. (9)-58 p.
CtSoP; InCW; MB; MH; MiGr.
47133

Turner's Comic Almanack for
1838. Boston, Mass., James
Huane, [1837]. MWA. 47134

---- New York, N.Y., Turner
& Fisher, [1837]. MWA. 47135

Turton, Thomas.
The Roman Catholic doctrines
of the Eucharist considered in
reply to Dr. Wiseman's argu-
ment from scripture. By Thomas
Turton, D.D. Cambridge, John
W. Parker, 1837. 338 p. IEG;
GDecCT. 47136

Tuson, Edward William, 1802-
1865.
The dissector's guide; or,
Student's companion ... By Edward William Tuson ... 2d American ed., with additions, by

Winslow Lewis, jr. ... Boston,
W. D. Ticknor, 1837. 220 p.
CtMW; KyLxT; MB; NNN; PPWa.
47137

[Tuttle, Henry].
The historical catechism:
comprising the important and interesting items in the history of
the United States. Ninth edition
- with additions. Newburyport,
Henry Tuttle, 1837. 31 p. CSmH;
MH; NN; NNC; OO. 47138

Tuttle, Sarah.
Female influence; or, the
temperance girl.... Written for
the Massachusetts Sabbath School
Society, and revised by the
committee of publication. 2nd ed.
Boston, Massachusetts Sabbath
School Society, 1837. 144 p.
IHi. 47139

---- The little soldier, a plea
for peace... Boston, Massachusetts Sabbath School Society,
1837. 122 p. RPB. 47140

Tyler, Bennet, 1783-1858.
Letters on the origin and progress of the New Haven theology
....New York, New York, Printed
by Robert Carter & Ezra Collier,
1837. 180 p. CtHC; GDecCT;
MBC; PPPrHi; WHi. 47141

Tyler, L. H.
Treatise on astronomy ...
Middletown, E. Hunt, 1837.
CtHWatk; CtY; CU; PHi. 47142

Tyng, Stephen Higginson, 1800-
1885.
The connexion between early
religious instruction and mature
piety; a sermon, preached in St.
Paul's church, Philadelphia, May
22, 1837. By Stephen H. Tyng
.... Philadelphia, American Sunday School union, 1837. 28 p.
CtY; ICP; MeB; NjPT; PPLT.
47143

Tyson, Job R[oberts], 1803-
1858.
    Lottery system in the United
States ... By Job R. Tyson.
3d ed. Philadelphia, F. L.
Carey & A. Hart, 1837. 114 p.
NjR; OO; PHi; PPA; ScC. 47144

U

Uncle Sam's Almanack for 1838.
Philadelphia, Pa., Griggs &
Co., (1837). MWA; NjR. 47145

Uncle Solomon and the Homan
family, or How to live in hard
times. By a poor man. Boston, printed by Cassady and
March, 1837. 23 p. CtY; MH;
MWA; NN.   47146

---- 3d ed. Boston, printed
by Cassady and March, 1837.
23 p. MB; MH; MWA; NN.
                            47147
Underhill, Samuel.
    An address, delivered Jan.
29, 1837. At Shalersville.
Portage Co. Ohio, on the centennial anniversary of the birth
of Thomas Paine, who was born
January 29, 1737. By Dr.
Samuel Underhill, of Cleveland,
Ohio. Cleveland, Sanford &
Lott, 1837. 24 p. OClWHi.
                            47148
Underwood, Joseph Rogers, 1791-
1876.
    Speech of J. R. Underwood,
of Kentucky, on reference of the
presidents message to the standing committees, as proposed by
Mr. Haynes, of Georgia. Delivered in Committee of the
whole, on Dec. 21, 1837. [n.p.,
1837.] 8 p. MiU-C.   47149

---- Speech of J. R. Underwood, on the bill to suspend
the payment of the fourth in-

stalment of the surplus revenue
to the states. Delivered in the
House of Representatives U.S.,
in Committee of the whole, September 20, 1837. Washington,
Printed by Gales & Seaton, 1837.
16 p. CtY; NjP; NN; P; ViU.
                            47150
Union bank of Tennessee.
    An act to charter the Union
bank of the state of Tennessee
.... Nashville, 1837. 16 p.
CSmH; NjP.   47151

The union Bible dictionary, for
the use of schools. See Packard,
Frederick Adolphus, 1794-1867.

Union College. Schenectady,
N.Y.
    Catalogue of the officers and
students in Union College, 1837-
38. Schenectady, S. S. Riggs,
Printer, 1837. [2], 32 p.
CSmH; NN; PPM.   47152

---- The charter of Union College together with the amendments to the same and the laws
of the state of New-York, relating to said college. Schenectady, Printed by S. S. Riggs,
1837. 49 p. MH; MWA; NN;
PPPrHi; PHi.   47153

Union Extra. Nashville, Tennessee, June 13, 1837. To the
Public. [16] p. MdHi. 47154

United Brethren in Christ.
    A collection of hymns for the
use of the United Brethren in
Christ. Adapted to public and
private worship. Circleville,
Ohio, The conference Office,
1837. 338 p. ODaB; OWerU;
Vi.   47155

---- Constitution of the United
Brethren's home-mission society
of N.C. Salem, Blum, 1837.
4 p. NcU; PNazMHi.   47156

---- Origin, constitution, doctrine & discipline. Circleville, Ohio, Printed at the Conference Office, 1837. 64 p. DLC; NcU; OClWHi; OHi; P; PPL-R.   47157

United Brethren's Home Mission Society of North Carolina.
Constitution of the United Brethren's home-mission society of North-Carolina. Salem, Blum & Son, 1837. PNazMHi.
47158

United Christians.
Constitution of the community of United Christians. ed. 2. Berea, 1837. 16 p. OO. 47159

United States.
Acts concerning the Sale of Public Lands. 1837. An appropriation was made, in the act approved October 16, 1837, of $25,000 to cover the expense of preparing and printing this and two other documents, all ordered by the Senate. [Washington, 1837] DNA.   47160

---- Annual Message, with Documents. President Martin Van Buren. Dec. 4, 1837. Ex. Docs., No. 3, 25th Cong., 2d sess., Vol. I. Condition of the country; Foreign relations; Northeastern boundary; Affairs with Mexico; Public deposits; Public lands; Indian hostilities in Florida; Removal of Indians westward; Post-Office Department; Affairs of the District of Columbia. [Washington, 1837] 870 p. DNA.   47161

---- Condition of Surveying Districts. June 8, 1837. Library of the Interior Department. Circular relating to general reports on the condition of each surveying district. [Washington, 1837] DNA.   47162

---- Congressional Directory, Twenty-fifth Congress, First Session. Sept. 5, 1837. Published by Thomas Allen. [Washington, 1837] 59 p. DNA.
47163
---- Congressional Directory, Twenty-fifth Congress, Second Session. Dec. 4, 1837. Edition published by Thomas Allen. 61 p. Jonathan Elliot, jr. 64 p. [Washington, 1837] DNA.
47164
---- Construction of a Preemption Act. June 9, 1837. Library of the Interior Department. Construction of act of June 19, 1834, and instructions thereunder relating to preemption rights. [Washington, 1837] 2 p. DNA.
47165
---- Deposits of Land Moneys. June 9, 1837. Library of the Interior Department. Circular relating to deposits in cases where banks heretofore depositories have suspended specie payments. [Washington, 1837] 1 p. DNA.   47166

---- Digest of Acts of Congress. Compiled by Thomas F. Gordon. 1837. Law Library of Congress. Second edition of Digest of 1837; Digest of the Laws of the United States; Abstract of judicial decisions relating to the constitutional and statutory law, with notes, explanatory and historical. [Washington, 1837] 884 p. DNA.
47167
---- Disbursements by Land Officers. Sept. 26, 1837. Library of the Interior Department. Circular relating to disbursements of appropriations. [Washington, 1837] DNA.   47168

---- Diplomatic and Consular List. April, 1837. Library of the State Department. Official list of diplomatic and consular officers of the United States. [Washington, 1837] 14 p. DNA. 47169

---- Disposition of Public Lands. June 9, 1837. Library of the Interior Department. Circular of Treasury sent to each receiver in regard to disposition of public lands. [Washington, 1837] DNA. 47170

---- Documents in Relation to the Claim of Loomis & Gay. Jan. 17, 1837. Senate Docs., No. 78, 24th Cong., 2d sess., Vol. II. Statements concerning the claim of Loomis & Gay, contractors, for performing work on Cumberland road. [Washington, 1837] 4 p. DNA. 47171

---- Documents on the Increase of Force in the Post-Office Department. Feb. 14, 1837. Ex. Docs., No. 153, 24th Cong., 2d sess., Vol. IV. Letter from the Postmaster-General recommending an increase in the clerical force of that Department and an addition to the salaries of his assistants; Letter from the Auditor of the Treasury for the Post-Office Department recommending an increase of the clerical force in that office. [Washington, 1837] 3 p. DNA. 47172

---- Documents relating to Duties on Goods Destroyed by New York Fire. Jan. 2, 1837. Senate Docs., No. 41, 24th Cong., 2d sess., Vol. I. List of claims entitled to drawback under Senate bill to remit duties on certain goods destroyed by the late fire in New York. [Washington, 1837] 5 p. DNA. 47173

---- Documents relative to

Appropriations. Dec. 28, 1837. Ex. Docs., No. 46, 25th Cong., 2d sess., Vol. II. Letters, estimates, etc., from various officers of the Government in relation to items in the civil and diplomatic appropriation bill. [Washington, 1837] 21 p. DNA. 47174

---- Documents relative to Blankets for Indian Trade. Jan. 26, 1837. Senate Docs., No. 106, 24th Cong., 2d sess., Vol. II. Copies of letters from John Jacob Astor and other documents relative to supply of blankets for the Indian trade. [Washington, 1837] 5 p. DNA. 47175

---- Documents relative to Claim of Dubuque and Chouteau. Dec. 28, 1837. Senate Docs., No. 51, 25th Cong., 2d sess., Vol. I. Petition, reports, etc., in relation to the claim of Dubuque and Chouteau to a certain tract of land in Missouri. [Washington, 1837] 4 p. DNA. 47176

---- Documents relative to Claim of Executor of John J. Bulow, jr. Dec. 16, 1837. Senate Docs., No. 36, 25th Cong., 2d sess., Vol. I. Petition, affidavits, etc., in relation to claim for property destroyed by the Seminole Indians in Florida. [Washington, 1837] 12 p. DNA. 47177

---- Documents relative to Duties on Imports. Jan. 27, 1837. Senate Docs., No. 111, 24th Cong., 2d sess., Vol. II. Statement showing articles proposed to be made free of duty and articles upon which a reduction of duty is proposed by the bill reported from the Finance Committee. [Washington, 1837] 8 p. DNA. 47178

---- Documents relative to
Fortifications. Dec. 22, 1837.
Ex. Docs., No. 39, 25th Cong.,
2d sess., Vol. II. Letters
recommending the fortification of
the mouth of the Connecticut
River and the harbor of New
London. [Washington, 1837]
7 p. DNA.   47179

---- Documents relative to Land
Claim of John Fletcher. Feb.
15, 1837. Senate Docs., No.
177, 24th Cong., 2d sess.,
Vol. II. Correspondence and
statements concerning claim of
John Fletcher for confirmation
of title to certain lands in
Mississippi. [Washington, 1837]
4 p. DNA.   47180

---- Documents relative to
Mississippi Congressional Elec-
tion. Dec. 29, 1837. Ex.
Docs., No. 54, 25th Cong., 2d
sess., Vol. II. Copies of writ
and certificates of election of
Congressmen from the State of
Mississippi to the Twenty-fifth
Congress. [Washington, 1837]
3 p. DNA.   47181

---- Documents relative to the
Tariff. Feb. 14, 1837. Senate
Docs., No. 173, 24th Cong., 2d
sess., Vol. II. Copies of various letters on the subject of
Senate bill to amend the several
tariff acts. [Washington, 1837]
7 p. DNA.   47182

---- Documents relative to
Treaty with Spain. Jan. 4,
1837. Senate Docs., No. 49,
24th Cong., 2d sess., Vol. I.
Copies of treaties, correspondence,
and other documents in relation
to Senate bill to give effect to
the eighth article of the treaty
of 1819 with Spain. [Washing-
ton, 1837] 19 p. DNA.   47183

---- Estimates for Indian Appropriations. Jan. 28, 1837. Ex.
Docs., No. 57, 25th Cong., 2d
sess., Vol. II. Estimates of
appropriations required for the
service of the Indian Department
for the year 1838. [Washington,
1837] 31 p. DNA.   47184

---- Estimates for Public Buildings and Grounds. Jan. 28,
1837. Ex. Docs., No. 109,
24th Cong., 2d sess., Vol. III.
Estimates of appropriations
needed for public buildings
and grounds in Washington for
the year 1837. [Washington,
1837. 6 p. DNA.   47185

---- Estimate of Expenses of
Foreign Missions. Jan. 13, 1837.
Ex. Docs., No. 78, 28th Cong.,
2d sess., Vol. II. Comparative
estimate of present expenses
of foreign missions, and of those
probable under provisions of
House bill No. 836. [Washing-
ton, 1837] 7 p. DNA.   47186

---- Examination of Land Moneys.
Sept. 30, 1837. Library of the
Interior Department. Circular
to registers instructing them to
examine the public moneys in
hands of receivers. [Washing-
ton, 1837] 1 p. DNA.   47187

---- Historical Documents concerning the District of Columbia.
1837. An appropriation was made
in the act approved October 16,
1837, of $25,000 to cover the ex-
pense of preparing and printing
this and two other documents,
all ordered by the Senate.
[Washington, 1837] DNA.
                             47188
---- House Documents, Twenty-
fifth Congress, First Session.
From Sept. 4, 1837. Vol. I,
Docs. Nos. 1 to 54, except 52;

also, Reports 1, 2, and 3, and
Resolutions 1, 2, and 3.
Printed by Thomas Allen. Doc.
No. 52, William B. Stokes et
al., report of the Solicitor of
the Treasury regarding.
Printed by Thomas Allen.
[Washington, 1837] DNA. 47189

---- House Documents, Twenty-
fifth Congress, Second Session.
From Dec. 4, 1837. [Washing-
ton] Printed by Thomas Allen,
[1837]. 12 v. DNA.   47190

---- House Journal, Twenty-
fifth Congress, First Session.
Sept. 4, 1837. Printed by
Thomas Allen, Washington.
From September 4, 1837, to
October 16, 1837. Speaker of
the House, James K. Polk, of
Tennessee; Clerk of the House,
Walter S. Franklin, of Pennsyl-
vania. [Washington, 1837]
273 p. DNA.   47191

---- House Journal, Twenty-
fifth Congress, Second Session.
Dec. 4, 1837. Printed by Thomas
Allen, Washington. From Decem-
ber 4, 1837, to July 9, 1838.
Speaker of the House, James
K. Polk, of Tennessee; Clerks
of the House, Walter S. Frank-
lin, of Pennsylvania, Hugh A.
Garland, of Virginia, elected
December 3, 1838. [Washington,
1837] 1,538 p. DNA.   47192

---- House Reports, Twenty-
fifth Congress, Second Session.
From Dec. 4, 1837. [Washing-
ton] Printed by Thomas Allen,
[1837]. 4 v. DNA.   47193

---- Inaugural Address. President Martin Van Buren. March
4, 1837. Senate Journal, 24th
Cong., 2d sess. [Washington,
1837] 8 p. DNA.   47194

---- Indian Treaties, 1778-1837.
By authority. Washington, 1837.
Library of Congress. Treaties
with the several Indian tribes.
[Washington, 1837] DNA.
     47195
---- Inquiry into System of
Public Accounts. P. G. Washing-
ton. Jan. 6, 1837. Ex. Docs.,
No. 71, 24th Cong., 2d sess.,
Vol. II. Statement showing the
present system of settling the
public accounts and a plan for
its simplification. [Washington,
1837] 10 p. DNA.   47196

---- Instructing Disbursing Land
Officers. June 20, 1837. Library of the Interior Department.
Circular relative to course to
be pursued by disbursing officers in consequence of suspension
of specie payments by banks
where they made deposits.
[Washington, 1837] DNA.
     47197
---- Laws of the United States.
George Sharswood, editor. Philadelphia, 1837. Law Library of
Congress. A continuation of the
edition of the statutes edited by
Judge Story. [Washington, 1837]
159 p. DNA.   47198

---- Letter on a Renewal of Duty
Bonds. Secretary Levi Woodbury. Sept. 28, 1837. Ex.
Docs., No. 35, 25th Cong., 1st
sess. Transmitting information
in relation to the number of duty
bonds which will be renewed
or extended should the Senate
bill on that subject become a
law, and to the fees to be charged
thereon. [Washington, 1837] 6 p.
DNA.   47199

---- Letter on Arkansas Land
Grant. Secretary Levi Woodbury.
Feb. 16, 1837. Senate Docs.,
No. 184, 24th Cong., 2d sess.,

Vol. II. Transmitting copies of communications from John Pope, late Governor of Arkansas, respecting land granted to that Territory for the erection of a public building at Little Rock. [Washington, 1837] 13 p. DNA.   47200

---- Letter on Certain Land Claims. Commissioner James Whitcomb. Dec. 12, 1837. Ex. Docs., No. 25, 25th Cong., 2d sess., Vol. II. Transmitting reports from the register and receiver of the land office at St. Stephen's Alabama, on the claims of John McGrew, Richard Cravat, Hardy Perry, and Beley Cheney. [Washington, 1837] 4 p. DNA.   47201

---- Letter on Charts of Massachusetts Harbors. Sec. ad interim B. F. Butler. Feb. 17, 1837. Ex. Docs., No. 165, 24th Cong., 2d sess., Vol. IV. Stating the impossibility at this session of complying with House resolution requiring charts of certain harbors on the Massachusetts coast. [Washington, 1837] 2 p. DNA.   47202

---- Letter on Claim of Eleazer W. Ripley. Sec. ad interim B. F. Butler. Feb. 28, 1837. Senate Docs., No. 214, 24th Cong., 2d sess., Vol. III. Stating the reasons which will prevent his making to the present session of the Senate a report on the claims of Eleazer W. Ripley, late a brevet major-general of the Army. [Washington, 1837] 1 p. DNA.   47203

---- Letter on Dry-Docks at New York. Secretary Mahlon Dickerson. Dec. 19, 1837. Ex. Docs., No. 35, 25th Cong.,

2d sess., Vol. II. Transmitting reports of examinations made with a view to the establishment of dry-docks in New York Bay or its vicinity. [Washington, 1837] 12 p. DNA.   47204

---- Letter on Due-Bills of Corporation of Washington. Mayor Peter Force. Feb. 28, 1837. Ex. Docs., No. 181, 24th Cong., 2d sess., Vol. IV. Transmitting statement of amount of due-bills of the corporation of Washington withdrawn from circulation and destroyed, and the balance still in circulation. [Washington, 1837] 2 p. DNA.   47205

---- Letter on Exploring Expedition. Secretary Mahlon Dickerson. Oct. 12, 1837. Ex. Docs., No. 50, 25th Cong., 1st sess. Transmitting information relative to causes of the detention in the sailing of the South Sea exploring expedition, amount of appropriation expended, and estimates for additional apporpriations required. [Washington, 1837] 28 p. DNA.   47206

---- Letter on Indian Department. Secretary ad interim B. F. Butler. Jan. 23, 1837. Ex. Docs., No. 108, 24th Cong., 2d sess., Vol. III. Transmitting estimates of additional appropriations required for the service of the Indian Department for the year 1837. [Washington, 1837] 10 p. DNA.   47207

---- Letter on Indian Hostilities, etc. Secretary J. R. Poinsett. Sept. 15, 1837. Ex. Docs., No. 19, 25th Cong., 1st sess. Recommending an appropriation for the prosecution of the Seminole war, and a further appropriation for the removal of

the raft on Red River. [Washington, 1837] 2 p. DNA.
47208

---- Letter on Navy-Yard Site. Secretary M. Dickerson. Feb. 1, 1837. Ex. Docs., No. 130, 24th Cong., 2d sess., Vol. III. Transmitting report of commissioners to examine and report upon the comparative advantages of harbors south of Chesapeake Bay for the establishment of a navy-yard. [Washington, 1837] 6 p. DNA. 47209

---- Letter on Report on Commerce and Navigation. Sec. Levi Woodbury. March 3, 1837. Senate Docs., No. 220, 24th Cong., 2d sess., Vol. III. Transmitting statement from the Register of the Treasury that the reports of the commerce and navigation of the United States for the year 1836 will not be ready for transmission to Congress at the present session, and recommending that authority be granted to transmit them to the Secretary of the Senate during the recess. [Washington, 1837] 3 p. DNA.
47210

---- Letter on Returns of Receivers of Public Moneys. Sec. Levi Woodbury. Oct. 3, 1837. Ex. Docs., No. 39, 25th Cong., 1st sess. States the impossibility of furnishing at the present session the copies of monthly returns from receivers of public moneys, and of certificates of deposit received from the late deposit banks, called for by the House of Representatives; Proposes to furnish the original papers. [Washington, 1837] 1 p. DNA. 47211

---- Letter on the Dutch Capture of American Vessel. Sec.

John Forsyth. Dec. 9, 1837. Senate Docs., No. 13, 25th Cong., 2d sess., Vol. I. Transmitting copies of instructions and correspondence relative to the seizure and sequestration of the ship Mary and cargo, of Baltimore, by the Dutch Government in 1800. [Washington, 1837] 11 p. DNA. 47212

---- Letter on the Establishment of Light-Houses. Sec. Levi Woodbury. Dec. 12, 1837. Ex. Docs., No. 21, 25th Cong., 2d sess., Vol. II. Transmitting reports of surveys of the coast south of Chesapeake Bay, with a view to the establishment of light-houses, etc. [Washington, 1837] 6 p. DNA. 47213

---- Letter on the Receivers of Public Moneys. Secretary Levi Woodbury. Dec. 11, 1837. Ex. Docs., No. 18, 25th Cong., 2d sess., Vol. II. Transmitting abstracts of monthly returns from receivers of public moneys, and abstract showing amount of money deposited by receivers, with the relative proportion of specie and bank notes. [Washington, 1837] 32 p. DNA.
47214

---- Letter on War Department Appropriations. Sec. ad interim B. F. Butler. Jan. 31, 1837. Ex. Docs., No. 119, 24th Cong., 2d sess., Vol. III. Transmitting statement of appropriations and expenditures for the War Department for the year 1836. [Washington, 1837] 17 p. DNA.
47215

---- Letter on Whale's Back Light-House. Secretary Levi Woodbury. Sept. 16, 1837. Ex. Docs., No. 19, 25th Cong., 2d sess., Vol. II. Transmitting information in relation to the necessity of constructing a breakwater for the protection of the Whale's Back light-house at Portsmouth, New Hampshire. [Washington, 1837] 7 p. DNA.   47216

---- Letter relative to Appropriations. Secretary Levi Woodbury. Dec., 1837. Ex. Docs., No. 20, 25th Cong., 2d sess., Vol. II. Transmitting estimates of appropriations necessary for the service of the Government for the year 1838. [Washington, 1837] 43 p. DNA.
47217

---- Letter relative to Army Appropriations. Secretary J. R. Poinsett. Dec. 20, 1837. Ex. Docs., No. 40, 25th Cong., 2d sess., Vol. II. Transmitting explanations relative to certain items in the estimates of appropriations for the support of the Army for the year 1838. [Washington, 1837] 15 p. DNA.
47218

---- Letter relative to Bounty Lands. Commissioner James Whitcomb. Dec. 29, 1837. Ex. Docs., No. 83, 25th Cong., 2d sess., Vol. V. Statements showing number of unsatisfied claims for bounty land, quantity and quality of land set apart for bounty land, etc. [Washington, 1837] 5 p. DNA.   47219

---- Letter relative to Convention with Spain. Secretary John Forsyth. Jan. 7, 1837. Ex. Docs., No. 73, 24th Cong., 2d sess., Vol. II. Transmitting communications from the commissioner appointed under the late convention with Spain, alleging the necessity of an extension of the time within which his duties shall terminate. [Washington, 1837] 3 p. DNA.   47220

---- Letter relative to Deposit Banks. Secretary Levi Woodbury. Jan. 9, 1837. Ex. Docs., No. 75, 24th Cong., 2d sess., Vol. II. Submitting statement of condition of two additional deposit banks selected since last annual report. [Washington, 1837] 2 p. DNA.   47221

---- Letter relative to District of Columbia Banks. Secretary Levi Woodbury. Jan. 10, 1837. Ex. Docs., No. 76, 24th Cong., 2d sess., Vol. II. Transmitting copies of returns made by the banks in the District of Columbia, showing their condition at the close of the year 1836. [Washington, 1837] 8 p. DNA.
47222

---- Letter relative to Fees of Gaugers. Secretary Levi Woodbury. Jan. 24, 1837. Ex. Docs., No. 117, 24th Cong., 2d sess., Vol. III. Transmitting communication from the gaugers at the port of New York in relation to the reduction of their fees, with statement showing the amount of fees paid, etc. [Washington, 1837] 6 p. DNA.
47223

---- Letter relative to Indian Hostilities. Secretary ad interim B. F. Butler. Feb. 11, 1837. Ex. Docs., No. 152, 24th Cong., 2d sess., Vol. IV. Recommending additional appropriations for the suppression and prevention of Indian hostilities in the South, and calling attention to the propriety of making some allowance to paymasters of militia and volunteers. [Washington, 1837] 3 p. DNA.   47224

---- Letter relative to Indian Hostilities, etc. Secretary J. R. Poinsett. Sept. 14, 1837. Senate Docs., No. 18, 25th Cong., 1st

sess. Recommending an appropriation for the prosecution of the war against the Seminole Indians, and a further appropriation for the removal of the raft on Red River. [Washington, 1837] 2 p. DNA.
47225

---- Letter relative to Indian Hostilities. Secretary J. R. Poinsett. Dec. 21, 1837. Ex. Docs., No. 65, 25th Cong., 2d sess., Vol. II. Asking additional appropriations for the prevention and suppression of Indian hostilities. [Washington, 1837] 3 p. DNA.   47226

---- Letter relative to Indian Reservations. Sec. ad interim B. F. Butler. Feb. 11, 1837. Senate Docs., No. 180, 24th Cong., 2d sess., Vol. II. Transmitting communication from the Commissioner of Indian Affairs, accompanied by a draft of a bill to carry out the treaty with the Creek Indians providing reservations for chiefs, heads of families, and others. [Washington, 1837] 8 p. DNA.
47227

---- Letter relative to Insolvent Debtors of United States. Sec. L. Woodbury. Dec. 21, 1837. Ex. Docs., No. 37, 25th Cong., 2d sess., Vol. II. Statement in relation to applicants for relief under the act for the relief of insolvent debtors of the United States; Names, nature of debt, etc. [Washington, 1837] 6 p. DNA.   47228

---- Letter relative to Intercourse with Barbary Powers. Sec. Levi Woodbury. Jan. 5, 1837. Ex. Docs., No. 69, 24th Cong., 2d sess., Vol. II. Transmitting statements of money disbursed from the

Treasury for expenses of intercourse with the Powers on the Barbary coast for the year 1836. [Washington, 1837] 3 p. DNA.   47229

---- Letter relative to Issue of Treasury Notes. Secretary Levi Woodbury. Oct. 3, 1837. Ex. Docs., No. 38, 25th Cong., 1st sess. Transmitting copies of correspondence with individuals, banks, and other corporations in relation to a proposed issue of United States Treasury notes. [Washington, 1837] 9 p. DNA.
47230

---- Letter relative to Land Claims. Secretary Levi Woodbury. Dec. 21, 1837. Senate Docs., No. 37, 25th Cong., 2d sess., Vol. I. Transmitting documents in relation to pre-emption rights and the other description of claims on the public lands commonly called floats. [Washington, 1837] 109 p. DNA.
47231

---- Letter relative to Land Claims in Louisiana. Secretary Levi Woodbury. Jan. 4, 1837. Ex. Docs., No. 64, 24th Cong., 2d sess., Vol. II. Transmitting report from the register and receiver of the land office for the southeastern district of Louisiana on certain claims to land in that district, with a communication from the Commissioner of the General Land Office on the same subject. [Washington, 1837] 13 p. DNA.
47232

---- Letter relative to Land Office at Fort Wayne. Secretary Levi Woodbury. Feb. 4, 1837. Ex. Docs., No. 142, 24th Cong., 2d sess., Vol. III. Transmitting information in relation to the examination and condition of the land office at Fort Wayne.

[Washington, 1837] 24 p. DNA.
47233

---- Letter relative to Navigation of Passaic River. Sec.
Levi Woodbury. Jan. 27, 1837.
Ex. Docs., No. 110, 24th Cong.,
2d sess., Vol. III. Transmitting a report of the survey of
obstructions to the navigation
of the Passaic River, New Jersey,
with plan and estimate for their
removal. [Washington, 1837] 3
p. DNA. 47234

---- Letter relative to New
England-Mississippi Land Co.
T. L. Winthrop. Jan. 25, 1837.
Senate Docs., No. 212, 24th
Cong., 2d sess., Vol. II.
Statement in explanation of the
claim of the said company against
the United States. [Washington,
1837] 2 p. DNA. 47235

---- Letter relative to Ordnance
Department. Sec. ad interim
B. F. Butler. Jan. 24, 1837.
Ex. Docs., No. 107, 24th Cong.,
2d sess., Vol. III. Transmitting
special estimate for additional
appropriations for the service
of the Ordnance Department
for the year 1837. [Washington,
1837] 5 p. DNA. 47236

---- Letter relative to Osage
Indians. Secretary J. R. Poinsett. Dec. 28, 1837. Senate
Docs., No. 59, 25th Cong., 2d
sess., Vol. I. Transmitting information of the distressed and
starving condition of the Osage
Indians, and recommending the
adoption of measures for their
relief. [Washington, 1837] 10
p. DNA. 47237

---- Letter relative to Pension
Appropriations. Commissioner
J. L. Edwards. Dec. 26, 1837.
Ex. Docs., No. 47, 25th Cong.,

2d sess., Vol. II. Explanatory
of increase in the estimates for
payment of pensions for year
1838. [Washington, 1837] 1 p.
DNA. 47238

---- Letter relative to Protection
of Western Frontier. Sec. J. R.
Poinsett. Dec. 30, 1837. Ex.
Docs., No. 59, 25th Cong., 2d
sess., Vol. II. Submitting a
plan for the protection of the
Western frontier against the
aggressions of the Indians, with
information as to the number
and available force of the Indians
beyond the frontier, etc. [Wash-
ington, 1837] 20 p. DNA.
47239

---- Letter relative to Public
Deposits. Secretary Levi Woodbury. Oct. 6, 1837. Ex. Docs.,
No. 43, 25th Cong., 1st sess.
Transmitting the last weekly
statement of the United States
Treasury, showing the amount
to his credit in the late deposit
banks by the returns last received; Amount drawn since the
commencement of the present
session of Congress, etc.
[Washington, 1837] 3 p. DNA.
47240

---- Letter relative to Quartermaster's Department. Sec. ad
int. B. F. Butler. Jan, 18, 1837.
Senate Docs., No. 90, 24th Cong.,
2d sess., Vol. II. Transmitting
information relative to the Quartermaster's Department, and recommending an increase in the force
of that department. [Washing-
ton, 1837] 4 p. DNA. 47241

---- Letter relative to Report on
Postmasters' Salaries. P. M. Gen.
Kendall. Jan. 16, 1837. Senate
Docs., No. 80, 24th Cong., 2d
sess., Vol. II. Stating that it
will be impracticable to furnish
to the present session of Congress

the report called for, showing the amount of emoluments received by each postmaster in the United States, but that it will be transmitted, if possible, at the next session. [Washington, 1837] 2 p. DNA. 47241a

---- Letter relative to Revenue-Cutter. Secretary Levi Woodbury. Feb. 1, 1837. Ex. Docs., No. 127, 24th Cong., 2d sess., Vol. III. Estimate of cost of revenue-cutter constructed so as to be used as a steam tow-boat. [Washington, 1837] 1 p. DNA. 47242

---- Letter relative to Subtreasury System. Secretary Levi Woodbury. Sept. 30, 1837. Ex. Docs., No. 36, 25th Cong., 1st sess. Transmitting an estimate of the probable expenses attendant upon the subtreasury system proposed by the bill now pending in the House of Representatives. [Washington, 1837] 2 p. DNA. 47243

---- Letter relative to Surplus Revenue. Secretary Levi Woodbury. Jan. 3, 1837. Ex. Docs., No. 62, 24th Cong., 2d sess., Vol. II. Transmitting statement of the surplus revenue of the United States to be deposited to the credit of the several States. [Washington, 1837] 2 p. DNA. 47244

---- Letter relative to Survey. Secretary M. Dickerson. Feb. 3, 1837. Ex. Docs., No. 132, 24th Cong., 2d sess., Vol. III. Informing the House of Representatives, in reply to a resolution asking for report of progress made in the survey of the coast from the Rigolets to Mobile Point, that no resolution of the House directing such survey to be made has been received. [Washington, 1837] 1 p. DNA. 47245

---- Letter relative to the John Paul Jones Prize-Money. Reg. T. L. Smith. Jan. 28, 1837. Ex. Docs., No. 115, 24th Cong., 2d sess., Vol. III. Transmitting statement relative to the prize-money due to the squadron under the command of the late John Paul Jones. [Washington, 1837] 4 p. DNA. 47246

---- Letter relative to the Militia. Secretary ad interim B. F. Butler. Feb. 7, 1837. Ex. Docs., No. 140, 24th Cong., 2d sess., Vol. III. Transmitting copies of orders issued by the War Department respecting calls for volunteers or militiamen for service in the Florida war, with a statement of the volunteer and militia force mustered into the United States service during the years 1835 and 1836. [Washington, 1837] 89 p. DNA. 47247

---- Letter relative to Treaty with Spain. Secretary Levi Woodbury. Jan. 3, 1837. Ex. Docs., No. 67, 24th Cong., 2d sess., Vol. II. Statement in relation to the causes which have prevented the payment of certain claims of inhabitants of Florida filed under the provisions of the ninth article of the treaty with Spain of February 22, 1819. [Washington, 1837] 2 p. DNA. 47248

---- Letter relative to United States Bank. Secretary Levi Woodbury. Feb. 27, 1837. Senate Docs., No. 208, 24th Cong., 2d sess., Vol. VI. Statement in relation to the offer of the directors of the United States

Bank to settle the claim of the
United States against the bank.
[Washington, 1837] 3 p. DNA.
                                    47249
---- Letter relative to War
Claim of Massachusetts. Secretary J. R. Poinsett. Dec.
23, 1837. Ex. Docs., No. 45,
25th Cong., 2d sess., Vol. II.
Statement of amount of claims
of Massachusetts for militia
services and expenditures
during the war of 1812. [Wash-
inton, 1837] 1 p. DNA. 47250

---- Letter relative to Wisconsin Territory. Secretary Levi
Woodbury. Jan. 14, 1837.
Ex. Docs., No. 98, 24th Cong.,
2d sess., Vol. III. Transmitting information on the subject
of an appropriation by Congress
to defray the expenses of the
Legislature of Wisconsin.
[Washington, 1837] 5 p. DNA.
                                    47251
---- Letter transmitting Diplomatic Correspondence. Sec.
John Forsyth. Feb. 16, 1837.
Ex. Docs., No. 167, 24th Cong.,
2d sess., Vol. IV. Copies of
correspondence of the late
William Tudor, jr., United
States consul, with the State
Department and with the Peru-
vian Government. [Washington,
1837] 207 p. DNA.   47252

---- Letter transmitting Diplomatic Correspondence. Sec.
John Forsyth. Sept. 26, 1837.
Ex. Docs., No. 32, 25th Cong.,
1st sess. Transmitting copies
of correspondence of the late
William Tudor, jr., chargé
d'affaires of the United States
at Rio Janeiro, with the State
Department and with the
Brazilian Government. [Wash-
ington, 1837] 261 p. DNA.
                                    47253

---- Letters on Deposit Banks.
Secretary Levi Woodbury. Dec.
5, 1837. Ex. Docs., No. 5,
25th Cong., 2d sess., Vol. I.
Transmitting statement showing
number, names, and condition
of banks employed as depositories
of public money. [Washington,
1837] 3 p. DNA.   47254

---- List of French Spoliation
Memorialists. March 3, 1837.
Ex. Docs., No. 184, 24th Cong.,
2d sess., Vol. IV. Names and
residences of memorialists to
Congress during the Nineteenth,
Twentieth, Twenty-first, Twenty-
second, and Twenty-third Con-
gresses on account of French
spoliations prior to 1800.
[Washington, 1837] 27 p. DNA.
                                    47255
---- List of Reports to be made
to Congress. Sept. 4, 1837.
Ex. Docs., No. 3, 25th Cong.,
1st sess. List of reports to be
made to Congress at the first
session of the Twenty-fifth Congress by public officers. [Wash-
ington, 1837] 18 p. DNA.
                                    47256
---- List of Reports to be made
to Congress. Dec. 5, 1837.
Ex. Docs., No. 1, 25th Cong.,
2d sess., Vol. I. List of reports to be made to the second
session of the Twenty-fifth Congress by public officers. [Wash-
ington, 1837] 19 p. DNA.
                                    47257
---- List of Senate Committees.
Sept. 8, 1837. Senate Docs.,
No. 8, 25th Cong., 1st sess.
Names and membership of Senate
committees for the first session
of the Twenty-fifth Congress.
[Washington, 1837] 2 p. DNA.
                                    47258
---- List of Senate Committees.
Dec. 7, 1837. Senate Docs., No.
4, 25th Cong., 2d sess., Vol. I.

Names and membership of the committees of the Senate for the second session of the Twenty-fifth Congress. [Washington, 1837] 2 p. DNA.   47259

---- Memorial asking a Land Grant for New Hagerstown Academy. Dec. 28, 1837. Ex. Docs., No. 160, 25th Cong., 2d sess., Vol. VII. Citizens of Ohio pray for a donation of public land to that institution. [Washington, 1837] 1 p. DNA.   47260

---- Memorial of a Delegation of the Cherokee Nation. Dec. 15, 1837. Ex. Docs., No. 99, 25th Cong., 2d sess., Vol. V. Protesting against the enforcement of the instrument purporting to be a treaty with the Cherokee Nation negotiated at New Echota in 1825. [Washington, 1837] 49 p. DNA.   47261

---- Memorial of Directors of Bank of the Metropolis. Washington. Jan. 24, 1837. Ex. Docs., No. 129, 24th Cong., 2d sess., Vol. III. Asking for a continuance of the charter of the bank and authority for an increase of its capital stock. [Washington, 1837] 2 p. DNA.   47262

---- Memorial of Heirs of Carlos de Villemont. Jan. 20, 1837. Senate Docs., No. 89, 24th Cong., 2d sess., Vol. II. Praying for confirmation of title to land in Arkansas claimed under Spanish grant. [Washington, 1837] 93 p. DNA.   47263

---- Memorial of President and Directors of Bank of Washington. Dec. 26, 1837. Senate Docs., No. 45, 25th Cong., 2d sess., Vol. I. Praying

for an extension of the charter of said bank. [Washington, 1837] 2 p. DNA.   47264

---- Memorial of President and Directors of the United States Bank. Feb. 24, 1837. Senate Docs., No. 201, 24th Cong., 2d sess., Vol. II. Stating the desire of the bank to settle its accounts with the United States, and making a final offer of settlement directly to Congress. [Washington, 1837] 3 p. DNA.   47265

---- Memorial of the Administrator of George Simpson. Dec. 21, 1837. Senate Docs., No. 90, 25th Cong., 2d sess., Vol. I. Praying the allowance of a commission on subscriptions procured to the United States loan in 1813. [Washington, 1837] 9 p. DNA.   47266

---- Memorial of the New York Pilots. Dec. 27, 1837. Senate Docs., No. 44, 25th Cong., 2d sess., Vol. I. Praying the repeal or modification of the act of Congress of March 2, 1837, regulating the pilot system. [Washington, 1837] 9 p. DNA.   47267

---- Memorial of the President and Directors of the United States Bank. Feb. 25, 1837. Ex. Docs., No. 172, 24th Cong., 2d sess., Vol. IV. Making a final offer of settlement of the claims of the United States against the United States Bank. [Washington, 1837] 3 p. DNA.   47268

---- Memorial of William A. Slocum. Dec. 18, 1837. Senate Docs., No. 24, 25th Cong., 2d sess., Vol. I. Praying compensation for his services in obtaining information in relation to the country and inhabitants in the neigh-

borhood of the Columbia River.
[Washington, 1837] 31 p. DNA.
47269
---- Memorial on a Bankruptcy
Law. Citizens of Maine. Dec.,
1837. Ex. Docs., No. 182, 25th
Cong., 2d sess., Vol. VI. Praying Congress to establish a uniform system of bankruptcy in
the United States. [Washington,
1837] 3 p. DNA.   47270

---- Memorial on a National
Bank. Citizens of Alabama.
Sept. 15, 1837. Ex. Docs.,
No. 16, 25th Cong., 1st sess.
Praying for the establishment
of a national bank. [Washing-
ton, 1837] 2 p. DNA.   47271

---- Memorial on a National
Bank. Citizens of Alabama.
Sept. 23, 1837. Senate Docs.,
No. 22, 25th Cong., 1st sess.
Praying for the establishment
of a national bank. [Washing-
ton, 1837] 10 p. DNA.   47272

---- Memorial on a National
Bank. Citizens of Baltimore.
Sept. 25, 1837. Senate Docs.,
No. 24, 25th Cong., 1st sess.
Praying for the establishment
of a national bank, For the ap-
pointment of the United States
Bank of Pennsylvania as the
fiscal agent to the Government.
[Washington, 1837] 2 p. DNA.
47273
---- Memorial on a National
Bank. Citizens of Florida.
Sept, 14, 1837. Ex. Docs., No.
15, 25th Cong., 1st sess.
Praying for the establishment
of a national bank. [Washing-
ton, 1837] 2 p. DNA.   47274

---- Memorial on a National
Bank. Citizens of Illinois.
Sept. 13, 1837. Ex. Docs.,
No. 8, 25th Cong., 1st sess.

Praying for the establishment
of a national bank. [Washing-
ton, 1837] 2 p. DNA.   47275

---- Memorial on a National
Bank. Citizens of Illinois.
Sept. 15, 1837. Senate Docs.,
No. 23, 25th Cong., 1st sess.
Praying for the establishment of
a national bank. [Washington,
1837] 3 p. DNA.   47276

---- Memorial on a National
Bank. Citizens of Indiana.
Sept. 12, 1837. Ex. Docs., No.
5, 25th Cong., 1st sess. Praying for the establishment of a
national bank. [Washington,
1837] 2 p. DNA.   47277

---- Memorial on a National
Bank. Citizens of Indiana.
Sept. 21, 1837. Ex. Docs., No.
26, 25th Cong., 1st sess. Praying for the establishment of a
national bank. [Washington,
1837] 2 p. DNA.   47278

---- Memorial on a National
Bank. Citizens of Mississippi.
Sept. 11, 1837. Senate Docs.,
No. 11, 25th Cong., 1st sess.
Praying for the establishment of
a national bank. [Washington,
1837] 2 p. DNA.   47279

---- Memorial on a National
Bank. Citizens of Mississippi.
Sept. 22, 1837. Senate Docs.,
No. 20, 25th Cong., 1st sess.
Praying for the establishment of
a national bank. [Washington,
1837] 5 p. DNA.   47280

---- Memorial on a National
Bank. Citizens of New Jersey.
Oct. 13, 1837. Senate Docs.,
No. 35, 25th Cong., 1st sess.
Praying for the establishment of
a national bank. [Washington,
1837] 2 p. DNA.   47281

---- Memorial on a National Bank. Citizens of New York. Sept. 28, 1837. Ex. Docs., No. 34, 25th Cong., 1st sess. Praying for the establishment of a national bank. [Washington, 1837] 2 p. DNA.   47282

---- Memorial on a National Bank. Citizens of Ohio. Sept. 13, 1837. Ex. Docs., No. 9, 25th Cong., 1st sess. Praying for the establishment of a national bank. [Washington, 1837] 2 p. DNA.   47283

---- Memorial on a National Bank. Citizens of Ohio. Oct. 2, 1837. Senate Docs., No. 28, 25th Cong., 1st sess. In opposition to the creation of a national bank, and in favor of the adoption of measures to increase the circulation of gold and silver. [Washington, 1837] 3 p. DNA.   47284

---- Memorial on a National Bank. Citizens of St. Louis. Sept, 14, 1837. Ex. Docs., No. 13, 25th Cong., 1st sess. Praying for the establishment of a national bank. [Washington, 1837] 2 p. DNA.   47285

---- Memorial on a National Bank. Citizens of Vermont. Sept. 13, 1837. Ex. Docs., No. 10, 25th Cong., 1st sess. Praying for the establishment of a national bank. [Washington, 1837] 2 p. DNA.   47286

---- Memorial on a National Bank. Citizens of Virginia. Sept. 18, 1837. Ex. Docs., No. 20, 25th Cong., 1st sess. Praying for the establishment of a national bank. [Washington, 1837] 2 p. DNA.   47287

---- Memorial on a National Bank. Citizens of Wheeling, Virginia. Aug., 1837. Senate Docs., No. 25, 25th Cong., 1st sess. Praying for the establishment of a national bank. [Washington, 1837] 4 p. DNA.   47288

---- Memorial on a National Bank. L. D. Teackle. Sept. 8, 1837. Senate Docs., No. 6, 25th Cong., 1st sess. Presenting to Congress a plan of a proposed national bank, and praying that it be considered and acted upon. [Washington, 1837] 13 p. DNA.   47289

---- Memorial on a National Bank. New Orleans Chamber of Commerce. Sept, 8, 1837. Senate Docs., No. 7, 25th Cong., 1st sess. Praying for the establishment of a national bank. [Washington, 1837] 4 p. DNA.   47290

---- Memorial on a National Bank. New Orleans Chamber of Commerce. Sept. 12, 1837. Ex. Docs., No. 4, 25th Cong., 1st sess. Praying for the establishment of a national bank. [Washington, 1837] 4 p. DNA.   47291

---- Memorial on a National Bank. St. Louis Chamber of Commerce. Sept. 11, 1837. Senate Docs., No. 9, 25th Cong., 1st sess. Praying for the establishment of a national bank. [Washington, 1837] 2 p. DNA.   47292

---- Memorial on a National Bank. St. Louis Chamber of Commerce. Sept, 14, 1837. Ex. Docs., No. 14, 25th Cong., 1st sess. Praying for the establishment of a national bank. [Washington, 1837] 2 p. DNA.   47293

---- Memorial on a National Road. Citizens of Pennsylvania.

Aug. 16, 1837. Ex. Docs.,
No. 56, 25th Cong., 2d sess.,
Vol. II. Praying for the construction of a road from some
point on the Cumberland road
to the harbor of Erie. [Wash-
ington, 1837] 2 p. DNA.
                                47294
---- Memorial on a National
Road. Citizens of Pennsylvania.
Aug. 16, 1837. Senate Docs.,
No. 4, 25th Cong., 1st sess.
Praying Congress to construct
a macadamized road from some
point on the Cumberland road
to the harbor at Erie, Pennsylvania. [Washington, 1837] 2
p. DNA.   47295

---- Memorial on Banks and
Currency. Citizens of Ohio.
Sept. 11, 1837. Senate Docs.,
No. 10, 25th Cong., 1st sess.
In favor of the adoption of
measures to increase the circulation of gold and silver and
opposing the charter of any
banking institution by the
United States. [Washington,
1837] 2 p. DNA.   47296

---- Memorial on Capital Punishment. Citizens of Pennsylvania.
Dec. 5, 1837. Ex. Docs., No.
53, 25th Cong., 2d sess., Vol.
II. Praying that persons condemned to death under the
United States laws may be executed within the prison yards.
[Washington, 1837] 2 p. DNA.
                                47297
---- Memorial on Capital Punishment. Citizens of Pennsylvania.
Dec. 5, 1837. Senate Docs.,
No. 6, 25th Cong., 2d sess.,
Vol. I. Praying that persons
hereafter condemned to death
under the United States laws
may be executed within the
prison yards. [Washington,
1837] 2 p. DNA.   47298

---- Memorial on Cession of Land
by Virginia. John Taliaferro.
Jan. 31, 1837. Ex. Docs., No.
117, 24th Cong., 2d sess., Vol.
III. Praying Congress to determine whether the stipulations
made by the State of Virginia in
ceding to the United States her
lands north and west of the Ohio
River have been faithfully com-
plied with. [Washington, 1837]
2 p. DNA.   47299

---- Memorial on Duty on Coal.
Citizens of Pennsylvania. Jan.
10, 1837. Senate Docs., No.
59, 24th Cong., 2d sess., Vol.
I. In opposition to any reduction of the duty on imported
coal. [Washington, 1837] 7 p.
DNA.   47300

---- Memorial on Grant of Land.
Corporation of South Hanover
College. Dec. 19, 1837. Senate
Docs., No. 28, 25th Cong., 2d
sess., Vol. I. Asking grant of
land for that institution. [Wash-
ington, 1837] 1 p. DNA.
                                47301
---- Memorial on Harbor on Lake
Michigan. Indiana Legislature.
Dec. 28, 1837. Ex. Docs., No.
105, 25th Cong., 2d sess., Vol.
V. Asking a further appropria-
tion for the improvement of the
harbor at Michigan City, Indiana.
[Washington, 1837] 1 p. DNA.
                                47302
---- Memorial on Harbors on Lake
Michigan. Indiana Legislature.
Jan. 10, 1837. Ex. Docs., No.
104, 24th Cong., 2d sess., Vol.
III. Asking an appropriation to
further the completion of the har-
bor at Michigan City, Indiana.
[Washington, 1837] 2 p. DNA.
                                47303
---- Memorial on Imprisonment for
Debt. Silas M. Stilwell. Dec. 11,
1837. Senate Docs., No. 7, 25th

Cong., 2d sess., Vol. I. Praying that the United States courts be prevented from issuing process for imprisonment for debt in States where it is not allowed by the State laws. [Washington, 1837] 2 p. DNA. 47304

---- Memorial on Indian Reservations. Arkansas Legislature. Dec. 1, 1837. Senate Docs., No. 53, 25th Cong., 2d sess., Vol. I. Against a selection of Indians reservations in Arkansas which shall conflict with the pre-emption rights of settlers. [Washington, 1837] 3 p. DNA. 47305

---- Memorial on International Arbitration. Citizens of Massachusetts. Dec. 13, 1837. Ex. Docs., No. 290, 25th Cong., 2d sess., Vol. VIII. In favor of the establishment of an international court of arbitration. [Washington, 1837] 2 p. DNA. 47306

---- Memorial on International Copyright. Certain British authors. Feb. 12, 1837. Ex. Docs., No. 162, 24th Cong., 2d sess., Vol. IV. Asking passage of a law securing to them the exclusive ownership in their respective writings in the United States. [Washington, 1837] 4 p. DNA. 47307

---- Memorial on Land Claim. Joseph Roby. Dec. 19, 1837. Senate Docs., No. 29, 25th Cong., 2d sess., Vol. I. Praying permission to locate a floating Indian reservation of land on any unappropriated lands of the United States in Illinois or Wisconsin Territory. [Washington, 1837] 8 p. DNA. 47308

---- Memorial on Louisiana Land

Claim. Representatives of Wade Hampton. Dec. 27, 1837. Senate Docs., No. 144, 25th Cong., 2d sess., Vol. III. Praying confirmation of title to certain land in Louisiana. [Washington, 1837] 31 p. DNA. 47309

---- Memorial on National Finance. Pennsylvania anti-bank convention. Sept. 13, 1837. Ex. Docs., No. 11, 25th Cong., 1st sess. Recommending the adoption of measures recommended by the President, and condemning the establishment of any national bank. [Washington, 1837] 2 p. DNA. 47310

---- Memorial on Naturalization. Citizens of New York. Nov., 1837. Ex. Docs., No. 154, 25th Cong., 2d sess., Vol. VII. Praying Congress to enquire whether an amendment of the naturalization laws is not needed to secure the free institutions and liberties of the country. [Washington, 1837] 3 p. DNA. 47311

---- Memorial on Ohio Canal Grants. Citizens of Ohio. Dec. 1, 1837. Senate Docs., No. 52, 25th Cong., 2d sess., Vol. I. Praying for the sale of the canal reservations in the State of Ohio, and the appropriation of the proceeds to the construction of certain roads. [Washington, 1837] 3 p. DNA. 47312

---- Memorial on Payment of Duties. New York merchants. Sept. 14, 1837. Ex. Docs., No. 24, 25th Cong., 1st sess. Praying for an extension of the time for the payment of bonds given for duties on merchandise. [Washington, 1837] 4 p. DNA. 47313

---- Memorial on Payment of

Duties. New York merchants.
Sept, 14, 1837. Senate Docs.,
No. 13, 25th Cong., 1st sess.
Praying for an extension of the
time for the payment of bonds
given for duties on merchandise.
[Washington, 1837] 5 p. DNA.
47314

---- Memorial on Pre-emption
Law. Citizens of Michigan.
Dec. 1, 1837. Senate Docs.,
No. 61, 25th Cong., 2d sess.,
Vol. I. Praying for the passage
of a general pre-emption law.
[Washington, 1837] 4 p. DNA.
47315

---- Memorial on Pre-emption
Rights. Citizens of McDonough
Co., Ill. Sept. 30, 1837.
Senate Docs., No. 27, 25th
Cong., 1st sess. Praying to
be granted pre-emption rights
to certain lands upon which they
have settled. [Washington,
1837] 7 p. DNA.   47316

---- Memorial on Pre-emption
Rights. Sundry settlers in
Illinois. Feb. 13, 1837. Ex.
Docs., No. 151, 24th Cong., 2d
sess., Vol. IV. Praying that
pre-emption rights be granted
to settlers on unsurveyed public lands. [Washington, 1837]
3 p. DNA.   47317

---- Memorial on Public Deposits. Citizens of Illinois.
Nov. 23, 1837. Ex. Docs.,
No. 203, 25th Cong., 2d sess.,
Vol. VIII. In opposition to
entrusting any bank with the
custody of the public money.
[Washington, 1837] 4 p. DNA.
47318

---- Memorial on Sales of
Public Lands. Citizens of Ohio.
Dec. 22, 1837. Senate Docs.,
No. 137, 25th Cong., 2d sess.,
Vol. II. Praying a modification
of the laws regulating the sale

of public lands, pre-emption
rights, etc. [Washington, 1837]
3 p. DNA.   47319

---- Memorial on Sculpture for
the Capitol. Philadelphia
Artists' Society. Feb. 1, 1837.
Ex. Docs., No. 159, 24th Cong.,
2d sess., Vol. IV. Recommending the appointment of Luigi
Persico to superintend the
sculptural decoration of the Capitol. [Washington, 1837] 3 p.
DNA.   47320

---- Memorial on Taxation of
Public Lands. Illinois Legislature. Jan. 23, 1837. Senate
Docs., No. 99, 24th Cong., 2d
sess., Vol. II. Praying for a
removal of the restrictions for
five years on the taxation of
public land sold in Illinois.
[Washington, 1837] 3 p. DNA.
47321

---- Memorial on Testimony before a House Committee. R. M.
Whitney. Feb. 6, 1837. Ex.
Docs., No. 156, 24th Cong., 2d
sess., Vol. IV. Complaining of
an assault made upon him by two
members of the committee appointed to investigate the affairs
of the deposit banks while he
was giving testimony before that
committee. [Washington, 1837]
2 p. DNA.   47322

---- Memorial on the Annexation
of Texas. Women of Boston.
Oct. 9, 1837. Ex. Docs., No.
45, 25th Cong., 1st sess.
Remonstrating against the annexation of Texas to the United
States as a slave-holding Territory. [Washington, 1837] 1 p.
DNA.   47323

---- Memorial on the Annexation
of Texas. Yearly meeting of
Friends. Sept. 9, 1837. Senate

Docs., No. 46, 25th Cong., 1st sess., Vol. I. Protesting against the annexation of Texas. [Washington, 1837] 1 p. DNA. 47324

---- Memorial on the Bank of the Metropolis. James H. Causten. Oct. 6, 1837. Ex. Docs., No. 53, 25th Cong., 1st sess. Praying the revocation of the charter of said bank. [Washington, 1837] 8 p. DNA. 47325

---- Memorial on the Bank of Milwaukee. Citizens of Milwaukee. Jan. 31, 1837. Senate Docs., No. 121, 24th Cong., 2d sess., Vol. II. Praying Congress not to confirm an act of the Legislature of Wisconsin to incorporate the stockholders of the Bank of Milwaukee. [Washington, 1837] 22 p. DNA. 47326

---- Memorial on the Coinage. Lewis Feuchtwanger. Sept. 13, 1837. Ex. Docs., No. 7, 25th Cong., 1st sess. Praying Congress to substitute a currency made of a metallic composition invented by him, and called "German silver," for the copper currency in use. [Washington, 1837] 1 p. DNA. 47327

---- Memorial on the Construction of a Harbor. Citizens of Wisconsin. Dec. 20, 1837. Ex. Docs., No. 159, 25th Cong., 2d sess., Vol. VII. Praying for an appropriation for the construction of a harbor at the mouth of the Kewaunee River, Wisconsin. [Washington, 1837] 2 p. DNA. 47328

---- Memorial on the Currency. L. D. Teackle. Sept. 12, 1837. Ex. Docs., No. 6, 25th Cong., 1st sess. Proposing the plan of a proposed national currency

and its distribution. [Washington, 1837] 38 p. DNA. 47329

---- Memorial on the Currency, etc. L. D. Teackle. Dec. 13, 1837. Ex. Docs., No. 30, 25th Cong., 2d sess., Vol. II. Presenting a plan for a national currency and the establishment of State banks. [Washington, 1837] 16 p. DNA. 47330

---- Memorial on the Currency. Thomas H. Baird. Oct. 13, 1837. Ex. Docs., No. 51, 25th Cong., 1st sess. Proposing a currency system for the relief of the present financial embarrassments of the country. [Washington, 1837] 6 p. DNA. 47331

---- Memorial on the Finances. Citizens of Philadelphia. Dec. 6, 1837. Ex. Docs., No. 69, 25th Cong., 2d sess., Vol. II. Praying for the adoption of a sub-treasury system, a return to a metallic currency, etc. [Washington, 1837] 3 p. DNA. 47332

---- Memorial on the Location of a Court, etc. Citizens of Florida. Dec. 16, 1837. Ex. Docs., No. 287, 25th Cong., 2d sess., Vol. VIII. Praying for the location of the superior court of Franklin County at St. Joseph, and for an appropriation to build a court-house and jail at that place. [Washington, 1837] 1 p. DNA. 47333

---- Memorial relative to a District Bank. Citizens of Georgetown. Jan. 2, 1837. Ex. Docs., No. 91, 24th Cong., 2d sess., Vol. III. Praying for the establishment of a bank in Washington, with branches in Georgetown and Alexandria. [Washington, 1837] 1 p. DNA. 47334

---- Memorial relative to a
National Bank. Citizens of
New York city. Jan. 27, 1837.
Ex. Docs., No. 113, 24th Cong.,
2d sess., Vol. III. [Washing-
ton, 1837] 17 p. DNA.   47335

---- Memorial relative to a Na-
tional Bank. Merchants of New
York. Jan. 4, 1837. Senate
Docs., No. 163, 24th Cong.,
2d sess., Vol. II. Praying
Congress to establish a national
bank in the city of New York.
[Washington, 1837] 18 p. DNA.
                              47336

---- Memorial relative to a Navy-
Yard. Citizens of Charleston,
S.C. Feb. 20, 1837. Senate
Docs., No. 195, 24th Cong.,
2d sess., Vol. II. Praying the
establishment of a navy-yard at
Charleston. [Washington, 1837]
6 p. DNA.   47337

---- Memorial relative to a Sys-
tem of Finance. John Golder.
Sept. 25, 1837. Ex. Docs.,
No. 33, 25th Cong., 1st sess.
Proposing for the consideration
of Congress a plan for an im-
proved system of finance.
[Washington, 1837] 4 p. DNA.
                              47338

---- Memorial relative to Breakwater. Indiana Legislature.
Jan. 10, 1837. Senate Docs.,
No. 108, 24th Cong., 2d sess.,
Vol. II. Praying for an additional appropriation for the
completion of the breakwater
at Michigan City. [Washington,
1837] 2 p. DNA.   47339

---- Memorial relative to Copyright. G. Furman et al. Feb.
20, 1837. Senate Docs., No.
192, 24th Cong., 2d sess., Vol.
II. Praying passage of an international copyright law. [Wash-
ington, 1837] 3 p. DNA. 47340

---- Memorial relative to Cumberland Road. Indiana Legislature. Jan. 18, 1837. Senate
Docs., No. 119, 24th Cong.,
2d sess., Vol. II. Praying for
the completion of the Cumberland road within the States of
Ohio, Indiana, and Illinois.
[Washington, 1837] 2 p. DNA.
                              47341

---- Memorial relative to Duty
on Coal. Citizens of Pennsylvania. Feb. 13, 1837. Ex.
Docs., No. 158, 24th Cong., 2d
sess., Vol. IV. Remonstrating
against a repeal of the duty on
foreign coal. [Washington,
1837] 2 p. DNA.   47342

---- Memorial relative to Duty on
Coal. Citizens of Virginia.
Jan. 20, 1837. Ex. Docs., No.
93, 24th Cong., 2d sess., Vol.
III. Opposing any reduction of
the duty on imported coal.
[Washington, 1837] 8 p. DNA.
                              47343

---- Memorial relative to Grant
of Land. Ohio Legislature.
Jan. 3, 1837. Senate Docs.,
No. 115, 24th Cong., 2d sess.,
Vol. II. Praying for a donation
of land in lieu of certain lands
granted the State of Ohio and
afterward sold by the United
States. [Washington, 1837]
2 p. DNA.   47344

---- Memorial relative to Grant
of Lands. Ohio Legislature.
Feb. 9, 1837. Senate Docs.,
No. 210, 24th Cong., 2d sess.,
Vol. II. Praying for a donation
to the State of Ohio of certain
tracts of land between the
Muskingum and Little Miami
Rivers. [Washington, 1837] 2
p. DNA.   47345

---- Memorial relative to Harbors
on Lake Michigan. Indiana

Legislature. Jan. 21, 1837.
Ex. Docs., No. 150, 24th Cong.,
2d sess., Vol. IV. Praying for
liberal appropriations for the
survey and construction of harbors on the southern coast of
Lake Michigan. [Washington,
1837] 2 p. DNA.   47346

---- Memorial relative to Harbors on Lake Michigan. Indiana Legislature. Jan. 21,
1837. Senate Docs., No. 133,
24th Cong., 2d sess., Vol. II.
Praying for the improvement of
the harbors on the southern
coast of Lake Michigan. [Wash-
ington, 1837] 3 p. DNA.
                          47347
---- Memorial relative to Improvement of Allegheny River.
Citizens of Pa. Jan. 16, 1837.
Ex. Docs., No. 84, 24th Cong.,
2d sess., Vol. III. Praying
for an appropriation to improve
the navigation of the Allegheny
River between Pittsburgh,
Pennsylvania, and Olean, New
York. [Washington, 1837] 5
p. DNA.   47348

---- Memorial relative to Improvement of Grand River. Mo. Legislature. Jan. 9, 1837. Ex. Docs.,
No. 165, 24th Cong., 2d sess.,
Vol. VII. Asking an appropriation for the improvement of the
navigation of Grand River.
[Washington, 1837] 1 p. DNA.
                          47349
---- Memorial relative to Indians.
Michigan Legislature. Jan. 10,
1837. Senate Docs., No. 112,
24th Cong., 2d sess., Vol. II.
Praying that Congress will make
an appropriation to provide for
holding treaties with Indian
tribes on the sources of the
Mississippi for the purpose of
acquiring the right to locate
the lake tribes in that quarter.

[Washington, 1837] 4 p. DNA.
                          47350
---- Memorial relative to Naval
Promotions. Lieutenants in the
Navy. Dec. 29, 1837. Senate
Docs., No. 254, 25th Cong., 2d
sess., Vol. III. Praying that
those lieutenants who entered the
Navy as midshipmen prior to and
during the war of 1812 may be
promoted. [Washington, 1837]
3 p. DNA.   47351

---- Memorial relative to New
Land District. Missouri Legislature. Feb. 6, 1837. Ex. Docs.,
No. 156, 24th Cong., 2d sess.,
Vol. VII. Asking for the establishment of a new land district
in the northwestern part of Missouri. [Washington, 1837] 1 p.
DNA.   47352

---- Memorial relative to Pension
Laws, etc. Illinois Legislature.
Jan. 23, 1837. Senate Docs.,
No. 98, 24th Cong., 2d sess.,
Vol. II. Praying extension of
the benefits of the pension laws
to those persons who served
three months prior to 1795, and
for grant of bounty land to
soldiers of the war of 1812.
[Washington, 1837] 2 p. DNA.
                          47353
---- Memorial relative to Post-
Routes. Mississippi Legislature.
May 12, 1837. Senate Docs.,
No. 3, 25th Cong., 1st sess.
Praying for the establishment by
law of a number of post-routes
in the State of Mississippi.
[Washington, 1837] 2 p. DNA.
                          47354
---- Memorial relative to Pre-
emption Law. Citizens of Indi-
ana. Dec. 15, 1837. Ex. Docs.,
No. 178, 25th Cong., 2d sess.,
Vol. VII. In favor of the pas-
sage of a law granting pre-
emption rights to actual settlers.

[Washington, 1837]   1 p.   DNA.
                                      47355
---- Memorial relative to Pre-
emption Law, etc. Wis. Legislative Council. Dec. 28, 1837.
Senate Docs., No. 50, 25th
Cong., 2d sess., Vol. II. Praying for the passage of a special
pre-emption law in favor of the
citizens of Southport, Indiana,
and for the construction of a
harbor at that place. [Wash-
ington, 1837]   2 p.   DNA.
                                      47356
---- Memorial relative to Pre-
emption Rights. Missouri
Legislature. Jan. 5, 1837.
Ex. Docs., No. 152, 25th Cong.,
2d sess., Vol. VII. Asking
grant of pre-emption rights to
settlers upon lands covered by
Spanish claims. [Washington,
1837]   2 p.   DNA.   47357

---- Memorial relative to Public
Lands. Alabama Legislature.
Dec. 23, 1837. Ex. Docs., No.
180, 25th Cong., 2d sess.,
Vol. VII. Praying passage of
a pre-emption law, a reduction
in the price of public lands,
that unproductive lands that
have remained for a certain time
unsold be granted to the States
in which they lie, etc. [Wash-
ington, 1837]   3 p.   DNA.
                                      47358
---- Memorial relative to Pub-
lic Lands. Alabama Legislature.
Dec. 23, 1837. Senate Docs.,
No. 171, 25th Cong., 2d sess.,
Vol. IV. Praying passage of a
pre-emption law, reduction in
price of public lands, and grant
of certain lands in Alabama to
that State. [Washington, 1837]
3 p.   DNA.   47359

---- Memorial relative to Public
Lands. Citizens of Illinois.
Feb. 21, 1837. Senate Docs.,

no. 198, 24th Cong., 2d sess.,
Vol. II. Praying passage of a
pre-emption law in favor of set-
tlers of unsurveyed public lands.
[Washington, 1837]   3 p.   DNA.
                                      47360
---- Memorial relative to Public
Lands. Citizens of Wisconsin.
Feb. 2, 1837. Senate Docs.,
No. 127, 24th Cong., 2d sess.,
Vol. II. Praying passage of a
law granting pre-emption rights
to public lands. [Washington,
1837]   4 p.   DNA.   47361

---- Memorial relative to Slavery,
Witchcraft, etc. Citizens of
Virginia. Sept. 28, 1837. Ex.
Docs., No. 49, 25th Cong., 1st
sess. Praying that the wisdom
of Congress may avert the horrors
of a religious crusade against
Southern citizens by the witch-
burners of Massachusetts and
other Northern States. [Wash-
ington, 1837]   2 p.   DNA.
                                      47362
---- Memorial relative to Surplus
Revenue. Citizens of Brooklyn,
N.Y. Feb. 7, 1837. Senate
Docs., No. 153, 24th Cong., 2d
sess., Vol. II. Praying for a
reduction of the revenues to the
wants of the Government. [Wash-
ington, 1837]   2 p.   DNA.
                                      47363
---- Memorial relative to Texas.
Citizens of District of Columbia.
Feb. 13, 1837. Senate Docs.,
No. 172, 24th Cong., 2d sess.,
Vol. II. Praying for the recog-
nition by the United States of
the independence of Texas.
[Washington, 1837]   2 p.   DNA.
                                      47364
---- Memorial relative to the Currency, etc. Citizens of Philadelphia. Dec. 18, 1837. Senate
Docs., No. 22, 25th Cong., 2d
sess., Vol. I. Praying Congress
to adopt the subtreasury system

and to establish an exclusive metallic currency. [Washington, 1837] 4 p. DNA.   47365

---- Memorial relative to the Currency, etc. L. D. Teackle. Dec. 18, 1837. Senate Docs., No. 23, 25th Cong., 2d sess., Vol. I. Presenting a plan for the establishment of a bank and a national currency. [Washington, 1837] 38 p. DNA.
47366

---- Memorial relative to the Establishment of Bank. Citizens of Dist. of Col. Jan. 16, 1837. Ex. Docs., No. 92, 24th Cong., 2d sess., Vol. III. Praying for the establishment of a bank in Washington, with branches in Georgetown and Alexandria. [Washington, 1837] 2 p. DNA.   47367

---- Memorial relative to the Finances. Citizens of Brooklyn. Aug. 18, 1837. Senate Docs., No. 36, 25th Cong., 1st sess. Condemning the present system of finance and favoring a separation of the trade of banking from affairs of state. [Washington, 1837] 2 p. DNA.
47368

---- Memorial relative to the Tariff. Citizens of Brooklyn. Jan. 30, 1837. Ex. Docs., No. 128, 24th Cong., 2d sess., Vol. III. Praying for a reduction of the duties on imports and a repeal of the duties on coal and salt. [Washington, 1837] 1 p. DNA.   47369

---- Memorial relative to the Tariff. Citizens of Massachusetts. Feb. 6, 1837. Ex. Docs., No. 135, 24th Cong., 2d sess., Vol. III. Against the passage of the bill to reduce the duty on imports now pending in the

House of Representatives. [Washington, 1837] 3 p. DNA.
47370

---- Memorial relative to the Tariff. Massachusetts Legislature. Feb. 24, 1837. Ex. Docs., No. 170, 24th Cong., 2d sess., Vol. IV. Remonstrating against the passage of the bill to reduce the tariff, now pending in the House of Representatives. [Washington, 1837] 3 p. DNA.
47371

---- Memorial relative to the Tariff. Massachusetts Legislature. Feb. 25, 1837. Senate Docs., No. 202, 24th Cong., 2d sess., Vol. II. In opposition to the bill pending in the House of Representatives to reduce the duties on imports. [Washington, 1837] 3 p. DNA.   47372

---- Memorial relative to the Tariff. New York manufacturers. Feb. 26, 1837. Senate Docs., No. 211, 24th Cong., 2d sess., Vol. II. In opposition to any reduction of the duty on imported hair-cloth. [Washington, 1837] 3 p. DNA.   47373

---- Memorial relative to Wyoming Claims. Citizens of Pennsylvania. Dec. 29, 1837. Ex. Docs., No. 52, 25th Cong., 2d sess., Vol. II. In behalf of the sufferers by the invasion of the Wyoming settlement by the British and Indians during the Revolutionary war; Praying for a grant of land to the survivors and to the heirs of those who are dead. [Washington, 1837] 8 p. DNA.
47374

---- Memorial that St. Joseph be a Port of Entry. Citizens of Florida. Dec. 16, 1837. Ex. Docs., No. 286, 25th Cong., 2d sess., Vol. VIII. Praying for the establishment of a port of entry at that place. [Washington, 1837] 3 p. DNA. 47375

---- Message on Affairs with Mexico. President Andrew Jackson. Jan. 18, 1837. Senate Docs., No. 84, 24th Cong., 2d sess., Vol. II. Transmitting copies of correspondence with General Santa Ana in relation to the troubles between Mexico and Texas. [Washington, 1837] 5 p. DNA. 47376

---- Message on Affairs with Mexico. President Andrew Jackson. Feb. 6, 1837. Senate Docs., No. 160, 24th Cong., 2d sess., Vol. II. Transmitting correspondence and documents in relation to affairs with Mexico, and recommending passage of a law authorizing reprisals and the use of the naval force of the United States by the Executive to enforce them in the event of a refusal by the Mexican Government to come to an amicable adjustment of the matters in controversy upon another demand thereof, made from on board of one of the vessels of the United States on the coast of Mexico. [Washington, 1837] 170 p. DNA. 47377

---- Message on Claims against Mexico. President Andrew Jackson. Feb. 6, 1837. Senate Journal, 24th Cong., 2d sess. Recommending the passage of an act authorizing reprisals to be made against Mexico in the event of her refusal to adjust claims of the United States. [Washington, 1837] 2 p. DNA. 47378

---- Message on Criminal Laws. President Andrew Jackson.

Jan. 17, 1838. Ex. Docs., No. 85, 24th Cong., 2d sess., Vol. III. Recommends repeal of statute of limitations in criminal cases, and a severer punishment for the wanton destruction of public property. [Washington, 1837] 3 p. DNA. 47379

---- Message on Indian Hostilities. President Andrew Jackson. Feb. 14, 1837. Ex. Docs., No. 154, 24th Cong., 2d sess., Vol. IV. Transmitting reports of the commissioners appointed to investigate the causes of the late hostilities of the Creek Indians. [Washington, 1837] 61 p. DNA. 47380

---- Message on the Annexation of Texas. President Martin Van Buren. Sept. 30, 1837. Ex. Docs., No. 40, 25th Cong., 1st sess. Transmitting copies of correspondence between the United States and Texas in relation to the annexation of that country to the United States. [Washington, 1837] 18 p. DNA. 47381

---- Message on the Case of General Wool. President Martin Van Buren. Oct. 9, 1837. Ex. Docs., No. 46, 25th Cong., 1st sess. Transmitting proceedings of the court of inquiry appointed to examine into the conduct of Brevet Brigadier-General Wool and others under his command in reference to his and their conduct in the Cherokee country. [Washington, 1837] 85 p. DNA. 47382

---- Message on the Claim of John Galphin. President Andrew Jackson. Jan. 18, 1837. Senate Docs., No. 83, 24th Cong., 2d sess., Vol. II. Transmitting copies of correspondence in relation to the claim of the heirs of John Galphin against the Cherokee Indians. [Washington, 1837] 12 p. DNA.   47383

---- Message on the Exploring Expedition. President Andrew Jackson. Feb. 6, 1837. Ex. Docs., No. 138, 24th Cong., 2d sess., Vol. III. Transmitting report of the Secretary of the Navy upon the progress made in the arrangements for the exploring expedition to the South Seas authorized by the last session of Congress. [Washington, 1837] 15 p. DNA.   47384

---- Message on the Mexican Boundary. President Martin Van Buren. Oct. 2, 1837. Ex. Docs., No. 42, 25th Cong., 1st sess. Transmitting copies of correspondence in relation to the boundary-line between the United States and Mexico, and to a proposed cession of territory by Mexico to the United States. [Washington, 1837] 94 p. DNA.   47385

---- Message on the Missouri Boundary. President Andrew Jackson. Jan. 17, 1837. Ex. Docs., No. 83, 24th Cong., 2d sess., Vol. III. Transmitting copy of act of State of Missouri assenting to the act of Congress extending the western boundary of that State. [Washington, 1837] 2 p. DNA.
47386
---- Message on the New Hampshire Claim. President Andrew Jackson. Feb. 11, 1837. Ex. Docs., No. 155, 24th Cong., 2d sess., Vol. IV. Transmitting letter from the Governor and resolutions of the Legislature of New Hampshire, claiming the reimbursement of certain ex-

penses incurred by that State in defending its title to a portion of territory claimed by Great Britain. [Washington, 1837] 4 p. DNA.   47387

---- Message on the Northeastern Boundary. President Martin Van Buren. Sept. 26, 1837. Ex. Docs., No. 31, 25th Cong., 1st sess. Transmitting correspondence between the United States and Great Britain, and between the United States and the State of Maine, in relation to the northeastern boundary of the United States. [Washington, 1837] 32 p. DNA.   47388

---- Message on the Public Buildings. President Martin Van Buren. Dec. 21, 1837. Ex. Docs., No. 38, 25th Cong., 2d sess., Vol. II. Transmitting information in relation to the Treasury building now in course of construction. [Washington, 1837] 9 p. DNA.   47389

---- Message on the Treaty with Morocco. President Andrew Jackson. Feb. 9, 1837. Ex. Docs., No. 145, 24th Cong., 2d sess., Vol. IV. Transmitting copies of treaty of peace and commerce between the United States and the Emperor of Morocco, concluded September 16, 1836. [Washington, 1837] 5 p. DNA.   47390

---- Message relative to Mexican Claims. President Martin Van Buren. Dec. 12, 1837. Senate Docs., No. 14, 25th Cong., 2d sess., Vol. I. Transmitting copy of a communication from the State Department to the Mexican Minister, enclosing additional documents relative to claims of citizens of the United States against Mexico. [Washington, 1837] 4 p. DNA.   47391

---- Message relative to Ship-Canal. President Andrew Jackson. Jan. 9, 1837. Senate Journal, 24th Cong., 2d sess. Relative to the construction of a ship-canal across the Isthmus of Panama. [Washington, 1837] 1 p. DNA.   47392

---- Message relative to the Maine Claim. President Andrew Jackson. Jan. 30, 1837. Ex. Docs., No. 125, 24th Cong., 2d sess., Vol. III. Transmitting communication from the Governor of Maine relative to the claim of that State for reimbursement of certain sums paid to John and Phineas R. Harford for losses and expenses incurred by them in the boundary disputes between Maine and New Brunswick. [Washington, 1837] 3 p. DNA.   47393

---- Message, with Documents. President Martin Van Buren. Sept. 4, 1837. Ex. Docs., No. 1, 25th Cong., 1st sess. Financial embarrassments of the country; Suspension of specie payments; Creation of a national bank; Public deposits; Measures of relief recommended. [Washington, 1837] 29 p. DNA.   47394

---- The Mine a la Motte and Mississippi Railroad Co. Legislature of Mo. Jan. 30, 1837. Senate Docs., No. 210, 26th Cong., 1st sess., Vol. V. Copy of act of incorporation granted the company. [Washington, 1837] 4 p. DNA.   47395

---- Navy Register. 1837. Published by the Navy Department. [Washington, 1837] 94 p.   47396

---- Payments for Land Sales. Oct. 25, 1837. Library of the Interior Department. Circulars relating to Treasury notes to be received in payment for sales of public lands. [Washington, 1837] 2 p. DNA.   47397

---- Petition for Grant of Land. Indiana Pottery Company. Dec. 20, 1837. Senate Docs., No. 70, 25th Cong., 2d sess., Vol. I. Asking for grant of land in Indiana to enable them to continue the manufacture of poettery in the United States. [Washington, 1837] 3 p. DNA.   47398

---- Petition for Half-Pay, etc. Nathan Williams. Nov. 28, 1837. Ex. Docs., No. 29, 25th Cong., 2d sess., Vol. II. Praying for an allowance of seven years' half-pay on account of Revolutionary services of his late father, Nathan Williams, and for remuneration for horse and equipments taken from him by the British. [Washington, 1837] 6 p. DNA.   47399

---- Petition for Increased Compensation. New York weighers. Feb. 4, 1837. Senate Docs., No. 149, 24th Cong., 2d sess., Vol. II. Praying that their annual compensation be increased to $2,000. [Washington, 1837] 1 p. DNA.   47400

---- Petition for Military Advancement. Non-commissioned Army officers. Jan. 16, 1837. Ex. Docs., No. 88, 24th Cong., 2d sess., Vol. III. Praying that non-commissioned officers may be granted an opportunity for promotion from the ranks. [Washington, 1837] 3 p. DNA.   47401

---- Petition for Pension.

Nathaniel Bird. Jan. 16, 1837. Ex. Docs., No. 95, 24th Cong., 2d sess., Vol. III. Praying allowance of arrears of pension. [Washington, 1837] 1 p. DNA.   47402

---- Petition for the Adoption of Financial Plan. William Brent, jr. Sept. 13, 1837. Senate Docs., No. 31, 25th Cong., 1st sess. Praying the Senate to adopt a plan suggested by him for relief of the country. [Washington, 1837] 2 p. DNA.   47403

---- Petition of Alexandria and Falmouth Railroad Company. Feb. 7, 1837. Senate Docs., No. 161, 24th Cong., 2d sess., Vol. II. Praying national aid in the construction of the road. [Washington, 1837] 5 p. DNA.   47404

---- Petition of Naval Surgeons and Assistant Surgeons. Feb. 15, 1837. Senate Docs., No. 176, 24th Cong., 2d sess., Vol. II. Praying the establishment of the office of Surgeon-General of the Navy. [Washington, 1837] 2 p. DNA.   47405

---- Petition of Tarlton Woodson. Dec. 25, 1837. Ex. Docs., No. 60, 25th Cong., 2d sess., Vol. II. Prays allowance of commutation pay for Revolutionary services. [Washington, 1837] 2 p. DNA.   47406

---- Petition on a Pre-emption Law. Settlers in Wisconsin. Aug. 24, 1837. Senate Docs., No. 30, 25th Cong., 2d sess., Vol. I. Praying for the passage of a general pre-emption law. [Washington, 1837] 3 p. DNA.   47407

---- Petition on Post-Office Building. Citizens of District of Columbia. Feb. 17, 1837. Senate Docs., No. 185, 24th Cong., 2d sess., Vol. II. Praying that the General Post-Office be rebuilt on its former site. [Washington, 1837] 3 p. DNA.   47408

---- Petition on Safety Steam-Boiler. Samuel Raub, jr. Jan. 16, 1837. Ex. Docs., No. 51, 24th Cong., 2d sess., Vol. II. Praying for the adoption on board of all United States vessels of his safety apparatus for steam-boilers. [Washington, 1837] 6 p. DNA.   47409

---- Petition on Sunday Mail Delivery. Harmon Kingsbury. Dec. 5, 1837. Senate Docs., No. 9, 25th Cong., 2d sess., Vol. I. Praying the repeal of that portion of the act of Congress which rquires postmasters to deliver letters, etc., on Sunday. [Washington, 1837] 12 p. DNA.   47410

---- Petition on the Culture of Tropical Plants. Henry Perrine. Sept. 8, 1837. Senate Docs., No. 26, 25th Cong., 1st sess. Asking that his former petition for a grant of land in Florida for the domestication of tropical plants be referred to the Committee on Agriculture. [Washington, 1837] 2 p. DNA.   47411

---- Petition on the Importation of Railroad Iron. S. B. Chandler et al. Jan. 25, 1837. Senate Docs., No. 105, 24th Cong., 2d sess., Vol. II. Praying to be allowed to import, free of duty, iron to be used in the construction of a railroad in Illinois. [Washington, 1837] 1 p. DNA.   47412

---- Petition on the Loss of Ship Alleghany. John Kurtz. Dec. 11, 1837. Senate Docs., No. 5, 25th Cong., 2d sess., Vol. I. Claiming for himself and the other owners, compensation for the ship Alleghany and her cargo, captured by the British in the war of 1812 while chartered by the United States. [Washington, 1837] 32 p. DNA.
47413

---- Petition relative to a Light-House. Seward Porter. Jan. 27, 1837. Senate Docs., No. 143, 24th Cong., 2d sess., Vol. II. Praying that a lighthouse may be erected on St. George's Shoals, Massachusetts. [Washington, 1837] 5 p. DNA.
47414

---- Petition relative to a Peace Congress. New York Peace Society. Dec. 18, 1837. Ex. Docs., No. 50, 25th Cong., 2d sess., Vol. II. Praying Congress to send forth a proposal to the various nations of the earth for a congress of nations or international board of arbitration. [Washington, 1837] 7 p. DNA.
47415

---- Petition relative to Banking. Citizens of New York. Jan., 1837. Senate Docs., No. 203, 24th Cong., 2d sess., Vol. II. Praying Congress to prohibit the issue of notes and bills by State banks. [Washington, 1837] 2 p. DNA.
47416

---- Petition relative to Copyright. Certain British authors. Feb. 2, 1837. Senate Docs., No. 134, 24th Cong., 2d sess., Vol. II. Praying the passage of a law granting them the exclusive right to their respective writings in the United States. [Washington, 1837] 4 p. DNA.
47417

---- Petition relative to Copyright. Citizens of the United States. Feb. 4, 1837. Senate Docs., No. 141, 24th Cong., 2d sess., Vol. II. Praying for a change in the present law of copyright, with a view to the liberal encouragement of American writers and the protection of others. [Washington, 1837] 2 p. DNA.
47418

---- Petition relative to Copyright. Professors of University of Virginia. Feb. 20, 1837. Senate Docs., No. 193, 24th Cong., 2d sess., Vol. II. Recommends passage of an international copyright law. [Washington, 1837] 3 p. DNA.
47419

---- Petition relative to Duty on Coal. Citizens of Maine. Jan. 23, 1837. Ex. Docs., No. 106, 24th Cong., 2d sess., Vol. III. Praying for a repeal of the duty on foreign coal. [Washington, 1837] 1 p. DNA.
47420

---- Petition relative to Entry on House Journal. Rep. William Brent, jr. Feb. 1, 1837. Ex. Docs., No. 166, 24th Cong., 2d sess., Vol. IV. Asking that an erroneous entry on the House Journal of a petition presented by him be expunged. [Washington, 1837] 7 p. DNA. 47421

---- Petition relative to Indian Land Claims. Citizens of Mississippi. Jan. 21, 1837. Senate Docs., No. 91, 24th Cong., 2d sess., Vol. II. Praying Congress to institute an inquiry into the claims of the Choctaw Indians to lands under the treaty of Dancing Rabbit Creek. [Washington, 1837] 3 p. DNA.
47422

---- Petition relative to Land

Claim. Oliver M. Spencer.
Dec. 25, 1837. Ex. Docs.,
No. 102, 25th Cong., 2d sess.,
Vol. V. Claiming refundment
of excess of purchase-money
paid for public land. [Washing-
ton, 1837] 2 p. DNA.   47423

---- Petition relative to Land
in Saint Louis. Corporation of
Saint Louis. Jan. 25, 1837.
Senate Docs., No. 171, 24th
Cong., 2d sess., Vol. II.
Praying for the rejection of
any claim for land within the
limits of the common in said
city. [Washington, 1837] 2 p.
DNA.   47424

---- Petition relative to Marine
Hospital. Citizens of Kentucky.
Dec. 11, 1837. Senate Docs.,
No. 108, 25th Cong., 2d sess.,
Vol. II. Praying for the erection of a marine hospital at
Smithland, Kentucky. [Wash-
ington, 1837] 2 p. DNA.
     47425
---- Petition relative to Mineralogical Collections. George
W. Hughes et al. Feb. 11,
1837. Senate Docs., No. 167,
24th Cong., 2d sess., Vol. II.
Praying Congress to establish
a mineralogical collection to be
attached to the Library of Congress. [Washington, 1837] 2
p. DNA.   47426

---- Petition relative to Naviga-
tion of Fox River. Citizens of
Wisconsin. Oct. 18, 1837.
Ex. Docs., No. 171, 25th
Cong., 2d sess., Vol. VII.
Praying for a grant of public
lands to aid in the improve-
ment of the navigation of the
Fox River. [Washington, 1837]
2 p. DNA.   47427

---- Petition relative to Niagara

River. John R. St. John.
Feb. 4, 1837. Senate Docs.,
No. 142, 24th Cong., 2d sess.,
Vol. II. Praying the removal
of the dam at Black Rock, in
the Niagara River, on account
of its having caused a rise in
the waters of Lake Erie and an
injury to the southern shores
of that lake. [Washington,
1837] 2 p. DNA.   47428

---- Petition relative to Patents.
Samuel Martin. Jan. 16, 1837.
Ex. Docs., No. 120, 24th Cong.,
2d sess., Vol. III. Praying
passage of a law requiring that
a specification model of every
patent granted shall be deposited with every State in the
Union. [Washington, 1837] 1
p. DNA.   47429

---- Petition relative to Port of
Entry. Selectmen of Jersey
City. Feb. 1, 1837. Senate
Docs., No. 140, 24th Cong., 2d
sess., Vol. II. Praying that
that city be made a port of en-
try. [Washington, 1837] 2 p.
DNA.   47430

---- Petition relative to Pre-
emption Claim. George Davenport. Dec. 20, 1837. Ex. Docs.,
No. 331, 25th Cong., 2d sess.,
Vol. X. Praying passage of a
law granting him a pre-emption
right to certain land in Illinois.
[Washington, 1837] 11 p. DNA.
     47431
---- Petition relative to Public
Documents. William Brent, jr.
Aug. 28, 1837. Ex. Docs., No.
386, 25th Cong., 2d sess., Vol.
X. Praying for the passage of
a law providing for the more
general distribution of public
documents. [Washington, 1837]
4 p. DNA.   47432

---- Petition relative to Public Documents. William Brent, jr. Sept. 14, 1837. Senate Docs., No. 30, 25th Cong., 1st sess. Praying for a more general distribution of the public documents and laws of the United States and of the several States. [Washington, 1837] 4 p. DNA.
47433

---- Petition relative to Public Lands. Citizens of Ohio. Dec. 22, 1837. Ex. Docs., No. 101, 25th Cong., 2d sess., Vol. V. Praying passage of a law allowing credit for the purchase-money of public lands to certain classes of actual settlers. [Washington, 1837] 3 p. DNA.
47434

---- Petition relative to Safety Steam-Boiler. A. B. Quinby. Dec. 14, 1837. Senate Docs., No. 17, 25th Cong., 2d sess., Vol. I. Praying for an appropriation to test the value of his invention for preventing the explosion of steam-boilers. [Washington, 1837] 9 p. DNA.
47435

---- Petition relative to Salt Manufacture. N. S. Von Shoultz. Jan., 1837. Ex. Docs., No. 89, 24th Cong., 2d sess., Vol. III. Offering to the United States, for a reward, his discovery of a method for purifying the salt water used for the manufacture of salt in the United States. [Washington, 1837] 3 p. DNA.
47436

---- Petition relative to Spanish Land Claims. Sherlock S. Gregory. Dec. 3, 1837. Ex. Docs., No. 67, 25th Cong., 2d sess., Vol. II. Praying Congress to institute an inquiry into the justice of their claim to the territory purchased of Spain. [Washington, 1837] 1 p. DNA.
47437

---- Petition relative to Telegraph Line. Samuel C. Reid. Jan. 25, 1837. Senate Docs., No. 107, 24th Cong., 2d sess., Vol. II. Praying for the establishment of a line of telegraph from New York to New Orleans. [Washington, 1837] 2 p. DNA.
47438

---- Petition relative to the Indians. Sherlock S. Gregory. Dec. 3, 1837. Ex. Docs., No. 66, 25th Cong., 2d sess., Vol. II. Praying that the Indians may be protected in their rights. [Washington, 1837] 1 p. DNA.
47439

---- Petitions relative to Claims against Mexico. Citizens of Massachusetts. March 26, 1837. Ex. Docs., No. 291, 24th Cong., 2d sess., Vol. VIII. In favor of the reference of the claims of of the United States against Mexico to a court of arbitration, and of the establishment of an international board of arbitration or congress of nations for the settlement of all international disputes. [Washington, 1837] 10 p. DNA.   47440

---- Receivers to Disburse Treasury Notes. Nov. 3, 1837. Library of the Interior Department. Circular relating to Treasury notes issued to receivers for disbursements. [Washington, 1837] DNA.   47441

---- Remonstrance on Anti-Slavery Petitions. Grand jury of Washington. Jan. 17, 1837. Senate Docs., No. 75, 24th Cong., 2d sess., Vol. II. Asking Congress to put a stop to the reception of petitions for the abolition of slavery in the District of Columbia. [Washington, 1837] 3 p. DNA.   47442

---- Report in Case of O. H.
Dibble. Secretary Levi Woodbury. Oct. 9, 1837. Ex. Docs.,
No. 48, 25th Cong., 1st sess.,
Transmitting additional papers
in relation to the claim of O. H.
Dibble for expenses incurred in
making preparations to execute
his contract for the construction
of the bridge across the Potomac. [Washington, 1837] 8 p.
DNA. 47443

---- Report of Clerks in Navy
Department. Secretary M.
Dickerson. Jan. 4, 1837. Ex.
Docs., No. 66, 24th Cong., 2d
sess., Vol. II. Statement
showing names and compensation
of clerks employed in the Navy
Department during the year
1836. [Washington, 1837] 2 p.
DNA. 47444

---- Report of Clerks in State
Department. Secretary John
Forsyth. Jan. 4, 1837. Ex.
Docs., No. 70, 24th Cong., 2d
sess., Vol. II. Statement show-
ing names, compensation, etc.,
of clerks employed in the State
Department during the year
1836. [Washington, 1837] 3 p.
DNA. 47445

---- Report of Clerks in Treasury Department. Secretary
Levi Woodbury. Jan. 17, 1837.
Ex. Docs., No. 86, 24th Cong.,
2d sess., Vol. III. Statement
showing the names, compensation, etc., of clerks employed
in the Treasury Department
during the year 1836. [Wash-
ington, 1837] 13 p. DNA.
47446

---- Report of Clerks in War
Department. Sec. ad interim
B. F. Butler. Jan. 13, 1837.
Ex. Docs., No. 79, 24th Cong.,
2d sess., Vol. II. Statement

showing names, compensation,
etc., of clerks employed in the
War Department during the year
1836. [Washington, 1837] 4 p.
DNA. 47447

---- Report of Debates, Twenty-
Fifth Congress, First Session.
Sept, 4, 1837. Register of De-
bates in Congress, by Gales &
Seaton. Vol. XXVIII, Proceed-
ings, pp. 1-1168. Vol. XXIX,
Proceedings, pp. 1160-1744.
Congressional Globe, by John C.
Rives. Vol. III, Proceedings.
[Washington, 1837] DNA.
47448

---- Report of Debates, Twenty-
fifth Congress, Second Session.
Dec. 4, 1837. Congressional
Globe, by John C. Rives. Vol.
IV, Proceedings, pp. 1-512,
and Appendix, pp. 1-641.
[Washington, 1837] DNA.
47449

---- Report of Examination of
Narragansett Bay. Secretary
M. Dickerson. Jan. 4, 1837.
Senate Docs., No. 56, 24th
Cong., 2d sess., Vol. I. Transmitting information concerning
an examination of Narragansett
Bay with a view to the establishment of a naval depot. [Wash-
ington, 1837] 2 p. DNA.
47450

---- Report of General Land
Office. Commissioner James
Whitcomb. Dec. 9, 1837. Ex.
Docs., No. 23, 25th Cong., 2d
sess., Vol. II. Statement of the
operations of the several land
offices during the year 1836 and
the first, second, and third
quarters of 1837; Supplemental
reports in relation to the preservation of the records of surveys
in the offices of the surveyors-
general. [Washington, 1837]
100 p. DNA. 47451

---- Report of Joint Com. to notify M. Van Buren of his Election as President. Feb. 11, 1837. Reports of Committees, No. 199, 24th Cong., 2d sess., Vol. I. Committee reports performance of the duty assigned it. [Washington, 1837] 1 p. DNA.   47452

---- Report of Louisville and Portland Canal Company. Dec. 30, 1837. Ex. Docs., No. 104, 25th Cong., 2d sess., Vol. V. Statement of the affairs of the company for the year 1837; Receipts and expenditures. [Washington, 1837] 13 p. DNA.   47453

---- Report of the General Land Office. Commissioner James Whitcomb. Dec. 9, 1837. Senate Docs., No. 11, 25th Cong., 2d sess., Vol. I. Statements showing the operations of the several land offices during the year 1836, and the first, second, and third quarters of 1837. [Washington, 1837] 74 p. DNA.   47454

---- Report on Acts of Wisconsin Territory. Finance Committee. Feb. 3, 1837. Senate Docs., No. 136, 24th Cong., 2d sess., Vol. II. Recommends confirmation of three acts passed by the Legislative Assembly of Wisconsin chartering certain banking companies in that Territory; Bill reported. [Washington, 1837] 1 p. DNA.   47455

---- Report on Additional Navy-Yards. Naval Committee. Feb. 20, 1837. Senate Docs., No. 196, 24th Cong., 2d sess., Vol. II. Adverse to any present increase in the number of navy-yards. [Washington, 1837] 1 p. DNA.   47456

---- Report on Agent for Deposit Banks. House select committee. March 1, 1837. Reports of Committees, No. 193, 24th Cong., 2d sess., Vol. III. Majority and minority reports relative to appointment by the deposit banks of an agent to transact their business with the Treasury Department, with journal of the proceedings of the committee. [Washington, 1837] 636 p. DNA.   47457

---- Report on American Seamen. Secretary John Forsyth. Jan. 27, 1837. Ex. Docs., No. 111, 24th Cong., 2d sess., Vol. III. Abstract showing the number of American seamen registered in each port of entry of the United States during the year 1836. [Washington, 1837] 5 p. DNA.   47458

---- Report on American Seamen. Secretary John Forsyth. Dec. 12, 1837. Ex. Docs., No. 24, 25th Cong., 2d sess., Vol. II. Abstract showing the number of American seamen registered in each port of entry of the United States from January 1 to October 1, 1837. [Washington, 1837] 5 p. DNA.   47459

---- Report on Appropriations, New Offices, etc. Clerk W. S. Franklin. March 13, 1837. Ex. Docs., No. 189, 24th Cong., 2d sess., Vol. IV. Statement of appropriations made during the second session of the Twenty-fourth Congress, new offices created, etc. [Washington, 1837] 41 p. DNA.   47460

---- Report on Armories. Col. G. Bomford. March 3, 1837. Senate Docs., No. 221, 24th Cong., 2d sess., Vol. III. Statement of operations of the United

States armories during the year 1836. [Washington, 1837] 7 p. DNA. 47461

---- Report on Army Officers on Detached Service. Adjutant-Gen. R. Jones. March 3, 1837. Ex. Docs., No. 187, 24th Cong., 2d sess., Vol. IV. List of officers of the Army so employed in the year 1836 as to separate them from their regiments or corps. [Washington, 1837] 15 p. DNA. 47462

---- Report on Banking Companies. House select committee. March 3, 1837. Reports of Committees, No. 306, 24th Cong., 2d sess., Vol. II. Recommends an amendment to the Constitution providing that no State shall authorize any incorporated company to issue any bank note or other paper for circulation. [Washington, 1837] 25 p. DNA. 47463

---- Report on Bursting of Cannon at Clarke's Foundry. Col. G. Bomford. July 13, 1837. Senate Docs., No. 19, 25th Cong., 1st sess. Statement of facts and correspondence in relation to the bursting of sixteen cannon at Major Clarke's foundry while being proved by the inspectors of cannon. [Washington, 1837] 69 p. DNA. 47464

---- Report on Case of Andrew Armstrong. Naval Committee. Jan. 27, 1837. Senate Docs., No. 113, 24th Cong., 2d sess., Vol. II. Recommends payment for expenses incurred while Navy agent at Lima, Peru; Bill reported. [Washington, 1837] 2 p. DNA. 47465

---- Report on Case of Charles G. Hunter. House Naval Committee. Feb. 28, 1837. Reports of Committees, No. 296, 24th Cong., 2d sess., Vol. II. Recommends rejection of Senate bill granting arrears of pay as midshipman to Charles G. Hunter. [Washington, 1837] 4 p. DNA. 47466

---- Report on Case of James Francher. House Rev. Pensions Committee. Jan. 14, 1837. Reports of Committees, No. 111, 24th Cong., 2d sess., Vol. I. Recommends allowance of pension; Bill reported. [Washington, 1837] 3 p. DNA. 47467

No entry 47468

---- Report on Case of Samuel Miller. House Claims Committee. Jan. 25, 1837. Reports of Committees, No. 155, 24th Cong., 2d sess., Vol. I. Recommends passage of Senate bill compensating claimant for apprehension of Indian charged with murder. [Washington, 1837] 1 p. DNA. 47469

---- Report on Charges against Judge Thruston. House Judiciary Com. March 3, 1837. Reports of Committees, No. 327, 24th Cong., 2d sess., Vol. II. Submitting testimony relative to charges of official misconduct against Buckner Thruston, one of the associate judges of the circuit court of the District of Columbia. [Washington, 1837] 194 p. DNA. 47470

---- Report on Chickasaw Fund. Secretary Levi Woodbury. Dec. 8, 1837. Ex. Docs., No. 17, 25th Cong., 2d sess., Vol. II. Statement of funds received under the treaties with the Chickasaw Indians from sales of lands, and of their investment and disbursement. [Washington, 1837] 2 p. DNA. 47471

---- Report on Claim against
United States Bank. Secretary
Levi Woodbury. Jan. 30, 1837.
Ex. Docs., No. 118, 24th Cong.,
2d sess., Vol. III. Submitting
statement and documents relative
to the proceedings taken for a
settlement of the claims of the
United States against the Bank
of the United States. [Washing-
ton, 1837] 137 p. DNA. 47472

---- Report on Claim for Mail
Transportation. Post-Office
Committee. Dec. 20, 1837.
Senate Docs., No. 32, 25th
Cong., 2d sess., Vol. I.
Recommends allowance of claim;
Bill reported; Name of claimant
not stated. [Washington, 1837]
1 p. DNA.   47473

---- Report on Claim of Alexander G. Morgan. House Claims
Committee. Dec. 14, 1837.
Reports of Committees, No. 50,
25th Cong., 2d sess., Vol. I.
Recommends that claim for loss
of horse and wagon in war of
1832 against the Sac and Fox
Indians be disallowed, and that
claim for pay as aide-de-camp
be referred to the accounting
officers of the Treasury to
make allowances claimant would
have received had his appointment been regular; Bill reported. [Washington, 1837]
3 p. DNA.   47474

---- Report on Claim of Augusta, Georgia. House Claims
Committee. March 3, 1837.
Reports of Committees, No.
319, 24th Cong., 2d sess.,
Vol. II. Adverse to claim for
expenses incurred in raising
troops for Florida war. [Wash-
ington, 1837] 1 p. DNA.
                               47475

---- Report on Claim of B. H.
Mackall. House Claims Committee. Dec. 14, 1837. Reports
of Committees, No. 13, 25th Cong.,
2d sess., Vol. I. Recommends
claim for house burned by the
British in 1814; Bill reported.
[Washington, 1837] 1 p. DNA.
                               47476

---- Report on Claim of Christopher Clarke. House Claims Committee. Dec. 14, 1837. Reports
of Committees, No. 40, 25th Cong.,
2d sess., Vol. I. Recommends
claim for provisions furnished
United States troops; Bill reported. [Washington, 1837] 1
p. DNA.   47477

---- Report on Claim of Citizens
of Wilkes County, Georgia.
March 3, 1837. Reports of Committees, No. 322, 24th Cong., 2d
sess., Vol. II. The House
Claims Committee reports adversely to claim for repayment of
money advanced by the corporation of Washington and other
citizens of Wilkes County to certain volunteers to aid in the suppression of Indian hostilities.
[Washington, 1837] 2 p. DNA.
                               47478

---- Report on Claim of City of
Mobile. House Claims Committee. March 1, 1837. Reports
of Committees, No. 304, 24th
Cong., 2d sess., Vol. II.
Recommends rejection of Senate
bill reimbursing the city of Mobile for expenses in equipping
soldiers to serve in the Creek
war. [Washington, 1837] 3 p.
DNA.   47479

---- Report on Claim of Conrad
Widrig. House Rev. Pensions
Committee. Feb. 14, 1837. Re-
ports of Committees, No. 211,
24th Cong., 2d sess., Vol. I.
Recommends allowance of pension;

Bill reported. [Washington, 1837. 2 p. DNA. 47480

---- Report on Claim of Cornelius Manning. House Foreign Affairs Com. Feb. 28, 1837. Reports of Committees, No. 291, 24th Cong., 2d sess., Vol. II. Recommends payment for servant taken by the British during the late war; Bill reported. [Washington, 1837] 1 p. DNA. 47481

---- Report on Claim of Crawford Johnson. House Rev. Claims Com. Dec. 22, 1837. Reports of Committees, No. 114, 25th Cong., 2d sess., Vol. I. Recommends issue of land warrant; Bill reported. [Washington, 1837] 1 p. DNA. 47482

---- Report on Claim of Don Juan Madrazo. House Claims Committee. Feb. 22, 1837. Reports of Committees, No. 250, 24th Cong., 2d sess., Vol. II. Adverse to allowance of claim for slaves taken by a vessel fitted out in the United States. [Washington, 1837] 6 p. DNA. 47483

---- Report on Claim of Eli Horton. House Claims Committee. Dec. 14, 1837. Reports of Committees, No. 37, 25th Cong., 2d sess., Vol. I. Recommends refunding sum paid into the Treasury for a patent which petitioner has never taken out; Bill reported. [Washington, 1837] 1 p. DNA. 47484

---- Report on Claim of Erastus and Thaddeus Fairbanks. House Claims Com. Feb. 22, 1837. Reports of Committees, No. 252, 24th Cong., 2d sess., Vol. II. Recommends refundment of overpayment made on issue of patent;

Bill reported. [Washington, 1837] 1 p. DNA. 47485

---- Report on Claim of Executor of J. Jordan. House Rev. Claims Com. Dec. 22, 1837. Reports of Committees, No. 123, 25th Cong., 2d sess., Vol. I. Recommends allowance of claim for commutation pay; Bill reported. [Washington, 1837] 5 p. DNA. 47486

---- Report on Claim of Ezekiel Burnham. House Invalid Pensions Com. Jan. 10, 1837. Reports of Committees, No. 82, 24th Cong., 2d sess., Vol. I. Adverse to allowance of pension. [Washington, 1837] 1 p. DNA. 47487

---- Report on Claim of Francis Allyn. House Claims Committee. March 3, 1837. Reports of Committees, No. 326, 24th Cong., 2d sess., Vol. II. Recommends rejection of Senate bill granting compensation to petitioner for services in bringing General La Fayette and his family to the United States in the year 1824. [Washington, 1837] 2 p. DNA. 47488

---- Report on Claim of George Allen. House Revolutionary Claims Com. Jan. 26, 1837. Reports of Committees, No. 160, 24th Cong., 2d sess., Vol. I. Adverse to claim for payment of sum alleged to be due him as administrator of John Reynolds and to have been paid to person not entitled. [Washington, 1837] 2 p. DNA. 47489

---- Report on Claim of H. W. Russel. House Claims Committee. Jan. 13, 1837. Reports of Committees, No. 87, 24th Cong., 2d sess., Vol. I. Recommends payment for forage purchased by

claimant, late assistant quartermaster, for the use of the Army;
Bill reported. [Washington,
1837] 2 p. DNA.   47490

---- Report on Claim of H. W.
Russel. House Claims Committee. Dec. 14, 1837. Reports
of Committees, No. 61, 25th
Cong., 2d sess., Vol. I.
Recommends claim for moneys
advanced in purchase of forage
for troops in Alabama in 1836;
Bill reported. [Washington,
1837] 2 p. DNA.   47491

---- Report on Claim of Heirs
of D. Warner. House Priv.
Land Claims Com. Dec. 22,
1837. Reports of Committees,
No. 142, 25th Cong., 2d sess.,
Vol. I. Recommends grant of
land warrant; Bill reported.
[Washington, 1837] 1 p. DNA.
                          47492
---- Report on Claim of Heirs
of Dr. T. Carter. Secretary
Levi Woodbury. Dec. 29, 1837.
Senate Docs., No. 58, 25th
Cong., 2d sess., Vol. I.
Transmitting report of the
First Auditor on claim for
balance of pay for Revolution-
ary services. [Washington,
1837] 4 p. DNA.   47493

---- Report on Claim of Heirs
of Henry Irwin. House Rev.
Claims Com. Dec. 22, 1837.
Reports of Committees, No.
107, 25th Cong., 2d sess.,
Vol. I. Recommends allowance
of commutation pay; Bill reported. [Washington, 1837] 1
p. DNA.   47494

---- Report on Claim of Heirs
of Thomas Carter. Rev.
Claims Committee. Feb. 13,
1837. Senate Docs., No. 170,
24th Cong., 2d sess., Vol. II.

Recommends that the Secretary
of the Treasury be directed to
examine and report on the accounts of Thomas Carter,
formerly a surgeon in the Revolutionary army. [Washington,
1837] 1 p. DNA.   47495

---- Report on Claim of Isaac
Austin. House Revolutionary
Pensions Com. Jan. 24, 1837.
Reports of Committees, No. 145,
24th Cong., 2d sess., Vol. I.
Recommends allowance of arrears
of pension; Bill reported. [Wash-
ington, 1837] 2 p. DNA.
                          47496
---- Report on Claim of James
Herron. House Claims Committee. Dec. 14, 1837. Reports
of Committees, No. 60, 25th
Cong., 2d sess., Vol. I.
Recommends claim for money deposited in the United States
Treasury for patent which
claimant did not take out; Bill
reported. [Washington, 1837]
1 p. DNA.   47497

---- Report on Claim of James
Kilgore. House Claims Committee. Jan. 27, 1837. Reports
of Committees, No. 162, 24th
Cong., 2d sess., Vol. I. Adverse to payment for buildings
burned by the British in the
war of 1812. [Washington, 1837]
2 p. DNA.   47498

---- Report on Claim of John B.
Perkins. House Claims Committee. Dec. 14, 1837. Reports
of Committees, No. 43, 25th
Cong., 2d sess., Vol. I. Recommends claim for horse lost in
1818 in the Seminole war; Bill
reported. [Washington, 1837]
1 p. DNA.   47499

---- Report on Claim of John J.
Bulow. Claims Committee. Jan.

27, 1837. Senate Docs., No. 109, 24th Cong., 2d sess., Vol. II. Recommends that claim for buildings destroyed by the Indians in the war of 1812 be referred to the Secretary of the Treasury; Bill reported. [Washington, 1837] 2 p. DNA. 47500

---- Report on Claim of John J. Bulow, jr. Claims Committee. Jan. 27, 1837. Senate Docs., No. 10, 24th Cong., 2d sess., Vol. I. Recommends that the Secretary of the Treasury be authorized to ascertain the value of buildings belonging to petitioner destroyed by the Indians in Florida, and to make payment for them; Bill reported. [Washington, 1837] 2 p. DNA. 47501

---- Report on Claim of John Krepps. House Claims Committee. Dec. 14, 1837. Reports of Committees, No. 32, 25th Cong., 2d sess., Vol. I. Recommends passage of a law directing settlement of claim for work done on Cumberland road; Bill reported. [Washington, 1837] 2 p. DNA. 47502

---- Report on Claim of John Vannethen. House Claims Committee. Feb. 22, 1837. Reports of Committees, No. 254, 24th Cong., 2d sess., Vol. II. Recommends that committee be discharged from consideration of claim for services of John Vannethen and his company during the war of 1812. [Washington, 1837] 1 p. DNA. 47503

---- Report on Claim of Loomis & Gay. House Claims Committee. March 2, 1837. Reports of Committees, No. 308, 24th

Cong., 2d sess., Vol. II. Adverse to passage of Senate bill allowing additional payment to claimants for work on Cumberland road. [Washington, 1837] 1 p. DNA. 47504

---- Report on Claim of Maine. House Foreign Affairs Committee. Feb. 22, 1837. Reports of Committees, No. 249, 24th Cong., 2d sess., Vol. II. Adverse to reimbursement for advances made to John and Phineas Harford on account of losses sustained in the conflict between Maine and the British provinces. [Washington, 1837] 2 p. DNA. 47505

---- Report on Claim of Moses Van Campen. House Rev. Claims Committee. Feb. 14, 1837. Reports of Committees, No. 204, 24th Cong., 2d sess., Vol. I. Recommending rejection of Senate bill allowing commutation pay to claimant. [Washington, 1837] 1 p. DNA. 47506

---- Report on Claim of Ransom Mix. House Invalid Pensions Committee. Feb. 2, 1837. Reports of Committees, No. 186, 24th Cong., 2d sess., Vol. I. Recommends passage, with amendments, of Senate bill granting him pension. [Washington, 1837] 1 p. DNA. 47507

---- Report on Claim of Richard W. Meade. Secretary John Forsyth. Feb. 13, 1837. Senate Docs., No. 169, 24th Cong., 2d sess., Vol. II. Transmitting copies of papers on file in the State Department having any relation to the claim of Richard W. Meade against the Government of Spain. [Washington, 1837] 11 p. DNA. 47508

---- Report on Claim of Samuel
Ferguson. Claims Committee.
Dec. 21, 1837. Senate Docs.,
No. 34, 25th Cong., 2d sess.,
Vol. I. Recommends passage
of bill allowing claim for horse
lost in the service. [Washing-
ton, 1837] 2 p. DNA.   47509

---- Report on Claim of Samuel
Warren. House Rev. Claims
Committee. Feb. 24, 1837.
Reports of Committees, No. 266,
24th Cong., 2d sess., Vol. II.
Recommends passage of Senate
bill allowing commutation pay to
claimant. [Washington, 1837]
1 p. DNA.   47510

---- Report on Claim of Sarah
Pemberton. House Rev. Pensions Com. Jan. 23, 1837.
Reports of Committees, No.
139, 24th Cong., 2d sess.,
Vol. I. Recommends allowance
of pension to petitioner as
widow of John Pemberton; Bill
reported. [Washington, 1837]
4 p. DNA.   47511

---- Report on Claim of Thomas
J. Lawler. House Claims Committee. Dec. 14, 1837. Reports
of Committees, No. 31, 25th
Cong., 2d sess., Vol. I.
Recommends claim for amount
paid Dr. S. M. Miles for medical attendance on slaves con-
fined in jail, and bill reported;
Recommends rejection of claim
for rations furnished slaves.
[Washington, 1837] 2 p. DNA.
                        47512
---- Report on Claim of Wiley
Harben. House Claims Committee. Jan. 17, 1837. Reports
of Committees, No. 116, 24th
Cong., 2d sess., Vol. I. Adverse to claim for provisions,
etc., furnished volunteers, and
for horses killed in the United

States service during the year
1836. [Washington, 1837] 2 p.
DNA.   47513

---- Report on Claim of William
H. Bell. House Claims Committee. Dec. 14, 1837. Reports
of Committees, No. 11, 25th
Cong., 2d sess., Vol. I. Recommends claim for services as assistant engineer at Delaware
Breakwater; Bill reported.
[Washington, 1837] 1 p. DNA.
                        47514
---- Report on Claim of William
Hogan. House Naval Committee.
Feb. 22, 1837. Reports of Committees, No. 273, 24th Cong.,
2d sess., Vol. II. Recommends
passage, with amendments, of
Senate bill granting compensation to William Hogan, as administrator of Michael Hogan, for
services and expenses of the latter as Navy agent at Valparaiso.
[Washington, 1837] 5 p. DNA.
                        47515
---- Report on Claims for Lost
Horses. House Claims Committee. Oct. 12, 1837. Ex. Docs.,
Report No. 3, 25th Cong., 1st
sess. Bill reported making payment for horses turned over to
the Government, by order of the
commanding officer, by persons
leaving the military service.
[Washington, 1837] 1 p. DNA.
                        47516
---- Report on Claims of Certain
Officers of Florida Militia. Feb.
14, 1837. Reports of Committees, No. 220, 24th Cong., 2d
sess., Vol. I. House Claims
Committee asks to be discharged
from further consideration of the
claims of officers of the Second
Regiment Florida militia for services during the Florida war.
[Washington, 1837] 2 p. DNA.
                        47517
---- Report on Claims of Certain

Tennessee Volunteers. House Claims Com. Feb. 8, 1837. Reports of Committees, No. 196, 24th Cong., 2d sess., Vol. I. Recommends payment for military services during the year 1836; Bill reported. [Washington, 1837] 8 p. DNA. 47518

---- Report on Claims of Indiana Militiamen. House Claims Committee. Feb. 8, 1837. Reports of Committees, No. 197, 24th Cong., 2d sess., Vol. I. Recommends payment of portion of claims for expenses incurred in protecting certain Indians on the Tippecanoe River in the year 1836; Bill reported. [Washington, 1837] 4 p. DNA. 47519

---- Report on Claims of Officers of Sloop of War Boston. House Naval Com. Feb. 22, 1837. Reports of Committees, No. 278, 24th Cong., 2d sess., Vol. II. Recommends rejection of Senate bill reimbursing officers of sloop of war Boston for losses occasioned by being paid in depreciated currency. [Washington, 1837] 2 p. DNA. 47520

---- Letter on Claims of Tennessee Volunteers. Secretary J. R. Poinsett. Dec. 18, 1837. Ex. Docs., No. 34, 25th Cong., 2d sess., Vol. II. Transmitting copies of documents relative to the claims for compensation of certain companies of Tennessee volunteers for services in 1836. [Washington, 1837] 40 p. DNA. 47521

---- Report on Claims to Indian Reservations. Commissioner C. A. Harris. Dec. 16, 1837. Senate Docs., No. 25, 25th Cong., 2d sess., Vol. I. Transmitting information relative to the proceedings of the board of commissioners to adjust claims to reservations of land made under the Choctaw treaty of 1830. [Washington, 1837] 29 p. DNA. 47522

---- Report on Clerks in Post-Office Department. P. M. Gen. A. Kendall. Feb. 20, 1837. Ex. Docs., No. 169, 24th Cong., 2d sess., Vol. IV. Names, compensation, etc., of persons employed in the Post-Office Department during the year 1836. [Washington, 1837] 3 p. DNA. 47523

---- Report on Clerks in Treasury Department. Secretary Levi Woodbury. Feb. 27, 1837. Senate Docs., No. 207, 24th Cong., 2d sess., Vol. II. Statement showing names, compensation, etc., of clerks employed in the office of the Auditor of the Treasury for the Post-Office Department for the year 1836. [Washington, 1837] 3 p. DNA. 47524

---- Report on Clerks in War Department. Secretary ad interim B. F. Butler. Jan. 10, 1837. Senate Docs., No. 68, 24th Cong., 2d sess., Vol. II. Statement giving the names and compensation of clerks employed in the War Department during the year 1836. [Washington, 1837] 5 p. DNA. 47525

---- Report on Commerce and Navigation. Secretary Levi Woodbury. April 4, 1837. Ex. Docs., No. 188, 24th Cong., 2d sess., Vol. IV. Statements respecting commerce and navigation between the United States and foreign countries during the year ending September 30, 1836, and tonnage of the United States for the same period. [Washington, 1837] 317 p. DNA. 47526

---- Report on Compilation of
Cong. Docs. Sec. of Senate
and Clerk of House. March 1,
1837. Ex. Docs., No. 180,
24th Cong., 2d sess., Vol. IV.
Stating that the compilation of
Congressional documents authorized by Congress has been com-
pleted. [Washington, 1837] 2
p. DNA.   47527

---- Report on Contingent Expenses of P. O. Dept. P.M.
Gen. A. Kendall. Dec. 9,
1837. Ex. Docs., No. 16, 25th
Cong., 2d sess., Vol. II.
Statement of expenditures from
the contingent fund of the Post-
Office Department since January
1, 1837. [Washington, 1837]
5 p. DNA.   47528

---- Report on Contingent Expenses of State Department.
Sec. J. Forsyth. Dec. 7, 1837.
Ex. Docs., No. 10, 25th Cong.,
2d sess., Vol. II. Transmitting
statements of expenditures from
the incidental and contingent
funds under the control of the
Department of State for the
year ending November 30, 1837.
[Washington, 1837] 49 p. DNA.
                           47529
---- Report on Contingent Expenses of the Navy. Secretary
M. Dickerson. Dec. 12, 1837.
Ex. Docs., No. 26, 25th Cong.,
2d sess., Vol. II. Statement of
expenditures from the contingent fund of the naval establishment for the year ending
September 30, 1837. [Washing-
ton, 1837] 10 p. DNA. 47530

---- Report on Contingent Fund
of the House. Clerk W. S.
Franklin. Dec. 6, 1837. Ex.
Docs., No. 7, 25th Cong., 2d
sess., Vol. I. Statement of expenditures from the contingent

fund of the House of Representatives from January 1 to
November 30, 1837. [Washing-
ton, 1837] 20 p. DNA. 47531

---- Report on Contingent Expenses of Treasury Dept. Sec.
Levi Woodbury. Dec. 12, 1837.
Ex. Docs., No. 22, 25th Cong.,
2d sess., Vol. II. Statement
of expenditures from the contingent funds of the Treasury
Department and its bureaus
during the year ending September 30, 1837. [Washington,
1837] 28 p. DNA.   47532

---- Report on Copyright. Se-
lect committee. Feb. 16, 1836.
Senate Docs., No. 179, 24th
Cong., 2d sess., Vol. II.
Recommends the extension of the
benefits of the copyright laws
to foreign authors; Bill reported.
[Washington, 1837] 3 p. DNA.
                           47533
---- Report on Court of Inquiry.
Adjutant-General R. Jones.
March 29, 1837. Senate Docs.,
No. 224, 24th Cong., 2d sess.,
Vol. III. Proceedings of a court
of inquiry held at Frederick,
Maryland; Case of Major-General
Scott (failure of the Florida cam-
paign in 1836); Case of Major-
General Scott (delay in opening
and prosecuting the Creek cam-
paign); Case of Major-General
Gaines; Proceedings in reference
to publications by officers of the
Army. [Washington, 1837] 734
p. DNA.   47534

---- Report on Culture of Silk.
House Manufactures Committee.
Feb. 25, 1837. Reports of Committees, No. 287, 24th Cong.,
2d sess., Vol. II. Submits as
part of the report of the com-
miteee a letter from Mr. Andrew
T. Judson in relation to, and

recommending, the promotion of the culture and manufacture of silk in the United States. [Washington, 1837] 13 p. DNA. 47535

---- Report on Customs Officers. Secretary Levi Woodbury. Feb. 27, 1837. Ex. Docs., No. 177, 24th Cong., 2d sess., Vol. IV. Abstracts of official emoluments and expenditures of officers of the customs for the year 1836. [Washington, 1837] 10 p. DNA. 47536

---- Report on Customs Officers. Secretary Levi Woodbury. Feb. 27, 1837. Senate Docs., No. 206, 24th Cong., 2d sess., Vol. II. Statement of emoluments and expenditures of officers of the customs for the year 1836. [Washington, 1837] 10 p. DNA. 47537

---- Report on Delaware Breakwater. Captain Richard Delafield. Jan. 10, 1837. Senate Docs., No. 79, 24th Cong., 2d sess., Vol. II. Statements showing sums already expended on the Delaware Breakwater, estimates of amount required for its completion, and of amount necessary to construct a pier near the breakwater. [Washington, 1837] 8 p. DNA. 47538

---- Report on Deposit Banks. Secretary Levi Woodbury. Sept. 25, 1837. Ex. Docs., No. 30, 25th Cong., 1st sess. Transmitting copies of orders issued and correspondence with the several deposit banks in relation to the payments to the State governments under the deposit act; Statement of condition of the deposit banks. [Washington, 1837] 146 p. DNA. 47539

---- Report on Disbursements for the Indians. Auditor W. B. Lewis. Feb. 6, 1837. Ex. Docs., No. 137, 24th Cong., 2d sess., Vol. III. Transmitting copies of accounts rendered by persons charged with disbursements for the Indians, and list of names of persons to whom money, goods, or effects for the benefit of the Indians have been delivered, from October 1, 1835, to September 30, 1836. [Washington, 1837] 126 p. DNA. 47540

---- Report on Disbursements in Indian Department. Com'r C. A. Harris. Feb. 10, 1837. Senate Docs., No. 165, 24th Cong., 2d sess., Vol. II. Transmitting information relative to commissions on disbursements of money in the Indian Department. [Washington, 1837] 8 p. DNA. 47541

---- Report on District of Columbia Banks. Secretary Levi Woodbury. Jan. 10, 1837. Senate Docs., No. 66, 24th Cong., 2d sess., Vol. II. Transmitting copies of returns of the banks of the District of Columbia, showing the state of their affairs at the close of the year 1836. [Washington, 1837] 8 p. DNA. 47542

---- Report on Drawback on Exported Hemp. House Commerce Committee. Feb. 16, 1837. Reports of Committees, No. 229, 24th Cong., 2d sess., Vol. I. Recommends passage of Senate bill allowing drawback of duties on exported hemp, with an amendment allowing drawback of duties on imported wheat exported after manufacture into flour. [Washington, 1837] 6 p. DNA. 47543

---- Report on Eastern Shore Railroad. Lieutenant-Colonel

J. J. Abert. March 2, 1837.
Senate Docs., No. 218, 24th
Cong., 2d sess., Vol. III.
Transmitting report and esti-
mate in reference to the Eastern
Shore Railroad of Maryland.
[Washington, 1837] 28 p. DNA.
47544

---- Report on Erection of
Bridge at Wheeling, Virginia.
Jan. 19, 1837. Reports of
Committees, No. 135, 24th Cong.,
2d sess., Vol. I. House Roads
and Canals Committee recom-
mends the completion of the
Cumberland road east of the
Ohio River by the erection of
a bridge at Wheeling, Virginia;
Bill reported. [Washington, 1837]
38 p. DNA.   47545

---- Report on Evasion of Tariff
Laws. House Commerce Committee. Dec. 28, 1837. Reports
of Committees, No. 200, 25th
Cong., 2d sess., Vol. I. Reports bill making regulations in
regard to certificates given by
consuls to invoices of goods
imported into the United States.
[Washington, 1837] 7 p. DNA.
47546

---- Report on Evasions of
Customs Laws. Commerce Committee. Feb. 3, 1837. Senate
Docs., No. 138, 24th Cong., 2d
sess., Vol. II. Recommends that
the Secretary of the Treasury
be instructed to investigate and
report whether abuses such as
charged by Mr. Dodge, American consul at Bremen, are practiced in the importation of goods
into the United States. [Wash-
ington, 1837] 2 p. DNA.
47547

---- Report on Examination of
Fire-Arms. Board of Army officers. Oct. 2, 1837. Senate
Docs., No. 29, 25th Cong., 1st
sess. Condensed report of in-

vestigations into the comparative
merits of improvements in fire-
arms made by Hall, Colt, Cochran,
and the Baron Hackett. [Wash-
ington, 1837] 15 p. DNA.
47548

---- Report on Exchange of Lands
with Indians. Commissioner
C. A. Harris. Jan. 9, 1837.
Ex. Docs., No. 82, 24th Cong.,
2d sess., Vol. III. In relation
to the expediency of holding
treaties with and purchasing
lands belonging to the Sac, Fox,
Sioux, and Winnebago Indians
in Wisconsin Territory, and to
provide for their removal west
of the Mississippi River. [Wash-
ington, 1837] 12 p. DNA.
47549

---- Report on Execution of
Osage Treaty. Commissioner
C. A. Harris. Dec. 30, 1837.
Senate Docs., No. 64, 25th Cong.,
2d sess., Vol. I. Statement of
progress made in survey of lands
to be granted to the Osage Indians under the treaty of 1825.
[Washington, 1837] 12 p. DNA.
47550

---- Report on Expenditures for
Public Buildings. March 2, 1837.
Reports of Committees, No. 312,
24th Cong., 2d sess., Vol. II.
The House Committee on Expenditures for Public Buildings
reports that the account of the
Commissioner of Public Buildings
has been examined and found
correct. [Washington, 1837] 7
p. DNA.   47551

---- Report on Expenses of Collecting the Revenue, etc. Sec.
L. Woodbury. Feb. 6, 1837.
Senate Docs., No. 148, 24th
Cong., 2d sess., Vol. II. Transmitting statements of net revenues
collected on the lakes, with expenses of collection, from January 1 to September 30, 1836, and

of expenditures in constructing harbors, etc., for the same period. [Washington, 1837] 4 p. DNA. 47552

---- Report on Finances of Post-Office Department. Treasurer John Campbell. Dec. 5, 1837. Ex. Docs., No. 9, 25th Cong., 2d sess., Vol. II. Statement of amounts deposited in the deposit banks used by the Post-Office Department, and amounts drawn, from July 1, 1836, to December 1, 1837. [Washington, 1837] 2 p. DNA. 47553

---- Report on Fire at Post-Office Building. House Post-Office Committee. Jan. 20, 1837. Reports of Committees, No. 134, 24th Cong., 2d sess., Vol. I. Reports testimony and results of investigation into the causes of the recent fire at the Post-Office building, with recommendations. [Washington, 1837] 49 p. DNA. 47554

---- Report on Fire in Patent Office. Select committee. Jan. 9, 1837. Senate Docs., No. 58, 24th Cong., 2d sess., Vol. I. Bill reported providing for the replacement as far as practicable of the records, drawings, and models destroyed by the recent fire in the Patent Office, and making additional regulations in regard to the issue of patents, fees, etc. [Washington, 1837] 17 p. DNA. 47555

---- Report on Fire in Post-Office Building. Post-Office Committee. March 2, 1837. Senate Docs., No. 215, 24th Cong., 2d sess., Vol. III. Submits statements received from the Postmaster-General, the

Superintendent of the Patent Office, and other officers in relation to the recent destruction by fire of the building containing the General Post-Office, the city post-office, and the Patent Office. [Washington, 1837] 16 p. DNA. 47556

---- Report on Foreign Duties on Tobacco. House select committee. Feb. 18, 1837. Reports of Committees, No. 239, 24th Cong., 2d sess., Vol. II. Recommends that the President be requested to instruct the representatives of this country in Europe to negotiate with the governments to which they are accredited for a modification of the duties and restrictions upon tobacco imported from the United States; Bill reported. [Washington, 1837] 15 p. DNA. 47557

---- Report on Foreign Mails. House Foreign Affairs Committee. March 2, 1837. Reports of Committees, No. 311, 24th Cong., 2d sess., Vol. II. Recommends that memorial of citizens of New Bedford praying that letters addressed to citizens of the United States residing in England may be forwarded free of postage be referred to the President. [Washington, 1837] 2 p. DNA. 47558

---- Report on Foreign Tobacco Trade. Secretary John Forsyth. Sept. 29, 1837. Ex. Docs., No. 41, 25th Cong., 1st sess. Statement of measures adopted in relation to the tobacco trade between the United States and foreign countries, and to the proposed negotiations for the benefit of that trade. [Washington, 1837] 7 p. DNA. 47559

---- Report on Frauds in Land
Purchases. Secretary Levi
Woodbury. Feb. 11, 1837.
Senate Docs., No. 168, 24th
Cong., 2d sess., Vol. II.
Submitting a report and docu-
ments in relation to frauds com-
mitted by means of "floats" in
the purchase of public lands.
[Washington, 1837] 57 p. DNA.
                                    47560
---- Report on Harbor of Havre
de Grace. Lieutenant-Colonel
J. J. Abert. Feb. 1, 1837.
Ex. Docs., No. 195, 25th Cong.,
2d sess., Vol. VII. Transmit-
ting report, plan, and estimate
for the improvement of the harbor of Havre de Grace. [Wash-
ington, 1837] 11 p. DNA.
                                    47561
---- Report on Harbor of Milwaukee. John M. Berrien.
Feb. 25, 1837. Senate Docs.,
No. 217, 24th Cong., 2d sess.,
Vol. VII. Transmitting plan,
report, and estimate for the improvement of the harbor of
Milwaukee, Wisconsin. [Wash-
ington, 1837] 6 p. DNA.
                                    47562
---- Report on Immigration.
Secretary John Forsyth. Feb.
15, 1837. Ex. Docs., No. 163,
24th Cong., 2d sess., Vol. IV.
Statement showing number and
designation of passengers arriving in the United States from
foreign countries during the
year 1836. [Washington, 1837]
27 p. DNA.   47563

---- Report on Immigration.
Secretary John Forsyth. Feb.
15, 1837. Senate Docs., No.
178, 24th Cong., 2d sess.,
Vol. II. Transmitting statement
showing number and designation
of passengers arriving in the
United States from foreign countries during the year 1836.

[Washington, 1837] 27 p. DNA.
                                    47564
---- Report on Imports, Exports,
Revenue, etc. Secretary Levi
Woodbury. Jan. 16, 1837.
Senate Docs., No. 74, 24th
Cong., 2d sess., Vol. II. Statement of imports and exports of
the United States for the year
1836; Estimated receipts from
customs and public lands for
the year 1837; Amount of money
in the Treasury, etc. [Washing-
ton, 1837] 7 p. DNA.   47565

---- Report on Imports of Grain.
Secretary Levi Woodbury. Oct.
6, 1837. Ex. Docs., No. 44,
25th Cong., 1st sess. Transmitting statement of quantity
and value of grain imported into
the United States from October
1, 1834, to June 30, 1837.
[Washington, 1837] 7 p. DNA.
                                    47566
---- Report on Impressment of
Property and Indian Depredations. March 1, 1837. Reports
of Committees, No. 301, 24th
Cong., 2d sess., Vol. II.
House Committee on Claims asks
to be discharged from further
consideration of so much of the
President's message as relates
to the taking of the property of
individuals for public use, and
the relief of sufferers by Indian
depredations or by the operations
of our own troops in Florida,
Alabama, and Georgia. [Wash-
ington, 1837] 7 p. DNA.
                                    47567
---- Report on Improvement of
Black River, N.Y. Lt. Col.
J. J. Abert. Jan. 6, 1837.
Ex. Docs., No. 74, 24th Cong.,
2d sess., Vol. II. Submitting
plan, report, and estimates for
the improvement of the mouth of
Black River, Jefferson County,
New York. [Washington, 1837]
7 p. DNA.   47568

---- Report on Improvement of Brunswick Harbor, Ga. Chief Eng. C. Gratiot. Jan. 20, 1837. Ex. Docs., No. 123, 24th Cong., 2d sess., Vol. III. Statement concerning the method of removing the obstructions to the entrance of Brunswick harbor, and recommendation for an increased appropriation. [Washington, 1837] 5 p. DNA. 47569

---- Report on Improvement of Road in Arkansas. Feb. 22, 1837. Reports of Committees, No. 251, 24th Cong., 2d sess., Vol. II. House Roads and Canals Committee recommends appropriation to complete the repair and improvement of the road from Memphis to Fort Gibson, Arkansas; Bill reported. [Washington, 1837] 2 p. DNA. 47570

---- Report on Improvements in Fire-Arms. Board of Army officers. Sept. 19, 1837. Senate Docs., No. 15, 25th Cong., 1st sess. Report on comparative merits of fire-arms invented or improved by Hall, Cochran, Colt, and the Baron Hackett. [Washington, 1837] 27 p. DNA. 47571

---- Report on Independence of Texas. House Foreign Affairs Committee. Feb. 18, 1837. Reports of Committees, No. 240, 24th Cong., 2d sess., Vol. II. Recommends recognition by the United States of the independence of Texas. [Washington, 1837] 1 p. DNA. 47572

---- Report on Indian Campaign in Florida. Sec. ad interim B. F. Butler. Jan. 20, 1837. Senate Docs., No. 100, 24th Cong., 2d sess., Vol. II. Transmitting copies of correspondence between the War Department and R. K.

Call, Governor of Florida, in relation to the Indian campaign there. [Washington, 1837] 24 p. DNA. 47573

---- Report on Indian Depredations. Com'rs L. T. Pease and J. M. Smith. Nov. 28, 1837. Ex. Docs., No. 127, 25th Cong., 2d sess., Vol. VI. Report on investigation of claims of citizens of Georgia and Alabama on account of depredations committed by the Seminole and Creek Indians. [Washington, 1837] 29 p. DNA. 47574

---- Report on Indians in Military Service. Secretary J. R. Poinsett. Sept. 21, 1837. Ex. Docs., No. 27, 25th Cong., 1st sess. Transmitting statement showing the number of Indians employed in the military service of the United States during the present Seminole war, with copies of orders and instructions under which employed. [Washington, 1837] 13 p. DNA. 47575

---- Report on Insolvent Debtors. Secretary Levi Woodbury. Jan. 10, 1837. Senate Docs., No. 67, 24th Cong., 2d sess., Vol. II. Transmitting statement giving information relative to applicants under the act for the relief of insolvent debtors of the United States. [Washington, 1837] 4 p. DNA. 47576

---- Report on Insolvent Debtors of the United States. Sec. Levi Woodbury. Jan. 13, 1837. Ex. Docs., No. 80, 24th Cong., 2d sess., Vol. III. Statement of applications for relief under the acts for the relief of insolvent debtors of the United States. [Washington, 1837] 4 p. DNA. 47577

---- Report on Light-Houses,
etc. Board of Commissioners.
Dec. 15, 1837. Ex. Docs., No.
41, 25th Cong., 2d sess., Vol.
II. Statement of proceedings
and reports of examinations made
in compliance with the act of
Congress making appropriations
for light-houses, beacons, etc.
[Washington, 1837] 99 p. DNA.
                                47578
---- Report on Light-Houses,
etc. Board of Navy officers.
Dec. 9, 1837. Senate Docs.,
No. 375, 25th Cong., 2d sess.,
Vol. IV. Statement of results
of their examination of certain
sites for light-houses, beacons,
etc., on the coast of New Jersey. [Washington, 1837] 5
p. DNA.   47579

---- Report on Light-Houses,
etc. Secretary Levi Woodbury.
Dec. 13, 1837. Ex. Docs., No.
27, 25th Cong., 2d sess., Vol.
II. Statement of progress
made in the construction of
light-houses, beacon-lights,
buoys, etc., since the passage
of the act of March 3, 1837.
[Washington, 1837] 27 p. DNA.
                                47580
---- Report on Light-Houses,
etc., in New Jersey. Board
of Navy officers. Dec. 9, 1837.
Senate Docs., No. 154, 25th
Cong., 2d sess., Vol. III. Report of examination of sites proposed for lights, buoys, and
beacons in the State of New
Jersey. [Washington, 1837]
4 p. DNA.   47581

---- Report on Little Egg Harbor. Chief Engineer C.
Gratiot. Nov. 6, 1837. Ex.
Docs., No. 32, 25th Cong., 2d
sess., Vol. II. Statement of
progress made on the works for
the preservation of Tucker's

Island, Little Egg Harbor.
[Washington, 1837] 5 p. DNA.
                                47582
---- Report on Louisiana Land
Claims. Commissioner James
Whitcomb. Feb. 21, 1837. Ex.
Docs., No. 168, 24th Cong., 2d
sess., Vol. IV. Statement relative to claims to land in Louisiana confirmed under different
acts of Congress. [Washington,
1837] 3 p. DNA.   47583

---- Report on Mail Contracts.
Postmaster-General Amos Kendall.
March 1, 1837. Ex. Docs., No.
182, 24th Cong., 2d sess., Vol.
IV. Statement of contracts
made between January 1 and July
1, 1836, for transportation of
the mail. [Washington, 1837]
16 p. DNA.   47584

---- Report on Marine Apprentice-
ship. Commerce Committee. Jan.
31, 1837. Senate Docs., No.
122, 24th Cong., 2d sess., Vol.
II. Recommends indefinite postponement of House bill requiring merchant vessels of the
United States to employ boys as
part of their crews. [Washing-
ton, 1837] 2 p. DNA.   47585

---- Report on Marine Hospitals.
Commerce Committee. Feb. 3,
1837. Senate Docs., No. 137,
24th Cong., 2d sess., Vol. II.
Recommends amendment of Senate
bill relative to marine hospitals
so as to suspend the tax on seamen for one year, and in lieu
thereof to appropriate $150,000
for the relief of sick and disabled
seamen and watermen; and adoption of resolutions requiring the
Secretary of the Treasury to report on cost of erection of additional hospitals, and on a plan
for their government, etc.
[Washington, 1837] 3 p. DNA.
                                47586

---- Report on Marine Hospitals. Secretary Levi Woodbury. Dec. 11, 1837. Senate Docs., No. 8, 25th Cong., 2d sess., Vol. I. Transmitting information as to the location and cost of marine hospitals, with recommendations as to the disbursement of funds for the relief of sick and disabled seamen, and for the government of hospitals erected for that purpose. [Washington, 1837] 17 p. DNA.   47587

---- Report on Memorial of Alexandria and Falmouth Railroad Company. Feb. 16, 1837. Reports of Committees, No. 238, 24th Cong., 2d sess., Vol. II. House Committee on Roads and Canals recommends national subscription to the stock of the company; Bill reported. [Washington, 1837] 29 p. DNA.   47588

---- Report on Memorial of Ambrose H. Sevier. Judiciary Committee. March 7, 1837. Senate Docs., No. 216, 24th Cong., 2d sess., Vol. II. Reports that memorialist is entitled to a seat in the United States Senate from the State of Arkansas under an appointment from the Governor of that State. [Washington, 1837] 2 p. DNA.   47589

---- Report on Memorial of Ann L. De Van Brun. Rev. Claims Committee. Jan. 18, 1837. Senate Docs., No. 82, 24th Cong., 2d sess., Vol. II. Adverse to allowance of claim for commutation pay on account of services of her late husband, John L. De Van Brun, in the Revolutionary War. [WAshington, 1837] 2 p. DNA.   47590

---- Report on Memorial of

Arkansas Legislature. House Pub. Lands Com. Dec. 22, 1837. Reports of Committees, No. 90, 25th Cong., 2d sess., Vol. I. Recommends donation of land to each head of family who resided west of present western boundary of Arkansas as an indemnity for loss of improvements ceded to Choctaw Indians; Bill reported. [Washington, 1837] 16 p. DNA.   47591

---- Report on Memorial of Austin & Taylor. House Claims Committee. Dec. 14, 1837. Reports of Committees, No. 49, 25th Cong., 2d sess., Vol. I. Recommends that the Secretary of War examine claim for damages sustained by suspending shipment of stone for construction of Fort Sumter, under orders from the Department, and that he adjust and settle the claim. [Washington, 1837] 1 p. DNA.   47592

---- Report on Memorial of Baltimore and Susquehanna Railroad Company. Feb. 14, 1837. Reports of Committees, No. 224, 24th Cong., 2d sess., Vol. I. Ways and Means Committee recommends remission of duties on certain railroad-iron imported; Bill reported. [Washington, 1837] 2 p. DNA.   47593

---- Report on Memorial of Baltimore Railroad Co. Ways and Means Com. Dec. 14, 1837. Reports of Committees, No. 2, 25th Cong., 2d sess., Vol. I. Recommends refundment of duty on railroad iron; Bill reported. [Washington, 1837] 2 p. DNA.   47594

---- Report on Memorial of Columbian Institute. House Pub. Buildings Com. Feb. 14, 1837. Reports of Committees, No. 226, 24th Cong., 2d sess., Vol. I.

Recommends reimbursement of
the Columbian Institute for
money expended on the improvement of public land in Washington temporarily granted to that
institution; Bill reported.
[Washington, 1837] 1 p. DNA.
                                 47595
---- Report on Memorial of Commodore C. G. Ridgeley. Jan.
17, 1837. Reports of Committees, No. 113, 24th Cong., 2d
sess., Vol. I. House Foreign
Affairs Committee recommends
reimbursement of expenses incurred in protecting and entertaining Spanish officers while
commanding officer of the naval
forces of the United States on
the South American station in
1820 and 1821; Bill reported.
[Washington, 1837] 2 p. DNA.
                                 47596
---- Report on Memorial of
Commodore Isaac Hull. Dec.
22, 1837. Reports of Committees, No. 147, 25th Cong., 2d
sess., Vol. I. House Committee
on Naval Affairs recommends
allowance of compensation for
extra services at the navy-
yard in Washington, and that
the sum paid for live-oak timber be refunded; Bill reported.
[Washington, 1837] 11 p. DNA.
                                 47597
---- Report on Memorial of Com-
mon Council of Alexandria.
District Com. Jan. 20, 1837.
Senate Docs., No. 86, 24th
Cong., 2d sess., Vol. II.
Recommends an appropriation
to aid in the completion to
Alexandria of the Chesapeake
and Ohio Canal; Bill reported.
[Washington, 1837] 1 p. DNA.
                                 47598
---- Report on Memorial of
Corporation of Alexandria.
House Dist. Com. Feb. 22,
1837. Reports of Committees,

No. 255, 24th Cong., 2d sess.,
Vol. II. Memorialists ask the
aid of Congress in the completion of the Chesapeake and Ohio
Canal to the city of Alexandria;
Committee submits a favorable
opinion on the memorial as a
basis for future legislation.
[Washington, 1837] 3 p. DNA.
                                 47599
---- Report on Memorial of D. G.
Farragut. House Naval Committee. Feb. 22, 1837. Reports of
Committees, No. 279, 24th Cong.,
2d sess., Vol. II. Adverse to
payment of extra allowance claimed
by memorialist in addition to his
pay as a lieutenant in the Navy.
[Washington, 1837] 1 p. DNA.
                                 47600
---- Report on Memorial of David
Melville. House Commerce Committee. Feb. 22, 1837. Reports
of Committees, No. 242, 24th
Cong., 2d sess., Vol. II. Memorialist protests against his recent
removal from the custom-house at
Newport, and asks Congress to
restrict the patronage of the
executive branch of the Government so as to secure the citizens in all their rights, etc.;
Committee reports that the appointment of memorialist expired
by operation of law, that he has
not been removed from office,
and that no further action ought
to be taken on his memorial.
[Washington, 1837] 5p. DNA.
                                 47601
---- Report on Memorial of
Econchattanico. Indian Committee. Feb. 2, 1837. Senate Docs.,
No. 131, 24th Cong., 2d sess.,
Vol. II. Recommends that the
papers of the memorialist, a
Seminole Indian, be transmitted
to the President, and that he
be requested to have prosecuted
the trespassers on the property
of the memorialist, with a view

to his indemnification. [Washington, 1837] 1 p. DNA. 47602

---- Report on Memorial of Executor of William T. Smith. March 2, 1837. Reports of Committees, No. 315, 24th Cong., 2d sess., Vol. II. The House Revolutionary Claims Committee recommends payment for Revolutionary loan-office certificates lost; Bill reported. [Washington, 1837] 1 p. DNA. 47603

---- Report on Memorial of Executor of William T. Smith. Dec. 22, 1837. Reports of Committees, No. 103, 25th Cong., 2d sess., Vol. I. House Revolutionary Claims Committee recommends allowance of claim for amount of loan certificates; Bill reported. [Washington, 1837] 2 p. DNA. 47604

---- Report on Memorial of Ferdinand Clark. House Commerce Committee. Jan. 4, 1837. Reports of Committees, No. 64, 24th Cong., 2d sess., Vol. I. Recommends reimbursement of duties paid by petitioner under the act imposing tonnage duties on Spanish vessels; Bill reported. [Washington, 1837] 8 p. DNA. 47605

---- Report on Memorial of Ferdinand Clark. House Commerce Com. Dec. 22, 1837. Reports of Committees, No. 88, 25th Cong., 2d sess., Vol. I. Recommends remission of duties paid under the act relating to tonnage duties on Spanish vessels; Bill reported. [Washington, 1837] 8 p. DNA. 47606

---- Report on Memorial of Francis Vigo. House Rev. Claims Committee. Dec. 22, 1837. Reports of Committees,

No. 118, 25th Cong., 2d sess., Vol. I. [Washington, 1837] 33 p. DNA. 47607

---- Report on Memorial of Gilbert S. Fish. House Invalid Pensions Com. Jan. 19, 1837. Reports of Committees, No. 126, 24th Cong., 2d sess., Vol. I. Recommends allowance of pension; Bill reported. [Washington, 1837] 1 p. DNA. 47608

---- Report on Memorial of H. Morfit. House Rev. Pensions Committee. Jan. 7, 1837. Reports of Committees, No. 76, 24th Cong., 2d sess., Vol. I. Adverse to allowance of Pension as widow of Henry Morfit. [Washington, 1837] 1 p. DNA. 47609

---- Report on Memorial of Heirs of Francis Cazeau. Judiciary Committee. Dec. 22, 1837. Senate Docs., No. 41, 25th Cong., 2d sess., Vol. I. Recommends allowance of claim for remuneration for supplies furnished the American Army during the Revolution; Bill reported. [Washington, 1837] 2 p. DNA. 47610

---- Report on Memorial of Illinois Central R. R. Co. House Pub. Lands Com. Jan. 17, 1837. Reports of Committees, No. 121, 24th Cong., 2d sess., Vol. I. Recommends grant of certain land to aid in the construction of the road; Bill reported. [Washington, 1837] 15 p. DNA. 47611

---- Report on Memorial of J. Kern and J. D. George. House Commerce Com. Feb. 22, 1837. Reports of Committees, No. 257, 24th Cong., 2d sess., Vol. II. Memorialists ask remuneration for amount expended in employment of extra clerks in the custom-house at Philadelphia; Committee recommends payment; Bill reported. [Washington, 1837] 5 p. DNA. 47612

---- Report on Memorial of John Downes. House Claims Committee. Dec. 14, 1837. Reports of Committees, No. 53, 25th Cong., 2d sess., Vol. I. Recommends that the accounting officers of the Treasury be required to allow memorialist a credit of $723.60 in settlement of his accounts, that sum having been erroneously charged to him. [Washington, 1837] 2 p. DNA. 47613

---- Report on Memorial of John Turner. House Rev. Claims Committee. Dec. 22, 1837. Reports of Committees, No. 105, 25th Cong., 2d sess., Vol. I. Recommends allowance of claim for commutation of half-pay for life for services of Philip Turner; Bill reported. [Washington, 1837] 1 p. DNA. 47614

---- Report on Memorial of Joshua Dodge. House Commerce Committee. Jan. 28, 1837. Reports of Committees, No. 163, 24th Cong., 2d sess., Vol. I. Recommends amendment of the laws relating to consular regulations and consuls' fees; Bill reported. [Washington, 1837] 4 p. DNA. 47615

---- Report on Memorial of Martha Piatt. House select committee. Feb. 14, 1837. Reports of Committees, No. 227, 24th Cong., 2d sess., Vol. I. Bill reported for relief of petitioner, granting her commutation of pay as daughter of Joshua Huddy, who suffered death for his services during the Revolutionary War. [Washington, 1837] 46 p. DNA. 47616

---- Report on Memorial of New York Chamber of Commerce. Feb. 11, 1837. Senate Docs., No. 166, 24th Cong., 2d sess., Vol. II. Committee on Commerce recommends that public vessels of the United States be directed to cruise on the coast during the winter prepared to afford aid in cases of shipwreck; Bill reported. [Washington, 1837] 1 p. DNA. 47617

---- Report on Memorial of R. Clay and J. Lowell. Ways and Means Com. Feb. 14, 1837. Reports of Committees, No. 208, 24th Cong., 2d sess., Vol. I. Adverse to remission of duties on molasses destroyed by fire. [Washington, 1837] 2 p. DNA. 47618

---- Report on Memorial of Richard Harrison. House Foreign Affairs Com. Feb. 22, 1837. Reports of Committees, No. 265, 24th Cong., 2d sess., Vol. II. Recommends allowance of compensation for services as consul in Spain. [Washington, 1837] 43 p. DNA. 47619

---- Report on Memorial of Thomas B. Parsons. House Naval Affairs Com. Dec. 22, 1837. Reports of Committees, No. 148, 25th Cong., 2d sess., Vol. I. Recommends allowing compensation for services in rescuing crew of United States gunboat in 1808; Bill reported. [Washington, 1837] 4 p. DNA. 47620

---- Report on Mexican Affairs. House Foreign Affairs Committee. Feb. 24, 1837. Reports of Committees, No. 281, 24th Cong., 2d sess., Vol. II. Reports that the indignities to the American flag and injuries to American citizens by officers of the Mexican Government, and the refusal of that government to make atonement, would justify Congress in taking measures to obtain redress by the exercise of its own power, but recommends that the President be respectfully requested to make another solemn demand upon Mexico for redress of grievances. [Washington, 1837] 4 p. DNA.   47621

---- Report on Military Academy. House select committee. March 1, 1837. Reports of Committees, No. 303, 24th Cong., 2d sess., Vol. II. Recommends abolition of education of cadets at the public expense, the organization at West Point of a military school for Army officers, etc.; Bill reported. [Washington, 1837] 200 p. DNA.   47622

---- Report on Military Contingent Expenses. Sec. ad interim B. F. Butler. Jan. 6, 1837. Ex. Docs., No. 72, 24th Cong., 2d sess., Vol. II. Transmitting statement showing the expenditure of the appropriation for the contingent expenses of the military establishment for the year 1836. [Washington, 1837] 6 p. DNA.   47623

---- Report on Military Depot in Mississippi. Military Committee. Jan. 4, 1837. Senate Docs., No. 53, 24th Cong., 2d sess., Vol. I. Reports that the bill to establish arsenals in States where there are none includes Mississippi, and that no separate bill is necessary. [Washington, 1837] 1 p. DNA.   47624

---- Report on Military Land Warrants. House Public Lands Committee. Jan. 13, 1837. Reports of Committees, No. 90, 24th Cong., 2d sess., Vol. I. Recommends extension of law authorizing issuance of scrip for military land warrants; Bill reported. [Washington, 1837] 2 p. DNA.   47625

---- Report on Mississippi Election. House Elections Committee. Sept. 25, 1837. Ex. Docs., Report No. 2, 25th Cong., 1st sess. Reports that Samuel J. Gholson and John F. H. Claiborne are duly elected members of the Twenty-fifth Congress from the State of Mississippi under the writ for a special election issued by the Governor of that State. [Washington, 1837] 10 p. DNA.   47626

---- Report on National Armories. Col. George Bomford. March 3, 1837. Ex. Docs., No. 186, 24th Cong., 2d sess., Vol. IV. Operations of the national armories during the year 1836. [Washington, 1837] 4 p. DNA.   47627

---- Report on Navy Appropriations. Secretary M. Dickerson. Feb. 1, 1837. Ex. Docs., No. 126, 24th Cong., 2d sess., Vol. III. Statement of appropriations and expenditures for the naval service for the year 1836. [Washington, 1837] 6 p. DNA.   47628

---- Report on Navy Contracts. Secretary M. Dickerson. Jan. 18, 1837. Ex. Docs., No. 90, 24th Cong., 2d sess., Vol. III. Transmitting statement of contracts made by the Commissioners of the Navy during the year 1836. [Washington, 1837] 9 p. DNA.   47629

---- Report on Navy Pensions.
Secretary Mahlon Dickerson.
Dec. 14, 1837. Senate Docs.,
No. 20, 25th Cong., 2d sess.,
Vol. I. Statements showing
condition and amount of Navy
pension fund, names of persons
on the Navy pension-list, etc.
[Washington, 1837] 14 p. DNA.
47630

---- Report on Navy-Yard at
Charleston. Secretary M.
Dickerson. Dec. 26, 1837.
Ex. Docs., No. 44, 25th Cong.,
2d sess., Vol. II. In favor of
the establishment of a navy-yard
at that city. [Washington, 1837]
2 p. DNA. 47631

---- Report on Niagara Ship-
Canal. House Roads and Canals
Committee. Feb. 14, 1837. Reports of Committees, No. 201,
24th Cong., 2d sess., Vol. I.
Recommends the construction of
a ship-canal around the Falls of
Niagara, to connect the waters
of Lake Erie and Lake Ontario;
Bill reported. [Washington,
1837] 40 p. DNA. 47632

---- Report on Paintings for the
Capitol Rotunda. House select
committee. Feb. 28, 1837. Reports of Committees, No. 294,
24th Cong., 2d sess., Vol. II.
Recommends that a contract be
made for the execution of four
historical pictures for the rotunda of the Capitol. [Wash-
ington, 1837] 1 p. DNA.
47633

---- Report on Patents. Secretary John Forsyth. Feb. 23,
1837. Ex. Docs., No. 174,
24th Cong., 2d sess., Vol. IV.
Statement relative to patents
for useful inventions granted
from January 1, 1836, to December 1, 1836; Names of
patentees; Nature of inventions,
etc. [Washington, 1837] 42 p.
DNA. 47634

---- Report on Patents. Secretary John Forsyth. Feb. 23,
1837. Ex. Docs., No. 175,
24th Cong., 2d sess., Vol. IX.
Statement of patents for inventions, etc., which have expired
within the year 1836. [Washing-
ton, 1837] 9 p. DNA. 47635

---- Report on Payment of Alabama Troops. House Claims
Committee. Feb. 22, 1837. Reports of Committees, No. 258,
24th Cong., 2d sess., Vol. II.
Recommends appropriation for
the payment of three companies
of Alabama troops for services
in the year 1836. [Washington,
1837] 1 p. DNA. 47636

---- Report on Persons Employed
in Indian Department. Com'r
C. A. Harris. Feb. 7, 1837.
Ex. Docs., No. 141, 24th Cong.,
2d sess., Vol. III. Names, compensation, and time employed of
persons in the service of the
Indian Department during the year
1836. [Washington, 1837] 14 p.
DNA. 47637

---- Report on Petitions for Half-
Pay. Revolutionary Claims Committee. Feb. 3, 1837. Senate
Docs., No. 135, 24th Cong., 2d
sess., Vol. II. Recommends
allowance of claims for half-pay,
with interest, to Mrs. Lucy Bond,
widow of William Bond, and Mrs.
Hannah Douglas, widow of William
Douglas; Bill reported. [Wash-
ington, 1837] 3 p. DNA.
47638

---- Report on Petition of A. B.
Quimby. Select committee. Feb.
1, 1837. Senate Docs., No.
125, 24th Cong., 2d sess., Vol.
II. Recommends an appropriation

for making experiments with index invented by petitioner, to be attached to steam-boilers; Bill reported. [Washington, 1837] 2 p. DNA. 47639

---- Report on Petition of A. Forbes. House Private Land Claims Com. Jan. 28, 1837. Reports of Committees, No. 170, 24th Cong., 2d sess., Vol. I. Recommends grant of bounty land for services in the war of 1812; Bill reported. [Washington, 1837] 1 p. DNA. 47640

---- Report on Petition of Abigail Appleton. House Naval Committee. Feb. 1, 1837. Reports of Committees, No. 180, 24th Cong., 2d sess., Vol. I. Recommends allowance of pension to petitioner as widow of Daniel Appleton; Bill reported. [Washington, 1837] 1 p. DNA. 47641

---- Report on Petition of Abraham Lansing. House Claims Committee. Dec. 14, 1837. Reports of Committees, No. 30, 25th Cong., 2d sess., Vol. I. Recommends claim for attendance at the Boston rendezvous as assistant to the commanding recruiting officer. [Washington, 1837] DNA. 47642

---- Report on Petition of Abraham Woodall. House Public Lands Com. Dec. 22, 1837. Reports of Committees, No. 98, 25th Cong., 2d sess., Vol. I. Recommends claim for exchange of land titles in Alabama; Bill reported. [Washington, 1837] 1 p. DNA. 47643

---- Report on Petition of Adam Hall. House Claims Committee. Feb. 22, 1837. Reports of Committees, No. 269, 24th Cong.,

2d sess., Vol. II. Recommends reference of claim for horse lost in the service of the United States during the Creek war to the Third Auditor. [Washington, 1837] 1 p. DNA. 47644

---- Report on Petition of Administrator of B. Laws. House Claims Com. Dec. 14, 1837. Reports of Committees, No. 19, 25th Cong., 2d sess., Vol. I. Recommends claim for brick furnished for fortifications at Old Point Comfort; Bill reported. [Washington, 1837] 2 p. DNA. 47645

---- Report on Petition of Administrator of E. Duval. House Claims Com. Dec. 14, 1837. Reports of Committees, No. 47, 25th Cong., 2d sess., Vol. I. Recommends claim for improvements made at the Cherokee agency; That the accounting officers of the Treasury, in settlement of accounts of Edward Duval, pass to his credit balance due him after deducting judgment rendered; Bill reported. [Washington, 1837] 3 p. DNA. 47646

---- Report on Petition of Administrator of J. Taylor. House Claims Com. Dec. 14, 1837. Reports of Committees, No. 23, 25th Cong., 2d sess., Vol. I. Recommends claim for interest on debt of United States, the debt having been liquidated but interest withheld; Bill reported. [Washington, 1837] 1 p. DNA. 47647

---- Report on Petition of Administrator of P. Quarles. Dec. 22, 1837. Reports of Committees, No. 106, 25th Cong., 2d sess., Vol. I. House Committee on Revolutionary Claims recommends allowance of claim for half-pay; Bill reported. [Washington, 1837] 1 p. DNA. 47648

---- Report on Petition of Albion T. Crow. House Claims
Committee. Dec. 14, 1837.
Reports of Committees, No. 22,
25th Cong., 2d sess., Vol. I.
Recommends claim for stable
burnt while occupied by United
States troops in 1832, and re-
jects claim for ornamental and
fruit trees. [Washington, 1837]
2 p. DNA.   47649

---- Report on Petition of Alexander Gillis. House Rev. Pensions Com. Dec. 22, 1837. Reports of Committees, No. 175,
25th Cong., 2d sess., Vol. I.
Recommends allowance of pension; Bill reported. [Washing-
ton, 1837] 2 p. DNA.   47650

---- Report on Petition of Alexandria and Falmouth Railroad
Company. Feb. 16, 1837.
Senate Docs., No. 181, 24th
Cong., 2d sess., Vol. II.
Roads and Canals Committee
recommends an appropriation to
aid in the construction of said
railroad within the District of
Columbia. [Washington, 1837]
1 p. DNA.   47651

---- Report on Petition of
Amelia Leach. House Priv.
Land Claims Com. Dec. 22,
1837. Reports of Committees,
No. 143, 25th Cong., 2d sess.,
Vol. I. Recommends exchange
of land warrant; Bill reported.
[Washington, 1837] 1 p. DNA.
                                    47652

---- Report on Petition of Allen
R. Moore. House Claims Committee. Dec. 14, 1837. Reports
of Committees, No. 26, 25th
Cong., 2d sess., Vol. I.
Recommends claim for use of
and damage to store by United
States troops in 1814; Bill
reported. [Washington, 1837]
2 p. DNA.   47653

---- Report on Petition of Amos
Thompson. House Rev. Pensions
Committee. Jan. 7, 1837. Re-
ports of Committees, No. 79,
24th Cong., 2d sess., Vol. I.
Recommends allowance of pension;
Bill reported. [Washington, 1837]
1 p. DNA.   47654

---- Report on Petition of Amos
Thompson. House Rev. Pen-
sions Com. Dec. 22, 1837.
Reports of Committees, No. 156,
25th Cong., 2d sess., Vol. I.
Recommends allowance of pension;
Bill reported. [Washington,
1837] 1 p. DNA.   47655

---- Report on Petition of Andrew
Lyman. House Rev. Pensions
Committee. Jan. 7, 1837. Re-
ports of Committees, No. 73,
24th Cong., 2d sess., Vol. I.
Recommends allowance of pension;
Bill reported. [Washington,
1837] 1 p. DNA.   47656

---- Report on Petition of Ann
Bloomfield. House Rev. Pensions Com. Feb. 16, 1837. Reports of Committees, No. 234,
24th Cong., 2d sess., Vol. II.
Recommends allowance of pension to petitioner as widow of
Thomas Bloomfield; Bill reported.
[Washington, 1837] 1 p. DNA.
                                    47657

---- Report on Petition of Ann
L. De Van Brun. House Rev.
Claims Com. March 1, 1837.
Reports of Committees, No. 302,
24th Cong., 2d sess., Vol. II.
Recommends remuneration for
Revolutionary services of her late
husband, John L. De Van Brun;
Bill reported. [Washington,
1837] 3 p. DNA.   47658

---- Report on Petition of Ann
S. Heileman. House Military
Committee. Feb. 14 1837. Re-

ports of Committees, No. 225, 24th Cong., 2d sess., Vol. I. Recommends allowance of half-pay pension to petitioner as widow of J. F. Heileman; Bill reported. [Washington, 1837] 2 p. DNA. 47659

---- Report on Petition of Ann W. Johnston. House Claims Committee. Dec. 14, 1837. Reports of Committees, No. 73, 25th Cong., 2d sess., Vol. I. Recommends allowance of claim for horse killed in the United States service in 1814; Bill reported. [Washington, 1837] 2 p. DNA. 47660

---- Report on Petition of Anthony Gale. Naval Committee. Feb. 4, 1837. Senate Docs., No. 145, 24th Cong., 2d sess., Vol. II. Recommends allowance of extra pay for services as Army quartermaster; Bill reported. [Washington, 1837] 3 p. DNA. 47661

---- Report on Petition of Apollos Cooper. House Rev. Claims Committee. Dec. 22, 1837. Reports of Committees, No. 126, 25th Cong., 2d sess., Vol. I. Recommends allowance of commutation pay; Bill reported. [Washington, 1837] 1 p. DNA. 47662

---- Report on Petition of Asa Merrill. House Rev. Pensions Committee. Jan. 24, 1837. Reports of Committees, No. 152, 24th Cong., 2d sess., Vol. I. Adverse to allowance of pension. [Washington, 1837] 1 p. DNA. 47663

---- Report on Petition of Avery, Saltmarsh & Co. House Post-Office Com. Feb. 23, 1837. Reports of Committees, No. 280,

24th Cong., 2d sess., Vol. II. Recommends that petitioners be indemnified for losses incurred in attack by Indians while engaged in the transportation of the mail; Bill reported. [Washington, 1837] 9 p. DNA. 47664

---- Report on Petition of Bailey & Delord. House Claims Committee. Feb. 2, 1837. Reports of Committees, No. 192, 24th Cong., 2d sess., Vol. I. Adverse to allowance of claim of petitioners, late sutlers, for payment of certain debts due from soldiers. [Washington, 1837] 1 p. DNA. 47665

---- Report on Petition of Baily & Delord. House Claims Committee. Dec. 14, 1837. Reports of Committees, No. 9, 25th Cong., 2d sess., Vol. I. Recommends claim for goods furnished United States soldiers in the war of 1812; Bill reported. [Washington, 1837] 2 p. DNA. 47666

---- Report on Petition of Benedict I. Heard. House Claims Committee. March 3, 1837. Reports of Committees, No. 325, 24th Cong., 2d sess., Vol. II. Adverse to payment for damages to plantation in the war of 1812. [Washington, 1837] 2 p. DNA. 47667

---- Report on Petition of Benjamin Gannett. House Rev. Pensions Com. Jan. 31, 1837. Reports of Committees, No. 172, 24th Cong., 2d sess., Vol. I. Recommends allowance of pension; Bill reported. [Washington, 1837] 2 p. DNA. 47668

---- Report on Petition of Benjamin Gannett. House Rev. Pensions Com. Dec. 22, 1837. Reports of Committees, No. 159, 25th Cong., 2d sess., Vol. I.

Recommends allowance of pension;
Bill reported. [Washington,
1837] 2 p. DNA.   47669

---- Report on Petition of Benj.
McCullock. House Invalid Pen-
sions Com. Jan. 7, 1837.
Reports of Committees, No. 72,
24th Cong., 2d sess., Vol. I.
Recommends allowance of pension;
Bill reported. [Washington, 1837]
1 p. DNA.   47670

---- Report on Petition of
Benjamin Mooers. House Claims
Committee. Dec. 14, 1837.
Reports of Committees, No. 36,
25th Cong., 2d sess., Vol. I.
Recommends claim for damages
done to crops while the United
States troops were camped upon
his farm in 1814; Bill reported.
[Washington, 1837] 2 p. DNA.
                          47671
---- Report on Petition of Bowie
and others. Claims Committee.
Jan. 21, 1837. Senate Docs.,
No. 92, 24th Cong., 2d sess.,
Vol. II. Refers to report of
Foreign Affairs Committee of
January 20, 1830, and recom-
mends payment for cargo of the
ship Alleghany, and disallowance
of the claim for value of ship;
Bill reported. [Washington,
1837] 1 p. DNA.   47672

---- Report on Petition of Bradley T. Jipson. House Invalid
Pensions Com. Dec. 22, 1837.
Reports of Committees, No.
185, 25th Cong., 2d sess.,
Vol. I. Recommends allowance
of pension; Bill reported.
[Washington, 1837] 2 p. DNA.
                          47673
---- Report on Petition of Caroline E. Clitherall. Claims Committee. Dec. 20, 1837. Senate
Docs., No. 33, 25th Cong., 2d
sess., Vol. I. Recommends re-

imbursement of amount paid for
quarters by her late husband,
George C. Clitherall, a surgeon
in the Army; Bill reported.
[Washington, 1837] 4 p. DNA.
                          47674
---- Report on Petition of Catherine C. Read. Naval Committee. Jan. 27, 1837. Senate
Docs., No. 110, 24th Cong., 2d
sess., Vol. II. Recommends
allowance of pension to petitioner
as widow of Benjamin F. Read;
Bill reported. [Washington, 1837]
2 p. DNA.   47675

---- Report on Petition of Catharine Hodges. House Foreign
Affairs Com. Feb. 18, 1837.
Reports of Committees, No. 241,
24th Cong., 2d sess., Vol. II.
Recommends compensation for
slave belonging to her late husband, Benjamin Hodges, taken by
the British in the war of 1812;
Bill reported. [Washington, 1837]
5 p. DNA.   47676

---- Report on Petition of Certain
Creek Indians. Jan. 12, 1837.
Senate Docs., No. 62, 24th Cong.,
2d sess., Vol. II. Private Land
Claims Committee recommends allowance of claims of Samuel
Smith, Semoice, Linn McGhee,
and Susan Marlowe for compensation for land taken from them
under the provisions of the
treaty with the Creek Indians;
Bill reported. [Washington,
1837] 1 p. DNA.   47677

---- Report on Petition of Charles
B. Bristol. House Claims Committee. Feb. 16, 1837. Reports
of Committees, No. 233, 24th
Cong., 2d sess., Vol. II. Adverse to reimbursement for
losses sustained by detention of
merchandise by the collector of
the port of Oswego during the

embargo of 1808. [Washington, 1837] 8 p. DNA.   47678

---- Report on Petition of Charles Benns. House Claims Committee. March 3, 1837. Reports of Committees, No. 324, 24th Cong., 2d sess., Vol. II. Recommends payment for baggage seized by deputy collector of customs; Bill reported. [Washington, 1837] 2 p. DNA.   47679

---- Report on Petition of Charles Benns. House Claims Committee. Dec. 14, 1837. Reports of Committees, No. 76, 25th Cong., 2d sess., Vol. I. Recommends payment to petitioner of value of baggage seized by United States customs officer; Bill reported. [Washington,1837] 2 p. DNA. 47680

---- Report on Petition of Charles Coffin. House Invalid Pensions Com. Jan. 13, 1837. Reports of Committees, No. 92, 24th Cong., 2d sess., Vol. I. Recommends allowance of pension; Bill reported. [Washington, 1837] 1 p. DNA.   47681

---- Report on Petition of Charles Coffin. House Invalid Pensions Com. Dec. 22, 1837. Reports of Committees, No. 188, 25th Cong., 2d sess., Vol. I. Recommends allowance of pension; Bill reported. [Washington, 1837] 2 p. DNA.   47682

---- Report on Petition of Charles F. Sibbald. House Claims Committee. March 3, 1837. Reports of Committees, No. 323, 24th Cong., 2d sess., Vol. II. Recommends that claim for damages incurred by being dispossessed of his land

by an agent of the United States be referred to the Secretary of the Treasury. [Washington, 1837] 2 p. DNA.   47683

---- Report on Petition of Charles Park. House Naval Committee. Feb. 24, 1837. Reports of Committees, No. 288, 24th Cong., 2d sess., Vol. II. Adverse to purchase of right to employ in the Navy machine invented by the petitioner for worming and serving ropes. [Washington, 1837] 2 p. DNA.   47684

---- Report on Petition of Charles S. Matthews et al. House Claims Com. Jan. 17, 1837. Reports of Committees, No. 117, 24th Cong., 2d sess., Vol. I. Adverse to additional payment on contract made with Charles S. Matthews, Charles Wood, and James Hall for the delivery of marble at the New York custom-house. [Washington, 1837] 5 p. DNA.   47685

---- Report on Petition of Charles Waldron. House Claims Committee. Feb. 14, 1837. Reports of Committees, No. 214, 24th Cong., 2d sess., Vol. I. Adverse to claim for losses sustained at Fort Defiance on account of destruction of property by United States troops. [Washington, 1837] 1 p. DNA.   47686

---- Report on Petition of Chastelain & Pouvert. Ways and Means Com. Dec. 14, 1837. Reports of Committees, No. 1, 25th Cong., 2d sess., Vol. I. Recommends that petitioners be relieved from payment of duty on goods destroyed by fire; Bill reported. [Washington, 1837] 1 p. DNA.   47687

---- Report on Petition of Chauncey

Rice. House Rev. Pensions
Committee. Jan. 3, 1837. Reports of Committees, No. 58,
24th Cong., 2d sess., Vol. I.
Recommends allowance of pension; Bill reported. [Washing-
ton, 1837] 2 p. DNA.   47688

---- Report on Petition of
Chauncey Rice. House Rev.
Pensions Committee. Dec. 22,
1837. Reports of Committees,
No. 180, 25th Cong., 2d sess.,
Vol. I. Recommends allowance
of pension; Bill reported. 3
p. DNA.   47689

---- Report on Petition of
Christopher Dennison. House
Rev. Pensions Com. Feb. 8,
1837. Reports of Committees,
No. 198, 24th Cong., 2d sess.,
Vol. I. Recommends allowance
of pension; Bill reported.
[Washington, 1837] 1 p. DNA.
                          47690
---- Report on Petition of
Christopher Dennison. House
Rev. Pens. Com. Dec. 22,
1837. Reports of Committees,
No. 171, 25th Cong., 2d sess.,
Vol. I. Recommends allowance
of pension; Bill reported. [Wash-
ington, 1837] 1 p. DNA. 47691

---- Report on Petition of
Christopher Moon. House Rev.
Claims Com. Jan. 10, 1837.
Reports of Committees, No. 85,
24th Cong., 2d sess., Vol. I.
Adverse to allowance of seven
years' half-pay as heir of Jacob
Moon. [Washington, 1837] 1
p. DNA.   47692

---- Report on Petition of
Christopher Werner. House
Claims Committee. Dec. 14,
1837. Reports of Committees,
No. 54, 25th Cong., 2d sess.,
Vol. I. Recommends claim for

amount deposited in the Treasury
for a patent; Bill reported.
[Washington, 1837] 1 p. DNA.
                          47693
---- Report on Petition of Citizens of Alabama. House Pub.
Lands Com. Jan. 23, 1837.
Reports of Committees, No. 137,
24th Cong., 2d sess., Vol. I.
Recommends that Elisha Moreland,
William M. Kennedy, Robert J.
Kennedy, and Mason E. Lewis,
whose lands have been included
in Indian reservations, be allowed
to locate land elsewhere; Bill reported. [Washington, 1837] 3
p. DNA.   47694

---- Report on Petition of Citizens of Alabama. House Public
Lands Com. Dec. 22, 1837. Reports of Committees, No. 92, 25th
Cong., 2d sess., Vol. I. Recommends that Elisha Moreland,
William M. Kennedy, Robert J.
Kennedy, and Mason E. Lewis
be allowed to enter land not occupied by other settlers, in lieu
of their several improvements;
Bill reported. [Washington, 1837]
3 p. DNA.   47695

---- Report on Petition of Citizens of St. Augustine, Florida.
Feb. 14, 1837. Reports of Committees, No. 218, 24th Cong.,
2d sess., Vol. I. House Claims
Committee report adversely to
claim for repairs of fortifications
of St. Augustine during the
Seminole war. [Washington, 1837]
1 p. DNA.   47696

---- Report on Petition of Conrad Widrig. House Rev. Pensions
Com. Dec. 22, 1837. Reports
of Committees, No. 169, 25th
Cong., 2d sess., Vol. I. Recommends allowance of pension; Bill
reported. [Washington, 1837]
2 p. DNA.   47697

---- Report on Petition of Converse & Rees. House Claims Committee. Feb. 22, 1837. Reports of Committees, No. 246, 24th Cong., 2d sess., Vol. II. Recommends allowance of interest on amount of drafts received in payment of mail transportation; Bill reported. [Washington, 1837] 2 p. DNA.
47698

---- Report on Petition of Curtis Grubb. House Claims Committee. Dec. 14, 1837. Reports of Committees, No. 42, 25th Cong., 2d sess., Vol. I. Recommends claim for damages sustained by having property used or consumed by United States troops in 1814; Bill reported. [Washington, 1837] 2 p. DNA.   47699

---- Report on Petition of D. W. Haley. House Claims Committee. Dec. 14, 1837. Reports of Committees, No. 72, 25th Cong., 2d sess., Vol. I. Recommends allowance of claim for horse lost in the United States service in 1814; Bill reported. [Washington, 1837] 2 p. DNA.   47700

---- Report on Petition of D. W. Haley. House Claims Committee. Feb. 14, 1837. Reports of Committees, No. 210, 24th Cong., 2d sess., Vol. I. Recommends that petitioner be allowed reward for apprehending slaves implicated in robbing the mails; Bill reported. [Washington, 1837] 2 p. DNA.   47701

---- Report on Petition of Daniel B. Perkins. House Invalid Pensions Com. Jan. 13, 1837. Reports of Committees, No. 89, 24th Cong., 2d sess., Vol. I. Bill reported for relief of petitioner on account of injuries received while saving public property from fire. [Washington, 1837] 1 p. DNA.   47702

---- Report on Petition of Daniel Davis. House Claims Committee. Dec. 14, 1837. Reports of Committees, No. 15, 25th Cong., 2d sess., Vol. I. Recommends claim for horse lost in the United States service in 1814; Bill reported. [Washington, 1837] 2 p. DNA.   47703

---- Report on Petition of Daniel Davis. House Revolutionary Pensions Com. Jan. 4, 1837. Reports of Committees, No. 61, 24th Cong., 2d sess., Vol. I. Recommends allowance of pension; Bill reported. [Washington, 1837] 2 p. DNA.   47704

---- Report on Petition of Daniel Davis. House Rev. Pensions Committee. Dec. 22, 1837. Reports of Committees, No. 157, 25th Cong., 2d sess., Vol. I. Recommends allowance of pension; Bill reported. [Washington, 1837] 2 p. DNA.   47705

---- Report on Petition of Daniel Rardon. House Invalid Pensions Com. Feb. 28, 1837. Reports of Committees, No. 292, 24th Cong., 2d sess., Vol. II. Recommends increase of pension; Bill reported. [Washington, 1837] 1 p. DNA.   47706

---- Report on Petition of Daniel Sellers. House Rev. Pensions Com. Jan. 28, 1837. Reports of Committees, No. 167, 24th Cong., 2d sess., Vol. I. Adverse to allowance of pension. [Washington, 1837] 2 p. DNA.
47707

---- Report on Petition of Daniel Steenrod. Claims Committee.

Dec. 27, 1837. Senate Docs.,
No. 48, 25th Cong., 2d sess.,
Vol. I. Recommends additional payment on contract for
work on Cumberland road; Bill
reported. [Washington, 1837]
3 p. DNA.   47708

---- Report on Petition of
Daniel W. Going. House In-
valid Pensions Com. Feb. 22,
1837. Reports of Committees,
No. 262, 24th Cong., 2d sess.,
Vol. II. Recommends allowance
of pension; Bill reported.
[Washington, 1837] 1 p. DNA.
                             47709
---- Report on Petition of
Daniel Rardon. House Invalid
Pensions Com. Dec. 22, 1837.
Reports of Committees, No. 186,
25th Cong., 2d sess., Vol. I.
Recommends allowance of addi-
tional pension; Bill reported.
[Washington, 1837] 1 p. DNA.
                             47710
---- Report on Petition of
Daniel Steinrod. Roads and
Canals Committee. Jan. 12,
1837. Senate Docs., No. 61,
24th Cong., 2d sess., Vol. II.
Recommends allowance of claim
for additional payment on con-
tract for work on Cumberland
road; Bill reported. [Washing-
ton, 1837] 2 p. DNA.   47711

---- Report on Petition of David
Goorley. House Naval Committee. Feb. 25, 1837. Reports
of Committees, No. 289, 24th
Cong., 2d sess., Vol. II. Adverse to claim of petitioner for
reimbursement of his expenses
to the United States after his
discharge from the United
States naval service at Leghorn.
[Washington, 1837] 1 p. DNA.
                             47712
---- Report on Petition of David
Stone. Claims Committee. Jan.

17, 1837. Senate Docs., No.
76, 24th Cong., 2d sess., Vol.
II. Recommends payment of claim
as assignee of certain persons
who served on the frontiers
during the war of 1812, and of
others whose property was
destroyed during that war; Bill
reported. [Washington, 1837]
1 p. DNA.   47713

---- Report on Petition of David
T. Patterson. House Claims Committee. Dec. 14, 1837. Reports
of Committees, No. 7, 25th Cong.,
2d sess., Vol. I. Recommends
claim for expenses incurred in
visiting different courts in countries bordering on the Mediter-
ranean as commander of the naval
forces of the United States; Bill
reported. [Washington, 1837]
6 p. DNA.   47714

---- Report on Petition of David
Wilson. House Invalid Pensions
Com. Dec. 28, 1837. Reports of
Committees, No. 226, 25th Cong.,
2d sess., Vol. I. Recommends
allowance of pension; Bill reported. [Washington, 1837] 2
p. DNA.   47715

---- Report on Petition of De
Forrest Marice. Finance Committee. Jan. 19, 1837. Senate
Docs., No. 85, 24th Cong., 2d
sess., Vol. II. Recommends
remission of duties paid on certain woolen goods imported; Bill
reported. [Washington, 1837] 4
p. DNA.   47716

---- Report on Petition of Delia
Tudor. House Foreign Affairs
Committee. Feb. 8, 1837. Reports of Committees, No. 200,
24th Cong., 2d sess., Vol. I.
Recommends allowance of claim
for compensation for services of
her late son, William Tudor, jr.,

as diplomatic agent at Lima, Peru; Bill reported. [Washington, 1837] 3 p. DNA. 47717

---- Report on Petition of Dr. David H. Maxwell. House Claims Committee. Dec. 14, 1837. Reports of Committees, No. 55, 25th Cong., 2d sess., Vol. I. Recommends that claim for medical attendance and medicines furnished United States troops in 1813 be referred to the accounting officers of the Treasury; Bill reported. [Washington, 1837] 2 p. DNA. 47718

---- Report on Petition of Duncan & Taylor. House Claims Committee. Feb. 14, 1837. Reports of Committees, No. 217, 24th Cong., 2d sess., Vol. I. Adverse to payment for goods seized in Indian country while engaged in Indian trade without a license. [Washington, 1837] 2 p. DNA. 47719

---- Report on Petition of E. Eastman. House Invalid Pensions Committee. Jan. 7, 1837. Reports of Committees, No. 70, 24th Cong., 2d sess., Vol. I. Recommends that petitioner be paid pension as guardian of his father, Eli Eastman; Bill reported. [Washington, 1837] 1 p. DNA. 47720

---- Report on Petition of Ebenezer A. Lester. House Claims Committee. Dec. 14, 1837. Reports of Committees, No. 8, 25th Cong., 2d sess., Vol. I. Recommends claim for storage of engine built for the United States at Charlestown navy-yard; Recommends that claim for interest due on sum for building engine be rejected. [Washington, 1837] 2 p. DNA. 47721

---- Report on Petition of Edward Burgess. House Claims Committee. DEc. 14, 1837. Reports of Committees, No. 6, 25th Cong., 2d sess., Vol. I. Recommends claim for compensation for enlisting men during the war; Bill reported. [Washington, 1837] 2 p. DNA. 47722

---- Report on Petition of Edward Kearney. House Rev. Pensions Committee. Feb. 24, 1837. Reports of Committees, No. 284, 24th Cong., 2d sess., Vol. II. Adverse to restoration to pensionlist. [Washington, 1837] 1 p. DNA. 47723

---- Report on Petition of Edward L. Young. House Naval Committee. Jan. 14, 1837. Reports of Committees, No. 108, 24th Cong., 2d sess., Vol. I. Adverse to allowance of pension for services in the Navy. [Washington, 1837] 1 p. DNA. 47724

---- Report on Petition of Eleanor Gardiner. House Claims Committee. Jan. 4, 1837. Reports of Committees, No. 63, 24th Cong., 2d sess., Vol. I. Adverse to payment for property destroyed by the British in the war of 1812. [Washington, 1837] 1 p. DNA. 47725

---- Report on Petition of Elias Johns. House Claims Committee. Dec. 14, 1837. Reports of Committees, No. 27, 25th Cong., 2d sess., Vol. I. Recommends claim for horse lost in the United States service in 1814; Bill reported. [Washington, 1837] 1 p. DNA. 47726

---- Report on Petition of Elias Wallen. House Claims Committee. March 2, 1837. Reports of Com-

mittees, No. 314, 24th Cong.,
2d sess., Vol. II. Adverse to
allowance of claim; Nature not
stated; Refers to report made
at last session. [Washington,
1837] 1 p. DNA.   47727

---- Report on Petition of Elijah Barden. House Rev. Pensions Committee. Jan. 24,
1837. Reports of Committees,
No. 146, 24th Cong., 2d sess.,
Vol. I. Recommends allowance
of arrears of pension; Bill reported. [Washington, 1837] 1
p. DNA.   47728

---- Report on Petition of
Elisha Eastman. House Rev.
Pensions Com. Jan. 23, 1837.
Reports of Committees, No.
138, 24th Cong., 2d sess.,
Vol. II. Recommends allowance
of pension to petitioner as
guardian of Eli Eastman; Bill
reported. [Washington, 1837]
1 p. DNA.   47729

---- Report on Petition of
Elisha Ely. House Revolutionary Claims Com. Jan. 28, 1837.
Reports of Committees, No. 166,
24th Cong., 2d sess., Vol. I.
Adverse to claim for commutation of pay. [Washington, 1837]
2 p. DNA.   47730

---- Report on Petition of
Elisha Smith. House Post-Office
Committee. Feb. 16, 1837.
Reports of Committees, No. 231,
24th Cong., 2d sess., Vol. II.
Adverse to additional payment
on contract for transportation
of mail. [Washington, 1837]
2 p. DNA.   47731

---- Report on Petition of
Elizabeth Burmer. House Rev.
Claims Committee. Feb. 14,
1837. Reports of Committees,

No. 209, 24th Cong., 2d sess.,
Vol. I. Adverse to payment
for blankets furnished by her
late husband, Jacob Burmer,
to his company of soldiers.
[Washington, 1837] 1 p. DNA.
                           47732
---- Report on Petition of Elizabeth Case. House Rev. Pensions
Committee. Feb. 14, 1837. Reports of Committees, No. 222,
24th Cong., 2d sess., Vol. I.
Recommends allowance of pension
to petitioner as widow of James
Case; Bill reported. [Washing-
ton, 1837] 1 p. DNA.   47733

---- Report on Petition of Elizabeth Case. House Rev. Pensions
Committee. Dec. 22, 1837. Reports of Committees, No. 177,
25th Cong., 2d sess., Vol. I.
Recommends allowance of pension
to widow of James Case; Bill
reported. [Washington, 1837] 1
p. DNA.   47734

---- Report on Petition of Elizabeth Hunt. House Rev. Claims
Committee. Dec. 22, 1837. Reports of Committees, No. 194,
25th Cong., 2d sess., Vol. I.
Recommends commutation pay to
heir of William Hendricks; Bill
reported. [Washington, 1837]
1 p. DNA.   47735

---- Report on Petition of Elizabeth Newman. Judiciary Committee. Feb. 23, 1837. Senate
Docs., No. 43, 24th Cong., 2d
sess., Vol. I. Recommends that
petitioner be released from payment of interest on amount found
due in the accounts of her late
husband, Francis Newman, as
collector of the revenue. [Wash-
ington, 1837] 2 p. DNA.
                           47736
---- Report on Petition of Elizabeth Newman. Judiciary Commit-

tee. Feb. 23, 1837. Senate Docs., No. 200, 24th Cong., 2d sess., Vol. II. Recommends that petitioner, executrix of Francis Newman, be released from payment of interest on amount due the United States in the accounts of the latter as collector of taxes; Bill reported. [Washington, 1837] 2 p. DNA. 47737

---- Report on Petition of Elizabeth W. Bacot. House Claims Committee. Dec. 14, 1837. Reports of Committees, No. 25, 25th Cong., 2d sess., Vol. I. Recommends claim for expenses incurred by Thomas W. Bacot in repairing post-office at Charleston, South Carolina; Bill reported. [Washington, 1837] 3 p. DNA. 47738

---- Report on Petition of Emanuel Srofe. House Invalid Pensions Com. Dec. 28, 1837. Reports of Committees, No. 220, 25th Cong., 2d sess., Vol. I. Recommends allowance of pension; Bill reported. [Washington, 1837] 1 p. DNA. 47739

---- Report on Petition of Empson Hamilton. House Naval Committee. Jan. 24, 1837. Reports of Committees, No. 149, 24th Cong., 2d sess., Vol. I. Recommends allowance of pension; Bill reported. [Washington, 1837] 1 p. DNA. 47740

---- Report on Petition of Executor of David Gelston. House Claims Com. Dec. 14, 1837. Reports of Committees, No. 38, 25th Cong., 2d sess., Vol. I. Recommends partial allowance of claim for expenses incurred and disbursements made by David Gelston, collector

of the port of New York, from 1807 to 1820; Bill reported. [Washington, 1837] 9 p. DNA. 47741

---- Report on Petition of Executor of E. Wood. House Rev. Claims Com. Jan. 14, 1837. Reports of Committees, No. 97, 24th Cong., 2d sess., Vol. I. Adverse to allowance of commutation pay and bounty land. [Washington, 1837] 4 p. DNA. 47742

---- Report on Petition of Executor of J. H. Peterson. House Commerce Com. Dec. 22, 1837. Reports of Committees, No. 90, 25th Cong., 2d sess., Vol. I. Recommends allowance of claim for services as surveyor at Petersburg, Virginia; Bill reported. [Washington, 1837] 23 p. DNA. 47743

---- Report on Petition of Executor of John Addoms. House Claims Com. Dec. 14, 1837. Reports of Committees, No. 24, 25th Cong., 2d sess., Vol. I. Recommends claim for damages done to premises in Plattsburg by United States troops in 1814; Bill reported. [Washington, 1837] 3 p. DNA. 47744

---- Report on Petition of Executor of T. Matthews. Rev. Claims Com. Jan. 2, 1837. Senate Docs., No. 46, 24th Cong., 2d sess., Vol. I. Adverse to allowance of claim for commutation pay. [Washington, 1837] 3 p. DNA. 47745

---- Report on Petition of Executor of T. Woodson. House Rev. Claims Com. Dec. 22, 1837. Reports of Committees, No. 136, 25th Cong., 2d sess., Vol. I. Recommends allowance of balance due Tarlton Woodson on account rendered by the Commissioner of Army Accounts, February 10, 1791; Bill reported. [Washington, 1837] 1 p. DNA. 47746

---- Report on Petition of Executors of James Roddy. House Claims Com. Feb. 4, 1837. Reports of Committees, No. 187, 24th Cong., 2d sess., Vol. I. Adverse to release as surety on the bond of Samuel Champlain, late paymaster in the Army. [Washington, 1837] 4 p. DNA. 47747

---- Report on Petition of Farron & Harris. House Claims Committee. Dec. 14, 1837. Reports of Committees, No. 66, 25th Cong., 2d sess., Vol. I. Recommends allowance of claim for additional payment for work done on fortifications at Dauphin Island; Bill reported. [Washington, 1837] 2 p. DNA. 47748

---- Report on Petition of Fielding Pratt. House Invalid Pensions Com. Jan. 5, 1837. Reports of Committees, No. 68, 24th Cong., 2d sess., Vol. I. Recommends allowance of pension; Bill reported. [Washington, 1837] 1 p. DNA. 47749

---- Report on Petition of Fielding Pratt. House Invalid Pensions Com. Dec. 22, 1837. Reports of Committees, No. 182, 25th Cong., 2d sess., Vol. I. Recommends allowance of pension; Bill reported. [Washington, 1837] 1 p. DNA. 47750

---- Report on Petition of Frances Gardner. House Claims Committee. Dec. 14, 1837. Reports of Committees, No. 35, 25th Cong., 2d sess., Vol. I. Recommends claim for property

destroyed in the military service of the United States; Bill reported. [Washington, 1837] 2 p. DNA. 47751

---- Report on Petition of Francis Allyn. Claims Committee. Jan. 13, 1837. Senate Docs., No. 64, 24th Cong., 2d sess., Vol. II. Recommends partial allowance of claim for payment for use of his vessel in the transportation to this country of General La Fayette. [Washington, 1837] 3 p. DNA. 47752

---- Report on Petition of Frederick Frey & Co. House Commerce Com. Jan. 26, 1837. Reports of Committees, No. 157, 24th Cong., 2d sess., Vol. I. Recommends the refundment of certain duties paid on playing-cards; Bill reported. [Washington, 1837] 2 p. DNA. 47753

---- Report on Petition of Frederick Hill. House Rev. Pensions Committee. Feb. 14, 1837. Reports of Committees, No. 223, 24th Cong., 2d sess., Vol. I. Recommends allowance of pension; Bill reported. [Washington, 1837] 1 p. DNA. 47754

---- Report on Petition of Frederick Hill. House Rev. Pensions Committee. Dec. 22, 1837. Reports of Committees, No. 168, 25th Cong., 2d sess., Vol. I. Recommends allowance of pension; Bill reported. [Washington, 1837] 1 p. DNA. 47755

---- Report on Petition of Frederick Wilheid. House Rev. Pensions Com. Dec. 22, 1837. Reports of Committees, No. 176, 25th Cong., 2d sess., Vol. I. Recommends restoration of petitioner's name to the pensionroll; Bill reported. [Washington, 1837] 2 p. DNA.   47756

---- Report on Petition of Freeman Brady. House Claims Committee. Jan. 18, 1837. Reports of Committees, No. 122, 24th Cong., 2d sess., Vol. I. Recommends allowance of claim for amount of payment withheld on contract for work on Cumberland road; Bill reported. [Washington, 1837] 2 p. DNA.   47757

---- Report on Petition of Freeman Brady. House Claims Committee. Dec. 14, 1837. Reports of Committees, No. 62, 25th Cong., 2d sess., Vol. I. Recommends claim for work on Cumberland road; Bill reported. [Washington, 1837] 2 p. DNA.   47758

---- Report on Petition of G. T. Rhodes. House Claims Committee. Jan. 10, 1837. Reports of Committees, No. 84, 24th Cong., 2d sess., Vol. I. Adverse to claim for extra compensation for services in the Engineer Department. [Washington, 1837] 5 p. DNA.   47759

---- Report on Petition of Gad Humphreys. Claims Committee. Feb. 7, 1837. Senate Docs., No. 162, 24th Cong., 2d sess., Vol. II. Recommends payment for property destroyed during the Seminole war. [Washington, 1837] 1 p. DNA.   47760

---- Report on Petition of George Barkley and John Weaver. Dec. 22, 1837. Reports of Committees, No. 190, 25th Cong., 2d sess., Vol. I. House Invalid Pensions Committee recommends allowance of pensions; Bills reported. [Washington, 1837] DNA.   47761

---- Report on Petition of George C. Johnston. Indian Committee. Senate Docs., No. 120, 24th Cong., 2d sess., Vol. II. Recommends reference of claim against the Shawnee Indians to the Secretary of War; Bill reported. [Washington, 1837] 1 p. DNA.   47762

---- Report on Petition of George C. Willard. House Public Lands Com. Dec. 28, 1837. Reports of Committees, No. 203, 25th Cong., 2d sess., Vol. I. Recommends the issue of land warrant; Bill reported. [Washington, 1837] 1 p. DNA.   47763

---- Report on Petition of George Dyer, jr. House Commerce Committee. Jan. 23, 1837. Reports of Committees, No. 136, 24th Cong., 2d sess., Vol. I. Recommends allowance of fishing bounty; Bill reported. [Washington, 1837] 1 p. DNA.   47764

---- Report on Petition of George Dyer, jr. House Commerce Committee. Dec. 22, 1837. Reports of Committees, No. 84, 25th Cong., 2d sess., Vol. I. Recommends allowance of fishing bounty; Bill reported. [Washington, 1837] 1 p. DNA.   47765

---- Report on Petition of George Geortner. House Rev. Claims Com. Jan. 26, 1837. Reports of Committees, No. 174, 24th Cong., 2d sess., Vol. I. Adverse to allowance of claim on account of services in the Army of his late father, Peter Geortner. [Washington, 1837] 1 p. DNA.   47766

---- Report on Petition of George Innes. House Commerce Committee. Feb. 22, 1837. Reports of Committees, No. 261, 24th Cong., 2d sess., Vol. II. Recommends allowance of compensation for services as deputy inspector of revenue at the port of New York; Bill reported. [Washington, 1837] 6 p. DNA.   47767

---- Report on Petition of George J. Knight. Claims Committee. Jan. 13, 1837. Senate Docs., No. 65, 24th Cong., 2d sess., Vol. II. Recommends payment for vessel impressed into the United States service and destroyed by the British in the war of 1812; Bill reported. [Washington, 1837] 3 p. DNA.   47768

---- Report on Petition of George McFadden. House Invalid Pensions Com. Dec. 28, 1837. Reports of Committees, No. 224, 25th Cong., 2d sess., Vol. I. Recommends allowance of arrears of pension; Bill reported. [Washington, 1837] 1 p. DNA.   47769

---- Report on Petition of George W. Brand. Indian Committee. Jan. 3, 1837. Senate Docs., No. 47, 24th Cong., 2d sess., Vol. I. Recommends remuneration for occupancy of his property by United States Indian agent; Bill reported. [Washington, 1837] 2 p. DNA.   47770

---- Report on Petition of George Wood. House Claims Committee. Feb. 22, 1837. Reports of Committees, No. 247, 24th Cong., 2d sess., Vol. II. Recommends reference of claim on account of military services in the war of 1812 to the Third Auditor. [Washington, 1837] 2 p. DNA.   47771

---- Report on Petition of Gersham Wakeman. Pensions Committee. Feb. 16, 1837. Senate Docs., No. 183, 24th Cong., 2d sess., Vol. II. Adverse to allowance of pension. [Washington, 1837] 1 p. DNA.   47772

---- Report on Petition of Gideon Sheldon. House Invalid Pensions Com. Feb. 14, 1837. Reports of Committees, No. 207, 24th Cong., 2d sess., Vol. I. Adverse to allowance of pension. [Washington, 1837] 1 p. DNA.   47773

---- Report on Petition of Gilbert S. Fish. House Invalid Pensions Com. Dec. 28, 1837. Reports of Committees, No. 221, 25th Cong., 2d sess., Vol. I. Recommends allowance of pension; Bill reported. [Washington, 1837] 1 p. DNA.   47774

---- Report on Petition of Gurdon Robbins. House Claims Committee. Jan. 28, 1837. Reports of Committees, No. 169, 24th Cong., 2d sess., Vol. I. Adverse to payment for destruction of vessel by the British in the war of 1812. [Washington, 1837] 2 p. DNA.   47775

---- Report on Petition of Hampton Lovegrove. House Rev. Pensions Com. Jan. 28, 1837. Reports of Committees, No. 168, 24th Cong., 2d sess., Vol. I. Adverse to allowance of pension. [Washington, 1837] 1 p. DNA.   47776

---- Report on Petition of Hannah Budlong. House Claims Committee. Dec. 14, 1837. Reports of Committees, No. 45, 25th Cong., 2d sess., Vol. I. Recommends half-pay pension for services of Elias Hyde in the volun-

teer service of the United States; Bill reported. [Washington, 1837] 2 p. DNA.
47777

---- Report on Petition of Hannah Eldridge. House Rev. Pensions Com. Jan. 18, 1837. Reports of Committees, No. 124, 24th Cong., 2d sess., Vol. I. Recommends allowance of pension to petitioner, widow of Daniel Littlefield; Bill reported. [Washington, 1837] 1 p. DNA.
47778

---- Report on Petition of Hannah Gordon. House Rev. Pensions Com. Jan. 14, 1837. Reports of Committees, No. 106, 24th Cong., 2d sess., Vol. I. Adverse to allowance of pension as widow of William Gordon. [Washington, 1837] 1 p. DNA.
47779

---- Report on Petition of Heirs of C. Sampson. House Rev. Claims Com. Dec. 22, 1837. Reports of Committees, No. 134, 25th Cong., 2d sess., Vol. I. Recommends the issue of duplicate land warrant; Bill reported. [Washington, 1837] 1 p. DNA.   47780

---- Report on Petition of Heirs of C. Snead. House Rev. Claims Com. Dec. 22, 1837. Reports of Committees, No. 111, 25th Cong., 2d sess., Vol. I. Recommends allowance of commutation pay; Bill reported. [Washington, 1837] 1 p. DNA.
47781

---- Report on Petition of Heirs of C. Taylor. House Rev. Claims Com. Dec. 22, 1837. Reports of Committees, No. 137, 25th Cong., 2d sess., Vol. I. Recommends allowance of commutation pay; Bill reported. [Washington, 1837] 1 p. DNA.
47782

---- Report on Petition of Heirs of David Caldwell. House Claims Com. Dec. 14, 1837. Reports of Committees, No. 12, 25th Cong., 2d sess., Vol. I. Recommends claim for fees due David Caldwell as clerk of the United States court for the eastern district of Pennsylvania; Bill reported. [Washington, 1837] 47 p. DNA.   47783

---- Report on Petition of Heirs of F. Jarvis. House Priv. Land Claims Com. Dec. 22, 1837. Reports of Committees, No. 145, 25th Cong., 2d sess., Vol. I. Recommends exchange of land warrant; Bill reported. [Washington, 1837] 1 p. DNA.
47784

---- Report on Petition of Heirs of Francis Taylor. House Rev. Claims Com. Dec. 22, 1837. Reports of Committees, No. 127, 25th Cong., 2d sess., Vol. I. Recommends allowance of commutation pay; Bill reported. [Washington, 1837] 1 p. DNA.
47785

---- Report on Petition of Heirs of Frederick Reze. House Commerce Committee. Dec. 22, 1837. Reports of Committees, No. 79, 25th Cong., 2d sess., Vol. I. Recommends remission of duties paid on articles imported for churches; Bill reported. [Washington, 1837] 3 p. DNA.
47786

---- Report on Petition of Heirs of G. Gibson. House Rev. Claims Com. Dec. 22, 1837. Reports of Committees, No. 113, 25th Cong., 2d sess., Vol. I. Recommends allowance of commutation pay; Bill reported. [Washington, 1837] 2 p. DNA.
47787

---- Report on Petition of Heirs of Henry Morfit. Rev. Claims

Committee. Jan. 23, 1837.
Senate Docs., No. 96, 24th
Cong., 2d sess., Vol. II.
Recommends allowance of com-
mutation pay; Bill reported.
[Washington, 1837] 2 p. DNA.
                                    47788
---- Report on Petition of Heirs
of J. Conway. House Invalid
Pensions Com. Dec. 22, 1837.
Reports of Committees, No.
191, 25th Cong., 2d sess.,
Vol. I. Recommends allowance
of pension; Bill reported.
[Washington, 1837] 1 p. DNA.
                                    47789
---- Report on Petition of Heirs
of J. De Treville. House Rev.
Claims Com. Dec. 22, 1837.
Reports of Committees, No. 133,
25th Cong., 2d sess., Vol. I.
Recommends allowance of com-
mutation pay; Bill reported.
[Washington, 1837] 2 p. DNA.
                                    47790
---- Report on Petition of Heirs
of J. Hayden. House Rev.
Claims Com. Jan. 17, 1837.
Reports of Committees, No. 119,
24th Cong., 2d sess., Vol. I.
Adverse to allowance of seven
years' half-pay. [Washington,
1837] 1 p. DNA.   47791

---- Report on Petition of Heirs
of J. Winston. House Rev.
Claims Com. Dec. 22, 1837.
Reports of Committees, No.
195, 25th Cong., 2d sess.,
Vol. I. Recommends allowance
of commutation pay; Bill reported. [Washington, 1837]
2 p. DNA.   47792

---- Report on Petition of Heirs
of Jacob Sammons. House Rev.
Claims Com. Feb. 7, 1837.
Reports of Committees, No. 228,
24th Cong., 2d sess., Vol. I.
Adverse to reimbursement of
advances made to United States

troops by Jacob Sammons during
the Revolutionary War. [Wash-
ington, 1837] 6 p. DNA.
                                    47793
---- Report on Petition of Heirs
of James Broadus. House Rev.
Claims Com. Feb. 22, 1837.
Reports of Committees, No. 276,
24th Cong., 2d sess., Vol. II.
Adverse to claim for Revolutionary services. [Washington, 1837]
1 p. DNA.   47794

---- Report on Petition of Heirs
of James Fay. House Rev. Pensions Com. Jan. 14, 1837. Reports of Committees, No. 103,
24th Cong., 2d sess., Vol. I.
Adverse to allowance of seven
years' half-pay. [Washington,
1837] 1 p. DNA.   47795

---- Report on Petition of Heirs
of James Purvis. House Rev.
Claims Com. March 1, 1837.
Reports of Committees, No.
298, 24th Cong., 2d sess., Vol.
II. Recommends allowance of
commutation pay; Bill reported.
[Washington, 1837] 1 p. DNA.
                                    47796
---- Report on Petition of Heirs
of James Purvis. House Rev.
Claims Com. Dec. 22, 1837.
Reports of Committees, No. 135,
25th Cong., 2d sess., Vol. I.
Recommends allowance of commutation pay; Bill reported. [Wash-
ington, 1837] 1 p. DNA.
                                    47797
---- Report on Petition of Heirs
of James Rumsey. House select
com. March 2, 1837. Reports
of Committees, No. 317, 24th
Cong., 2d sess., Vol. II. Recommends distribution of money and
lands among the heirs of James
Rumsey, claimed to be the original inventor of steam navigation.
[Washington, 1837] 7 p. DNA.
                                    47798

---- Report on Petition of Heirs of John Campbell. Jan. 24, 1837. Reports of Committees, No. 153, 24th Cong., 2d sess., Vol. I. House Private Land Claims Committee recommends issue of patent for land claimed in Michigan; Bill reported. [Washington, 1837] 2 p. DNA.
47799

---- Report on Petition of Heirs of John Chilton. House Rev. Claims Com. Dec. 22, 1837. Reports of Committees, No. 109, 25th Cong., 2d sess., Vol. I. Recommends allowance of commutation pay; Bill reported. [Washington, 1837] 1 p. DNA.
47800

---- Report on Petition of Heirs of John Davis. House Rev. Claims Com. Jan. 6, 1837. Reports of Committees, No. 60, 24th Cong., 2d sess., Vol. I. Adverse to allowance of commutation of pay and bounty land. [Washington, 1837] 1 p. DNA.
47801

---- Report on Petition of Heirs of John Hawkins. Rev. Claims Committee. Jan. 23, 1837. Senate Docs., No. 95, 24th Cong., 2d sess., Vol. II. Adverse to allowance of commutation pay. [Washington, 1837] 1 p. DNA.
47802

---- Report on Petition of Heirs of John Marks. House Rev. Claims Com. Dec. 22, 1837. Reports of Committees, No. 132, 25th Cong., 2d sess., Vol. I. Recommends allowance of commutation pay; Bill reported. [Washington, 1837] 2 p. DNA.
47803

---- Report on Petition of Heirs of John Stokes. House Rev. Claims Com. Jan. 28, 1837.

Reports of Committees, No. 165, 14th Cong., 2d sess., Vol. I. Adverse to claim for commutation pay. [Washington, 1837] 2 p. DNA.
47804

---- Report on Petition of Heirs of John Waters. House Rev. Claims Com. Feb. 14, 1837. Reports of Committees, No. 203, 24th Cong., 2d sess., Vol. I. Adverse to issue of land scrip to petitioners in lieu of Virginia military land warrants. [Washington, 1837] 1 p. DNA.
47805

---- Report on Petition of Heirs of L. Allen. House Rev. Claims Com. Dec. 22, 1837. Reports of Committees, No. 131, 25th Cong., 2d sess., Vol. I. Recommends allowance of commutation pay; Bill reported. [Washington, 1837] 2 p. DNA. 47806

---- Report on Petition of Heirs of Larkin Smith. House Rev. Claims Com. Feb. 24, 1837. Reports of Committees, No. 285, 24th Cong., 2d sess., Vol. II. Adverse to allowance of commutation of half-pay. [Washington, 1837] 3 p. DNA. 47807

---- Report on Petition of Heirs of Lathrop Allen. House Rev. Claims Com. Jan. 13, 1837. Reports of Committees, No. 91, 24th Cong., 2d sess., Vol. I. Recommends allowance of commutation of five years' full pay; Bill reported. [Washington, 1837] 2 p. DNA. 47808

---- Report on Petition of Heirs of Levi Todd. House Rev. Claims Com. Feb. 14, 1837. Reports of Committees, No. 202, 24th Cong., 2d sess., Vol. I. Adverse to allowance of claim for half-pay. [Washington, 1837] 2 p. DNA. 47809

---- Report on Petition of Heirs
of Miles King. House Rev.
Claims Com. Jan. 14, 1837.
Reports of Committees, No. 98,
24th Cong., 2d sess., Vol. I.
Adverse to allowance of commutation pay. [Washington,
1837] 1 p. DNA.   47810

---- Report on Petition of Heirs
of Oliver Parrish. House Rev.
Pensions Com. Jan. 3, 1837.
Reports of Committees, No. 55,
24th Cong., 2d sess., Vol. I.
Recommends allowance of pension; Bill reported. [Washing-
ton, 1837] 2 p. DNA.   47811

---- Report on Petition of Heirs
of P. Helphenson. House Rev.
Claims Com. Dec. 22, 1837.
Reports of Committees, No.
193, 25th Cong., 2d sess., Vol.
I. Recommends allowance of
commutation pay; Bill reported.
[Washington, 1837] 2 p. DNA.
                          47812
---- Report on Petition of Heirs
of Philip Johnston. Rev.
Claims Committee. Jan. 23,
1837. Senate Docs., No. 94,
24th Cong., 2d sess., Vol. II.
Adverse to claim for commutation
of half-pay. [Washington, 1837]
1 p. DNA.   47813

---- Report on Petition of Heirs
of R. Campbell. House Rev.
Claims Com. Dec. 22, 1837.
Reports of Committees, No. 108,
25th Cong., 2d sess., Vol. I.
Recommends allowance of com-
mutation pay; Bill reported.
[Washington, 1837] 1 p. DNA.
                          47814
---- Report on Petition of Heirs
of R. Chapman. House Rev.
Claims Com. Jan. 5, 1837.
Reports of Committees, No. 67,
24th Cong., 2d sess., Vol. I.
Adverse to allowance of claim;

Nature not stated. [Washing-
ton, 1837] 1 p. DNA.   47815

---- Report on Petition of Heirs
of R. Farmer. Dec. 22, 1837.
Reports of Committees, No. 139,
25th Cong., 2d sess., Vol. I.
House Private Land Claims Committee recommends confirmation
of land claim in Alabama; Bill
reported. [Washington, 1837]
3 p. DNA.   47816

---- Report on Petition of Heirs
of Reuben Butler. House Rev.
Claims Com. Jan. 14, 1837.
Reports of Committees, No. 101,
24th Cong., 2d sess., Vol. I.
Adverse to allowance of commutation pay. [Washington, 1837]
2 p. DNA.   47817

---- Report on Petition of Heirs
of Robert Fulton. House Claims
Com. March 1, 1837. Reports
of Committees, No. 300, 24th
Cong., 2d sess., Vol. II.
Recommends allowance of claim
of petitioners for money expended by Robert Fulton in torpedo experiments, for the use of
his patent right for constructing
steam-frigates, for use of steam-
boat Vesuvius, and for personal
services; Bill reported. [Wash-
ington, 1837] 5 p. DNA.
                          47818
---- Report on Petition of Heirs
of Robert Fulton. House Claims
Committee. Dec. 14, 1837. Reports of Committees, No. 68,
25th Cong., 2d sess., Vol. I.
Recommends compensation to
petitioners for money expended
by Robert Fulton in torpedo experiments, for use of his patent
right for constructing steam
frigates, for use of steamboat
Vesuvius, and for personal services; Bill reported. [Washing-
ton, 1837] 5 p. DNA.   47819

---- Report on Petition of Heirs of Sawney York. House Rev. Pensions Com. Jan. 4, 1837. Reports of Committees, No. 62, 24th Cong., 2d sess., Vol. I. Recommends allowance of arrears of pension; Bill reported. [Washington, 1837] 1 p. DNA.
47820

---- Report on Petition of Heirs of Sawney York. House Rev. Pensions Com. Dec. 22, 1837. Reports of Committees, No. 173, 25th Cong., 2d sess., Vol. I. Recommends allowance of pension; Bill reported. [Washington, 1837] 1 p. DNA.   47821

---- Report on Petition of Heirs of T. Feely. House Rev. Claims Com. Dec. 22, 1837. Reports of Committees, No. 116, 25th Cong., 2d sess., Vol. I. Recommends allowance of commutation pay; Bill reported. [Washington, 1837] 1 p. DNA.   47822

---- Report on Petition of Heirs of T. Houghton. House Rev. Claims Com. Jan. 26, 1837. Reports of Committees, No. 159, 24th Cong., 2d sess., Vol. I. Adverse to claim for bounty land. [Washington, 1837] 1 p. DNA.   47823

---- Report on Petition of Heirs of T. Knowlton. House Rev. Claims Com. Dec. 22, 1837. Reports of Committees, No. 130, 25th Cong., 2d sess., Vol. I. Recommends allowance of commutation pay; Bill reported. [Washington, 1837] 1 p. DNA.   47824

---- Report on Petition of Heirs of W. B. Bunting. House Rev. Claims Com. Dec. 22, 1837. Reports of Committees, No. 115, 25th Cong., 2d sess., Vol. I.

Recommends allowance of commutation pay; Bill reported. [Washington, 1837] 2 p. DNA.
47825

---- Report on Petition of Heirs of W. Bailey. Revolutionary Claims Com. Jan. 2, 1837. Senate Docs., No. 44, 24th Cong., 2d sess., Vol. I. Adverse to allowance of claim for commutation pay. [Washington, 1837] 1 p. DNA.   47826

---- Report on Petition of Heirs of W. H. Smith. House Rev. Claims Com. Dec. 22, 1837. Reports of Committees, No. 112, 25th Cong., 2d sess., Vol. I. Recommends allowance of commutation pay; Bill reported. [Washington, 1837] 1 p. DNA.
47827

---- Report on Petition of Heirs of W. Johonnot. House Rev. Claims Com. Dec. 22, 1837. Reports of Committees, No. 117, 25th Cong., 2d sess., Vol. I. Recommends allowance of commutation pay; Bill reported. [Washington, 1837] 2 p. DNA.
47828

---- Report on Petition of Heirs of W. Noyes. House Rev. Claims Com. Dec. 22, 1837. Reports of Committees, No. 192, 25th Cong., 2d sess., Vol. I. Recommends allowance of commutation pay; Bill reported. [Washington, 1837] 1 p. DNA.
47829

---- Report on Petition of Heirs of W. Reddick. House Rev. Claims Com. Dec. 22, 1837. Reports of Committees, No. 119, 25th Cong., 2d sess., Vol. I. Recommends allowance of claim for house burned by the British in 1779; Bill reported. [Washington, 1837] 2 p. DNA.
47830

---- Report on Petition of Heirs

of W. Vawter. House Rev.
Claims Com. Jan. 26, 1837.
Reports of Committees, No.
156, 24th Cong., 2d sess.,
Vol. I. Recommends allowance
of five years' full pay; Bill reported. [Washington, 1837]
5 p. DNA.   47831

---- Report on Petition of Heirs
of W. Vawter. House Claims
Com. Dec. 22, 1837. Reports
of Committees, No. 121, 25th
Cong., 2d sess., Vol. I.
Recommends allowance of commutation pay; Bill reported.
[Washington, 1837] 5 p. DNA.
                             47832
---- Report on Petition of Heirs
of William Camp. House Rev.
Claims Com. Jan. 14, 1837.
Reports of Committees, No.
102, 24th Cong., 2d sess.,
Vol. I. Adverse to allowance
of commutation of five years'
full pay. [Washington, 1837]
2 p. DNA.   47833

---- Report on Petition of Heirs
of William Johnston. House Rev.
Claims Com. Jan. 9, 1837.
Reports of Committees, No.
410, 24th Cong., 2d sess.,
Vol. II. Adverse to allowance
of commutation pay. [Washing-
ton, 1837] 1 p. DNA.   47834

---- Report on Petition of Heirs
of William Jones. Rev. Claims
Committee. Jan. 23, 1837.
Senate Docs., No. 101, 24th
Cong., 2d sess., Vol. II.
Recommends payment for Revo-
lutionary loan-office certificates
destroyed; Bill reported.
[Washington, 1837] 1 p. DNA.
                             47835
---- Report on Petition of Heirs
of William Oliver. House Rev.
Claims Com. Feb. 22, 1837.
Reports of Committees, No.

277, 24th Cong., 2d sess., Vol.
II. Adverse to allowance of
commutation pay. [Washington,
1837] 1 p. DNA; R.   47836

---- Report on Petition of Henry
Beamish. House Commerce Committee. Dec. 22, 1837. Reports of Committees, No. 78,
25th Cong., 2d sess., Vol. I.
Recommends allowance of claim
for property seized by revenue
officers; Bill reported. [Wash-
ington, 1837] 9 p. DNA.
                             47837
---- Report on Petition of Henry
F. Lamb. House Claims Committee. March 2, 1837. Reports
of Committees, No. 305, 24th
Cong., 2d sess., Vol. II. Adverse to allowance of claim; Nature of claim not stated; Refers
to report made at last session.
[Washington, 1837] 1 p. DNA.
                             47838
---- Report on Petition of Henry
J. Pickering. Finance Committee. Feb. 18, 1837. Senate
Docs., No. 191, 24th Cong., 2d
sess., Vol. II. Recommends
refundment of duties paid by
petitioner on certain machines
for the manufacture of paper;
Bill reported. [Washington,
1837] 5 p. DNA.   47839

---- Report on Petition of Henry
J. Pickering. Finance Committee. Dec. 14, 1837. Senate
Docs., No. 18, 25th Cong., 2d
sess., Vol. I. Recommends refundment of duties paid on the
importation of certain machines
for the manufacture of paper;
Bill reported. [Washington,
1837] 10 p. DNA.   47840

---- Report on Petition of Hezekiah L. Thistle. Military Committee. Feb. 25, 1837. Senate
Docs., No. 204, 24th Cong., 2d

sess., Vol. II. Petitioner asks compensation for the use by the United States of an improved saddle invented by petitioner; Committee reports adversely to any present action on the petition. [Washington, 1837] 2 p. DNA. 47841

---- Report on Petition of Hiner Stigermire. House Public Lands Committee. Jan. 3, 1837. Reports of Committees, No. 57, 24th Cong., 2d sess., Vol. I. Recommends exchange of land entered by petitioner; Bill reported. [Washington, 1837] 1 p. DNA. 47842

---- Report on Petition of Hiram Saul. House Invalid Pensions Committee. Feb. 14, 1837. Reports of Committees, No. 205, 24th Cong., 2d sess., Vol. I. Recommends allowance of pension on account of injuries sustained by explosion of gun; Bill reported. [Washington, 1837] 1 p. DNA. 47843

---- Report on Petition of Hugh M. Pettus. House Rev. Claims Committee. Dec. 22, 1837. Reports of Committees, No. 208, 25th Cong., 2d sess., Vol. I. Recommends allowance of commutation pay to the heirs of Samuel O. Pettus; Bill reported. [Washington, 1837] 1 p. DNA. 47844

---- Report on Petition of Hugh McDonald. House Claims Committee. March 3, 1837. Reports of Committees, No. 318, 24th Cong., 2d sess., Vol. II. Recommends payment for horse lost in the United States service in the war of 1812; Bill reported. [Washington, 1837] 1 p. DNA. 47845

---- Report on Petition of Hugh McDonald. House Claims Committee. Dec. 14, 1837. Reports of Committees, No. 71, 25th Cong., 2d sess., Vol. I. Recommends allowance of claim for horse taken for express by the United States; Bill reported. [Washington, 1837] 1 p. DNA. 47846

---- Report on Petition of Huldah Pennyman. House Rev. Pensions Com. Feb. 16, 1837. Reports of Committees, No. 235, 24th Cong., 2d sess., Vol. II. Recommends allowance of pension to petitioner as widow of Bethuel Pennyman; Bill reported. [Washington, 1837] 1 p. DNA. 47847

---- Report on Petition of Huldah Taylor. House Rev. Pensions Committee. Dec. 22, 1837. Reports of Committees, No. 161, 25th Cong., 2d sess., Vol. I. Recommends allowance of pension to widow of Augustin Taylor; Bill reported. [Washington, 1837] 1 p. DNA. 47848

---- Report on Petition of Ichabod Beardsly. House Rev. Pensions Com. Dec. 22, 1837. Reports of Committees, No. 170, 25th Cong., 2d sess., Vol. I. Recommends allowance of pension; Bill reported. [Washington, 1837] 1 p. DNA. 47849

---- Report on Petition of Ichabod Bearsly. House Rev. Pensions Com. Jan. 26, 1837. Reports of Committees, No. 158, 24th Cong., 2d sess., Vol. I. Recommends allowance of pension; Bill reported. [Washington, 1837] 1 p. DNA. 47850

---- Report on Petition of Isaac Austin. House Rev. Pensions Committee. Dec. 22, 1837. Re-

ports of Committees, No. 155,
25th Cong., 2d sess., Vol. I.
Recommends that the name of
petitioner be restored to the
pension-roll; Bill reported.
[Washington, 1837] 2 p. DNA.
47851
---- Report on Petition of Isaac
Barker. House Rev. Pensions
Committee. Dec. 28, 1837. Reports of Committees, No. 213,
25th Cong., 2d sess., Vol. I.
Recommends allowance of pension; Bill reported. [Washing-
ton, 1837] 2 p. DNA.   47852

---- Report on Petition of Isaac
Hilton. House Rev. Pensions
Committee. Jan. 24, 1837.
Reports of Committees, No. 143,
24th Cong., 2d sess., Vol. I.
Recommends allowance of pen-
sion; Bill reported. [Washing-
ton, 1837] 2 p. DNA.   47853

---- Report on Petition of Isaac
Hilton. House Revolutionary
Pensions Com. Dec. 22, 1837.
Reports of Committees, No.
153, 25th Cong., 2d sess.,
Vol. I. Recommends allowance
of pension; Bill reported.
[Washington, 1837] 2 p. DNA.
47854
---- Report on Petition of Isaac
Parker. House Rev. Pensions
Committee. Feb. 22, 1837.
Reports of Committees, No.
264, 24th Cong., 2d sess.,
Vol. II. Recommends allowance
of arrears of pension; Bill re-
ported. [Washington, 1837] 1
p. DNA.   47855

---- Report on Petition of Isaac
Satterly. House Rev. Claims
Committee. Jan. 17, 1837. Reports of Committees, No. 120,
24th Cong., 2d sess., Vol. I.
Adverse to allowance of compensation for secret service during

the Revolutionary War. [Wash-
ington, 1837] 1 p. DNA.
47856
---- Report on Petition of Isaac
Satterly. House Revolutionary
Claims Com. Dec. 28, 1837.
Reports of Committees, No. 21,
25th Cong., 2d sess., Vol. I.
Adverse to claim for services as
a spy during the Revolutionary
War. [Washington, 1837] 1 p.
DNA.   47857

---- Report on Petition of Isaac
Wellborn, jr. House Public
Lands Com. Dec. 22, 1837.
Reports of Committees, No. 91,
25th Cong., 2d sess., Vol. I.
Recommends confirmation of land
title in Alabama; Bill reported.
[Washington, 1837] 2 p. DNA.
47858
---- Report on Petition of Isaiah
Parker. House Invalid Pensions
Com. Dec. 22, 1837. Reports
of Committees, No. 187, 25th
Cong., 2d sess., Vol. I.
Recommends allowance of ar-
rearages of pension; Bill re-
ported. [Washington, 1837]
1 p. DNA.   47859

---- Report on Petition of J. A.
Williams. House Public Lands
Committee. Dec. 22, 1837. Reports of Committees, No. 97,
25th Cong., 2d sess., Vol. I.
Recommends claim for exchange
of land titles in Alabama; Bill
reported. [Washington, 1837]
1 p. DNA.   47860

---- Report on Petition of J. H.
Bradford. House Invalid Pensions
Com. Dec. 28, 1837. Reports
of Committees, No. 227, 25th
Cong., 2d sess., Vol. I. Recom-
mends allowance of pension.
[Washington, 1837] 2 p. DNA.
47861
---- Report on Petition of J. M.

Edwards. House Invalid Pensions Com. Dec. 28, 1837. Reports of Committees, No. 216, 25th Cong., 2d sess., Vol. I. Recommends allowance of pension; Bill reported. [Washington, 1837] 1 p. DNA.
47862

---- Report on Petition of J. P. Converse and H. Rees. House Claims Com. Dec. 14, 1837. Reports of Committees, No. 67, 25th Cong., 2d sess., Vol. I. Recommends claim for amount paid for protest on draft, and report bill; Recommends that claim for interest on drafts be disallowed. [Washington, 1837] 2 p. DNA.
47863

---- Report on Petition of J. P. Hutchinson. House Foreign Affairs Com. Jan. 17, 1837. Reports of Committees, No. 115, 25th Cong., 2d sess., Vol. I. Recommends compensation for services while acting as chargé d'affaires at Lisbon. [Washington, 1837] 1 p. DNA. 47864

---- Report on Petition of J. S. Douglass. House Priv. Land Claims Com. Dec. 22, 1837. Reports of Committees, No. 198, 25th Cong., 2d sess., Vol. I. Adverse to claim of James S. George, Stephen, and Alfred Douglass, Samuel House, William House, and James Tant to land in Louisiana. [Washington, 1837] 2 p. DNA. 47865

---- Report on Petition of J. Wiley and J. Greer. House Public Lands Com. Dec. 28, 1837. Reports of Committees, No. 205, 25th Cong., 2d sess., Vol. I. Recommends allowance for improvements made on public lands; Bill reported. [Washington, 1837] 2 p. DNA. 47866

---- Report on Petition of Jacob Houseman. House Claims Committee. Feb. 14, 1837. Reports of Committees, No. 215, 24th Cong., 2d sess., Vol. I. Adverse to claim for expenses incurred in raising troops for the defence of Indian Key, Florida. [Washington, 1837] 2 p. DNA. 47867

---- Report on Petition of Jacob Schade. House Invalid Pensions Com. Dec. 28, 1837. Reports of Committees, No. 222, 25th Cong., 2d sess., Vol. I. Recommends allowance of pension; Bill reported. [Washington, 1837] 1 p. DNA. 47868

---- Report on Petition of Jacob Shade. House Invalid Pensions Com. March 2, 1837. Reports of Committees, No. 316, 24th Cong., 2d sess., Vol. II. Recommends allowance of pension; Bill reported. [Washington, 1837] 1 p. DNA. 47869

---- Report on Petition of James and William Crooks. House Claims Com. Dec. 14, 1837. Reports of Committees, No. 64, 25th Cong., 2d sess., Vol. I. Recommends claim for damages for seizure of vessel in 1812; Bill reported. [Washington, 1837] 3 p. DNA. 47870

---- Report on Petition of James B. Rice. House Rev. Pensions Committee. Feb. 3, 1837. Reports of Committees, No. 185, 24th Cong., 2d sess., Vol. I. Recommends allowance of pension; Bill reported. [Washington, 1837] 1 p. DNA. 47871

---- Report on Petition of James Baker. House Claims Committee. Dec. 14, 1837. Reports of Com-

mittees, No. 16, 25th Cong.,
2d sess., Vol. I. Recommends
claim for horses and wagon
lost in the United States service in 1832; Bill reported.
[Washington, 1837] 2 p. DNA.
47872
---- Report on Petition of James
Barron. House Naval Affairs
Committee. Dec. 22, 1837.
Reports of Committees, No.
151, 25th Cong., 2d sess.,
Vol. I. Recommends compensation for use of invention called
"a ventilator of ships" upon relinquishment of patent right to
the United States; Bill reported.
[Washington, 1837] 1 p. DNA.
47873
---- Report on Petition of
James Callan. House Claims
Committee. Feb. 22, 1837.
Reports of Committees, No. 244,
24th Cong., 2d sess., Vol. II.
Recommends payment for services as draughtsman in General Land Office; Bill reported.
[Washington, 1837] 2 p. DNA.
47874
---- Report on Petition of James
Callan. House Claims Committee.
Dec. 14, 1837. Reports of Committees, No. 65, 25th Cong.,
2d sess., Vol. I. Recommends
claim for allowances as draughtsman in the Land Office; Bill reported. [Washington, 1837]
2 p. DNA.   47875

---- Report on Petition of James
Day and Mary Perkins. Naval
Committee. Jan. 31, 1837.
Senate Docs., No. 123, 24th
Cong., 2d sess., Vol. II. Adverse to renewal of pensions
formerly paid from privateer
pension fund. [Washington,
1837] 1 p. DNA.   47876

---- Report on Petition of James
Dutton. Public Lands Commit-

tee. Jan. 23, 1837. Senate
Docs., No. 93, 24th Cong., 2d
sess., Vol. II. Recommends exchange of land entered by petitioner; Bill reported. [Wash-
ington, 1837] 1 p. DNA.
47877
---- Report on Petition of James
Hunter. House Invalid Pensions
Com. Feb. 1, 1837. Reports
of Committees, No. 178, 24th
Cong., 2d sess., Vol. I.
Recommends allowance of pension;
Bill reported. [Washington,
1837] 2 p. DNA.   47878

---- Report on Petition of James
J. Coffin. House Rev. Pensions
Committee. Jan. 3, 1837. Re-
ports of Committees, No. 59,
24th Cong., 2d sess., Vol. I.
Recommends allowance of pension;
Bill reported. [Washington,
1837] 2 p. DNA.   47879

---- Report on Petition of James
J. Pattison. House Claims Committee. Dec. 14, 1837. Reports
of Committees, No, 14, 25th
Cong., 2d sess., Vol. I.
Recommends claim for house
burned by the British in 1814;
Bill reported. [Washington,
1837] 3 p. DNA.   47880

---- Report on Petition of James
L. Kenner. House Claims Committee. Dec. 14, 1837. Reports
of Committees, No. 59, 25th
Cong., 2d sess., Vol. I.
Recommends that claim for horse
lost in the Seminole war be referred to the accounting officers
of the Treasury to ascertain
value of horse; Bill reported.
[Washington, 1837] 2 p. DNA.
47881
---- Report on Petition of James
M. Edwards. House Invalid Pensions Com. Jan. 19, 1837. Reports of Committees, No. 129,

24th Cong., 2d sess., Vol. I. Adverse to allowance of pension. [Washington, 1837] 1 p. DNA. 47882

---- Report on Petition of James McMahon. House Claims Committee. Jan. 4, 1837. Reports of Committees, No. 65, 24th Cong., 2d sess., Vol. I. Adverse to allowance of interest on claim for reimbursement of money expended for the United States service while a deputy postmaster. [Washington, 1837] 1 p. DNA. 47883

---- Report on Petition of James McMahon. House Claims Committee. Dec. 14, 1837. Reports of Committees, No. 28, 25th Cong., 2d sess., Vol. I. Recommends claim for services and expense incurred in the arrest of Charles B. Rouse, postmaster at Mayville, New York, for robbing the mail; Bill reported. [Washington, 1837] 3 p. DNA. 47884

---- Report on Petition of James McPherson. House Claims Committee. Feb. 22, 1837. Reports of Committees, No. 267, 24th Cong., 2d sess., Vol. II. Adverse to claim for house-rent, fuel, and subsistence for Indians, and for property taken by United States troops in the war of 1812. [Washington, 1837] 2 p. DNA. 47885

---- Report on Petition of James Moor. House Private Land Claims Com. Dec. 22, 1837. Reports of Committees, No. 138, 25th Cong., 2d sess., Vol. I. Recommends exchange of land certificate; Bill reported. [Washington, 1837] 1 p. DNA. 47886

---- Report on Petition of James Rigden. House Military Affairs Com. Dec. 28, 1837. Reports of Committees, No. 232, 25th Cong., 2d sess., Vol. I. Adverse to allowance for services as spy in 1813. [Washington, 1837] 3 p. DNA. 47887

---- Report on Petition of James Tongue. House Claims Committee. March 3, 1837. Reports of Committees, No. 321, 24th Cong., 2d sess., Vol. II. Adverse to payment for building destroyed during the war of 1812. [Washington, 1837] 2 p. DNA. 47888

---- Report on Petition of James Witherell. House Rev. Claims Com. Dec. 22, 1837. Reports of Committees, No. 124, 25th Cong., 2d sess., Vol. I. Recommends allowance of commutation pay; Bill reported. [Washington, 1837] 1 p. DNA. 47889

---- Report on Petition of James Wyman. House Invalid Pensions Com. Jan. 14, 1837. Reports of Committees, No. 110, 24th Cong., 2d sess., Vol. I. Adverse to allowance of pension. [Washington, 1837] 1 p. DNA. 47890

---- Report on Petition of Jehu Hollingsworth. House Public Lands Com. Dec. 23, 1837. Reports of Committees, No. 93, 25th Cong., 2d sess., Vol. I. Recommends claim for exchange of land titles in Alabama; Bill reported. [Washington, 1837] 1 p. DNA. 47891

---- Report on Petition of Jennett Willis. House Private Land Claims Com. Jan. 13, 1837. Reports of Committees, No. 95, 24th Cong., 2d sess., Vol. I.

Petitioner, assignee of James
Minnie, owner of a pre-emption
right to land taken by United
States for light-house, prays
grant of land elsewhere; Committee reports bill for relief.
[Washington, 1837] 1 p. DNA.
47892

---- Report on Petition of Je-
rusha Ripley. House Rev. Pensions Committee. Jan. 7, 1837.
Reports of Committees, No. 77,
24th Cong., 2d sess., Vol. I.
Recommends allowance of pension to petitioner, widow of
Samuel Sturtevant; Bill reported. [Washington, 1837]
1 p. DNA. 47893

---- Report on Petition of Jesse
E. Dow. House Claims Committee. Dec. 14, 1837. Reports
of Committees, No. 5, 25th
Cong., 2d sess., Vol. I.
Recommends claim for services
as witness for the United
States against W. A. Christley
for theft of goods from Charlestown navy-yard; Bill reported.
[Washington, 1837] 5 p. DNA.
47894

---- Report on Petition of Jesse
Potts. House Rev. Claims Committee. Feb. 22, 1837. Reports of Committees, No. 275,
24th Cong., 2d sess., Vol. II.
Adverse to allowance of commutation pay. [Washington,
1837] 1 p. DNA. 47895

---- Report on Petition of Joel
Chandler. House Public Lands
Committee. Dec. 22, 1837.
Reports of Committees, No.
96, 25th Cong., 2d sess., Vol.
I. Recommends claim for ex-
change of land titles in Alabama;
Bill reported. [Washington,
1837] 1 p. DNA. 47896

---- Report on Petition of John

B. Ashe. House Rev. Claims
Committee. Dec. 22, 1837. Reports of Committees, No. 122,
25th Cong., 2d sess., Vol. I.
Recommends allowance of commutation pay. [Washington,
1837] 1 p. DNA. 47897

---- Report on Petition of John
Bostworth. House Invalid Pensions Com. Dec. 22, 1837. Reports of Committees, No. 183,
25th Cong., 2d sess., Vol. I.
Recommends allowance of pension;
Bill reported. [Washington,
1837] 1 p. DNA. 47898

---- Report on Petition of John
Brooks. Revolutionary Claims
Committee. Feb. 16, 1837.
Senate Docs., No. 182, 24th
Cong., 2d sess., Vol. II.
Recommends allowance of com-
mutation pay; Bill reported.
[Washington, 1837] 1 p. DNA.
47899

---- Report on Petition of John
Broome. House Claims Committee. Feb. 22, 1837. Reports
of Committees, No. 260, 24th
Cong., 2d sess., Vol. II. Adverse to payment for house
destroyed by the British in the
war of 1812. [Washington, 1837]
1 p. DNA. 47900

---- Report on Petition of John
Brunson. Claims Committee.
Dec. 20, 1837. Senate Docs.,
No. 31, 25th Cong., 2d sess.,
Vol. I. Adverse to claim for
property destroyed by the British in the war of 1812. [Wash-
ington, 1837] 1 p. DNA.
47901

---- Report on Petition of John
Cayford. House Claims Committee. Jan. 31, 1837. Reports
of Committees, No. 176, 24th
Cong., 2d sess., Vol. I. Adverse to allowance of claim for

expenses while acting as agent for obtaining mechanics for arsenal station in Florida. [Washington, 1837] 2 p. DNA.
47902

---- Report on Petition of John Clark. House Rev. Claims Committee. Dec. 22, 1837. Reports of Committees, No. 196, 25th Cong., 2d sess., Vol. I. Recommends allowance of commutation pay; Bill reported. [Washington, 1837] 2 p. DNA.
47903

---- Report on Petition of John De Wolf. House Claims Committee. Jan. 23, 1837. Reports of Committees, No. 141, 24th Cong., 2d sess., Vol. I. Adverse to allowance of additional compensation as United States assessor. [Washington, 1837] 2 p. DNA.
47904

---- Report on Petition of John F. Wiley. House Invalid Pensions Com. Dec. 28, 1837. Reports of Committees, No. 228, 25th Cong., 2d sess., Vol. I. Recommends allowance of pension; Bill reported. [Washington, 1837] 1 p. DNA.
47905

---- Report on Petition of John Forsyth. Claims Committee. Jan. 3, 1837. Senate Docs., No. 51, 24th Cong., 2d sess., Vol. I. Adverse to claim for payment for crop of cotton destroyed by United States troops. [Washington, 1837] 1 p. DNA.
47906

---- Report on Petition of John H. Hall. Military Committee. Jan. 14, 1837. Senate Docs., No. 69, 24th Cong., 2d sess., Vol. II. Recommends compensation to the petitioner for use

by the United States of his improvements in the manufacture of fire-arms; Bill reported. [Washington, 1837] 17 p. DNA.
47907

---- Report on Petition of John H. Hall. Military Committee. Dec. 21, 1837. Senate Docs., No. 35, 25th Cong., 2d sess., Vol. I. Recommends remuneration to petitioner for the use of his inventions and improvements in the manufacture of fire-arms; Bill reported. [Washington, 1837] 2 p. DNA.
47908

---- Report on Petition of John H. McIntosh. Claims Committee. Feb. 7, 1837. Senate Docs., No. 158, 24th Cong., 2d sess., Vol. II. Recommends payment for buildings destroyed by the Indians during the Florida war; Bill reported. [Washington, 1837] 2 p. DNA.
47909

---- Report on Petition of John Kelly. House Claims Committee. Feb. 28, 1837. Reports of Committees, No. 293, 24th Cong., 2d sess., Vol. II. Adverse to claim for services in apprehending the Whites, charged with having destroyed the Treasury building. [Washington, 1837] 1 p. DNA.
47910

---- Report on Petition of John M. Jewell. House Invalid Pensions Com. Jan. 20, 1837. Reports of Committees, No. 131, 24th Cong., 2d sess., Vol. I. Recommends allowance of pension; Bill reported. [Washington, 1837] 1 p. DNA.
47911

---- Report on Petition of John M. Oliver. House Claims Committee. Dec. 14, 1837. Reports of Committees, No. 39, 25th Cong., 2d sess., Vol. I. Recom-

mends removal of charge on
the books of the Treasury
against petitioner for deficiency
in work on Cumberland road;
Bill reported. [Washington,
1837] 2 p. DNA.   47912

---- Report on Petition of John
McArann. House Public Buildings Com. Feb. 25, 1837. Reports of Committees, No. 290,
24th Cong., 2d sess., Vol. II.
Recommends that certain public
grounds near the Capitol be
enclosed for the purpose of
being improved as a botanic
garden and for the establishment of a national museum, and
that the President be requested
to cause the collection of plants
and natural curiosities belonging
to petitioner to be examined by
competent judges for the purpose of ascertaining their value.
[Washington, 1837] 5 p. DNA.
                             47913
---- Report on Petition of John
McCarthy. House Claims Committee. Dec. 14, 1837. Reports of Committees, No. 10,
25th Cong., 2d sess., Vol. I.
Recommends claim for house
burned by the British in 1814;
Bill reported. [Washington,
1837] 2 p. DNA.   47914

---- Report on Petition of John
McClelland. House Rev. Pen-
sions Com. Jan. 24, 1837.
Reports of Committees, No.
144, 24th Cong., 2d sess.,
Vol. I. Recommends allowance
of pension; Bill reported.
[Washington, 1837] 1 p. DNA.
                             47915
---- Report on Petition of John
McClellan. House Rev. Pensions
Com. Dec. 22, 1837. Reports
of Committees, No. 172, 25th
Cong., 2d sess., Vol. I.
Recommends allowance of pen-

sion; Bill reported. [Washing-
ton, 1837] DNA.   47916

---- Report on Petition of John
McCormick. House Rev. Pensions Com. Jan. 19, 1837. Reports of Committees, No. 127,
24th Cong., 2d sess., Vol. I.
Recommends allowance of pension;
Bill reported. [Washington,
1837] 2 p. DNA.   47917

---- Report on Petition of John
McDowel. House Rev. Claims
Committee. Dec. 22, 1837. Reports of Committees, No. 197,
25th Cong., 2d sess., Vol. I.
Recommends allowance of commutation pay; Bill reported.
[Washington, 1837] 1 p. DNA.
                             47918
---- Report on Petition of John
P. Briggs. House Naval Committee. Jan. 24, 1837. Reports
of Committees, No. 148, 24th
Cong., 2d sess., Vol. I. Recommends allowance of pension; Bill
reported. [Washington, 1837]
2 p. DNA.   47919

---- Report on Petition of John
R. Williams. House Claims Committee. Feb. 14, 1837. Reports
of Committees, No. 219, 24th
Cong., 2d sess., Vol. I. Adverse to payment for loss of
property at Buffalo during the
war of 1812. [Washington, 1837]
2 p. DNA.   47920

---- Report on Petition of John
Stevens. House Rev. Claims
Committee. Jan. 5, 1837. Reports of Committees, No. 66,
24th Cong., 2d sess., Vol. I.
Adverse to allowance of claim
for payment of Revolutionary certificates as executor of Albert
Stevens. [Washington, 1837]
1 p. DNA.   47921

---- Report on Petition of John Sutton. House Rev. Claims Committee. Jan. 14, 1837. Reports of Committees, No. 99, 24th Cong., 2d sess., Vol. I. Adverse to allowance of commutation pay. [Washington, 1837] 2 p. DNA.   47922

---- Report on Petition of John Whitsitt. House Public Lands Committee. Dec. 28, 1837. Reports of Committees, No. 206, 25th Cong., 2d sess., Vol. I. Recommends granting petitioner right to land forfeited, upon payment of balance due; Bill reported. [Washington, 1837] 2 p. DNA.   47923

---- Report on Petition of John Wilson. House Claims Committee. Dec. 14, 1837. Reports of Committees, No. 52, 25th Cong., 2d sess., Vol. I. Recommends claim for services in the Black Hawk war; Bill reported. [Washington, 1837] 2 p. DNA.   47924

---- Report on Petition of Jonathan Boone. House Public Lands Committee. Jan. 3, 1837. Reports of Committees, No. 56, 24th Cong., 2d sess., Vol. I. Recommends exchange of land entered by petitioner; Bill reported. [Washington, 1837] 1 p. DNA.   47925

---- Report on Petition of Jonathan Boone. House Public Lands Com. Dec. 28, 1837. Reports of Committees, No. 207, 25th Cong., 2d sess., Vol. I. Recommends change of land entry; Bill reported. [Washington, 1837] 1 p. DNA.   47926

---- Report on Petition of Jonathan Davis. House Claims Committee. Dec. 14, 1837. Reports of Committees, No. 21, 25th Cong., 2d sess., Vol. I. Recommends claim for horses and cow taken by United States troops in 1813; Bill reported. [Washington, 1837] 2 p. DNA.   47927

---- Report on Petition of Jonathan Eliot. House Claims Committee. Dec. 14, 1837. Reports of Committees, No. 51, 25th Cong., 2d sess., Vol. I. Recommends claim for hay and grain taken for use of United States troops in 1813; Bill reported. [Washington, 1837] 3 p. DNA.   47928

---- Report on Petition of Joseph Deshields. House Commerce Committee. Dec. 22, 1837. Reports of Committees, No. 86, 25th Cong., 2d sess., Vol. I. Recommends claim for remission of fine or neglect to obtain clearance papers; Bill reported. [Washington, 1837] 1 p. DNA.   47929

---- Report on Petition of Joseph Hall. House Claims Committee. Dec. 14, 1837. Reports of Committees, No. 20, 25th Cong., 2d sess., Vol. I. Recommends claim for restoration of money paid to obtain a patent; Bill reported. [Washington, 1837] 1 p. DNA.   47930

---- Report on Petition of Joseph Henderson. House Public Lands Com. Dec. 28, 1837. Reports of Committees, No. 301, 25th Cong., 2d sess., Vol. I. Recommends change of land entry; Bill reported. [Washington, 1837] 1 p. DNA.   47931

---- Report on Petition of Joseph Nourse. House Claims Committee. Jan. 17, 1837. Senate Docs., No. 77, 24th Cong., 2d

sess., Vol. II. Adverse to allowance of claim for extra services in disbursing money while Register of the Treasury. [Washington, 1837] 5 p. DNA.
47932

---- Report on Petition of Joseph Nourse. House Claims Committee. Dec. 14, 1837. Reports of Committees, No. 58, 25th Cong., 2d sess., Vol. I. Recommends claim for extra services distinct from official duties as Register of the Treasury in disbursing certain funds; Bill reported. [Washington, 1837] 5 p. DNA.
47933

---- Report on Petition of Joseph Pardee. Claims Committee. Dec. 29, 1837. Senate Docs., No. 55, 25th Cong., 2d sess., Vol. I. Adverse to claim for indemnity for losses on Treasury notes received in payment on contract for the Navy in the war of 1812. [Washington, 1837] 2 p. DNA.
47934

---- Report on Petition of Joseph Radcliffe. House Claims Committee. Feb. 22, 1837. Reports of Committees, No. 266, 24th Cong., 2d sess., Vol. II. Recommends allowance of additional payment on contract for furnishing lumber to navy-yard at Washington; Bill reported. [Washington, 1837] 5 p. DNA.
47935

---- Report on Petition of Joseph Radcliff. House Claims Committee. Dec. 14, 1837. Reports of Committees, No. 75, 25th Cong., 2d sess., Vol. I. Recommends allowance of claim for timber delivered at the navy-yard in the District of Columbia; Bill reported. [Washington, 1837] 5 p. DNA.
47936

---- Report on Petition of Joseph Veazie. House Naval Committee. Jan. 24, 1837. Reports of Committees, No. 150, 24th Cong., 2d sess., Vol. I. Recommends allowance of pension; Bill reported. [Washington, 1837] 1 p. DNA.
47937

---- Report on Petition of Joseph Veazie. House Rev. Pensions Committee. Dec. 22, 1837. Reports of Committees, No. 166, 25th Cong., 2d sess., Vol. I. Recommends allowance of pension; Bill reported. [Washington, 1837] 1 p. DNA.
47938

---- Report on Petition of Josiah Clark. House Rev. Pensions Committee. Jan. 17, 1837. Reports of Committees, No. 114, 24th Cong., 2d sess., Vol. I. Recommends allowance of pension; Bill reported. [Washington, 1837] 1 p. DNA; R.
47939

---- Report on Petition of Josiah Clark. House Rev. Pensions Committee. Dec. 22, 1837. Reports of Committees, No. 174, 25th Cong., 2d sess., Vol. I. Recommends allowance of pension; Bill reported. [Washington, 1837] 1 p. DNA.   47940

---- Report on Petition of Josiah Strong. House Invalid Pensions Com. Dec. 28, 1837. Reports of Committees, No. 302, 25th Cong., 2d sess., Vol. I. Recommends allowance of additional pension; Bill reported. [Washington, 1837] 1 p. DNA.
47941

---- Report on Petition of Josiah West. House Rev. Pensions Committee. Jan. 19, 1837. Reports of Committees, No. 125, 24th Cong., 2d sess., Vol. I. Recommends allowance of pension;

Bill reported. [Washington, 1837] 1 p. DNA.   47942

---- Report on Petition of Josiah West. House Rev. Pensions Committee. Dec. 22, 1837. Reports of Committees, No. 163, 25th Cong., 2d sess., Vol. I. Recommends allowance of pension; Bill reported. [Washington, 1837] 1 p. DNA. 47943

---- Report on Petition of Josiah Westlake. House Invalid Pensions Com. Dec. 22, 1837. Reports of Committees, No. 189, 25th Cong., 2d sess., Vol. I. Recommends allowance of pension; Bill reported. [Washington, 1837] 3 p. DNA.   47944

---- Report on Petition of L. Bissel. House Claims Committee. Feb. 24, 1837. Reports of Committees, No. 283, 24th Cong., 2d sess., Vol. II. Adverse to payment for timber cut from his land by Captain Hinkley, of the Engineer Corps. [Washington, 1837] 4 p. DNA.   47945

---- Report on Petition of L. W. Stockton et al. Judiciary Committee. Jan. 20, 1837. Senate Docs., No. 88, 24th Cong., 2d sess., Vol. II. Recommends payment of claim of petitioners for extra compensation for transportation of the mail. [Washington, 1837] 3 p. DNA.   47946

---- Report on Petition of Leonard Joines. House Invalid Pensions Com. Feb. 14, 1837. Reports of Committees, No. 206, 24th Cong., 2d sess., Vol. I. Adverse to allowance of pension. [Washington, 1837] 1 p. DNA.   47947

---- Report on Petition of

Leonard Loomis. House Invalid Pensions Com. Feb. 2, 1837. Reports of Committees, No. 181, 24th Cong., 2d sess., Vol. I. Recommends allowance of pension; Bill reported. [Washington, 1837] 2 p. DNA.   47948

---- Report on Petition of Leslie Malone. House Rev. Pensions Com. Jan. 14, 1837. Reports of Committees, No. 105, 24th Cong., 2d sess., Vol. I. Adverse to allowance of pension. [Washington, 1837] 1 p. DNA.   47949

---- Report on Petition of Levi Chadwick. House Rev. Claims Committee. Dec. 22, 1837. Reports of Committees, No. 129, 25th Cong., 2d sess., Vol. I. Recommends the issue of duplicate land warrant; Bill reported. [Washington, 1837] 1 p. DNA.   47950

---- Report on Petition of Levy Court of Maryland. House Claims Com. Dec. 14, 1837. Reports of Committees, No. 70, 25th Cong., 2d sess., Vol. I. Recommends claim to indemnity for court-house and jail destroyed by the British in 1814; Bill reported. [Washington, 1837] 2 p. DNA.   47951

---- Report on Petition of Lewis B. Williams. House Commerce Committee. Dec. 28, 1837. Reports of Committees, No. 201, 25th Cong., 2d sess., Vol. I. Recommends allowance for services as deputy surveyor of the port of New Orleans; Bill reported. [Washington, 1837] 2 p. DNA.   47952

---- Report on Petition of Lewis Hatch. House Rev. Pensions Committee. Jan. 14, 1837. Reports of Committees, No. 104,

24th Cong., 2d sess., Vol. I.
Adverse to allowance of pension. [Washington, 1837] 1 p.
DNA.   47953

---- Report on Petition of
Martha McKee. House Claims
Committee. March 3, 1837.
Reports of Committees, No.
320, 24th Cong., 2d sess.,
Vol. II. Adverse to allowance
of claim for land located under
Virginia military land warrant.
[Washington, 1837] 1 p. DNA.
                                  47954
---- Report on Petition of Mary
O'Bannon. House Rev. Claims
Committee. Jan. 19, 1837. Reports of Committees, No. 173,
24th Cong., 2d sess., Vol. I.
Adverse to payment for team
belonging to her late husband,
Andrew O'Bannon, wagon-
master, and taken by the Brit-
ish in the Revolutionary War.
[Washington, 1837] 2 p. DNA.
                                  47955
---- Report on Petition of Mary
Sronfe. House Private Land
Claims Com. Jan. 24, 1837.
Reports of Committees, No.
147, 24th Cong., 2d sess.,
Vol. I. Recommends that petitioner be allowed to purchase
public land upon which she
has settled at the minimum
price; Bill reported. [Washing-
ton, 1837] 2 p. DNA.   47956

---- Report on Petition of Matilda Drury. House Claims
Committee. Feb. 22, 1837.
Reports of Committees, No. 253,
24th Cong., 2d sess., Vol. II.
Adverse to payment for buildings destroyed in the war of
1812. [Washington, 1837] 4
p. DNA.   47957

---- Report on Petition of
Matthew Arbuckle. Private Land

Claims Com. Jan. 16, 1837.
Senate Docs., No. 73, 24th Cong.,
2d sess., Vol. II. Recommends
confirmation of title to land in
Arkansas; Bill reported. [Wash-
ington, 1837] 5 p. DNA.
                                  47958
---- Report on Petition of
Melancthon T. Woolsey. House
Claims Committee. Dec. 14,
1837. Reports of Committees,
No. 57, 25th Cong., 2d sess.,
Vol. I. Recommends that the
accounting officers of the
Treasury be authorized to settle
the accounts of petitioner and
make such allowances as they
are satisfied would be just and
would have been proved if his
vouchers had not been lost;
Bill reported. [Washington,
1837] DNA.   47959

---- Report on Petition of Miami
Exporting Company. House
Claims Com. March 2, 1837.
Reports of Committees, No. 310,
24th Cong., 2d sess., Vol. II.
Adverse to claim of petitioners;
Nature of claim not stated; Re-
fers to Report 373, first session
Twenty-first Congress. [Wash-
ington, 1837] 1 p. DNA.
                                  47960
---- Report on Petition of Milley
Yates. House Indian Affairs
Committee. Dec. 22, 1837. Re-
ports of Committees, No. 146,
25th Cong., 2d sess., Vol. I.
Recommends passage of act au-
thorizing the location of two sections of land in name of petitioner; Bill reported. [Washington,
1837] 2 p. DNA.   47961

---- Report on Petition of Moses
Merrill. House Commerce Committee. Dec. 22, 1837. Reports
of Committees, No. 85, 25th
Cong., 2d sess., Vol. I. Recommends allowance of fishing bounty;

Bill reported. [Washington, 1837] 1 p. DNA. 47962

---- Report on Petition of Moses Van Campen. Revolutionary Claims Com. Jan. 2, 1837. Senate Docs., No. 43, 24th Cong., 2d sess., Vol. I. Recommends allowance of commutation pay; Bill reported. [Washington, 1837] 1 p. DNA. 47963

---- Report on Petition of Nathan Adams. House Revolutionary Claims Com. Dec. 22, 1837. Reports of Committees, No. 104, 25th Cong., 2d sess., Vol. I. Recommends renewal of land warrants; Bill reported. [Washington, 1837] 1 p. DNA. 47964

---- Report on Petition of Nathan Levy. House Commerce Committee. Dec. 22, 1837. Reports of Committees, No. 87, 25th Cong., 2d sess., Vol. I. Recommends payment of judgment obtained against petitioner for acts done in discharge of his duty as United States consul at St. Thomas; Bill reported. [Washington, 1837] 1 p. DNA. 47965

---- Report on Petition of Nathan Smith. House Commerce Committee. Dec. 22, 1837. Reports of Committees, No. 83, 25th Cong., 2d sess., Vol. I. Recommends allowance of fishing bounty; Bill reported. [Washington, 1837] 1 p. DNA. 47966

---- Report on Petition of Nathaniel Goddard et al. House Claims Com. Dec. 22, 1837. Reports of Committees, No. 109, 25th Cong., 2d sess., Vol. I. Recommends that petitioners be allowed a remission of the forfeiture on the ship Ariadne, captured by United States vessel and condemned as prize of war, and a return of the avails so far as they have been realized by the United States; Bill reported. [Washington, 1837] 17 p. DNA. 47967

---- Report on Petition of Nathaniel Holmes. House Rev. Pensions Com. Jan. 14, 1837. Reports of Committees, No. 107, 24th Cong., 2d sess., Vol. I. Adverse to allowance of claim for arrears of pension and bounty land. [Washington, 1837] 1 p. DNA. 47968

---- Report on Petition of Nathaniel Patten. House Post-Office Committee. Feb. 22, 1837. Reports of Committees, No. 271, 24th Cong., 2d sess., Vol. II. Adverse to allowance in his accounts as postmaster for public moneys stolen. [Washington, 1837] 1 p. DNA. 47969

---- Report on Petition of Nathaniel Perry. Pensions Committee. Feb. 15, 1837. Senate Docs., No. 175, 24th Cong., 2d sess., Vol. II. Adverse to allowance of pension. [Washington, 1837] 1 p. DNA. 47970

---- Report on Petition of Neil McNeil. House Rev. Pensions Committee. Jan. 20, 1837. Reports of Committees, No. 133, 24th Cong., 2d sess., Vol. I. Recommends allowance of pension; Bill reported. [Washington, 1837] 4 p. DNA. 47971

---- Report on Petition of Neil McNeil. House Rev. Pensions Committee. Dec. 22, 1837. Reports of Committees, No. 154, 25th Cong., 2d sess., Vol. I. Recommends allowance of pension;

Bill reported. [Washington, 1837] 4 p. DNA.   47972

---- Report on Petition of New England-Mississippi Land Company. Feb. 20, 1837. Senate Docs., No. 197, 24th Cong., 2d sess., Vol. II. Petitioners claim balance of amount due on land granted them by the State of Georgia, and by them released to the United States; Judiciary Committee reports bill for relief. [Washington, 1837] 10 p. DNA.   47973

---- Report on Petition of New England-Mississippi Land Co. Judiciary Com. Dec. 26, 1837. Senate Docs., No. 42, 25th Cong., 2d sess., Vol. I. Recommends payment for tract of land in Georgia conveyed to the United States; Bill reported. [Washington, 1837] 7 p. DNA.   47974

---- Report on Petition of Nicholas Hedges. House Claims Committee. Dec. 14, 1837. Reports of Committees, No. 33, 25th Cong., 2d sess., Vol. I. Recommends claim for services as crier of the United States circuit court of the District of Columbia; Bill reported. [Washington, 1837] 2 p. DNA.   47975

---- Report on Petition of Northam & Whitehorne. Ways and Means Com. Feb. 22, 1837. Reports of Committees, No. 256, 24th Cong., 2d sess., Vol. II. Adverse to refundment of amount paid for license to distil liquors on account of suspension of distilling. [Washington, 1837] 2 p. DNA.   47976

---- Report on Petition of Oliver H. Perry. House Claims Committee. Feb. 14, 1837. Reports of Committees, No. 212, 24th Cong., 2d sess., Vol. I. Adverse to payment for use of schooner owned by his late father, Samuel Perry, during the war of 1812. [Washington, 1837] 5 p. DNA.   47977

---- Report on Petition of Oliver Peck. House Revolutionary Pensions Com. Feb. 14, 1837. Reports of Committees, No. 221, 24th Cong., 2d sess., Vol. I. Recommends allowance of pension; Bill reported. [Washington, 1837] 1 p. DNA.   47978

---- Report on Petition of Oliver Peck. House Rev. Pensions Committee. Dec. 22, 1837. Reports of Committees, No. 158, 25th Cong., 2d sess., Vol. I. Recommends allowance of pension; Bill reported. [Washington, 1837] 1 p. DNA.   47979

---- Report on Petition of Oliver Welch. House Priv. Land Claims Com. Dec. 22, 1837. Reports of Committees, No. 144, 25th Cong., 2d sess., Vol. I. Recommends exchange of land warrant; Bill reported. [Washington, 1837] 1 p. DNA.   47980

---- Report on Petition of P. Yarnall and S. Mitchell. House select com. Feb. 16, 1837. Reports of Committees, No. 236, 24th Cong., 2d sess., Vol. II. Recommends that petitioners be released from payment of judgment obtained against them on account of failure to fulfil their contract for furnishing subsistence to the Army; Bill reported. [Washington, 1837] 7 p. DNA.   47981

---- Report on Petition of Parker Cole. Senate Pensions Committee. Jan. 25, 1837. Senate

Docs., No. 104, 24th Cong., 2d sess., Vol. II. Adverse to allowance of pension. [Washington, 1837] 1 p. DNA. 47982

---- Report on Petition of Patrick Green. House Post-Office Committee. Jan. 4, 1837. Reports of Committees, No. 60, 24th Cong., 2d sess., Vol. I. Petitioner asks compensation for injuries received in defending the United States mail from stage robbers; Committee reports bill for relief. [Washington, 1837] 2 p. DNA. 47983

---- Report on Petition of Patrick Green. House Post-Office Committee. Dec. 22, 1837. Reports of Committees, No. 102, 25th Cong., 2d sess., Vol. I. Recommends compensation for defending the United States mail; Bill reported. [Washington, 1837] 2 p. DNA. 47984

---- Report on Petition of Peter Yarnell. House select committee. Dec. 22, 1837. Reports of Committees, No. 230, 25th Cong., 2d sess., Vol. I. Recommends allowance for subsistence stores furnished the Army in 1828 and 1829; Bill reported. [Washington, 1837] 5 p. DNA. 47985

---- Report on Petition of Philip Lightfoot. House Rev. Claims Com. Feb. 22, 1837. Reports of Committees, No. 274, 24th Cong., 2d sess., Vol. II. Adverse to allowance of commutation pay to petitioner as son of Philip Lightfoot. [Washington, 1837] 1 p. DNA. 47986

---- Report on Petition of Philip Marshall. House Claims Com-

mittee. Dec. 14, 1837. Reports of Committees, No. 41, 25th Cong., 2d sess., Vol. I. Recommends claim for full pay and emoluments of lieutenant; Bill reported. [Washington, 1837] 2 p. DNA. 47987

---- Report on Petition of Physicians of Portland. House Commerce Com. Dec. 22, 1837. Reports of Committees, No. 82, 25th Cong., 2d sess., Vol. I. Recommends appropriation for erection of a marine hospital at Portland, Maine; Bill reported. [Washington, 1837] 4 p. DNA. 47988

---- Report on Petition of Presley N. O'Bannon. House Claims Committee. Dec. 14, 1837. Reports of Committees, No. 34, 25th Cong., 2d sess., Vol. I. Recommends claim for horse lost in the United States service in 1813; Bill reported. [Washington, 1837] 1 p. DNA. 47989

---- Report on Petition of Presly Gray. House Rev. Pensions Committee. Jan. 3, 1837. Reports of Committees, No. 54, 24th Cong., 2d sess., Vol. I. Recommends allowance of pension; Bill reported. [Washington, 1837] 1 p. DNA. 47990

---- Report on Petition of R. Gilmore et al. House Foreign Affairs Com. March 1, 1837. Reports of Committees, No. 299, 24th Cong., 2d sess., Vol. II. Adverse to claim for payment for vessel captured in 1808 by a French privateer. [Washington, 1837] 3 p. DNA. 47991

---- Report on Petition of R. Peebles and J. Graham. House Claims Com. Dec. 14, 1837.

Reports of Committees, No. 46,
25th Cong., 2d sess., Vol. I.
Recommends that petitioners be
relieved from liability of contract to furnish beans at Fort
Crawford, Fort Armstrong,
and Fort Snelling; Bill reported. [Washington, 1837]
4 p. DNA.   47992

---- Report on Petition of Ran-
dolph Carter. House Invalid
Pensions Com. Dec. 28, 1837.
Reports of Committees, No.
229, 25th Cong., 2d sess.,
Vol. I. Recommends allowance
of pension; Bill reported.
[Washington, 1837] 2 p. DNA.
                             47993

---- Report on Petition of
Representatives of Farrow &
Harris. Feb. 22, 1837. Reports of Committees, No. 245,
24th Cong., 2d sess., Vol. II.
House Claims Committee recommends additional payment on contract for work performed on
fortifications at Dauphin's Island; Bill reported. [Wash-
ington, 1837] 2 p. DNA.
                             47994

---- Report on Petition of
Representatives of Henry
Richardson. Dec. 22, 1837.
Reports of Committees, No.
149, 25th Cong., 2d sess.,
Vol. I. House Committee on
Naval Affairs recommends allow-
ance of prize-money; Bill re-
ported. [Washington, 1837]
1 p. DNA.   47995

---- Report on Petition of
Representatives of S. Claggett.
Rev. Claims Com. Jan. 2,
1837. Senate Docs., No. 45,
24th Cong., 2d sess., Vol. I.
Adverse to allowance of claim
for commutation pay. [Wash-
ington, 1837] 2 p. DNA.
                             47996

---- Report on Petition of Reuben Gentry. House Indian Affairs Committee. Dec. 28, 1837.
Reports of Committees, No. 212,
25th Cong., 2d sess., Vol. I.
Recommends allowance for property destroyed by the Sac and
Fox Indians; Bill reported.
[Washington, 1837] 5 p. DNA.
                             47997
---- Report on Petition of Richard Allen. House Rev. Pensions
Committee. Jan. 7, 1837. Reports of Committees, No. 78,
24th Cong., 2d sess., Vol. I.
Adverse to allowance of pension
to petitioner on account of Revolutionary services of his late
father, Richard Allen. [Wash-
ington, 1837] 1 p. DNA.
                             47998
---- Report on Petition of Richard Frisby. House Claims Committee. Dec. 14, 1837. Reports
of Committees, No. 48, 25th
Cong., 2d sess., Vol. I.
Recommends claim for buildings
and grain destroyed by the
British in 1814; Bill reported.
[Washington, 1837] 2 p. DNA.
                             47999
---- Report on Petition of Robert
Keyworth. House Claims Committee. Feb. 4, 1837. Reports
of Committees, No. 188, 24th
Cong., 2d sess., Vol. I.
Recommends allowance of additional compensation for the manufacture of ornamental swords
ordered under a resolution of
Congress; Bill reported. [Wash-
ington, 1837] 11 p. DNA.
                             48000
---- Report on Petition of Robert
Keyworth. House Claims Committee. Dec. 14, 1837. Reports
of Committees, No. 74, 25th Cong.,
2d sess., Vol. I. Recommends
additional compensation for making swords; Bill reported.
[Washington, 1837] 12 p. DNA.
                             48001

---- Report on Petition of Robert Lucas. House Invalid Pensions Com. Jan. 7, 1837. Reports of Committees, No. 75, 24th Cong., 2d sess., Vol. I. Recommends allowance of pension; Bill reported. [Washington, 1837] 1 p. DNA. 48002

---- Report on Petition of Robert Lucas. House Invalid Pensions Com. Dec. 28, 1837. Reports of Committees, No. 225, 25th Cong., 2d sess., Vol. I. Recommends allowance of pension; Bill reported. [Washington, 1837] 1 p. DNA. 48003

---- Report on Petition of Robert McBride. House Invalid Pensions Com. Dec. 28, 1837. Reports of Committees, No. 219, 25th Cong., 2d sess., Vol. I. Recommends allowance of pension; Bill reported. [Washington, 1837] 1 p. DNA. 48004

---- Report on Petition of Robert Murray. House Public Lands Committee. Dec. 28, 1837. Reports of Committees, No. 204, 25th Cong., 2d sess., Vol. I. Recommend change of land entry; Bill reported. [Washington, 1837] 1 p. DNA. 48005

---- Report on Petition of Roswell Lee. House Claims Committee. Dec. 14, 1837. Reports of Committees, No. 17, 25th Cong., 2d sess., Vol. I. Recommends claim for services as inspector of arms at the United States armory at Springfield, Massachusetts; Bill reported. [Washington, 1837] 8 p. DNA. 48006

---- Report on Petition of S. B. Hugo. House Invalid Pensions Committee. Dec. 28, 1837.

Reports of Committees, No. 217, 25th Cong., 2d sess., Vol. I. Recommends allowance of pension; Bill reported. [Washington, 1837] 1 p. DNA. 48007

---- Report on Petition of S. Burton, jr. House Private Land Claims Com. Feb. 4, 1837. Reports of Committees, No. 190, 24th Cong., 2d sess., Vol. I. Adverse to grant of bounty land for services in the war of 1812. [Washington, 1837] 1 p. DNA. 48008

---- Report on Petition of S. La Lande. House Private Land Claims Com. Dec. 22, 1837. Reports of Committees, No. 141, 25th Cong., 2d sess., Vol. I. Recommends confirmation of land title in Alabama; Bill reported. [Washington, 1837] 2 p. DNA. 48009

---- Report on Petition of S. T. Winslow. House Invalid Pensions Com. Jan. 7, 1837. Reports of Committees, No. 71, 24th Cong., 2d sess., Vol. I. Adverse to allowance of pension. [Washington, 1837] 2 p. DNA. 48010

---- Report on Petition of Samuel B. Hugo. House Invalid Pensions Com. Feb. 2, 1837. Reports of Committees, No. 183, 24th Cong., 2d sess., Vol. I. Recommends allowance of pension; Bill reported. [Washington, 1837] 1 p. DNA. 48011

---- Report on Petition of Samuel Cozad. House Claims Committee. Feb. 14, 1837. Reports of Committees, No. 213, 24th Cong., 2d sess., Vol. I. Adverse to allowance of claim; Refers to report made at first session Twenty-fourth Congress. [Washington, 1837] 1 p. DNA. 48012

---- Report on Petition of
Samuel Brown. House Claims
Committee. Jan. 23, 1837.
Reports of Committees, No.
140, 24th Cong., 2d sess.,
Vol. I. Adverse to allowance
of additional compensation as
United States assessor in Rhode
Island in 1816 and 1817.
[Washington, 1837] 2 p. DNA.
48013

---- Report on Petition of
Samuel Brown. House Invalid
Pensions Com. Dec. 22, 1837.
Reports of Committees, No.
184, 25th Cong., 2d sess.,
Vol. I. Recommends allowance
of pension; Bill reported.
[Washington, 1837] 1 p. DNA.
48014

---- Report on Petition of
Samuel Edgcomb. House Rev.
Pensions Com. Dec. 22, 1837.
Reports of Committees, No. 152,
25th Cong., 2d sess., Vol. I.
Recommends allowance of pension;
Bill reported. [Washington,
1837] 1 p. DNA. 48015

---- Report on Petition of
Samuel Edgecomb. House Rev.
Pensions Com. Feb. 1, 1837.
Reports of Committees, No.
177, 24th Cong., 2d sess., Vol.
I. Recommends allowance of
pension; Bill reported. [Wash-
ington, 1837] 1 p. DNA.
48016

---- Report on Petition of
Samuel J. Smith. House Invalid
Pensions Com. Dec. 28, 1837.
Reports of Committees, No.
218, 25th Cong., 2d sess., Vol.
I. Recommends allowance of
pension; Bill reported. [Wash-
ington, 1837] 1 p. DNA.
48017

---- Report on Petition of
Samuel Jones. House Rev.
Claims Committee. Dec. 22,
1837. Reports of Committees,

No. 125, 25th Cong., 2d sess.,
Vol. I. Recommends allowance
of commutation pay; Bill reported. [Washington, 1837] 1
p. DNA. 48018

---- Report on Petition of Samuel
Miller. Claims Committee. Dec.
19, 1837. Senate Docs., No. 27,
25th Cong., 2d sess., Vol. I.
Recommends payment of claim
for apprehension of escaped
prisoners; Bill reported. [Wash-
ington, 1837] 1 p. DNA.
48019

---- Report on Petition of Samuel
Raub, jr. Roads and Canals
Committee. Feb. 7, 1837. Senate
Docs., No. 159, 24th Cong., 2d
sess., Vol. II. Recommends an
appropriation of $5,000 to be ex-
pended in making experiments
with mode of preventing explosions of steam-boilers invented
by petitioner. [Washington,
1837] 7 p. DNA. 48020

---- Report on Petition of Samuel
S. Marcy et al. Commerce Committee. Dec. 29, 1837. Senate
Docs., No. 56, 25th Cong., 2d
sess., Vol. I. Adverse to payment for wharf destroyed by a
storm while in use by the United
States. [Washington, 1837] 1
p. DNA. 48021

---- Report on Petition of Samuel
Sanderson. House Claims Committee. Dec. 14, 1837. Reports
of Committees, No. 4, 25th Cong.,
2d sess., Vol. I. Recommends
claim for salvage in saving lives
of slaves; Bill reported. [Wash-
ington, 1837] 3 p. DNA.
48022

---- Report on Petition of Samuel
Warren. Revolutionary Claims
Com. Jan. 2, 1837. Senate
Docs., No. 39, 24th Cong., 2d
sess., Vol. I. Recommends al-

lowance of commutation pay;
Bill reported. [Washington, 1837]
1 p. DNA. 48023

---- Report on Petition of
Samuel Weeks. House Rev.
Pensions Committee. Jan. 14,
1837. Reports of Committees,
No. 100, 24th Cong., 2d sess.,
Vol. I. Adverse to allowance
of increase of pension. [Washington, 1837] 1 p. DNA.
48024

---- Report on Petition of
Samuel Young. House Rev.
Claims Committee. Dec. 22,
1837. Reports of Committees,
No. 128, 25th Cong., 2d sess.,
Vol. I. Recommends allowance
of claim for house and barn of
Joseph Young, destroyed by
the British in 1778; Recommends
disallowance of claim for services as guide to the Continental
troops. [Washington, 1837]
3 p. DNA. 48025

---- Report on Petition of
Sarah Murphy. House Claims
Committee. Dec. 14, 1837.
Reports of Committees, No. 29,
25th Cong., 2d sess., Vol. I.
Recommends claim for services
in whitewashing and cleaning
the Arch street prison in Philadelphia in 1815; Bill reported.
[Washington, 1837] 1 p. DNA.
48026

---- Report on Petition of Sarah
Rogers. Pensions Committee.
Feb. 4, 1837. Senate Docs.,
No. 146, 24th Cong., 2d sess.,
Vol. II. Adverse to allowance
of pension to petitioner, widow
of Jedediah Rogers. [Washington, 1837] 1 p. DNA. 48027

---- Report on Petition of
Satterlee Clark. House Claims
Committee. Jan. 28, 1837. Reports of Committees, No. 164,

24th Cong., 2d sess., Vol. I.
Adverse to claim for certain allowances in his accounts as an
Army officer. [Washington,
1837] 10 p. DNA. 48028

---- Report on Petition of Simeon
Moss. House Rev. Pensions Committee. Dec. 22, 1837. Reports
of Committees, No. 178, 25th
Cong., 2d sess., Vol. I. Recommends allowance of pension; Bill
reported. [Washington, 1837]
1 p. DNA. 48029

---- Report on Petition of Simeon
Smith. House Rev. Pensions
Committee. Jan. 25, 1837. Reports of Committees, No. 154,
24th Cong., 2d sess., Vol. I.
Recommends allowance of pension;
Bill reported. [Washington, 1837]
1 p. DNA. 48030

---- Report on Petition of Simeon
Smith. House Rev. Pensions
Committee. Dec. 22, 1837. Reports of Committees, No. 167,
25th Cong., 2d sess., Vol. I.
Recommends allowance of pension; Bill reported. [Washington, 1837] 1 p. DNA. 48031

---- Report on Petition of Solomon Ketcham. House Rev. Pensions Com. Jan. 10, 1837. Reports of Committees, No. 80,
24th Cong., 2d sess., Vol. I.
Recommends allowance of pension;
Bill reported. [Washington,
1837] 1 p. DNA. 48032

---- Report on Petition of Solomon Ketcham. House Rev. Pensions Com. Dec. 22, 1837.
Reports of Committees, No. 162,
25th Cong., 2d sess., Vol. I.
Recommends restoration of the
name of petitioner to the pensionroll; Bill reported. [Washington,
1837] DNA. 48033

---- Report on Petition of Spencer C. Gist. House Naval Affairs Com. Dec. 22, 1837. Reports of Committees, No. 150, 25th Cong., 2d sess., Vol. I. Recommends allowance of difference of pay and rations between the grades of midshipman and lieutenant; Bill reported. [Washington, 1837] 5 p. DNA.   48034

---- Report on Petition of Squire Stearns. House Commerce Committee. Dec. 22, 1837. Reports of Committees, No. 80, 25th Cong., 2d sess., Vol. I. Recommends allowance of claim for losses sustained in consequence of wrongful seizure by custom-house officer; Bill reported. [Washington, 1837] 3 p. DNA.   48035

---- Report on Petition of Sureties of James Mouncy. Finance Committee. Feb. 18, 1837. Senate Docs., No. 190, 24th Cong., 2d sess., Vol. II. Adverse to release of petitioners from liability as sureties of James Mouncy, late collector of customs in North Carolina. [Washington, 1837] 2 p. DNA.   48036

---- Report on Petition of Sylvester Tiffany. House Invalid Pensions Com. Jan. 13, 1837. Reports of Committees, No. 88, 24th Cong., 2d sess., Vol. I. Recommends allowance of pension; Bill reported. [Washington, 1837] 1 p. DNA.   48037

---- Report on Petition of T. H. Perkins. Commerce Committee. Jan. 5, 1837. Senate Docs., No. 54, 24th Cong., 2d sess., Vol. I. Recommends that petitioner be released from liability on certain custom-house

bond; Bill reported. [Washington, 1837] 15 p. DNA. 48038

---- Report on Petition of T. T. Triplett. House Indian Affairs Committee. Dec. 28, 1837. Reports of Committees, No. 211, 25th Cong., 2d sess., Vol. I. Recommends partial allowance of claim for services in carrying into effect the treaty with the Creek Indians; Bill reported. [Washington, 1837] 3 p. DNA.   48039

---- Report on Petition of Tabitha Bosworth. House Rev. Pensions Com. Jan. 20, 1837. Reports of Committees, No. 132, 24th Cong., 2d sess., Vol. I. Recommends allowance of pension to petitioner, as widow of Samuel Bosworth; Bill reported. [Washington, 1837] 1 p. DNA.   48040

---- Report on Petition of the Calvert County Levy Court. House Claims Com. March 2, 1837. Reports of Committees, No. 313, 24th Cong., 2d sess., Vol. II. Recommends payment for court-house and jail destroyed by the British in the war of 1812; Bill reported. [Washington, 1837] 2 p. DNA.   48041

---- Report on Petition of Thomas Collins. House Invalid Pensions Com. Jan. 13, 1837. Reports of Committees, No. 93, 24th Cong., 2d sess., Vol. I. Adverse to allowance of pension. [Washington, 1837] 2 p. DNA. 48042

---- Report on Petition of Thomas Cushing. House Commerce Committee. Dec. 22, 1837. Reports of Committees, No. 89, 25th Cong., 2d sess., Vol. I. Recommends allowance of fishing bounty; Bill reported. [Washington, 1837] 2 p. DNA.   48043

---- Report on Petition of Thomas F. McCanless. House Claims Committee. Dec. 14, 1837. Reports of Committees, No. 18, 25th Cong., 2d sess., Vol. I. Recommends claim for horse lost in the Creek war, 1812; Bill reported. [Washington, 1837] 1 p. DNA. 48044

---- Report on Petition of Thomas Fillebrown. House Claims Committee. Dec. 14, 1837. Reports of Committees, No. 69, 25th Cong., 2d sess., Vol. I. Recommends claim for services as secretary of the Board of Naval Commissioners of Navy Hospitals in the disbursement of funds; Bill reported. [Washington, 1837] 3 p. DNA. 48045

---- Report on Petition of Thomas Fillebrown, jr. House Claims Com. March 2, 1837. Reports of Committees, No. 307, 24th Cong., 2d sess., Vol. II. Recommends allowance of commission on disbursements made from Navy hospital fund; Bill reported. [Washington, 1837] 2 p. DNA. 48046

---- Report on Petition of Thomas Graves. House Rev. Claims Committee. Jan. 10, 1837. Reports of Committees, No. 81, 24th Cong., 2d sess., Vol. I. Adverse to allowance of claim, nature not stated. Refers to previous report. [Washington, 1837] 1 p. DNA. 48047

---- Report on Petition of Thomas Tyner. House Claims Committee. Dec. 14, 1837. Reports of Committees, No. 56, 25th Cong., 2d sess., Vol. I. Recommends claim for work on Cumberland road; Bill re-

ported. [Washington, 1837] 2 p. DNA. 48048

---- Report on Petition of Thomas West. House Rev. Pensions Committee. Feb. 1, 1837. Reports of Committees, No. 179, 24th Cong., 2d sess., Vol. I. Recommends allowance of pension; Bill reported. [Washington, 1837] 2 p. DNA. 48049

---- Report on Petition of Thomas West. House Rev. Pensions Committee. Dec. 22, 1837. Reports of Committees, No. 179, 25th Cong., 2d sess., Vol. I. Recommends allowance of pension; Bill reported. [Washington, 1837] 2 p. DNA. 48050

---- Report on Petition of W. Moor. House Private Land Claims Com. Dec. 22, 1837. Reports of Committees, No. 140, 25th Cong., 2d sess., Vol. I. Recommends exchange of land certificate; Bill reported. [Washington, 1837] 1 p. DNA. 48051

---- Report on Petition of Ward Peck. Pensions Committee. Jan. 11, 1837. Senate Docs., No. 60, 24th Cong., 2d sess., Vol. II. Adverse to allowance of pension. [Washington, 1837] 1 p. DNA. 48052

---- Report on Petition of William A. Poor. House Naval Committee. Jan. 31, 1837. Reports of Committees, No. 171, 24th Cong., 2d sess., Vol. I. Adverse to allowance of claim for compensation for extra services as purser in the Navy. [Washington, 1837] 2 p. DNA. 48053

---- Report on Petition of William and James Crooks. House Claims Com. Feb. 22, 1837. Reports

of Committees, No. 243, 24th
Cong., 2d sess., Vol. II.
Recommends payment of interest on value of vessel taken
by United States officer in
1812; Bill reported. [Washing-
ton, 1837] 3 p. DNA.   48054

---- Report on Petition of Wil-
liam Arnel. Revolutionary
Claims Com. Jan. 23, 1837.
Senate Docs., No. 97, 24th
Cong., 2d sess., Vol. II.
Adverse to claim for value of
house accidentally destroyed
by United States troops.
[Washington, 1837] 1 p. DNA.
48055

---- Report on Petition of Wil-
liam Barclay. Private Land
Claims Com. Feb. 7, 1837.
Senate Docs., No. 157, 24th
Cong., 2d sess., Vol. II.
Adverse to confirmation of
title to tract of land claimed.
[Washington, 1837] 1 p. DNA.
48056

---- Report on Petition of William Bowman. House Invalid
Pensions Com. Jan. 20, 1837.
Reports of Committees, No.
130, 24th Cong., 2d sess.,
Vol. I. Recommends allowance
of pension; Bill reported.
[Washington, 1837] 1 p. DNA.
48057

---- Report on Petition of William Bowman. House Invalid
Pensions Com. Dec. 28, 1837.
Reports of Committees, No. 223,
25th Cong., 2d sess., Vol. I.
Recommends allowance of pension; Bill reported. [Washing-
ton, 1837] 1 p. DNA.   48058

---- Report on Petition of Wil-
liam C. Parker. House Foreign
Affairs Com. March 1, 1837.
Reports of Committees, No.
297, 24th Cong., 2d sess., Vol.
II. Recommends that the Presi-

dent be requested to negotiate
with the Court of Denmark for
the purpose of obtaining indemnification for the value of three
prizes sent by John Paul Jones
into Bergen, Norway, in 1799
and delivered up by the Crown
of Denmark to the English.
[Washington, 1837] 3 p. DNA.
48059

---- Report on Petition of William Davis. House Rev. Pensions Committee. Dec. 28, 1837.
Reports of Committees, No. 214,
25th Cong., 2d sess., Vol. I.
Recommends allowance of pension;
Bill reported. [Washington,
1837] 1 p. DNA.   48060

---- Report on Petition of William Eadus. House Claims Committee. Dec. 14, 1837. Reports
of Committees, No. 44, 25th Cong.,
2d sess., Vol. I. Recommends
claim for house and furniture
burnt by the British in 1813;
Bill reported. [Washington,
1837] 2 p. DNA.   48061

---- Report on Petition of William Farris. House Rev. Pensions
Com. Dec. 28, 1837. Reports
of Committees, No. 215, 25th
Cong., 2d sess., Vol. I. Recommends an increase of pension;
Bill reported. [Washington,
1837] 1 p. DNA.   48062

---- Report on Petition of William Fitzgerald. House Rev. Pensions Com. Jan. 18, 1837. Reports of Committees, No. 123,
24th Cong., 2d sess., Vol. I.
Recommends allowance of pension;
Bill reported. [Washington,
1837] 5 p. DNA.   48063

---- Report on Petition of William Fitzgerald. House Rev. Pensions Com. Dec. 22, 1837. Reports of Committees, No. 164,

25th Cong., 2d sess., Vol. I.
Recommends allowance of pension; Bill reported. [Washing-
ton, 1837] 5 p. DNA.   48064

---- Report on Petition of William G. Sanders. House Claims
Committee. Feb. 14, 1837.
Reports of Committees, No.
216, 24th Cong., 2d sess.,
Vol. I. Adverse to payment
for property destroyed by
United States troops. [Wash-
ington, 1837] 2 p. DNA.
                        48065

---- Report on Petition of William Graham. House Claims
Committee. Jan. 10, 1837.
Reports of Committees, No. 83,
24th Cong., 2d sess., Vol. I.
Adverse to claim of petitioner
as assignee of Thomas Dowler,
a soldier of the war of 1812,
for arrears of pay, etc.
[Washington, 1837] 7 p. DNA.
                        48066

---- Report on Petition of William Harper. House Rev. Pensions Com. Jan. 13, 1837.
Reports of Committees, No.
94, 24th Cong., 2d sess., Vol.
I. Recommends allowance of
pension; Bill reported. [Wash-
ington, 1837] 2 p. DNA.
                        48067

---- Report on Petition of Wil-
liam J. Aarons. House Public
Lands Com. Dec. 22, 1837.
Reports of Committees, No. 94,
25th Cong., 2d sess., Vol. I.
Recommends claim for exchange
of land title; Bill reported.
[Washington, 1837] 1 p. DNA.
                        48068

---- Report on Petition of William Jenkinson. House Rev.
Pensions Com. Jan. 24, 1837.
Reports of Committees, No. 151,
24th Cong., 2d sess., Vol. I.
Recommends allowance of pension; Bill reported. [Washing-
ton, 1837] 2 p. DNA.   48069

---- Report on Petition of William Jenkinson. House Rev.
Pensions Com. Dec. 22, 1837.
Reports of Committees, No. 165,
25th Cong., 2d sess., Vol. I.
Recommends allowance of pension; Bill reported. [Washing-
ton, 1837] 2 p. DNA.   48070

---- Report on Petition of William Jones. House Claims Committee. Feb. 22, 1837. Reports
of Committees, No. 270, 24th
Cong., 2d sess., Vol. II.
Recommends that claim for horse
lost in the United States service
during the war of 1812 be referred to the Third Auditor.
[Washington, 1837] 1 p. DNA.
                        48071

---- Report on Petition of William Marbury. House Public
Lands Com. Dec. 28, 1837. Reports of Committees, No. 209,
25th Cong., 2d sess., Vol. I.
Recommends compensation for
loss of land claim; Bill reported.
[Washington, 1837] 1 p. DNA.
                        48072

---- Report on Petition of William Purcell. House Claims Committee. Feb. 22, 1837. Reports of Committees, No. 268,
24th Cong., 2d sess., Vol. II.
Adverse to payment for horse
lost in the service of the United
States during the Creek war.
[Washington, 1837] 3 p. DNA.
                        48073

---- Report on Petition of William R. Custis. House Rev.
Claims Com. Feb. 4, 1837. Reports of Committees, No. 189,
24th Cong., 2d sess., Vol. I.
Adverse to allowance of commutation of half-pay. [Washing-
ton, 1837] 1 p. DNA.   48074

---- Report on Petition of William Shaw. House Claims Committee. Feb. 24, 1837. Reports

of Committees, No. 282, 24th
Cong., 2d sess., Vol. II.
Adverse to the claim of the
petitioner, keeper of light-
house near Baltimore, for
property destroyed by burning
of the light-house. [Washing-
ton, 1837] 1 p. DNA.   48075

---- Report on Petition of Wil-
lis Stephans. House Indian
Affairs Committee. Dec. 28,
1837. Reports of Committees,
No. 210, 25th Cong., 2d sess.,
Vol. I. Recommends relinquish-
ment of title of the United
States to land reservation;
Bill reported. [Washington,
1837] 2 p. DNA.   48076

---- Report on Petition of William Tharp. House Claims Committee. Feb. 15, 1837. Reports of Committees, No. 230,
24th Cong., 2d sess., Vol. II.
Recommends that claim of petitioner for reimbursement on account of judgment obtained
against him as endorser of a
draft drawn on the Secretary
of War by James Read, military
agent, be referred to the Secretary of War for settlement;
Bill reported. [Washington,
1837] 1 p. DNA.   48077

---- Report on Petition of William Tharp. House Claims Committee. Dec. 14, 1837. Reports
of Committees, No. 63, 25th
Cong., 2d sess., Vol. I.
Recommends that claim for fee
paid by petitioner to attorney
to defend suit for recovery on
protested draft be referred to
the Secretary of the Treasury;
Bill reported. [Washington,
1837] 1 p. DNA.   48078

---- Report on Petition of William Vanderveer. House Rev.

Pensions Com. Jan. 17, 1837.
Reports of Committees, No. 118,
24th Cong., 2d sess., Vol. I.
Adverse to allowance of pension.
[Washington, 1837] 1 p. DNA.
                        48079
---- Report on Petition of William Vaughan. House Naval
Committee. March 2, 1837. Reports of Committees, No. 309,
24th Cong., 2d sess., Vol. II.
Adverse to claim of petitioner,
a sailing master in the Navy, for
pay while on furlough. [Wash-
ington, 1837] 2 p. DNA.
                        48080
---- Report on Petition of William Walker. House Public Lands
Committee. Dec. 22, 1837. Reports of Committees, No. 95,
25th Cong., 2d sess., Vol. I.
Recommends claim for exchange
of land titles in Alabama; Bill
reported. [Washington, 1837]
DNA.   48081

---- Report on Petition of William York. House Rev. Pensions
Committee. Dec. 22, 1837. Reports of Committees, No. 160,
25th Cong., 2d sess., Vol. I.
Recommends allowance of pension;
Bill reported. [Washington,
1837] 1 p. DNA.   48082

---- Report on Petition of Wilson
Thorpe. House Public Lands
Com. Jan. 17, 1837. Reports
of Committees, No. 112, 24th
Cong., 2d sess., Vol. I. Adverse to grant of land to petitioner on account of his blindness
and other infirmities. [Washing-
ton, 1837] 1 p. DNA.   48083

---- Report on Petition of Winthrop Sears. House Commerce
Committee. Dec. 22, 1837. Reports of Committees, No. 77,
25th Cong., 2d sess., Vol. I.
Recommends allowance of fishing

bounty; Bill reported. [Washington, 1837] 1 p. DNA.
48084

---- Report on Petition of Wright Groom. House Claims Committee. Feb. 16, 1837. Reports of Committees, No. 237, 24th Cong., 2d sess., Vol. II. Recommends reference of claim for furnishing horse equipment to the Army to the Quartermaster-General for settlement. [Washington, 1837] 2 p. DNA.
48084a

---- Report on Petition of Zebulon Wade. House Naval Committee. Jan. 14, 1837. Reports of Committees, No. 109, 24th Cong., 2d sess., Vol. I. Adverse to allowance of pension for naval services. [Washington, 1837] 1 p. DNA. 48085

---- Report on Petition relative to Public Lands. House Public Lands Com. Dec. 28, 1837. Reports of Committees, No. 202, 25th Cong., 2d sess., Vol. I. Recommends reduction and graduation of price of public lands; Bill reported. [Washington, 1837] 5 p. DNA. 48086

---- Report on Petitions for Pension. House Rev. Pensions Committee. Jan. 7, 1837. Reports of Committees, No. 74, 24th Cong., 2d sess., Vol. I. Recommends allowance of pension to Primus Hall and Elias Trask; Bill reported. [Washington, 1837] 2 p. DNA.
48087

---- Report on Petitions of Thomas Coolins. House Invalid Pensions Com. Dec. 22, 1837. Reports of Committees, No. 181, 25th Cong., 2d sess., Vol. I. Adverse to allowance of pension. [Washington, 1837] 2 p. DNA.
48088

---- Report on Memorial of Heirs of Francis Cazeau. Judiciary Committee. Jan. 16, 1837. Senate Docs., No. 72, 24th Cong., 2d sess., Vol. II. Recommends allowance of claim for supplies furnished the Army during the Revolutionary War; Bill reported. [Washington, 1837] 1 p. DNA.
48089

---- Report on Pilot Regulations. House Commerce Committee. Feb. 22, 1837. Reports of Committees, No. 263, 24th Cong., 2d sess., Vol. II. Recommends that the subject of pilot regulations be left to the several States. [Washington, 1837] 9 p. DNA.
48090

---- Report on Post-Office Balances. P. M. General Amos Kendall. March 3, 1837. Ex. Docs., No. 185, 24th Cong., 2d sess., Vol. IV. Statement of balances due by late postmasters prior to July 1, 1836. [Washington, 1837] 147 p. DNA.
48091

---- Report on Post-Office Contracts. P. M. General Amos Kendall. March 3, 1837. Senate Docs., No. 13, 24th Cong., 2d sess., Vol. III. Statement of contracts for transportation of the mails made by the Post-Office Department from January 1 to July 1, 1836. [Washington, 1837] 13 p. DNA. 48092

---- Report on Pre-emption Rights. House Public Lands Committee. Jan. 3, 1837. Reports of Committees, No. 53, 24th Cong., 2d sess., Vol. I. Recommends extension of the benefits of the pre-emption laws to actual settlers who have been prevented from obtaining their pre-emptions under the act of 1834; Bill reported. [Washington, 1837] 1 p. DNA.
48093

---- Report on Privateer Pension Fund. House Naval Committee. Feb. 14, 1837. Reports of Committees, No. 232, 24th Cong., 2d sess., Vol. II. Recommends that permanent provision be made for the payment of pensions chargeable to the privateer pension fund; Bill reported. [Washington, 1837] 7 p. DNA.   48094

---- Report on Proposed Constitutional Amendments. House select com. Feb. 28, 1837. Reports of Committees, No. 296, 24th Cong., 2d sess., Vol. II. Committee reports adversely on proposed amendments to the Constitution limiting the veto power, changing the present mode of appointing the Secretary of the Treasury, to that of an annual election by Congress, and otherwise restricting the power of the President. [Washington, 1837] 14 p. DNA.
48095

---- Report on Protections to American Seamen. House Commerce Com. Feb. 2, 1837. Reports of Committees, No. 182, 24th Cong., 2d sess., Vol. I. Recommends repeal of laws authorizing issue of protections to American seamen and charging fees for same; Bill reported. [Washington, 1837] 14 p. DNA.
48096

---- Report on Public Buildings. Commissioner W. Noland. Dec. 15, 1837. Ex. Docs., No. 28, 25th Cong., 2d sess., Vol. II. Statement of progress made in the construction of public buildings, etc., in Washington during the year 1837. [Washington, 1837] 6 p. DNA.   48097

---- Report on Public Deposits. Secretary Levi Woodbury. Sept.

22, 1837. Ex. Docs., No. 29, 25th Cong., 1st sess. Transmitting information as to the different methods adopted since the organization of the Government for the safe-keeping of the public funds. [Washington, 1837] 4 p. DNA.   48098

---- Report on Public Expenditures. Secretary Levi Woodbury. Sept. 21, 1837. Ex. Docs., No. 17, 25th Cong., 1st sess. Statement of amount of unexpended appropriations required to fulfil existing engagements; Objects of public expenditure that can be either dispensed with or materially reduced during the present year. [Washington, 1837] 101 p. DNA.   48099

---- Report on Public Money in Deposit Banks. Secretary Levi Woodbury. Jan. 10, 1837. Ex. Docs., No. 77, 24th Cong., 2d sess., Vol. II. Submitting statement showing amounts of public moneys in deposit banks on the first day of each quarter in the years 1833, 1834, 1835, and 1836. [Washington, 1837] 11 p. DNA.
48100

---- Report on Pursers in the Navy. House Naval Committee. Jan. 23, 1837. Reports of Committees, No. 142, 24th Cong., 2d sess., Vol. I. Recommends revision of the laws regulating the compensation of pursers in the Navy; Bill reported. [Washington, 1837] 4 p. DNA.   48101

---- Report on Railroad Survey in Georgia. S. H. Long. Nov. 7, 1837. Senate Docs., No. 57, 25th Cong., 2d sess., Vol. I. Statement of progress made in the reconnaissance and survey of the Western and Atlantic Railroad. [Washington, 1837] 40 p. DNA.   48102

---- Report on Receipts and
Disbursements. P. M. Gen.
Amos Kendall. Oct. 13, 1837.
Ex. Docs., No. 54, 25th Cong.,
1st sess. Statement of receipts and disbursements of
the Post-Office Department
since May 1, 1837; Estimated
receipts and disbursements for
the remainder of the year;
Balances on hand. [Washing-
ton, 1837] 4 p. DNA. 48103

---- Report on Receipts from
Public Lands. Commissioner
James Whitcomb. Jan. 27,
1837. Senate Docs., No. 114,
24th Cong., 2d sess., Vol. II.
Statement of amount of money
received for public lands during
the year 1836 and the amount
expended in the transportation
of gold and silver from land
offices to the deposit banks.
[Washington, 1837] 8 p. DNA.
48104

---- Report on Reissue of Notes
of United States Bank. House
select com. Feb. 22, 1837. Reports of Committees, No. 272,
24th Cong., 2d sess., Vol. II.
Bill reported providing for the
punishment of the reissue of
the notes of the United States
Bank once redeemed, and joint
resolution excluding such notes
from circulation so far as re-
gards the collection of the public revenues. [Washington,
1837] 10 p. DNA. 48105

---- Report on Relations with
Mexico. Foreign Relations Committee. Feb. 19, 1837. Senate
Docs., No. 189, 24th Cong., 2d
sess., Vol. II. Recommending
that the Senate concur in the
opinion of the President that another demand ought to be made
upon Mexico for the redress of
grievances, and that the mode

of making the demand be left to
the discretion of the President.
[Washington, 1837] 4 p. DNA.
48106

---- Report on Relations with
Mexico. Secretary John Forsyth.
Jan. 25, 1837. Ex. Docs., No.
105, 24th Cong., 2d sess., Vol.
III. Transmitting copies of
papers on file in the State Department showing the present
state of the political relations
between the United States and
Mexico. [Washington, 1837]
59 p. DNA. 48107

---- Report on Resignations of
Army Officers. Sec. ad interim
B. F. Butler. March 1, 1837.
Ex. Docs., No. 183, 24th Cong.,
2d sess., Vol. IV. Transmitting
information relative to Army officers who resigned during the
year 1836, and to the number
of companies operating during
the past year against the Creeks
and Seminoles. [Washington,
1837] 9 p. DNA. 48108

---- Report on Revenue from
Imports. Secretary Levi Woodbury. Jan. 20, 1837. Ex.
Docs., No. 94, 24th Cong., 2d
sess., Vol. III. Statement exhibiting amount of duties accruing on merchandise imported and
of drawbacks payable on re-
exportation during 1832, 1833,
1834, and 1835. [Washington,
1837] 8 p. DNA. 48109

---- Report on River and Harbor Improvements. Sec. ad int.
R. B. Taney. Jan. 23, 1837.
Senate Docs., No. 115, 24th
Cong., 2d sess., Vol. II. Transmitting statements showing what
river and harbor improvements
have been commenced by the
United States; Original estimate
of cost; Amount expended; Pres-

ent condition of work; List of reports of surveys, etc. [Washington, 1837] 53 p. DNA.

48110

---- Report on River and Harbor Improvements. Secretary of War. 1837. An act approved October 16, 1837, made an appropriation of $25,000 to cover the expense of preparing and publishing this and two other documents, all ordered by the Senate. [Washington, 1837] DNA.

48111

---- Report on River and Harbor Improvements. Ways and Means Com. Jan. 31, 1837. Reports of Committees, No. 175, 24th Cong., 2d sess., Vol. I. Reports bill making appropriations for improvements of certain rivers and harbors. [Washington, 1837] 32 p. DNA.

48112

---- Report on Rules of the House. House select committee. Sept. 13, 1837. Ex. Docs., Report No. 1, 25th Cong., 1st sess. Recommends adoption of various amendments to the rules. [Washington, 1837] 5 p. DNA.

48113

---- Report on Salaries of Department Clerks. Ways and Means Com. Jan. 27, 1837. Reports of Committees, No. 161, 24th Cong., 2d sess., Vol. I. Recommends reorganization of the Executive Department and new classification of the clerks and an increase of their salaries. [Washington, 1837] 35 p. DNA.   48114

---- Report on Sale of Arkansas Lands. Private Land Claims Committee. Jan. 2, 1837. Senate Docs., No. 42, 24th Cong., 2d sess., Vol. I. Recommends confirmation of title to purchasers from the Governor of Arkansas of certain public lands granted to that Territory; Bill reported. [Washington, 1837] 2 p. DNA.   48115

---- Report on Seizure of Slaves on Board American Vessels. Feb. 14, 1837. Senate Docs., No. 174, 24th Cong., 2d sess., Vol. II. Report of Secretary John Forsyth transmitting copies of correspondence relative to the seizure by the British authorities of slaves on board of the American brigs Encomium and Enterprise, which were wrecked on the Bahama Islands. [Washington, 1837] 58 p. DNA. 48116

---- Report on Senate Bills granting Commutation pay. Feb. 22, 1837. Reports of Committees, No. 259, 24th Cong., 2d sess., Vol. II. House Revolutionary Claims Committee recommends rejection of Senate bills granting commutation pay to Samuel Y. Keene, Moses Elmer, Gustavus B. Horner, William Cogswell, Benjamin J. Porter, and Isaac Bronson, surgeons' mates. [Washington, 1837] 5 p. DNA.   48117

---- Report on Senate Contingent Fund. Secretary of Senate A. Dickins. Dec. 7, 1837. Senate Docs., No. 3, 25th Cong., 2d sess., Vol. I. Statement of expenditures from the contingent fund of the Senate for the year ending December 3, 1837. [Washington, 1837] 7 p. DNA.   48118

---- Report on Specie Payment. Secretary Levi Woodbury. Sept. 14, 1837. Ex. Docs., No. 18, 25th Cong., 2st sess. Transmitting information in relation to the offer to pay members of Congress in specie, to what other claimants on the Treasury a similar offer has been made, and to the principles of discrimination adopted in the payment of public creditors; Statement of specie received since May 1, 1837, persons to whom paid, etc. [Washington, 1837] 20 p. DNA. 48119

---- Report on Survey of Cape May Roads. H. Bache. Dec. 1, 1837. Senate Docs., No. 155, 25th Cong., 2d sess., Vol. III. Report, plans, and estimate in reference to the survey of Cape May roads, including Crow Shoal. [Washington, 1837] 17 p. DNA. 48120

---- Report on Survey of Connecticut River. Captain Swift. Jan. 31, 1837. Ex. Docs., No. 252, 25th Cong., 2d sess., Vol. VIII. Survey, plan, and estimate for the improvement of the harbor and mouth of Connecticut River. [Washington, 1837] 11 p. DNA. 48121

---- Report on Survey of George's Shoal. Lieutenant Charles Wilkes. Oct. 20, 1837. Ex. Docs., No. 247, 25th Cong., 2d sess., Vol. VIII. Report on the practicability of erecting a light-house on George's Shoal and Bank, off the coast of Massachusetts. [Washington, 1837] 6 p. DNA. 48122

---- Report on Survey of Harbor of Havre de Grace. George W. Hughes. Jan. 30, 1837. Ex. Docs., No. 134, 24th Cong., 2d sess., Vol. III. Survey of harbor of Havre de Grace, with estimates for its improvement. [Washington, 1837] 10 p. DNA. 48123

---- Report on Survey of James River. Howard Stansbury. Jan. 25, 1837. Ex. Docs., No. 133, 24th Cong., 2d sess., Vol. III. Survey of James River from Richmond, Virginia, to its mouth; Estimates of cost of improvement of navigation. [Washington, 1837] 12 p. DNA. 48124

---- Report on Survey of Mississippi River. Chief-Engineer C. Gratiot. Feb. 24, 1837. Ex. Docs., No. 173, 24th Cong., 2d sess., Vol. IV. Transmitting reports on the survey and the improvement of the navigation of the Mississippi River. [Washington, 1837] 17 p. DNA. 48125

---- Report on Survey of St. Francis River. W. B. Guion. Jan. 17, 1837. Senate Docs., No. 219, 24th Cong., 2d sess., Vol. III. Account of a survey of St. Francis River and statement as to the expediency of removing the natural rafts thereon. [Washington, 1837] 5 p. DNA. 48126

---- Report on Surveys of Public Lands. Commissioner James Whitcomb. Feb. 25, 1837. Ex. Docs., No. 178, 24th Cong., 2d sess., Vol. IV. Relative to surveys of public lands in the States of Illinois and Missouri. [Washington, 1837] 19 p. DNA. 48127

---- Report on Tariff on Coal. Senate Committee on Manufactures. Jan. 23, 1837. Senate Docs., No. 102, 24th Cong., 2d sess., Vol. II. Recommends repeal of duties on foreign coal; Bill reported. [Washington, 1837] 12 p. DNA. 48128

---- Report on Telegraph System. Secretary Levi Woodbury. Dec. 6, 1837. Ex. Docs., No. 15, 25th Cong., 2d sess., Vol. II. Recommending the adoption of a system of telegraphs for the United States, and transmitting information relative to the subject. [Washington, 1837] 37 p. DNA.   48129

---- Report on Tennessee School Lands. House Public Lands Committee. Dec. 22, 1837. Reports of Committees, No. 100, 25th Cong., 2d sess., Vol. I. Recommends authorizing the State to sell; Bill reported. [Washington, 1837] 3 p. DNA.   48130

---- Report on Tennessee Vacant Lands. House Public Lands Committee. Dec. 22, 1837. Reports of Committees, No. 101, 25th Cong., 2d sess., Vol. I. Recommends ceding to the State of Tennessee the vacant lands within the limits of the State; Bill reported. [Washington, 1837] 26 p. DNA.   48131

---- Report on the Bank of Missouri. Secretary Levi Woodbury. Sept. 20, 1837. Ex. Docs., No. 25, 25th Cong., 1st sess. Stating date on which the Bank of Missouri was made a deposit bank, with information in relation to its condition and the deposits therein. [Washington, 1837] 1 p. DNA.   48132

---- Report on the Coast Survey, Weights and Measures. Supt. F. R. Hassler. Nov. 18, 1837. Senate Docs., No. 79, 25th Cong., 2d sess., Vol. I. Statement of progress made in the survey of the United States coast, and in the fabrication of standard weights and measures. [Washington, 1837] 16 p. DNA.   48133

---- Report on the Electoral Vote. Joint committee on part of House. Feb. 4, 1837. Reports of Committees, No. 191, 24th Cong., 2d sess., Vol. I. Recommends adoption of certain rules governing the counting of the votes cast for President and Vice-President at the last Presidential election. [Washington, 1837] 2 p. DNA.   48134

---- Report on the Electoral Vote. Joint committee on part of Senate. Feb. 4, 1837. Senate Docs., No. 144, 24th Cong., 2d sess., Vol. II. Recommends adoption of certain rules governing the counting of the votes cast for President and Vice-President at the last Presidential election. [Washington, 1837] 2 p. DNA.   48135

---- Report on the Executive Departments. House select committee. March 3, 1837. Reports of Committees, No. 194, 24th Cong., 2d sess., Vol. III. 472 p. Majority and minority reports on the condition of the various Executive Departments, their discharge of the public business, and the complaints of the manner in which they have fulfilled the objects of their creation, with journal of the proceedings of the committee. [Washington, 1837] 472 p. DNA.   48136

---- Report on the Finances. Secretary Levi Woodbury. Sept. 5, 1837. Ex. Docs., No. 2, 25th Cong., 1st sess. Condition of the Treasury; Payment of customs duties; Public deposits and former deposit banks; General causes and remedies of the present financial embarrassments of the country. [Washington, 1837] 88 p. DNA.   48137

---- Report on the Finances. Secretary Levi Woodbury. Dec.

4, 1837. Ex. Docs., No. 4,
25th Cong., 2d sess., Vol. I.
Statement of revenues and expenditures from January 1,
1836; Public debt; Estimated
revenues and expenditures for
the year 1838; Banks and public deposits. [Washington,
1837] 76 p. DNA.   48138

---- Report on the General
Brahan Case. Secretary Levi
Woodbury. Feb. 27, 1837.
Senate Docs., No. 205, 24th
Cong., 2d sess., Vol. II.
Transmitting copies of cor-
respondence relative to the
debt due the United States by
the late General Brahan, re-
ceiver of the land district of
Huntsville, Alabama. [Washing-
ton, 1837] 32 p. DNA.   48139

---- Report on the Memorial
of Choctaw Indians. Private
Land Claims Com. Jan. 18,
1837. Senate Docs., No. 81,
24th Cong., 2d sess., Vol. II.
Memorialists ask further grant
of land under the Choctaw
treaty of September 27, 1830;
Bill for relief reported. [Wash-
ington, 1837] 2 p. DNA.
                          48140

---- Report on the Militia.
Secretary ad interim B. F.
Butler. Feb. 6, 1837. Ex.
Docs., No. 136, 24th Cong.,
2d sess., Vol. III. Abstract
of the general returns of the
militia of the United States,
and of their arms, accoutre-
ments, and ammunition, for the
year 1836. [Washington, 1837]
9 p. DNA.   48141

---- Report on the Militia.
Secretary ad interim B. F.
Butler. Feb. 6, 1837. Senate
Docs., No. 147, 24th Cong.,
2d sess., Vol. II. Transmitting

abstract of annual returns of
the militia for the year 1836.
[Washington, 1837] 10 p. DNA.
                          48142
---- Report on the Mint. Direc-
tor R. M. Patterson. Jan. 17,
1837. Ex. Docs., No. 96, 24th
Cong., 2d sess., Vol. II. Statement of the operations of the
Mint during the year 1836, and
of the progress made toward
completion of the branch mints
in North Carolina, Georgia, and
Louisiana. [Washington, 1837]
9 p. DNA.   48143

---- Report on the Surplus
Revenue, etc. Ways and Means
Committee. Jan. 11, 1837. Reports of Committees, No. 86,
24th Cong., 2d sess., Vol. I.
Adverse to the distribution of
the surplus revenue of the United
States; Recommends a revision
and reduction of the duties on
imports. [Washington, 1837]
24 p. DNA.   48144

---- Report on the Territory on
the Columbia River. Sec. John
Forsyth. Dec. 23, 1837. Ex.
Docs., No. 43, 25th Cong., 2d
sess., Vol. II. Submitting information in relation to the occupancy by the Hudson Bay Company of a portion of the territory
of the United States on the Columbia River. [Washington,
1837] 2 p. DNA.   48145

---- Report on the Treasury
Department. House Commerce
Committee. Dec. 22, 1837. Reports of Committees, No. 81,
25th Cong., 2d sess., Vol. I.
Recommends reorganization; Bill
reported. [Washington, 1837]
45 p. DNA.   48146

---- Report on Transfer of Appropriation. Secretary Levi

Woodbury. Dec. 6, 1837. Ex. Docs., No. 12, 25th Cong., 2d sess., Vol. II. Submitting information of a transfer of appropriation from a particular branch of expenditure to another. [Washington, 1837] 1 p. DNA.   48147

---- Report on Treasury Accounts. Treasurer John Campbell. Dec. 6, 1837. Ex. Docs., No. 8, 25th Cong., 2d sess., Vol. I. Transmitting copies of accounts of the Treasurer of the United States as settled by the accounting officers of the Treasury for the third and fourth quarters of 1837. [Washington, 1837] 141 p. DNA.
48148

---- Report on Treasury Balances. Comptroller George Wolf. Feb. 2, 1837. Ex. Docs., No. 131, 24th Cong., 2d sess., Vol. III. Statement of balances on the books of the revenue remaining unsettled for more than three years prior to September 30, 1836. [Washington, 1837] 7 p. DNA.   48149

---- Report on Treasury Balances. Comptroller George Wolf. Feb. 8, 1837. Ex. Docs., No. 144, 24th Cong., 2d sess., Vol. IV. Statement of balances on the books of the Treasury which have remained unsettled by receivers of public moneys more than three years prior to September 30, 1836. [Washington, 1837] 8 p. DNA.
48150

---- Report on Treasury Balances. Comptroller George Wolf. Dec. 5, 1837. Ex. Docs., No. 2, 25th Cong., 2d sess., Vol. I. Statement of accounts remaining unsettled on the books of the Fourth Auditor

for more than three years prior to September 30, 1837. [Washington, 1837] 35 p. DNA.
48151

---- Report on Treasury Balances. Comptroller George Wolf. Dec. 6, 1837. Ex. Docs., No. 6, 25th Cong., 2d sess., Vol. I. Statement of accounts remaining unsettled on the books of the Second Auditor for more than three years prior to September 30, 1837. [Washington, 1837] 7 p. DNA.   48152

---- Report on Treasury Balances. Comptroller George Wolf. Dec. 28, 1837. Ex. Docs., No. 48, 25th Cong., 2d sess., Vol. II. Statements of accounts remaining unsettled on the books of the Third Auditor for more than three years prior to September 30, 1837; Officers who have not rendered their accounts within the year. [Washington, 1837] 114 p. DNA.   48153

---- Report on Treasury Contracts. Secretary Levi Woodbury. Jan. 18, 1837. Ex. Docs., No. 87, 24th Cong., 2d sess., Vol. III. Statements of contracts relative to light-houses, etc., of payments for miscellaneous claims for the year 1836, of expenditures from the marine hospital fund for the year 1835, and of contracts authorized by the Secretary of the Treasury for the year 1836. [Washington, 1837] 15 p. DNA.   48154

---- Report on Undrawn Appropriations. Secretary Levi Woodbury. Jan. 14, 1837. Senate Docs., No. 71, 24th Cong., 2d sess., Vol. II. Transmitting statement of appropriations undrawn on January 1, 1837, with the dates of acts making such appropriations. [Washington, 1837] 18 p. DNA. 48155

---- Report on Unexpended Appropriations. Secretary Levi Woodbury. Sept. 14, 1837. Ex. Docs., No. 17, 25th Cong., 1st sess. Statement of unexpended appropriations of the past and present years; Estimate of proposed reduction in public expenditures. [Washington, 1837] 3 p. DNA. 48156

---- Report on Unpaid Duties, etc. Secretary Levi Woodbury. Sept. 21, 1837. Ex. Docs., No. 28, 25th Cong., 1st sess. Amount of unpaid duties accrued and when payable; Amount due from United States Bank and when payable; Data on which accruing revenues for the last half of the present year were founded. [Washington, 1837] 4 p. DNA. 48157

---- Report on War Department Contingent Fund. Secretary J. R. Poinsett. Dec. 6, 1837. Ex. Docs., No. 11, 25th Cong., 2d sess., Vol. II. Statement of expenditures from the contingent funds of the War Department and its bureaus for the year ending September 30, 1837. [Washington, 1837] 22 p. DNA. 48158

---- Report on War Department Contracts. Sec. ad interim B. F. Butler. Jan. 23, 1837. Ex. Docs., No. 99, 24th Cong., 2d sess., Vol. III. Transmitting statements of all contracts made by the War Department during the year 1836. [Washington, 1837] 58 p. DNA. 48159

---- Report on Warehouse System, etc. Ways and Means Committee. Feb. 8, 1837. Reports of Committees, No. 195, 24th Cong., 2d sess., Vol. I. Reports bills authorizing deposit of imported merchandise in warehouses, changing the time at which goods may be sold for nonpayment of duties, and allowing drawbacks on certain merchandise exported. [Washington, 1837] 6 p. DNA. 48160

---- Report on Washington Penitentiary. Board of inspectors. Jan. 18, 1837. Ex. Docs., No. 97, 24th Cong., 2d sess., Vol. III. Statements showing number of convicts now in the penitentiary, receipts and expenditures of the institution, estimate of expenditures for the present year, etc. [Washington, 1837] 12 p. DNA. 48161

---- Report on Works at Black Rock. Chief Engineer C. Gratiot. Sept. 15, 1837. Senate Docs., No. 21, 25th Cong., 1st sess. Stating that the want of an appropriation has prevented the making of a survey to ascertain whether the works at Black Rock raise the waters of Lake Erie to the injury of property on its shores. [Washington, 3 p. DNA. 48162

---- Report relative to Consular Certificates. Secretary Levi Woodbury. Dec. 14, 1837. Senate Docs., No. 21, 25th Cong., 2d sess., Vol. I. Information and recommendations as to a modification of the law requiring consular certificates on invoices of merchandise imported. [Washington, 1837] 4 p. DNA. 48163

---- Report relative to Navy Officers. Secretary M. Dickerson.

Jan. 14, 1837. Ex. Docs., No.
81, 24th Cong., 2d sess., Vol.
III. Statement of names of
officers of the Navy who have
received orders for service
during the year 1836, and have
asked to be excused, with the
reasons. [Washington, 1837]
6 p. DNA. 48164

---- Report relative to Survey
of Crow Shoal. Lieut. Col.
J. J. Abert. Jan. 25, 1837.
Senate Docs., No. 124, 24th
Cong., 2d sess., Vol. II. Informing the Senate of the
reasons which have prevented
the completion of the survey of
Crow Shoal, in the Delaware
River. [Washington, 1837] 2
p. DNA. 48165

---- Resolution on a National
Bank. Representative Cambreleng. Sept. 25, 1837. Ex.
Docs., Resolution No. 2, 25th
Cong., 1st sess. That it is
inexpedient to charter a national bank; Amendments offered
by Representatives Wise, Bell,
Pope, and Ewing. [Washing-
ton, 1837] 2 p. DNA. 48166

---- Resolution on School Lands.
Representative Johnson, of
Maryland. Dec. 22, 1837. Reports of Committees, Resolution
No. 3, 25th Cong., 2d sess.,
Vol. IV. That a committee of
one from each State be appointed to inquire into the
propriety of reporting a bill
to appropriate an increased portion of the public lands for the
benefit of the States and Territories. [Washington, 1837] 1
p. DNA. 48167

---- Resolution on the Censure
of the President. Senator Bayard. Dec. 14, 1837. Senate

Docs., No. 19, 25th Cong., 2d
sess., Vol. I. That the resolution expunging from the Senate
Journal the resolution censuring
the late President Jackson for
his action in relation to the
public deposits be rescinded.
[Washington, 1837] 2 p. DNA.
48168

---- Resolution on the Price of
Public Lands. Representative
Lawler. Dec. 22, 1837. Reports
of Committees, Resolution No.
4, 25th Cong., 2d sess., Vol.
IV. That it is expedient to
reduce, according to some equit-
able scale of gradation, the price
of such public lands as will
not sell within a reasonable time
at one dollar and twenty-five
cents per acre. [Washington,
1837] 1 p. DNA. 48169

---- Resolution relative to Public Lands. Representative
Chilton Allan. Jan. 7, 1837.
Reports of Committees, Resolution No. 1, 24th Cong., 2d sess.,
Vol. II. That a select committee be appointed to inquire into
the justice and expediency of
making to each of the thirteen
original States, together with
each of the State of Maine, Vermont, Kentucky, and Tennessee, grants of land for education
proportionate to those made to
new States and Territories;
Amendment proposed by Mr.
Vinton. [Washington, 1837]
2 p. DNA. 48170

---- Resolutions on a National
Bank. New Hampshire Legislature. July 7, 1837. Senate
Docs., No. 19, 25th Cong., 1st
sess. In opposition to any
proposition to charter a bank of
the United States. [Washing-
ton, 1837] 1 p. DNA. 48171

---- Resolutions on a National
Bank. Representative Sher-
rod Williams. Sept. 28, 1837.
Ex. Docs., Resolution No. 3,
25th Cong., 1st sess. In favor of the establishment of a
national bank. [Washington,
1837] 1 p. DNA. 48172

---- Resolutions on Boundary-
Lines. Missouri Legislature.
Dec. 2, 1837. Senate Docs.,
No. 63, 25th Cong., 2d sess.,
Vol. I. In favor of the appointment by Congress of
commissioners to settle the
boundary-line between Missouri and Wisconsin. [Wash-
ington, 1837] 3 p. DNA.
48173

---- Resolutions on Censure of
President and Election of Vice-
President. Feb. 13, 1837.
Ex. Docs., No. 157, 24th Cong.,
2d sess., Vol. IV. Resolutions
of Rhode Island Legislature instructing the Senators from
Rhode Island to vote to expunge
from the Journal of the Senate
the resolution censuring the
President for his action relative to the public deposits, and
to vote for Richard M. Johnson
for Vice-President, should the
election of that officer devolve
upon the Senate. [Washington,
1837] 1 p. DNA. 48174

---- Resolutions on Censure of
the President. Delaware
Legislature. Jan. 21, 1737.
Senate Docs., No. 152, 24th
Cong., 2d sess., Vol. II. In
favor of restoring to the Senate
Journal the resolutions censuring
the President for his action to
the public deposits, expunged
from the Journal by order of
the Senate. [Washington, 1837]
2 p. DNA. 48175

---- Resolutions on Censure of
the President. Michigan Legislature. Jan. 19, 1837. Senate
Docs., No. 128, 24th Cong., 2d
sess., Vol. II. In favor of expunging from the Senate Journal
the resolutions censuring the
President for his action in regard to the public deposits.
[Washington, 1837] 3 p. DNA.
48176

---- Resolutions on Financial
Condition of the Country. Citizens of Ohio. Sept. 23, 1837.
Senate Docs., No. 33, 25th Cong.,
1st sess., Vol. I. Approving
the measures proposed by the
Executive, etc. [Washington,
1837] 5 p. DNA. 48177

---- Resolutions on Government
Finances. New Jersey Legislature. Nov. 15, 1837. Ex.
Docs., No. 88, 25th Cong., 2d
sess., Vol. V. Disapproving
the measures of the President
in relation to the currency, the
public deposits, appointments
to office, etc. [Washington,
1837] 3 p. DNA. 48178

---- Resolutions on Improvement
of Navigation. New Jersey
Legislature. Jan. 18, 1837.
Ex. Docs., No. 100, 24th Cong.,
2d sess., Vol. III. In favor of
improving the navigation of
Newark Bay, and of removing
the obstructions to the navigation of Staten Island Sound.
[Washington, 1837] 2 p. DNA.
48179

---- Resolutions on Internal Improvements. Board of Public
Works of Ill. Oct. 13, 1837.
Senate Docs., No. 34, 25th
Cong., 1st sess. Requesting
donations of public lands in aid
of internal improvements in Illinois. [Washington, 1837] 1 p.
DNA. 48180

---- Resolutions on Louisville and Portland Canal. Indiana Legislature. Jan. 10, 1837. Ex. Docs., No. 101, 24th Cong., 2d sess., Vol. III. In opposition to the purchase by the United States of the stock of the Louisville and Portland Canal Company. [Washington, 1837] 1 p. DNA.   48181

---- Resolutions on Pre-emption Law. Convention of Illinois settlers. Dec. 11, 1837. Senate Docs., No. 248, 25th Cong., 2d sess., Vol. III. In favor of circulating for signatures among the people of the northern part of Illinois copies of a memorial asking the passage of a pre-emption law. [Washington, 1837] 4 p. DNA.   48182

---- Resolutions on Slavery and Right of Petition. Massachusetts Legislature. April 12, 1837. Ex. Docs., No. 21, 25th Cong., 1st sess. Condemning the action of the House of Representatives in ordering that all petitions, etc., relative to slavery be laid on the table without further action, and asserting the right of Congress to abolish slavery in the District of Columbia. [Washington, 1837] 2 p. DNA.   48183

---- Resolutions on State Rights and Slavery. Senator Norvell. Dec. 28, 1837. Senate Docs., No. 49, 25th Cong., 2d sess., Vol. I. Asserting the sovereignty of the States and condemning any interference by one State with the domestic institutions of any other. [Washington, 1837] 1 p. DNA.   48184

---- Resolutions on Surplus Revenue. Indiana Legislature. Feb. 16, 1837. Ex. Docs., No. 160, 24th Cong., 2d sess., Vol. IV. In favor of the relinquishment by the United States of any claim to the surplus revenue deposited with the several States. [Washington, 1837] 1 p. DNA.   48185

---- Resolutions on Texas, Slavery, etc. Vermont Legislature. Nov. 1, 1837. Ex. Docs., No. 182, 25th Cong., 2d sess., Vol. VII. Protesting against the annexation of Texas to the Union, and of any State whose constitution tolerates domestic slavery, and affirming the right of Congress to abolish slavery in the District of Columbia and in the Territories, and to prohibit the slave trade between the States. [Washington, 1837] 4 p. DNA.   48186

---- Resolutions on the Delaware Piers. Delaware Legislature. Feb. 13, 1837. Ex. Docs., No. 147, 24th Cong., 2d sess., Vol. IV. Asking an appropriation for the construction and repair of certain piers on the Delaware Bay and River. [Washington, 1837] 2 p. DNA.   48187

---- Resolutions on the Electoral Vote. Indiana Legislature. Feb. 3, 1837. Ex. Docs., No. 171, 24th Cong., 2d sess., Vol. IV. In favor of various amendments to the Constitution in relation to the election of President and Vice-President, and the appointment of Senators or Representatives to office by the Executive. [Washington, 1837] 1 p. DNA.   48188

---- Resolutions on the Franking Privilege. Maryland Legislature. Jan. 16, 1837. Ex. Docs., No. 103, 24th Cong., 2d sess., Vol. III. In favor of extension of the franking privilege to Governors of States and to the members and chief clerks of the State Legislatures. [Washington, 1837] 2 p. DNA.   48189

---- Resolutions on the Franking Privilege. Mississippi Legislature. May 13, 1837. Senate Docs., No. 5, 25th Cong., 1st sess. In favor of extending the franking privilege to Governors of States, and opposed to extending it to members of State Legislatures. [Washington, 1837] 1 p. DNA.   48190

---- Resolutions on the Franking Privilege. Virginia Legislature. Feb. 15, 1837. Ex. Docs., No. 179, 24th Cong., 2d sess., Vol. IV. In favor of extending the franking privilege to members and chief clerks of the various State Legislatures if it can be done without interfering with the proposed reduction in private postage. [Washington, 1837] 1 p. DNA.   48191

---- Resolutions relative to Annexation of Florida. Alabama Legislature. Dec. 23, 1837. Ex. Docs., No. 163, 25th Cong., 2d sess., Vol. VII. In favor of the annexation to Alabama of that part of West Florida lying south of said State. [Washington, 1837] 1 p. DNA.   48192

---- Resolutions relative to Annexation of Texas. Rhode Island Legislature. Dec. 29, 1837. Ex. Docs., No. 55, 25th Cong., 2d sess., Vol. II. In opposition to the annexation of Texas to the Union. [Washington, 1837] 2 p. DNA.   48193

---- Resolutions relative to Bridge in Indiana. Indiana

Legislature. Jan. 21, 1837. Ex. Docs., No. 149, 24th Cong., 2d sess., Vol. IV. Asking a grant of land to aid in the construction of a bridge over the Kankakee River. [Washington, 1837] 1 p. DNA.   48194

---- Resolutions relative to Certain Land Claims. Indiana Legislature. Feb. 3, 1837. Senate Docs., No. 186, 24th Cong., 2d sess., Vol. II. Recommends passage of a law to ascertain the justice of the land claims of certain French Canadian inhabitants of Vincennes. [Washington, 1837] 1 p. DNA.   48195

---- Resolutions relative to Certain Public Lands. Indiana Legislature. Feb. 2, 1837. Ex. Docs., No. 161, 24th Cong., 2d sess., Vol. IV. Asking passage of a law selling to Indiana, at the minimum price, certain public lands on the line of the Wabash and Erie Canal. [Washington, 1837] 1 p. DNA.   48196

---- Resolutions relative to Construction of Piers. Delaware Legislature. Feb. 2, 1837. Senate Docs., No. 129, 24th Cong., 2d sess., Vol. II. Asking an appropriation for the construction of piers in Delaware Bay and River. [Washington, 1837] 2 p. DNA.   48197

---- Resolutions relative to Dry-Dock. New Jersey Legislature. Jan. 26, 1837. Senate Docs., No. 150, 24th Cong., 2d sess., Vol. II. Asking that surveys be made for the construction of a dry-dock within the State of New Jersey. [Washington, 1837] 1 p. DNA.   48198

---- Resolutions relative to Foreign

Duty on Tobacco. Md. Legislature. Jan. 23, 1837. Senate
Docs., No. 132, 24th Cong.,
2d sess., Vol. II. Requesting
measures to obtain a reduction
of the duty imposed by foreign
governments on the introduction of tobacco within their
respective limits. [Washington,
1837] 2 p. DNA.   48199

---- Resolutions relative to Harbors on Lake Michigan. Indiana Legislature. Jan. 26, 1837.
Ex. Docs., No. 148, 24th Cong.,
2d sess., Vol. IV. Asking
that surveys be made for construction of harbors at Indiana
City and City West, on Lake
Michigan. [Washington, 1837]
1 p. DNA.   48200

---- Resolutions relative to Harbors on Lake Michigan. Indiana Legislature. Jan. 26, 1837.
Senate Docs., No. 151, 24th
Cong., 2d sess., Vol. II. Asking survey of two harbors on
Lake Michigan, one at City West
and one at Indiana City. [Wash-
ington, 1837] 1 p. DNA.
                           48201
---- Resolutions relative to Hospital Tax. Delaware Legislature.
Feb. 13, 1837. Ex. Docs., No.
146, 24th Cong., 2d sess.,
Vol. IV. In favor of repealing
the tax of hospital-money on
persons engaged in the coasting trade and the fisheries.
[Washington, 1837] 1 p. DNA.
                           48202
---- Resolutions relative to
Louisville and Portland Canal.
Ind. Legislature. Jan. 10,
1837. Senate Docs., No. 117,
24th Cong., 2d sess., Vol. II.
In opposition to the purchase by
the United States of the stock of
the Louisville and Portland Canal.
[Washington, 1837] 1 p. DNA.
                           48203

---- Resolutions relative to
Newark Bay. New Jersey Legislature. Jan. 17, 1837. Senate
Docs., No. 116, 24th Cong., 2d
sess., Vol. II. In favor of an
appropriation for the removal of
sand bars in Newark Bay.
[Washington, 1837] 2 p. DNA.
                           48204
---- Resolutions relative to President's Message. Representative
Cushing. Dec. 19, 1837. Reports of Committees, Resolution
No. 2, 25th Cong., 2d sess.,
Vol. IV. Directing reference of
the portion of the President's
message relating to the collection
and safe-keeping of the public
money to a committee, with instructions to report on a method
of keeping the public treasure
which shall promote the welfare,
etc., of the people, and other
reforms in the administration of
the Government. [Washington,
1837] 1 p. DNA.   48205

---- Resolutions relative to President's Message. Representative
Haynes. Dec. 7, 1837. Reports
of Committees, 25th Cong., 2d
sess., Vol. IV, Resolution No.
1. Committing to the different
committees of the House the consideration of the various matters
alluded to in the message of the
President. [Washington, 1837]
2 p. DNA.   48206

---- Resolutions relative to Public Lands. Indiana Legislature.
Feb. 2, 1837. Senate Docs.,
No. 187, 24th Cong., 2d sess.,
Vol. II. Asking passage of law
allowing the State of Indiana to
purchase at minimum price certain public lands on the Wabash
and Erie Canal. [Washington,
1837] 1 p. DNA.   48207

---- Resolutions relative to Road

in Ohio. Ohio Legislature.
Jan. 10, 1837. Senate Docs.,
No. 154, 24th Cong., 2d
sess., Vol. II. In favor of
an appropriation for the repair
of the Maumee and Western Reserve road. [Washington,
1837] 2 p. DNA.   48208

---- Resolutions realtive to
School Lands. Illinois Legislature. Feb. 1, 1837. Senate
Docs., No. 126, 24th Cong., 2d
sess., Vol. II. In favor of
passage of law authorizing selection of other lands in lieu of
such school sections as may be
unavailable for the purpose for
which they were granted.
[Washington, 1837] 1 p. DNA.
                        48209
---- Resolutions relative to Ship-
Canal. Ohio Legislature. Jan.
23, 1837. Senate Docs., No.
156, 24th Cong., 2d sess., Vol.
II. Asking the construction of
a ship-canal around the Falls of
Niagara. [Washington, 1837]
4 p. DNA.   48210

---- Resolutions relative to Specie
Payments. Representative Biddle. Sept. 7, 1837. Ex. Docs.,
Resolution No. 1, 25th Cong.,
1st sess. Directing Secretary
of the Treasury to report whether he has offered to pay members
of Congress in specie, and to
what other claimants a similar
offer has been made, etc.
Amendment offered by Representative Robertson asking general information as to receipts
and disbursements of specie.
[Washington, 1837] 1 p. DNA.
                        48211
---- Resolutions realtive to State
Rights and Slavery. Senate
Calhoun. Dec. 27, 1837. Senate
Docs., No. 47, 25th Cong., 2d
sess., Vol. I. Asserting the

rights of the States over their
own domestic institutions, and
condemning any interference by
Congress or any of the States
with the institution of slavery.
[Washington, 1837] 2 p. DNA.
                        48212
---- Resolutions relative to State
Rights and Slavery. Senator
Morris. Dec. 29, 1837. Senate
Docs., No. 54, 25th Cong., 2d
sess., Vol. I. Asserting the
right of the people of any State
to discuss the domestic instituions
of any of the States, the right of
Congress to prohibit the slave
trade between the States, or to
abolish slavery in the District
of Columbia, etc. [Washington,
1837] 3 p. DNA.   48213

---- Resolutions relative to Tax
for Hospitals. Delaware Legislature. Feb. 2, 1837. Senate
Docs., No. 130, 24th Cong., 2d
sess., Vol. II. In favor of repeal of laws imposing taxes for
hospital money on persons engaged in the coasting trade.
[Washington, 1837] 1 p. DNA.
                        48214
---- Resolutions relative to the
Subtreasury Bill. Citizens of
New Jersey. March 29, 1837.
Senate Docs., No. 391, 25th
Cong., 2d sess., Vol. V. In
opposition to the passage of the
subtreasury bill pending in Congress. [Washington, 1837] 2
p. DNA.   48215

---- Resolutions relative to the
Tariff. New Hampshire Legisla-
ture. Jan. 13, 1837. Ex. Docs.,
No. 113, 24th Cong., 2d sess.,
Vol. III. In favor of a reduc-
tion of the tariff to meet the
actual wants of the Government.
[Washington, 1837] 2 p. DNA.
                        48216
---- Resolutions relative to the

Tariff. Rhode Island Legislature. Jan. 28, 1837. Senate Docs., No. 118, 24th Cong., 2d sess., Vol. II. In opposition to any reduction of the duties on imports. [Washington, 1837] 1 p. DNA.   48217

---- Resolutions relative to West Florida. Alabama Legislature. Dec. 23, 1837. Senate Docs., No. 107, 25th Cong., 2d sess., Vol. II. In favor of the annexation to Alabama of that portion of West Florida lying south of that State. [Washington, 1837] 1 p. DNA.   48218

---- Rules of the House. 1837. Printed by Thomas Allen. Constitution of the United States, Rules of the House of Representatives, Joint Rules of the two Houses, and Rules of the Senate, with Jefferson's Manual. Printed by order of the House of Representatives. [Washington, 1837] 222 p. DNA. 48219

---- Senate Documents, Twenty-fifth Congress, Second Session. From Dec. 4, 1837. Vol. I, Docs., Nos. 1 to 92, inclusive. Printed by Blair & Rives. Vol. II, Docs. No. 93 to 138, inclusive. Printed by Blair & Rives. Vol. III, Docs. Nos. 139 to 261, inclusive. Printed by Blair & Rives. Vol. IV, Docs. Nos. 262 to 387, inclusive. Printed by Blair & Rives. Vol. V, Docs. Nos. 388 to 470, inclusive. Printed by Blair & Rives. Vol. VI, Docs. Nos. 471 to 509, inclusive. Printed by Blair & Rives. [Washington, 1837] DNA.   48220

---- Senate Journal, Twenty-fifth Congress, First Session. Sept. 4, 1837. Printed by Blair & Rives, Washington. From September 4, 1837, to October 16, 1837. Vice-President, Richard M. Johnson, of Kentucky; President of the Senate pro tempore, William R. King, of Alabama, elected March 7, 1837, at special session, again elected October 13, 1837; Secretary of the Senate, Asbury Dickins, of North Carolina. [Washington, 1837] 92 p. DNA.   48221

---- Senate Journal, Twenty-fifth Congress, Second Session. Dec. 4, 1837. Printed by Blair & Rives, Washington. From December 4, 1837, to July 9, 1838. Vice-President, Richard M. Johnson, of Kentucky; President of the Senate pro tempore, William R. King, of Alabama, elected March 7, 1837, at special session, again elected October 12, 1837, again elected July 2, 1838, and again elected February 25, 1839; Secretary of the Senate, Asbury Dickins, of North Carolina. [Washington, 1837] 770 p. DNA.   48222

---- State Action on Suspension of Specie Payments. Clerk W. S. Franklin. Nov. 25, 1837. Ex. Docs., No. 13, 25th Cong., 2d sess., Vol. II. Transmitting copies of laws enacted by State Legislatures in relation to the suspension of specie payments by the banks. [Washington, 1837] 26 p. DNA.   48223

---- Statement of Appropriations, New Offices, etc. Oct. 17, 1837. Senate Docs., No. 37, 25th Cong., 1st sess. Appropriations made during the first session of the Twenty-fifth Congress; New offices created and salaries thereof. [Washington, 1837] 3 p. DNA.   48224

---- Statement of Condition of the Treasury. Sept. 18, 1837. Ex. Docs., No. 23, 25th Cong., 1st sess. Estimated state of the Treasury on October 1, 1837; Probable state of the Treasury in the last quarter of 1837, excluding unavailable funds. [Washington, 1837] 2 p. DNA. 48225

---- Statement of Imports and Exports of Specie. McClintock Young. Oct. 2, 1837. Senate Docs., No. 32, 25th Cong., 1st sess. Imports and exports of specie, according to returns received at the Treasury, since September 19, 1837. [Washington, 1837] 1 p. DNA. 48226

---- Statement of Mode of Collecting Revenue in Great Britain and France. Sept. 14, 1837. Ex. Docs., No. 12, 25th Cong., 1st sess. Mode in which the revenues of Great Britain are carried into the exchequer; Mode of collecting, keeping, and transferring public money in France. [Washington, 1837] 3 p. DNA. 48227

---- Statement of Persons Imprisoned for Debt in the District of Columbia. 1837. Statement of persons imprisoned for debt in the District of Columbia since 1820, by George Watterson, under direction from the House. An act approved March 3, 1837, appropriated $600 for the payment of Mr. Watterson. [Washington, 1837] DNA. 48228

---- Statement of Potomac Bridge Claim. O. H. Dibble. Dec. 11, 1837. Ex. Docs., No. 33, 25th Cong., 2d sess., Vol. II. Statement relative to his claim for damages on account of the annulling by the United States

of his contract for building bridge across the Potomac at Washington. [Washington, 1837] 9 p. DNA. 48229

---- Statement of the Condition of the Treasury. Sept. 30, 1837. Ex. Docs., No. 37, 25th Cong., 1st sess. Estimate of the state of the Treasury and of its outstanding resources and liabilities on the 1st of January, 1838. [Washington, 1837] 1 p. DNA. 48230

---- Statements of Appropriations, New Offices, etc. Secretary of Senate. March 27, 1837. Senate Docs., No. 223, 24th Cong., 2d sess., Vol. III. Appropriations made during the second session of the Twenty-fourth Congress; Offices created and the salaries thereof; Offices the salaries of which have been increased. [Washington, 1837] 40 p. DNA. 48231

---- Statements of Gold Coinage and Imports and Exports of Specie. Sept. 19, 1837. Senate Docs., No. 17, 25th Cong., 1st sess. Amount of gold coined at the United States Mint from January 1 to August 31, 1837; Imports and exports of specie since September 30, 1836, from returns received up to September 19, 1837. [Washington, 1837] 1 p. DNA. 48232

---- Supplemental Land Instructions. Oct. 1, 1837. Library of the Interior Department. Supplemental to instructions of 9th of June, 1837. [Washington, 1837] 3 p. DNA. 48233

---- Surveyor-Generals' Estimates. May 28, 1837. Library of the Interior Department. Circular relating to surveyor-

generals' annual estimates, etc.
[Washington, 1837] DNA. 48234

---- Synopsis of Laws, etc.,
relative to Revolutionary Claims.
Dec. 27, 1837. Ex. Docs., No.
42, 25th Cong., 2d sess., Vol.
II. Digest of laws, opinions,
etc., on the subject of allowing
interest on Revolutionary claims.
[Washington, 1837] 12 p. DNA.
                                    48235
---- Township Plats. June 13,
1837. Library of the Interior
Department. Circular to the
surveyor-generals, instructing
them to furnish registers and
receivers plats of townships not
heretofore furnished. [Washing-
ton, 1837] DNA.   48236

---- Treasury Circular to Land
Receivers. May 17, 1837. Library of the Interior Department.
Circular of the Treasury Department to receivers relative
to drafts to be hereafter issued. [Washington, 1837] 1
p. DNA.   48237

---- Western Academy of Natural Sciences. Officers of
Academy. Dec. 28, 1837.
Senate Docs., No. 71, 26th
Cong., 2d sess., Vol. III.
Prays aid of Government in
purchase of library, instruments, and building, and purchase of ground for botanic
garden. [Washington, 1837]
3 p. DNA.   48238

---- Circuit Court (4th Circuit).
Reports...John Marshal...
1837.   48239

---- ---- Reports of cases decided
by the honourable John Marshall
... in the Circuit court of the
United States, for the district
of Virginia and North Carolina,

from 1802 to 1833 inclusive,
edited by John W. Brockenbrough
...Philadelphia, James Kay, Jun,
and Bro., etc., 1837. 2 v.
IaUL; Mi-L; Nj; OCLaw; PU.
                                    48240
---- Congress. House. Select
Committee Relative to the Bank
of the United States.
   Report of the Select Commit-
tee Relative to the United States
Bank, together with the testi-
mony taken in relation thereto.
Mr. Hill, chairman. Read in the
House of Representatives March
24, 1837. Harrisburg, printed
by S. D. Patterson, 1837. 55
p. MH; P; PHi; PP; PPN; MiD-B.
                                    48241
No entry   48242

---- ---- Senate....
   ... Report on a bill to settle
and establish the Northern
Boundary line of the state of
Ohio, ... Washington, Gales
& Seaton, [1836]. 53 p. OT.
                                    48243
---- Constitution.
   Constitution of the United
States of America: rules of the
House of representatives,
joint rules of the two Houses,
and rules of the Senate, with
Jefferson's Manual...Washington,
T. Allen, printer to the House,
1837. [9]-222 p. IaK; MW;
ViU.   48244

---- ---- Constitutions of the
United States, and State of
Michigan; with the Ordinance of
1787, and the Act admitting
Michigan into the Union, etc.

Detroit, Published by Bagg,
Barns and Co., 1837. 74 p.
Mi.   48245

---- District Court. Pa. (East-
ern district).
Reports of cases adjusted in
the District Court of the United
States for the Eastern district
of Pennsylvania, [1828-1836].
By Henry D. Gilpin. Phila-
delphia, P. H. Nicklin and T.
Johnson, 1837. 656 p. DLC;
KyU; NcD; NN; WaU-L.   48246

---- Office of Indian Affairs.
Board of Indian Commissioners.
Report of the board of com-
missioners, assembled at
Michilimackinac, September,
1836, on the claims of creditors,
of the Ottawas and Chippewas,
presented under the Treaty of
Washington, concluded with
those tribes March 28th, 1836.
Detroit, Printed by Geo. L.
Whitney, 1837. 66 p. MBC;
MiD-B; MiGr.   48247

---- Post Office Department.
Tables of the post offices in
the United States, on the
fifteenth July 1837, arranged in
alphabetical order, exhibiting
the states and countries in
which they are situated-the
names of the postmasters-and
the distance of each office as
far as satisfactorily ascertained
from the Capital, of the United
States, and the state capitals
respectively. Washington,
Langtree and O'Sullivan,
1837. 190 p. MMedHi.   48248

---- President, 1829-1837 (Jackson).
The farewell address of
Andrew Jackson: and the
inaugural of Martin Van Buren,
president of the United States.

Published and delivered on the
fourth of March, one thousand
eight hundred and thirty-seven.
Raleigh, N.C., T. Loring, printer, 1837. 36 p. DLC.   48249

---- ---- Farewell address of
Andrew Jackson to the people
of the United States ... Harrisburg, Printed by S. D. Patterson, 1837. 16 p. DLC; ICN;
MiD-B; MoKU; NcU; P; PHi (14
p.); PU; PPeSchw; PPi.   48250

---- ---- Farewell address of
Andrew Jackson to the people
of the United States: and the
inaugural address of Martin Van
Buren, president of the United
States. Washington, Blair and
Rives, printers, 1837. 23 p.
ICN; MiGr; MnU; NjR; TCh; WHi.
                              48251
---- ---- Message from the
President of the United States,
to both Houses of congress, at
the opening of the first session
of the twenty-fifth congress.
Washington, Thomas Allen, 1837.
29, (1) p. MoSU; Nj.   48252

---- ---- Messages of Gen. Andrew Jackson: with a short
sketch of his life. Concord,
N.H., J. F. Brown and W. White,
1837. 429 p. InU; LNH; MiU;
RBr; WHi.   48253

---- President, 1837-1841 (Van
Buren).
Message from the President
of the United States, to the two
houses of Congress, at the commencement of the second session
of the Twenty-fifth Congress.
[Washington, Printed by Blair
and Rives, 1837] 16 p. CoCsC;
DLC; MB; Nj; WHi.   48254

---- Treaties, etc.
Treaties between the United

States of America and the several Indian tribes, from 1778
to 1837: with a copious table
of contents. Compiled and
printed by the direction, and
under the supervision, of the
commissioner of Indian affairs.
Washington, D.C., Langtree
and O'Sullivan, 1837. 699 p.
CSansS; ICHi; KyLoF; MdHi;
WHi.   48255

---- ---- Two treaties made
and concluded at forks of the
Wabash in the state of Indiana
between the United States of
America ... and the Miami
Tribe of Indians. Q. Wash.,
1837-39. In.   48256

United States Almanac for 1838.
     Calculations by Charles
Frederick Egelmann. Philadelphia, Pa., George W.
Mentz, [1837]. MWA; PPeSchw.
                              48257
The United States register,
geographical, historical, and
statistical. New York, Published by Phelps & Squire,
1837. 54 p. CSmH; IaDaP;
MWA; PHi; RPL.   48258

Unity Scientific and Military
Academy.
     Catalogue of The Officers
and Students of Unity Scientific & Military Academy, for
the year ending November 21,
1837. Claremont, N.H., Printed
at the Book Office, by N. W.
Goddard, 1837. 12 p. MeB;
Nh.   48259

Universal Lyceum.
     First report... Philadelphia,
1837. PPL.   48260

Universalist Church in America.
Convention.
     Annual report of the general

convention of Universalists, for
the United States of America,
for the year 1837,...together
with the proceedings of the Universalist Historical Society.
New York, published by P.
Price..., 1837. MiD-B; MMet-Hi;
NCoS; PPL; RPB.   48261

Universalist Sabbath School
Association.
     Proceedings and constitution
of the Universalist Sabbath
School Association; with the report of the Committee on the
best method of conducting sabbath schools; and the sermon
delivered before the association,
Boston, Abel Tomkins, ...
(J. N. Bang, Printer...), 1837.
23, (1) p. MHi; MiD-B; MMeT;
MMeT-Hi.   48262

The Universalist Year Book.
     Universalist register and al-
manac for 1838: containing statistics of the denomination of
Universalists in the United
States, and the British Provinces;
together with various articles illustrative of Universalism. O.
Whiston and G. Sanderson, publishers. Rochester, Printed at
the office of the Herald of
Truth, [1837]. 36 p. MWA;
NRU; WHi.   48263

Upham, Thomas Cogswell, 1799-
1872.
     Elements of mental philosophy,
embracing the two departments
of the intellect and the sensibil-
ities, by Thomas C. Upham ...
2d ed. Portland, [Me.], W.
Hyde, 1837. 2 v. InNd; MH;
NhPet; NNUT; ViU.   48264

Utica, N.Y. Directories.
     Utica directory....1837-8;
containing 1st--an account of the
various institutions of the city;

2nd--a directory of the streets
of Utica, with their commencement and termination; 3d--a
directory of the citizens of
Utica to which is added an
advertising list. Utica, G.
Tracy, publisher, Eli Maynard,
printer, (1837?). 156 p.
MH; NUt; NUtSC.   48265

---- Female Academy.
Circular of the Utica Female
Academy. Schenectady, 1837.
11 p. NUt.   48266

V

Vale, Gilbert, 1788-1866.
A companion to Vale's United
Globe and Celestial Sphere.
New York, 1837. 52 p. MB;
PHi; PU; RPB.   48267

---- A compendium of the life
of Thomas Paine By G. Vale.
... New York, Published by
the author, 1837. 4-32 p.
CSmH; MdHi; MiU-C; NN; OC.
                          48268
[Vallejo, Mariano G., 1808-1890.
Dios y libertad, Sonoma,
Febrero 20 de 1837. Broadsheet.
CHi; CSmH; CSt; CU-B.   48269

---- Dios y libertad, Sonoma,
Enero 7 de 1837. Broadsheet.
CHi; CSmH; CSt; CU-B.   48270

---- Dios y libertad, Sonoma,
Enero 24 de 1837. Broadsheet.
CHi; CSmH; CSt; CU-B.   48271

---- Ecspocision [!] que hace el
comdanante [!] general interino
de la Alta California al gobernador de la misma. [Sonoma,
Cal., 1837]. 21 p. CSmH;
CSt; CU; DLC.   48272

---- Proclama Mariano G. Vallejo

comandante general de la Alta
California, a sus habitantes.
[Monterey, February 24, 1837].
Broadside. CU-B.   48273

Valley Railroad in Vermont.
Report of the engineer on
the survey. Montpelier, Clark,
1837. 40 p. NN; PPFrankI.
                          48274
Valpy, Richard, 1754-1836.
... The elements of Greek
grammar, by R. Valpy ... 12
ed. New York, W. E. Dean,
1837. 301 p. CU; DLC; ICU;
KyU; NNG.   48275

Valton, John, 1740-1794.
The life and labours of the
late Rev. John Valton. By John
Valton; new ed. with many
additions and letters to Jos. Sut-
cliffe.... New York, T. Mason
& G. Lane, 1837. 163 p. DLC;
ICBB; NjMD; OrU; TxU.   48276

The Value of the Soul from Its
Nature and Faculties. Methodist
Tracts. New York, 1837. IEG.
                          48277
Van Cott, Joshua Martin.
A discourse upon the life,
character and services of James
Madison, late ex-president of
the United States, delivered before the "Hamilton literary association" of the city of Brooklyn,
(the Common Council and citizens being invited) on the
twenty-eight day of July, 1836.
Brooklyn, 1837. 26 p. Ct; MH;
PHi; RPB; WHi.   48278

Van Heythuysen, Frederick Miles.
(The) Equity draftsman, being
a selection of forms of pleadings
in suits in equity.... Revised
and enlarged, with numerous
additional forms and practical
notes, by Edward Hughes, Esq.
From the 2d London edition. New

York, Halsted & Voorhies, Law
Booksellers, 1837. 952 p.
In-SC; LNT-L; MH-L; NRAL;
OCLaw.   48279

Vanarsdale, Cornelius Cornell.
The Christian patriot. An
oration, before the alumni of
Rutger's College; pronounced
in the college chapel, at New
Brunswick N.J... Hartford,
Printed by Case, Tiffany and
Burnham, 1837. 32 p. MH-
And; NjR; PPPrHi; RPB; VtU.
                          48280
Vanderpoel, Aaron, 1799-1871.
Speech of Mr. Vanderpoel,
of New York, on the resolution
declaring that slaves have no
right to petition Congress.
Delivered in the House of
Representatives. Feb. 11,
1837. Washington, Printed
at the Globe office, 1837. 7 p.
MBC; MiGr; N; OClWHi; WHi.
                          48281
Vans, William, b. 1763.
A statement of facts, con-
firmed by records of the
Legislature...with the account
against John and Richard Cod-
man as partners. Boston,
January 1837. 10 p. DLC;
MB; MBAt; MH; NHi.   48282

No entry   48283

No entry   48284

Vassa, Gustavus. See Equiano,
Olaudah, b. 1745.   48285

[Velde, Karl Franz van der],
1779-1824.

Tales from the German ...
Boston, American stationers'
company, J. B. Russell, 1837.
2 v. MB; MBL; MH; Mi; MnU.
                          48286
Vergilius Maro, Publius.
Publius Virgilius Maro, Bucolica,
Georgica, et Aeneis, Accedurt
clavis metrica, notulae anglicae
et quaestiones, cura B. A. Geuld
...Bostoniae, Hilliard, Gray et
soc., 1837. 491 p. MoKCM;
MWH; NbU.   48287

---- Publii Virgilii Maronis opera:
or, The works of Virgil, with
copious notes...in English,
comp. from the best commentators
with many that are new, together with an ordo of the most in-
tricate parts of the text...by
J. G. Cooper. Ed. 9. New
York, White, 1837. 615 p.
MH; NcU; PU; TxU.   48288

---- Virgil. The eclogues translated by Wrangham, the georgics
by Soteby, and the Aeneid by
Dryden. In two volumes. Published by Harper & Brothers,
1837. 2 v. IJI; MdBLC; RPB.
                          48289
Vermilye, Thomas Edward, 1803-
1893.
Funeral discourse occasioned
by death of Abraham Van Vech-
ten, delivered in Reformed Prot.
Dutch Church, Albany, Jan. 15,
1837...Albany, 1837. 21 p.
PHi; PPPrHi.   48290

---- An introductory address to
the course of lectures, before
the young men's association for
mutual improvement in the City
of Albany.... By Thomas E.
Vermilye ... Albany, printed by
J. Munsell, 1837. 37 p. MH;
MiD-B; NjR; PPPrHi; WHi.
                          48291
Vermont. General Assembly.

House of Representatives.
Journal of the House of
representatives, of the state
of Vermont, Oct. session,
1837. Published by authority. Montpelier, E. P. Walton
& son, 1837. 293 p. CSmH;
ICU; MH; NhD; WHi.   48292

---- ---- ---- Report of the
Committee on the location of
Franklin county buildings.
October 16, 1837. n.p.,
[1837]. 23 p. NN; VtU.
                          48293
---- ---- Senate.
Journal of the senate of the
state of Vermont, Oct. session,
1837. Pub. by authority.
Montpelier, E. P. Walton &
son, 1837. 131 p. ICU;
MH; MnU; NhD; WHi.   48294

---- Laws, statutes, etc.
Acts passed by the legisla-
ture of the State of Vermont,
at their October session, 1837.
Published by authority. Mont-
pelier, E. P. Walton & Son,
printers, 1837. [3]-112 p.
CU-Law; IaHi; MdBB; Nj; TxU-L.
                          48295
Vermont Year Book, 1838...
Astronomical calculations by
Zadock Thompson, A.M. Mont-
pelier, Published by E. P.
Walton & Son, [1837]. MHi; MWA.
                          48296
View of Iron Mountains of Mis-
souri... Hartford, 1837. PPL.
                          48297
The village school geography.
... By a teacher. Third edi-
tion. Hartford, Published by
Reed and Barber, 1837. 128 p.
NNC.   48298

Vincent, Thomas.
Christ's sudden and certain ap-
pearance in judgment. Chambersburg, Printed for the Publisher by
Thomas J. Wright, 1837. 352 p.

PAnL; WvShT.   48299

The Violet; a Christmas and
New Year's gift. Philadelphia,
Carey and Hart, 1837. NjR;
PPL; TxU; WU.   48300

[Virey, Julien Joseph], 1775-
1846.
Natural history of the negro
race. Extracted from the French.
By J. H. Guenebault...Charles-
ton, S.C., D. J. Dowling, 1837.
162 p. DLC; MdBE; MH; ScC;
ViU.   48301

Virginia. General Assembly.
House of delegates.
... Abstract of the returns
of clerks of courts....1836/37- .
Richmond, 1837-19. LU. 48301a

---- Abstract of the laws relating
to the appointment, powers and
duties of school commissioners...
3rd. ed. Richmond, Shepherd,
1837. 44 p. DHEW; PPPrHi;
Vi.   48302

---- ---- Acts of the General
assembly of Virginia passed at
the extra session, commencing
on the 12th, and terminating on
the 24th June, 1837, in the 61st
year of the commonwealth. Richmond, T. Ritchie, 1837. 11 p.
IaU-L; MdHi; Nj.   48303

---- ---- Acts of the general
assembly of Virginia, passed at
the session of 1836-37, commencing December 5, 1836 and ending
March 31, 1837. ... Richmond,
Thomas Ritchie, printer to the
commonwealth, 1837. 338 p.
IaHi; Ky; Nj; R; ViL; WvW-L.
                          48304
Virginia and Maryland, Or the
Lord Baltamore's printed case,
uncased and answered. Shewing
the illegality of his patent and
usurpation of royal jurisdiction

and dominion there ... London,
1655, [Washington, P. Force,
1837]. 47 p. CSt; IU; MdBP;
MH; TxWB.   48305

Virginia and North Carolina
Almanack for 1838. By David
Richardson. Richmond, Va.,
John Warrock, [1837]. MWA.
                             48306
Der Volksfreund und Hager-
stauner calender, 1838....By
Carl F. Egelmann. Hagerstown,
Maryland, Johann Gruber, n. pr,
[1837]. (20) p. MWA; NjR.
                             48307
Voltaire, [Francois Marie Arouet]
de.
....Histoire de Charles XII,
roi de Suede. Par Voltaire.
Nouvelle edition, revue et cor-
rigee, par J. et P. Mouls....
New-York, Collins, Keese & co.,
1837. 287 p. MH; TJaU; ViNew.
                             48308
---- The history of Charles
the Twelfth, king of Sweden.
By M. de Voltaire. A new
translation, from the last Paris
edition. Hartford, Andrus,
Judd, & Franklin, 1837. 276 p.
Ct; ICP; PU; TNP.   48309

Vyse, Colonel Howard.
Operations carried on at the
pyramids of Gezeh in 1837. v.
1-3. GMM.   48309a

W

Wabash College (Crawfords-
ville, Indiana).
A catalogue of the officers
and students of Wabash College
and Teachers' Seminary. Craw-
fordsville, Ia., Snyder & Holmes,
printers, July 1837. 12 p. MoSM.
                             48310
Wading River Manufacturing
and Canal Co.
First Report...Philadelphia,
printed by L. R. Bailey, 1837.

16 p. MH-BA.   48311

Wakefield, Samuel, 1799-1895.
The Christian's Harp, containing a choice selection of
psalm and hymn tunes....de-
signed for the use of public &
family worship. By Samuel Wakefield, Esq. Corrected & enlarged by Lazarus M'Lain. Pittsburgh, Pub. by Johnston &
Stockton, 1837. (208) p.
InLogCM; PPiHi.   48312

Walch, Johannes Heinrich, 1775-
1855.
Watermans quick step. Boston, 1837. MB.   48313

Waldie's literary omnibus. News,
books entire, sketches, reviews,
tales, miscellaneous intelligence.
V. 1: 1837. Philadelphia, A.
Waldie, 1837. 300 p. CtHWatk;
DLC; IaLB; MdBP; PHi.   48314

Walker, Donald.
British manly exercises containing rowing and sailing, rid-
ing & driving, etc. etc. By
Donald Walker. Philadelphia,
T. Wardle, 1837. 285 p. ICJ;
MB-FA; MoS; MWiW; OCX; RWe.
                             48315
Walker, George, 1803-1879.
Chess made easy; being a
new introduction to the rudiments of that scientific and popular game. ... Baltimore, Published by Bayly & Burns, 1837.
[ix]-x, 94 p. C-S; MH; NbHi;
OCl; WU.   48316

Walker, James, 1794-1874.
"To the law and to the testimony." A discourse on the
deference paid to the scriptures
by Unitarians. Printed for the
American Unitarian association.
Boston, James Munroe & co.,
1837. 32 p. CBPac; DLC;
ICMe; MBAU; MeBat.   48317

Walker, John, 1732-1807.
Cobb's abridgment of J.
Walker's critical pronouncing
dictionary...for the use of
schools...Ithaca, N.Y.,
Mack, Andrus and Woodruff,
1837. 440 p. CSt; NIC; PP.
48318
---- Walker's critical pronouncing dictionary and expositor of
the English language, abridged
for the use of schools. To
which is annexed, an abridgment of Walker's key to the
pronunciation of Greek, Latin,
and Scripture proper names.
Boston, R. S. Davis, etc.,
1837. MH.   48319

---- ---- [New York, Collins
and Hannay, 1837]. 609,
70 p. MiAlbC.   48320

---- ---- Standing edition,
greatly improved. Philadelphia,
printed by Grigg & co. For
Joseph M'Dowell, 1837. 410,
3 p. NNC; OMC.   48321

Walker, Robert James, 1801-
1869.
Speech of Mr. Walker, of
Mississippi. In Senate, September 27, 1837 - On the bill for
the collection, safe keeping, and
disbursement of the public
moneys. [n.p., 1837]. 16 p.
DLC; MBAt; OClWHi; PPM.
48322
---- Speech of Mr. Walker, of
Mississippi, on the bill presented by himself, limiting
the sale of the public lands to
actual settlers. Delivered in
the Senate of the U.S. January 14, 1837. Washington,
Printed at the Globe office,
1837. 8 p. PPL; ViU; WHi.
48323
Walker, Thomas, 1784-1836.
The art of dining; and, The

art of attaining high health.
With a few hints on suppers, by
Thomas Walker ... Philadelphia,
E. L. Carey & A. Hart, 1837.
267 p. CU; MdBP; NjP; PPA;
RBr.   48324

Walker, Timothy, 1806-1856.
Introduction to American law,
designed as a first book for
students. By Timothy Walker,
one of the professors in the law
department of the Cincinnati College. Philadelphia, P. H. Nicklin & T. Johnson, 1837. 679 p.
KyU-L; LNX; NcU; PPB; RPA.
48325
---- Introductory lecture on The
dignity of the law as a profession, ... Cincinnati, Printed at
the Daily gazette office, 1837.
26 p. IaB; MB; MH-L; OClWHi;
PPAmP.   48326

Wall, Garret Dorset, 1783-1850.
Speech ... on the petition of
Col. P. Johnston's heirs, paying
compensation for revolutionary
services ... Senate ... 1836.
Wash., 1837. 7 p. MiD-B; NjR.
48327
[Wallace, William Ross], 1819-
1881.
The Battle of Tippecanoe;
Triumphs of science, and other
poems.... Cincinnati, Published
by P. McFarlin, [Kendall and
Henry, Prs.], 1837. 105, [1]
p. CSmH; In; NBuG; PHi; WHi.
48328
Walley, Samuel Hurd, 1805-1877.
Report of the superintendent
of Mason Street Sabbath School,
1836. Boston, 1837. 10 p.
MH-AH.   48329

---- A superintendent's offering;
being a memoir of two scholars
in the Mason St. Sabbath School.
Boston, 1837. MB; MBC; MH-AH.
48330

Walton, Izaak.
The complete angler. By
Izaak Walton and Charles Cotton...London, C. Tilt; Philadelphia, T. Wardle; (etc., etc.),
1837. 2 v. ICN; MH.   48331

Walz, E. L.
Allgemeine Beschreibung der
Welt oder kurzgefaszte Dar-
stellung des Wissenswverdigsten
aus der Sternkunde, natur-
geschichte und Erdbeschreibung.
Von E. L. Walz, Philadelphia,
J. G. Wesselholft, 1837. 428 p.
                         48332
Wanostrocht, Nicolas, 1745-1812.
Grammer of the French lan-
guage with practical exercises
.... By N. Wanostrocht, L.L.D.
.... Also a Treatise on French
Versification. By M. De Wailly
... Boston, American Stationers
Company, John B. Russell, 1837.
447 p. MeHi.   48333

---- ---- Philadelphia, Barrington & Geo. D. Haswell, [1837].
[16]-447 p. InI; LNL; MH.
                         48334
---- ... Recueil choisi de traits
historiques et de contes moraux.
Avec la signification des mots en
anglais au bas de chaque page
... Par N. Wanostrocht ... Rev.
by Joseph Mauls...New York,
W. E. Dean, 1837. vi, [7]-
298 p. InEuW; MH; MsNF; ViU;
WOccR.   48335

Ward, Jonathan, 1769-1860.
Father Ward's letter to Pro-
fessor Stuart. [Newburyport?
Mass., C. Whippel, 1837]. 10
p. DLC; MB; PHi; OClWHi;
TxU.   48336

Ward, Robert Plumer, 1765-1846.
Fielding; or, Society Atticus;
Or The Retired Statesman: and
St. Lawrence. By the author of

"Tremaine" and "De Vere." Pub.
E. L. Carey & A. Hart. Phila-
delphia, 1837. 3 v. CtHT; MB;
MdW; OCh; ViAl.   48337

---- Tremaine; or, The man of
refinement. Phila., 1837. MBAt.
                         48338
Ward, Samuel, 1786-1839.
Address delivered at the opening of the Stuyvesant Institute
of the City of New-York, on the
4 November, 1837, by Samuel
Ward, Junior. New-York, Published by The Stuyvesant Institute, Geo. F. Hopkins & Son,
Printers, 1837. 34 p. MiD-B;
NNU; PPL-R; RPB; WHi. 48339

Ward, Thomas, 1652-1708.
Errata of the protestant Bible;
or, The truth of the English
translations...New ed. rev.
Philadelphia, 1837. PPL. 48340

[Ward, Thomas], 1807-1873.
A month of freedom....New
York, Published by George Holley,
1837. 90 p. ICU; MWA; NBuG;
NN; RPB.   48341

Ward, William, 1836-1837.
A treatise on Legacies, or re-
quests of personal property. By
William Ward, Esq....Barrister
at Law. Philadelphia, John S.
Littell, Publisher....1837. DLC;
MdBB; OO; PP; WaU-L.   48342

Wardlaw, Ralph, 1779-1853.
Discourses on the principal
points of the Socinian controversy.
Ed. 5. New York, 1837. PPiRPr.
                         48343
Wardrop, James, 1782-1869.
On the curative effects of
blood-letting in the treatment of
diseases, by James Wardrop.
Philadelphia, Published by A.
Waldie, 1837. 73 p. ICU; MeB;
PPM; RNR; ViU.   48344

[Ware, Henry], 1794-1843.
The duties of young men in
respect to the dangers of the
country. (Cambridge, Metcalf,
Torry, and Ballou, 1837?) 21
p. MB; MH; MH-AH.   48345

---- Education the business of
life. Two discourses preached
in the Chapel of Harvard University .... By Henry Ware,
Jr. Cambridge, Metcalf, Torry,
and Ballou, 1837. 28 p. CPBac;
ICMe; MBC; MiD-B; RPB. 48346

---- The nature, reality, and
power of Christian Faith, by
Henry Ware Jr., D.D. Printed
for the American Unitarian association. Boston, James Munroe & co., 1837. 15, (1) p.
ICMe; MCON; MH; MMeT; RP.
                           48347
---- The object and means of
Christian ministry. A sermon,
preached at the ordination of the
Rev. Cyrus A. Bartol, as junior
pastor of the West church in
Boston, Wednesday, March 1,
1837. ... With a charge of
the right hand of fellowship,
and an appendix. Cambridge,
(Mass.), Folsom, Willis, &
Thurston, 1837. 48 p. CPBac;
ICMe; MB; PHi; RPB.   48348

---- Two discourses preached in
the chapel of Harvard University, on the last Sabbath of
the Academical year, 16 July,
MDCCCXXXVII. By Henry
Ware, Jr.,...Cambridge Press,
Metcalf, Torry and Ballou,
1837. 28 p. MBAU.   48349

Ware, William, 1797-1852.
Letters of Lucius M. Piso,
from Palmyra, to his friend
Marcus Curtivs, at Rome. Now
first translated and published.
New-York, C. S. Francis; Bos-

ton, Joseph H. Francis, 1837.
2 v. CSmH; KPea; MB; MH;
RPB.   48350

Warne, Joseph Andrews, 1795-
1881.
The comparative advantages
of written and extemporaneous
sermons. By Joseph A. Warne,
A.M. Boston, Published by
Whipple and Damrell; New York,
Scofield & Voorhies, 1837. 48 p.
CBPac; CtHC; MBC; MH-And;
PPPrHi.   48351

---- A Concise Introduction to
The Study of The Holy Scrip-
tures, ... By the Rev. Joseph
A. Warne. Published by the
Brattleboro Typographic Company,
... Brattleboro, Vermont, 1837.
82, (20), xxiv, 705, 54 p.
KNB; KNnB; MeAu; VtMidSM.
                           48352
Warren, John Collins, 1778-1856.
Circular letter placing his
practise in the hands of his son,
Dr. Mason Warren, Boston, June
1, 1837. 1 p. MHi.   48353

---- Surgical observations on
tumors, with cases and operations.
By John C. Warren, Boston,
Crocker and Brewster, 1837.
207 p. GU-M; KyLxT; MnU;
NhD; PU.   48354

Warren, Samuel, 1807-1877.
Passages from the diary of a
late physician. New York,
Harper, [1837]. 3 v. ArU-M;
MB; OCl.   48355

---- ---- 5th ed. New York,
G. Routledge and sons, [1837].
503 p. DNLM; PAlt; PPP; WMMU-
M.   48356

---- A popular and practical introduction to law studies. By
Samuel Warren.... New York,

Law press, 1837. 552 p. Ct;
Lu-L; MHL; NR; OClW.   48357

Warren academy, Litchfield.
Catalogue of the instructors
and students of Warren academy ... Litchfield, n. pub.,
printed by Henry Adams, 1837.
12 p. NjR.   48358

Warrington, Joseph.
An oration on the improvements in medicine, ... by Joseph
Warrington, M.D. ... Philadelphia, Joseph & William Kite,
printers, 1837. 28 p. NNNAM;
PHC; PHi; PPL.   48359

Washburn, John.
The confession of John Washburn....under sentence of death
for the murder of Mr. Wm. Beaver,
Cincinnati, Ohio, ordered for
execution on the 6th day of
January, 1837, dictated by himself and written by a fellow
prisoner. Cincinnati, np., 1837.
(5), 24 p. MoU; OCHP; PHi.
        48360
Washington, George, 1732-1799.
Washington's abschieds ad-
dresse an das volk der Vereinigten Staaten; bekannt gemacht im
September, A.D. 1796. Gedruckt
in folge eines am 22sten Februar,
A.D. 1837, angenommenen
beschlusses im Hause der repre-
sentanten von Pennsylvanien.
Harrisburg, Jacob Baab, 1837.
16 p. CSmH; MB; NRCR; PHi;
PPCP.   48361

---- The farewell addresses of
General George Washington and
General Andrew Jackson, to the
people of the United States.
Frankfort, Frankfort Argus
office, 1837. 185 p. LPL.
        48362
---- Washington's farewell ad-
dress to the people of the United

States. Published in Sept. 1796.
Printed in pursuance of a reso-
lution of the House of Representa-
tives adapted on the 22nd of
February 1837. Harrisburg,
S. D. Patterson, 1837. MB.
        48363
---- Valedictory address to the
people of the United States.
Published in September, A.D.
1796. ...Harrisburg, S. D. Pat-
terson, 1837. 16 p. CSmH;
DLC; MB; NN; PU.   48364

---- The Writings of George
Washington; being his correspondence, addresses, messages
and other papers, official and
private, selected and published
from the original manuscripts;
with a life of the author, notes
and illustrations. By Jared
Sparks. Boston, American Stationer's Company. John B. Russell, 1837. 12 v. KyLx; LU;
MdAN; ViSwc.   48365

Washington, George Corbin,
1789-1854.
Letters from Geo. C. Washing-
ton, President Chesapeake &
Ohio Canal Company, to the
Governor of Maryland. Annapolis,
William M'Neir, printer, 1837.
(3)-17 p. MBAt; MdHi; MiD-B;
ViU.   48366

Washington College, Washington,
Pa.
Catalogue of the officers and
students of Jefferson College,
Canonsburg, July 1837. Washington, Pa., Printed by John Grayson, 1837. 15 p. PWW. 48367

Washington Insurance Company,
Cincinnati.
Charter and by-laws of the
Washington Insurance Company.
Cincinnati, [Smith, Day & Co.,
printers, No. 4, Main Street],

1837. 12 p. IU; MH-BA;
MiU-C; OCHP.   48368

Washington Medical College of
Baltimore.
Circular of Washington medical college of Baltimore. September 1837. Baltimore, Printed
by William Wooddy, 1837. 8 p.
CtY; DNLM; MdBP; NNN. 48369

Washington Wharf Company,
Boston.
An Act to incorporate the
Washington Wharf Company.
[Boston, 1837]. 4 p. MH.
                       48370
Wasson's Troy Almanac for
1838. Calculated by C. H.
Anthony. Troy, N.Y., N.
Tuttle, [1837]. MWA; NhHM.
                       48371
Watertown, New York.
Black River Literary &
relig. institute. Cat. of
trustees...[Watertown, 1837].
MB; MH.   48372

Waterville college, Woodstock,
Vt.
Catalogue of the officers and
students of Waterville college,
and of the Clinical school of
medicine, at Woodstock, Vt.
connected with the college.
1837-38. Woodstock, Vt.,
Printed by Haskell & Palmer,
1837. (12) p. NNNAM.   48373

Watson, Richard, 1737-1816.
An apology for the Bible, in
a series of letters, addressed
to Thomas Paine, author of the
"Age of Reason" by R. Watson.
New York, Carlton and Porter,
[1837?]. ICRL; NNU-W; ViU.
                       48374
---- ---- New York, Mason and
Lane, 1837. [5]-187 p. ICU;
MdBD; MnSH; TNS.   48375

---- A biblical and theological
dictionary; explanatory of the
history, manners, and customs
of the Jews, and neighboring
nations....An exposition of the
principal doctrines of Christianity....New York, T. Mason and
G. Lane, pub.; J. Collard,
printer, 1837. 1004 p. Ia;
IaHA; MnSH; TxDaM; ViFre.
                       48376
---- The nature, subjects, and
mode of Christian Baptism. By
Rev. Richard Watson. New
York, Published by T. Mason
and G. Lane, for the Methodist
Episcopal Church at the conference office....J. Collord, Printer, 1837. 65 p. IEG; MBC;
MBNMHi; MoKU; NNMHi.   48377

[Watt, Archibald.]
Conveyances on record in the
Register's office, By Archibald
Watt, ... Printed by Alexander
S. Gould, 1837. 40 p. NNMuCN.
                       48378
Watts, Charles.
A discourse on the life and
character of the Hon. George
Mathews, late presiding judge
of the Supreme court of the
state of Louisiana....New Or-
leans, Printed by B. Levy, 1837.
15 p. NIC; RPB; TxU. 48379

Watts, F.
A few simple instructions in
the veterinary Art. By F.
Watts. West Walton Norfolk,
n.p., 1837. 118 p. MoCgS.
                       48380
Watts, Isaac, 1674-1748.
Divine and moral songs for
children. Birmingham, T.
Groom, 1837. 31 p. IaU; ICU;
NjP; PPPrHi.   48381

---- ---- N.Y., Mahlon Day,
1837. MLow.   48382

---- Divine songs. Pt. 1.
Northampton, J. Metcalf, 1837.
24 p. CtY; MH.   48383

---- Divine songs attempted in
easy language for the use of
children. By I. Watts...
New York, Mahlon Day, 1837.
105 p. CtY; MnU; MWbor.
                              48384

---- The improvement of the
mind; or, a supplement to the
art of logic. Containing a variety of remarks and rules for
the attainment and communication of useful knowledge in religion, in the sciences and in
common life. Baltimore, N.
Hickman, 1837. 281 p. MH;
NN.   48385

---- The psalms and hymns of
Dr. Watts, arranged by Dr.
Rippon....Corrected and improved by Rev. C. G. Sommers
...and Rev. John L. Dagg...
Philadelphia, Clark and Lippincott, 1837. ScU.   48386

---- Psalms, hymns, and spiritual songs of the Rev. I.
Watts, to which is added select hymns, from other authors
...by S. Worcester. New ed...
improved by S. M. Worcester...
Boston, Crocker and Brewster,
1837. 28, 51-776 p. GDecCT;
MBC; NN; PPPrHi; PU.   48387

---- Wiconi Owihanke Wannin...
Dr. Watts' second Catechism
for children, in the Dakota language. Boston, printed for the
American Board of Commissioners for Foreign Missions. By
Crocker and Brewster, 1837.
23 p. CtY; DLC; ICN; MBGCT;
MH.   48388

Watts, Marshall.
Organic chemistry adapted for
students for use in science
classes and higher and middle
class schools....M. Watts. New
York, N.Y. Printed by Putnam,
1837. 130 p. UPB.   48389

Wayland, Francis, 1796-1865.
Elements of moral science:
by Francis Wayland, D.D. ...
Third edition revised. Boston,
Gould, Randall, and Lincoln,
1837. 239 p. InU; KMcpC;
NhPet.   48390

---- ---- 4th ed. Boston, Gould,
Kendall, and Lincoln, 1837.
239 p. KAS.   48391

---- ---- Fourth edition, re-
vised and stereotyped. Utica,
Bennett and Bright; Boston,
Gould, Kendall and Lincoln,
1837. 398 p. CtMMHi; CtMW;
NCH; NjR; NUt.   48392

---- ---- Fifth edition. Revised
and stereotyped. Boston, Gould,
Kendall and Lincoln. (etc., etc.),
1837. [2], 4-30, [1], 24-398,
[6] pp. GEU-T; IaDuU; MH;
OUrC; PPM.   48393

---- The elements of political
economy. By Francis Wayland
... New York, Leavitt, Lord &
Company, 1837. 472 p. LU;
MnU; NjP; OWoC; ViRU. 48393a

---- The Elements of political
economy, abridged for the use of
academies. Boston, Gould, Kendall, and Lincoln, 1837. 254 p.
CtHT; InNd; MeB; MoS; WBeloC.
                              48394

---- ---- 6th ed. Boston, Gould,
Kendall and Lincoln, 1837. 406
p. OKentU.   48395

---- The Limitations of Human
Responsibility. 2 ed. New York,
D. Appleton & Co.....1837. 196
p. OrPWB.   48396

---- The moral law of accumulation, the substance of two discourses, delivered in the First Baptist meeting house, Providence, May 14, 1837. Providence, [R.I.], John E. Brown, 1837. 35 p. CSmH; ICN; MB; NNG; OClWHi.   48397

---- ---- 2nd ed. Boston, Gould, Kendall and Lincoln, 1837. 32 p. DLC; MH; NUt; PPL; RPB.   48398

---- ---- Second edition. Utica, Bennett & Bright, printers, 1837. 32 p. DLC; KyLoS; MBC; PPM; ViRU.   48399

Weatherhead, George Hume, 1790-1853.
A practical treatise on the principal diseases of the lungs,, ...by G. Hume Weatherhead, M.D. Philadelphia, Haswell, Barrington, and Haswell, 1837. 89 p. CSt-L; KyU; NBMS; PP; RPM.   48400

Webb, George James, 1803-1887.
The odeon; a collection of secular melodies, arranged and harmonized for four voices, designed for adult singing schools, and for social music parties, by G. J. Webb and Lowell Mason... Boston, J. H. Wilkins and R. B. Carter, 1837. xi, 304 p. CtHT; MB; NUtHi; OO; PPL.   48401

Webb, Thomas Hopkins.
Rheumatism, its cause and treatment, by Thomas H. Webb, M.D. ... Boston, D. Clapp, jr. Office of the medical and surgical journal, 1837. 24 p. IEN-M; MBAt; NNN; RHi; RPB.   48402

Weber, Edward, & company.
Map shewing the connection of the Baltimore and Ohio rail-road with other rail roads executed or in progress throughout the United States. Baltimore, Ed. Weber & co., [1837?]. MdBP.   48403

Webster, Benjamin Nottingham, 1797-1882.
My young wife, and my old umbrella. A farce. In one act. Adapted from the French by Benjamin Webster .. New York, London, Samuel French, [1837]. 16 p. OCl.   48404

---- The swiss swains, an original operetta, in one act. By B. Webster ... the music by Alexander Lee ... New York, Samuel French, [1837]. 20 p. OCl.   48405

Webster, [Daniel], 1782-1852.
Extract's from Mr. Webster's Speeches in the Senate, in 1834, on the subject of the currency. Washington, 1837. 43 p. MiD-B; PHi.   48406

---- The protest against expunging. In the Senate of the United States, Jan. 16, 1837. [Washington, 1837]. 7 p. CU; MB; MBAt; MH.   48407

---- The specie circular. Speech of Mr. Webster, (of Massachusetts) in the Senate, Dec. 21, 1836. [Washington, 1837]. 16 p. CU; ICN; MB; MBAt; MH.   48408

---- ("We Have One Country-One Constitution-One Destiny.") Speech delivered by Daniel Webster, at Niblo's Saloon, in New York on the 15th March 1837. [New York? 1837]. 32 p. DLC; MB; MMal; PHi; TxU.   48409

---- ---- New York, Printed by Harper & Brothers, 1837. 35 p.

IaHi; MH; Nh; RPB; WHi.

48410

---- Mr. Webster's speech on Mr. Ewing's resolution to rescind the Treasury order of July 11, 1836. Delivered in the Senate of the United States, December 21, 1836. Washington, printed by Gales and Seaton, 1837. 37 p. CU; MBAt; MdBJ; OClWHi; PHi.

48411

---- Mr. Webster's speech on the currency, and on the new plan for collecting and keeping the public moneys. Delivered in the Senate of the United States, September 28, 1837. Washington, Printed by Gales and Seaton, 1837. 26 p. KHi; MDeeP; Nh-Hi; OClWHi; RPB.

48412

Webster, Josiah.

The church triumphant: A sermon delivered at the North church, Newburyport, at the ordination of Rev. John Calvin Webster, pastor of the Congregational church in Hampton, N.H. ... Newburyport, press of Hiram Tozer, 1837. [3]-32 p. CtSoP; MBC; Nh-Hi; PPPrHi; RPB.

48413

Webster, Mathew Henry.

Annual address delivered before the Albany institute, April 28th, 1837, by Mathew Henry Webster, A.M.....Albany, Packard and Van Benthuysen, printers, 1837. 24 p. CtHWatk; MB; NjR; PPM.

48414

Webster, Noah, 1758-1843.

An American dictionary of the English language exhibiting the origin, orthography, pronunciation and definitions of words ... Abridged from the quarto ed. of the author. To which are added a synopsis of words differently pronounced by different orthoepists and Walker's key to the classical pronunciation of Greek, Latin and scripture proper names. 15th ed. New York, N. & J. White, 1837. 1011 p. ArCH; C-S; OClW.

48415

---- The American spelling book; containing the rudiments of the English language,....(N.pl.) Stereotyped by the publisher. Sandborton power press, Samuel G. Hayes, 1836. 144 p. NN; NRU-W.

48416

---- A dictionary for primary schools. New York, N. & J. White, 1837. 341 p. MH.

48417

---- The elementary spelling book. Cincinnati, Burgess and Crane, [1837?]. 168 p. CtY.

48418

---- ---- Concord, Published by Roby, Kimball & Merrill, 1837. 168 p. CtHWatk; MeHi; MH; MiU; RPaw.

48419

---- ---- New Haven, S. Babcock, [1837]. 168 p. 319 p. CtY.

48420

---- History of the United States to which is prefixed a brief historical account of our English ancestors...and of the conquest of S. America by the Spaniards. New Haven, S. Babcock, 1837. IaHA; NN; PPL; NBLiHi.

48421

No entry

48422

---- A letter to the hon. Daniel Webster, on the political affairs of the United States. By Marcellus. Philadelphia, printed by

J. Crissy, 1837. 34 p. CtB;
MBC; MH; PHi; PPM.   48423

---- Mistakes and corrections
.... Improprieties and errors
in the common version of the
Scriptures; with specimens of
amended language in Websters
edition of the Bible. Explanations of prepositions, in English,
and other languages these con-
stutute a very difficult part of
philology. Errors in English
grammars.... By Noah Web-
ster. New Haven, B. L. Hamlen; pr., 1837. 3-8 p. MH;
NjR; OMC; PU; VtU.   48424

---- The teacher: a supplement
to the Elementary spelling book
... New Haven, S. Babcock,
1837. 156 p. Ct; MB; MH;
MaToN; P.   48425

Webster's Calendar, or the Albany Almanack for 1838. By
Edwin E. Prentice. Albany,
N.Y., E. W. & C. Skinner,
[1837]. MWA; NAI; NT.   48426

Weeks, (John M.), 1788-1858.
A Manual; or, An Easy Method of Managing Bees, in the
most profitable manner to their
owner, with infallible rules to
prevent their destruction by the
moth. Second Edition. Middlebury, Elan R. Jewett, 1837.
74 p.   48427

Weems, Mason Locke, 1759-1825.
The life of George Washington; with curious anecdotes,
... honourable to himself, and
exemplary to his young country-
men...six engravings. By
M. L. Weems, formerly rector
of Mount Vernon parish...Phila-
delphia, J. Allen, 1837. 228 p.
MdHi; MiU; NjT; PPi; WGr.
                            48428

Weiser, Daniel.
Lichtsdinautze oder Hulfe zur
Wahrheit Eine Enirderung auf
"Das Licht aud dem dunkeln
Eck." Philadelphia, Pa., 1837.
PPeSchw.   48429

Weiss, John.
Song written for the senior
class of 1837. By John Weiss,
jr. (Cambridge, Mass., 1837).
Broadside. MH.   48430

Weisz, George.
Short instruction in the
Christian religion according to
the Heidelberg catechism, in
German and English; an abstract.
Lancaster, Ohio, 1837. 58 p.
OHi.   48431

Welch, B. T.
A discourse addressed to the
First Baptist church and congregation, in the city of Albany,
occasioned by the death of their
pastor, Elder Alanson L. Covell,
Sept. 22nd. 1837. Albany,
printed by Hoffman & White,
1837. 28 p. MBC; MH-And;
NHC-S; NjR; PPPrHi.   48432

Welch, Oliver.
Welch's Improved American
Arithmetic, adapted to the cur-
rency of the United States. To
which is added a concise Treatise
on the mensuration of planes and
solids. Compiled by Oliver
Welch...Concord, (N.H.), Oliver
L. Sanborn, 1837. 218 p.
MBilHi.   48433

[Weld, Theodore Dwight], 1803-
1895.
The Bible against slavery.
An inquiry into the patriarchal
and Mosaic systems on the subject
of human rights. New York,
The American Anti-Slavery Society, 1837. 81 p. DLC; ICN;
OClWHi; OO; TxU.   48434

Wells, E. M. P.
Liturgy of the day for the
School of Moral discipline. By
the rector. E. M. P. Wells.
Boston, Cassady and March,
1837. 12 p. MdBD.   48435

Wells, George W.
The dangers and duties of
those whose faith is misunder-
stood. A discourse delivered
at the Unitarian Church, Nov.
26, 1837.... Savannah, 1837.
12 p. PHi; MBAU.   48436

Wesley, John, 1703-1791.
A collection of hymns for the
use of the Methodist Episcopal
church, principally from the
collection of the Rev. John Wesley, Cincinnati, J. F. Wright
and L. Swormstedt, 1837.
623 p. OClWHi; ODaB.   48437

---- The journal of the Reverend John Wesley. First complete and standard American
ed. from the latest London ed.
with the last corrections of the
author: Comprehending also
numerous translations and notes,
by John Henry. New York, B.
Waugh and T. Mason, 1837. 2 v.
IaDmD; NcD; NNUT; PBa; TJo.
48438
---- A plain account of Christian
perfection, by John Wesley, from
1725 to 1777, with his own notes.
From the London edition 1837.
New York, J. S. Taylor, 1837.
153 p. CtMW; GDecCT; ICU;
MH; OO; PPL.   48439

---- ---- New York, Published
by T. Mason and G. Lane,
1837. 175 p. KBB.   48440

---- Sermons on several occasions. By the Rev. John Wesley A.M....In two volumes.
New York, Published by T.

Mason & G. Lane, for the Methodist Episcopal Church, 1837.
ILM; MdHi; NcD; OFM; TJaL.
48441
Wesleyan Methodist Church.
Catechism. English.
The catechisms of the Wesleyan Methodists comp. & pub.
by the order of the British Conference, rev. & adapted to the
use of families & schools connected with the Method. Episcopal ch. with an apx. containing
a short catechism of Scripture
names & prayers for little
children. New York, N. Bangs
& J. Emory, 1837. AmSSchU;
MdBAM; PPAmS.   48442

Wesleyan university, Middletown,
Conn. Library.
Catalogue of the library of
the Wesleyan University. Middletown, W. D. Starr, print., 1837.
50 p. CtHT.   48443

West, George Montgomery.
Hear both sides; being a
statement of the controversy respecting the destruction of the
church in Kensington. Philadelphia, 1837. 52 p. PHi.
48444
West, Nathaniel, 1794-1864.
The substance of a charge,
delivered 13th Oct., 1836, to
the united churches and congregations of Greenville and Salem,
Mercer Co., Pa., at the ordination and installation of Rev.
James G. Wilson. Pittsburgh,
Allinder, 1837. 15 p. CSmH;
MiU-C; PPPrHi.   48445

West, William S.
A few interesting facts respecting the rise, progress and
pretensions of the Mormons. By
Wm. S. West...(Warren?O.),
1837. 16 p. NN.   48446

West Boylston, Mass., Baptist
Church.
Articles of faith, Covenant,
and list of members, of the
Baptist Church in West Boylston, Mass. Worcester, Printed
by Henry J. Howland, 1837.
15 p. MB; MBC; MNtCA; MWA.
48447
West Chester Rail Road Company
& the West Chester Extended
Railroad Company.
Case stated. Philadelphia,
1837. 20 p. PHi.   48448

West Philadelphia.
Copy of acts of Assembly
and Ordinances, passed by the
Council of the Borough of West
Philadelphia; with by-laws.
Philadelphia, 1837. 39 p. PHi.
48449
West Philadelphia Rail Road
Company.
Communication from the
president and managers...in
relation to the report of Henry
R. Campbell,...Read in the
Senate March 4, 1837. Harris-
burg, Emanuel Guyer, 1837.
16 p. PPAmP.   48450

---- Message from the governor
transmitting a communication
from the president and managers
of the ... co. relative to avoiding the Schuylkill inclined
planes of the Philadelphia and
Columbia Railroad, read in the
House of Representatives, March
4, 1837. Harrisburg, Patterson,
1837. 7 p. PPAmP.   48451

West Virginia Iron Mining and
Manufacturing Company.
Prospectus of the West Virginia iron mining and manufacturing company, incorporated
by the Legislature of Virginia,
March 15, 1837. [Richmond?
1837] 29 p. MBC; MH; Vi.
48452

Western, Henry M.
An address delivered in be-
half of the Tailoresses' and
Seamstresses' Benevolent Soci-
ety at the Broadway Tabernacle,
December 28th, 1836. New York,
Craighead & Allen, 1837. 12 p.
MH.   48453

The Western academician and
journal of education and science.
Ed. by J. W. Picket. v. 1;
Mar. 1837-Feb. 1838. Cincinnati,
J. R. Allbach, 1837-38. 704 p.
ICJ; MHi; OCHP; OT; TxU.
48454
... Western Almanac for the
year of our Lord 1838: 2d after
bissextile or leap year, and,
till July 4th, the 62d of Ameri-
can independence. Adopted to
the meridian of Rochester, Mon-
roe County, N.Y. Lat. 43°8'17"
N. - Lon. 49'12" W. from Wash.
City. (vignette) Rochester,
Published and sold, wholesale
and retail, by Hoyt & Porter,
Rochester, (1837?). (24) p.
NRHi; NRU.   48455

Western Almanack for 1838.
Cazenovia, N.Y., Henry &
Severance, [1837]. MiD-B; MWA.
48456
---- 2d after bissextile or leap
year, and, till July 4th, the 62d
of American independence.
Adopted to the meridian of Ithaca, N.Y., and will answer for
the northern part of Pennsylvania. Ithaca, N.Y., Published
and sold by Mack, Andrus &
Woodruff, [1837.] [24] p.
MWA; NHi; NIC; NN; WHi.
48457
The Western Emigrants' Magazine,
and Historian of the Times in the
West. Carthage, Ill., Th. Gregg.
Vol. 1., No. 1 for May, 1837.
NN.   48458

The Western farmers' almanac, for 1838: being the 62d-63d of American independence. Calculated for the meridian of Auburn, and will serve for the western part of New York and Pennsylvania, northern part of Ohio, Michigan, Upper Canada, &c. Astronomical calculations by Lyman Abbot, Jr. Auburn, Published and sold, wholesale and retail, by Oliphant & Skinner. Oliphant & Skinner, printers, [1837.] [24 p. MiD-B; MWA; NBu.   48459

The Western "Patriot" and Canton Almanack, for the Year of our Lord 1838; being the second after Bissextile, or Leap Year: containing 365 days, and after the 4th of July, the sixty second of American Independence. arranged after the system of the German Calendars.... Canton Stark County, Ohio, Published and sold by Peter Kaufman, [1837]. OHiHL.   48460

The Western primer, or introduction to Webster's spelling book...Columbus, O., I. N. Whiting, 1837. 35 p. O; OClWHi.   48461

The Western quarterly journal of practical medicine....No. 1.- June 1837. Cincinnati, J. A. James & Co., 1837. vi, 163 p. DNLM; ICJ.   48462

Western Railroad Corporation.
    Proceedings of the Western rail-road Corporation, November 23rd. Including an address to the people of the Commonwealth of Mass., on the application for a loan of the state credit. Boston, Dutton & Wentworth, printers, 1837.

11 p. CtY; IU; InU; MB; MeHi; VtU.   48463

Western Reserve University. Cleveland, O.
    Catalogue of the Officers and Students of the Western Reserve College, January 1837. Hudson, Ohio. Printed by James Lowry, 1837. 14 p. MWA; WBeloC.
                                    48464
Westmoreland, N.Y. Second Baptist Church.
    Circular letter of some of the members to their beloved brethren. Rome, 1837. 28 p. MBC.
                                    48465
Westtown School. Committee.
    Report to the yearly meeting. Philadelphia, 1837. 3 p. PHi.
                                    48466
Weymouth, Massachusetts.
    Names of the several streets, lanes and squares, in the town of Weymouth as adopted by said town May 8, 1837. ... printed at the Patriot Office, Quincy, Mass., [1837]. Broadside. MWeyHi.   48467

Whales and whaling for little readers. New Haven, S. Babcock, 1837. 16 p. MH. 48468

Wharton, William Harris, 1802-1839.
    Reasons why the Independence of Texas should be immediately recognized by the government of the United States. ... [Jefferson] [Washington, Tex., 1837]. 12 p. CtY; TxU.   48469

"What is Man?" or errors in theology examined: a polemic discourse, by a layman in a town in Connecticut where "new divinity" prevails. Boston, 1837. 25 p. MBC.   48470

Whately, Richard, 1787-1863.

Christianity independent of
the civil government. By
Richard Whately. New York,
Harper and brothers, 1837.
(3), 180 p. IaB; MB; MPiB;
NjPT; Vt.   48471

---- Elements of Logic comprising the substance of the
articles in the encyclopedia
metropolitans: with additions
etc by Richard Whatley, D.D.
New York, pub. by William
Jackson; Boston, James Munroe
Co., 1837. 359 p. CtSoP;
MB; MH; NCaS; PReaAT. 48472

---- Letters on the church.
By Richard Whately. New York,
Harper, 1837. 180 p. NcU.
                             48473
Wheatley, Charles, 1686-1742.
Rational illustration of the
book of common prayer, of the
Church of England. By Charles
Wheatley, A.M....improved by
additions and notes,....Boston,
Benjamin B. Mussey, 1837.
572, (15) p. CtHT; InID;
MdBD; OC; PU.   48474

Wheaton College. Norton, Mass.
Catalogue for two years ending April, 1837. Boston, 1837.
12 p. MHi.   48475

---- Catalog of the officers and
members. Boston, Crocker,
1837-1913. MBC; MNotnW.
                             48476
Wheeler, Jacob D.
A practical treatise on the
law of slavery. Being a
compilation of all the decisions
made on that subject, in the
several courts of the United
States, and state courts. With
copious notes and references to
the statutes and other authorities, systematically arranged.

By Jacob D. Wheeler ... New
York, A. Pollock, jr.; New Or-
leans, B. Levy, 1837. 476 p.
CSmH; GAU; MiU; MWA; TU.
                             48477
Wheeler, Noyes.
Lecture on education and
school keeping. Hartford, N.
Wheeler, 1837. CtHC; CtSoP;
MB.   48478

Whelpley, Samuel, 1766-1817.
A compend of history... By
Samuel Whelpley, A.M. Eleventh
edition. With corrections and
important additions and improvements. By Rev. Joseph Emerson. Two volumes in one. Boston, American Stationers' Company, 1837. 2 v. OBerB.
                             48479
Whewell, William.
History of the inductive sciences. New York, D. Appleton
and company, 1837. 3 v. LNT.
                             48480
Whig Almanac for 1838. 3rd ed.
New York, N.Y., H. Greeley,
[1837]. MWA.   48481

Whig Party. Massachusetts.
Boston.
Whig ticket. Ward II. For
Mayor, Samuel A. Eliot. For
alderman, Henry Farnam, Thomas
Wetmore,...[Boston, 1837?].
Broadside. MHi.   48482

---- ---- Bristol County.
Proceedings of a Whig county
convention of delegates from all
the towns in Bristol County,
held at Taunton Oct. 11, 1837.
New Bedford, 1837. 16 p. M;
MHi; MNBedf.   48483

---- ---- Central Committee.
To the Electors of Massachu-
setts. At a convention com-
posed of the Whig members....
(Worcester, 1837). DLC; ICN;
MBC; NcD; WHi.   48484

---- ---- Worcester.
Address of R. C. Winthrop
and others, to the electors of
Massachusetts, at Worcester,
Oct. 4, 1837. n.p. (1837?)
40 p. M.   48485

Whipple, John, 1784-1866.
Mr. Whipple's speech. Sub-
stance of a speech delivered at
the Whig meeting held at the
Town house, Providence, R.I.
August 28, 1837... [Providence,
1837]. 16 p. DLC; MH; RHi.
                            48486
Whipple, Thomas J.
Eulogy on James Madison,
Ex-President of the United
States, delivered at the annual
commencement of the Norwich
University, August 18, 1836.
By Thomas J. Whipple, ...
Woodstock, Vt., J. B. & S. L.
Chase and Co., 1837. 12 p.
Nh.   48487

Wisconsin.
Memorial praying for a pre-
emption law [in Wisconsin.]
Washington, 1837. PPL.   48488

[Whitaker, Daniel Kimball],
1801-1881.
Sidney's letters to William E.
Channing, D.D., occasioned by
his letter to Hon. Henry Clay,
on the annexation of Texas to
the United States. ... Charleston, S.C., printed by E. C.
Councill, 1837. 84 p. CU;
DLC; MB; ScU; ViU.   48489

---- ---- 2d ed. 1837. MH.
                            48490
White, Carleton.
Narrative of the loss of the
steam-packet Home, Carleton
White, master, on a voyage
from New York to Charleston,
with affidavits disproving the
charges of misconduct against

the master. New York, Printed
by J. Ormond, 1837. 36 p.
LNH; MB; MH; MHi; NN. 48491

White, Edward.
Reports on the proposed
Cheraw and Waccamaw Rail-road
by Edward White, Engineer, and
Messrs. Harlee, Ellerbe and
Evans, Commissioners appointed
by the Convention held at Marion,
C. H. S. C. Jan. 24, 1837.
Fayetteville, E. Hale, 1837. 24
p. ScC.   48492

White, Elipha.
Education: an introductory
discourse, before the American
Institute of Instruction, de-
livered in Worcester, Mass.,
Aug. 24, 1837. Boston, I. R.
Butts, 1837. 21 p. MH-AH;
PPPrHi; ScC.   48493

---- The genius and moral
achievements of the spirit of
foreign missions. A sermon
preached in the Presbyterian
church. John's Island, S.C.
Dec. 18, 1836. By Rev. Elipha
White, pastor. Boston, Crocker
& Brewster, 1837. 22 p. MBC;
NcMHi; OO; PPPrHi; RPB.
                            48494
White, Henry Kirke, 1785-1806.
The Beauties of Henry Kirke
White, consisting of selections
from his poetry and prose. By
Alfred Howard, Esq. Stereotyped
by David Hills, Boston. Hart-
ford, Conn., Andrus, Judd, &
Franklin, 1837. 214 p. MAnA;
TNP.   48495

White, John, 1575-1648.
The planters plea; or, the
grovnds (sic) of plantations examined and vsuall (sic) answered
.... By John White. Washington, P. Force, 1837. 2, (2), 47
p. CtMW; NjP; OCL; TxWB; WHi.
                            48496

White, Joseph M., 1781-1839.
Legal opinions of J. M.
White of the House of Representatives, Daniel Webster,
senator in Congress and Edward Livingston late Secretary
of State in relation to the title
of the Duke of Alagon. New
York, E. S. Mesier, 1837.
26 p. FTaSU; LNT; MH; NN;
PPL.   48497

---- Letter to the people of
Florida. Washington, 1837.
PPL.   48498

Whitman, Bernard, 1796-1834.
On denying the Lord Jesus.
By the Bernard Whitman.
Printed for the American Uni-
tarian Association. Boston,
James Munroe and Co., 1837.
46 p. CBPac; IaPeC; MeB;
MMeT-Hi; N.   48499

---- What is it to deny our Lord?
The question fairly stated and
answered. A sermon on "denying the Lord Jesus." delivered
before his church and society,
in Waltham. Boston, Weeks,
Jordan, 1837. 46 p. CBPac;
KyHi; MH-AH; MNF; RPB.
                                    48500
Whitman, Jason, 1799-1848.
The hard times; a discourse
delivered in the Second unitarian church ... January 1st,
1837. By Jason Whitman ...
Portland, Arthur Shirley,
printer, 1837. 22 p. MBAt;
MeHi; MWA; NNG; RPB.   48501

---- Memoir of the Rev. Bernard Whitman. Boston, Tuttle,
Weeks and Dennet, School St.,
1837. 215 p. CtY; ICMe; ICP;
MB; MH.   48502

---- Our Public Schools. An Address, delivered at the opening

of the New School House, for the
West Female Grammar School,
Portland, December 4, 1837. By
Jason Whitman. Portland, 1837.
16 p. MeB; MeHi; MWA. 48503

Whitney, George, 1804-1842.
The moral and religious uses
of mechanical exhibitions. A
sermon preached before the religious society worshiping at
Jamaica Plain,...by George Whitney,...Boston, printed and published by I. R. Butts, 1837.
20 p. CtY; ICMe; MBAU; MWA;
RPB.   48504

Whitney, Peter.
A Sermon, delivered at Quincy,
January 1, 1837. By Rev. Peter
Whitney, Senior Pastor of the
First Congregational Society in
that Town. Published by re-
quest. Quincy, Printed by
Green & Osborne, 1837. 12 p.
MB; MBAt; MBC; MWA.   48505

Whitney, Reuben M.
Protest against the proceedings of the select committee of
the House of Representatives to
investigate the executive departments, Jan. 25, 1837. Washington, Printed at the Globe Office,
1837. 15 p. PPi.   48506

Whitridge, Joshua Barker.
An address to the candidates
for the degree of Doctor of Medicine, delivered at the annual commencement of the Medical College
of South Carolina, March 15th,
1837. Charleston, 1837. 23 p.
Ct; MB; MH; MHi; ScCC. 48507

Whittemore, Thomas, 1800-1861.
Sermon... New York, 1837.
PPL.   48508

---- Songs of Zion, or, the
Cambridge collection of sacred

music, etc. comprising a rich
variety of the most popular
tunes, anthems, etc. with many
pieces from various authors
never before published, written
expressly for this work; arranged with a figured bass for
the organ or pianoforte, etc.
Boston, 1837. 357 p. ICN;
MHi; MPeHi.   48509

Whittier, John Greenleaf, 1807-
1892.
Poems written during the
progress of the abolition question in the United States, between the years 1830 and 1838
... Boston, I. Knapp, 1837.
103 p. DeWi; MHa; PPL; TxH;
ViU.   48510

Whittingham, William R.
An address on the Pursuit
of Knowledge, before The
Orange Lyceum, Orange, N.J.
by William R. Whittingham ...
Newark, printed at the Daily
and Sentinel Office, 1837. 19
p. MdBD.   48511

Whittington and his cat. Baltimore, Published by Bayly and
Burns, 1837. [2] p., 6 ℓ.,
[2] p. MdHi.   48512

Whitwell, Bond and Co., firm.
Boston.
Catalogue of a collection of
valuable books, principally in
foreign languages to be sold by
auction, on Thursday, May 25th,
1837...Whitwell, Bond and Co.,
auctioneers...Boston, John Eas-
burn, printer, 1837. MiU-C.
                           48513
(Wicklifee, Robert), 1815?-1860.
Letters to James T. Morehead
on Transylvania University, and
the necessity of a system of education in Kentucky by "William
Pitt," (pseud.). Smithland, Ky.,

C. A. Fuller, 1837. Pamphlet.
MH.   48514

---- A plea for the education of
the people of Kentucky. An address, delivered before the Mayor
and Common Council of Lexington,
on the 29th of July, 1837, the
anniversary of the public school
of that city. Lexington, Ky.,
Finnell & Zimmerman, 1837. 17
p. KyU; MB; MH; PHi.   48515

Wild flowers culled for early
youth. By a lady. New York,
Published by John S. Taylor,
1837. 257 p. CSmH; InRv;
NjP; NRU.   48516

Wilde, Richard H.
Letter from the Hon. Richard
H. Wilde, to the Governor of
Maryland. Annapolis, William
M'Neir, printer, 1837. 5, [2]
p. MdHi.   48517

Wilkes, Charles, 1798-1877.
Chart of Georges shoal and
bank.... New York, 1837.
PPAmP; RPA; RPB.   48518

---- ---- Washington, 1837.
MB; PHi; PPAmP; RPA; RPB.
                           48519
Wilkins, T. E.
Lessons for children of the
New Church. Boston, Otis Clapp,
1837. 96 p. MB; PBa; OUrC.
                           48520
Wilks, Thomas Egerton, 1812-
1854.
... The seven clerks; or, The
three thieves and the denouncer;
an original romantic drama in
two acts. New York, T. H.
French, London, Samuel French,
[1837?]. 27 p. OCl.   48521

---- Sudden thoughts; an original farce, in one act. New York,
London, Samuel French, [1837?].
19 p. OCl.   48522

Willard, Emma (Hart), 1787-
1870.
History of the United States,
or republic of America: designed
for schools and private libraries.
5th ed. Emma Willard, principal
of Troy Female Seminary. New-
York, M. & J. White, 1837.
424 p. CaNSWA; DLC; MdW;
MNBedf; NTEW.   48523

Willard, Samuel, 1776-1859.
The general class-book, or
interesting lessons in prose &
verse on a great variety of subjects, combined with an epitome
of English Orthologhy & pronunciation. Published by
Phelps & Ingersoll. Greenfield, Mass., 1837. InLogCM.
                              48524
---- The Popular reader, or
complete scholar; intended as a
reading book for the higher
classes in Academies and other
schools in the United States.
Fourth edition. Greenfield,
Mass., A. Phelps; Boston,
Crocker & Brewster; New York,
M. Day and D. Felt & Co.,
1837. 353 p. MPiB; MTem;
NHi.   48525

Willcox, H. P.
Irving, on Lake Erie.
Buffalo, Charles Faxon, print-
er, 1837. 47 p. MH; MMeT;
N.   48526

Willetts, Jacob, 1785-1860.
... The scholar's arithmetic,
designed for the use of schools
in the United States. By Jacob
Willetts...45 ed. Poughkeepsie,
Potter and Wilson; Philadelphia,
S. Potter & co., 1837. [iv],
[5]-191 p. CSt.   48527

William and Mary College.
Williamsburg, Va.
Laws and regulations of the

College of William and Mary in
Virginia. Petersburg, Printed
at the office of the Farmers
Register, 1837. 28 p. M; MeBa.
                              48528
William Prince and sons.
Annual Catalogue, of fruit
and ornamental trees and plants,
cultivated at the Linnaean botanic
garden and nurseries. William
Prince & sons, proprietors,
Flushing, Long Island, near
New-York. Thirtieth edition.
New York, Printed by George P.
Scott and co., 1837. iv, [5]-
88 p. MdHi.   48529

Williams, Catherine Read (Arnold).
Religion at home; a story,
founded on facts.... By Mrs.
Williams. Providence, B. Cranston and Co., 1837. (7)-312 p.
NPV; RHi-RP; RPB; RShaw.
                              48530
---- ---- 2d ed. Providence,
printed by B. Cranston & Co.,
1837. 312 p. DLC; MNS;
NWatt.   48531

---- ---- 3d ed. Providence,
printed by B. Cranston & Co.,
1837. 312 p. GDecCT; MB;
RNHi; RPB.   48532

Williams, John, 1796-1839.
A narrative of missionary en-
terprises in the South Sea islands ... 1st American ed. New
York, D. Appleton and co.,
[1837]. [2], [25]-525 p. CtHC;
MH; NjR; PPP; RPA.   48533

Williams, John Lee.
Territory of Florida; or,
sketches of the topography, civil
and natural hsitory, of the country, the climate and the Indian
tribes, from the first discovery
to the present time. New York,
Published by Goodrich, 1837.
304 p. A-GS; FU; MB; MiU;
OrP.   48534

Williams, R. G.
Human rights; a paper on
anti-slavery. By R. G. Williams, publishing agent. New
York, Dec. 1837. 4 p. MA.
48535
Williams, Stephen West, 1790-
1855.
Biographical memoir of the
Rev. John Williams, first minister of Deerfield, Mass., with
a slight sketch of ancient Deerfield ... & papers relating to
Indian wars in Deerfield. Ingersoll, Greenfield, Mass., 1837.
127 p. ICN; MDeeP; Me; PPM;
WHi.   48536

Williams, Thomas, 1779-1876.
A sermon on the conclusion
of the second century from the
settlement of the State of Rhode
Island and Providence Plantation.
By Thomas Williams.... Provi-
dence, Printed by Knowles, Vose
& Co., 1837. 32 p. Ct; MHi;
PCA; RNHi; WHi.   48537

Williams college. Williamstown,
Mass.
Catalogue of the officers
and students of Williams college,
and of the Berkshire Medical
institution connected with it,
Oct. 1837. Albany, Printed
by Packard, Van Benthuysen
and co., 1837. 16 p. NNNAM.
48538
Williamsburgh Fire Insurance
Company, Williamsburgh, N.Y.
The Act of Incorporation and
Bye-Laws of the Williamsburgh
Fire Insurance Company. New-
York, Printed by J. Booth &
Son, 1837. 14 p. NN.   48539

Willis, Anson.
The emblematical table-book
.... with the definitions of all
the common geometrical figures
.... By Anson Willis .... New-

York, Howe & Bates, n.pr.,
1837. 72 p. NjR.   48540

Willis, Nathaniel Parker, 1806-
1867.
American scenery, by N. P.
Willis, esq. Illustrated in a
series of views, by W. H. Bart-
lett. London, G. Virtue; New
York, R. Martin, (1837-38).
V. 1. NhD.   48541

---- Melanie and other poems
by N. P. Willis. New York,
Published by Saunders and Otley, 1837. 242 p. CtMW; ICU;
MH; NCH; PU.   48542

---- ---- 2 ed. New York,
Saunders & Otley, 1837. 242 p.
KyBC; NjP; NN; OO; TxU.
48543
Willis, Robert.
The Lexington Cabinet and
Repository of Sacred Music.
... Louisville, Ky., 1837. 200
p. MHi.   48544

Williston, Seth, 1770-1851.
Discourses on the temptations
of Christ. By Seth Williston ...
Utica, [N.Y.], Press of W. Wil-
liams, 1837. 152 p. DLC; ICBB;
KyBC; MPiB; NUt.   48545

Willoughby University. Medical
department.
Annual catalogue and circular, 1837- . DNLM; MB; OCIW;
PPC.   48546

Willson, James N.
Address on...African slavery
....Chambersburg, n. pub.,
printed by J. Pritts, 1837. 44
p. NjR; PHi.   48547

---- Address, on the subject of
African Slavery, delivered in
Fayetteville, Sept. 14, 1837.
(Published by Request). (Fay-

etteville, Ind.), 1837. 32 p.
FC; TNF.   48548

Wilson, Caroline (Fry), 1787-
1846.
The Listener. By Caroline
Fry....Fifth edition. From the
last London edition, revised.
Philadelphia, Published by G. W.
Donohue, 1837. 2 v. MB;
MeBat; MoS; PHi; PWW.   48549

Wilson, Hugh Nesbitt, 1813-1878.
An address, delivered at the
late anniversary meeting of the
sabbath schools of Suffolk
County, showing the duties and
responsibilities of parents, in
the right improvement of sabbath
school instruction. By Rev.
H. N. Wilson, of Southampton,
L.I. Published by request.
Sag Harbor. Printed at the
Watchman-Office, and for sale
by O. O. Wickham, 1837. 8 p.
NjP; NSmb.   48550

[Wilson, John].
An oration on superstition,
delivered at the annual commencement of Williams College, August
1836. Andover, printed by
Gould and Newman, 1837. 12
p. MH.   48551

Wilson, John, 1804-1875.
The life of John Eliot, the
Apostle of the Indians, Re-
vised by the editors. New
York, Published by T. Mason
and G. Lane, for the Sunday
School Union of the Methodist
Episcopal Church, at the Con-
ference Office, 1837. 8-120 p.
MPiB.   48552

Wilson, John Grover.
Both sides reviewed, in rela-
tion to the Union Wesleyan church,
Kensington: with account of the
Methodist Protestant church.

Philadelphia, 1837. 52 p. PHi.
                            48553
Wilson, Joshua Lacy, 1774-1846.
Wilson's plea in the case of
Lyman Beecher, made before the
synod of Cincinnati, October,
1835, Cincinnati, O., Printed by
R. F. Brooks, 1837. 120 p.
CtHC; ICP; MH; NNUT; OClWHi;
PHi.   48554

Wilson, Samuel, 1763-1827.
A Scripture manual, or, a
plain representation of the ordinance of baptism. Philadelphia,
published by the Baptist general
tract society, 1837. 24 p.
NHC-S; NjR.   48555

Wilson, Thomas, 1663-1755.
Sacra privata; meditations
and prayers of the Right Rev.
Thomas Wilson...accommodated
to general use. New York, J. S.
Taylor, 1837. 108 p. CtHT;
MdBD; PPWa; RPB; WHi. 48556

---- A short and plain instruction for better understanding of
the Lord's Supper. By Thomas
Wilson, D. D., Late Lord Bishop
of Sodor and Man. Charleston,
A. E. Miller, 1837. 40 p.
MBNMHi.   48557

Winchester, Samuel Gover, 1805-
1841.
Pastoral letter to the Sixth
Presbyterian Church and congregation of Philadelphia. Philadelphia, Merrihew, 1837. 16 p.
PHi; PPPrHi.   48558

---- The sinner's inability is no
excuse for his impenitency ...
Philadelphia, Presbyterian tract
and Sunday school society, 1837.
24 p. MiU; MsSC; OMtv; PPPrHi;
WHi.   48559

Windham, William, 1750-1810.

Select speeches of the right
Honourable William Windham,
and the right Honourable William Huskisson; with preliminary
biographical sketches. Ed. by
Robert Walsh. Philadelphia,
E. C. Biddle, 1837. 37-39,
616 p. CtMW; LU; RPA;
TxDaM; WaPS. 48560

Winebrenner, John, 1797-1860.
Reasons for not embracing
the doctrine of universal salvation, in a series of letters to a
friend. Harrisburg, Pa.,
Author, 1837. 132 p. PPLT.
48561
(Wines, Enoch Cobb), 1806-
1879.
A trip to Boston, in a series
of letters to the editor of the
United states gazette. By the
author of "Two years and a
half in the Navy." Boston,
Charles C. Little and James
Brown, 1837. (13), 224 p.
MA. 48562

Winnisimmet Academy. Chelsea,
Mass.
An abstract of the annual
report of Winnisimmet Academy
for 1837, with some considerations relating to the institution,
Chelsea, 1837. Boston, Press
of John Putnam, 1837. (3), 4-
14 p. M; MH; MHi. 48563

Winslow, Benjamin.
Trial of Benjamin Winslow
and George B. Stearns, on an
indictment for a conspiracy to
defraud Gordon & Stoddard.
Boston, John H. Eastburn,
printer, 1837. 24 p. Nh.
48564
Winslow, Hubbard, 1799-1864.
The appropriate sphere of
woman. A discourse, delivered
in the Bowdoin Street church,
July 9, 1837. Boston, Weeks,

Jordan & Company, 1837. 16 p.
ICMe; MB; MiD-B; RPB; WHi.
48565
---- Are you a Christian? or
aid to self-examination...4th ed.
Boston, D. K. Hitchcock, 1837.
61 p. MBC. 48566

---- Rejoice with trembling. A
discourse delivered in Bowdoin
Street Church, Boston, on the
day of Annual Thanksgiving,
November 30, 1837. Boston,
Published by Perkins & Marvin,
1837. 32 p. MB; MeHi; MiD-B;
MWA; RPB. 48567

---- The relation of natural sci-
ence to revealed religion: an
address delivered before the
Boston natural history society,
June 7, 1837. Boston, Pub. by
the society. Weeks, Jordan &
Co., 1837. 20 p. MH; MiD-B;
MnU; PPAmP; WHi. 48568

---- The young man's aid to
knowledge, virtue, and happiness... Boston, D. K. Hitchcock, 1837. (13)-408 p. InCW;
MCanHi; MB; MH; RP. 48569

Winslow, Miron.
Memoir of Mrs. Harriet L.
Winslow .... By Rev. Miron
Winslow. New York, Published
by the American Tract Society,
[1837]. 479, [1] p. PCA.
48570
Winslow, Octavius.
The English Bible as it is.
New York, 1837. NbCrD.
48571
Winthrop, Robert Charles.
Address to the electors of
Mass. Oct. 4, 1837. (Boston,
1837). 40 p. MHi. 48572

Wirt, Elizabeth Washington
(Gamble).
Flora's dictionary by Mrs.

E. W. Wirt of Virginia. Embellished by Miss Ann Smith. Baltimore, Fielding Lucas, Jr., [1837]. 223 p. MdBP; MiDU; MSN; NcAS.   48573

Wirt, William, 1772-1834.
Letters of the British Spy .... to which is prefixed a biographical sketch of the author. Edition 10, revised. New York, Harper and Brothers, 1837. 260 p. GMM; IaU; NBuU; OClWHi; ViU.   48574

Wisconsin (Ter.).
Territory of Wisconsin documents, 1837-1848. [n.p.] 1837-1848. 2 v. WHi.   48575

---- Adjutant General.
Order...[issued from Regimental headquarters, Green Bay, by J. Wheelock, colonel 2d regiment, Wisconsin militia]. Green Bay, 1837. No. 1, Jan. 17, 1837. WHi.   48576

---- District Court (3d District).
Rules of the Territorial and United States District Court for the County of Brown and Territory of Wisconsin, Green Bay, 1837. 7 p. DLC.   48577

---- Governor (Henry Dodge).
Governor's message, November 7th, 1837. [Burlington, W. T., James Clarke, 1837.] [10 p.] WHi.   48578

---- Legislative Assembly, Council.
Rules for the government of the council of Wisconsin territory, Second session, commenced Nov. 6, 1837. Burlington, James Clarke & co., printers, 1837. [3]-11 p. WBeloc; WGr; WHi.   48579

---- ---- House.
Journal of the House of representatives, of the legislative assembly of Wisconsin; being the second session, begun and held at Burlington, on the sixth day of November, one thousand eight hundred and thirty-seven, Green Bay, W.T., Charles C. Sholes, 1837. 450 p. DLC; MH; W; WBeloC; WS.   48580

Wisconsin Mining Company.
Articles of agreement and association of the Wisconsin Mining Company. Instituted 15th March, 1837. Chicago, T. O. Davis, 1837. 8 p. NN; PPRF.   48581

Wise, Henry Alexander.
Speech of Mr. Wise, of Virginia, on the resolution to refer so much of the president's message as relates to the finances, and every thing connected therewith, to the committee of ways and means. Delivered in the house of representatives of the United States, December 15, 1837. Washington, printed by Gales and Seaton, 1837. 7 p. MdHi; MH; PHi.   48582

Wiseman, Nicholas Patrick Stephen, 1802-1865.
Lectures on the Principal Doctrines & Practices of the Catholic Church. Delivered at St. Mary's, Moorfields. During the lent of 1836. By Nicholas Wiseman, D.D.... In two volumes. 1st. American from the 1st. London edition. Philadelphia, Eugene Cummisky, 1837. 2 v. ArLSJ; LNL; MdW; OO; ViHop.   48583

---- Twelve lectures on the connexion between science and revealed religion. Delivered in Rome by Nicholas Wiseman... First American from the first

London edition. Andover, Gould & Newman, 1837. (9)-404 p. IaGG; MdBD; RPB; ScCC; ViW.   48584

The witches: a tale of New-England.... See Stone, William Leete.

No entry.   48585

Withington, Leonard, 1789-1885.
Cobwebs swept away; or, Some popular deceptions exposed. A sermon .... By Leonard Withington .... Newburyport, n. pub., press of Hiram Tozer, 1837. 25 p. CtSoP; ICMe; MPiB; NjR; WHi.   48586

Wolff, Joseph, 1795-1862.
Researches and missionary labours among the Jews, Mohammedans, and other sects, by the Rev. Joseph Wolff, during his travels between the years 1831 and 1834. ...First American edition, revised and corrected by the author. Philadelphia, Orrin Rogers, 1837. 338 p. ArCH; IaMp; NbCrD; PHi; WNaE.   48587

Wolff, Oskar Luwdig Bernhard, 1799-1851.
The German tourist. Illustrated with seventeen engravings from drawings. By H. E. Lloyd, Esq. London and Berlin, A. Asher; Philadelphia, De Silver, Thomas and Co., 1837. 200 p. PPPCity.   48588

No entry.   48589

Wood, George Bacon, 1797-1879.
Introductory lecture to the course of materia medica, delivered in the University of Penna. Nov. 6, 1837. Phila-

delphia, J. G. Auner, 1837. DSG; MBAt; NBuU-M; PHi; PU.   48590
---- Syllabus of the course of lectures on materia medica and pharmacy, delivered in the University of Pennsylvania, in the winter of 1837-38. Philadelphia, 1837. 69 p. WU.   48591

Wood, James, 1799-1867.
Facts and observations concerning the organization and state of the churches in the three synods of western New-York and the Synod of Western Reserve. By James Wood. Saratoga Springs, [N.Y.], Printed by G. M. Davison, 1837. 48 p. CSmH; KyDC; NjR; TxHuT; ViRut.   48592

Wood, Samuel.
Letters from Boston, on Harvard University, by the Rev. Samuel Wood. [From the Christian Reformer for November, 1837.] 12 p. DLC; ICU; PPAmP; PPL.   48593
Wood, Thomas.
Germs of thought; or, Rudiments of knowledge: intended to promote the mental and religious improvement of youth. By Thomas Wood... New York, Published by T. Mason and G. Lane, J. Collard, printer, 1837. 214 p. GDecCT; IaU; MiU; MWHi.   48594
Woodbridge, John.
Practical religion recommended and enforced in a series of letters, from Epsilon to his friend. By John Woodbridge, D.D. New York, Pub. by John S. Taylor, 1837. 316 p. InCW; MWiW; NbOP; PCC; OSW.   48595

Woodbury, Levi, 1789-1851.
A discourse pronounced at the Capitol of the United States, in the Hall of Representatives,

before the American Historical
Society....By the Hon. Levi
Woodbury, ... Washington,
Printed by Gales & Seaton,
1837. 67 p. KyDC; Nh;
OCHP; PPi; TxDaM. 48596

Woodhouselee, Alexander Fraser
Tytler, 1747-1813.
Elements of General History.
Ancient and Modern. By Alex-
ander Fraser Tytler. With a
continuation, terminating at
The Demise of King III. By
Rev. Edward Nares. To which
are added a succinct History of
The United States.....Concord,
N.H., John H. Brown, 1837.
527, 44 p. MB; MiPaw; MsJS;
ScU; TNP. 48597

---- Universal history, from
the creation of the world to
the beginning of the eighteenth
century. Boston, Hilliard,
Gray and Company, 1837. 2 v.
MB; MH; NcDaD. 48598

Woodland cottage, or Henry
and Emma Acton's conversations
to their children, on the animal
and vegetable world. Compiled
by a mother for her children.
3d ed., with additions and corrections by the compiler. Salem,
Ives and Jewett, 1837. DLC;
MB; MH. 48599

Woods, Alva, 1794-1887.
Valedictory address, de-
livered December 6, 1837, at
the close of the seventh collegiate
year of the University of the
state of Alabama. By Alva
Woods...Tuscaloosa, Marmaduke
J. Slade, Printer, 1837. 52 p.
AU; MAnP; MH; NcD; NCH; ScU.
48600
Wood's Almanac.
By Joshua Sharp. New York,
S. S. T. W. Wood, 1837. MWA.
48601

Woodward, John.
Argument and observations
on the empresario contracts of
Texas; by John Woodward,
trustee for compromising with
the government. New York, J.
Narine, 1837. 35 p. CU; NN;
PHi; TxU; TxWFM. 48602

Woodward College. Cincinnati.
Catalogue of the Woodward
College, and of the High School
with an Address by the President, (Rev. B. P. Aydelott)
American Education or the education we need. Cincinnati, 1837.
23 p. OCHP. 48603

Woolman, John, 1720-1773.
A Journal of the life, gospel
labours, and christian experience of that faithful minister of
Jesus Christ, John Woolman, late
of Mount Holly, in the province
of New Jersey. Philadelphia,
published by T. E. Chapman,
1837. 396 p. CSmH; IU; NcD;
OCU; PU. 48604

Woolsey, Theodore Dwight, 1801-
1889.
A selection of Greek tragedies,
with notes, for the use of colleges, and for private reading.
Boston, James Munroe and co.,
1837. 2 v. CtMW; InCW; MB;
MH-AH; NjP. 48605

Worcester, Henry Aikin.
Sermons on the Lord's Prayer.
To which are added three sermons on other subjects. By Henry A. Worcester. Boston, published by Otis Clapp, 1837. 187
p. IEG; KyHe; MCNC; MsJMC;
PBa. 48606

Worcester, Joseph Emerson, 1784-
1865.
Elementary dictionary for ...
schools. Boston, Russell, 1837.
324 p. OHi; OMC. 48607

---- Elements of history, ancient
& modern. Boston, 1837. 403
p. OO; TNP; UPB.   48608

Worcester, Samuel, 1793-1844.
Fourth book of lessons for
reading. Stereotype edition.
Boston, C. J. Hendee, 1837.
408 p. DLC; MB; MH; MoU;
PHi.   48609

---- A third book for reading
and spelling, with simple rules
and instructions for avoiding
common errors. 16th ed.
Boston, C. J. Hendee, 1837.
MH.   48610

Worcester, Mass. First church.
Articles of faith and cove-
nant adopted by the First
church of Christ in Worcester.
Worcester, Mirick, 1837. 16 p.
ICN; MWHi.   48611

Worcester Academy, Worcester,
Mass.
Petition and report relating
to the Worcester Co. Manual Labor High School. (Boston,
1837.) 11 p. MH.   48612

Wordsworth, William, 1770-1850.
The complete works of William
Wordsworth, together with a
description of the country of
the lakes in the north of Eng-
land.... Edited by Henry
Reed.... Philadelphia, James
Kay, Jun. and Brother; Boston,
James Munroe and Company;
Pittsburgh, John I. Kay & Co.,
1837. 25-551 p. ArCH; CtMW;
GHi; Phi; RPA.   48613

The works of Cowper and Thomson. Including many letters
and poems never before published in this country....Phila-
delphia, T. Grigg, 1837. x,
404, 133 p. CtHT; InCW; OCY;
PNt; WGr.   48614

World affairs; continuing the
Advocate of peace through justice.
Washington, D.C., American
Peace Society, v. 1-. 1837-.
DLC; IU; LU; MH; WaSp.
                          48615
Wraxall, Nathaniel William, 1751-
1831.
Historical memoirs of my own
time. Part the first, from 1772
to 1784, by Sir N. William Wrax-
all, Bart... Philadelphia, Carey,
Lea, and Blanchard, 1837.
[11]-494 p. FOA; MdBG; PPA;
ScCC; WNaE.   48616

The wreath, designed as a token
for the young. New York, N. B.
Holmes, 1837. MB; MH; RPB.
                          48617
(Wrifford, Anson).
Traits of character, pursuits,
manners, customs and habits,
manifested by the inhabitants of
the North-eastern States, in
their common pursuits of life.
By Uncle Daniel (pseud.). Portland, [Me.[, Arthur Shirley,
printer, 1837. 68 p. MBC;
MeHi; MWA; Nh-Hi.   48618

Wright, David.
Memoir of Alvan Stone, of
Goshen, Mass...Boston, Gould,
Kendall & Lincoln, 1837. 256 p.
CtY; DLC; ICN; MB; MiD-B.
                          48619
Wright, Silas, 1795-1847.
Speech of Mr. Wright, of New
York, [on the bill imposing addi-
tional duties as depositories of
the public money upon certain
public officers[. [Washington?
D.C., 1837]. 16 p. DLC; MiU.
                          48620
Wright, Thomas, 1711-1786.
The universe and the stars,
being an original theory on the
visible creation, founded on the
laws of nature, by Thomas
Wright. 1st American ed. from

the London ed. of 1750, with
notes by C. S. Rafinesque.
... Philadelphia, Printed for
C. Wetherill, 1837. 158, [2] p.
MBAt; NjP; OMC; PHi; WHi.
                            48621
Wright, Thomas, 1785-1855.
  A good life, extracted from
the true plan of a living temple,
or man considered in his proper
relation to the ordinary occu-
pations and pursuits of life.
By the author of The Morning
and Evening Sacrifice, etc.
With an introductory essay by
John Brazer. 2d. ed. Bos-
ton, Joseph Dowe, 1837. MB;
MBC; MH; MH-AH; RBr.   48622

Wylie, Andrew, 1789-1851.
  Address on the subject of
common school education. Delivered before the Convention
of the friends of education, in
Indianapolis, January 3, 1837,
by Andrew Wylie, D.D. Indianapolis, Douglass & Noel, printers, 1837. 19 p. DLC; In;
PPPrHi; MWA.   48623

---- The danger and duty of
the young; a sermon preached
to the senior class on the Sabbath previous to commencement
...Indiana College. Pittsburgh,
Allinder, 1837. In; InU; PPPrHi.
                            48624
Wyoming, Pa.
  Petition of the sufferers at
Wyoming during the Revolutionary War for relief, Dec. 29th,
1837. (Washington, 1837). 8
p. NIC.   48625

Y

Yale University.
  Catalogue of the Officers and
Students in Yale College, 1837-
38. [New Haven? 1837?]. 35 p.

Ct; NBuU; PHi; RNR; WMA.
                            48626
---- The laws of Yale College,
in New Haven, Connecticut: enacted by the president and fellows. New Haven, B. L. Hamlen, 1837. 43 p. ICU; NN; PU;
OKentU.   48627

---- Calliopean society. Library.
  Catalogue of the library of
the Calliopean society, Yale university, February 16, 1837. New
Haven, Hitchcock & Stafford,
1837. 56 p. MB; NN; PU; TNV.
                            48628
---- Divinity School.
  Order of exercises at the anniversary of the theological department in Yale College, August
15, 1837. New Haven, (Conn.),
printed by B. L. Hamlen, (1837).
3 p. MoS; NNUT.   48629

---- Linonian society. Library.
  Catalogue of the library of
the Linonian society, Yale Col-
lege, July, 1837. New Haven,
Hamlen, 1837. 82 p. CtY; ICN;
MB; MiD-B; PPAmP.   48630

Yandell, Lunsford P.
  A Lecture on the duties of
physicians. Delivered before
the Medical Class of Transylvania
University, on the 4th and 10th
of February, 1837... Lexington,
Intelligencer Print, 1837. 26 p.
KyLxT; LexPL.   48631

---- A narrative on the dissolu-
tion of the medical faculty of
Transylvania university, by
Lunsford P. Yandell. Nashville,
W. Hasell Hunt, printer, 1837.
31, 10 p. InU; KyDC; MH;
PPPrHi; TxU.   48632

The Yankee; or, Farmer's Almanac for the Year of Our Lord
and Saviour, 1838, etc. By

Thomas Spofford, Boston, [1837]. MWA; MWo; WHi. 48633

Yates, Emma.
System of universal history in perspective... N.Y., Huntington, 1837. 459 p. VtB. 48634

Yates, John Van Ness, 1779-1839.
A collection of pleadings and practical precedents, with notes thereon, and approved forms of bills of costs: containing, also, references, &c. to Graham's practice, 2d edition. By John V. N. Yates....Albany, W. & A. Gould & co.; New York, Gould, Banks & co., 1837. 866 p. CLSU; MnU; NcD; NIC; WU-L. 48635

[Yonge, Francis].
A narrative of the proceedings of the people of South Carolina, in the year 1719: and of the true causes and motives that induced them to renounce their obedience to the lords proprietors, as their governors, and to put themselves under the immediate government of the Crown. London, 1726. [Washington, P. Force, 1837]. 39 p. CtHT; ICU; MBBC; NcU; TxU. 48636

No entry. 48637

Young, Alexander, 1800-1854.
The Good Merchant. A discourse delivered in The Church on Church Green March 26, 1837. The Sunday after The Decease of William Parsons, Esq. By Alexander Young. Boston, Hilliard, Gray & Co., 1837. 30 p. CBPac; ICMe; MNe; NCH; RPB. 48638

---- Manual of phrenology. A

pleasing, concise yet a connected view of that science... Philadelphia, 1837. 36 p. PHi. 48639

Young, Edward, 1683-1765.
The complaint and consolation, or Night thoughts on life, death and immortality. To which is added, The force of religion. A new ed. Boston, T. H. Carter, 1837. 288 p. MH. 48640

---- The complaint: or, Night thoughts. By Edward Young, D.D. Baltimore, Published by N. Hickman, 1837. 293 p. IaHA; MdHi; MsNF; TJaU. 48641

---- ---- Boston, T. H. Carter, 1837. 299 p. MWHi. 48642

---- ---- Concord, N.H., published by Oliver L. Sanborn, 1837. 288 p. CtHWatk; NH-Hi; TxElpL. 48643

---- ---- Hartford, Conn., Judd Loomis & Co., 1837. 324 p. IaGG; MNS. 48644

Young, James Hamilton, 1793- .
Map of Indiana. Philadelphia, Mitchell, 1837. InLPU. 48645

---- New map of Texas, with the contiguous American and Mexican states. By J. H. Young. Philadelphia, Published by S. Augustus Mitchell, 1837. 1 fold. map. MB; TKL-Mc. 48646

---- The tourist's pocket map of the state of Illinois, exhibiting its internal improvements, roads, distances, etc. Philadelphia, Mitchell, 1837. UU. 48647

---- Tourists' pocket map of the State of Virginia. Philadelphia, Mitchell, 1837. NBuG; PHi; RPB. 48648

Young, Samuel.
Suggestions on the best mode of promoting civilization and improvement; or, The influence of woman on the social state; a lecture.... By Hon. Samuel Young. Albany, Hoffman and White, pr., 1837. 36 p. ICT; MBC; MdBP; NjR; OClWHi.   48649

The Young lady's book; A manual of elegant recreations exercises and pursuits, 6th ed. Boston, published by C. A. Wells, 1837. 505, (1) p. MB; MHolliHi; NBuG; NcAS.
                               48650
The young lady's book of elegant prose, comprising selections from the works of British and American authors. Philadelphia, Biddle, 1837. 320 p. DLC.   48651

The young man's evening book. ... New York, Charles H. Francis; Boston, Joseph H. Francis, 1837. 9-336 p. DLC; MH; MNe.
                               48652
Young man's manual. The genuineness and authenticity of the New Testament, by Timothy Dwight, and an answer to the question. Why are you a Christian, by John Clarke, Hartford, 1837. MBC.   48653

Young Men's Association. Albany.
Catalogue of Books in the Library of the Young Men's Association ... Albany, MDCCCXXXVII. Albany, 1837. 33 p. MHi; NAl.   48654

---- Constitution of the Young Men's Association for Mutual Improvement in the City of Schenectady; together with the Rules and Regulations of the Executive Committee. Schenectady, Printed by Thos W. Flagg,

1837. 11, (1) p. NSchHi.
                               48655
---- A catalogue of books in the library of the Young Men's Association of the city of Buffalo, founded February 22, 1836... Buffalo, Oliver G. Steele, 1837. ICLaw.   48656

---- First annual report of the Executive committee of the Young ... reported and adopted Feb. 8, 1837. Buffalo, press of Oliver G. Steele, 1837. 13 p. M; WV.   48657

The Youth's Cabinet; a weekly paper. v. 1- 1837- . New York, 1837- . PPL-R.   48658

The youth's friend. 1837. Revised by the committee of publication. Philadelphia, American S. S. Union, 1837. 192 p. PAtM.   48659

Youth's lyseum. v. 1- . 1837- . New-Lisbon, [O.[, 1837- . OClWHi.   48660

The Youth's magazine, v. 1, no. 1- . Cincinnati, 1837- . 3 v. OClWHi.   48661

The youth's natural history of birds. Concord, Published by Atwood & Browne, 1837. 16 p. MH; OCl.   48662

Z

Zerah, the believing Jew. Published in aid of laying the corner stone of Jesus church, a protestant church, in the valley of the Mississippi. New York, Protestant Episcopal press, 1837. CtY; MB-FA; ViU.   48663

Zeuner, Charles, 1795-1857.

The American harp; being a
collection new and original
church music, under control of
the Musical Professional Society
in Boston. Arranged and composed by Ch. Zeuner, Organist
to St. Paul's Church, and to
the Handel and Hayden Society.
Stereotype ed. Boston, Published by Hilliard, Gray and
Company, 1837. (15), 7-407 p.
MHi; MPiB; NN.   48664

---- The ancient lyre, a collection of old, new and original church music, under the
approbation of the Professional
music society in Boston,
Crocker, 1837. 358 p. ICN;
MBU-T; MH-AH.   48665

---- The Feast of Tabernacles,
a poem for music. In two parts.
By Henry Ware, Jr. Cam-
bridge, Folsom, Wells and
Thurston, Printers, 1837.
38 p. CBPac; ICMe; MH-And;
OO; RNR.   48666

---- ---- Cambridge, [Mass.],
J. Owen, 1837. 38 p. CSmH;
DLC; MB; PU; ViU.   48667

---- The Feast of tabernacles,
an oratorio. The music by
Charles Zeuner, the words by
Henry Ware, jr.... [Boston?],
1837. 12 p. CtY; MH; NcU;
WHi.   48668

Zion's Hill, being a choice collection of hymns, selected from
different denominations, for the
use of pious Christians. Concord, N.H., John F. Brown,
1837. 128 p. CtY-D.   48669

Zollikofer, Johannes, 1633-1692.
    A newly opened treasury of
heavenly incense, or Christian's
companion, containing instruc-

tions and devotional exercises
....Translated and compiled
chiefly from the...work...of...
J. Z.... To which are prefixed
three...sermons, by...J. M.
Mason and...A. M'Clelland...
(Edited) By J. S. Ebaugh.
Philadelphia, New-York (printed),
1837. ICP; NN; OO; PLERG-Hi.
                         46870
Zoological Institute, New York.
    Zoological Institute and
reading room...a delineated
description and history of all
the beasts, birds, & reptiles,
contained therein. New-York,
J. W. Bell, 1837. 32 p. MB;
MH; MH-Z; NNC; NN.   48671

Zschokke, Heinrich, 1771-1848.
    Abellino, the bravo of Venice.
Translated from the French by
M. G. Lewis... Ithaca, Mack,
Andrus and Woodruff, 1837.
107 p. MiU.   48672